THE
ALASTAIR CAMPBELL
DIARIES

THE
ALASTAIR
CAMPBELL
DIARIES

Volume 2
POWER AND THE PEOPLE
1997–1999

Edited by
ALASTAIR CAMPBELL
and
BILL HAGERTY

HUTCHINSON: LONDON

Published by Hutchinson 2011

1 3 5 7 9 10 8 6 4 2

First published in Great Britain in 2011 by
Hutchinson
Random House, 20 Vauxhall Bridge Road,
London SW1V 2SA

www.rbooks.co.uk

Addresses for companies within The Random House Group Limited can be found at:
www.randomhouse.co.uk/offices.htm

The Random House Group Limited Reg. No. 954009

A CIP catalogue record for this book
is available from the British Library

ISBN 9780091797317 (hardback)
ISBN 9780091937379 (paperback)

The Random House Group Limited supports The Forest Stewardship
Council (FSC), the leading international forest certification organisation.
All ourtitles that are printed on Greenpeace approved FSC certified paper
carry the FSC logo. Our paper procurement policy can be found at
www.rbooks.co.uk/environment

Typeset in Palatino by Palimpsest Book Production Limited,
Falkirk, Stirlingshire

Printed and bound in Great Britain by Clays Ltd, St Ives plc

To my mother, Betty Campbell, Fiona's mother,
Audrey Millar, and the friendship between them

Contents

Acknowledgements

Many thanks once more to Bill Hagerty, who took over the task of editing these diaries after the sad death of our friend and colleague Richard Stott, and to Mark Bennett, who was with me in Downing Street and has also been with me on the long and sometimes tortuous road to publication.

Both through my diaries, and the two novels I have published, I have come to appreciate the professionalism and kindness of many people at Random House. I would like to thank Gail Rebuck, Susan Sandon, Caroline Gascoigne, Joanna Taylor, Charlotte Bush, Emma Mitchell and the team of 'spin doctors', Martin Soames for his legal advice, David Milner, Mark Handsley, Vicki Robinson, Helen Judd, Sue Cavanagh, and Jeanette Slinger in reception for always ensuring one of my books is at the front of the display cabinet downstairs – at least when I am visiting the building. My thanks, as ever, to my literary agent Ed Victor, to his PA Linda Van and to his excellent team.

I want to thank Tony Blair for giving me the opportunity he did, and thank the many friends and colleagues who have helped me in good times and bad.

Finally, thanks to my family. As these diaries show, the pressures of the job I did also fell on Fiona and the children, and I thank them for their love and support.

Introduction

The driving narrative in Volume 1 of my full diaries, *Prelude to Power*, was relatively straightforward: though with many ups and downs along the way, it was basically the story of how Tony Blair became leader of the Labour Party, shaped New Labour, and led the party to a landslide victory which put him in Downing Street.

That is where *Power and the People* begins, the long years of opposition over, the huge challenges of government about to begin, helped not just by the scale of victory, but by the mood in the country it engendered. Most British voters, on seeing the picture on the front cover today, will know instantly where and when it was taken – Downing Street, Friday, May 2, 1997 – and perhaps remember something of what they felt at the time.

As I recorded in the closing pages of *Prelude to Power*, with those challenges looming, the sense of euphoria is not something in which either TB or I were sharing. Tony has since confirmed that he felt distant from the happiness of others, and real fear about what lay ahead. Outwardly, he was the ultimate modern politician, youthful and energetic, with a clear programme of major change to implement, and the favourable wind of public opinion in his sails. But inside, he knew that the euphoria would pass, that many lonely and difficult moments lay ahead, and that nothing can really prepare you for a job that so few get to do. Only five people alive at the time of writing know what it is like to be British Prime Minister – Margaret Thatcher, John Major, Tony Blair, Gordon Brown and David Cameron. And only a handful of people – Tony's wife Cherie obviously, Jonathan Powell, Anji Hunter, Sally Morgan, myself, one or two others – really know what it was like for Tony Blair to be one of those five; the pressures he had to contend with minute by minute, hour by hour, day by day, week by week, year by year; the different, often difficult characters he had to deal with at home and abroad, the myriad policy issues he had to master, or at least look and sound as if he had mastered sufficiently to deal with anyone and anything that came at him in the 'terrifying' forum of Prime Minister's Questions.

Think about it. He had been a student, a lawyer, then an MP, who became leader of the Labour Party in unexpected circumstances, namely following John Smith's sudden death from a heart attack, and the equally sudden reversal of opinion about who was John's likelier successor, himself or Gordon Brown. He had never been a minister, let alone run a department. He had spent the previous few months careering round the country in constant campaign mode, the last day or two virtually without sleep and now, on the back of the votes of the people, he is whisked off through cheering crowds to see the Queen, becomes prime minister, is immediately required to make decisions large and small, expected and unexpected, day and night; is now responsible not just for the words that form a manifesto, but the actions that turn those words into real change for Britain and the world.

It is often said that we didn't do enough in the first term, with that huge parliamentary majority and the hopes that had created it. Yet there were times during the editing process of *Power and the People*, not least when we were writing the little 'running feet' which give a flavour of the content of each page, when I felt a sense of genuine astonishment remembering how much happened during the two years covered by this volume. Many of the most significant and enduring parts of the Blair government's legacy stem from this period – Bank of England independence, the minimum wage after a century of Labour campaigning for it, devolution to Scotland, Wales and London, the New Deal jobs programme, Sure Start, the beginnings of the reversal in the underinvestment in schools and hospitals, the first steps of welfare reform and the anti-government protests to match – the policy programme certainly rolls forward.

Yet so often it is the unexpected which comes to dominate. The seemingly inevitable personal and political scandals that come along: our first sex scandal, when Foreign Secretary Robin Cook's private life was exposed; TB's role in supporting Bill Clinton through an alto-gether bigger and more potent sex scandal which threatened to destroy his presidency; problems over party funding brought into sharp relief by the donation from Formula One boss Bernie Ecclestone; 'Ron Davies' 'moment of madness' on Clapham Common which led to his resignation as Welsh Secretary; and the resignation of Peter Mandelson soon afterwards, when details of his misguidedly taken loan from Geoffrey Robinson became known, just as TB was dealing with a crisis concerning Iraq. Given the scale of the controversy generated by military action against Saddam Hussein in Labour's third term, it is perhaps easy to forget that TB's first authorisation of military action in his first term was also against Iraq, far less controversially.

The sudden death of Princess Diana was perhaps most unexpected of all, and her loss was felt throughout the world. The outpouring of mourning which followed is now part not just of political history, but cinematic folklore thanks to the hugely successful film *The Queen*, one of many dramatisations of the Blair era which have confirmed New Labour's strong and in many ways continuing hold on the political culture of recent times. Then there is the Northern Ireland peace process, so often overlooked in the media commentary about TB but surely one of his greatest achievements, especially considering the relentless toing and froing with the province's notoriously difficult politicians, and then the terrible, grave blow of the Omagh bombing as the extremists tried to tear the Good Friday Agreement apart.

But characters well beyond the UK fill these pages as TB tries to forge a more proactive and positive foreign policy, not least when taking up the presidency of the EU and the G8. Helmut Kohl and Gerhard Schroeder, Jacques Chirac, Boris Yeltsin, Nelson Mandela and above all Bill Clinton become major players in the Blair premiership. Behind all the smiles and the bonhomie there were some fairy brutal EU summits, not least over the setting up of the European Central Bank. The handover of Hong Kong to the Chinese, and King Hussein's funeral in Jordan, were among the more extraordinary official events. Chile's former dictator General Pinochet landed the government with an unexpected diplomatic hand grenade. We created a few of our own in trying to get Japanese and Argentine leaders to say sorry for past war activities. We see in this volume TB's early attempts to make a difference in the Middle East, still continuing today. And the volume ends, halfway through our first term, with the Northern Ireland peace process again in trouble, and Britain at the heart of a difficult and messy war to reverse Slobodan Milosevic's ethnic cleansing of Kosovo, in my view another of TB's finest hours.

Not that British politicians – including those on his own side – didn't give TB enough headaches from time to time. The so-called 'Big Guns' from those often ghastly meetings in opposition did not always fire in the same direction once we got into government either. Though TB respected Robin Cook's intellect and passion, 'diddling' became one of his favourite descriptions for his Foreign Secretary's activities. As in *Prelude to Power*, for all his chippiness and temper, John Prescott is shown once more to be fundamentally decent and loyal. That doesn't stop him, however, from trying to slow the New

Labour train, not least when TB is trying to get the Liberal Democrats on board.

The very worst of the tensions between Tony and Gordon Brown come later. But just as they existed in *Prelude to Power*, so they emerge from time to time in these first two years of government covered by *Power and the People*. There is a point where TB expresses the fear that GB is 'deliberately destabilising' the government. We hear of GB's 'catatonic rage' that a reshuffle saw some of his supporters sacked or demoted. We endure the fiasco of our handling of policy on the single European currency, not my greatest moment, but in part driven by attempts to bring TB and GB to the same place.

I thought TB dealt with his relationship with GB pretty fairly in his own memoir, *A Journey*, which was published while I was preparing this volume. So much has been written and said about relations between the two of them, but it was good to get, finally, TB's own version of events. As with all of us who were there, it is only one perspective, but his is perhaps more important than anyone else's, with the possible exception of GB's, for which we will have to wait some time I think.

A Journey didn't hide the difficulties they had in reaching the decision as to which of them should stand for the leadership, nor the significance of the tensions which then developed. But it was one of TB's strengths as a leader that he never feared – indeed he positively welcomed – there being other big players in the government beyond himself. Nor did he resent the idea that a part of GB's mind would always be on when and how he might follow TB as prime minister. This volume shows how, more than his inner team perhaps, he was able to ignore, or at least live with, the manoeuvrings of some of the Chancellor's most zealous supporters who seemed genuinely to believe that GB was the real strength in the government, and that he would make a better PM than TB, and the sooner the better. Tony seemed fairly relaxed about all of that. It was only later, when he sensed the personal ambition was beginning to translate into regular and unnecessary policy differences, that he felt the sometimes positive effect of 'creative tension' crossed a line into something more damaging.

In part as a result of various published accounts, TB's and mine included, and perhaps even more so Peter Mandelson's insufferably self-indulgent account, some have asked why we all played the role we did in helping GB to take over as prime minister, and indeed, in going back to work on his 2010 election campaign. In short the argument goes like this: you've all had some pretty terrible things to say about him, or shown him behaving in a way that aroused a lot of concern about his all-round abilities and personality, so why didn't you do more to stop him? I think this volume of my diaries, perhaps more than any other, shows why that question is too simple in a world – the world of politics – which is often more complicated than it seems even to those living inside it. In the books written about and by us all, it is certainly possible to go to this page or that page and see GB behaving badly, or selfishly, or in a way that seems to show he is unsuited to playing as part of a team. But it is also possible to look elsewhere and see a very different side to him – brilliant, driven, committed to great causes, with a range and scale on policy and argument that justified TB's pretty consistent view of him as the second most talented and important minister in the government; a view, incidentally, which did not offend his actual deputy, John Prescott, who would generally agree with that assessment. TB often said, when things were really bad with GB, that he was 'brilliant but impossible'. If he were just brilliant, he would say, that would be great. Had he just been impossible, then those who urged TB to replace or remove him could have had their wishes granted. But the combination made it a more difficult decision than is sometimes understood. Even with the benefit of hindsight, it is not entirely clear that TB could or should have moved or sacked Gordon. This is not just about whether it was better to have him pissing inside the tent, as it were, rather than from outside, important though that calculation may have been. It is also the case that it was not clear, to him or many others in the party, me included, that there was anyone capable either of beating Gordon in a leadership election, or doing a better job as prime minister. There was a fear, too, that the process of finding out might have left us in a worse not better position.

In a way, all that is for future volumes, and there will be plenty of it. But in these first two years in government, GB, while sometimes difficult, and with his sidekicks often a screaming pain, was at least delivering on establishing a sense of real economic strength and credibility, and so addressing what was historically one of Labour's biggest perceived weaknesses.

I have always believed history will judge TB and his government more kindly than the day-to-day commentary of a media whose right wing don't much care for him because he kept the Tories out for so long, whose left wing aren't too keen because he wasn't left wing enough for their tastes, and many of whose broadcasters will never forgive him for Iraq. I think TB's book, reminding people as it did of the scale of change in Britain over which he presided, and the qualities and characteristics which made him Labour's most successful ever leader, will be an important part of a reassessment within that debate.

I hope *Power and the People*, with its immediate account of those heady early days of government, will also be a contribution to that historical debate. Once all my diaries are published, it will certainly be the longest, and possibly the most complete, single account of life at the heart of the Blair team. But mine too is just one perspective, that of a diarist, often exhausted at the end of another long day, recording what he saw, heard, said, thought and felt, day by day, through an extraordinary period in British political and social history.

As with *Prelude to Power*, the text that follows contains no benefit of hindsight and, other than in this introduction, there is no context-ualisation of today. Amid all the scandals, the crises and the unex-pected events sometimes knocking us off course, a lot went right in these first two years. Britain began to change for the better and many of those changes will endure. I was pleased and proud to be part of the team that helped TB to make it happen, and am glad now to be able to share my account of it all.

Alastair Campbell
London, Wednesday, September 29, 2010

Who's Who

May 1997–April 1999

The Cabinet

Tony Blair	Prime Minister (TB)
John Prescott	Deputy Prime Minister and Secretary of State for the Environment, Transport and the Regions (JP)
Gordon Brown	Chancellor of the Exchequer (GB)
Robin Cook	Foreign Secretary (RC)
Jack Straw	Home Secretary (JS)
David Blunkett	Education and Employment Secretary (DB)
Margaret Beckett	Trade and Industry Secretary 1997–98, Leader of the Commons 1998 onwards (MB)
Jack Cunningham	Minister of Agriculture, Fisheries and Food 1997–98. Chancellor of the Duchy of Lancaster 1998 onwards (JC)
Donald Dewar	Scottish Secretary 1997–99 (DD)
George Robertson	Defence Secretary 1997–99 (GR)
Frank Dobson	Health Secretary 1997–99 (FD)
Ann Taylor	Leader of the House of Commons 1997–98, Chief Whip from 1998
Chris Smith	Culture Secretary
Harriet Harman	Social Security Secretary 1997–98
Mo Mowlam	Northern Ireland Secretary 1997–99 (Mo)
Ron Davies	Welsh Secretary 1997–98
Clare Short	International Development Secretary
Lord (Derry) Irvine	Lord Chancellor
Lord (Ivor) Richard	Leader of the House of Lords 1997–98
David Clark	Chancellor of the Duchy of Lancaster 1997–98
Gavin Strang	Minister of Transport 1997–98
Alistair Darling	Chief Secretary to the Treasury 1997–98, Social Security Secretary 1998 onwards

Nick Brown	Chief Whip 1997–98, Minister of Agriculture 1998 onwards

Additional Cabinet Changes 1998–99

Stephen Byers	Chief Secretary to the Treasury 1998, Trade and Industry Secretary 1998 onwards
Baroness (Margaret) Jay	Leader of the House of Lords 1998 onwards
Peter Mandelson	(Minister without Portfolio 1997–98) Trade and Industry Secretary July–December 1998 (PM in index only)
Alun Michael	Welsh Secretary 1998–1999
Alan Milburn	Chief Secretary to the Treasury 1998–99
John Reid	Minister of Transport 1998–99

10 Downing Street

Alex Allan	Principal private secretary (to August 1997) (AA)
Tim Allan	Special adviser, Press Office
Philip Barton	Private secretary, Foreign Affairs
Mark Bennett	AC's researcher
Alison Blackshaw	AC's senior personal assistant
Cherie Blair	Wife of TB (CB)
David Bradshaw	Special adviser, Strategic Communications Unit
Julian Braithwaite	Press officer, Foreign Affairs
Sir Robin Butler	Cabinet Secretary (to 1998)
Alastair Campbell	Chief press secretary and prime minister's official spokesman (AC)
Magi Cleaver	Press officer, overseas visits
Hilary Coffman	Special adviser, Press Office (HC)
Kate Garvey	Diary secretary
Bruce Grocott MP	Parliamentary private secretary
Jeremy Heywood	Private secretary, Economic Affairs
John Holmes	Principal private secretary and Foreign Affairs adviser (1997–99)
Anji Hunter	Presentation and planning
Peter Hyman	Strategist and speechwriter
Angus Lapsley	Private secretary, Home Affairs

Liz Lloyd	Special adviser, Policy Unit
Pat McFadden	Special adviser, Policy Unit
David Miliband	Head of Policy Unit (DM)
Fiona Millar	AC's partner, aide to CB (FM)
Sally Morgan	Political secretary
Allan Percival	Deputy press secretary (1997–98)
Jonathan Powell	Chief of staff
Roz Preston	Assistant to CB
Lance Price	Special adviser, Press Office
Terry Rayner	Driver, Government car service
John Sawers	Foreign Affairs adviser (from January 1999)
Godric Smith	Press officer (Deputy Press Secretary from 1998)
Sir Richard Wilson	Cabinet secretary (from 1998)

HM Treasury

Ed Balls, Ed Miliband, Sue Nye, Charlie Whelan	Special advisers
Geoffrey Robinson	Paymaster General

Northern Ireland

Gerry Adams	President, Sinn Fein
Bertie Ahern	Prime Minister of Ireland (BA)
General John de Chastelain	Chair, Independent International Commission on Decommissioning
Sir Ronnie Flanagan	Chief Constable, Royal Ulster Constabulary
John Hume	Leader, SDLP
Tom Kelly	Northern Ireland Office spokesman (from 1998)
Seamus Mallon	Deputy Leader, SDLP
Martin McGuinness	Sinn Fein chief negotiator
Senator George Mitchell	US special envoy for Northern Ireland
Ian Paisley	Leader, Democratic Unionist Party
John Taylor	Deputy Leader, Ulster Unionist Party
David Trimble	Leader, Ulster Unionist Party

The Royal Households

The Earl of Airlie	Lord Chamberlain (LC)
Mark Bolland	Press secretary to the Prince of Wales
Geoffrey Crawford	Press secretary to the Queen

Sir Robert Fellowes	Private secretary to HM Queen Elizabeth II
Michael Gibbins	Private secretary to Diana, Princess of Wales
Sir Robin Janvrin	Deputy private secretary to the Queen

The White House
Sandy Berger	National security advisor
Bill Clinton	42nd President of the United States (BC)
Hillary Clinton	First Lady (HC)
Al Gore	Vice-President
Joe Lockhart	White House press secretary (from 1998)
Mike McCurry	White House press secretary (to 1998)
Jim Steinberg	Deputy national security advisor

Kosovo
General Wesley Clark	SACEUR (Supreme Allied Commander Europe)
General Sir Charles Guthrie	Chief of the (UK) Defence Staff
Slobodan Milosevic	President of Yugoslavia
Jamie Shea	NATO spokesman
Javier Solana	NATO Secretary General

The Labour Party
Lord (Charlie) Falconer	Solicitor General 1997–98, later Cabinet Office minister
Frank Field	Welfare Reform minister 1997–98
Philip Gould	Political pollster and strategist, adviser to TB (PG)
David Hill	Director of Communications
Tessa Jowell	Health minister 1997–99
Neil Kinnock	Labour Leader 1983–92, European commissioner
Michael Levy	Businessman, Labour Party fundraiser
Margaret McDonagh	Deputy General Secretary, General Secretary from 1998

Parliament

Paddy Ashdown	Leader of the Liberal Democrat Party 1989–99
Betty Boothroyd	Speaker of the House of Commons
Alan Clark	MP for Kensington and Chelsea 1997–99. Controversial diarist, friend of AC
Viscount Cranborne	Shadow Leader of the Lords 1997–98
William Hague	Leader of the Conservative Party 1997–2001
John Major	Conservative Prime Minister 1990–97 (JM)
Alex Salmond	Leader of the Scottish National Party 1990–2000

The Media

Tony Bevins	*Independent* political editor
Michael Brunson	ITN political editor
Paul Dacre	*Daily Mail*
Sir David English	Chairman, Associated Newspapers
Sir David Frost	Broadcaster, *Breakfast with Frost* presenter
Andrew Grice	*Sunday Times* political editor
Stuart Higgins	*Sun* editor
Trevor Kavanagh	*Sun* political editor
Donald Macintyre	*Independent* political commentator
Piers Morgan	Editor, *Daily Mirror*
Rupert Murdoch	Chairman, News Corporation
Denis Murray	BBC Northern Ireland correspondent
Robin Oakley	BBC political editor
Peter Riddell	*Times* political commentator
Paul Routledge	*Mirror* commentator
Jon Sopel	BBC political correspondent
Philip Webster	*Times* political editor
Michael White	*Guardian* political editor
Patrick Wintour	*Guardian* political correspondent

The Diaries

Friday, May 2, 1997

TB went off with [Sir] Robin Butler [Cabinet Secretary] to the Cabinet Room for a security briefing. Jonathan [Powell, chief of staff], Sally Morgan [political secretary], David Miliband [head of policy] and I went up to the dining room, where a buffet lunch had been laid on. Jonathan Haslam [John Major's press secretary] showed me around, introduced me to a few people, and it was all a bit weird. Jonathan was being very pleasant and doing what he had to do, but I felt for him. He was being kicked out of the job, and having to guide me as to what to do next. I sensed very mixed feelings in the staff. The messengers seemed friendly and helpful. The press office people were nervous, I could tell. I guess they only had what they read and heard to go on, and they were worried about the Tim [Allan] and Hilary [Coffman] [special advisers] situation. They also sensed, rightly, that I had not been impressed by the JM press operation and would want to make changes. Jonathan had left me a note on the strengths and weaknesses of all of them. It was odd having such a big office, PAs and the like, when I had been pretty much used to operating anywhere from a mobile phone. I was introduced to Alison [Blackshaw], my new PA, who seemed a bit dizzy, told me how much she had liked Major and every time I wandered off, she said she had to know where I was and she was worried I would be too 'independent' for her to be able to do her job.

TB seemed to be in his element. We were in the Cabinet Room, working through the Cabinet and some of the junior jobs, and he was clear and decisive, had found new reserves of energy. Butler and Alex Allan [principal private secretary] seemed to take to him. Butler said later all the machine wanted was clear direction. I told him I had not been too impressed with the way the government media machine worked, and nor had TB. I asked if I was within my rights to get them all in and emphasise the need for change and he said no problem. That was what they expected. I was still feeling a bit flat and deflated, and the atmosphere of the place didn't help. The children helped lift things a bit, Euan and Nicky in particular running a bit wild. Butler – or 'Buttleshanks' as TB had decided to christen him when talking to us – was fussing around the whole time. Once lunch was out of the way, TB started to see everyone to appoint the Cabinet. JP [John Prescott, Deputy Prime Minister] came in first and was really happy with his lot. Robin [Cook, Foreign Secretary] went straight out and did a doorstep and TB said we had to keep a very wary eye on him. 'He is playing the old games.' Derry [Irvine, Lord Chancellor] was happy enough. [David] Blunkett [Education and Employment Secretary] came in and I introduced him to Haslam, who was going to be his top press man. It was interesting how quickly the idea settled that they were now in government and off to do real jobs as opposed to all the Shadow stuff we had been doing for years; listening to TB set out priorities, and then talk about detail of policies which were now going to be put into practice.

Margaret [Beckett, Trade and Industry Secretary] and Jack S [Straw, Home Secretary] in particular made the point they just couldn't wait to get started. I did a briefing on the Cabinet, and some background on the mood etc., and again it was odd how quickly it came to seem and feel normal that I was there, doing it. I went down to the briefing room with my new team, walked in to a few 'Hear, hears' and then just got going. Tony Bevins [*Independent*] asked if I was going to scrap the lobby and I said no. I got home reasonably early and watched the news, which was all about mood and euphoria and the rest, and I still didn't feel it, felt flat and anticlimactic. There was also a real problem looming because CB [Cherie Blair] was clearly dead set against Anji [Hunter, head of TB's office] being there. I thought it was unfair to Anji if she was now kicked aside, but also that she would be very good at watching his back.

Saturday, May 3

TB was pretty knackered but he had to keep going on appointments. We started at 9 and he was keen for a very New Labour element to the reshuffle. He called Frank Field and offered him Number 2 to Harriet [Harman] at Social Security. We were in the Cabinet Room, TB, Jonathan and I on one side, Butler and Alex Allan on the other. Those two seemed absolutely fine about me and Jonathan, no problem at all. I got the feeling that Alex had found the last stages of the JM government really draining. He has a very quiet, unassuming manner, but there is a sharpness and energy there and I sense he really wants to help. RB is very smiley and friendly, but more old-fashioned, more naturally Establishment. The one I was keeping a close eye on was Mark Adams [private secretary with responsibility for Prime Minister's Questions], who I sensed trying to get barriers up early on. I took a pretty instant dislike. He was cocky without having the obvious talent to justify it and when he was giving it large about how we should prepare for PMQs, I couldn't help pointing out that Major's PMQs was one of his biggest weaknesses. We got through the appointments quicker than any of us thought possible. Mo [Mowlam] and I had a very friendly chat before she headed straight for Northern Ireland. TB had been slightly dreading telling Derek Foster, Tom Clarke and Michael Meacher [Shadow Cabinet Labour MPs] that they would not be in the Cabinet, but they all took it as well as they could be expected to. I had a meeting with Tim and Hilary, plus Allan Percival [AC's Civil Service deputy] and the rest of the press office. Allan was very quiet and ponderous, and clearly saw himself as the guardian of propriety. The press officers were a mixed bunch, but gave off the sense of being terrified. I tried to assure them I would listen to any of their concerns as the new government bedded in. I said it should be an exciting time for them because the PM values communications. But I did say I intended to change the way things were done.

I did a briefing for the broadcasters on the appointments, and then for the Sundays. I gave them the story about TB and family living in Number 11 not 10, which had them going on for ages. Also, re the official residences – RC Chevening, GB [Gordon Brown, Chancellor] Dorneywood, JP access to both plus Admiralty House. Jack S wanted to stay at home so Mo was using South Eaton Place. Flat for Margaret B. Derry came over for a chat re his own press and profile. I said he had huge strengths, particularly the intellectual support he gave to TB, as he had during the campaign. I thought he should do all the things he had to do, but not generate profile. He should establish himself as a big figure in the government without shouting about it. Derry is a lovely guy but part of his strength is his old-fashionedness and it doesn't lend itself to dealing with the media too closely. He said he was worried about CB; he feared she would find it hard to balance everything. GB came round to see me and we talked about how he would put up interest rates and simultaneously announce an independent Bank of England. He would work on the script today and have everything in place. Secrecy was paramount.

We talked about Charlie [Whelan] who had come to see me earlier to say he was alarmed that TB didn't want him, that he would work as my deputy if that was what I really wanted. I said TB was wrong to suggest that because I had to have a civil servant as a deputy. GB asked me to agree that Charlie stayed at the Treasury, but kept in regular communication with me. Charlie looked very low, though Ed Balls [special adviser to GB] was looking even more smug than usual. TB left at 6 for a meeting of the Privy Council. I had a session with Alison Blackshaw who said she was really anxious. 'The trouble is you are so independent,' she said, yet again, and I laughed and said 'Is that code for wanting me in my box?' The press office were baulking at the idea of Tim and HC briefing for the government as well as the party. I raised it with Butler and Alex, who said it was fine; they could brief for the government, and be political, but not party political. They seemed to be fine about pretty much anything I was putting forward, and I got them to come round to the press office to tell everyone there was no problem Tim and HC speaking for HMG. I could tell they were all a bit jumpy.

The Anji problem was still running on and I was worried it would get out there before it was sorted. I was still not totally convinced I wanted to do the job. I told Fiona [Millar, AC's partner] I thought I was more cut out for campaigning than government. I'd raised it with TB, who was having none of it. I wrote a letter to the heads of information in departments, making clear we would be wanting a lot of change. I wanted all bids co-ordinated through the Number 10 press office, and we wanted a log of all contacts with the media. I know the second part of that won't be observed, but they need a pretty firm message from the word go.

Sunday, May 4

TB was at home working on more appointments. Peter M [Mandelson, Minister without Portfolio] did a photocall at the Cabinet Office without clearing it with us, which pissed me off, particularly as he was simultaneously saying that people should not be doing things without clearance through Number 10. We had to establish quickly, even with Peter, that things had to be routed through Number 10. It was going to be more important in government than in opposition, because there are so many different places that can make news. The message was getting through pretty quickly though. JP called to let me know he was doing an interview with the *Guardian*, Frank Dobson [Health Secretary] with the *Mirror*. These are Cabinet ministers and they can easily get coverage without resort to me. We must have proper systems.

TB went off later to play tennis. He was anxious about Anji. I called her, and she said she was determined to stay. Sally M was anxious that we had not yet briefed on the job she would be doing, and was not going to be messed around. She was clearly worried if Anji did come back in, she would not be so influential. Both Cherie and Fiona were opposed to Anji coming in, but TB was insistent. In the morning, they were filmed at church, all very casual. TB called later, worried we could easily lose the initiative quickly if we were not careful, and said we had to have a steady flow of new Labour initiatives. We were planning union rights at GCHQ [Government Communication Headquarters], and of course the Bank of England.

I spoke to Doug Henderson [minister for Europe] who was due to go to Brussels tomorrow, and said he needed the Foreign Office to get briefing on a new approach in Europe. TB asked Michael Levy [Labour peer, businessman, Labour Party fund-raiser] to try to sort out the Cherie/Anji situation. Eventually it was agreed Anji would come in, work on presentation ['Special Assistant for Presentation and Planning'], and share an office with Fiona and Roz [Preston, assistant to CB]. Fiona said she got the sense Tony needed Anji as much as Cherie needed Carole [Caplin, friend and adviser to CB]. TB called again, and said we all needed some rest. I said I had not been fantastically impressed by what I had seen so far from the government machine. Alan Clark [Conservative politician, diarist and friend of AC] called. 'Fan-bloody-tastic,' he said. Nick Soames [Conservative MP, grandson of Churchill] called, said we deserved it, we had run a great campaign, but they would be back straight away.

Monday, May 5

It was a bank holiday, but a normal working day. I went round to TB's, who was livid at RC who had briefed hard on the Social Chapter. 'I could cheerfully kill the little bugger,' he said. He called him in the car on the way in and said he was now involved in running the country and representing Britain, not winning a few rounds of applause at a conference. These things have to be done according to an overall plan, not just spilled out when people feel like it. As he came off the phone, he said 'Unbelievable,' and laughed. 'He said "You are going to need me as much as I need you."' There was a bit of light relief on appointments when he was appointing Bernard Donoughue [Labour peer, former adviser in Wilson and Callaghan governments] to a job [at the Ministry of Agriculture, Fisheries and Food] and the switchboard got Brian Donohue [Labour MP] instead. TB said he was already well on the way to appointing him when he realised he had got the wrong Donohue. My letter to heads of information was already causing a bit of a stir in Whitehall. Whelan told me it was being called 'the fascist letter' in the Treasury. It was clear some departments weren't happy with it, but with others I felt we were getting there slowly.

At Richmond Crescent [the Blairs' Islington home], I chatted to CB re Anji. She had reconciled herself to the fact that he wanted her there. TB asked me what I thought of my Civil Service team. It was mixed. I wrote a briefing note on Sally's position for the heavies and Bevins came back straight away and said they were splashing on TB using political appointments like me and her to strengthen the centre. We got a few more appointments out for the lunchtimes but were holding back on Tony Banks [Labour MP] until Tom Pendry [former Shadow sports minister] was told he wouldn't be getting sport. When he was told, apparently he was weeping.

I had a meeting with GB, Ed B, Charlie W, Jill Rutter [Treasury head of press] and HMT officials to go over tomorrow's plan on the Bank. It was going to be big and bold and I said to GB he really had to capture the sense of history, set it in the bigger context of making Britain strong and competitive for the long term, building long-term prosperity. He was scribbling madly and I could see some of the Treasury officials realising they had never worked with anyone like this before. I had another session with CB to work on the letter I was sending to editors re the kids not being fair game as they came and went. They were due to move in today, and Nicky [Blair, younger son] said he was looking forward to it because they were getting goalposts in the garden. TB called a political meeting at 5.30 – AC, Jonathan, Bruce [Grocott MP, parliamentary private secretary], SM, DM, Kate Garvey [TB's diary secretary] and Anji on her first day, largely to work out issues of how to manage his time. He had decided to work mainly in the little room off the bit outside the Cabinet Room, which was pretty small but he said it was the best of what was on offer. He was pressing for something to move forward re us and the Liberals. I said I was worried he would get swallowed by the machine and he had to maintain visibility in the country as well as here. GB came over again to go over interest rates and the Bank. TB had been pressing on the Bank for a while and I was keen for him to be involved in some way, but now he was doing it, it was clear GB was going to present it as very much his thing. TB said he didn't mind as long as we were doing it. We put together a plan for telling the Cabinet one by one tomorrow. GB didn't believe it would hold if too many people were told today. It was big, bold, genuinely historic and would give us a real sense of momentum.

Tuesday, May 6

There were loads of CB moving-in pictures. Charlie was tipping off people from 7.55 that the Governor of the Bank was seeing GB at 8. The BBC were pretty slow off the mark. The assumption was interest-rate rise full stop. I listened to the news in the office. John Holmes [private secretary, foreign affairs] came in to say he was worried the news was overblowing TB's Irish visit. It was unlikely to produce much at this stage. He wanted me to play it down. Allan Percival came to see me and said he was worried people would no longer think this was a good place to work. He felt the last few days had not been handled well. I said I had been trying to give people re-assurance whilst at the same time making clear we would be making change. He had to understand that seen from opposition, the govern-ment media machine had seemed hopeless. The media thought it was hopeless and we had to change the way it worked. I wanted people to work with me but they had to understand change had to happen. Peter M chaired a meeting, me, Jonathan, Allan P, Alex, HC, David Hill [chief spokesman, Labour Party], CW, largely about handling of the Bank. He said he wanted to chair morning meetings, which was fine.

I went over to GB's office for a pre-meeting on the Bank independ-ence. There was a real buzz in there, and GB was tense and fidgety, firing off questions and then answering them himself. It was genuinely exciting, a really big moment. The Treasury officials looked a little bit shell-shocked. I sensed GB was taking far less care at keeping them sweet than TB. He was making very clear, in word and deed, who was in charge. The room was packed, GB had a real authority there, and dealt well with questions. GB was much more relaxed than he had been in the latter stages of the campaign. He was clearly taking to the Treasury like a duck to water.

TB was seeing Cabinet committees, e.g. on the Constitution. Equally annoyingly, the decisions reached were out in the press within half an hour. We had to get a grip of this. Referendum [on devolution] by September. It was TB's birthday and there was a little do for him in the Cabinet Room, to which lots of the Garden Room Girls [Prime Minister's secretarial staff] and other staff came. It could have been a really good scene for him, but he didn't really rise to it, which was a pity. All felt a bit flat. I did the lobby in the afternoon and I sensed that they sensed we had quickly established control and were setting the agenda as promised. David Rose [Welsh journalist] asked if it was a deliberate snub that there were no Welsh speakers in the Welsh team and I said yes. They were asking a lot about so-called presidential style. Mark Adams chaired a meeting on PMQs. He set out how they did it with JM and I said that had not exactly been a great success. These were the same people who had been responsible for one of the weakest parts of his whole operation. I said we should use it to make more announcements and set a new tone.

I had to square Derek Foster re his words about resigning from the Minister of State job he'd been given – quickest resignation yet – to go for Deputy Speaker.[1] I worked on notes for a speech to my first meeting to heads of information, who we invited over to a drink in the White Room at Number 10. Peter M came too and we both emphasised the importance TB attached to information and communication, and we wanted a more proactive approach. I said TB barely read the papers but he was a believer in strategic communications and they needed to be involved in that. I sensed that some of them didn't have a clue what I was talking about. But some did, and were clearly happy with their new bosses.

Wednesday, May 7

The main event for today was TB at the PLP [Parliamentary Labour Party], with a big New Labour message, and the re-election of the Speaker. GB got a terrific press re Bank of England independence, deservedly, though there was too much 'it was Ed Balls' idea' around. Derek Scott [TB's special adviser on economics] told me that at the meeting with Eddie George [Governor of the Bank of England], Ed rather than Alistair Darling [chief secretary to the Treasury] had sat next to GB. Peter M said well done to the HMT [Her Majesty's Treasury] team on the handling of the Bank announcement. TB was worrying about Ireland, wanting quickly to take an initiative but worrying whether he could do it without upsetting too many parts of the equation. MB called to bend my ear on the need to get a trade union rights bill. Jack Cunningham [Agriculture Secretary] called to bend my ear about the need to go early for a Food Standards Agency. He was scathing about MAFF [Ministry of Agriculture, Fisheries and Food], said the place was a total shambles.

The PLP meeting was at Church House and there was a terrific atmosphere, a real sense of excitement. There was a lot of yearning and ambition in there. TB got a great reception and it was a good speech, translating some of the messages of the campaign into a language for government, warning of the additional responsibility of

[1] Derek Foster MP, former Shadow Chancellor of the Duchy of Lancaster, resigned as parliamentary secretary, Cabinet Office, after two days in post.

a large majority. 'There were a lot of illusions floating around in there,' he said on the way back.

The Civil Service had done a not bad job writing the Queen's Speech based on the advice we had given in advance re early priorities, but I rewrote it to make it a bit less frumpy and to get in a bit of message. The Palace were fine about most of the changes but one or two they pushed back on. TB met the Northern Ireland Office people for a briefing, and then [Sir] David English [chairman, Associated Newspapers] with [Lord] Rothermere [chairman, Daily Mail and General Trust]. English popped round for a chat and said what a brilliant campaign it had been. He said he would try to keep [Paul] Dacre [editor, *Daily Mail*] in line, and would be helped if they felt they knew what was going on. Jonathan told me that Butler had said he did not think I should attend Cabinet. I did a little note to TB saying if we were to get clarity of briefing out of Cabinet I had to be there. He said in writing there was no question of me not attending Cabinet meetings. I was unimpressed that Butler had tried to get it done through Jonathan, rather than come to me or raise it with TB. He said nothing more about it. We were getting lots of calls about whether Cherie liked the Downing Street cat ['Humphrey']. I got home and caught the news. Fantastic pictures of TB with all the women MPs. We got a flurry of late calls after Clare Short [International Development Secretary] on Channel 5 talking about the age of consent and saying she wasn't happy we didn't have a women's ministry.

Thursday, May 8

I sensed we were really beginning to motor. In less than a week, we had established momentum and a sense of competence and we were getting broadly positive reactions to most things we were doing. The picture of TB and the women MPs was pretty mega everywhere and again was adding to the sense of a breath of fresh air. The only ragged-ness was that there were too many stories around about the Queen's Speech. It was partly my fault in that I had probably talked too much in the margins of the briefing, but also people were chattering around the place the whole time. The *Indy* went big on Freedom of Information being delayed, and the *Guardian* on the idea it was because Peter M and I were basically against. Peter was terribly miffed about it, whereas I was not terribly fussed. He went off and did a round of interviews saying he was in favour.

TB was seeing [Paddy] Ashdown [Lib Dem leader] who, helpfully, volunteered the view that there should be reform of PMQs. This was great news because TB was intending to announce change tomorrow, and it was good that Paddy raised it rather than being pushed into backing it. Elsewhere, however, TB was unimpressed, because Paddy was not keen on merger talks and was instead asking for stuff like a privy councillorship for Bob Maclennan [Lib Dem MP and party president], more peers. We agreed he should be there next week and accept a couple of Cabinet committee places, and we should go public on it next week. Today was unbelievably busy, with relentless interest in every detail of the Cabinet, Queen's Speech, plus the John Bruton [Irish Prime Minister] meeting.

The Cabinet started arriving fairly early and there was a good mood around the place. They gathered outside and were drinking tea and chatting. I agreed with JP that he would do clips in the street afterwards, but nobody else. We had to stop the notion Robin had tried to start that people just wander over and talk to whoever is out there. We did the official photo, and it was only after they were all there that I realised there was only one woman in the front row, which didn't look great. GB looked very tense and bunched up. There was something about team photos that made people nervous and a bit silly. Alex Allan told me TB had said he would dispense with all the titles in Cabinet and just use Christian names. TB told me later it had been AA who first suggested it. I briefed the *Standard* on the [London] mayor and the Assembly commitment. The Cabinet Office had done a seating plan and they took ages to settle down. TB had made absolutely clear to Butler I would be attending and I sat at the back with Alex and John Holmes and the other private secretaries. Jonathan sat directly behind Butler and TB. Bruce was sitting in the other chair to the side of the fireplace. The Civil Service were getting the message that TB would not allow his political team to be undermined, let alone broken up.

TB said the last government had been a shambles and we had to learn from that. He said we will sink or swim together. There was too much chattering to the media going on. It was a bit like first day at school. TB was on great form but he looked tired. He said 'Good morning everyone,' sat down and then said he had been thinking what they should call each other at these meetings; that they had been together so long that it would be odd suddenly to start using titles, so we should carry on calling each other by our Christian names. Hear, hears. He was serious about proper co-ordination through the centre, on policy and on press. Clare asked if every interview had to be cleared through me and he said yes. He said there was too much chattering going on, and pointed to the *Scotsman* account of the constitutional committee meeting. He said he expected ministers to have a grip of their special advisers who again should only be speaking to the media in a co-ordinated, disciplined way.

GB raised the pay review bodies and said he thought it was difficult for the Cabinet to take their full salary rises when they were urging restraint on others. TB and JP (less enthusiastically) weighed in with support. Donald [Dewar, Secretary of State for Scotland] raised the issue of how pension entitlements were affected and TB said it made no difference. Later Clare was asking for rail renationalisation, more trade union rights. JP gave her one of his withering looks. TB basically ignored her. They went through the bills for the Queen's Speech, TB explaining why some which might seem a bit odd had to be in there. Ministers were still pressing for their own projects but largely as a way of letting their own people know they were having their say in Cabinet. That's how it felt at any rate. Donald said he needed more Scottish bills. TB said 'You'll have to drop the referendum bill to get them,' and DD laughed and that was that. TB saw the education team after Cabinet, then part of the day was taken dealing with BSE [bovine spongiform encephalopathy]. GB had said it was a disaster that could cost us billions. There was a MAFF/Health turf war over who should lead on the Food Standards Agency. TB had indicated Jack C should get it, but that would go down badly with consumer groups. Jack and now Jeff Rooker [junior agriculture minister] were both complaining that MAFF was a total shambles. Jeff said they were useless from the permanent secretary down. I asked whether anyone had thought about sacking the people at the top. I did a note for the four o'clock [lobby briefing], and was fairly downbeat, covered Cabinet, twenty-two bills, pay, meeting with Bruton. On most of the bulletins, we had the first three stories. The Bruton meeting was fine, and TB was clearly up for a big push on it. He didn't want to do media and so we left it all to Bruton and Mo.

Friday, May 9

We got good coverage out of Cabinet – 'Call me Tony' – and on Ireland. The *Telegraph* had a leak of sorts on TB's plan to move PMQs. TB spoke to Paddy about it again and he was fine. Then he spoke to [John] Major who was clearly minded to attack it. TB went over some of the arguments, saying he felt fifteen minutes wasn't long enough; that neither of them ever came out of it well. In the end, he said, you'll have to decide whether to attack it or not, but he believed one longer session per week was better than two shorter ones. I had prepared a written briefing on PMQs, which I revised. We had Wim Kok [Dutch Prime Minister] coming in for lunch, and I was also organising a picture of Cherie and Humphrey the cat because of the stuff about her hating cats. Peter M was getting more and more pompous at the morning meetings, and I feared we were heading for a spat fairly soon. Charlie Whelan was as usual totally vague about GB's plans; said he had a couple of interviews coming up but hadn't decided what he would be saying yet. PMQs reform was the main issue at the eleven o'clock, and though some thought there should have been more consultation, it went fine.

At 11.45 we had a strategy meeting – TB, GB, Peter M, AC, Jonathan, CW. It meandered really though GB was in better form than of late, and a bit more engaged. I relayed the call I had from Nick Brown [chief whip] re BSE, who said 'Don't let TB take charge of it because it is insoluble.' GB said he was more worried about the public finances. Also, that he feared there was too much ill discipline among MPs. And he was worried, as ever, about JP. 'Why on earth did you give him the regions as well?' 'That was your idea,' said TB. 'No it wasn't.' GB said RC was fucking up on Europe. I'd had words with RC about the TV shots of him kissing Oskar Lafontaine [chairman, Social Democratic Party of Germany (SPD)]. TB said our objectives for the IGC[1] were to protect borders, relax the veto where we said we would, not allow an inner core of countries to go ahead at different pace, reweighting of votes, flexible labour markets, CAP [Common Agricultural Policy] reform. I did the Sunday lobby at 1.20. I said I did not intend to have a fixed slot for them every week, and it would depend on whether there was anything to say. They were by and large not a serious bunch and it was largely a waste of time. The serious ones would demand more time outside the briefing anyway. It went on a bit and I was late for the Kok lunch. TB was saying we intended to be constructive but there were certain things we could not cede. The Dutch [EU] presidency were publishing a new draft treaty in the next few days. The current game appeared to be that we would get it into the new treaty that we kept border controls, something the last government failed to get. TB emphasised no weakening of the veto on foreign and defence policy. He said the whole third pillar[2] (justice and home affairs) could not become intergovernmental. It was like learning a new language and TB took to it easily, better than I did. Variable geometry? IGC, multi-speed, third pillar. He said it was

[1] The 1996–97 Intergovernmental Conference led to the signing of the Treaty of Amsterdam in October.
[2] The 1992 Maastricht Treaty divided EU policy into three pillars: European community, common foreign and security policy, and justice and home affairs.

May '97: Learning the language of Eurospeak

important we stamped our mark on the IGC. Kok and TB had a private session then Kok came out to do a doorstep. We left our media to RC, who was so puffed up it was comic.

TB was heading off to Chequers [Prime Minister's official country residence]. We had a chat before he left and he said I had to try to get some rest. He said we had had a good first week and we had to keep on establishing grip and competence. I was missing PG's [Philip Gould, pollster, strategist and adviser to TB] notes but he sent one through today saying the mood was overwhelmingly positive and the first week had been great. He had played an absolute blinder during the campaign. There had been times when it felt like he and I had held the thing together. He had a lot of the qualities needed for a long campaign like that – work ethic, perseverance, enthusiasm and not getting too fussed when things went a bit wrong. It annoyed me that he was virtually written out of the post-election script, partly because he was not in the government, but also because Peter was so busy taking credit.

Saturday, May 10
The first quiet day in ages. Godric [Smith, press officer] called about an *Indy on Sunday* story, Friends of the Earth saying Jack C should be moved because of his outside interests. I gave a robust statement defending Jack and saying it was a preposterous attempt to gain publicity, and would not be taken seriously.

Sunday, May 11
The papers were basically fine, though there was far too much chatter about the Budget. I went for a swim and then a lunch at Fredericks for TB's birthday organised by Maggie Rae [partner of Alan Haworth, PLP secretary] and Katie Kay [former neighbour of the Blairs, later an aide]. Lots of his family were there and it was an OK event. I was sitting next to a relative of Cherie's who runs a B&Q store. TB arrived in a rather poncy four-buttoned suit. He said he felt rested. He liked Chequers. He was worried about changing PMQs, felt it would come back and hit us at some time. We were only getting away with it because of the honeymoon effect. He felt once that ended, we would have to raise the game another gear.

Monday, May 12
The Tory leadership was fairly dominant. Our main focus was GB in Brussels insisting we could cut VAT on fuel, and RC doing his 'mission

statement' for a new foreign policy. Things had settled down fairly quickly and I was missing the intensity of the campaign. I had a lot of challenges and problems but many of them were dull, administrative kind of things, making change that should have been made yonks ago. TB was seeing Ian Paisley [Democratic Unionist leader], John Hume [nationalist SDLP leader] and David Trimble [Ulster Unionist leader] and it was interesting to watch them put their own spin not just on the meetings, but the bigger picture. TB said he reckoned he could see a way of sorting the Northern Ireland problem. I loved the way he said it, like nobody had thought of it before. I said what makes you think you can do it when nobody else could? I had a long session with him and John Holmes, who looked after Ireland as well as Europe and all the big foreign policy stuff. He was not your typical Foreign Office man. He was from Preston, had a very dry sense of humour and had been totally grown up about the main changes. He worked fantastically hard and quickly established a rapport with Tony, and an ability to speak his mind without bullshit. I could tell he was a bit quizzical about TB's optimism, but willing to give it a good go. TB was thinking of going to NI at the end of the week, making a basically pro-Union speech but at the same time saying that officials could talk to Sinn Fein. John said it was not guaranteed to produce a ceasefire but it was probably the best way to try. I could see TB getting really seized of it. Every time I saw him today, whatever the issue, he would say something about Ireland. 'I can see a way on this.'

We were briefing on the small business payments bill, carved up between me, Siobhan [Kenny, Number 10 press officer] and Jean Caines [DTI press officer]. DTI were being incredibly slow about it and when I chased it up Jean said she hadn't got 'presidential approval'. Presidential! As in president of the Board of Trade. I called Margaret Beckett and said could she tell her press people that she didn't need to authorise every briefing that went out, provided it was based on policy. I told Jean MB and I had a very good relationship because she was one of the real grown-ups. There were one or two little problems that led to the private office getting pissed off with me. Peter Hain [junior minister, Welsh office] had wanted to announce the abolition of nursery vouchers in Wales [Labour scrapped the previous government's nursery provision scheme] and checked with me from a media point of view and I said no problem. But he hadn't cleared it on the policy front, and when Blunkett went mad about it later, Peter used the line that I had cleared it on TB's behalf. Also Jack Straw came through me on an immigration appeal case that was going to get a bit of play. These were just teething problems really.

I had a look round the Number 11 flat with Fiona and Roz. It was a bit musty and not terribly homely. The main living room felt more like an overpriced hotel than a home. The pictures were pretty dire. The kitchen was awful. I felt a bit sorry for them, having to move in, but the kids seemed fine enough with it. I was beginning to work on the planning of the [US President Bill] Clinton visit, which clearly had to go well. I had the first formal heads of information meeting, which was not as successful as the drinks do. There was definitely a culture gap here. I said things that I felt were blindingly obvious, e.g. about planning of events coming up, and they didn't seem to get it. I said it was important to think about backdrops so that they helped communicate a message, or at the least did not provide a distraction, and you'd have thought I was asking the earth. I said the FCO [Foreign and Commonwealth Office] launch today at least looked like some thought and energy had gone into it but in opposition we used to be amazed at how amateur some of the government events looked. What was clear was that they had very little clout within departments. They looked a bit ground down. They were a pretty dull and uninspiring lot. They felt a bit bruised by some of the stuff in the papers at the weekend, but anyone would think they had been a great success story that we were trying to destroy.

Tuesday, May 13

Of all the press officers, Godric struck me as the most naturally gifted in the black arts. I didn't bother with an eleven o'clock, instead working on the speech for tomorrow, and ploughing through paper-work. TB called me round for a chat on his speech for the Queen's Speech debate. What did I think the theme should be? One Nation; the future; delivering what we promised; ran as New Labour, govern as New Labour. On the Tory leadership, he was happy for us to push the line that [Kenneth] Clarke [ex-Chancellor] was the one we feared, but in truth he thought he was the past, and too close politically to be able to offer a distinctive agenda. On balance he felt [William] Hague [ex-Welsh Secretary] was the one to want the least. [Michael] Howard [ex-Home Secretary] seemed to be dead in the water because Ann Widdecombe [ex-Home Office minister] was doing him in so heavily. He was waxing lyrical re the team he had brought in from outside, saying we were far better than most of the civil servants – 'And these are supposed to be the best.' His worry at the moment was devolution. He still felt there were too many unanswered questions, and he hadn't been impressed by the policy work done so far. Re GB he said he had a great intellect but he was hopeless at taking advice about himself. We went for a walk round the garden. He gave me a few thoughts for the speech which I went off and turned into passages.

Very funny piece of Peter M-ery today. I had done a strategic overview note for the Queen's Speech. DM and Peter Hyman [strategist and speech-writer] had done individual briefing notes on the various bills. Peter M took the lot, did a little introduction, stuck it on the front and sent the whole thing round to ministers as though he'd done it all. PH was affronted. I said life's too short. Who cares who wrote it? Blunkett threw a wobbly because he thought he was going to be on the *Today* programme but we put on GB. Alex Allan sent a note to Peter Hain's office with a clear bollocking re the vouchers business. I called Frank Field re a *Sun* page 1 story that looked like it came from him; which he denied. Fiona, Anji, Magi [Cleaver, press officer] and I met the Clinton visit pre-advance team. This was the team that would set up the visit before the real advance team came in. Talk about overmanning. There were about fifteen of them to our four. We agreed Clinton would go to Cabinet, and speak, and that we should have coverage of that. There would be a TB/BC lunch. They were also keen for what they called a 'fun event', but they were totally divided on what it should be. Someone suggested a big crowd in the street. I said it would look too much like TB after the election. The Foreign Office wanted a visit to the Globe theatre. Fiona said CB would be doing a separate programme when TB/BC were doing the talks etc. We went round in circles, and I sensed there would be lots of planning that came to nothing. But we had the main bits in place.

I had a meeting with Jonathan and John Holmes re the NI visit. John felt it was important we set the visit up as an act of reassurance to the Unionists, maybe TB say he didn't expect a united Ireland in our lifetime, but give the go-ahead for talks with Sinn Fein. I said, so we want the spin for the Unionists; the substance for the nationalists. I said come the day, the move to talks would be the bigger thing. He said the last government didn't do it because of the fear of the reaction, and because of their tiny majority, but we had a chance. He said this was a big step, and the spin operation would be very difficult. I said I would need to immerse myself in this. It was important we did the two main lines together and avoid any briefing before it was ready; and make sure it came from here. There was a reception for ministers, the traditional pre-QS drinks do. Neil [Kinnock, former Labour leader] was invited and I could tell he was a bit uncomfortable with it, because he was laughing over-loudly the whole time. TB was very nice about him in his little speech. He also did a little tribute to the

Civil Service. JP took me to one side and said he wanted to say thanks for all the help I'd given him in the campaign, which was nice of him, and also helping him since with his own profile. GB wanted a chat too and we went into TB's little den. He said he still feared Peter M was a menace. His latest thing was to go round saying he was in charge of chairing policy development. He said all he did was talk himself up at the expense of everyone else. 'I don't know how you put up with it.' He also thought Europe was a disaster waiting to happen, because the media were obsessed and we didn't have our own clear agenda on it. Tony Banks was upstairs, full of himself having kept his fingers crossed when he took the oath in the House. Widdecombe's big attack on Howard was the main news of the day. TB said we were doing well on the general tone of government – firm leadership, driving the agenda, populist touch.

Wednesday, May 14

Queen's Speech day. There was lots of toing and froing on the visit to Belfast on Friday. We were working on the speech to the last minute, as ever scrabbling round at the last for a few half-decent jokes. TB was thinking a lot about the Libs at the moment. He was due to see Paddy tomorrow to offer him a couple of seats on the Constitution committee but his instinct was to push it further. He said he wasn't sure what Paddy's endgame was, but he felt on instinct it was the right thing to do. He wanted to bind them into a position where they would back us on most of what we did. DD called me, said he felt he had a real problem with the press. He said his Civil Service people were hopeless. His own problem was that he was far too defensive with the media.

I put to TB the idea of walking to the House and the Special Branch said fine and planned it out. He and CB set off and we got terrific pictures out of it, very good mood in the crowds, and then to his new office in the House. How many times had I walked past the outer office, seen the secretaries and the security people hanging around, and wondered whether we would ever make it? Now we had. TB's new office was similar in style to the one down the corridor, but a bit grander, with a full Cabinet-sized table in there, bigger paintings and mirrors. Mark Adams had done a good job on the mechanics of the speech. TB and I had another chat re the Tories. His hunch had changed again – he now thought they would go for Clarke. He said he thought we had a really good first Queen's Speech. 'If we actually do this now, we will achieve a hell of a lot.' He went off, first to the Commons, then to the Lords, where they all watched the Queen deliver the speech. I watched on TV and I loved hearing her read out the more political bits we had added in: for the whole nation ... education the number one priority ... excess profits. She didn't look at all comfortable reading out the bit on banning handguns. [Michael] Brunson [ITN political editor] talked about her delivering her first New Labour sound bites. Little did he know.

The debate in the House was pretty flat. Major's heart wasn't in it, for fairly obvious reasons. I said to TB it all felt a bit flat and he said we should make that part of a new politics; steady delivery now on a programme of change. We went to Millbank Tower where TB and Tom Sawyer [Labour Party general secretary] did little speeches thanking them for their work in the campaign. It felt flat there too, because they didn't really know what they were for now, and we were going to have to find ways of keeping the party machine involved and motivated. We had a meeting in the Cabinet Room on Ireland – TB, Jonathan, John H, RB, AA and me. JH had done a draft and it was in tone very Unionist but I felt the offer of talks with Sinn Fein was sufficiently big and bold for that to be the main story out of it, and so it was OK. TB said he was sure we had only a brief window of opportunity and we had to take it. He said he intended to sleep on it before making a final decision to do it. He was seeing Paddy in the morning and he would speak to JM tomorrow night, and tell him he intended to get officials to talk to SF. He admitted that the effect of what we were proposing was that SF would get into talks without a ceasefire. It was hard to see how the Unionists would do anything other than go mad at that, which is why the tone had to be heavily weighted in their favour.

TB asked for a few beers to be brought in. He clearly liked JH and AA, but RB was clearly of another age. I spoke to Anji about setting up the visit without actually pressing the button. We really had to think about mood, tone, backdrop, pictures. My hunch was he was definitely going to do it and go for another bold move early on. RC called to get the go-ahead to do GCHQ tomorrow. Earlier, I bumped into Hezza [Michael Heseltine, ex-Deputy Prime Minister]. 'How are you and Powell getting on?' he said. Fine, I said. We'll see, he said. They were clearly going to try to get up the politicisation of the Civil Service charge.

Thursday, May 15

Our two big problems for the day would be Paddy A, and Ireland. TB squared JP, MB and RC pre-Cabinet that we should offer the Libs a couple of places on Cabinet committees. But then Jack Straw persuaded him that it would be better to offer a special general purposes committee. Derry, post-Cabinet, was of the view we should not do anything with them. We were doing a school visit in Brixton, so we set off at 8.45. I was with Moira Wallace [private secretary] who was pretty hoity-toity. We had quite a good laugh though. I asked her if she and her colleagues took any of the blame for the last government being so useless. On the *Today* programme, Iain Vallance [British Telecom chairman] said BT would mount a legal challenge against the windfall levy.[1] It was perfectly good news on one level but could become a bit of a mess. I asked GB as he arrived for Cabinet what we should say. 'The man's an idiot,' he barked, and walked on. TB had been urging him to consult properly but he hadn't. BAA [British Airports Authority] went for it later in the day too. TB did an all-purpose doorstep at the school, then back for Cabinet. Beforehand Ron Davies [Welsh Secretary] was bending my ear re his campaign on nursery vouchers. Blunkett was complaining about his office. Tim Allan was complaining at being frozen out and not having enough to do.

At Cabinet, TB said he was pleased at the way things were going, that people had settled in well. He said we had to keep an iron grip on public spending. GB started to say much the same thing. Clare's contribution to the debate was to say she would give up her car. JP was directly in my eyeline at the time and we rolled eyes, as did most people in the room. TB, knowing it would just put pressure on her colleagues, gave her a patronising little look and just said 'Er, keep the car.' Jack C gave a very gloomy assessment of the beef situation. He said the last lot's claim that the beef ban would be lifted by November was a total fraud. RC did a big spiel on GCHQ, ditto George [Robertson, Defence Secretary] on Zaire. TB briefed them, fairly elliptically it has to be said, on his plans for the Libs. He said he wanted to ease them out of knee-jerk opposition-itis. Jack S said they were terrible leakers and nothing we discussed would stay private. Ann Taylor [Leader of the Commons] said they not only leak, they leak inaccurately. TB said he would approach it all with immense care. The strategic objective was to get them, a couple of years down the track when we were established, as being more supportive. DD said, mysteriously, to a laugh, 'The dark forces will be at work.' I think he meant the press. On Ireland, Mo emphasised that TB would make the UUs [Ulster Unionists] feel secure. Magi Cleaver was meeting

[1] Sir Iain Vallance threatened to block any attempts to impose a windfall levy on excess profits of the privatised utilities, including BT.

trouble at the NIO [Northern Ireland Office], with Andy Wood [head of press] seemingly briefing already that it was on.

TB went through the demands on peers, PCs [privy councillors] etc. He explained his plan for a strategy committee. Ashdown was clearly keen. TB was worried that 1. on a real committee they would leak, and 2. they would eventually find something to disagree about, and walk out. This approach was meant to bind them in more closely. TB said he had been surprised at some of our people who had been fine about co-operation. Paddy said he intended to support the Queen's Speech and would say so on *On the Record* [BBC]. We then had another meeting on Ireland. I had written a few passages trying to distil the whole thing. TB was clear that if he was saying, basically, 'I am a Unionist,' then he had to do the other side. The feedback from the NIO on the draft was OK, up to a point. TB said he was aware of the objections but he instinctively felt he had a very brief window of opportunity, that the election was the only change in the landscape, and we had to do it now. He knew the talks would end up as the main thing out of it, and it was tricky without the ceasefire, but he felt it was a risk worth taking. He clearly liked John Holmes, who had a really good manner with him. He clearly knew the issue inside out, and was not afraid to say when he thought one or other of us was talking crap. He strikes me as a very good bloke, straight and trustworthy, and very clever. Having read the latest draft, TB looked up at him and said 'You're not the Master of the Grand Orange Order, are you?' JH said needs must. TB spoke to John Major who was supportive and said he would say so publicly. The US, the Irish and SF would also be supportive. The problem, despite the warm words, would be the Unionists.

I did the four o'clock and got a lot of questions about Tony Banks. He'd kept the fingers crossed, and he was now saying Eric Cantona and Gianfranco Zola [footballers] should be eligible for England. Later TB called me at home and said he was worried Banks was a bit of a loon and I had to speak to him. I did, said TB was worried he had made a mistake; that he had upset a few people by appointing him not Tom Pendry and he didn't want to be let down. He did not want a court jester, and it was better he got down to some hard graft and less publicity. He said the hard work was going on too but it would take some time to come through. BT and BAA was the main story by the end of the day.

Friday, May 16

I really enjoyed today, for all sorts of reasons. Northern Ireland was a big story, announcing government officials talking to SF without delivering a ceasefire. A bold move, full of risks which by and large we handled pretty well. We spent a lot of time getting the words right, the details of the visits; there was a lot of sophisticated spinning had to be done, and it paid off. The Northern Ireland Office had been far too gabby about the visit, but nobody had a sniff of the scale of what TB would say. Terry [Rayner, TB's driver] collected me at half six and I got in to hear the visit leading the news, but without much detail. I wrote a briefing note and Q&A based on the conversations with TB, JH and Jonathan. The difficult balancing act would be to reassure the Unionists while signalling a major change. Before we left, he spoke to Trimble and he was pretty candid with him, but he seemed OK-ish. In the car to Northolt, he spoke to Hume, who was fine. We got driven to the RAF plane, which was more comfortable than I expected, and the four of us went through the last-minute changes and the difficult questions. I was picking JH's brains in order to be sure I would be able to handle any question at a briefing. I was pretty clear that no matter how warm the words for the Unionists, there was only one story in it come the end of the day. We agreed TB would let his words speak for themselves, I would brief, Mo would do all the interviews.

We landed, then flew by helicopter to Armagh. TB met what Mo called 'the holies', namely the Protestant and Catholic top guys, then did a fantastic walkabout, really good mood, really friendly and warm. I called Denis Murray [BBC's Ireland correspondent] on his mobile just before the lunchtimes and briefed him fully on the speech. 'Bloody hell,' he said. He was impressed. He said it was a great story. I liked Denis, had always liked his reporting, and I felt I could trust him to put both parts of the equation. He did. The first reports were important, and they were word-perfect for us when I listened down the phone a bit later. TB felt buoyed up after the walkabout. He said those people are desperate for something good to happen. He did the troops, then back into the helicopters to head for the agriculture show where he was doing the speech. By now there was an enormous media presence to match the expectations. We were as happy as we were ever going to be with the text. I was a bit alarmed hearing Trimble's overwhelmingly enthusiastic response, so briefed Denis again, who emphasised at the end of the lunchtime bulletin that the big thing here was the offer of talks, and Mo would be writing to Gerry Adams [Sinn Fein]. Again, we were getting credit for being big and bold and ballsy.

TB did another walkabout on the way out. It was a very rural, very Ulster event, but he seemed to have a natural empathy. As he walked along shaking hands I told him Hume and Trimble had been fine,

Paisley very hostile. TB put his foot in an enormous cowpat but just carried on till we got to the car. None of the media seemed to have noticed. Bill Lloyd [protection officer] gave him a packet of tissues and I said what a glamorous life I led, sitting alongside the prime minister as he cleaned bullshit off his shoes. He was worried that the over-positive Trimble reaction would make SF hostile and unable to play along. Martin McGuinness [Sinn Fein] reacted with a very churlish response but did at least say they would enter the talks. TB was waxing lyrical about his team again. He said he was always amazed to learn how much we had to do behind the scenes to keep the show on the road. It had gone pretty much perfectly.

Anji and I were now trying to talk him out of going to Malmo [in Sweden] for a meeting with Kok and a few others because it would mean pulling out of the *Sun* police bravery awards. I said to him it was imperative we never lost sight of opportunities to stay in touch with real people, not just world leaders and politicians. The dangers of getting out of touch were all too apparent as we headed to Chequers, through beautiful scenery, up the long driveway, that unique sound of wheel on gravel. It was a lovely building but didn't feel very homely. TB and I chatted away as we waited for CB, FM and the kids to arrive. The food was terrific and one or two of the staff said it was nice having children around. We were taken upstairs and told we were sleeping in Winston Churchill's bed. TB said he was getting exasperated at GB's refusal to move into Number 10 after they had agreed he, CB and the kids would take the bigger flat in Number 11. We talked over the Clintons' visit and what we might do on the social/private front. TB was really on a bit of a high after the success of the Irish trip. Fiona said we would have to work really hard to keep our feet on the ground. Peter M was getting loads of publicity out of an interview he'd done with a psychiatrist, in which he started crying. The attention-seeking was becoming absurd. There were a few funny moments when we were driving to Chequers and tuned in to the 6pm news. Every time the newsreader said 'the government', 'the Home Secretary' or whatever, we were on tenterhooks as to what they were up to that was making news.

Saturday, May 17

I weighed myself – fifteen stone five. Bloody hell. It didn't stop me eating an enormous breakfast served up by the Wrens. The *Sun* had a poll saying we were the most popular government ever! Even the *Telegraph* praised the 'sure-footed' Ulster initiative. I went for a swim and was called out to take a call from Charlie Whelan. He said they had a Vallance letter dated May 2 which accepted we had a mandate and accepting they would be hit by the levy. GB, Charlie, and to a lesser extent I, were quite keen to leak it on condition it did not have our fingerprints on it. TB was against. He wanted Jonathan to speak to Vallance and put out something conciliatory. We played football with the kids, then TB and I went for a stroll. He was wearing his Newcastle shirt. He said he was clear what had to be done. Work on the pledges and see results quickly. A proper business strategy. Welfare reform – though he said he was worried that Frank Field was too much of a maverick. Get the welfare-to-work programme up. Get some results in Europe. Devolution. Bind in the Liberals. He suddenly said he thought PR [proportional representation] may be OK. What? He said you could maybe have eighty per cent first past the post and then PR for a hundred extra seats, bind in the Liberals for a generation, genuinely a new era in politics. It was amazing how he came up with new ideas just when I felt like I was running out of steam. I said do you really think that you can get both parties to go for it? Worth thinking about, he said.

He was worried about JP, felt that some of his policy stuff would end up as interfering nonsense. He was worried about Robin diddling around. He felt GB was coming into his own, though even now GB occasionally said to him that we could have got away with a higher top rate of tax. We sat out on the veranda, and went through the next stages, which sadly involved an awful lot of travel. He said we would have to go to Hong Kong [for handover to Chinese] even though it was a total humiliation. He said I had to keep an eye on making sure we kept setting our agenda, whatever the events around us. The most interesting stuff was when he came out with that on the Libs and PR. He clearly wanted to do something to help Paddy and he was confident it will work.

I got him to talk to Andy Grice [*Sunday Times*] on the way to the FA Cup Final [Chelsea beat Middlesbrough 2-0]. He said things were going well because we had thought about it, and we were driving an agenda, but that there would be very hard times ahead. We set off for the Cup Final, with a police escort through the crowds, which always embarrassed him but they didn't seem to mind. The match was dull though TB had a chance to talk to UEFA about the [2006] World Cup bid. Jarvis Astaire [sport and property entrepreneur] was very nice about the campaign. Ditto Dickie Attenborough [Lord Attenborough, actor and director]. As the players came up for their medals, TB was pretty much in shot, though holding himself back. But some of the players were clearly really pleased to see him. I met

Bob Ayling and Colin Marshall [British Airways chief executive and chairman] in the car park on the way out and Bob seemed thrilled that we had won. We got the Tube home, and I started to get calls about the *News of the World* splash – Mohammad Sarwar [Labour MP] allegedly trying to bribe another candidate. It was clearly the first serious sleaze test and we were going to have to pass it. I called TB who was pretty downcast about it. He said we had to try to turn it to our advantage but both he and GB then felt we should try to play it down. It would be hard. I could tell from the nature and volume of calls it was going to be big. Trying to play it down was not possible. It made the splash in other later editions. TB asked me to get Nick Brown to summon Sarwar down to see him tomorrow and it was fixed for 2pm at Number 12. David Hill was on the case, saying we would deal with it thoroughly and toughly if wrongdoing had taken place, but neither of us had much confidence in NB to deal with it.

Sunday, May 18

I was totally knackered and had a lie-in. Sarwar was the main story. First, Geoff Crawford [press secretary to the Queen] called to say that Simon Walters' [*Mail on Sunday*] story that the Queen was worried about TB's presidential style was total fiction. Sally spoke to DD and agreed that when Sarwar saw Nick Brown, it should be the aim to get the whip suspended pending a police inquiry. That was TB's view as well, and it was impressed upon Nick. TB was back from Chequers and feeling that this was a real pain, which it was. David Hill went in to see Nick. The press had heard about the meeting at Number 12 and it was important we got a grip on this straight away. Nick called me after the meeting, said his view was that he could not withdraw the whip. He'd also agreed that Sarwar should say that he too had asked for the procurator fiscal to report into this. Next PA [Press Association] ran a story giving the impression that no action was being taken and that the procurator inquiry was his idea. Donald called to agree a statement calling on the Crown Office to investigate. He also felt Nick had acted too softly. Nick disappeared straight after the meeting to go to Glyndebourne of all places. 'I like opera even though I don't know anything about it,' he said. Not a very good start.

DH called me to say that the press were not impressed. I called TB to say NB was fucking this up, and that the whole thing was going wrong for us. Both Sally and I tried to track down NB but he had disappeared for a while. Eventually we got the message to him to call TB at Michael Levy's. TB called me back and said this should not be a problem because 1. we have called in the police, 2. we got him straight down to see the chief whip, and 3. we are making it clear that if he has done wrong then he will be kicked out of the party. TB said the trouble was that Sarwar could see nothing wrong in any of this. But it was the lead story and I was getting too many calls saying we had not done enough about it, and that we were just the same as the Tories, which was a real problem. I had been deeply unimpressed by Nick, ponderous and pompous, and I could see none of the political nous he was supposed to have. We went round to Philip Gould's with the kids, from where I called all the papers to stress the lines TB had set. Siobhan Kenny called re a *World in Action* enquiry into arms dealing and a claim that TB promised a businessman dealing with Indonesia that he would continue to grant export licences. TB had no recollection of it at all. I had a long discussion with Siobhan about the need to modernise the Government Information Service [GIS] without making everyone feel they were useless.

Monday, May 19

DH had done a pretty good job on the [parliamentary press] gallery, and combined with the calls I made from Philip's, it wasn't as bad as it might have been. Most of the papers gave us the benefit of the doubt that we were dealing with it but TB was still angry with Nick Brown. He met him early on and told him that he and I had better judgement on how these things played out and he should have kept more closely in touch through the day. At the morning meeting, I quizzed Nick on whether Sarwar gave a proper explanation. Nick was very defensive, citing natural justice. I said to him that if there were fresh allegations conflicting with what he had been told, we had to have a contingency plan. I still felt, as did even Bruce, that we should have suspended the whip pending inquiry. GB was going to be big news tomorrow with his statement on the Bank of England and his CBI [Confederation of British Industry] speech. We agreed to bring forward the Martin Taylor [chief executive of Barclays bank, charged by GB with proposing tax and benefits reform] announcement to today. I met with TB, GB, Peter M, Jonathan and Charlie in the Cabinet Office re strategy. We had to press on the economy all week, leading up to Europe. We had to get back to Europe on Britain's terms. TB was now focusing on Friday, and said the [European] Council would be a big test for us. He intended to try to get up an agenda around competitiveness, the single market, CAP reform, flexible labour markets, enterprise. 'There is a lot right about Europe, and a lot that is wrong about Europe too.'

The BBC led on a Frank Dobson speech to the RCN [Royal College of Nursing] and a complete surprise, to us that is, his announcement that the ban on tobacco advertising would also include sports sponsorship. 1. this was a potentially bad story, and 2. there had been no real flagging up to us of it. Health said there was nothing new in it. I said news is what people decide is news, and anyone could have worked out this would have been seen as news. In any event, we should have known it was coming. We still needed to tighten up on internal co-ordination. The paperwork was really coming at me now. I could not believe how much there was to read. TB was seeing minor Irish party leaders. At the diary meeting, we emphasised to the FCO the need to keep down foreign visits. At the lobby, questioning was mainly Sarwar and Martin Taylor. TB was worried about Sarwar and also determined there should be more definition of the government. Dobson's stuff was a problem.

Tuesday, May 20

I stayed at home all day, the first day off in weeks. I slept in, had a bath, went for a massage. GB's statement on the Bank and SIB [Strategic Investment Board] reform was leading the news all day, and going fine, as was DB on shutting down bad schools.

Wednesday, May 21

First PMQs day. But first we had the NEC [National Executive Committee] re Sarwar. Yesterday went very well. GB's statement had gone well despite the usual lack of consultation. The morning meeting was brief. We went over Sarwar pre-NEC, and we agreed we had a potential big problem on this because the sense was we were no different and he was seeming to get away with it. Peter M wondered if we could not persuade him to stand aside. Donald and Nick were doubtful. Donald said he believed he was likely to be getting support from George Galloway [maverick Labour MP], who was well liked in the Pakistani community. TB said this was the one blot on the landscape at the moment. He wondered if we should not get proper legal advice, explaining that it could prejudice a trial if we were to take disciplinary action now. Sally was worried that would set a bad precedent. We agreed with TB he had to have very harsh words to say at the start of the NEC, to the effect that even if the police investigation did not lead to charges, there could still be disciplinary action up to and including loss of the whip.

Then a meeting on PMQs. TB went over the areas we needed lines on. He decided to do it without notes, though he had all the briefing from Mark Adams, which was working well. I felt quite nervous about it but TB was on good form. We left for the NEC where Greg Cook [Labour Party polling expert] did a polling presentation. TB said we must not lose sight of why we won – New Labour, good organisation, a united party, a clear message. He said the Tories would rebuild themselves, however long it took, and we had to remain united and disciplined, and always ahead of the game. No doubt we would have disagreements, but the tone of disagreement matters. The One Nation message was even more important given the size of the majority. Nobody should get drunk on power. We are here to serve. On Sarwar, he said we had set high standards and we have to maintain them in government. TB left the NEC early and it emerged later others wanted tougher action on Sarwar.[1] TB denied he was nervous pre-Questions. We left for the House. In the car on the way over, he was starting to go over some of the possible answers. He was more nervous now. He locked himself away in the office to write out answers on the tough questions, calling me in every now and then to try them out on me, then asking for help on sharpening lines. The civil servants told me Jonathan Haslam always said 'good luck' to Major as he went through to the chamber. I said my job was not to say 'good luck'. It was all of our jobs to make sure he didn't need it. It went fine in the end. If anything it was a bit of an anticlimax. Our lot were quite excited and there were maybe too many soft questions. The Tories' hearts weren't really in it. At the four o'clock briefing, they were all a bit disappointed.

I got back for a meeting with the next Clinton advance team. It was hard to make progress because Clinton had apparently said he wanted to go shopping, eating and didn't know whether he wanted to make a speech or not. They're all very nice, but very vague and didn't really know what they wanted. They thought Clinton wanted to go for an Indian meal. Then to a meeting with Peter, Jonathan, John Holmes, Brian Bender [head of European Secretariat, Cabinet Office] on Europe and our plan for the EU leaders' summit in Noordwijk. I was keen on the big-picture messages. Europe was a total minefield, and I was concerned to make sure it was not the one that blew me up. I had been reading as much as I could to get on top of the detail, but it was really complicated. I wanted to get the line 'Europe on Britain's terms'. They were not confident that would work. We were still completely dominating the news. Ban on landmines leading. Jack Straw speech

[1] Sarwar was subsequently charged with election offences but acquitted in 1999.

on youth crime, Northern Ireland talks between SF and NIO were under way, the first PMQs. Maybe there was too much but we had to keep the momentum going.

Thursday, May 22

The honeymoon was still going on, with the press overwhelmingly favourable again. But the *Mail*, probably wound up by Ed Balls, splashed on GB vs Eddie George. The *Telegraph*, probably briefed by Peter M (which he denied), led on flexible labour markets. I got in early to work up a briefing note on Europe, which with the summit tomorrow was my current nightmare. I went through it with John Holmes, who made one or two changes, but it was basically fine. I got RC to agree it, though he clearly felt it was too UK-centric. Cabinet was mainly Europe, Ireland and discussion of draft bills. TB gave them another little lecture about co-ordination. RC said we were making progress on border controls and said he was confident of the deal we would get. He said we had legal authority for retaining border controls and so achieving something the Tories never had. Defence was the other tricky area, with the French-Germans pushing for something that we would regard as undermining NATO. He said the smaller countries were on our side. TB said there were all sorts of areas for greater co-operation but we should not roll over and have our tummies tickled. On spending, he said he did not want a great outbreak of departmentalitis. Then we had a meeting with RC re Noordwijk. I then did a briefing with Nigel Sheinwald [Foreign Office press secretary] and Paul Lever [FCO official]. There was a huge turnout and a lot of interest in what approach TB was intending to take. I was emphasising a more co-operative approach, but also saying we would argue for Europe on Britain's terms. Yes to more QMV[1] in certain areas, but border controls sacrosanct.

Then a strategy meeting, TB, GB, Peter M, PG, Jonathan, CW. GB was going over some of the approach re the Budget but was clearly holding a fair bit back. He stressed fiscal tightening but when pushed on tax would not be drawn. He wanted to focus on welfare reform, and savings that way. He said public spending was going to be a real battle because they all thought they would get more than they would, and we wanted to focus any extra spending on health and

[1] Qualified majority voting. Each member state has a fixed number of votes. The number allocated to each country is roughly determined by its population, though favouring smaller countries.

May '97: TB sets out approach to Europe

education. We had to do more to get over the economic problems we had inherited – inflation back in the system, interest rates too high. I said the Tories never let us forget the bad side of our record and we should now do the same to them. We agreed July 2 was probably the best date for the Budget because there were so many foreign trips coming up. GB was on good form but TB was not happy at the Eddie George rumblings. Also Margaret Thatcher had said GB was arrogant. We had a meeting of the Big Four. They had come from a Cabinet committee meeting on Bosnia where Clare had apparently said to the defence chiefs that our policy was 'shameful', and she spoke for the PLP. JP said she was bonkers. Big Four was mainly about public spending and the need to bear down on it. GB said departments were just putting in ever bigger demands for more money in a very old-fashioned way. He said there were big savings to be made on fraud, loopholes etc., but we still had a problem. RC said we had to be wary of a winter crisis. I was unconvinced the Big Four forum would last in government.

Then I got back for the end of TB's meeting with Thatcher. Nobody saw her go in though there were people – e.g. GB – who saw her inside the building. I doubted it would stay quiet. I had real doubts about the need for it but he was adamant it made sense to involve her, make her feel her advice was valued. She struck me as a bit unhinged, over-hamming it all a bit, reminiscing loudly. Then the two of them went off for a session on their own, where he picked her brains on foreign affairs. He said afterwards she was still very sharp, though sometimes her determination to make a point got in the way of a broader understanding. I went in at the end to move him on for the next meeting and she was in full flow, warning him to keep an eye on the Foreign Office, saying Germany will follow if TB gives a real lead. The French cannot be trusted, and the Italians make nice clothes. Then a long lecture on single parents, illegitimacy etc. They were sitting on the sofas in the Green Room and she was complaining at the way loose threads were hanging off. To be fair, they did look a bit shabby. She told him he should do lots of receptions for the voluntary sector, then paused as if she was about to make a huge point, looked him in the eye and said 'And don't forget to invite the Lord-Lieutenants.' We agreed that if we had press enquiries we should simply say he wanted to talk to her re foreign affairs. 'Quite so,' she said, and off she went.

'God, she is so strong,' he said as she went. I was more struck by how obvious it was that she missed the place. Her reminiscences had been less about the big things than the little routines that she got into. There was a group of party people waiting to see TB and their eyes almost dropped out when they saw her walking past the Cabinet Room with TB. Alison [Blackshaw] was getting more into the swing of things and I was warming to her. She was desperate to be helpful but had never really met people like us before. 'I really think you should have a proper briefcase rather than that old bag,' she said. I agreed and she took great delight in showing me how to set the lock, etc. David English called re Vere Rothermere coming out for Labour. I asked David if VR would ever think about sitting as a Labour peer.

I took home a stack of reading on Europe, ready for tomorrow's 6am start. I'd never got nervous about a briefing before but I was slightly dreading the first one at a European summit. I could remember from my hack days what a bastard they were.

Friday, May 23

TB's main worry when I went to the flat, just before 7, was the Eddie George situation. Thatcher had said to TB she thought GB was arrogant and insensitive, that you could not treat a Bank Governor with anything but respect and that was not coming over. TB asked me to speak to Charlie W and get some support for George in the papers. I had to rush him out to set off to Heathrow for Holland. TB sat reading his papers, getting briefed and trying to work out a proper strategy on border controls, saying that that was the one we had to win. But basically today was as much about tone and demeanour. There is no doubt TB was the big story. I wrote a couple of sound bites on the plane, new era, new Europe type of thing, focusing less on ourselves and institutions, more on people and their concerns. Robin, according to Jonathan, had sacked his diary secretary for Gaynor [Regan, his eventual wife], which could be a real problem. RC was clearly on top of the detail, and was trying to get TB to be a little less sceptical. I sensed that Robin was going native very quickly. We got plenty done on the plane out, arrived, did a doorstep, and then TB began a series of bilaterals. First Santer and Prodi [Jacques Santer, European Commission president; Romano Prodi, Prime Minister of Italy]. Prodi was still sulking over Robin saying that Britain will be part of the big three with Germany and France. I mean literally sulking. He came round eventually and when TB asked him if he could ask about something specific, Prodi says 'Yes, even my sexual habits.' Weird. I split off after a while to brief some of the hacks.

TB went into lunch and both Kohl and Chirac [Helmut Kohl,

Chancellor of Germany; Jacques Chirac, President of France] went straight up to him, whilst others queued to have pictures taken with him. The body language was fascinating. Kohl was enormous and yet I sensed he was a bit nervous of TB, keen to get him onside. Chirac was effusively over the top. He stretched his arms out, gave him a warm welcome and launched into a great thing about how important he now was to Europe. Nigel Sheinwald and I went down to the briefing, which was absolutely heaving, hundreds of people. The venue was clearly not going to be big enough for TB's press conference later, so we set about trying to get it changed. The Dutch agreed we could use the presidency briefing room. The briefing went fine. I was pushing the main lines, sidestepping questions about whether we would compromise on immigration, hitting hard on flexible labour markets. There were a number of very attractive woman in there, which made it very different to the lobby. I went back to TB after lunch. He said he had enjoyed it so far. He got the impression they were desperate for new leadership in Europe. This theme developed as the day wore on. He said Kohl was impressive but very broad-brush and did not seem at all interested in detail. He said Chirac was all over the shop, and had made a series of ludicrous points, all delivered as though they were great revelations. Robin warned me 'he's enjoying it'.

The rules of the Council were that only two, the head of state or government, and the foreign minister, could go in and we could only take in messages. It was quite hard to follow what was going on in there. They spoke. People listening in took notes which were then faxed up to the delegation rooms. A ridiculous way to work. TB came out at 6.30. We walked straight to the press conference. We had agreed he would do without notes and just make very short remarks, and then take questions. The questions were reasonably easy, he did the necessary clips that would get used on the news. There were two bad moments, though, which revealed cockiness I didn't like. First, Tony Bevins asked how the other leaders had reacted and TB said 'A bit like the British electorate.' He got away with it but I hated it. Then an Italian journalist, clearly planted so TB could say something nice about Prodi, asked what he thought of the day and TB said that if he was told to stay on for another twenty-four hours he would not be too happy. In another time, this would be a bad scene, 'Blair bored after six hours', but the honeymoon was still on. Otherwise it was OK. I gave him a real monstering and on the way back I said he got in there with the big boys and they were taking him seriously, quite rightly, but that was no reason to get all cocky. He agreed, said he didn't quite know why he said what he did, and promised not to do it again.

He went into the dinner, so I went back to the press centre to push hard the line that he had been able to stamp himself on proceedings straight away. They were all going pretty much on new Europe, and there was no real downside to the coverage. There was clearly a way to go though, and the hard stuff would come at Amsterdam. I had a run-in with Santer's spokesman who had briefed TB's words, as if verbatim, but inaccurately. I didn't take to a lot of these Euro people. Earlier, at the family photo, TB held back a bit but Kohl made sure he came forward to the front. Kohl came across as being the main man, not Chirac. I had a nice friendly chat with Dick Spring [Irish minister for foreign affairs], who told me it was obvious I was important to 'yer man' and it was really important I got proper rest. On the flight back, TB was going over a strategy for Amsterdam. He sat down with a Scotch, a pad and pen and just scribbled out the various areas – borders, CFSP [Common Foreign and Security Policy], flexibility in the employment chapter, EU/WEU [Western European Union, defence organisation set up in 1954] merger, single market, fishing, and then drew out detailed stuff on each. He believed that we could get a deal to keep border controls. He was straight into the language, pillar three this, 3bis pillar that, QMV, reweighting, blah. He loved this stuff, the harder the better in a way. He said he been less impressed by Kohl and Chirac than he thought he would be. RC came up with the idea of 'Six gains in six weeks of a Labour government, six things the Tories could not get' for Amsterdam. Earlier I spoke to Trevor Kavanagh [political editor, *Sun*] who said, like so many others no doubt, he was amazed at how easily people had taken to the existence of a Labour government.

Saturday, May 24

TB was worried there was too much cockiness in the press, admitting it was his fault. We decided not to do the story of the Thatcher meeting but someone, possibly Peter M, gave it to the *Sunday Times*, and someone else, possibly Charlie, as GB knew about it, gave it to Tom Baldwin [*Times*]. GB had mentioned in a Cabinet committee meeting on Thursday that he had seen Thatcher in Number 10. Andy Grice also had the story that Clinton was to address the Cabinet. Frank Dobson called, worried about Simon Walters chasing a story that Peter M and I were pissed off that he had gone off-message on tobacco advertising. It suggested someone was briefing out of the morning meetings.

May '97: Kohl more 'main man' than Chirac

Sunday, May 25

It was my birthday, and I got really nice letters from both Mum and Dad, with a cheque, saying how proud they were at what I'd done in helping win the election. I really must get up to see them soon. I'd been anxious throughout the campaign about Dad, and would never forgive myself if he suddenly died and I had not been up there enough. It was a fairly quiet day, though the Thatcher meeting went even bigger than I thought it would, leading the bulletins most of the day. I got a lovely call from Jim Callaghan, saying he would like to help and we fixed for him to do *The World This Weekend*, saying it was very sensible of TB to see her. TB called, worried I had stuck the Thatcher story in the paper, which I hadn't. I was pretty sure Peter had put the Clinton/Cabinet story to Grice and once he realised the *Sunday Telegraph* had the Thatcher story, he gave that to Andy Grice as well. He was talking to the press far too much and was getting on my nerves again. TB was still thinking away re the European agenda and worrying about how we would get a deal in Amsterdam that would be a clear-cut success. He was at Chequers having a couple of quiet days before we headed for Paris.

Monday, May 26

NATO summit. There was lots of Thatcher follow-up and an odd *Telegraph* splash about the Labour Party press office taking precedence over the government media machine. I got David Hill to write a letter rebutting it. The car to take me to Northolt was due at 2, but it didn't arrive and Fiona had to drive me to Northolt. The FCO team was already there, waiting to collect RC at Teesside. TB arrived looking tanned after a couple of days in the sun at Chequers, and began working on the little NATO speech he had to make tomorrow. He would have to sit there for hours listening to all the others and he would be last. He was due to sit next to Clinton, so at least we could get some work done on the visit. We worked on the speech on the plane, trying to put in some emotion and personality. We arrived in Paris and were driven to the embassy. Up the steps where Thatcher did her dramatic 'I'm staying' and out into the garden with [Sir] Michael Jay [UK ambassador]. The garden was absolutely stunning, and there were butlers on hand doling out champagne. Dinner, TB, Jay, AC, Jonathan, John Holmes. Michael Jay was friendlier and more intelligent than in my dealings with him as a hack.

The main focus for discussions re Amsterdam was how to make Europe relevant to people. I suggested we publish something about the ten things we wanted to win in Amsterdam and explain their relevance in advance. We had to reconnect on Europe. Europe was distant and people did not feel we got anything out of it. TB said he did actually believe in integration but you could not say that. He believes in Europe because 1. greater prosperity through free trade, 2. it helped keep peace, 3. the world was breaking down into blocs and we had to be in one. We could not just stand alone, a glorified Norway. He said he'd pressed Thatcher on the alternative and she could not say. It was basically Norway. Jay said Europe did feel remote. It was a game being played. JH said yes, but it was a serious game. TB said that between now and the summer only three things mattered: Europe, the Budget and definition. He was keen to see as many leaders as possible if it helped get us what we wanted. He said he understood why they wanted common borders but we had to win on that. He was also determined to get support for NATO in there. He suggested a Royal Commission on organised crime with European ramifications. I said be wary of Royal Commissions. The general feeling was that only if you are clear about a desire for greater integration can you begin to drive the European agenda. We had a meeting then with our ambassador to NATO, John Goulden, and FCO experts, then joined by RC, to go through tough questions for tomorrow. Later TB and I had a chat in his bedroom and he said don't worry, I'm very well aware of the dangers in this job – lost contact between feet and ground. I said I would make it part of my job to stop it happening.

Tuesday, May 27

I didn't sleep at all well, and went down for breakfast just after 6, soon afterwards joined by TB. The first big thing of the day was the bilateral with Boris Yeltsin [President of Russia] at the Russian ambassador's residence. I took an instant liking to him. He was all the things you expected – big, a bit clumsy, a bit gauche, larger than life – but a few things I hadn't expected – witty, very warm, tactile and sensitive to mood and moment. We had been warned he would be very vague on detail but that wasn't the case at all. He started the meeting by saying he was pleased TB had won the election, which was a good start. He said 'My heart is open to you,' that he wanted to have friendly relations, that Europe was stronger if Britain and Russia were together. TB praised Yeltsin's transformation of Russia, and said that as one of the youngest PMs on the scene, he looked up to him. 'Not one of the youngest,' barked Boris, 'THE youngest.' We were served up with blinis and caviar and great mounds of salmon. 'Eat,' he said, something he did with difficulty. I noticed he had a finger missing. On trade, he said he had brought in new people, Anatoly Chubais and

Boris Nemtsov [pro-capitalist reformers and supporters of Yeltsin]. TB said he admired the appointments and the manner in which they were made. 'Fast,' said Yeltsin. They joked about sacking Robin. 'Your foreign minister is excellent – so let him work.' They spent a lot of time on NATO-Russia and Yeltsin asked if he favoured him going to Madrid, which TB did. Chirac supported it too, said Yeltsin. He said he would talk to Clinton and do some hard thinking. He asked TB to visit Moscow, then asked for support in moving from G7 to G8. Then they agreed to a joint agreement on dealing with organised crime. RC said he and Jack Straw would meet opposite numbers. Boris suddenly looked at TB and said 'You have good eyes, very bright. That says a bright mind. You are the right age. I think Great Britain is in good hands.' TB tried to steer it to economic reform but Boris was back on the personal – talking about his grandson at Millfield [School]. TB said he played tennis near there. Yeltsin said he would get fit and challenge him. 'I used to beat other leaders.' He could not have been warmer or more friendly and they genuinely seemed to hit it off.

I briefed on NATO, trade, crime agreement, tennis/personal stuff and said TB would be accepting the visit invite. TB headed to the Elysée in a not very big Citroën, the Roller apparently having broken down. The event itself was a series of sixteen speeches which tended to say much the same thing. TB and I had written his on the plane out and though there was an inevitable platitude count, his was easily one of the best, and he delivered it well. Bill C gave him a big thumbs up when he finished. But Yeltsin stole the show by saying he was removing warheads from weapons aimed at NATO countries, something he had hinted at in the breakfast. Anne Edwards [White House staff] was there and the Yanks seemed to be in chaos about what they actually wanted him to do on the UK visit. I told him at one point that his advance team had said he wanted to go to an Indian restaurant and he said that was bullshit; nobody had asked him, and he didn't. He just wanted to hang out. At the family photo, TB was supposed to be in the front row next to Clinton, but when it came to it he was at the end of the second row. Magi Cleaver discovered that it was Chirac who had insisted on the move, seemingly reckoning that the right having suffered heavy parliamentary election losses yesterday, and [Alain] Juppé [French Prime Minister] having been forced to resign, there was no point in drawing attention to successful left-of-centre party leaders.

TB said the leaders' lunch was an extraordinary event. 'If people had seen it, they would be terrified these people were running the world.' At one point Clinton, clearly in jest (or so TB thought), said to Yeltsin that he would get on with Ian Paisley and it would be a good idea if they met. Yeltsin appeared to take it seriously and twice asked TB when he wanted him to go. He said a lot of drink was taken, not just by Boris, and that Chirac could not stop making grand little speeches. Clinton told TB that Kohl said he saw TB as his natural successor as the main leader in Europe. Boris and Bill were all over him for the time I saw them together. Chirac was looking a bit unsettled, probably by the elections, but I don't think he much liked having TB as the centre of attention among the big guys.

A rather irritating Dutch official did most of the talking in the hour-long meeting with Kok, and TB had to say, look, he just could not live with what they were proposing. They were being obstinate and so were we but he wanted them to understand that we concede in some areas but not re border controls. This was going to be diffi-cult. They felt that one Europe, with one border, and everyone inside it, was central to what they wanted to achieve. It was a matter of pride almost. TB also stressed they were being too ambitious on defence and foreign policy. TB and Kok got on fine. Kok was a straight talker and it was a tough meeting but they understood each other better at the end. At one point, as we discussed the media, TB said of me to Kok 'He's worth his weight in gold,' to which I replied 'In which case I look forward to being paid.' On the plane home I started to draft a note – ten reasons we had to win at Amsterdam. Earlier Jonathan said TB had said he felt he (Jonathan) and I needed to show him more respect in front of other officials. Feet and ground, I wondered.

Wednesday, May 28

Though Yeltsin was the main show in the broadsheets, TB got a great press out of yesterday. The media could sense the impact he was making at these foreign affairs gatherings and it was coming through. God knows how long the honeymoon can last, but it is definitely still going on. I discovered I was not being paid. Jonathan said nor was he, and that Butler was complaining about the cost of SpAds [special advisers]. Donald D came around with Murray Elder [special adviser], Pat [McFadden, special adviser] and Jonathan and said he had to get rid of the press person he had, and get someone good. Even though DD was not a natural at modern media management, it was clear they were not giving him basic support and were refusing to do things that they had no grounds to refuse.

TB called a meeting on BSE, felt he should go to Brussels himself and put together a new strategy for dealing with it. He wanted to do it in a fairly low-profile way which I said was unrealistic. Alex Allan and Angus Lapsley [private secretary, home affairs] basically wanted him to forget BSE but given the issue we had made it in opposition, that was not realistic either. Various Americans were in during the day and they were becoming a real pain. They all spoke as if they had the absolute authority of the president but he himself had exposed the bullshit factor. I wondered how often some of them met him, if indeed they did. They were obsessing about what they called his 'fun time with the Blairs', but also now wanted a 'romantic interlude' for Bill and Hillary [Clinton], doubtless because the Paula Jones sexual harassment case was back in the headlines.[1] I did a Clinton visit briefing, which was OK, but we were going to end up with 'The Bill and Tony show' whether we liked it or not. TB was keen to use it for definition, a sense of new politics, and above all a progressive new politics, that the ideas of the left of centre were the most relevant for today. GB had worked up a G7 initiative and was pressing hard for a meeting with BC. I was working on TB's words for the Clinton press conference, which he really wanted to fly. I was also dealing with [Culture Secretary] Chris Smith's joke response to the massive pay rises for Camelot [National Lottery company] directors. I said he should call them in and express real outrage.

Thursday, May 29

The Clinton visit was well set up, with papers and broadcasts pretty much set according to the overnight briefing. I got in early to work on TB press conference words, when Cherie called and said André [Suard, CB's hairdresser] was there and I should go up and get a haircut. TB was in the bath but came through and we went over what we wanted to get out of today. As ever he was keen to get a phrase that summed it all up. I quite liked 'new generation politics' because it suggested the generation was not so much about age as about a change in politics. In truth, we were getting such a good press at the moment that the Americans stood to gain far more than we did, especially as Bill C was being done in by the Paula Jones sexual harassment case again. TB wanted it to be a day of definition so we went through the various areas where we could say a new politics was being forged, neither old left nor new right, and once I'd had my hair cut I went down and worked on a whole stack of lines beginning

[1] Jones, a former Arkansas civil servant, filed a sexual harassment case against Clinton in 1994.

'This is the generation which . . .'. It was OK if a bit heavy on the cliché front, but as a device it could carry a fair number of strong policy messages on jobs, growth, inclusion.

TB put Cabinet back to 10.45 because he wanted some more time to think through the tricky questions they might get at the press conference. But we had little to worry about. The press basically wanted it to go well. The weather was terrific so my idea of an open-air press conference in the garden was on. The lecterns were a bit second rate and shabby so we got two better ones sent down from the US Embassy. Cabinet was incredibly brief, and barely anyone but TB spoke. RC wasn't there so TB just ran through a few of the foreign policy issues, briefed on Europe, NATO etc. and then said he was well aware there was someone else due to speak to them today and they were probably impatient for that. They were. There was a real sense of anticipation at the idea of Clinton speaking to the Cabinet in the Cabinet Room. We waited for him to arrive and got word he was a few minutes away. Cherie came down, looking great. She was on good form at the moment and had got a good press in the run-up, largely because of comparisons with Hillary. Fiona had to get a lot of the credit for the advice and for the outcome in the press. TB was nervous, fussing about tiny details, like where on the step to stand when he arrived, should he kiss Hillary – we decided not – whether he and BC should stand in the middle or put the wives in the middle. He was talking very quickly, a sure sign of nerves. I had a brief chat with JP re the choreography for Cabinet, and we agreed they should applaud but stay seated. Then the car pulled up. It was a lovely sunny day, there were hundreds of photographers there and the mood between them was great. The pictures went straight on to the front of the *Standard* – 'Best of pals' – which BC loved when he saw it and later he asked if he could get a copy. By then we were at Le Pont de la Tour restaurant and Hilary Coffman had to go and buy one from a punter for ten quid!

TB's kids had come down to say hello just inside the door and he chatted to them as the rest of the American party piled in. There were too many of them and it was a bit crowded and hard to manage. BC's operation was overmanned and there were too many people claiming to have his ear who didn't. We had had the nonsense about the Indian. Now we were reliably informed he wanted the four of them to go to a pub. Anji had even got Jon Mendelsohn and Ben Lucas [Labour staff] to stay in the Anchor Tap pub literally all day, and when TB mentioned it to BC, just as when we had mentioned the Indian, he looked at us like we were mad. He sparkled at the Cabinet. 'I'm so

May '97: TB's nerves as Clinton arrives

thrilled to be here. It is very exciting for an American president to be in this room.' He spotted Mo and said he had seen her speeches on TV, and you could see her melt. He said he had read the policy handbook and went into the mantra – many not the few, future not the past, leadership not drift, education the number one priority. I said to him afterwards I wish our own people could express it as fluently. His main point was that we had faced up to change, been professional, seized the future. We could show the world that it was possible to have an advanced economy and a humane society. Upstairs, GB muscled in for a few minutes to talk about the G7 jobs idea. I liked Clinton. He had a great sense of humour, was clever, very political in almost everything he said and did. He was a master of the pause in public speaking. I'd noticed that watching him on TV but it was even more powerful in meetings. He could hold a room with a pause and a nod, and so control events. He had enormous, beautifully manicured hands and he used these too to powerful communications effect. TB was very nice about me in public again. I don't know whether this was just flattery or whether it was a way of sending a signal to the Civil Service machine. He said to BC that I was 'something of a political legend', who scared our opponents.

The main bilateral was in the White Room. As they settled down to talk TB said he wanted no officials in there at all for the first bit, so I went to the street to brief for the lunchtimes. They stayed in there together for ages, mainly doing Bosnia, Ireland and politics. BC showed he knew a fair bit about the UK political scene. He asked about the Hamiltons [Tory MP Neil and his wife Christine], and sleaze generally. He wanted to know about our PMQs reforms and whether we had got opposition to it. On the foreign affairs issues, he had a really detailed command of the arguments, e.g. on NATO expansion, and who should come in, he would summarise other countries' views then explain his own. They did Iran, EU defence, Iraq/MEPP [Middle East peace process]. They had a longish session on Hong Kong, where BC was fascinated by the politics of it all. He said the Chinese would try to be seen to be honouring the two-systems approach whilst squeezing it their way as much as they could. He said change will only come if we are able to shape their psychology like we did the Russians. TB said we felt a deep sense of obligation to the people there and had to make it work. BC said he would 'stick with you on this because we have a big dog in the sun.' I presume he meant China. On EMU, BC was keen to get TB's analysis, and what he said was on the sceptic end of the market. Said he was not against in principle but felt some of them were being over-romantic about the whole thing. BC said he had sidestepped all questions on it so far.

After the lunch TB and I went to the den to prepare for the press conference while BC etc. went back to the White Room. TB didn't want anyone in the room but the two of us. We had agreed the script and now were going over tricky questions. Bundesbank – row with Germans over Maastricht conditions; Lottery, after the pay-rise headlines. But in the end, maybe because of the sun shining, the press were fairly soporific and the questions were fairly easy to deal with. The mood was great. BC came down to see us ten minutes before we were due out, and we had a real laugh about the prospect of the whole thing being taken over by Paula Jones questions. He was able to laugh at himself, which was always a good sign. We had hoped Hillary and CB would join them at the end but they were yacking away in the Cabinet Room and didn't want to stop. So after eight or ten rounds of questions, which anyway were becoming a bit repetitive, we wound it up. We waited a few minutes for the snappers to get back into the street and then they went off to the residence. It had gone as well as anyone could have hoped, on the personal chemistry front as much as on substance and policy. Afterwards I said to TB I was surprised how formal it was at times, Mr President, Mr Prime Minister. He said if it had been any less formal, it would have seemed gimmicky. But at both the meetings and the press conference he felt there were times when what they said was interchangeable. He really felt he was someone on his wavelength. Jobs, welfare, education, citizenship, that whole agenda he felt was shared by a kindred spirit.

We left for Le Pont de la Tour at 6.15, having finally cancelled the pub plan. A small crowd had gathered because word had got out. I wanted good clean shots out of it and my experience of the way the US pools fucked up pictures led me to get Mike McCurry [BC's press secretary] to buy into us doing one outside their system. I tipped off one TV crew and three stills to be there and called them in one by one, with the agreement their stuff went everywhere. BC noticed it was not a full pool and asked what was going on. When I explained he said to TB 'This man's worse than McCurry.' TB said 'He's mad, bad and dangerous but he's mine so it's fine by me.' BC said he felt the whole visit had been handled well and he was grateful. Hillary said she had really enjoyed meeting Fiona. 'She is quality,' she said. I then left them, joined some of his people further down the restaurant and they embarked on what quickly became known as the dinner that doesn't end. I interrupted them when we got a front-page proof from the *Sun* sent through which had the restaurant picture splashed

May '97: TB and Clinton 'interchangeable' on policy

all over the paper. He said he was impressed we got the papers before the public. TB said afterwards that Hillary was more into strategy than he had expected. BC was much more political. They went out at one point for a little walk down towards the bridge and a whole lot of people gathered at the windows of the yuppie flats, waving and cheering. BC said these are your people and you must make sure they stay bound in. He also advised him to get out and about with real people at least once a week, because it would stand him in good stead when the harder times came. TB called after BC and HC had left and he was on his way back to Chequers. He felt today had been really important, and a great success whichever way you looked at it. BC had said to him that he – TB – would be the real leader of the left in many ways because he [BC] could not win again; he would be history by the time of the next election in 2000. TB said he [BC] had blazed the trail and now they had to set a new agenda for the left and centre left that made progressive politics dominant in the way conservative politics had been. I also felt we had shown them a thing or two about media management and I was more convinced than ever that it can only work if you are clear you are working for the politician, not for the press.

Friday, May 30

The papers were terrific. I joked to TB that his press was so good it can only be a matter of time before we read Peter M planned it all from his holiday in Italy. Even the massive restaurant bill was not seen as an enormous problem. The truth was we had planned it well, executed it well, and that was that. TB was at Chequers, and said he wanted to build on this. I said I was on the lookout for 'world-stage-itis'. I was working on a script for the Sunday lobby on welfare reform, with his welfare-to-work speech on Monday. Butler called and asked me to see him. We sat down in the big chairs over by the fireplace. It was about the Scottish Office situation [Civil Service media staff feeling they were being required to do work that was political]. I said I felt things were going reasonably well; that we had bent over backwards to avoid any semblance of political pressure; and that there had been some good feedback to some of the changes. But some of them were using the politicisation argument to avoid doing a proper professional job. He said he felt, judging from the permanent secretaries, that things were going pretty well. He said he was worried about the Treasury, where GB did not much talk to officials, and lesser versions in other departments, but by and large it was OK. I felt Butler was reasonably friendly but Jonathan was pretty sure he would have been at least in part responsible for some of the stirring in the press against us. I had a good meeting with Mike Granatt [head of Government Information Service (GIS) and Home Office press] who went through who he thought was good and who not. He said Downing Street had been more open in the last few weeks than any time for decades and people appreciated that. 'The good people are rolling with it and the bad ones are a pain in the arse,' he said.

Then Frank Field came to see me, clearly keen to hype up plans for a Green Paper. I advised against raising expectations too high and felt until proper policy work had been done, it was better he make speeches setting out analysis rather than promising solutions straight away. I found my initial concerns about Frank hardening as we spoke. It was very much about him, and his place in the firmament. I don't doubt he knows a lot but there is something creepy about the way he puts his case, as if he is the only person with the wisdom. TB was working on his speech for Monday and keen to get it up on values rather than policy mechanics. He shared Jonathan's suspicions re Butler and stuff in the press. I had another desk-clearing session and got home reasonably early. Fiona was getting a bit anxious about us being strapped for cash but I assumed the pay thing would get sorted.

Saturday, May 31

Tim was looking after the Sundays and was fairly confident they were not going too hard on the 'single parents to lose benefits' line after my briefing. However, the *Observer* splashed on it, which was a real pain. I complained at length to them when I saw how big they'd done it, and how they had flammed it up. The other broadsheets did it pretty big too. Black Dog [*Mail on Sunday* column] had a fictitious piece of crap about me writing to civil servants saying their jobs were safe for now. The *Sunday Times* diary had a story that Peter M had the idea of the garden press conference and the restaurant. TB said he had dealt with a lot of different pressures during the campaign and he was probably still working that all through.

Sunday, June 1

TB called early, saying he did not like the *Mail on Sunday*'s story that the Queen was not happy about lack of consultation over the Clinton visit. I said they were going to do this kind of thing the whole time. He said he wanted it dealt with. Geoff Crawford was a great help, privately in saying I could assure him on her behalf it was nonsense; and publicly by killing it early. I was busy on the phone all day trying to get the welfare speech back on track, but it was hard. The broad-

May '97: AC unconvinced by Frank Field on welfare

casters could not be budged off the single-parent tack now it had been in the papers. TB had Pat McFadden and Angus Lapsley down to Chequers to go over the devolution plans in real detail. He said he was determined to get it right, and he was not happy with the work he had seen on this so far and he was determined to put it right. It included cutting the number of MPs and a whole series of changes that would make the two-question referendum look like a tea party.

Monday, June 2

We got TB's welfare speech in a better place, much more focused on general message. He had barely looked at the speech, and was beginning to have doubts about the quality. I felt the basic message was fine. The *Mail on Sunday* story of yesterday, re me warning people they had three months to prove themselves, had been pretty nasty and produced a lot of comments through the day. Peter M was back from holiday for the morning meeting and was incredibly long-winded. The *Mail* splashed on a leaked memo from TB to the Cabinet urging them to be more co-ordinated and not float ideas in public. It was yet another big-stick story and a pain, but TB was happy enough for the centralising message to sink in. There was still far too much gabbing around the place. At the eleven o'clock, I went through the speech and their focus was very much on the single-parent element, though as I took them through it I tried to emphasise there was a lot more to it than that. I sensed myself getting very ratty at the endless questioning about it and started to get rude to one or two of them. They were also beginning to get wound up re special advisers and I did a very hard attack on that, said it was ridiculous considering how many senior civil servants there were. TB was seeing Pat re devolution again. Anji advanced to the Aylesbury estate [large and deprived council estate in Walworth, South London]. TB and I went through the speech on the way there. It was very windy and there were one or two Trots yelling abuse as we arrived. It was carried live on Radio 5, and there was a lot of interest from the broadcasters. The papers felt we had oversold it and had nothing much to do with it today. I got back for the briefing and all I got was me and Jonathan, what our status was, how much we were being paid, and I pushed back on that. Alison came to see me again, complaining she never knew where I was, how she had to know, and I said she had to be more flexible. I had the weekly MIO [meeting of information officers] meeting which I was quickly coming to see as a waste of time. They all seemed so beaten, and by what? They were full of problems, and very few ideas. The majority were well meaning, but the culture in which they had grown up was just way behind the times.

Tuesday, June 3

The Jonathan issue was picking up, as people focused on what would happen when Alex Allan went. I assumed John Holmes would become principal private secretary and Jonathan would stay chief of staff. The *Guardian* ran a story saying TB had blocked Jonathan becoming PPS after a protest from Butler. Jonathan was getting fed up with it. TB was also fed up and said he intended to send Butler a warning shot about it all. Whether he did or not, I don't know, but he did see him. Before the 11, I got agreement from TB, RB, Jonathan and AA to say that Jonathan was chief of staff and would remain so. There was no row. That, allied to endless questions about the list of special advisers we put out yesterday, which was getting a ridiculous amount of coverage, was all we were getting. Fiona and Roz made the list and were dubbed 'Cherie-maids'. TB was working on health, and later met Chris Woodhead [Chief Inspector of Schools], and I went in at the end to agree a line stressing the importance of the chief inspector in the whole educational process. There was something very creepy about him, but TB felt he was tough and did the job well. Butler came to see me and said he was sure Peter M was behind a lot of this stuff in the press re Jonathan. I said that struck me as unlikely. TB was not too fussed about it all, said he would rather we were accused of being arrogant at this stage than of being incompetent.

The best scam of the day came from Fiona. Cherie had the idea of inviting kids to Trooping the Colour and getting in the Kid's Club Network on Budget day, so I dropped it in at the four o'clock briefing and Brunson [ITN] loved it. He went straight for it and the other stuff was dropped. He asked if he could do a live two-way from the garden and we agreed, and he also filmed upstairs. I slightly lost it with George Jones [*Telegraph* political editor] at the four o'clock, when I had a total rerun of all the questions from the morning and said if he can't be bothered to turn up at the eleven o'clock, when I dealt with this ten times over, I didn't see why I should have to go over it all again. I was bothered later on because George had a story that political honours had been axed and we had blocked Major's political honours. Gus O'Donnell [former press secretary to John Major, senior Treasury official] came to see me and recommended radical reform of the GIS. He said it needed root-and-branch change.

June '97: TB keen on 'creepy' Chris Woodhead

Wednesday, June 4

Fiona did a terrific job yesterday and we got great CB coverage. GB was planning to do a briefing at 11.30 on his jobs initiative and I sent the lobby on to him from me. They didn't think there was much in it, but it was still a good thing to do. Honours was becoming a real problem, as I felt we had inadvertently misled them on it. I sort of got away with it at the eleven o'clock. TB said he may at some stage want to give honours out. There was a bad story in the *Independent*, which David Hill was dealing with, re using Fees Office [House of Commons finance office] money to get more agents [Labour Party staff]. TB was not happy at the way PMQs was being prepared. All the private secretaries came into the meeting, as with JM, and he was not impressed by them. He said to me later these top Civil Service people are not as good as they think. He said he wanted a much smaller briefing team, and mainly the political people. He said he was fed up seeing his name attached to stories he knew nothing about, most recently lottery, and now honours. We left for the House and he spent ages on his own. Major did five questions on devolution and something TB misspoke two weeks ago. I got a bit of a mauling outside and the four o'clock was livelier than usual. I decided to play it for laughs and had them laughing all over the shop. Archie Hamilton [Conservative MP] raised a point of order about whether political appointees, who were not yet positively vetted, could see classified material. It was all very silly but then Major wrote to TB about it and there was a brief flurry about that. TB was still worrying about definition. He didn't think he had done well today. He felt the Tories were picking up a bit. He said we had to watch arrogance. Tonight was Peter M crying on TV night.[1] TB just rolled his eyes when Anji showed him the pictures in one of the papers.

Thursday, June 5

TB was doing the *Sun* police bravery awards, lots of pictures with outstanding police officers, which would get to just about every local paper in the country. JP's transport White Paper was the main story. On the way to the morning meeting, I was locked in the lift with Alex [Allan], Charlie [Whelan], Nick Brown, Allan Percival, Siobhan [Kenny] and Jonathan. We were stuck in there for five minutes before rescue. Jonathan and I learned we had identical thoughts afterwards – how unpleasant it would be to die stuck inside a lift with Nick

[1] On BBC2's *The Chair*, psychiatrist Oliver James had asked Mandelson about the death of his father.

Brown. Meeting with TB and Alex, and we agreed it would be bad news for him to see Diana before Charles. The idea of a meeting had come from her, and he did not believe she was out to exploit it, but I was not so sure and thought it was better to be safe than sorry. The Big Guns meeting was largely about Europe, with Robin, fresh from yet another picture of himself flirting with Jacques Santer, really starting to go native. GB was pushing his jobs idea and saying we must think long term. At Cabinet, TB did a little speech on the political scene, said Clinton said his big mistake was he was so busy governing he stopped communicating and you cannot afford to do that. Trust depends on constant communication. He said a few weeks in, we were always going to be accused of being arrogant or incompetent. He would prefer arrogant to incompetent as a charge. He said we had to be careful to be proper in the procedures that we followed, and at the same time never lose sight of the importance of communicating to the public. We must always be setting the agenda and focusing on the big picture. There must always be a clear message. The country must know it is their government. And we should constantly emphasise the themes of One Nation, partnership, government in the radical centre, particularly if Ken Clarke becomes Tory leader. We had to show we understood the nature of change. Be seen as a government that is engaged and internationalist, not isolationist. At the strategy meeting we were focusing largely on Europe. GB and I seemed to share the view it was a bit of a nightmare but TB was confident re the outcome at Amsterdam. GB as ever had a stack of cuttings, and had marked up various quotes in them, and was saying they were not from the Treasury.

As we arrived at Northolt, Jonathan opened a red box and dozens of papers flew away in the wind. It was one of the most extraordinary things I have ever seen. The breeze literally sucked the papers out of the box, almost in slow motion and then they flew away like in a cartoon. He was unbelievably embarrassed as we joined the RAF guys chasing the papers all over the runway. We got most of them, but I was winding him up for hours about all the intelligence stuff that would end up in some Northolt allotment. What on earth would it have looked like if we had been at Heathrow, with cameras allowed on the runway, rather than the RAF base? On the plane, TB was working on the speech, me on the briefing note. I gave TB the line 'modernise or die' and he was later surprised that it ran bigger than his line about a third way for Europe. On arrival at Malmo, TB was again the centre of attention and the international media interest was enormous. Tim came through on the mobile with a *Telegraph* poll showing we were more popular than any government in history, and TB more popular than any prime minister. TB was seeing Kok and it was a bad scene on JHA [justice and home affairs] and defence. They could not really get their act together on this. TB did a doorstep, clips on the speech and then to the meeting of the Party of European Socialists [PES] leaders. The speech was going big and as always when I told him that, he got worried, or pretended to be worried, assuming badness in their desire to do it big. At the meeting [Lionel] Jospin [new Prime Minister of France] admitted he wasn't clear what to do now he was elected. TB had us in hysterics as he impersonated him later. They went to the dinner while Jonathan and I worked on the speech. TB came back and rewrote it, commenting that it was very hard, which it was. He was into major rewrite mode, covering the text with PTOs, As and Bs as inserts. It was a total origami job.

Friday, June 6

The 'modernise or die' briefing didn't go as big as it might, with just a couple of them leading on it, but the *Today* programme led on it and even took part of TB's speech live. I also briefed out a line re him saying there could be no fiddling re the EMU conditions. RC was worried our approach was a bit isolationist. TB felt we had to watch we were not saying we alone had the right agenda. We had a meeting with Pauline Green [Labour MEP] and it was the usual Euro-media wank-in, far too many cameras, no organisation, total chaos. How anyone thought any purpose was served by these media free-for-alls was beyond me. Rudolf Scharping [SPD] came with Oskar Lafontaine for a meeting that was largely a photocall and we got *On the Record* in to film it. Scharping was at his most oleaginous, whilst Lafontaine was trying too hard to delineate himself as being different, Old Labourish. Then Jospin came in and the pleasantries never stopped. TB had done an absolutely cutting impersonation of him and it was hard now not to laugh when I heard him speak – 'Ay av bin med prime ministaire and ay don't know what to do. Eet es terrible. Ay am een a mess.' TB definitely won the battle of the speeches, I would say. In the car from the conference centre to the Sheraton, he claimed he said to Clinton that he didn't know how he would survive without me, that he relied on me more than any other individual. He said I had to live with Peter M, use the good bits, ignore the irritating side to him. He said he knew all Peter's weaknesses, and in particular his constant need to exaggerate his own status and position, but he still had something to give, and we should take it. He was convinced we could get a better deal out of Europe and said we had to start talking up the language of co-operation. He was worried RC was a bit tricky at the moment.

We left for the airport and immediately started to work on Kohl. We had an ITN crew and Tom Bradby [political reporter] for the flight [to Berlin]. I found Bradby quite irritating and sensed it was mutual. TB was going through the briefs on Kohl, read them then sat down and made a few brief notes to himself. John Holmes was getting used to his ways more quickly than some of the others were. Major obviously relied very heavily on Civil Service information and advice. TB was more interested in raw data and fact, and then would use his own judgement and test it against others. JH was dutifully writing up his checklists, etc., but TB was then doing his own, often simply committing what he wanted to memory. The aim today had to be simply to come out of it as a major European player. Kohl had such a reputation and was physically so enormous that it was not automatic. But he was in a spot of political bother, with 4.4 million out of work and a sense in the German media that TB overshadowed him, certainly in relation to the relationship with Clinton. We had a sandwich lunch in [UK ambassador to Germany] Chris Meyer's office – JHA, defence, Eurofighter, NATO, EMU. Chris said Kohl had never committed himself publicly to Eurofighter and if we made some pointing noises that could be the story for the day. Otherwise we were looking at borders again. We were beginning to take an interest in the exchange of gifts that went with all these big meetings. Jonathan and I fell about when Chris told us the gift to Kohl was a framed fax of a schools exchange deal. Chris said it could have been worse – George Foulkes [junior minister, Department for International Development (DFID)] was once given a priceless Ming vase and George produced a bottle of Scotch.

We arrived at the Kanzleramt where there was more ceremony than we expected, bands, troops, pretty much the works, big media turnout. I asked Kohl's press guy what their line on Eurofighter was and he said there would be a positive decision in three weeks. I told Chris who said we should push that hard. TB looked fine doing the troops etc. then they did a rather pointless doorstep inside, no questions, and then up to Kohl's office while I got banjaxed by the press. We were trying to create a positive mood and avoid the issue being differences over EMU or borders. Above all we were trying to get Kohl to support more sensible language in the employment chapter at Amsterdam. The German media pushed me hard on the single currency but it was all fairly easy. The German officials kept moving us on until eventually I was virtually outside, at the very spot where in opposition I said for the first time we would be unlikely to join the first wave. TB got good mood music out of him on Eurofighter, not bad on frontiers and jobs. Meyer said there was a feel of the older man passing on wisdom to the young man he saw taking over one day. Yet I sensed almost the reverse, that Kohl was slightly in awe of TB on account of his charisma and his majority, about which he was intrigued. TB did a fairly brief and tame doorstep. They were mostly going on the 'TB big in Europe' angle. On the plane back, I chatted with Meyer re the GIS. Like O'Donnell, he felt it needed radical change if not abolition. 'You have the political clout at the centre. Use it,' he said. 'They are so set in their ways and so out of date. They are cynical and sullen.' TB was in great form on the way back, cracking jokes and saying he was more confident than ever re Amsterdam. He said the key was to win in argument. If someone put forward a bum idea, we had to expose it as such. John H said he marvelled at the way I had the press asking a stack of tame questions of TB today.

Saturday, June 7

Interesting little interlude today. It was the day Diana was supposed to go to Chequers. She had been insistent that it was there, rather than at Maggie Rae's house as before.[1] She had also been saying to her office that she would bring Harry. But it turned out in fact she was intending to bring William. Yet when Alex checked with the Palace, the time of the meeting did not coincide with a time when she would be with the boys at all. It was all a bit odd and reinforced in me and AA the view that he would do better to wait. TB felt we were being harsh, did not think she would exploit it, but it was not a risk worth taking. If it emerged he had seen her before Charles it would set off all sorts of bollocks. I think in part he just fancied having a bit of time with her, but it was risky. Alex and I both pressed him to cancel and eventually he agreed. In the end we got the duty clerk to call her office and to say there had been a message from Germany that he had to cancel.

Sunday, June 8

I was up at Mum and Dad's and more or less managed to avoid work. Neil Wallis [deputy editor of the *Sun*] called and said they had found out about TB selling Richmond Crescent. I persuaded him

[1] Maggie Rae, legal adviser to Diana, Princess of Wales, during her divorce from Prince Charles. Partner of Parliamentary Labour Party secretary Alan Haworth. Rae previously held a dinner for Diana, the Blairs, AC and Fiona Millar.

that it was because of security, the fact it would cost so much to secure, and the inconvenience to neighbours so it made sense they moved out.

Monday, June 9

A lot of the focus was starting to shift from us to the Tory leadership. I used the breather to read up more on the Europe/IGC issues. It was both fascinating and headache-inducing at the same time, but I had to get on top of it all pre-Amsterdam. It was pretty clear that TB, to get borders, was going to have to concede that some of the things we wanted to keep in the third pillar, intergovernmental, would have to shift to the first. It would give us a few presentational problems and TB wanted me to get Peter Riddell [*Times*] in to go over it and start to lay the ground, namely frontiers sacrosanct but we opt in to other Community procedures as we see fit. TB was very hard line on frontiers. On EMU, he said we had to play cleverly; it would be folly to be anything other than enthusiastic for it to work. Otherwise we have no influence. We have to argue from a pro-European perspective to be able to have influence. The Major government approach was a disaster. I was trying to speak to GB and Ed [Balls] to find out what was happening in Luxembourg but their meeting was thrown into chaos when the new French finance minister suddenly announced they wanted to delay the single currency.

TB was not happy at the (we assumed Ed- or Blunkett-inspired) *Guardian* splash that we would not have money for teachers' pay. When I spoke to DB re the teachers story, he sensed I was saying TB thought he may have been the source, and got very steamed up, later writing to TB and GB to say how angry he was at the story. The eleven o'clock was low key, I had meetings with TB, Butler, Jonathan, Peter M and AA re Europe coming problems, then re planning for the New York trip, and we were having to deal with written questions re me and Jonathan. We published the list of ministerial committees, which had them obsessing at the four o'clock, counting who was on what – JP on twelve, Peter M on eleven, Ann Taylor on ten. I got back for MIO which was as dispiriting as the last time. I was beginning to think the majority were useless. I had tried to be fair and friendly and co-operative but we were met by sullenness and blank looks. I met Alex Allan to go over how bad it was and also to say I may want to change my Number 10 team too. I went for a walk round the garden with TB who was really beginning to focus on Amsterdam now.

Peter Riddell did a good job on TB's IGC briefing. TB was pissed off at the *Sun*, my briefing to Kavanagh used on the front on the line TB saying Ken Clarke was lazy. He said he would have to write to KC to apologise, which he did. It put him in a jumpy and distracted mood all day. He didn't like it when he got involved, through others – in this case me – in slanging with MPs he took seriously like Ken. I went over to the FCO to a meeting Robin had called on the IGC. I remembered the office from interviewing Douglas Hurd [former Conservative Foreign Secretary] in there years ago, but somehow it looked even bigger and grander with RC in it. He was absolutely loving it, surrounded by public schoolboy diplomats he could order around, dealing with huge issues on which he could pontificate at will. I like to think part of him is overdoing it out of a sense of self-parody, but you can never be sure. But for all his diddling and pomposity, I find it hard not to like him. He was also clearly on top of the detail, and clear about what we needed to achieve. RC went through his own plan – win on borders; focus on jobs; aim for more votes for Britain; keep the veto on CFSP; NATO established as bedrock of European defence; tough action on fraud; CAP reform; fish. I used the four o'clock to keep going on frontiers and the opt-out/opt-in argument as per TB's Riddell briefing. Godric [Smith] came for a chat, said that he felt most people felt really energised by the change, but it was hard to carry out the fundamental review we needed. He was too nice to say out loud what he meant but I know what it was – some of the old guard were so set in their ways they could not really make the change needed.

I went off with TB to do the [Lord] Snowdon [photographer, former husband of Princess Margaret] picture. On the way TB complained he was feeling tired. He was enjoying it, and felt on top of things, but the workload was relentless. Snowdon put him in a blue shirt from Turnbull & Asser [London tailors] and put some weird kind of moulding in his hair, but at least he knew what he wanted and was reasonably quick. The Tory leadership results came through – could hardly have been better. Clarke forty-nine, Hague forty-one, the other three split. So it looked like Hague would win. TB on balance felt Clarke would have been better for us, and that Hague was about the best choice they could make, but I still felt we would get the better of him. I went to [Rupert] Murdoch's [Head of News Corps] do. There were a few ministers – GB, Nick Brown, Frank Field, DB. JP didn't want to go. CB was clearly giving the cold shoulder to Mary Ann Sieghart [*Times*]. The mood was pretty good, but whenever I was with them en masse, it always struck me as if for the first time how right wing they were. It was as if they all thought the same thing – the same as RM thought.

TB was seeing the Queen, then called Clinton re Northern Ireland. He thought he might have upset the Queen who was wearing a green dress. She said she was going to Northern Ireland tomorrow. 'I hope you're not wearing that dress,' he said, and for a moment she thought it was a comment on the dress, not Irish politics. 'I think she got the point,' he said. 'But I couldn't be too sure.'

Wednesday, June 11

TB saw Neil [Kinnock] who said re him meeting Thatcher 'Why did you do it, Tony?' Mark Adams had prepared the PMQs brief and we didn't realise that [the Department for] Education seemed to have reneged on one part of the assisted places scheme plan, re kids going through for thirteen years. There were only about 2,000 of them affected. DB was slithering a bit to get round the fact Peter Kilfoyle as Shadow schools minister had said we would honour these places. There was endless toing and froing with DB's office and then TB said he would write the line himself. Hezza was standing in for Major and I said to TB even if he didn't go on this, we should get out of it straight away. We sent TB's line over to Education. DB wanted to change it again. TB asked me to say no. I'd earlier told TB that David was doing the best of the lot, press-wise, but this was a fuck-up and he was livid. The other issue for us was Hong Kong. After all the dither, it was agreed he would definitely go to the handover. TB announced it to a planted question from Jim Cousins [Labour MP]. TB was relaxed and humorous at PMQs. Our lot were less sycophantic than previously, which was a lot better. Trevor Kavanagh called and asked if the kids were going to Balmoral [Queen's Scottish summer residence] with TB and CB. TB told me they had been invited but he was unsure. I said that to Trevor, but later discovered they were going to do a big number on 'The Famous Five'. When I told TB he said it confirmed his feeling they shouldn't go. The kids were not that keen anyway and he felt it looked like they were saying their kids were like royal kids. I called the Palace, agreed a line on it, and got it out through PA after dealing with Trevor.

Paris. We arrived and were driven straight to the Elysée. Chirac was so over the top in his welcome it was almost comical. He slightly exaggerated everything. Handshake firmer than most, and longer than most. Hand movements slightly more expansive than most. He was a slow walker so he walked very slowly. He read from notes printed

June '97: TB makes a crack re Queen's dress

on little postcards and when he consulted them, he really looked at them, picked them up slowly, read them as everyone looked at him, put them down, then spoke. He said everything as though it was a grand statement. TB at times looked like he was about to burst out laughing. By comparison with TB, he was very much a no-detail merchant, even after looking at the cards. So the impression he gave, on JHA, defence, anything, was that he agreed, but in fact most of the time he was saying something slightly different. TB said we wanted to take a new approach in Europe, but emphasised the importance of keeping border controls. TB said in passing we had no ID cards in Britain, and Chirac was shocked. 'No identity cards! You have no identity cards. Mmmm.' Exaggerated nodding and shaking of head. TB said he was in favour but they were considered a breach of civil liberties. On *coopération renforcée* [enhanced co-operation] and some of his QMV areas, Chirac said '*C'est une bonne idée. Si non, je ne la proposerais pas.*' ['It is a good idea. If it wasn't, I wouldn't put it forward.'] Exaggerated looking around for amused responses. He did have a fine sense of humour. When TB raised jobs, Chirac said '*Ah, là on va nous accorder, nous les hommes de gauche.*' ['There we are going to be in agreement, we men of the left.']

JC kept pushing TB on his support for the French position on the Stability Pact [agreement by EU member states relating to conduct of fiscal policy]. TB kept qualifying it. JC kept saying 'So I count on your support. It is a delicate subject. There must be solidarity.' Then on to Bosnia, security co-ordination, defence, Strasbourg-Brussels, Turkey, NATO, CAP. We went to prepare for the doorstep and TB was making a habit of making comments about me to these guys. He said to Chirac 'He is a very bad man but he is very good at it.' It was fairly straight-forward, then I did a huddle with the press, which made me late arriving for the dinner, which had the protocol guy in a total strop. I said I would be one moment. '*Monsieur Campbell, j'ai dit que le Président vous attend.*' ['Mr Campbell, I said that the president is waiting for you.'] I walked in and literally they were waiting for me to start. Chirac seemed fine but his people were a bit hoity-toity. They had a long discussion about Romania and John Holmes got really energised, made it clear he totally disagreed with what Chirac was saying. TB said he thought Chirac was a likeable rogue.

Thursday, June 12

There was fairly quiet coverage of the Chirac meeting and only the *Telegraph* did a line on me being late for the dinner. I took the morning off for the boys' sports day. I got in at 12 for the strategy meeting. TB later said Peter M had complained I was snubbing him and hardly asked his opinion any more. I said it was probably because he had become so grand. We were walking round the garden and he said I was at fault. 'Why me?' I said. 'Because you are the grown-up and he knows no better.' I said he was great when he was great, but a total pain when he was going through one of his prima donna phases, as he was. He was like a caricature of himself at morning meetings, pontificating, saying what he thought of ministers. Cabinet was mainly IGC and public spending, but I ducked out to prepare for my Amsterdam briefing. TB and I talked over the Tory leadership again. He said if they did not go for Clarke they were insane, but Hague was not useless. If he had a sense of project and saw it through, he could be dangerous. I thought he was OK but had a lot of weaknesses to attack.

Friday, June 13

I woke up to a problem leading the news, Frank Dobson's warning from his speech yesterday that nothing could be ruled in or out in the spending review, a fairly innocuous statement that had got mangled into screaming headlines about charges to see a doctor, visit a hospital etc. TB called, said this could be the end of the honeymoon. I got hold of Frank, who said he had spoken to Peter M last night and agreed not to go on the *Today* programme. But it was now leading the news and I persuaded him he should go on and try to calm it down. He said he had done no more than stick to the Treasury line. There was a theory that he had done it deliberately so that we came straight out and ruled it out but that might be a bit sophisticated I thought. He eventually came on at 8.30 and did OK though we had by then had wall-to-wall cries of betrayal from the Tories, doctors etc. It soured the first of TB's regional tours and public Q&A meetings. He was a bit fed up with Dobbo. He had his usual chat with GB who was now backtracking on it. I said we either had to knock it down or stand it up, or attack the media for questioning the commitment and whipping up something out of nothing. In the end we agreed he should do a clip making a clear commitment to NHS but saying there were tough choices to face. Then we set off for the Q&A in Worcester, which was being called People's Question Time. TB was fretting re Dobson still. He did a party meeting first and recalled election night when we were watching the results come in and he said 'I said we had to beat them, not destroy them.' I spent half an hour persuading first GB and then AD that Alistair should do *World at One*. They were worried it would add a third voice, and possible confusion, after TB and FD. But we needed some calming down doing and AD did it well. The Q&A went OK, though he waffled at the start, and the sound quality wasn't great, but as an event it worked and made good TV. There were a couple of good ideas in the questions, like pagers for court witnesses, sequestration of crime assets for victim support, which I got GS to work up into a script for the Sundays, so that we would look at them seriously. On the train back we had another chat on Hague, Amsterdam and also the Millennium Dome exhibition which was coming over as TB vs GB. We had a reception for the TB election on-the-road team. It was great to see all the old team together. Even though it was just a few weeks ago, it felt like ages.

Saturday, June 14

The Sundays were quiet, though there was quite a lot of TB and [Prince] Charles, clearly spun by Charles' people to get a bit of reflected glory out of the new government. They're pretty sassy at this. Like they'll be when things go against us, no doubt.

Sunday, June 15

I had to go into Number 10 for a pre-Amsterdam meeting with TB, Jonathan, JH, Alex, Brian Bender and MAFF re quota hopping.[1] We were clearly not going to get agreement and had to work out a communications plan. I felt we should be talking up the real Spanish anger at the draft declaration, stressing other economic benefits and emphasising proper enforcement on catching cheats. TB was totally immersed in the detail not just on this but right across the European piece. He was clearly going to go for them on detail. The main media issue of the day was the Stability Pact so I got my head round that on the plane out and talked it through with GB and his team. GB wanted us to pitch ourselves as somehow mediating between France and Germany, stressing we were not being destructive, aware of the political capital invested, and officials were talking to other governments. GB was keen to say his jobs initiative was at the top of the agenda and should be consistent with the Stability Pact, and there should be no fiddling of the criteria. TB went straight to see Kok while I went to do an hour-long briefing, JHA, defence, jobs, Stability Pact, quota hopping. I left thinking there was something to be said for our broad-brush, trivial media. This lot were so serious and intense and detail-obsessed.

[1] The Common Fisheries Policy between member states and markets enabled EU ship owners to purchase vessels and use national quotas in other EU countries – called 'quota hopping' by British fishermen.

The security was a nightmare and it took ages to get back to the hotel and meet up with TB. He wanted to go for a walk so we wandered off with the cops and found a canalside and walked for half an hour or so. He said he was confident on borders after seeing Kok, less so on defence or fish. I sensed a real tension between RC and GB, and Robin was amazed at how clear GB made it that he did not want to be around TB. He went off and did his own thing most of the time, preferring to be with his own people. Jonathan had the idea of projecting TB as like the sensible brother trying to sort out feuding members of the family. I called Phil Webster [political editor, *The Times*] who was already on to that kind of approach. He said it was extraordinary that we were not even going to be in the euro but we were central to this story. It showed the honeymoon was still on. Of course, with Nigel Wicks [second permanent secretary to the Treasury] as chairman of the monetary committee, there was a clear UK focus in there. GB called after the Ecofin [EU Economic and Financial Affairs Council] dinner and said they were issuing a separate text on jobs alongside the Stability Pact and we should welcome it. JP called in a bit of a state, having left some documents in the BBC studio where he did *Panorama*. They had read the papers and now wanted to redo the interview. I said attack them for theft and make clear you've said nothing in public you have not said in the stolen correspondence.

Monday, June 16

The media were running with TB as peacemaker between France and Germany, which was a real surprise to TB when I raised it at the breakfast meeting. The European media was very much on the theme of TB as a real power in the land. There was big coverage of JP's lost papers. TB was not sure about us attacking the BBC but Peter M agreed they would not have done it had it been a Tory. At the summit, we were on course for showing that we could get a better deal than the Tories by being more positive. Securing the right deal on frontiers was crucial if we were signalling greater co-operation elsewhere.[1] In the breakfast meeting, he was going through the text line by line with officials, really into the detail. That too was an asset for us. I had been surprised at some of the meetings with the other big cheeses how totally broad-brush they were. At my first briefing, I really hammered

[1] At the Amsterdam summit Blair established frontier controls in that the UK retained control of immigration, asylum and visas while other countries chose other arrangements.

the frontiers issue, saying that though on the surface, the words in the text looked fine, we wanted them even clearer. TB was confident we would do that. We wanted any doubt removed that the European Court would have the power to question the decision on frontiers. I argued it could lead to our independent stance being scuppered by the back door. It was a fundamental point of principle, which had to be met.

TB did a brief doorstep as we left, good pictures, and then on to the summit, met by Kok. In the car, he said he was ready to go for them on defence, and the other JHA issues. I now felt on top of things, confident in the argument and the detail, and that we would win. At the next briefing I hit the frontiers message again, but also briefed on various contributions TB was making on the single currency, no fiddling of the criteria, jobs. I was enjoying using Boris Johnson [*Telegraph*] as a foil. He asked how many jobs the new schemes we were proposing would create and I said eight. The briefings were becoming something of a draw among the European media, who were more used to very po-faced reverential briefings. On the way in, I asked Bevins to ask me if there had been any contact with Tory MPs worried about William Hague's leadership, and whether they might come to us if he ruled out a single currency. He asked me the question, and I mumbled a few platitudes about the kind of contact we had, as if I had been embarrassed to be asked. It was enough. Afterwards I was surrounded by all the Brits asking more about who I was talking about. They probably realised it was basically a scam, but they couldn't resist it and went for it, though it was rather undermined when Robin Oakley [BBC political editor] went on and said it all came from me. Then news came through that two RUC [Royal Ulster Constabulary] officers had been killed in Lurgan [County Armagh].

TB looked sick at the lunch. He said it was clearly a deliberate sabotage, that they knew the plan we had to get them into talks with a date next week and this was the signal that they intended to scupper it. It was pretty grim. John Holmes and I put some words together, while we tried to contact the Americans, John Hume etc., to get them on the same line. I saw TB just after lunch, and he really was in a grim mood about the killing of the policemen. He was keen to go straight out, really go for the IRA, reveal that they were close to getting something, but we persuaded him against. We organised a joint doorstep with John Bruton [Irish Prime Minister], who was at his last summit. They had a brief meeting, then did the doorstep together. Bruton was really powerful, particularly in his attack on

Gerry Adams and weasel words. TB was quite strong too, but the impact was all the more powerful coming from the Irish PM. Afterwards, in the car, TB said 'What on earth do you do? We do everything we can. Clearly they don't want to know.' Meanwhile we were getting problems with the Commission on quota hoppers. The Spanish had gone mad and the Commission were now backtracking. I went for a drink with the broadcasters who were all buying the idea that we were getting more out of it than Major ever could have done, that TB was being taken more seriously. GB was off doing his own thing most of the time. He was really pushing his own agenda. The *Sun* splashed on what they called 'TB's blind spot' with the headline: 'Dump the Dome'.

Tuesday, June 17

TB was preoccupied by Ireland and the shooting and wondering whether to reveal the exchange of letters he had with Sinn Fein, to show that they were beyond the pale and also that they were acting in bad faith. Tim phoned with the Tory leadership results which I was able to pass on and say they were perfect from our point of view. They would clearly set up splits for good. TB met Santer to tie him down on exchanges of letters re fish/quota hopping. He struck me as a particularly flabby character, dull and drab, rather surprised to be in the position he was. We did the exchange, but agreed we would say nothing until tomorrow because the Spaniards would go mad. That was all fine until I learned that the *Guardian* were going to say the deal we had was crap, so I briefed John Palmer [*Guardian*] that we had a deal far better than the one he understood to have been struck, but we must keep it quiet until we got back. I gave the same line to the other heavies. I popped into the negotiations five or six times, and I got the impression TB was speaking, or at least involved, every time I went in. They were due to leave for the lunch and we discovered for the first time that the leaders were expected to ride a bike. I grabbed TB as he came out and said he should grab a proper-looking bike, get out there, turn it into a race, and win. We had to walk over a bridge to where the bikes were and on the way there were a number of girls screaming at him, Tony, Tony. The others looked on incredibly jealous, including Kohl. TB said how the hell is he going to ride a bike? This is a bit ridiculous, isn't it? I said it may be, but they will be fantastic pictures, if he wins. Winning in Europe, get it? He went for it, pedalling away madly while trying to look cool, and he got over the bridge first. We then watched the others come over, including [Lamberto] Dini [Italian foreign minister] who fell off.

Kohl didn't go on the bike and looked thoroughly pissed off. But he and TB had a good one-on-one re defence, and again, TB was winning on NATO, and watering down the commitment to the WEU/EU merger. The lesson was to state bottom lines and stick to them.

There was a lot of hanging around now, especially after the second briefing, and our media were doing loads on the Tory leadership. I went in and eventually got TB out for a doorstep on the defence deal, avoiding fish, and then I did the rounds, pushing our line. TB kept going on the detail, while Chirac was just making grand statements: 'La France vous propose . . .'. ['France proposes . . .'] Kohl was on the attack now too, but TB felt they were getting on fine. I went in at one point and TB was sat there with documents galore on his desk, and he was firing on all cylinders. It eventually broke up at 3. We did a press conference and then decided to stay over again. I enjoyed it a lot more than I did covering summits from the other side. It helped that we had pretty much won everything we had come to win. TB was tired, as we all were, but it had gone really well. James Robbins [BBC] did a summary, saying it was a great success for Blair, not so good for Europe. TB was getting a bit arrogant again, told me he had been the main man in there, nobody else would have been able to get as good a deal as he did, and none of the others would have been cheered the way he was. I said feet and ground.

Wednesday, June 18

I was up early, feeling totally exhausted, but the press was very positive again. The only exception was the stuff on the Dome, which was becoming a real problem. There was too much briefing going on about who was in favour and who wasn't – the majority. Perversely, I was beginning to wonder whether we should go for it as a way of showing he was not going to get pushed around and blow in the wind. TB's own instincts were still very much in favour of something big for the Millennium. I said fine, but it had to be something viable. We had to reach a decision by tomorrow. On the plane home, we worked on PMQs, and the statement on the summit. TB had not had much sleep but was running on adrenaline, really pleased with himself, clear he was a big player and could end up taking the whole show over. The *Times* leader said the bike ride was a parable as well as a photo op. Brian Bender wrote a list of twenty-seven positive achievements. I asked Robin his view of the Greenwich [Dome] exhibition and he gave me a long list of reasons why it should be dumped. 'So you agree with Gordon?' I said. He paused, smiled and said 'On the other hand . . .'. PMQs and the statement both went fine. The four o'clock was largely about the Millennium Exhibition, and we had a meeting on it later. All the arguments are against, but TB was still in favour. He said he didn't mind the press being against him on this, that he preferred the visionary route. The concerns to address were costs, concept, legacy and management. I was worried that every time there was an issue of public spending, the line will be run against us – you can spend money on the Dome but not on etc. etc. He was still keen. Peter M was not sure either, though at the same time angling to be in charge of it. Heseltine called me to say he hoped we weren't backtracking on the Dome.

Thursday, June 19

We started the day thinking TB was going to make a statement on Northern Ireland, announcing that Sinn Fein had a timetable for coming into talks. We ended it saving the Millennium Exhibition. TB was now against an NI statement, not least because there was a possibility it would clash horribly with yesterday's funeral of the policemen, one of whose sons was absolutely heartbroken on the TV news last night. On the Dome, he had pretty much decided to go ahead. He seemed genuinely split but felt the pros outweighed the cons. Peter M was in favour, not least because he was going to be centrally involved in the relaunch, and had helped get us to where we were. He was less bullish than before, however, which unsettled TB. I had moved marginally in favour only because everyone else had come out against and I didn't want him to be seen to give in to pressure. TB was due for a bilateral with JP and he was clearly in favour as well. He went into one of his great loud speeches in a quiet, small room, a mix of mania and enthusiasm, said it will be great to pull it off, it will be made to work, he was leader and if his instincts say do it, we should do it. I called Heseltine to ask him to be around to say something positive. TB then, pre-Cabinet, squared GB, who came up with another approach. He said that rather than say we were going ahead per se, we should say there were five tests that had to be met. Costs, legacy, new management structure, educational role, the whole nation enjoying and taking part. I sensed this was a sensible media strategy, but also that he may be suggesting it as a way of slowing and then scuppering like his tests on EMU. But it became clear in Cabinet there was going to be a real problem.

TB spoke, gave away one or two little doubts, but basically made clear he thought it was a good thing for Britain, provided costs, legacy, etc. were all sorted. GB said it was fine, subject to the tests. Chris Smith agreed with the overall approach. Jack Straw said he remembered the Festival of Britain and the great impact on kids at that time. 'Absolutely,' boomed JP. Then Blunkett said he was deeply against it. Dobson said on balance, so was he. Ann Taylor thought there should be some independent cost analysis. Jack Cunningham said people are against it and the management is crap. Donald D said it was a leap in the dark. George Robertson was more supportive. Harriet was in favour. Clare said she was vehemently opposed. Ron Davies couldn't see how we could make it an event for the whole nation. Robin was worried it would be seen as a white elephant and every time anything went wrong, it will be our problem. Darling was against. Mo came over to me during the discussion and said 'He's not going to get this.' Coincidentally, TB had to leave early to go to the church blessing of Parliament, so JP took the chair. I could see TB was thinking he would not win, and seemed resigned to it. JP chaired the rest of the meeting in a very JP way, let everyone ramble on for ages, but it was very effective. It meant enough supportive points were made for him to sum up by saying that he would say to TB that there was a long discussion, but they recognised the decision had to be his, and the clear message from Cabinet was they would support him whatever that decision was.

GB summed up in a very different way, saying that the five tests had to be passed. JP said 'Hold on, let's be clear in this. Are we saying yes if, or yes but? I'm for telling Tony it is yes but.' In other words, we are going ahead and we will do everything to make sure those tests are met. JP was not going to be budged. I think he was showing two things – his loyalty to TB, but also his ability to swing decisions. The truth is that he could easily have taken the discussion and said to TB 'Sorry, Tony, there is no way we can do this.' TB came back from the church, saying he had been worried leaving JP in charge, but the truth is that it was JP, helped by Margaret B above all, who really swung it round. The nine in favour were TB, JP, GB, Margaret, Mo, JS, GR, HH, Chris S. TB said he was less bothered by the press reaction, than whether the thing could actually be made to work, whether we will be left with a white elephant or not. We agreed I should brief at 2pm, announce we were going ahead, and that TB was going straight to Greenwich. It went OK, though some were incredulous. George Pascoe-Watson [*Sun*] just sat shaking his head. I came back and Anji told me Peter M and Chris Smith were also going, which I thought was madness. I felt at this stage it was best left restricted to TB. He had not even sorted Peter M's and CS' respective roles. I went to TB's room, where he was talking to Peter. Peter was already in full flow, protesting that we used him but did not treat him like a politician. He was winding himself up more and more and eventually directly accused me of trying to keep him off TV and undermine him. I said I thought it was wrong for him to be there when TB had not yet told Chris Smith that Peter was to get the single share that would put him in charge of the project. Peter said nobody would even notice if he went, at which point TB said he was being absurd and ridiculous. He said I think we can be fairly sure you'll make sure they notice. 'What does that mean?' asked Peter. If ever anything showed he saw everything as being about him, this did, and given the continuing sensitivities, we could do without it. Peter went on and on. TB was tearing his hair out. Jonathan had a smile on his face that said this is a madhouse. Eventually, Peter started shouting and bawling that he was fed up to the back teeth, had been treated like dirt and went to the door as if to walk out. TB warned him not to, and told him to come back and sit down. We tried to resume a normal conversation. I said if he went JP should go to give broader cover to it all, and stop so many questions being asked. In the end all four went in convoy. TB did clips on the site, then back for a strategy meeting with TB, GB, AC, Peter M, and Jonathan, during which the Hague result came through. I said we should do him as being in charge of two parties, not sure which one he was leading. GB thought we should go straight for him as extremist.

Friday, June 20

We were due to leave for the G8 in Denver and I was up much of the night working on the briefing. The Clinton bilaterals were falling into place and the Northern Ireland story was coming together. Mo had wanted to do an article for the *Belfast Telegraph*, revealing that Sinn Fein had the chance to come into talks six weeks after a cease-fire, and they sabotaged it with the killing of the policemen. TB, JH, Jonathan and I had a conference call and agreed he would be wrong to do it in that way. Better to do it with Clinton tomorrow, and get his support for our approach. I briefed in the Denver briefing how important Ireland would be to the Clinton talks. Then John Holmes came through. We had a problem. The draft *Belfast Telegraph* article had gone through, allegedly for production purposes. It meant they had the information even though we had decided to pull the article. It was classic Mo – give them the article before it was finished, or before it had been decided. I spoke to Mo and agreed we would speak to the editor, to see if they would do it in a way to cause least trouble, e.g. we were seeing Clinton to tell him there had been progress, what we had done to get it, and to say we were looking at new ways of taking it forward. He was terrific, and agreed only to speculate on the fact that the timetable idea was on the table.

TB chatted to Hume on the way to the airport. We were getting Concorde to New York before flying to Denver. We had the front of the plane for ministers, officials etc., with the press at the back. TB and I chatted re Peter's outburst yesterday. He said the good still outweighed the bad, and it was a small price to pay. He knew what a pain he could be but I had to try to use him properly. TB did a session with the press, and the main focus was Ireland. He was looking forward to seeing BC again, and was hoping for some time to continue their political discussions. GB kept himself to himself pretty much though we had a chat about free TV licences for pensioners. RC seemed a bit down. At Denver, there were lots of ceremonials and we had barely arrived at the hotel when TB had to do his first bilaterals with [Ryutaro] Hashimoto [Japanese Prime Minister], then [Jean] Chrétien [Canadian Prime Minister]. Hashimoto had an army of officials with him and all the formalities went on a bit. He was keen to know our pitch on EMU. TB said we were in favour, but there were 'political and economic' reasons why we were staying out for now. He felt it was not clear it would start on time because of the French budget deficit. Hashimoto said the Japanese wanted the European currency to be as strong as possible. He was also very iffy about the French figures. 'The euro must be created in the strongest manner possible.' They had a long discussion re Hong Kong and China. TB said the brutal truth was that our leverage on our own re China was very limited, which is why the broader international support for seeing that they honour the HK agreement was so important. Hashimoto was clearly suspicious of Jiang [Zemin, Chinese President], but also did not believe he had full control over the military. 'One piece of advice,' he said, 'Asian countries are watching to see how the UK will draw the curtain on this affair. The British Empire should leave the stage in a proud and graceful manner. Best to leave gracefully so that the noisier the Chinese are, the more difficult it is for them, not you.' TB said he was determined to bind China in to see the thing through properly but it would need the help of others.

Chrétien was a more languid and laid-back kind of leader. They talked politics and elections first, then Quebec, welfare reform. They had a fascinating discussion on pensions. Chrétien said the rich in Canada do not receive pensions, nothing at all, and that they went from universal to non-universal provision a lot more easily than they thought they would. The lower end of the scale now do a lot better.

The discussion bounced around; one minute NATO enlargement, the next asbestos, then Hong Kong. I went to the press centre and did a briefing on the whole summit agenda, but again our lot were focusing on Ireland. I pretty much confirmed that three weeks before the shootings they were offered a place in the talks after six weeks. This was OK but I gave the impression it was not equivocal, and the story was rather running away. I had to ring round to try to calm them down. Back at the hotel, TB was back in his 'how important and brilliant I am' mode. He came back from the dinner to say there had been a barely comprehensible conversation re Bosnia, which Yeltsin dominated. He said Kohl was warm and Chirac very chilly. He said Kohl had taken him aside, said how pleased he was they got on, that it was important there was another big player in Europe because he would not be there forever. Whereas with Chirac, TB said things were pretty bad. Kok (there as EU president) had told TB Chirac said TB was just another Thatcher and we should not deal with him. Meanwhile the mood with Clinton was great. He was looking for more time with TB, ditto Hillary and CB, and Hillary clearly took to Fiona as well.

Saturday, June 21

We had the bilateral planned for 11 with Clinton, and I was trying to fix up a picture and joint doorstep. We left the hotel after doing the Sundays and then to Denver library. TB had a few minutes with Clinton on arrival and JH saw [Sandy] Berger [Clinton's national security adviser], and news came back that there would be no press. Eventually they agreed there could be a pool at the end, but it was not what we needed. Brunson was hanging around outside with Godric on the off chance I got him in. I briefed him, Oakley, [Adam] Boulton [Sky political editor] and Phil Murphy [Press Association] with the details of the aide-memoire, in particular that before the Lurgan killings, Sinn Fein were offered a place in the talks after six weeks. They ran big with the story but to hammer home the message that SF were in the wrong, it needed TB and BC side by side saying the same thing.

The main G8 discussions were leaders plus sherpas, so I hung around for the meeting to break. TB and Bill C were talking about the aide-memoire and what Bill C called Adams' 'stupid response' to the killings. Jonathan and John Holmes joined us and Clinton said to me 'OK, what do you want me to do?' I said what would be great from our point of view, as the aide-memoire is now public, is if you and TB stand side by side, say the same message, and that you in particular say 'The ball is now in Sinn Fein's court.' He said that sounded right to him. By now, a rather nervous-looking Mike McCurry had joined us. He said 'Mr President, don't you think you should discuss this with your policy advisers first?' BC said get them down here then, and someone went to get Berger and Jim Steinberg [senior Clinton aide]. They went into a little huddle, but I think I had won the argument with Clinton that this was the right thing to do. He came back and said OK, where are we doing this? I got word to Godric to bring Brunson and his lot in, and we did a little pooled doorstep. Mike was almost hyperventilating by the time we got there. Clinton asked one more time 'Right, what do I say? Ball in their court. OK.' He did it brilliantly, looked the part, sounded the part, and it led our news all day. I could tell that Sandy was pissed off that we'd got Clinton to do it, but if it was the right thing to do, and the president thought so, I couldn't quite see the problem.

Then we heard David Trimble had gone mad because far from hearing an attack on Sinn Fein, he just heard the offer of a place at the talks. I was acutely conscious of the fact we were dealing with issues so sensitive that life and death sometimes depended on what we were saying. It was always a difficult balance we were trying to strike. I called Mo and she said it was coming over fine; the main impression was TB was trying hard to make it work, but one side was always upset, and often both sides were. At my next briefing, I was a bit more low-key about the offer [to Sinn Fein] and did not go into detail. We did some stuff on organised crime, TB having been asked to prepare something for our G8 next year. I went for lunch and then briefed myself on decommissioning. It was all tricky, sensitive stuff, but we were doing OK. TB was due to do ABC at the Capitol building tomorrow and I went over to check it out. TB wanted to go for a walk so we were driven out to a park. He said it was clear he had the chance to be a major player and that gave us a great opportunity. 'It's just a shame Britain is so small, physically.' I said we needed a bigger-Britain policy, and we then joked around about taking over Denmark, Belgium, then France. Joking aside, I warned him against world-leader-itis, said all this stuff was hugely important, but we mustn't lose sight of the domestic, never. We were walking around in a little bubble, surrounded by heavies, which underlined literally how easy it would be to get out of touch. He said he was doing really well with Kohl, badly with Chirac. I went off with Godric to the hacks' hotel to brief on changes we hoped to bring to summits next year when we had EU and G8 presidencies. I was also briefing on the environment speech, which was going bigger than I thought it would. Adam Boulton and I had a row about whether organised crime was important. Afterwards Fiona and I, JH, Jonathan went for dinner with Mike McCurry, Dee Dee Myers [press secretary], Jim Steinberg and a few others from the White House. McCurry was very funny, had everyone in hysterics describing how he came into the meeting room to find the American president being kidnapped by the UK delegation.

Sunday, June 22

I was up at 6 to prepare for ABC. TB was full of himself again, especially having met Chuck Berry [musician] with Clinton. He was also full of how much BC and Kohl liked him. Kohl clearly saw him as a kind of successor in Europe. So did Chirac, which is presumably why he had not taken to him. We went over some of the tough questions then left for the interview. I saw the questions by accident, knew they were going straight in on Northern Ireland. He was relaxed, competent, no real story but he talked about a letter he got from a young Northern Irish girl, and I knew the press would be on to it so we were tearing the Garden Rooms[1] apart trying to find it. He was tough on Bosnia, strong on Hong Kong. He didn't deliver one of the lines he wanted to push about us being a bridge over the Atlantic. I then went to Gordon's press conference, where I inadvertently turned the lights out leaning on the wall. GB was still very much doing his own thing. He didn't like these big foreign events, and he especially didn't like them when TB was the main man. I felt he tried too hard to be making news separate from TB. He'd do better to be part of a team. I went back to the library where our private office was based to work on the environment speech for the Earth Summit at the UN tomorrow. BC asked me how I thought yesterday went on Ireland. I said it went well. Media-wise, could not have been better. I said he had carried the thing. He said TB was all over the US networks. I said he was all over the British ones. Of all of them, he was the warmest and the friendliest. Mike McCurry told me he had been really appreciative of how we handled his visit to London, and managed to blow the Paula stuff away. Maybe the stuff yesterday was a bit of a payback. TB pointed out it was interesting how Bill asked my view on media stuff. I really liked him. Clinton was clearly a great politician and communicator, but had not been that impressive chairing the meeting.

TB did fine at the press conference, and then we walked back to the hotel. He was presented with a photo album of himself at the

[1] Downing Street home of the prime minister's secretarial staff.

summit then he went for a brief kip. He was thinking more and more about Ireland, trying to find a way forward. We left for the airport where he had a little false bonhomie chat with the press. I was feeling a bit fed up, and think the reason was I felt myself totally submerging my own personality into his, and that meant most of the time getting a lot of the problems, and very little of the credit or the upside. The ABC interview was going down well. I was surprised how many Americans recognised him, for example leaving church earlier he got a round of applause. On the plane Trevor Kavanagh was pushing on Japanese pressure on the single currency, presumably taken from my briefing. We were now on to working flat out on the environment speech, and I wrote in a couple of paragraphs clearly aimed at the US, Canada and Japan. TB was suddenly worried that the carbon dioxide twenty per cent cut was leading the news and even though it was a manifesto commitment, he was worried whether we could say it with conviction. I underestimated the level of interest in the Earth Summit which was leading the news all day. We eventually found the letter mentioned in the interview, which was actually sent to CB, from the young girl in Northern Ireland. I tried to sleep, failed, worked on the speech, and was winding up TB on his bigger-Britain plans. 'I wonder if we could get India or China. Maybe both. Britain would be so big then.' I was sitting behind Cherie and Fiona, who were dreaming up more and more plans to open up Number 10. They wanted to get kids from every region in with their local MPs. We arrived in New York, and Cherie changed in the loo. UN ambassador John Weston came on and from then on, he was never more than six inches behind TB. We left in the Rolls-Royce, CB and FM chatting about how they didn't want to go to [journalist] Tina Brown's party. Magi Cleaver called to say it was hideous and heaving. We got there and were really tired and wanted to leave straight away. But TB was enjoying himself. TB made a totally over-the-top speech talking about how much Tina and Harry [Harold Evans, US-based former *Sunday Times* editor] had done for us. Harry said he wanted to praise me, Jonathan and Clare [Short]. I said don't dare put her in the same breath as me, not realising she was right next to me.

Monday, June 23
TB woke me up and asked me to go to see him. He wasn't happy with the clips he had done on the environment late last night and wanted to redo them. He thought both on the environment and Ireland, the story was running away from us. I assured him it was fine, there

was no point redoing it because events would overtake what he said anyway. We left for the UN, Weston trailing just behind him as he went. We had a meeting with Kofi [Annan, UN Secretary General], which was fine. Jonathan said afterwards if Robin puffs himself up any more he will blow away. Clare arrived with JP and was arguing for a line re halving poverty in Africa by 2015. TB was fine about it. Weston was pressing for TB to do a press conference, and I said no, JP, Robin and Clare should do it. It was classic watching them preparing for it. Clare said 'I'll do world poverty, Robin can lead on water and the UN, then John can do the rest.' I went to brief the Brits, who were all complaining they didn't get the speech or the itinerary, so I briefed hard on the environmental measures. There was also a line in there about his kids complaining he was never home, which I'd had my doubts about leaving in, as it was bound to get attention on the children. JP later said can he make any policy without having to go through his children? JP also said he had to rein in Peter on the Millennium front as he was putting Cabinet noses out of joint. 'If he gets any more puffed up with his own importance, he won't fit inside the bloody Dome,' he said. 'Anyone would think it was a real job!'

TB had a brief bilateral with John Bruton, which didn't go into much detail but would come back to hit us later. We went into the chamber at the UN with JP, RC, Clare. TB's speech went fine. Then we heard Bruton was doing a big doorstep. Magi came and told me that the media were saying Bruton had said we had reached an agreement on decommissioning. The impression some of them had was that this was an agreement with Sinn Fein. We had a few days to go and were saying this was a big breakthrough. I had the twenty-five minutes of the Al Gore [US Vice President] bilateral to think it through and then talked to Jonathan, John and TB. TB said we should play it down. He was more interested in telling me how intently they listened in the UN chamber, which they had. Gore said, only half in jest, 'You really gave it to us with both fists in there.' TB was very much playing it down as an attack but Gore said, off the record, it was quite helpful to be under pressure on this, from us and Germany. Gore was much more impressive than the last time we saw him, when he seemed to rely totally on his cue cards and didn't really engage in dialogue. This was very different. On energy policy in particular, he was right on top of detail. He was worried that the demands pre-Kyoto were unrealistic, that agreement would only come if there was compromise. TB said he would support a compromise. He felt though that we would be able to get support for a radical approach. They had a long session on Ireland and again Gore was fairly impressive in his knowledge. Bill C seemed to have talked to him about who was who.

He and TB had a private session while I was bounced by the press re Bruton. He said there had been agreement reached. I said there was not. An agreement was something all the parties signed up to and this was not the case because Sinn Fein were not there and it was vital the Unionists were totally on board. I was basically suggesting Bruton was overstating things. It was very irritating. We had agreed we should play down the significance of the meeting, and here we were with all hell breaking loose. We went over to meet TB. Weston was really getting on my nerves, now inserting himself into the discussions on Northern Ireland. He really was joined to TB's shoulder. TB did a doorstep to get it in a better place, emphasising no agreement reached etc., and what the issues were, namely the governments were close to agreement on the way forward on decommissioning but we needed Unionist support. We were getting a big hit from his green speech, but I was really tired and starting to feel depressed. At the airport I couldn't be bothered with all the false bonhomie and the joshing and joking that always happens when we bump into the media at airports. CB joking about shopping, RC posing. TB took me aside and said we had to keep working on the *Sun*. He said it was obvious Kavanagh was pursuing a very right-wing agenda and would want them back to the Tories if he could.

Tuesday, June 24

We were back in the office just after 8 and the day was mainly given over to Northern Ireland. Both the briefings were almost exclusively about that, even though TB had a Commons statement on the G8, Hague's first as leader, after which he met TB to get briefed on Ireland. The main meetings were with Trimble, John Taylor [deputy leader, Ulster Unionists] and Ken Maginnis [Ulster Unionist MP] – not great but outside they were not as bad as they were in the meeting – and John Hume. In between briefing that it was positive and upbeat, I was fixing up for the twelve-year-old girl TB had mentioned in the ABC interview to come in tomorrow. Trimble was pretty difficult though, at one and the same time said he did not like the document, whilst claiming he had not been allowed to see it, and said we were conceding too much to the IRA because there was no mechanism to throw them out. The UUs were overemotional and saw conspiracies everywhere. 'It's all a pattern, always the same pattern,' said DT. TB said it was a moment of decision. He wanted to make a statement saying it was time to get substantial negotiations under way, leading to a devolved Assembly plus North-South dialogue. He said the mood in the US vis-à-vis SF had changed. It was time they got a move on. TB said they had to recognise there had always been the prospect of them getting into talks without giving up actual weapons. He talked up the independence of the commission on decommissioning under de Chastelain,[1] which would review the situation every eight weeks. He had always felt the Tories bound themselves in too hard on decommissioning, and DT kept coming back to it, again and again, saying the mechanics were not strong enough. TB said there had to be inclusive talks with SF, and meanwhile build from the centre with the SDLP. He said there was a brief window of opportunity with the Irish and US governments together with us on this now.

Trimble said the paper gave the IRA most of what they wanted and they would now push for more. There is no real pressure on them to pursue only peaceful means. TB said there was an emergency brake. Maginnis said they would not be thrown off once they were in because the pressures would be to keep them on board. DT said they needed 1. a firm commitment to decommissioning happening alongside talks, 2. machinery put in place to prevent SDLP and the Irish government putting a spanner in the works, 3. no 'guns for concessions'. Once we got on to 'confidence-building measures', they were all 'another sop to the IRA'. Prisoners, plastic bullets, changes to policing, they saw them all as a sop to the IRA. Any change must have the acceptance of both traditions. DT said we cannot survive in the same room unless SF are in parallel building confidence through decommissioning. Maginnis said Paisley would be able to create mayhem with this. TB said there would be sanctions on SF. DT said they were too weak. TB said if we didn't go for this now, we would miss the opportunity that was there. He knew it was a risk. He knew that SF had acted in bad faith. He knew all the obstacles, but he felt they had to move it forward now. Ken Maginnis kept underlining just how deep the mutual suspicions were. The IRA had infiltrated many parts of their national life. This proposal would let them infiltrate top-level political life without any real demand being made on them. DT said Hume would never cut his links with Adams and McGuinness.

On one level, it was a terrible meeting in that every time TB made a specific point, they had strong arguments against it, and put them

[1] General John de Chastelain. Canadian former soldier and diplomat, head of the Independent International Commission on Decommissioning in Northern Ireland. Born a British subject and, like Blair, an old Fettesian.

June '97: Decommissioning of IRA weapons a big problem

very emotionally. On another level, they were positive in public and TB felt they wanted to do something. Some of the civil servants found the UUs a pain to deal with, but TB said he thought Trimble was fair. He said it makes quite a powerful impact when Maginnis tells you he has personally met people who he knows had plotted to kill him. Taylor was keen to have the documents and in the end we gave them, and they did a pretty positive doorstep in the street. Hume came in, was just as emotional, said he was authorised to say he could set up a meeting between Martin McGuinness and Quentin Thomas [senior Northern Ireland Office official]. TB said that was not possible and he had to say that if SF did not come on board as a result of the decommissioning paper, and the IRA declare a ceasefire, he would acknowledge that we had to move on without them.

Hume felt we were close to something, though John Holmes warned me he always said that. But he had seen Adams and McGuinness and they had not dismissed the decommissioning paper out of hand. The prisoners issue was important. He said one meeting between him, Quentin Thomas and McGuinness would lead to a ceasefire. 'The prize is enormous but so is the danger.' TB felt he had gone as far as he could in pushing the UUs. He would tip them over the edge if he went much further. 'I'd get torn limb from limb.' It was again, on one level, a good meeting, on another it was not. They were miles apart, but the one thing TB took out that was positive was a shared desire to make progress, even if both sides were basically saying the other would make it impossible.

Wednesday, June 25

Ireland statement day. We had agreed yesterday to get in the twelve-year-old girl TB mentioned in America, so that was the focus early on. I was in late, having taken the boys to school for once, and worked on Ireland most of the day. TB was worrying both about Northern Ireland and Hague. It was his first PMQs and we thought he would do either devolution or health charges. He went on devolution. Hague was OK without being terrific. TB was in a fury over the story about their new £3,500 bed, which was on the front page of the *Sun*. Following her shopping in New York, there was a touch of the Imeldas [Imelda Marcos, extravagant former 'first lady' of the Philippines] about the coverage surrounding CB. He knew nothing about it, was livid and said he would pay for it himself. It was only then I realised it was meant to be paid for out of public money. CB then called and said on the basis of this, they could not possibly spend any money doing up the kitchen as planned, or anything else. Later it emerged, to nobody's surprise, that Carole Caplin had bought the bed. It can't have been easy moving into a new 'house', and then finding you have very limited control over what you can and cannot do in there, but I think the problem was it is only just beginning fully to dawn on CB how un-private her life is going to be. Then another Clare Short fiasco to deal with. She had 'accidentally' invited Adams and McGuinness to a reception at Lancaster House [mansion in St James's used for government functions]. This only came to light when Adams called to say he could not make it and could he send someone else? I told TB, who said he needed an explanation. I said we should announce what she had done, and how, and at such a sensitive time, and he should sack her. He said no. My view of Clare was that she was nothing but trouble, had virtually no redeeming features and would give him more grief than any upside from her merited. But he had a more favourable view. He had yet another chat with me about working too hard, not using Peter enough. Peter was doing the Millennium relaunch tomorrow. TB said he was worried that he was so dependent on me, which is why I had to get a stronger team. He said, I am more dependent on you than anyone, which is why Peter finds it so difficult at the moment and you have to be sympathetic about that. 'We go round the world together, all the time on big stuff, see all the big players, and he is stuck back here not as involved as he wants to be.' I said I couldn't be bothered with all the emotionalism.

Saturday, June 28

Today I caught up on paperwork, mainly Ireland and Hong Kong. The HK trip was going to be tricky, and I needed to get on top of the detail. We had a fairly big press pack coming, who would need briefing before we left, which meant today and first thing tomorrow. I called TB, who was also working his way through the briefing papers from the FCO. There were two main lines to push, that there must be adherence to the Joint Declaration [Chinese-British Joint Declaration in 1984 on Hong Kong's future], but also a new start in relations with China. We had dinner at Philip and Gail's [Gail Rebuck, publisher and wife of Philip Gould]. He said Hague was not making an impact, but there was a sense of the government now being taken for granted, and that was potentially a problem.

Sunday, June 29

I spent much of the morning reading all the briefings on Hong Kong to get up to speed. On the flight we had FCO expert Graham Fry who was clever and funny. 'I speak fluent Japanese so they put me on

China.' TB was worrying mainly about the Budget, but also about definition, whether we were really getting over a sense of identity about the government. He was also stressing the need for a stronger foreign policy. The VC10 was slow and it was a long, long flight. We had a good session with Fry, several meals, lots of chat about where we were on Ireland, the Budget. We had a bizarre stopover in Siberia, where we were not allowed to get off the plane until the refuelling was done, and were then allowed off to stretch our legs, but had to stay within ten yards of the plane.

Monday, June 30

We arrived at 11am local time. Chris Patten [former Conservative Cabinet minister, last governor of Hong Kong] and his wife came on. Chris went over what they should say and we left the plane to do the arrivals and a doorstep. TB praised CP's time as governor, said the Joint Declaration must be stuck to but we needed a new start with China. I felt Patten was overdoing the emotional side of things. It was easy to see why he'd taken to the place so much. But even so, everyone knew this day was going to come, and the handover would happen, yet he kind of gave the impression it was a personal act being committed against him. We had a working lunch at which he and our ambassador in China, Len Appleyard, ran over the meetings TB was due to have. When someone referred to the Chinese as the 'Dewhursts of Peking' there was a mild laugh around the table. I looked at CP a bit bemused. 'Dewhurst as in butchers,' he said. When someone said TB had Shakespeare's works to present as a gift to President Jiang Zemin, someone asked what about something for Li Peng [Chinese Prime Minister]. One of the officials, picking up on the theme, said 'What about a blue and white apron?' They were really wound up, far too emotional. They had negotiated every last detail of the handover and the ceremonies. The Chinese were insisting that as Jiang was a head of state, Prince Charles go to see him. They said that if they met on neutral territory, then Jiang had to sit on the left, as he was host. Eventually they went for parallel lines. There was a discussion about whether TB could leave early from the farewell ceremony tonight. I saw no problem, but CP was aghast. The general sense from CP was total doom and gloom, corruption of the business community, worries about democracy. I sensed a lot of it was personal; that he was giving up a job he liked, his family leaving a lifestyle he liked. I reread all the briefs and got filled in by Jonathan in London on the row between Peter and Charlie re the pre-Budget briefing that was going on. Peter was spitting, according to Jonathan, and Whelan was spitting back.

We left for a walkabout at the Majestic Palace shopping centre. The crowds were enormous. From the floor, he looked up to three different levels, three galleries, all lined with people cheering. I said to CP that the prime minister was the prime minister and it must be clear who the cheering was for. Though I said it with some good humour, he got the message and stayed back a bit. There was clearly a real affection for him, whereas with TB it was as much the celebrity factor as anything.

We then left for a meeting with Prince Charles on board *Britannia*. He strikes me as a fairly decent bloke, surrounded by a lot of nonsense and people best described as from another age. He and TB had a private session while CB, Bill, Katie [TB's brother and sister-in-law] and I were taken on a tour of *Britannia*. Then TB got the same tour as well, 'Oh you must, Prime Minister, it's fascinating,' while we made small talk with Charles. He said the more I travel the more I realise how marvellous Britain is. We drank very weak tea in very thin china, and little cakes that looked nicer than they tasted. There was something a bit sad about him. All his life, even on big issues, he had to make small talk, surrounded by luxury, as here, people fawning on him, and yet somehow obviously unfulfilled. People might look on and think how fantastic to live on a boat like that, waited on hand and foot, but if it is all you know, and you are basically not fulfilled, and your private life is a mess, it did not strike me as a very happy existence. I travelled with TB to the meeting with C.H. Tung [Tung Chee Hwa, chief executive of Hong Kong], and TB said as we drove away 'We must keep *Britannia*.' I knew he would. 'What an asset,' he said.

TB did the new-start bit, subtly warned re his worries about the corrupting of the Civil Service, said elections were key. Tung said May was the earliest they could be held. TB raised worries re the Chinese putting their own security people in place. Then free press. Economy. Human rights. Tung came back fairly bullish about it all. It was clear when it came to the two systems, one country, he wanted us to understand the country was China. He said the West had to develop better relations with China. TB repeated the new start was linked to adherence to the Joint Declaration. He did not want a great confrontation but international opinion would look to us to ensure it was upheld. Tung said, in answer to every point just about, that he was confident. By the time we got to the farewell ceremony it was pouring with rain and the poor organisation was such that we were left stranded without an umbrella or a way to our seats, other than by walking in front of the bigwigs. Eventually we were led to the steps and I was between Paddy Ashdown and Geoffrey Howe [former Conservative Chancellor and Foreign Secretary], two down from Hague and Ffion, who had chosen today to name their wedding day in December. I had a good look at them both. Hague looked the part. He didn't look at all out of place. She looked nervous. Geoffrey Howe gave me a running commentary, and his main theme was that we had to be nicer to China. The handover ceremony was poor, a mix of orchestral and military music. CP's speech again overdid the emotion, and as he sat down, he was close to tears and his daughters behind him were crying. TB looked embarrassed. Eventually we escaped and were driven to the police launch taking us over the river to the meeting with Jiang Zemin, Li Peng and others. It was quite a dramatic journey, as the weather was now pretty stormy. On their side, the crowds were smaller and less enthusiastic. TB got quite a good reception, but it was not a good meeting. We went in, TB met Jiang, shook hands, posed for the cameras, and then it began. There were a lot of hangers-on. Jiang had a fixed look on his face, half smile, half frown. TB did his now well-rehearsed line – new start, adhere to JD – a few clichés on it being a historic day, how we wanted to build bridges between each other, between China and the future. As the tea came round, Jiang said the handover removed a shadow from the relationship. The Labour Party does not have the historic burden. He said there was a Chinese saying – we can all wear our light uniform or march forward in a light manner. We all nodded knowingly, without having much of a clue what he meant. They did a bit on the economy and trade, again not very deep though. TB slipped in a very brief mention of human rights, and John Holmes wrote 'phew' on his notes as I had been briefing for days that obviously he would press them on human rights. Robin C and Derek Fatchett [FCO minister] looked very unimpressed. We all gave each other little 'Was that it?' looks. He did it so gently it was barely noticeable, added to which Li Peng kept spitting loudly into his hankie, and one of his spits coincided with the human rights bit. Li Peng said we had lost out economically because of bad relations. TB praised their economic reforms. Jiang slipped in a reference to non-interference as a key to building mutual respect. He said TB was a young man and would be around for a long time. 'The old give way to the new.' HK can be a bridge not a barrier between UK and China. Best sound bite of the meeting. The meeting ended fairly abruptly when some of the hangers-on started stirring. TB knew he had not been at his best. He said later he had suddenly felt jet-lagged and tired, a bit disorientated.

We got back to the boat and TB was a bit downcast because he knew he had fucked up. I went to the Conrad Hotel to brief the (drenched) lobby. They asked how much of the conversation had been devoted to human rights. Sufficient for them to know he was pressing them, I said. They pressed for detail but as there wasn't any I just pushed the same line. I got back as the banquet was ending. Robin was doing the toasts, more puffed up than ever. I bumped into Heseltine and his wife and kissed her to annoy him. 'Put her down,' he said. 'You've stolen enough from us.' Meanwhile TB was with Charles sorting out another bilateral. It was eventually agreed Charles and TB would go through one door as Jiang and Li Peng came through the other. We then went to the final ceremony. It was pretty grim. It was when the Chinese troops did their goose-stepping march that you sensed the full awfulness of what CP had been going on about. Charles' speech was OK. Jiang was more triumphalist and full of 'Motherland' references. Then the flag came down, and theirs went up and it was all pretty sick. TB hated it and it showed a little. Charles and Patten left for *Britannia*. TB said he found the whole thing humiliating. I can't believe that we could not have kept it. Did anyone realise the Chinese soldiers were all the same height? On the plane out, TB had a long session with Paddy to take forward the Lib-Lab stuff. I slept straight through for thirteen hours. I even slept through Siberia.

Tuesday, July 1

TB was now totally focused on the Budget and we got back to a series of meetings and chats with GB all day. Moira Wallace and Derek Scott were both complaining that they could not get anywhere on the detail, that they didn't know what was going on, and GB would only speak to TB and instructed officials not to speak to them. Moira said it was making it impossible. TB was alarmed that GB would not let others know what was going on, also insisting on conditions re cash and improved structures in health and education. Jonathan said Phil Stephens [FT] had told him Gordon's people were briefing the line that GB was the domestic prime minister, TB was the foreign affairs PM. Trevor Kavanagh quizzed me on the Royals. Diana and the kids were due to go to Chequers on Sunday and it was clearly getting out that she was going. I said there were meetings planned but they would not go ahead if it got out. TB was keen to see both and not just Charles. I also said he was pushing close to the limits re his own children. If it pops up they are hanging round with the royal kids, I think they have a problem.

Budget day. Charlie had briefed out a fair bit of Budget background and detail, too much in fact, but thankfully the cut in corporation tax and the boost for health and education spending were not yet public. This was a big day, and not just for GB. A lot of the landscape for the whole term was being set. Peter Hyman was worried that any tax increases would become a trust problem for TB not GB. Syd Young [former *Mirror* colleague] came in for a cup of tea, having told me during the campaign that having tea at Number 10 was a lifetime's ambition. I was really conscious, both with him and at [former *Mirror* reporter] Tom Merrin's memorial service later, of the different life I now lead. For example, having to clear away all the Budget papers before Syd came in, or being at the service and knowing that by the time I got back, work would have piled up whilst they all then trooped off to the pub.

I had a brief meeting with GB on the Budget, at which we agreed the key strategic lines to push in the immediate aftermath. We wanted to get the focus on health and education spending while also making clear the goal was long-term stability and old-style tax and spend was gone. We should emphasise that we were always going to do something with the windfall tax other than the jobs programme. He was pretty hyper. He briefed the Cabinet and got a good response, particularly for the extra money on health and education, and for the shift on pensions. He rattled through the figures and the forecasts, and then emphasised the key themes – investment, welfare to work, stability, education and skills. Some of the tax changes were straightforward, like petrol prices, and others less so. You sensed he was using the Cabinet presentation pretty much as a warm-up to his performance in the House. His style was very rat-tat-tat, very little light and shade, powering his way through it as if he was desperate to get it over with. But the Cabinet liked it.

At TB's PMQs preparation, he was annoyed that he was not getting information he needed quickly enough. Betty [Boothroyd, Speaker of the House of Commons] had allowed a Private Notice Question on the fact that details of the Budget seemed to have been leaked to the *Financial Times*. It was pretty obvious Hague would come at TB on it, which he did. TB did fine. It was odd, when we left Number 10, to have so many media in the street but this time all trained on Number 11. GB was doing a photocall with his new red box, and then driven to the Commons with Sue Nye [adviser to GB]. TB was fine at PMQs, but there was never going to be much interest in it, other than as a warm-up to the Budget. GB went down well with the back benches, and with the journalists I spoke to, though the broadcasters were very sniffy all night and we had to work on them, particularly to push health and education spending. Mike Brunson even said there were no surprises. I went back for a meeting during which I said to TB that GB would get a good press, but they were on to some of the long-term problems. I went briefly to GB's party, and he was much more relaxed now, laughing as he did the rounds. TB came through, and felt the thing was going OK.

Thursday, July 3

GB got a pretty good press though the BBC were still running it fairly negatively, focusing on the opposition and the scrapping of tax credits for pension funds, which [Peter] Lilley [Shadow Chancellor] had used to call it 'the Robert Maxwell budget'.[1] TB felt it had gone brilliantly in the press, though he still worried about some of the long-term issues. He gave a lecture to the Cabinet about where we were going with this. We had to emphasise that the government approach was to make Britain 'fair, modern and strong' and he wanted them to make speeches on that theme, related to their own briefs. He was very warm re GB and then said the four things to emphasise were 1. prudence, financial responsibility for the long term, 2. schools and hospitals, 3. it was New Labour – pro business, pro enterprise, 4. it was a One Nation Budget. It was all fine, but slightly different to how GB pitched it himself, and people picked up on that. He said by the end of July we need to get domestic definition through winning the arguments on the Budget, and also pushing home the arguments re Amsterdam. GB said the Tories looked ridiculous. He defended his pensions changes, said it was a much-needed reform and this was the right time to make it. Pension funds are now on the same footing as others. At the strategy meeting later TB said the only moment of Hague's speech that concerned him was when he went for the windfall tax. The main event of the day was his meeting with Bertie Ahern [Irish Prime Minister, having succeeded John Bruton on June 26]. TB had a private session first, and then the broader meeting with a clear difference in mood between Bruton and Ahern. BA was a nice enough bloke, and very affable, but TB felt he was basically putting the Sinn Fein line most of the time. Bruton had basically been hostile to SF. Ahern was not.

[1] Following the death in 1992 of former Labour MP and Mirror Group Newspapers proprietor Robert Maxwell it was discovered that he had plundered company pension funds.

TB said after they went he was worried the peace process had taken a setback. I bumped into GB in the Commons after my briefing on the Ahern meeting and he gave me a lift back. He was a lot friendlier than usual, obviously felt yesterday had gone well, and that we had helped.

Friday, July 4

I left with TB for Sedgefield and worked on the speech for tomorrow. Philip [Gould] did a very good note on the focus groups after the Budget. We clearly had to watch it. The published polls were going well, but there had been nothing like universal approval. Phil Stephens said in his *FT* column that I was the second most powerful figure in the government after GB. Bollocks. TB's main focus on the plane was how to keep going on education and health, with the pensions story still going strong. Andy Grice called saying that one of their reporters was on to a story about friction between the old guard and the new guard, some of which was very near the mark, for example CB having rows with the staff, me not getting on with some of the permanent civil servants. Alex Allan agreed he would speak to him, say it was crap. CB was convinced that someone in the household was briefing against her. TB did a phone call with Thatcher on Bosnia and NATO enlargement, much to the annoyance of John Burton [TB's constituency agent]. Myrobella [TB's constituency home] had changed markedly. There were armed police at the barber's shop as we approached, new fences, a new little police station, cops everywhere. André [Suard] called to say he was being hounded by the *Sunday Times*. That was clearly the next story and it would be a bad one. CB put him on to Hilary [Coffman] who said he was to say nothing.

CB and I travelled back to London together and had a nice enough chat about things. CB talked very loudly on her mobile and as she came off it I said I hope nobody in the carriage is a hack. She said she was finding it hard to get her head round the fact that anything they said or did was considered fair game, and also all the stuff that wasn't true. I said she had to be really heavy with Diana re no publicity out of Chequers. Fiona had spoken to Diana's office who seemed to take offence at the intimation that we thought they might.

Saturday, July 5

Andy Grice called to say the *Sunday Times* were doing a story about CB having a hairdresser, make-up artist and stylist in Denver. I talked to Fiona, Peter M and Alex Allan and we agreed a line that these were personal arrangements and she met the bill. It turned out, however, that in Denver and Hong Kong, some of the costs were met by the government, which was what happened with Norma Major and Thatcher. But I said she would pay. TB called a couple of times. He hated this type of thing, partly because it was personal re her, but also because he knew they felt they could get at him through the family. He said it had been her first big trip and she wanted to look her best. It took the wind out of the *Sunday Times* sails to say there was no taxpayers' money involved, but it was still a bad story. CB called from the car, and again was very loose on the phone and I said to be careful what she was saying in front of pool drivers etc. who I knew from my *Mirror* days were capable of gossip. She said 'If I end up having to pay for all this, I'll be broke pretty quickly.'

Peter M called and said that there was a lot of chatter around that he and I, and even TB, were responsible for leaking details of the Budget. There was even a story that GB told me and Peter what was in the Budget some weeks ago, including with a specific false trail to see if it ended up in the *Sunday Times*, which they were sure it would. This was bonkers-ville. I spoke to CW who of course denied all knowledge. Fiona and I went to the dance at the school at which there was another spat between groups of working-class and middle-class parents. TB called after I'd gone to bed to say that the Drumcree march was going ahead on strict conditions and if they were not met it would be banned next year.[1] He said it could be a bloodbath but the overwhelming advice of the army and the RUC was that it would be worse if it was called off. I spoke to Mo who said she thought it was the wrong decision; that it showed Unionism would win these arguments by being more vocal in complaining. This would set us right back with the nationalists who would feel they were never listened to in dialogue, a mindset that fuelled a belief in terrorism. She said Ronnie Flanagan [chief constable, RUC] had been dithering all day but the plan was to move to Garvaghy Road at 4am, make it secure, let the marchers go down with no music, a few flags, then wait for riots

---

[1] The troubled annual parade by Orangemen from Drumcree Parish Church, Portadown (County Armagh) through the Catholic Garvaghy Road area. The parade was a key event in the Protestant marching season, marking the victory of William of Orange over the Catholic James II at the Battle of the Boyne, culminating on July 12 each year. In 1998 the Northern Ireland Parades Commission banned the Drumcree march because of the Protestant/Catholic clashes. In following years the march was prevented from using Garvaghy Road as a route.

around the province, and SF saying we were the same as the Tories, always kowtowing to Unionism. She said she really believed it was a crazy decision but if this was the army and RUC advice she would go along with it.

Sunday, July 6

The violence overnight [in Northern Ireland following the Drumcree decision] was bad though as yet there were no deaths. I got next to no sleep as I was speaking to TB, Mo and others. Mo was really fed up with things, but she accepted not to have gone along with the overwhelming security advice would have been a very big step to take, especially if things then went wrong in a different direction. TB was really pissed off at the hairdresser story, said he should have known this was going on. He said if I had strong views on things like this, I must speak to him and CB and that she would take it from me. TB was at Chequers entertaining Diana and William. We chatted about it briefly on Sunday, more extensively on the way to the airport on Monday. He said she was more gorgeous than ever and 'Yes, before you ask, she did ask for you.' But he admitted the conversation was hard and it might have been better had I been there to jolly things along. She had been a bit miffed that we had suggested she might leak. William played football with the boys and went for a swim with them, while she and TB went for a walk in the woods. Fiona and I went for dinner at the Molloys' [former *Mirror* editor Mike Molloy, friend of celebrity chef Delia Smith]. Delia Smith had been floating in and out of the working-peer list, and I'd asked Mike to check whether she would like to be a peer or not. She decided she would only do it if she could do it full time so it was a no. Peter Hain called to say the Spice Girls were going to invite TB to appear in their next video. Were they now?

Monday, July 7

Mo was taking a few knocks, but in briefings all day I stressed support and how she was doing well in very difficult circumstances. As ever when Northern Ireland was in the news, the papers were desperate to splash on something else. CB was done over in several places, and I sensed the Tories were going to start piling in on her. I had a chat with TB as soon as I got in and said there was something here that only he could deal with. It was hardly my place to say I thought she had a problem with money. He suggested the four of us sat down to talk it over and put together a strategy for her, based on clarity about financing and extending her charity work. He said she had to be well presented, and she felt the need to look her best and Carole [Caplin] did a good job for her. We were doing a school visit with DB. TB did a doorstep, first on schools, and also on Drumcree, saying the search for peace goes on. The eleven o'clock was mainly about Ireland, and also CB.

I started to brief myself on Madrid and the NATO summit. Robin Butler was seeing TB and telling him that in his view Charlie was definitely responsible for Budget leaks. I had a positive vetting [security clearance] session. The guy was very nice and didn't actually push me terribly hard. He was interested in the drinking days, university, sex. In the car to the airport, we went over our plans re Libs on Cabinet committees. It was not made easier by them saying there was a £5 billion black hole in the Budget finances. We were back on the VC10, mainly reading up on Madrid, and I wrote a briefing note on [NATO] enlargement, how we were at odds with the French, and totally with the US on this. We got there and TB headed off for the dinner. We hung around for ages waiting for it to finish and then got a call from the cops saying he had gone off for an unscheduled bilateral with Clinton, which looked like it would go on for a while. They had gone back to Bill's hotel and asked for some beers to be sent up. Godric worked out we had now gone round the world in forty-eight days, having topped 25,000 miles. The press was straight on to the special relationship story, with TB and Clinton off together again till the early hours. Mo called me at midnight, said there was no violence on the streets, but Denis Murray [BBC Ireland correspondent] had produced a leaked document in which an official said that forcing the march through would be the least worst option. She was obviously worried it would lead to renewed attacks on her from people saying the deal had been stitched up, but I said she should be robust, say of course we looked at all the options. The real worry was that now there was leaking going on from inside.

Tuesday, July 8
Yesterday ended at 2.30 this morning, when we were debriefing TB re his session with Bill. He was wearing nothing but underpants and a wide-open dressing gown, and telling us cheerfully he had forgotten to raise Ireland. He was worried Clinton was wobbling on Slovenia and Romania and saying we could end up being more Catholic than the Pope in holding out firmly re NATO entrants. He said it had been mainly social, drinking beer together, talking politics. He thought Clinton was basically a dealmaker and was going to make a deal on

NATO enlargement. The working breakfast was a bit more subdued, allied to which Robin irritatingly brought in an STV crew doing a profile of him. In the session, TB and Bill were dominant. Robin was taking notes for me which I was using to brief. He said TB was on form, emphasising that we could live with the applicant countries being named as long as we didn't actually have to commit ourselves to tie them in.

Unbelievably gorgeous hostesses. During the break, it became clear that Clinton and TB felt exactly the same. There was a bizarre scene during a break, in the Gents. Several leaders, including Clinton, TB, Prodi, Kok and Kohl, were all having a pee in a row of stand-up urinals. Clinton turned around and said 'Isn't this the greatest picture that was never taken?' TB told him the story of the time Churchill moved away from Attlee while they were peeing together. Attlee looked hurt. Churchill explained: 'Every time you see something big you want to nationalise it.' TB spoke well, Robin said, and was winning the argument. TB said we were winning the arguments on NATO and you could see there was real panic among the French delegation, with Chirac having clearly overstated what he intended to get out of this. I briefed again, and during the briefing word came through that it had all wound up. I briefed hard re the special relationship and how we had worked with the Americans to get what we wanted, and also RC's negotiating abilities. On the drive back to the hotel, I told TB the Uxbridge by-election was set for July 31.[1] He didn't believe we could lose. He said he still doesn't fear Hague. He was also serious about the need for a new foreign policy and believed we had to use our history better to shape the future.

Wednesday, July 9

The hard NATO work was all done, just a little clearing up left, plus the Ukraine signing ceremony. I briefed on Clinton backing us on Ireland. TB was raving about the palace in which they had dinner last night and said again that we needed a more clearly thought-through approach to foreign policy. He was worrying about the fox-hunting bill. He had allowed it to go ahead because he claimed we'd been told Mike Foster [anti-hunting Labour MP] would not do anything else as a Private Member's Bill. TB was sure we were heading for disaster, especially as we were on the eve of a massive

---

[1] Conservative MP Sir Michael Shersby had died suddenly on May 8, after holding his seat with a narrow majority over Labour.

demonstration on the subject. We prepared for PMQs on the plane home. He was sure Hague would go for him on pensions. He did, and for the first time got the better of TB. He then had the NATO statement. At the four o'clock I was getting irritated about the line of questioning on Drumcree. The leaked memo had suddenly taken off and Mo was under attack from all sides on the grounds that it suggested the decision on the march to go ahead was taken three weeks ago. I defended her strongly, as had TB in the House. Then TB met Hume, Seamus Mallon [deputy leader, SDLP] and Eddie McGrady [SDLP MP] in his office at the House. He was very firm re Mo, said he felt for her but he was sure the right decision was taken – you cannot ignore the head of the police and the army. They were more reasonable today, though Mallon made the point that those who made threats the loudest tended to be the ones who got their way, and it was neither fair nor sensible. Hume said we were sitting on a tinderbox. McGrady said it was always the nationalists who were not listened to. TB said that was not fair. He was downcast afterwards, said some days it was impossible to see the way forward. Blunkett came round for dinner. He was very down about the Civil Service, found them too slow, not imaginative enough. TB felt after the bed and hair stories that we could not allow much money to be spent on the kitchen.

Thursday, July 10

It was a dull day, but two big bad stories were upon us. First, the rise in interest rates, then the massive rally for the countryside in Hyde Park, expected to attract 100,000 people. We did not have much to compete with it because we had delayed the announcement of the Lib-Lab Cabinet committee on PR for the European elections. Jonathan then said we had another problem. The SAS had tried to capture three Bosnian war criminals in the early hours. One was captured, successfully, one was killed after a gun battle, one was not there. NATO in the build-up had referred to the group as the Prijedor 3. I said they had to become known as the Prijedor 2. I felt we should get the story out on our terms. TB was in a meeting with JP. He agreed and said I should call George [Robertson] to get the line out. I spoke to GR who said it must be announced by the NATO operation, first so as not to offend our allies, second to minimise risk to British soldiers there – far better it was seen as a NATO operation, not just British. I saw the point but he was being very George-ish about it. I passed on what he said to the meeting of the Big Four. Robin was gung-ho and wanted us to go straight out and say what a success this had been. So was JP. GB was desperate to get it out, not least because interest-rate rises were so dominant. TB and I were pushing it because it was one of those situations where it was clearly going to get out – these were big catches they were talking about – and it was better we get it out on our terms and not theirs. Then George came in with Robin Butler. Butler made the point about the need to protect British people in Bosnia. George said it was important that Javier Solana [NATO Secretary General] made any announcement along with SACEUR [NATO Supreme Allied Commander in Europe]. The problem was Solana was on a plane and SACEUR was speaking at a podium in Stuttgart. George was being very George-ish now, and beginning to get on TB's nerves a bit. TB said what would happen if NATO was attacked by the Russians and everyone was on a plane or at a podium? Would the NATO governments be able to speak? I said if we allowed the other side to present the story it would be cock-up not success, because the story would be the one that got away. But GR was very firm and TB agreed with him eventually. But he was not impressed. As we walked through to Cabinet, he said 'We've got to get some steel into George.'

John Holmes said Reuters were beginning to snap on it, and it was all a bit garbled. I knew this would happen. It meant that the story was in the public domain and not on our terms. I suggested that we say TB, RC and GR briefed the Cabinet on the operation and George was to make a statement and we would at this stage just give bare details and name the two war criminals. After Cabinet, there was another meeting with George, Butler, TB and RC and we finally agreed we should do it now. I was due to brief at 11.30 and George was going on about the need to inform his private office beforehand, etc. TB was getting very impatient. 'Get on with it, Ali,' he said. 'I've heard enough about this.' So at the start of the briefing, I said there would be a statement in the Commons on Bosnian war criminals. Unbelievably, nobody asked about it during the briefing, so I got a note slipped to Adam Boulton saying ask me about Bosnia for God's sake. Then I gave out some of the details. One or two immediately made comments about interest-rate rises. RC did a doorstep, pumping himself up nicely. Nelson Mandela [President of South Africa] came in at 4, and chatted to a group of school-children in the street. I missed the meeting, because I was doing the four o'clock, mainly on Ireland, with Mo still under pressure, and Bosnia. I got back to the end of the Mandela meeting, and we then had a strategy meeting on the terrace. TB was emphasising that we have to build a sense of the government for the long term in every message. Philip was worried about the lack of strategic grip. Peter and I were barely speaking at the moment, nor were Peter and Gordon. TB was going on about 'fair, modern and strong' and I felt we should simply be doing delivery, focusing on keeping promises.

Friday, July 11

We had a problem on Freedom of Information. David Clark [Chancellor of the Duchy of Lancaster] had lunch with John Pienaar [BBC] and told him it was being delayed because of civil servants. The truth was it was being delayed because the work he'd done was so poor. There was massive coverage of the countryside rally and interest-rate rise, and the Bosnian situation. We had a policy awayday at Chequers but were late leaving and then we stopped for a cup of tea at a takeaway near Paddington, people gobsmacked to see us walking in to get a cup of tea. TB was worried about definition and the fox-hunting bill. He wanted us to get Mike Foster to agree to push it to a joint committee of the Commons and Lords. Chequers was a good place for these kinds of meetings. Very quiet. Mobiles didn't work. Good food. Long walks and all that. Geoff Mulgan [policy adviser] and Peter Hyman were going through some of the big questions coming up, particularly on welfare, education and the economy. There were various presentations by Mulgan, Roger Liddle [European policy adviser] on Europe. TB was impressive but it was notable that he would react instinctively with a right-wing response. Geoff Mulgan threw up some moral choices we had to face, and TB instinctively leaned to the right. E.g. TB said he was in favour of gay marriages but would skirt around it in public. What about cannabis? asked Geoff. TB shook his head.

During the health discussion in the afternoon, led by Robert Hill [policy adviser], he was very interested in whether we could do more with charges in the NHS. But when someone suggested defence cuts, it was a clear no go. On schools, he said we were not being radical enough. On Europe he was really concerned about the politics of it all. On EMU he was clear the French and Germans were going to go ahead and we had to work out a strategy re the criteria. Down on the European institutions, CAP a total disgrace. It was a good lively discussion and there were some bright people in the policy team. Lunch was interrupted by a call with Bertie Ahern. The news that the Orange Order had agreed to reroute the Drumcree march vindicated Mo and gave a real sense of lift and hope. The big disagreement with

Bertie was still decommissioning. Bertie did not think [George] Mitchell [independent chairman of the negotiations that led to the Good Friday Agreement] meant decommissioning during talks. TB did. We had a football match, my team against TB's, and we lost 3-2. TB missed a totally open goal though. After the fuss over a new bed/hair scenes, TB was worried re the new kitchen plans for Number 10. He told me to tell the office it should be middle of the range not top of the range and no more than 15k. But he didn't speak to CB so when someone spoke to her about it, she thought it was me laying down the law on her bloody kitchen, not TB.

Sunday, July 13

We had a very nice lunch at Derry Irvine's. Peter M and I had our first proper conversation in ages. He felt that I had been deliberately excluding him, not seeking his views and ignoring them if he volunteered them. I felt he had slightly lost the plot and was too grand and hoity-toity. We were able to speak very frankly to each other and agreed that TB relied on both of us in different ways, and wanted us to work together, which we had to do. It cleared the air, but he had got more out of touch, and more concerned about his own profile than the effectiveness of the government.

Monday, July 14

After a quiet weekend, I woke up to find gay sex at sixteen leading the news. The decision to drop the ECHR case had been made public.[1] It meant, as I said to the MIO meeting with Peter M later, that in forty-eight hours we had two bad stories that simply came up and hit us, the other being the 'People's Panel', an idiotic idea from David Clark.[2] Even more bizarrely, that one had come from a briefing Clark did for American correspondents! Why? We were losing our grip of events. We also had to keep an eye on the nanny-state stuff. On the one hand, we wanted gay sex at sixteen, on the other, Tessa Jowell [health minister] was holding a so-called smoking summit and the idea of a ban on smoking was around. I saw TB before the nine o'clock meeting and said we did not want to give

[1] The European Court of Human Rights found that the existence of different ages of consent for heterosexuals and homosexuals in the UK was discriminatory. As a result, the UK government would propose a bill to Parliament to reduce the age of consent for homosexual sex to sixteen.
[2] The People's Panel, a giant focus group formed to examine a wide range of public issues, was billed as Blair's hotline to the nation. It was wound up in 2002.

the sense that these were the kinds of issues we really cared about, and we should be focusing on the things that won us the election. The mixture of political correctness and nanny-state interference, not helped by fox hunting, could become pretty difficult. The liberals in the office, like Liz Lloyd [policy adviser] and Peter Hyman, said I was just being old-fashioned, but I was trying to forestall the end of the honeymoon.

I had a meeting with Robin Butler about whether TB could take an RAF plane on holiday. TB was nervous but was assured it was the safest way. The *Irish Times* had the story of resumed contact with the IRA which put me on the spot, and I had to confirm it. It was difficult not to. The 'People's Panel' story got the response I expected it to. I think they could tell that I was defending it without any enthusiasm at all. I had a couple of calls during the day with Ryan Giggs [footballer, Manchester United and Wales]. Alex [Ferguson, Manchester United manager and friend of AC] had squared him to help with the Welsh Assembly campaign, and he agreed first he would do a visit and also a *Mirror* article, which we drafted. By lunchtime, the age-of-consent story was being run alongside raising the age for buying cigarettes. TB was fairly relaxed, said yes, it was bad, and we would get hit, but we were bound to take hits, and we had to see it in its proper perspective. I met the guy from MI6 who liaised with the press, said his work was mainly about keeping things out of the press, but they did some proactive work too. I said he should feel free to use me to get out anything he wanted to. FM and I had dinner with Michael and Gilda Levy. He was really pissed off with Peter M, said he always came to him when he needed something but he had heard that Peter tried to stop him getting a peerage. We talked a lot about CB, felt the money thing would become a problem. Gilda felt it was a basic insecurity. Michael was also very insecure, but basically a decent man. He constantly needed to be told how well he was doing, how nobody else could raise the kind of money he did.

Tuesday, July 15

TB, Jonathan and I all complained of feeling tired today. We were bound to make mistakes when we all felt like this. I saw TB early on. He was alarmed at some of the nanny-state stuff coming out. We took the expected hammering on the age of consent. The problem dominating the eleven o'clock briefing was the DUP [Democratic Unionist Party] attacking Mo over the revelation that we were engaged in contact with Sinn Fein. Peter M and I had a meeting with heads of information, at which we stressed the need to get a strategic message around stories, so they did not just pop up out of the blue. It was a really moribund event. Those who spoke complained there was little feedback from the centre and we were constantly making demands of them. I said this was not about centralisation, but proper co-ordination. I said if government communications was invented now, it would not be invented with the system we have. How much money was being spent and wasted on departments all doing the same things in their own way, e.g. media monitoring, computer systems. I don't think some of them had any idea how out of date they were. I was called to a meeting with TB, Donald D and Derry and later Peter M re the devolution White Paper. Donald had agreed to cuts in Scottish MPs, and they were arguing about numbers. Finally it was agreed that yes, we would cut the numbers, but we had to watch that we didn't inflame the campaign. The big worry was low turnout and we had to get the party more engaged. TB said we now had strong language on sovereignty, strong language on tax and a clear signal that there will be a reduction of Westminster MPs. Then to lunch with a group of Welsh editors and Ron Davies. It showed why we were likely to be in trouble. They just had no real interest in it. TB did his best and gave them a semi-convincing impression that he was really up for it. They were a pretty unappealing bunch.

We got back for a meeting with the UDA/PUP [Ulster Defence Association, Progressive Unionist Party]. I asked John Holmes to do me a left-to-right. He scribbled David Ervine, John White, Hugh Smyth and Gary McMichael [elected peace-talks delegates, PUP and UDA]. When I put a question mark over John White's name, JH scribbled back 'double murderer'.[1] TB did a long spiel about why he was so engaged in it, why he made the speech he did, emphasised consent and no entry to the political process without giving up violence. If they didn't come in, he would move ahead with SF. He said he was determined on it. They were suspicious – as were the press – re us claiming the SF contacts were about clarification. They said it made it difficult for them, and gave Paisley etc. another stick with which to beat everyone. PR for European elections was running quite hard at the four o'clock, and I let them run with it, stressing

---

[1] White had confessed to the 1973 murders of Catholic councillor Paddy Wilson and his female friend, Irene Andrews, and he was sentenced to life imprisonment in 1978. Released in 1992, he joined the Ulster Defence Association. Following an internal feud, he was expelled from the UDA in 2002.

that we were likely to do it through the Lords and that it made no difference to PR for Westminster. Indeed, yesterday, TB and JP had met in the garden and JP said he would support TB, reluctantly, on PR for European elections because he'd already decided we should bind in the Liberals, but he would not back PR for Westminster. TB said he could tell him there was no way we were having PR for Westminster.

Wednesday, July 16

I was feeling a mix of boredom, tiredness and irritation, not least with Peter M who was continuing to focus more on personal profile than real co-ordination. The latest thing was Derek Draper [lobbyist, former Mandelson aide] who had sent me extracts from his book on the election and the *Sunday Times* serialisation and I was very blunt, told him it was crap but the real big problem was that it was all the Peter M story. I was also bored, in that so much of the work was becoming almost managerial. I was in early, felt through the day I was involved in dozens and dozens of bitty things, but we lacked strategic shape at the moment. TB was immersed in devolution, and then spent a couple of hours on his own preparing for PMQs. GB suddenly decided to do a big speech tomorrow, 'starting a debate' on the single currency, so I spent much of the afternoon agreeing briefing notes with Charlie. It worked out fine but Moira Wallace in particular was alarmed that GB was doing another big move without really keeping TB informed. I was called to a meeting with GB and Donald to talk over where we thought the limits for Scottish MP numbers should be. DD looked very nervous about the whole thing.

Thursday, July 17

TB's main focus was devolution again. I went into a meeting with TB, Donald, GB on tax and how to handle the tax question, and the numbers issue. GB was putting in a few last-minute ideas. He had only just caught up with the detail. As Donald explained that the electoral system meant there would never be an overall Labour majority, GB started shaking his head. 'Do we know what we are doing here?' TB again gave Cabinet a little lecture about the importance of co-ordination and not letting junior ministers make silly statements. Cabinet was dull, and discussion seemed to meander. We were not the only ones who were tired. Afterwards Harriet and Frank Dobson were bending my ear about various things, and thankfully the duty clerk rescued me and said TB wanted to see me. It was for yet another meeting on the devolution White Paper. I did an interview with David Butler and Dennis Kavanagh for their election book and their very first question was whether there was now such a thing as 'Mandelsonisation'. I had to emphasise the driving role TB played not just in campaigning but strategy, and debunk some of the Peter M mythology. I went in for the end of the Trimble meeting which had clearly gone badly. Trimble was in a foul mood and the atmosphere was terrible. TB was really tired. We had a strategy meeting with GB and PG which was very bitty and reactive, then Alex Allan's farewell. He and his wife sang some very funny songs about the place. It was a nice do but I was by now feeling totally exhausted.

Friday, July 18

Another day that brought back memories of the election campaign. Anji and Hilary having advanced, TB and I set off for Wales. I was getting irritated at the Lib Dems who on the one hand wanted to be sitting around with ministers agreeing an approach on the Constitution but on the other were constantly attacking us for not spending enough on any issue anyone cared to mention. We had to start identifying them more clearly as irresponsible, old-fashioned tax-and-spend merchants. On the way down, TB was reading up all the local info for his Q&A. I was reading up on the devolution White Paper. GB and DD were trying to get TB to water down the wording on tax and on cutting the number of Scottish MPs at Westminster. TB had pretty much laid down the law that they should be cut from seventy-two to fifty-nine. He said it was absurd to argue for the same number when we were creating a new parliament dealing with many of the issues Westminster had dealt with till now. He said GB was realising that if the party nationally had fewer Scots in Parliament, he might be less likely to make it as leader in a future election.

We also discussed whether he should go to the Uxbridge by-election. The convention was PMs did not do by-elections, but was it a sensible one? The argument was you got the blame if you lost but that happened whether you went or not. JP was in favour. PG said it was neck and neck and he might tip it our way. TB said we needed a shake-up of the private office. Alex was great but he had allowed them all to get a bit cocky. He was minded to put Anji in charge of a plan to get Number 10 going, get a bit more energy through the place. It needed it, but it would drive Cherie crazy. As we arrived in Wales, Jonathan called to say overnight intelligence was suggesting a Northern Ireland ceasefire was imminent. This was clearly going to dominate the agenda for a while. The only glitch was that it was following attacks from Trimble about us conceding too much to the nationalists so it was bound to prompt the charge that we had done some kind of deal, even though we hadn't. It was difficult. This was clearly going to be seen as tactical. Hospital visit in Gwent went fine, then to Caerphilly for a walkabout and we got good coverage on the Beeb and ITN. The Welsh *Mirror* had done us proud, splashing on TB's article, having splashed with Giggs' article yesterday. On the way to the Q&A, he was worrying the Unionists would respond the wrong way to a ceasefire. 'It will be seen as positive, won't it?' I said of course it will. He was dead serious about this stuff.

John Holmes called and said Downtown Radio were reporting Hume and Mallon saying the prospects for a ceasefire were good, so it was moving in the right direction. TB did a series of interviews, stressing the positive case for devolution in Wales, almost convincingly. Earlier in his doorstep he fucked up when he listed the things it would do and got them wrong, but nobody but one or two of the more anal Scots noticed. The best moment of the Q&A was Ron Davies stepping to the lectern with 'Prime Minister' written on it. TB and I were going through one of our hysteria sessions, reading the Welsh road signs to each other. 'Heddlu' (police) on the side of the police cars provoked a particularly bonkers response. Then the Jag broke down and we were driven in the police back-up car. On the train home he decided we should go all out for Uxbridge. He and Anji were both at me for not involving Peter enough. Anji said it looked like we were in some kind of war about who got the credit for the election victory. I said it was more that his profile was becoming a negative because it was about him not the government and what we were trying to do. TB said he was getting fed up with the inability of his key people to work together and he was looking to me to sort it. Peter M was in Paris at a seminar to assess the election. I got home in time for the news and there was fourteen minutes on the BBC re Northern Ireland. The ceasefire was clearly coming, which was good news, but I agreed with Mo we should say nothing until it was announced. Tony Wright [Derry Irvine's parliamentary private secretary] gave an interview in which he talked about Charles and Camilla and sparked a rash of stories about TB giving the nod to them as a couple. I got a message to Tony Wright to shut up but he had already agreed to do *Newsnight*.

Saturday, July 19

The ceasefire was the main story. It finally came at 9.30 and I called TB, who was unaware of it. He was worried about the line being run at us that we were giving too much to IRA/SF. He asked me to emphasise that the approach on decommissioning had not changed, that we were clear there must be some decommissioning during negotiations. John [Holmes] told me John de Chastelain, the Canadian general, was probably going to chair the independent decommissioning body. I talked that up as something that should reassure the Unionists, but the noises coming from their briefings all day were not good. TB said Trimble was not good at standing up to his own people. But he had to be kept onside. We fixed a pooled TB doorstep at 2pm, which we agreed should be with fields rather than Chequers in the background. TB did it in an open-necked shirt which was just about OK. His statement was fine. He said we should not appear overly euphoric because our main problem in this was going to be the UUs in advance of Monday's meeting with Trimble before Wednesday's vote on the decommissioning paper. TB was worried. He called on and off all day to ask how it was going, and to keep emphasising the points he wanted me to emphasise.

Sunday, July 20

TB called early, worried about Ireland. He felt the way the coverage was leaning could add to the pressure on Trimble to pull out. There was a sense that the IRA ceasefire was a tactic to secure exactly that, so that the Unionists would be the ones blamed for screwing it up. TB suggested that I sprinkle around references to the UUs surely not wanting to be seen to throw away the best prospect of peace for years. He wanted it made clear that we had not changed the line on decommissioning, and there was far too much of that around in the Sundays. We had both to reassure the Unionists, but also make clear how much was at stake if they pulled out now. We went down to Robert Harris' [novelist, columnist and friend of Mandelson] for the day. He was in very good form, clearly enjoying life. I was probably a bit too down on Peter, as they were good friends, but I explained Peter was not really doing the job TB asked him to do. Robert said Peter felt frustrated because he was not really being allowed to be a politician. I understood that but he had been given a job and I felt I ended up doing a lot of the work he was meant to be doing, while he swanned around pretending to be in the same league as GB or JP. Chris Smith did an extraordinary interview in the *Sunday Times* on which ministers he fancied, with TB and Jack

Cunningham apparently top. We got home at 9.30 to discover that we had been burgled. The video and some cash had gone. Very upsetting all round.

Monday, July 21

Ireland was leading the news in the morning because of the Trimble meeting. I briefed very hard on him not wanting to be the man who scuppered the peace talks. But we were in a difficult position. You have the sense that DT brings his own enemies with him, meaning John Taylor and Ken Maginnis. TB was worried about the whole thing, but said that at the eleven o'clock briefing I should be robust, making clear that we resented the suggestion by Trimble that we had done a deal with the IRA. I stressed that decommissioning meant during the negotiations. TB was becoming more and more preoccupied with Northern Ireland. He felt that if Trimble showed more strength, he could blow out Paisley. The mood was cautious and realistic. The problem was that the Irish government probably did tell Sinn Fein there would be no need for actual decommissioning, and we were saying the opposite to the Unionists. I didn't flam up but I didn't flam it down either. I spoke to Mo to suggest a doorstep hitting back at Trimble over the 'deal with the IRA' suggestion. We should stress that two weeks ago we were being accused of betrayal by the other side, because of Drumcree. George Robertson called me to complain about his press office, the latest in a long line.

We had an office meeting on Uxbridge and TB agreed to go. The argument against was that it would set a precedent and he would be expected to go to all by-elections. But the problem was the by-election was not taking off because after the general election people did not want to vote so soon again. We felt TB could make a difference. I had a meeting with DD and Murray Elder who were clearly worried I would brief a different line on the devolution plans, that I would be pushing the reduction of MPs as a big thing and would be saying definitively it would be down to fifty-nine. Donald wanted to be very vague about it. He felt it would harm us in the referendum. I said to TB we should be able to let it go on numbers and we should be relaxed about the timing.

The meeting with Trimble and Co. was friendlier than the noises around suggested it would be. Maginnis was the only one who lost it really. The problem was that Trimble was not really in charge of the show, and you sensed he was constantly worrying what they were thinking. He had a naturally red face which turned redder and redder as the meeting wore on. He had a mildly priggish smile which got more priggish the more nervous he got. Jeffrey Donaldson [UUP MP] was the quietest but he spoke with considerable force. Taylor was quite languid. Maginnis was the ranter today. But he too could be subtle while being tough. When we were discussing the decommissioning line, he said very nicely, but menacingly, 'I'm very worried that if we take that approach, it will be very damaging to you personally, David.' TB was pretty firm, admitting he could not deliver the Irish government to say what we understood by decommissioning happening. He started the meeting by saying it was 'high noon' and laughing. He said the problem was they wanted a guarantee that SF would be kicked out after a certain period if there was no actual decommissioning and he could not get the Irish signed up to that. They said that it was intolerable for them to have to sit round a table with these people, knowing that they would not give up a bomb or a bullet and yet there would be no way of kicking them out. Trimble said SF were making it clear they had a guarantee they would not be kicked out. They do not believe they need to decommission. TB said there had to be some acceptance of good faith. Maginnis scoffed. DT said you can be acting in good faith and not reach an agreement. TB said the principle of consent was paramount. The greatest difficulty for SF will come when it is clear this is not necessarily going to lead to a united Ireland. He said decommissioning had become symbolic. He said he wanted a timetable, September to May. He did not want this dragging on forever. He said it felt like swimming through blancmange. We went round and round in circles over the various problems. TB was looking exasperated at points and explained that two weeks ago he had the SDLP telling him he was guilty of the most monstrous betrayal, and now *they* were saying it. In the end we felt it might be better if Wednesday's vote on decommissioning did not take place and we got more time. Donaldson said it was always the Unionists being asked to help out, and there was nothing to show for it. He said he had lost members of his family to the IRA. 'We understand these people. They will go back to violence any time they feel like it.'

Mo was getting fed up with them, pulling faces etc. Eventually we agreed that there were some points of clarification we could try to meet in relation to the issue of arms being given over, how and when. I sensed Trimble was trying to be helpful, but it was clear he had to watch his back the whole time. TB said it had to be worth trying. He said he could not promise but he would try to get 1. clarification that Mitchell means decommissioning during negotiations, 2. UK and Irish governments to agree words on decommissioning, 3. schemes in place by the time we talk on September 15, and 4. agreement that consent is the fundamental principle. DT said there was an operation to build confidence in the nationalist community. The government needed an equivalent process with the Unionist population. He said he would not be able to support the decommissioning paper this side of the summer. Later, I wrote up a briefing note on the Lib Dem committee story for tomorrow. TB had been getting more and more pissed off about the Libs because they were attacking us so much on spending, but nonetheless we were committed to this. Of course he hadn't spoken to any of his colleagues about this and we were having to do the politics on it too late. He was also unsettled, because he had seen Jim Callaghan who said he was worried about Michael Levy going to the Lords.

Tuesday, July 22

Welsh devolution day, which went fine and was leading the news most of the day. TB was preoccupied with Ireland while I was working on the Cabinet committee announcement re the Libs, and also preparing for devolution. I was meeting DD the whole time, and he seemed very nervous and worried. It was hard at times to keep his spirits up. He was clearly suspicious we were going to brief this as a victory for the English. I assured him that we were not. TB agreed that we would make clear the reduction of MPs would be for the election after next. He spoke to Trimble before the eleven o'clock and they agreed that the vote on the decommissioning paper would go ahead, that the Unionists would vote against but stay in the talks. We agreed to use the eleven o'clock briefing, which I would be doing as TB saw Paisley, to make it clear the vote would be lost, but to stress that we would continue to try to find a way forward, keep on talking. It was a straightforward news management operation and worked fine so that on Wednesday when the vote was lost, the BBC said it had been so well trailed it was virtually an anticlimax.

I also briefed the lobby cold on the Lib Dem Cabinet committee. It was one of those that prompted an immediate intake of breath. They knew that personally I was not so keen on this Lib Dem stuff, and though I was stressing the 'new era' bit, there were one or two remarks about us gobbling up the Liberals. What was also clear was that they saw it as a good story. I agreed with the Liberals the basic line, then Paddy Ashdown was doing a press conference later. They were wetting themselves with excitement. It ran big on the news and ran well in the papers. It gave us back boldness and initiative. Paisley walked out as expected but we were managing expectations on this

OK. Philip called from Uxbridge and said it was not looking brilliant. I got home and had a terrible scene with the boys, who were really angry and shouting and generally misbehaving. It was pretty grim at the moment. Fairly bored at work, depressed at home, and we were desperately in need of a holiday.

Wednesday, July 23

I was getting depressed, worried that the boys were unhappy because I was at work so much, travelling too much, and bringing too much work home with me. The campaign had been bad enough, but it had been just as intense since. Hague's office called to say he would be doing Ireland at PMQs. JH told me I had worked miracles on the press on Ireland, and it definitely helped shape the outcome of the meeting yesterday. TB was in a foul mood and it took me ages to get him to agree to a simple 'thumbs up' picture for the *Daily Record*. I got a nice picture sent through by the White House, with a hand-written message from Clinton, suggesting I do a job swap with Mike McCurry. I told TB I intended to take it unless he snapped out of his mood. PMQs was OK but in general we were not handling Hague terribly well. TB called as I was coming back from the afternoon briefing and agreed we didn't get Hague right, we had to think more deeply about it. He said he didn't fear Hague at all, except in the chamber, where he was good. He didn't feel he was making an impact anywhere apart from the House, and that is where we had to weaken him. He was a debating-point merchant, not a strategist.

I established that Ewen MacAskill [*Guardian*] was writing that there would be a review of Scottish representation at Westminster. I called DD and said that there would be a repeat of the referendum story disaster if it came out in a London newspaper. Donald said he was very depressed but after much toing and froing, he agreed it would be better to brief the Scottish papers too. We agreed that Brian Wilson [Scottish Office minister] would call the *Herald*, *Scotsman* and *Record* to say the *Guardian* had the story and they should have it too. Ewen was livid, needless to say, and I was up-front with him, apologised, said it was political necessity and promised another story soon to make up for it. He was very pissed off, and rightly said in future there was no reason why he should bounce stories off us. I agreed, and I said this was a needs-must situation and he would just have to understand that. He didn't. Of course I couldn't really blame him. As well as having him angry, I also had Donald suspicious that we had given the story to Ewen in the first place, which we hadn't.

Thursday, July 24

The devolution stories came out OK. Ewen was very pissed off for obvious reasons. The Scots papers were fine and even Donald said to me before Cabinet that it was a news management triumph. TB was fretting we had to stress that it was a UK settlement. DD was in good form, at the right time. The Scots press made good use of the pooled pictures we did with TB yesterday, as did TV this morning. There was a meeting of the Big Guns. I went in with JP and Robin. GB was late. Robin was talking about the need to respond post-Uxbridge. I raised arms sales. JH had asked TB to resist strongly some of the excesses in Robin's suggested changes re arms sales criteria. TB said he felt we were in danger of opening the door to a disaster that would hit jobs and foreign relations. Robin tried to argue that the impact would be small, that we had promised a review and had to see it through. TB was adamant regimes like Indonesia or Saudi Arabia would withdraw trade if they felt they were on trial. JP and I were exchanging looks as Robin tried to talk his way through. It was so obviously a piece of pure leftism. He said there would be a furore if Hawk fighter-jet sales went to Indonesia, and we didn't have stricter criteria.[1] I said TB had given a clear signal in the House yesterday that Hawk sales would go ahead and it didn't make a line anywhere in the press.

Cabinet was mainly devolution, and BSE. TB congratulated DD and Ron Davies on what he called a 'sensible, balanced package'. He said it was important they all got involved in the 'yes, yes' campaign. DD thanked Derry in particular for the hard work that had gone into the policy. He said there had been a good spirit to it. He said we were putting the whole package firmly within the context of the UK, and the sovereignty of the Westminster Parliament. He and GR both spoke of the 'untenable' seventy-two MPs situation and said it would be reduced. Robin then did a long presentation on our coming presidency of the EU. He said it would take up an enormous amount of our time and energy but was an opportunity to show the benefits of a new direction and take opinion in a different direction on Europe. He said we had to show we were focused on issues of concern to people, not the institutional obsessions of politicians. Jobs, crime, environment, greater openness.

The lobby was mainly devolution and also a story that there was

[1] MPs called for a review of UK policy because the British-made aircraft were employed against separatists in the run-up to East Timor's independence referendum.

July '97: TB resists RC 'leftist' pitch on arms sales

a secret meeting of union leaders – so secret that Jon Cruddas [TB's deputy political secretary and Downing Street union link] was there so I laid into the BBC and the *Independent*, the only two to run with it. I saw Steve Evans [BBC] doing a piece in the street and really laid into him, said it was agenda-driven journalism – how can it be a secret meeting, somehow bad for us, when the PM's representative was there? At the strategy meeting, TB said he was not hopeful re Uxbridge. GB was clearly of the view that we were operating without a clear strategy at the moment, and we had to get up health and education initiatives. He felt we were running out of steam a bit. TB felt we were doing quite well, but lacked strategic focus. I called Piers Morgan [editor, *Mirror*] and said TB would do his first interview with him after Uxbridge, in the car to Chequers. He was happy enough. I called Neil Wallis [deputy editor, *Sun*] who was livid, said Stuart Higgins [editor, *Sun*] and Les Hinton [News International executive] would go mad. I was quite shaken by the vehemence and the viciousness. He said it was a total kick in the teeth. TB said he was amazed at the way I kept both papers sweet. The truth was I didn't. I decided we would have to do both.

Friday, July 25

The devolution press came out fine, and DD did well. As we set off for Uxbridge, we heard the Tories were revealing a defector from Labour. It turned out to be someone who tried to be the candidate and failed and was a friend of Bill Cash [Conservative MP], so not many dead. TB kept going over whether we thought the government is doing OK. On balance he does. He spoke to RC in the car and agreed a holding line on arms sales. RC was due to do a big number on Bosnia. We had a chat about a first reshuffle. He was thinking in terms of Peter M, Stephen Byers [education minister], Alan Milburn [health minister], maybe Tessa [Jowell]. We stopped for a cup of tea on the way and ended up doing a picture for the guys in a local motorbike shop. The visit went OK, though I had yet another wretched BBC documentary crew following me around. I briefed the general line that we welcomed the extra attention the defector would bring to the by-election but in truth it was going to be very hard to win here. TB did a crap doorstep, very ummy and aahy, a few interviews and we set off back to Number 10 while he went off to Chequers.

Jonathan called to say Derek Draper's serialisation in the *Sunday Times* had a couple of problems. There were two big problem areas – first, some of the detail of the TB/Paddy dinners in Number 10, and second, Diana's visit to Chequers and the kids playing football. I called Draper who was fishing for more detail and I would not even confirm the Diana meeting had taken place. The truth was he had put together what he knew from Peter with other stuff gleaned from media and gossip, but both were clearly big stories and would keep us busy over the weekend.

Saturday, July 26

Good coverage from Uxbridge but it was clear Draper's book was going to be a problem and the *Sunday Times* were going to milk it. Even though the material Draper provided was poor, they had enough to generate big news coverage. I spoke to Diana's and Paddy's offices to warn them. TB was worried they would think we were behind it. I doubted it. Draper claimed that the Diana story came from the Royals. I doubted that too. My suspicion re the Liberals was obviously Peter, though the fact there was also stuff about a defence committee meeting suggested it could have been [Roger] Liddle, who would have been at it. I called TB at Chequers. He was livid. As far as he was concerned, Draper was 'finished', and he could happily kill Peter. He said he had no doubt at all Peter had given a lot of this to Draper. As to what we say, I should say there was no talk of a merger with the Liberals and re Diana that of course he saw her from time to time, but all the detail that was claimed as fact was fantasy. Peter M called from Belfast, clearly worried that TB thought he was involved. He said it was obvious the Diana story came from the Royals – I said what Royals does Derek Draper know?

He did not sound terribly convincing. His complaint that I should have warned him earlier that these stories were coming cut little ice as I still suspected he was behind at least some of them. We killed them as best we could but then when we saw the paper, there was worse. Draper had given them material re Peter seeing Camilla and Tony being relaxed re Charles and Camilla getting married. TB was even more hacked off when I told him. He said the problem was that part of the press felt they could say whatever they wanted about the Royals. He said he had given both barrels to Peter and Peter gave both barrels back. He clearly thought I was winding up TB against him. Tony Benn [left-wing MP, former minister] and Roy Hattersley [former deputy leader of the Labour Party] were both attacking TB which was good in one way, bad in another. Benn said the Lib-Lab idea was the beginning of the end of the Labour Party, which was total nonsense, but we would be getting a lot of this in the run-up to conference. I called Tony Banks and we agreed to float the idea of

July '97: Problems from Derek Draper's book

David Mellor [former Conservative Cabinet minister] as chairman of the Football Task Force.

Sunday, July 27

TB was tired and fed up at the Draper stuff. I used the line that he had never expressed a view re Charles/Camilla and it was a non-story flammed up to boost the serialisation. He had never mentioned Charles/Camilla even to his closest advisers and all that had happened was Draper was forced to give a pound of flesh and this was it. I also made clear if Peter M saw Camilla, it was never on TB's behalf or at his behest. Peter called to say he had only ever met Camilla once. These royal stories could so easily run out of control. There was definitely a feeling among parts of the media that they could say what the hell they wanted, without comeback.

Robin Butler called to say Barbara Mills [Director of Public Prosecutions] was getting really worried at all the undermining of her in the press and could I help her? She called me later and I agreed at a minimum to get something out very supportive of her. There was next to no interest in the Libs merger story. It was all about the Royals. We had Calum's birthday party skating at the Sobell [leisure] centre and then to Peter M's party. Any doubts I had about Liddle's discretion were blown away as I heard him regaling Don Macintyre [*Independent* political editor and later biographer of Mandelson] with stories about the intelligence services spending review. Peter and I barely spoke. I got home to calls re the Mellor story, which I had given to David Bradshaw at the *Mirror*, though I pleaded ignorance with the *Sun*, whilst simultaneously confirming it. The *Sun/Mirror* situation was becoming a nightmare. Both of them felt we somehow owed them big stories day after day. Anything that appeared in one sent the other into a rage. TB claimed to have sympathy for my predicament but was happy to let me do all the dirty work on it. Mellor was really pleased to be doing the task force and we agreed he would do something with Banks on Wednesday. TB had [film director] Steven Spielberg (and seven kids), Sean Connery [Scottish film actor] and GB at Chequers to talk about Spielberg setting up studios in the UK, and Connery getting involved in the devolution campaign.

Monday, July 28

There were too many Camilla stories for my liking, including the *Sun* repeating the Draper quote as though it were new. TB called me just before 9 and said he wanted me to make clear once more that he'd never expressed a view, publicly or privately, about Charles and

Camilla. He was also pissed off at the story in the *Sun* and elsewhere that he was selling his house for £700k, which was not true, allied to him living in Number 10 for free – when it was a taxable benefit – and that he had no mortgage in Sedgefield, which he does. We were still working out how to deal with the *Sun* and *Mirror* interviews, and we decided he should do a personal-type interview with Piers and a more policy-focused interview with Kavanagh and [Chris] Roycroft-Davis [*Sun* leader writer]. The *Mirror* seemed more relaxed about us doing both on the same day, as long as they could trail it as his first as prime minister. The *Sun* were more pissed off and I just had to deal with that. There was a bit of interest, though not as much as Robin C said there would be, in Hawk sales going ahead. Ann Clwyd [Labour MP] attacked us on the news later. TB had a meeting with Butler, Jonathan and John Holmes to go over some areas we were looking at, like a reorganisation of how jobs at the centre [of government] were done. Derry had been proposing a split so that you had a head of the Civil Service and a Cabinet Secretary. TB was due to have dinner tomorrow night with the permanent secretaries, along with Peter M, Derry and Jonathan. Butler also asked for John Holmes to go. Butler struck me as very amiable but very out of date. He didn't really get what was going on inside TB's head, I don't think.

TB was very agitated at the royal stuff, and claimed to have had very heavy words with Peter M. He was also worried about Derry and later both of us told Derry to watch himself with the press. He was being a bit too clever by half, for example in his interview in the *Observer* yesterday, which admittedly had been my idea, saying that we could get a back-door privacy law through the European Court. The Royals dominated my morning briefing, and then TB did the *Mirror* interview. He was strong on message but because the Royals were in the news, it was clear to me straight away Piers wanted Diana to be the story. I later tried to talk him out of it being the splash [front page lead story], but failed. I suppose it was OK, not least because I could say to the *Sun* that Piers flammed it up. TB and I went for a walk round the garden to run over a few things. He was worried about the capability of the Civil Service. Re the *Sun*, I said he should have a go back at Benn and Hattersley and also float the idea of knighthoods for teachers. When Trevor Kavanagh raised Benn and Hattersley, TB delivered, but he was hopeless on Ks for teachers and I had to brief it hard afterwards. It was a different sort of interview, more political than the *Mirror*. They were surprisingly reverential. When they raised the Royals, TB played a dead bat and on the personal stuff he didn't really open up. We were still just about walking the tabloid diplomatic tightrope OK, and both interviews were fine. TB still felt the *Sun* would turn against us if it could. Piers had been a lot softer, going through all the various lines in pursuit of a story – CB, GB, Royals, feelings, family. Jonathan came to see me about [Peter] Temple-Morris [Conservative MP]. He was in despair at the Tories, and willing to defect, but not stay in Parliament. The obvious options were ambassador, Welsh Assembly, the Lords.

Tuesday, July 29

TB was worrying about Michael Levy's peerage, having been wound up by Peter M who wanted to delay a year. TB also instructed Peter to get a grip of Draper's book. I did the morning briefing early then we left for the Jimmy Young programme [BBC Radio 2]. TB said about the attacks on David Simon [former BP chairman appointed a Labour peer and trade minister in May], and about Michael Levy's peerage – 'I don't know why but I felt discombobulated by this.' The interview was fine then back to see Robin Butler. He was totally opposed to Derry's idea of splitting the Cabinet Secretary job. Butler was fine in many ways, though not a moderniser. TB was worried that Noel Gallagher [rock star] was coming to the reception tomorrow. He said he had no idea he had been invited. It had been Jonathan's idea to put him on the list, and TB felt he [Gallagher] was bound to do something crazy. The honours scrutiny committee was meeting today. Lord [Francis] Pym was not happy about [David] Sainsbury, because of recent large donations to the party; or Levy, and they wanted assurances about donations, and Mike Watson, because of the troubles in Glasgow Govan.[1] We were out for dinner for Calum's birthday when Godric called to say Roy Hughes [former Labour MP] had announced his peerage in the local press. Unbelievable. Almost comic. TB called me as he left Robin Butler's thing. He said is it a problem? No, but it could become one.

Wednesday, July 30

TB was doing *GMTV* and I was dealing with the Palace early on, to rubbish the *Guardian* story that the Queen did not want to open the Welsh Assembly. The Roy Hughes story didn't really fly but for some

---

[1] David Sainsbury, chairman and chief executive of the retail chain, Michael Levy and Mike Watson, Labour MP for Glasgow Central 1989–97. Watson's seat was abolished when the Glasgow Govan seat was created. He lost the nomination to Mohammad Sarwar. Baron Watson of Invergowrie was jailed for 'wilful fire-raising' in 2005.

reason it gave TB his first sleepless night. He said I hate these things that have the potential to go at my integrity. He was completely over the top about it. I picked him up and we set off for *GMTV*, who did a very soft interview trailed by a nice little film of our achievements so far. He was getting up the theme of long-term tough decisions. Philip [Gould] called to say how good he was and we should do a lot more like that. The story rumbling away was Lord Simon again with another front-page story, this one on alleged tax avoidance. I started to write, but eventually did not send, a letter to Peter M going through why I felt it was so difficult to work with him at the moment. TB was robust about David Simon at PMQs and determined to see the Tories off on this, and I was equally robust at the four o'clock, though clearly the press felt this was something to get their teeth into. I went back for a meeting on the referendum campaigns. We agreed we would have to keep the campaign momentum going through the summer. TB said it would be different in Scotland, which was about Scottish nationhood. In Wales it was going to be about getting a powerful voice. These were going to be major, full-scale campaigns.

I spoke to Alan McGee at Creation Records, who was coming to the Number 10 reception with Noel Gallagher, and said can we be assured he would behave OK? Alan said he would make sure he did. He was not going to mess around. He said if we had invited Liam [Gallagher], it might have been different. Sinead Cusack arrived with Kevin Spacey [actor] and asked me to go out for dinner, which I couldn't. Gallagher arrived with his wife Meg [Mathews], McGee and his girlfriend [Kate Holmes], loads of photographers outside, then Cherie met them and took them upstairs to see Kathryn and Nicky, who was pretty gobsmacked when Gallagher walked in. He said he thought Number 10 was 'tops', said he couldn't believe there was an ironing board in there. He was very down to earth, very funny. I took them up to do pictures with TB, then Lenny Henry, Maureen Lipman [actors], a few others.

As a social event, it was a rarity in that I quite enjoyed it. There was a good mix of people and it worked. Fiona and I then joined TB and CB for dinner in the flat. TB and I had a chat in the kitchen re Peter M. He accepted he was a problem at the moment but he asked me not to let my irritation prevent me working with him. Power some-times goes to people's heads at first but he will be fine. We talked about the need for pretty big reform in the Civil Service. The place was pretty inefficient but apart from TB, none of us were overconfi-dent we could change it much. He said we would come back after a holiday re-energised. We talked about CB's role. Everyone agreed she had done well, but needed more support and we should be more upfront about the fact she should get it.

Thursday, July 31

There was huge coverage out of last night, and not just Gallagher. In the morning meeting, Peter M wanted to get David Simon out to do an interview. I was not so sure. It was not his kind of thing. He was very diffident and would not be experienced at that kind of interview. At the eleven o'clock, the press were pretty ferocious about it and I had to be very robust defending him. I felt it was OK, but it was clear we were going to have to fight back. We agreed he should do an article for *The Times*, and Tim [Allan] did a very good draft. At the Big Guns meeting, we went over what we needed to do post-Uxbridge result. We now expected to lose. Cabinet was fairly brief. TB gave them a pep talk about how August was usually a disaster area and it was important they made sure their departments were still functioning properly and co-ordinating through Number 10. He also wanted everyone getting involved in the devolution campaigns and he wanted them to start focusing on the party conference, showing we were delivering on our promises, showing why we are the party of the future. He was worried that the combination of Simon, by-election defeat and honours would combine to end the honeymoon effect, and set up a bad summer. I brought forward the four o'clock to 3.30 to do the new code of conduct for ministers, QPM [Questions of Procedure for Ministers]. I got more grief over the Simon situation. Sheila Thompson [Lord Chancellor's press officer] came to see me and said Derry was very overbearing with journalists. She felt he could become an embarrassment and thought I should have a word.

Friday, August 1

What should have been a complex but fairly routine day turned into one of those rare days when, rather than scribbling into a notebook late at night, I thought I should sit down and type it all up while it stayed fresh in my mind, before leaving for home. We woke to defeat in Uxbridge [Conservative John Randall won with a 7.8 per cent swing]. That fact itself was not surprising but the 4,000 majority was, even though we had been talking down our prospects. Still, we had the arguments to explain it, and in any case we had taken a decision not to do the usual Tory excuse-making, just take it, accept it, explain it, move on. TB called me in the car and was in fairly jocular mood, said provided we stuck to messages about the long term, the media would quickly move on. His other concern today was the honours scrutiny committee, who had taken some persuading that Sainsbury and Mike Watson should go to the Lords. Eventually they accepted they should. Michael Levy had sent me over another copy of his CV and was virtually begging me to handle the press on his peerage. We also had the announcement of Richard Wilson as Butler's replacement as Cabinet Secretary, which at first we said should be embargoed but then agreed it should be done as a straight-up announcement at the eleven o'clock. TB wanted him sold as a moderniser, which Jonathan thought was a joke. He felt he was a classic Establishment Civil Service appointment with not that great a track record on the modernising front.

I had a meeting with Peter M at my request to assess why we had been working so badly together. I said it was beginning to harm the effectiveness of the operation. I felt he was exclusive and haughty and too concerned with his own profile. He said I was unsettled for the usual reasons – I was not sure if I was a spin doctor or a politician; not sure if I was in charge of events or responding to them. Maybe, I said, but cited one or two instances where I felt I was justified to complain about his behaviour. Likewise he came back with a number of occasions when he felt I should have consulted him. He said I had stopped asking for his advice, so he had happily stepped away from that side of his role. He was sure that he did not want to be a spin doctor. He enjoyed the policy side of things, co-ordinating, reading papers, discussing, watching for errors. But he didn't enjoy the other side of the job, didn't want to do it, and that meant a lot fell to me. I said not a lot, but all of it, and a lot of it was drudge. He reeled off the list of places I had been to and said how can that be drudge? He said he thought I was jealous of his profile and his relationship with TB. I said that wasn't the case, but I did resent the way he talked about the election as though he had single-handedly won it. It had been a team effort but he talked up nobody but himself. Peter said he still felt we were very close but our friendship had been damaged. That saddened him, he said, but he also knew I was a rock on which everything rested. He said TB had said as much to him. He also knew that if he landed himself in a crisis, I would be his first port of call. He was saddened that Fiona appeared to hate him. We agreed to reflect and seek to improve things after the break. I had a long chat with Liz [Lloyd] who said a lot of people were unhappy at Number 10.

I got a message to call Phil Hall at the *News of the World*. I said I hope you are not going to unleash a scandal while I am on holiday.

He said no, I'm going to do it now. I said what? He said 'Robin and Gaynor.' He said a couple of freelances had come in with a set of pictures which showed they had spent several nights together last week. He said they were bang to rights. I let on that I knew nothing. He said he didn't know whether to run it, in a way he didn't want to, but if he didn't these guys would take it somewhere else, so it might as well be him. He said could I talk to RC and say they could either do it as an exposé, or they could do it with something from him, and they would do it as sympathetically as they could. I said I promised him a proper response of some kind tomorrow if he would give me a guarantee not to approach any of the people involved, or their families. He said that was fine. What was extraordinary was that I called him immediately after coming back from a meeting with TB, Butler and Jonathan, where we said it was going to be very hard to do a reshuffle of the Big Guns unless one of them had to quit. I went back to see TB, who was with Jonathan. I said I bring you your first sex scandal. I went through the facts as Phil had told me. TB said what are the chances of persuading them not to run it? I said somewhere between zero and five per cent. The chances of it not being run somewhere were closer to the zero end. We called Butler back and went over various options. He said the [David] Mellor drama was not the main blow, it was the later ones.[1] We made a lot of bad-taste jokes, which is the usual sign of nervousness. Butler's main advice was to be aware of the clear difference between private and public morality, and the need not to make a rod for our backs. If he were to resign over an affair, that might seem the right thing now, but it might not always be so. He then left the room. TB was clearly a bit thrown by this one. He hated this personal stuff. It was why he was always so loath to get involved in Tory sleaze stories. 'What the hell do I do about this?' he said. We talked it round and round. Maybe RC would make our minds up for us. Maybe he would want to go. I doubted it. So did TB. Maybe he would be able to make a case for it being ludicrous even to think in those terms. TB said what is clear is that there will be a lot of interest in how we handle it. I called Peter M, who said we should dig out TB's *Spectator* lecture in '95, which made clear that morality to him was not about private lives.

I checked out RC's whereabouts without letting his office know

---

[1] Details of Mellor's extramarital affairs were made public in July 1992, but he did not resign his position until September, after a number of other stories about him were published.

why I wanted him. He was on the flight from Scotland to Heathrow to get the connection to Boston as he was going off for a holiday with Margaret [RC's wife and mother of his two sons]. He was due in London at 4.15 but the plane was delayed by half an hour. I said a lot will depend on how RC reacts and what he himself feels about this. We did talk over some of the worst-case scenarios, and were chewing over who should be Foreign Secretary if he went. Jack C, Beckett, JP possibly. TB and I then went round the entire Cabinet thinking of skeletons we either knew of, or could imagine. I said if you're not careful you'll be left with Dewar and [Gavin] Strang [transport minister]. I had left messages for RC and he called on his mobile after landing at Heathrow. He was being driven from the shuttle to the Boston plane. I asked if he was alone. He said no, I'm with Margaret and Dave Mathieson [RC's special adviser]. I said given what I am about to say, you might want to go to a private phone and call me back. I said a bad story was about to break and I needed to speak to him privately. 'Is it about me?' he asked. And I said yes it is. I could now hear Margaret chatting away happily in the background. I said are you sure you don't want to find a private phone? He said no, you speak, and I will listen. I suspected he knew what was coming. I said it's you and Gaynor. A freelance has seen you coming from her flat, having staked it out through the night, and they have pictures. He asked me to go through the dates, which I did. 'Yes,' he said, 'I can see how that could be a problem.' I was, I must say, quite impressed at how cool he was. There he was, just been told he was about to get done over for an affair, his wife was sitting next to him, and he was successfully communicating to me in a weird kind of code. 'Mmm, I can see why you think this could be a problem. Just remind me of the dates you have in mind.'

I explained the deal I had made with Hall, that nobody would be approached until I got back to them to explain how he intended to react. He said I assume you've discussed it with Tony. I said I had and I was sure he would be supportive, that it was not per se a resignation issue. We had to decide how to handle it. He said that was good to know. He said what would your own advice be? I said I didn't know what the situation was, with Margaret or with Gaynor, but in pure media terms, and I think in political terms too, the most important thing was clarity. He said it would be hard to maintain a clear line for long, which I didn't fully understand, but I took it to mean something dramatic. He was then cut off, clearly going through a bad mobile area. He came back a few minutes later and sounded a lot less confident. He had told Margaret and he was with her as he spoke. He sounded very emotional. I said I really feel for you. He said we are swimming in a fair amount of emotional turmoil. We are talking things over, and I cannot be precise when I will get back to you. You must give me some time. I said that was fine. TB was with me and had a word. He was very sympathetic but also firm, and backed my view that the best thing was to have a clear line. We then sat around for ages, talking it over. Then the FCO called – clearly still unaware of the whole thing – and said the Foreign Secretary had cancelled his holiday and was on his way to London. I called him again and he said he could not go away at a time like this 'and leave Gaynor to face two weeks of hell'. That was a pretty clear signal he was going to leave Margaret. In the way he talked, he certainly seemed to be thinking more about Gaynor than Margaret. He said it was much more than a fling, more than a romance. He said he was planning to talk things over with Margaret and he would call me in the morning, hopefully with a decision. He said Margaret did not want him to leave. TB spoke to him again, and said that if he wanted to remain Foreign Secretary, he would support him. The most important thing, whatever the emotions flying around, was that he was clinical about this, and clear about what he intended to do. He [TB] said elements of the media were ghastly, and this whole thing would be horrible, but AC would negotiate as sympathetic a line as could be achieved in what were bound to be horrible circumstances. RC asked me again what I thought. I said I felt we should have something clear to say tomorrow, and then follow up with a Paddy Ashdown-type bare-all statement, then say no more will be said. I said a lot depended on what they decided, how they felt, but we would support him whatever, and help make the story as unsleazy as we could. I told him I was due to go on holiday. He said he would really appreciate it if I could help him through the next few days. I said I would.

TB was more relaxed about things once RC explained that he and Margaret had not really been man and wife for some time, that Margaret knew about Gaynor, though not that it was still going on, that he had been trying to end things, but it had been very difficult. I spoke to him a couple of times through the evening, trying to cheer him up. I said he had been unlucky. No, Alastair, he said, very firmly, I have been incredibly foolish. He asked me to get a pledge tonight from the *News of the World* that they would not approach Gaynor. TB and I were drafting RC and TB spokesman statements for tomorrow, but the truth was it entirely depended on their decision. I was pretty clear he was going to call and say he was leaving Margaret and setting up home with Gaynor. In my last call of the day, he said something that made that pretty clear. I said presentationally that was the cleanest, easiest way. He said he was doubtful he could persuade Margaret to go along with it. He sounded very down now. He had gone from the emotional to the rational and now the painful. Tim [Allan] said we did not have so many good ministers that we could afford to lose RC. TB said it was ridiculous. He said maybe it is possible to love two people at the same time. Oh yeah, I said, and Cherie would accept that, would she? What would Fiona do if it was me, I said. Mmm, he said, chew your balls off. Kill you probably. Cherie would be the same. I felt for Robin though. I had only met Margaret once as far as I could recall, at [*Observer* editor] Will Hutton's, and I really hadn't taken to her. It was clear Robin had been with Gaynor for some time, and kept it fairly quiet, but now he was in a different league and these things would get out. RC asked me not to let Peter M get too closely involved in the handling of it. I said I would deal with it myself, at least through to the start of next week.

Saturday, August 2

I made one last call to Robin at 1 Carlton Gardens [Foreign Secretary's London residence] before going to bed. He sounded even more depressed. He said he expected to say his marriage was over in the morning. There was no real way of knowing where this would go but we were better placed with the *NoW* than the Tories were during their sex scandals. Fiona and I were up by 4.30am and we were on the road by 5. By the time we got through the Channel Tunnel, I called TB, who was in the bath. He had not changed his basic view. I then called Robin, who had Margaret with him. He said that he was going to have a statement by 9, in which he would be saying his marriage was over. I said that was exactly what I expected. He said Margaret was insisting that the statement said 'I am leaving my wife.' He said they had both had a wretched night for obvious reasons but they had sorted things out and he had drafted a short statement setting out the facts, making it clear he was to blame and calling for the privacy of others to be respected. I said I would alert the *NoW* and underline that they should approach none of the other parties. I called TB, who by now was in the car on the way to the airport and had been talking to Peter. I read him the statement and later read it to Peter. Neither of them liked those parts of the statement which admitted blame and responsibility, and TB wanted it to sound much more like a formal announcement. TB was also looking to say they had been trying to sort things out for some time. I fed all this through to Robin and also made one or two changes myself. By now, Margaret was leaving so he said he would call back.

During the day, we spoke several times, as we drove through France. The kids in the back were following it like some kind of soap opera. Where's Gaynor, what's Margaret doing now, is Robin going to live with Gaynor? It all made the journey go by a lot quicker than it otherwise would have done. Margaret got the eleven o'clock shuttle to Scotland, and Robin got the three o'clock, wanting to see his son, his mother and others up there, and also to get some things out of his house before coming back. He veered during the day between being very matter-of-fact and very depressed. There was a little part of me sensed that he was almost enjoying the fact he was involved in something like this – I don't mean the facts of it, which were grisly, but the fact that it was clearly going to be such a big thing reflected on his new status. For example, when I said we had to sort out the *News of the World*, and then deal with the fallout, he interrupted: 'Which will be very considerable of course.' He also spoke somewhat in the language of another age, like he was delivering lines in a drama. 'Will you move in with Gaynor' I asked. 'My future is Gaynor,' he said. We were about an hour or so into France when I called Phil Hall, first to tell him the statements were coming, then to give him them, one from Robin, one from me. There was something almost surreal about me and TB talking on mobiles en route to holidays, with RC back in the UK wanting me to do all the dealings with the paper. TB and I agreed I should do the statement on the record, named, as a way of making absolutely clear this was TB sticking by him. It also helped me in the moves I was beginning to make to put my briefings on the record.

As the day wore on, Robin seemed to get himself into better shape, maybe relieved Margaret was gone, perhaps just psyching himself up for what was to come. I had got a deal from Hall that they would let me see the copy in advance, and consult on headlines, even if I couldn't change them. It barely read like a *News of the World* exposé at all. It was very sympathetic, the headlines were basically onside, and totally based on the statements. They allowed us to make a couple of changes, for example talking of meetings rather than 'trysts'. I also asked them to take out of couple of things that I thought would provoke Margaret, either because it suggested she was in any way to blame, or it rubbed her nose in it. I also persuaded them to use just two pictures and leave out lurid detail. The only discussion now was the headline for the splash. They had 'Cabinet minister and his secret love' with 'Cook: my marriage is over' as a strap. I would have preferred the other way around, with 'Cook: my marriage is over' as the main headline. I suggested 'Cabinet minister leaves wife for secretary' which was more tabloid, but absolutely factual. Rebekah [Wade, deputy editor] came back and said the fact that the back bench cheered with delight made her think I should go back to her idea. It showed just how much we had changed our relations with the *NoW* and the Murdoch papers generally that they were willing to let us change the text. The inside pages consisted of Robin's statement, my statement, the background and then a glowing profile of Robin. It was so not the *News of the World*. I spoke to him after his arrival in Edinburgh and said that it was about as good as we could hope for. For what seemed like the hundredth time he thanked me for the help I was giving him. I said he had been unlucky. He repeated that he had been very foolish. Fiona was wondering whether GB would be pleased.

Sunday, August 3

First thing I called Robin who said 'You've worked wonders, and I'm very grateful.' The other papers took their lead from the *News of the World*, and only the *Sunday Mirror* got nasty, running a poll of readers asking who on earth would want to have an affair with Robin. *GMTV* led on it, the BBC ran it with no mention of Gaynor. Chris Patten was leading the BBC all day, re the inquiry into whether he leaked classified material. Robin was now worried about the editorials and also the *Mirror* doorstepping his mother. George Pascoe-Watson called and it was clear the *Sun* could go anti on this, lots of questions about whether the first Margaret knew really was Friday, whether there were other skeletons ready to tumble out, whether Robin duped TB or deceived anyone else. He mentioned, for example, that Margaret was photographed with him at his count on election night. Oh for fuck's sake, I said, what are you saying, that the minute a man starts an affair he tells his wife and then is never seen with her again? I don't think it quite works like that. I called Robin from a service station and said that whether he first told Margaret on Friday was a potential point of vulnerability. I did not want to lie, I said. I needed to know the truth before I could deal with all the questions, and I wanted to put this particular line of enquiry to bed. I asked if he had been having an affair with Gaynor for most of the five years they were together, and he said I probably would not find the answer to that question very helpful. He said, what I can say is that Margaret was aware of what was going on and I had been trying to end the marriage for some time. I told her last summer and she wanted to give it another go. Then again in December, I wanted to leave but

Margaret was keen to keep the marriage going. She hoped RC would be scared of the kind of publicity he was now getting.

It was clear Robin didn't mind at all. He sounded much more concerned about Gaynor than Margaret and was still worried whether it damaged TB, but he sounded very calm indeed now. Part of him was clearly relieved, whatever the media were doing, that the situation was resolved. I got Tim to ring round the papers and brief that RC had been trying to end the marriage for some time. Now I was desperate for a holiday. Then David Simon called. He said on Tuesday, BP results will be published and it could be a good time to say that he would sell his shares and donate profits made to charity. This seemed like a good idea. We got to our village finally and went for dinner at the restaurant. RC called again. I said the aim now should be low-profile. I said if possible get Margaret to issue a statement that they would remain friends and intended to get divorced. I'm aware of the utility of such a statement, said Robin. I'm also aware that I could not possibly achieve it. I also suggested to him that after a reasonable gap, and done in a way that would not provoke Margaret, he should emerge to be photographed with Gaynor.

Monday, August 4

I was winding down pretty well. I saw various papers. No wonder RC was grateful. Generally, the news management operation on Robin was textbook. There was very little that was permanently damaging and he had performed well. Nobody was calling for his resignation and he almost came out of some of them well. Bevins did a number on a hundred days in which he said GB, Derry, Peter and I were the four musketeers around TB and that we were ruthless in a way that would shock. The office called a few times and things had calmed down, with the exception of the [Chris] Patten story. Jon Sopel [BBC] had gone on World at One and given the most detailed briefing of how a 'Labour spin doctor' handled the Cook and Patten stories. Sopel, according to Tim and Peter, was apologetic and felt unable to explain why he did it. He basically said Downing Street were fanning the story about Patten as a way of taking attention away from Robin's affair. Peter said he had never been more shocked by a BBC report. That was a bit over the top, but Tim said he would never speak to Sopel again. I said we should not be too sanctimonious. The truth was we had all been hoping they did Patten ahead of RC. Peter also called about David Simon. He felt we were taking a hit and it was time to change tack and eat a bit of humble pie. We should use BP results day to say he was selling shares and donating profits to charity.

I said my only worry was the Tories feeling they had drawn blood. He said they already had.

Tuesday, August 5

Calum and I went up Mont Ventoux and RC called as we were heading back. 'To be honest, I'm rather depressed today,' he said. Margaret had put out a nice statement yesterday, saying she did not question RC's ability as an MP or minister. But then she apparently exploded on seeing an editorial favourably comparing him with Cecil Parkinson [former Conservative Party chairman, involved in an extramarital affair during the Thatcher era]. She demanded, on seeing it, apparently in the Scottish *Daily Express*, that he put out an apology to her. He tried to persuade her that this would just give the story fresh legs at a time it appeared to be dying away. He felt we had got through things as well as we could but that he now wanted to plan Gaynor's 're-entry'. They were likely to be going on holiday together so he felt, probably rightly, that they should do something sooner rather than later together. I was surprised he thought this was worth interrupting my holiday for, but I guess I had sold the pass in dealing with it all over the weekend. His idea was that they go to dinner at Frank Dobson's. I felt that would look furtive, if they were photographed leaving there. Better to go to a restaurant and we will ensure a photographer is there. He sounded very down. He had not left Carlton Gardens and was clearly feeling a bit cooped up and claustrophobic. Finally, he got round to what I suspected was the reason for the call. 'Have you spoken to Tony since the weekend?' I said I hadn't, not since the story was out in the open and he seemed to be OK about it.

Wednesday, August 6

Peter M called a few times. The David Simon exercise had gone fine. There was a sense of a U-turn but also a feeling that a line could be drawn. We also discussed how to organise the RC/Gaynor 'coming out' situation. I said I was worried RC was being too proactive to promote Gaynor and it would provoke Margaret and keep the thing going. I suggested we organise a photographer to go to the restaurant where they were meeting Dobbo and wife, but then as we discussed it, I moved against the idea, feeling it would only provoke Margaret. I was also called by Alex [Ferguson] who was being asked by Mellor to go on his Football Task Force and wanted to know how much work it would entail. I called Mellor who said it would probably be a couple of meetings a month. Alex said he was keen to do this, but really worried it would take up too much time. He said if they failed

August '97: RC begins to ruin AC's holiday

in Europe, people would be looking for reasons to blame him, and this would be one of them. He said there was some disappointment Mellor was in charge, that people in the game felt he had a big ego and would have his own agenda. Mellor called me on the Sunday from Germany, obviously disappointed Alex couldn't do it, and said he was going to go for Peter Robinson [chief executive] at Liverpool.

Friday, August 8

PG felt that some of our people were not translating well from opposition to government and that apart from me we lacked political big hitters with the media. He shared a lot of my frustrations with Peter, felt he talked a better game than he played and lacked any sense of playing in a team. He had changed. He also felt the way Peter took so much credit for the election was damaging to TB as well as untrue. He was also worried we were lacking strategic grip. I felt that we had neither the systems nor the will across the board to make it happen. Too many ministers were being captured by departments and too few departments operated strategically on their own, let alone as part of a bigger operation across government.

Monday, August 11

After the initial flurry, things calmed down and the flow of calls slowed. Tim was keeping me in touch most days and RC called from time to time, worried about whether TB had said anything, or whether the *News of the World* were planning any follow-up. He said he had written TB a note saying the support he had received from Number 10, and particularly me, had been magnificent, and he would not forget it. He was worried his career and reputation might have taken a hit, though, and was clearly desperate for some kind of reassurance from TB. I assured him that if TB was not happy about it, we would have heard. I filled in Philip [Gould] on the whole episode as we drove down to Nimes one day and he said 'Ah, well you've got Robin in your pocket now, I'd say.' Unlike JP and GB, he added. The main problem at home, according to Tim, was Peter. The hundred-day exercise, headed by him and JP, was fine at one level, but at the press conference, and later on *World at One*, Peter lashed out at journalists, and it led to the Tories mounting an attack that he was a megalomaniac who had gone mad. It led to the Sundays doing a big number on 'Who's in charge?', while I noticed a letter in someone's *Telegraph* I picked up at a cafe, asking when exactly did he become prime minister? I know that I had been feeling particularly hostile in the last bit but it was precisely because of all this kind of thing. He was a media problem for himself, and a political problem for TB, and it was all about ego.

Thursday, August 21

St Tropez was not quite what I had in mind for a relaxing end of holiday, but the kids enjoyed it and we had a lot of laughs with PG and Gail. One thing for sure, it was a much better holiday than last year. I was relaxed enough not to get involved when Tim phoned, as we drove down to the South, to say he was having trouble with Nick Brown, who would not let him know what was going on in the McMaster inquiry, because, he claimed, Tim had been briefing against him.[1] In the second week at Flassan, the only thing I had really had to deal with was the fallout from the Football Task Force. Alex told me there had not been a good reaction to Mellor's appointment. Mellor called to say it was all sorted but there were problems. He was particularly pleased he'd got three black people on board. Robin called again to thank me, but I suspected an ulterior motive this time, because stories had started to appear that I had given him one hour to decide whether he was staying with his wife or moving in with his mistress. He sounded variously chirpy and depressed. Reading the papers, on the rare occasion I got them, had been a bit of a depressing affair. Peter M was the only story in town. He had given a very good impression of having masterminded the Robin scenario, and much else besides. The letters pages were full of him. Then he did his big social exclusion speech to the Fabian Society, the delivery of which was the first we knew about it. I was even beginning to wonder whether we can work together.

I was also toying with the idea of going absolutely upfront on the record with briefings, both as a new challenge, but also as a freedom of information and centralisation move. It would give the centre more clout and allow us to get some message control. Philip was in favour when I discussed it with him. I tried to be dispassionate about Peter and work out whether my troubles were provoked by jealousy that he was a major news-making figure or whether, as I stated to him and to TB, I felt he was becoming a problem to TB and potential embarrassment to the government. It got so bad I was envisaging not voting for him in the NEC elections in which he was going head to

[1] Chief Whip Nick Brown had been tasked with inquiring into the circumstances of the suicide of Gordon McMaster, Labour MP for Paisley South, following personal criticism of him within the Scottish Labour Party.

head with [Ken] Livingstone [Labour MP]. I would in the end but it showed how bad it had got. His profile grew so much during the holiday when JP made a joke about a crab called Peter, it was front-page news and no amount of joking could hide the fact it was a bad story. As ever, PG and I spent ages talking re TB, GB, Peter M, where we were going. He appeared to agree with me, though less violently, about Peter. He said even with him he was very different, and oblivious to public opinion. He didn't really listen any more. He was interested in policy and power, and his influence in both. He was also a bit worried about TB. He felt we had lost grip. There was no fear, certainly not among the big guys. And he felt TB had ceded too much on control of the economy.

Friday, August 22

I caught a train to Nice and went round some of my old haunts, the cafes down the Avenue Masséna, the Méridien, the pizza place where I first played the pipes when I lived here, some of my old busking pitches, and back to Place Garibaldi through the old town. All the other names had changed and the woman I rented from, Mme Rinaudo, had died. Her own flat was bolted up and empty and just had 'M. et Mme Rinaudo' on a card. She must have left it to her son who was doing nothing with it. I checked with a neighbour who said she died a while back, left it to her family but they hardly ever came. There were a couple of Nazi symbols daubed on one of the walls, which shocked me.

I walked down to the port and there was a funeral going on in the big church there, for someone called Jacques who had died aged fifty-two. There were just eight people at the funeral. I went in and sat at the back, then signed the condolence book. I asked one of the women there who he was and she said he was a mental patient. He had been a fisherman. He didn't have many friends or family. I went round to the school where I'd taught and it was being done up by builders and though there were no pupils or teachers there I was able to wander around. I went to the classroom where I had done most of my so-called lessons, then to the office where I found M. Martini, the deputy head. I ran through all the teachers I could remember and most of them had gone.

Monday, August 25

I had a long chat with TB about his and our holiday. He sounded fine, said he had not read a single paper while he was away but was aware that things had not been particularly smooth. 'Can we not leave the country for two weeks without everything falling apart?' he said. I suppose that was the only upside. It reminded people how professional we were. People were beginning to say that the whole show was his, and the summer holiday stuff underlined how good he was. I gave him a relatively uncoloured assessment of what had been going on, saying the papers were bad and Peter had let his ego run out of control. He said, I'm not sure if Peter hasn't done himself in. I said if he was not brought under proper control then he would have three, not just two, people on his hands who felt they could do what they wanted. Of course GB had loved the summer, with Robin, JP and Peter all having fucked up in various ways. TB said he'd avoided the papers as it was the only way to relax.

TB said he hadn't wanted to bother me, but if he had known how bad things had been, he would have got more involved. But he felt we would soon be back on big-picture stuff and we can dismiss most of the silly season. We talked about doing a résumé speech, particularly focused on the economy. He asked me to go to Chequers tomorrow to work things out. We have almost four years to get the big things right, and if we do, the rest will go away. He said there had been massive interest in him in both France and Italy, and he felt a real opportunity to put Britain on the map politically. He was also back on his theme that we could make the press more positive, that they were only being negative because it was the mode, but could be put into a more positive frame. I spoke to several journalists during the day to catch up and most felt the summer had been a disaster area, which JP and Peter had handled badly, and that TB had to come back with a bang.

Tuesday, August 26

For the 11, I put together a few lines on TB activity to come, and his determination to focus on the big picture, and the issues on which we were elected. I was also doing a TB piece for the *Sun*, and trying to get a sense of perspective about the stuff over the summer. Higgins and Pascoe-Watson were desperate for a big number doing in Peter M and JP for their handling of the summer but I felt it best to ignore and put behind us. I spoke to TB before he left for home and then went to meet him at [RAF] Northolt. He was tanned, very smiley and chirpy, bounced down the [plane] steps carrying a red box, into the car and off we went. He said he had avoided papers but even reading today's papers on the plane, he could see the mood had changed. But he felt the actual events of the summer would be quickly forgotten. I stressed that it was hard to overstate just how high-profile Peter had been. We spent most of the journey, and then dinner at Chequers, small-talking re holiday, etc.

TB was on to the notion that our biggest enemy was cynicism. Once the mood really turns, they'll all turn together. GB will be the only one smiling, he said. He felt JP was fundamentally loyal but worried about his running of the department [Environment, Transport and the Regions]. Re the reshuffle, TB had decided on [David] Clark and [Gavin] Strang pretty much [for dismissal], but it didn't give him that much room for manoeuvre. He still had his mind on getting a couple of Liberals in. He was musing re the Millennium and felt maybe Peter M should be full-time in charge of it. He said of Peter that he had 'got too grand, had to learn some humility'. He said he wanted to push Europe up the agenda again, on our terms. He felt we could win the arguments and that it would test Hague. He also said he had written to Margaret Cook to say how sorry he was and how he hoped she would rebuild her life and she wrote back an odd letter saying she found it odd that he didn't say he was sad the marriage was over. He was clearly worried she would come back to cause us trouble at some point. We wanted to get up on education fairly quickly. He mentioned he had met a guy called Maurice Hatter [electronics tycoon and Labour donor] who said he would fund a schools computer project. We tried to track him down through Levy and others, got him and TB persuaded him that we could go ahead immediately. It would help for the school visit we were planning for Thursday. Over dinner, he was telling us how odd he now found it being recognised not just here but abroad as well. He said he was confident we could sell the benefits of the single currency. 'We won't be in the first wave but we will almost certainly be in within a decade.'

Wednesday, August 27
Over breakfast, TB said he sometimes despaired at the quality of some of his ministers. Even the ones we thought were good were not that good. GB and Peter M were the only ones who fully understood the way the media was changing politics. We spent the morning planning out the speech and interview programme for the next few weeks. He was going to get back into Ireland. He wanted a series of speeches on the theme of modernisation again – on the economy, constitution, unions, at the TUC [Trades Union Congress], public services, etc. He was clearly up for some major change. He also wanted more work done on defining the Tories. He felt we were slightly losing politics in the operation. He was on OK form, but troubled by the change in mood. He said he was angry with Peter because the worst thing was

that it was a moderniser who had fucked up and let that mood change. I spoke to Mo who wanted to do the announcement on Sinn Fein talks tomorrow and wanted TB involved. TB was adamant that it was a no. He went to play tennis and I headed to the office. The main thing to deal with was MI5, Shayler and what to do.[1] TB was not keen on building it up. I was of the view we should not blow it up, but Paul Martin [Security Service] felt it was damaging already and the damage had to be countered. Peter M wrote me an embarrassing note, claiming I had briefed against him, and defending the way he had conducted himself. I was fairly robust in response. If he had behaved less like a tit in the summer, there would have been no need to say anything to anyone.

Thursday, August 28

We were slowly getting a grip. Mo was at the end of her tether with the UUs, who were being really vile about her. She came into a meeting with TB and filled him in. TB was not too downbeat. Afterwards we had a long discussion on how to deal with the MI5 situation, Shayler and the *Mail on Sunday*. The school visit went fine, though Brunson tried to get TB going on 'Awful August', but he stuck to the education script. CB was there looking bored. He did an OK doorstep though it was pouring with rain. I could not have organised better 'end of honeymoon' pictures myself. After the Trimble meeting, TB said after Sinn Fein came into the talks we had to get more positive stories published for the Unionists. JP spoke to TB and was really worried that TB felt he screwed up. But TB had decided Peter, more than JP, had been the problem. To be fair to JP, he stuck up for Peter, said he had helped him on a number of personal things. I had a meeting with Brendan Barber [deputy general secretary, TUC], and they were really worried that TB would go over the top on the unions at the TUC.

The MI5 situation was taking up a fair bit of time. I had long chat with Jack Straw who was putting the case for being quite heavy. TB was not keen to make Shayler a martyr but Jack said damage had already been done. We agreed I would speak to Jonathan Holborow [editor, *Mail on Sunday*]. He kept saying he would do nothing to damage national security. I said he was not in a position to know whether it did or not. I said, for example, there were concerns that Shayler knew stuff re Libya and the IRA and could do considerable

---

[1] David Shayler, a former MI5 officer whose 'revelations' to the *Mail on Sunday* led to the government seeking an injunction to prevent publication.

damage. He said he would try to be sensible and came back to me to say there was nothing about the IRA or Libya. I said we still needed headline material to know what was going to be damaging or not. The main story was likely to be in keeping files on our people, like Jack and Peter M. JS seemed quite chuffed, kept telling me how he wasn't bothered about that. Paul Martin called, and they appeared very unfocused. He said the MI5 people were getting worried that we were getting nearer and nearer to Sunday and it was still not resolved.

Friday, August 29

I was up early to get to Heathrow to meet TB. He was worrying about the MI5 situation, and not impressed by the way the government machine dealt with it. He did not feel we had got all the information we wanted, and was keen that we made an effort to reach an agreement before injuncting. My sense was that Holborow wanted us to get heavy. I spoke to Holborow before and after his meeting with lawyers. He finally said that he could not help us any further. This was a journalistic editorial decision. He then gave me his solicitor's number. While he was touring his constituency, TB asked me to stay at the house [Myrobella] and deal with the MI5 situation. The Treasury Solicitor's letter came through. I made some changes, as did TB when I tracked him down at the training centre. He was not impressed. Who the hell drafted this? His concern was that we should not let the *Mail on Sunday* play on public sympathy. We stressed that we had no trouble with critical articles about the security services. We gave the *MoS* a 5pm deadline. There would be more legal wrangle overnight and then probably injunction. The Andy Grice interview on the plane went OK, but we didn't really have a story and he was pushing very hard to get TB to whack the unions harder.

I got Alex [Ferguson] lined up to do stuff for the referendum campaign. He'd just got the European Cup draw and was really up for it. On the train back, the phone and pager never stopped. Grice was with me and said he didn't know how I coped. He was surer than ever that he was right not to take the job [Grice had been offered the job as TB's press secretary before AC]. He said he could never have done it like I did. But the truth was I was feeling stressed and tired and beginning to hate Fridays because you tried to wind down for the weekend but you also knew the weekend would take over and it would be impossible to stop working. On the way back I was dealing with the speech, the lawyers, MI5, Ireland, a problem with an interview Clare had done attacking the FCO, a Tessa [Jowell] article for the *NoW*. I also had Spice Girls film people pushing for TB to appear, £50k to charity. I don't think so.

Saturday, August 30

A pretty extraordinary weekend, dealing with MI5 and the *Mail on Sunday*, then Diana's death in the early hours. The day started with Calum in tears when I said I might not be able to go to Burnley vs Bristol Rovers. I was worried I would not be able to deal with the Shayler situation properly, but he was so upset we set off. We then learned that in the exchange of letters Holborow was saying that I threatened to 'call in the heavies'. TB was a bit exercised that I was 'tootling off to a football match' and it was hardly ideal. I spent most of the journey on the phone. We prepared a statement on the injunction and got people lined up. We also had a problem with the *Sunday Times* interview. As we hadn't had a story, he was going on 'Blair backs Mandelson's power bid'. TB was pissed off and called him to say so. As the injunction hearing began at 11.30, we started to get out the line that far from being heavy, we had done everything we could to help them publish, but they had not co-operated. I was so busy and distracted that I missed the M6 turn-off, and we took ages to get there. News of the injunction came through just before the kick-off, when Nick the duty clerk[1] called and said government 1, *Mail on Sunday* 0. I spoke to TB at half-time, and we agreed that Jack [Straw] had to go up and be robust. It was the first game I had been to, part of which I had missed, because of constantly being on the phone. We were home by half nine, and the *Mail on Sunday* had a ridiculous account of my conversations with Holborow.

I got to bed, and at around 2 I was paged by media monitoring: 'Car crash in Paris. Dodi [al-Fayed] killed. Di hurt. This is not a joke.' Then TB came on. He had been called by Number 10 and told the same thing. He was really shocked. He said she was in a coma and the chances are she'd die. I don't think I'd ever heard him like this. He was full of pauses, then gabbling a little, but equally clear what we had to do. We started to prepare a statement. We talked through the things we would have to do tomorrow, if she died. By now the phones were starting from the press, and I didn't sleep. Then about an hour later Nick called and said simply 'She's dead. The prime minister is being told now.' I went through on the call. Angus

---

[1] Nick Matthews, senior duty clerk. The Number 10 duty clerks handle the prime minister's most confidential filing, calls, etc.

Lapsley was duty private secretary and was taking him through what we knew. But it was hard to get beyond the single fact of her death. 'I can't believe this. I just can't believe it,' said TB. 'You just can't take it in, can you?' And yet, as ever with TB, he was straight on to the ramifications. By the end of the call we had sorted all we had to do practically.

There was also the issue of the chasing photographers. He said we should say that is not for now. We agreed to say nothing until a formal announcement but then Robin in Manila was about to get on a plane and was unable to resist making the announcement first, and raised the issue of the press. TB's mind was whirring. We had I don't know how many conversations, and they went round and round, veering from the emotional – I can't believe this – to the practical – what we were doing in Paris, when should he speak to the Queen? – to the political – what impact would this have? He thought he should probably speak to the Queen and Charles. 'Those poor boys.' It seemed an age between us being told of the death and the French interior minister and Michael Jay [UK ambassador to France] announcing it. PA finally broke it through 'British sources'. TB had been late learning of the actual accident because he hadn't heard the phone and then when the cops were asked to wake him up, they thought it was a hoax. Number 10 had to go through Scotland Yard to get on to Durham and explain it was serious and the cops would have to bang on his door.

Once we knew she was dead, we were into a seemingly never-ending round of calls. At about 4, I got a flavour of the royal Establishment's approach when Angus and I had a conference call with Robert Fellowes [private secretary to the Queen]. 'You know about Diana, do you? She's dead.' I said yes. We were sorting when TB should speak to the Queen. It was all very matter-of-fact and practical, though he too, like TB earlier, said 'Those poor boys.' TB and I agreed a statement to put out as soon as it was confirmed that she was dead. It was pretty emotional. TB was genuinely shocked. It was also going to be a test for him, the first time in which the country had looked to him in a moment of shock and grief. We went round and round in circles about what he should say, and also how. I didn't like the idea of him walking out to do something just for this purpose and we agreed to do nothing until he went to the church in Trimdon in the morning. Anything before that would look tacky. I didn't want TB to pile in too much. I was pissed off with RC at having jumped the gun on the official announcement. The phones were going all the time and then at around 4 I got a rash of calls asking if it was true that she was dead, then the dreadful wait for the official announcement. I didn't like the position of knowing she was dead and having to fob people off the whole time. The journalists calling were breathless with excitement. Eventually, I turned off the phone, and just used the other one to speak to TB and Number 10. Just after 7 TB called again. He'd been working on the words for his doorstep at the church and he was going over some lines he'd drafted. We agreed that it was fine to be emotional, and to call her the People's Princess. Talk about the good she did, how people were feeling. He kept saying 'I can't really believe this has happened. People will be in a state of real shock. There will be grief that you would not get for anyone else.' He said that if the Queen died there would be huge sadness and respect but this will lead to an outpouring of grief. 'She will become an icon straight away. She will live on as an icon.' He felt that it happened as she was fairly close to the height of her appeal. Dodi was probably a step too far for a lot of people. Had she got married, had another child maybe, she'd have started to fall in popularity. But this will confirm her as a real icon. He kept coming back to his words. 'What I have to do today is try to express what the country is feeling. There will be real shock.' We talked about the last time they met at Chequers and the letters she sent afterwards. She was a real asset, a big part of 'New Britain'. But somehow he knew it was going to end like this, well before her time. He asked me to fix up for him to speak to the Queen and Charles. Nick [Matthews] called to say the Palace was saying official mourning and a state funeral. I started to get calls from the FA about whether Newcastle against Liverpool should be cancelled.

I went down for breakfast and seeing it on TV made it harder to take in. I was tired and felt really emotional now, and drained, and started crying. TB called again, and said he felt absolutely devastated. We went through what he would say one more time and he headed to the church. I called Phil Wilson [Labour organiser in Sedgefield and friend of TB] to go with him and get the cops to organise barriers. TB spoke to the Queen. Then he came on the TV as he and the family arrived at church. It was a very powerful piece of communication. The People's Princess was easily the strongest line and the people in the studio afterwards were clearly impressed, and felt he really had caught the mood. The question about the role of the press was gradually moving up the agenda. Chris Smith called and we agreed he would not do interviews. John Holmes was worried about the doorstep, felt it was too close to Di. We have to be careful, he said. I took the kids to [Fiona's mother] Audrey's, riding their bikes, me trying to talk to people on the way, and we then had a series of conference calls, e.g. TB, Donald Dewar, Angus [Lapsley] and me. Donald was reluctant to cancel campaigning on devolution because of the proximity. Hague had said he was suspending campaigning indefinitely and we agreed that we would say we were suspending now and would assess later. The Scots were not so wound up by it all. The word had come through that the Royals thought it would be appropriate for TB to be there when the plane came back with the body, so we had to sort the logistics on that. Very careful thought was going to have to be given to every detail of the funeral and already some of the problems were becoming apparent. There was a suggestion the Spencers [Diana's family] might want a private funeral, which people would inevitably take as a bit of a hit on the Royals, and in any event the public were clearly going to be expecting a really big event.

I got home to change and then left for the office. The cab driver was a Jewish woman, in tears. I had a catch-up meeting with Angus at Number 10 and then we left for RAF Northolt, to be greeted by an extraordinary array of Establishment figures. Several were in uniform but the only one I recognised was Field Marshal Bramall [former Chief of Defence Staff]. The Lord Chamberlain [Lord Airlie] arrived in his enormous Rolls-Royce. He had quite the shiniest toecaps I'd ever seen, impressive white hair. The mood was a bit edgy. I sensed the concerns they all had about where it was heading. TB arrived with George Robertson, and again I was struck by how, in this company, they emanated a sense of being very different. Yet in these circumstances they knew that they maybe lacked the skills to navigate through. The LC said as much. Diana's former private secretary, Michael Gibbins, came later and he seemed a bit upset and withdrawn, and said she wouldn't have liked all these people sitting around talking about her funeral. He spoke to her a few days ago and she was really happy. 'This Dodi character may have been a bit odd but he certainly made her happy.' I was hovering near TB as he chatted to the Lord Chamberlain and they called me over. The LC was clear that this was an extraordinary situation and they would find it useful if we could be involved in the discussions about this. TB volunteered me for the next few days and said we would do whatever they asked of us. They had been discussing the idea doing the rounds of a private funeral. I said nobody would understand. Some would think it was her family putting up two fingers to the Royals. Some would say it was a royal plot to do her down. But basically people wouldn't understand. On one level, I found it odd to think

I would be helping the Royals work their way through a difficult public opinion situation. On the other hand, it was bound to be a fascinating period, and a genuinely interesting professional challenge.

Finally, the plane arrived carrying the body. There were hundreds of journalists kept behind barriers. TB et al. went out on to the tarmac. There was absolute silence as the coffin was carried from the plane, and then driven away. Charles came in with Diana's sister. He looked sad, and not surprisingly was finding the never-ending small talk difficult. TB set off for Chequers, then Angus and I headed back to London. TB called from the car and said he felt they didn't really know what had hit them, and genuinely wanted help and support. He felt we had to make sure the funeral was not a classic Establishment event, but a different kind of funeral that united the country around her personality. Today, he said, his job had been to express the feelings of the nation. Tomorrow it would be setting direction and shape. He said the Lord Chamberlain at least understood it had to be different, but none of us yet knew for sure what that might mean. He said he felt drained and cancelled most of his meetings for tomorrow, though he would be seeing GB there.

Monday, September 1

The coverage was enormous of course. TB's contribution had gone down really well. The *Herald Tribune*'s main headline was 'World Mourns the People's Princess'. The phrase had really taken hold, and was becoming part of the language immediately. We had to be careful though that it doesn't look like we are writing our script, rather than hers. TB said the two things that people saw in her above all were compassion and modernity. But what was clear was that we would shape the event. He called from Chequers early on and said it had to be clear quickly whether it was a state funeral or not. It needs to be a real memorial to her. There was a fair bit of play in the media for the fact that they had not said prayers specifically for her at Balmoral. He felt they would be reluctant to stray far beyond what they know, and what tradition would dictate, but it was important they did this differently. He felt the Queen and Charles were the key to this: that they would actively have to want to do something different. Allan Percival said later he was worried it was looking like a Labour thing, not a people's thing.

TB wanted us to be right into the details on this, and Angus Lapsley and I were called to a meeting at the Lord Chamberlain's office. We walked down through the growing crowds who were laying flowers and just milling. I don't think we were spotted going in, though later some of the photographers saw us coming out. Airlie chaired the meeting, which was also attended by Robert Fellowes, Michael Gibbins from Diana's office, Mark Bolland [deputy private secretary to the Prince of Wales], Penny Russell-Smith [press secretary to the Queen], Dickie Arbiter [Buckingham Palace press officer] and Lt Col Malcolm Ross [Comptroller of the Lord Chamberlain's office], who sat to the Lord Chamberlain's left and appeared to be the main man. I was asked to sit opposite the LC, with Fellowes to his right. It took some time to get going as they took ages to link a conference call to [Sir] Robin Janvrin [deputy private secretary to the Queen] and Stephen Lamport [private secretary to the Prince of Wales] at Balmoral. It was clear that everyone was already thinking on the same lines, that there must be a mix of tradition and modernity which captured her uniqueness. Airlie said at the outset that everyone was agreed we had to be open to new thinking. There was no way they were just going to implement a 'dusty old plan'. They were clearly desperate to do this right and felt it could be a great healing event. But the real instincts came through regularly. When they were talking about the procession, the Lord Chamberlain said it would be important to consult the Queen and Charles. Fellowes added 'And her family.' The Lord Chamberlain coughed and said yes, in that order. We agreed on a gun carriage, not a hearse, and that there should be a procession of 300 or so people from the charities behind it. I said it was important they were not just the suits, chief executives, etc., but people at all levels of the charities, above all the beneficiaries.

We discussed a possible Pied Piper effect, the idea that people should start behind barriers then come in behind the procession, but this was later vetoed by the police. I stressed the need for a racial mix. I had noticed on the way down how many black people were paying tributes. The crowds were growing through the day. The Lord Chamberlain struck me as far more switched on than when we first met last night. Every detail was going to have to be thought through. Every issue had the potential to bring its own difficulties. Fellowes said there was a dispute: who should go to the interment at Althorp [the Spencers' family home]? Who should walk behind the coffin? Janvrin was clear there had to be a royal element behind the coffin. Would the boys be able to do it? Lamport said he wasn't sure Charles would want to do it. Fellowes said, what would happen if Charles walked and someone in the crowd turned on him? Janvrin was clear you could not do it without Charles Spencer [Diana's brother]. We agreed he should be kept informed of all these discussions. Nothing could be agreed finally without the family. Then there were the questions of balance and tone in the service itself. Often they seemed to want to take a lead from me on the issues they were not used to dealing with. Who should be invited? Stars? Children? What we meant by a light touch, how to combine ceremony with modernity. Someone asked if all the Lord-Lieutenants would be asked to the funeral and there was a fairly immediate chorus of NO. Do we invite the al-Fayeds? Yes. We discussed foreigners. It would be hard to stop world leaders and diplomats wanting to come but we should send out discouraging signs. Fellowes said he thought it would be good if TB went to Balmoral on Sunday. The referendum campaign issue was getting difficult. Hague called for a delay, opportunistic little sod. The pressure to do something about the press was growing. Major did an interview and said as much and one or two MPs were clearly thinking we were staying out of this because of closeness to Murdoch.

Back at Number 10, I did a briefing on the discussions re funeral arrangements, and they were pressing for every little detail they could. I had been seen coming out of the Palace so there was no point pretending we weren't involved and we had to make sure people understood we were there because they asked us to be. I got up the People's Funeral line, and stressed they had been thinking on the same lines and that we were just offering help. I didn't sense any political difficulty in the briefing. I was in a seemingly never-ending round of meetings with Angus, John Holmes and people from the Palace. John came through with news the driver may have been drunk. At the second Palace meeting, Anji came too and we went to the meeting where Malcolm Ross briefed the relevant departments on thinking so far. He said 'the People's Princess' was the main theme and it would be a People's Funeral. He emphasised the role of her charities, said they wanted a proper ethnic mix. He and I saw the police who were clear we could not do the Pied Piper thing. I had a meeting with Fellowes, Ross and Penny Russell-Smith. I said the pressure for a minute's silence was growing and we could put it into the service at the end. Re overseas visitors, I said they should feel free to use us to put out the signal that we did not want countries to send people for the sake of it. There was a case for inviting Clinton, Mandela and Chirac for special reasons but making clear it was not a traditional 'all countries to be represented' event. We also agreed there should only be a small number from government, TB and JP perhaps, CB the only spouse. There must be as much space as possible for the non-traditional.

Wandering around the building, it was bigger than Number 10, quieter, with fewer people. It was better kept in many ways but once you were into the working bits, very old-fashioned. They had a little tower of baskets as their in and out trays. The staff tended to be of a certain type, women with Alice bands and big skirts. As we left the Palace, Fellowes said: 'It's quite fun breaking the mould from time to time – as long as you don't do it too often.' He struck me as a kind person, but one who had worked out this had to be different, and had to be successful, and he had no qualms about letting us take the lead where that might help make it happen. The Queen and Charles had decided the boys should walk behind the coffin. Charles Spencer said that was fine, so long as they wanted to and were not being dragooned.

Tuesday, September 2

As I feared, there were the beginnings in the coverage of problems. For example, the *Telegraph* editorial suggested that we were politicising the funeral, and I wrote to Charles Moore [editor, *Daily Telegraph*] to explain how our involvement came about. Fellowes called early about public access to the Palace and I suggested they compromise by allowing the pre-booked parties. What was interesting was that they were telephoning about things like this, partly for advice, partly cover. TB said later they may think their problems are over with her death, but it is possible they are really just beginning. He said there is a crisis now, not far below the surface. If they do not respond with some change, they could be in real trouble. He was clear that how they dealt with this now would dictate the extent of any problems they faced in the future. We were meant to be seeing Murdoch but after a bit of dithering, I felt it was a risk not worth taking. He was already on his way when I called Jane Reed [News Corporation executive] while TB was seeing Lord Alderdice [Liberal Democrat peer], and said I thought it was a bad idea, that it would get a whole thing going about privacy/paparazzi etc. if we were not careful and it emerged he was there, which almost certainly it would.

TB said the pressure on Charles as king might be to make way for William whilst still fairly young. It was clear from the calls from Janvrin in the afternoon that they wanted constant assurance that they were keeping in step. He asked where I thought they were in relation to public opinion. I said slightly ahead of the game but we need a few more big announcements as the days wear on. I also felt it was important that Charles made some sort of gesture towards the boys, a touch, a hug, something that said father and son, not just Royal Family. He asked if people would understand if only William, not Harry, followed the coffin. I said yes. The problem was the diet on the Royals had been so negative for so long that people didn't believe in good royal stories as they used to, but there was a basic sympathy there at the moment. I spoke to Penny Russell-Smith and agreed our office should take a back seat on the briefing re the funeral. Yesterday had established a legitimate role but they should be doing the basic briefing on this. I could sense some of the civil servants were not happy at our involvement but TB clearly felt we had to stay on top of this the whole way through. He wished he had got on to Clinton and asked him to come. The White House had picked up on our signals and said Hillary would be coming, not BC. It was a good signal though, and would help as we persuaded others not to feel they had to come. They were happy for us to take the diplomatic hit by effectively saying people were not wanted if they were purely representative. There had to be a connection.

At the 10am meeting, the police explained why we could not do the Pied Piper thing. My other idea, the minute's silence at the end, was accepted. It was still not clear whether Charles would follow the coffin. The Lord Chamberlain stressed that it was not a state funeral. He said the theme had been agreed. Condolence books had been organised. We would have screens along the route of the funeral procession. We had got through a phenomenal amount in not too long – general outlines, theme, who would sing, condolences, other services, etc. Sounding rather embarrassed on the speakerphone, Janvrin said some of the Balmoral team wondered whether 500 people behind the coffin was not too many. Fellowes said no. Ross went through the groups that would normally be expected to attend and it was huge so we had to pare it down where we could. The media were already moving into a more questioning mode and there were lots of rumours doing the rounds about splits between the families, between the Palace and the government, etc., and it will be a job to see them properly addressed. Fellowes and I had a discussion afterwards and agreed we had to watch the politicisation problem. They seemed fine but it was clear there were those who felt TB was cashing in. There were some worries about how it would look if TB did a reading and Charles didn't. Michael Gibbins was clear that TB should do it, and she would have wanted that. Also the issue of the flag not flying at half mast was beginning to pick up.

Robin C called, worried that the Ministry of Defence were pushing for us to exempt JP 233 bombs from the Oslo landmine talks. These were like bomblets, landmines dropped as part of another bomb. When Anji and I were having lunch with TB in the small dining room, Angus came in and said the family wanted RC to go to the funeral because of his work on landmines. TB elaborated on the current challenge to the Palace, said that he felt we really could help them but they would have to change. We discussed Peter. He said we had to get on. Anji said that she felt it was irretrievable. He said Peter had good judgement about most things and I should use it. He admitted he screwed up in the summer, and said Peter was useless at self-advice. GB had said he was an egotistical maniac. But we had to take the pros and cons. He still felt on balance the pros outweighed the cons. I said Peter was interfering and using his position to build a new social life rather than focus on the job in hand.

I went for dinner at David Mellor's, where he was meeting his Football Task Force people. He was an enthusiast and had got a good group of people from the sport, police, media, etc. and I said TB really wanted them to think big on this, and come up with big ideas for change. Everyone was saying how well TB did yesterday, and how badly Hague had done in his tribute to Diana. 'People's Princess' was the phrase everyone was using.

Wednesday, September 3

Some of the papers were beginning to turn against the Royals. The issue of no flag at half mast, the family staying in Balmoral, it all had the *Sun* fulminating for example. Fellowes called early and asked what we could do about it. I felt we had to keep making major announcements about the planning and build up towards the funeral as a healing event. Today, for example, we would be saying that we were having to reroute the procession to meet the size of the crowds expected. Janvrin called and said he was pretty depressed. They had clearly put to the Queen the issue of lowering the flag but it was a broken tradition too far. I put out words putting pressure on the Scottish Football Association, who were refusing to call off Saturday's game against Belarus. I proposed that TB do some media, maybe *Frost*, maybe a doorstep later. But every step of this was fraught. What looks like helping can look like interfering. Also, there was a sense of there being Di people and Charles people and it was not easy to bridge.

I went to the LC morning meeting and [Sir] Paul Condon [Metropolitan Commissioner of Police] was there for the Yard. He said they could handle anything really but they did have to know if the princes were going to follow the cortège. He led off the meeting with a bit of a bumbling presentation on crowd safety. They were having to work out how to ensure the dignity of the event while also ensuring security. The problem was the route had to be long to let the crowds see the cortège pass, but that created extra policing problems and also meant if the princes followed it was a very long walk. I asked if there were any religious or protocol reasons why if the coffin was followed it had to be followed the whole way. One or two seemed unsure, but Michael Gibbins got the point straight away and said it could go from Kensington Palace. Then pennies dropped all round. Problem solved. It would be put to the Queen then we could announce it later, along with all the extra detail that was being firmed up. On the service itself, there was nothing much new. Janvrin reported on the conference call that they wondered if the princes could go by car whilst the charities could walk, but quickly agreed with the view our end that it wouldn't work. Condon agreed to go up and do interviews. Penny Russell-Smith, Sandy Henney [press secretary to the Prince of Wales] and Mark Bolland kept me back and said they had a real fear this was becoming 'the people against the family'. Sandy said that somebody should go up to speak for the family, to say they were grieving and sharing the grief of the people. Sandy said who do we put up? 'What about the Lord Chamberlain?' said Penny. 'Dare I say wrong image?' I asked. Everyone fell about. We agreed Sandy should do it in the first instance, say the press were being unfair, there was no reason why they should not stay at Balmoral, it's where the children want to be, etc.

I spoke to TB several times to go over whether he should say something. I felt there was a case for it, that I should do a briefing ostensibly to announce the government attendance, but also to bolster the Palace. The Palace agreed and then we had a ready-made excuse for TB doing a doorstep as he arrived back from Chequers, namely the rerouting announcement. I walked back through the park. Flowers everywhere. It was heaving with people, yet quiet. The piles of flowers were now vast. I talked to a group of five youngish people, three men, two women, who had come up from Croydon. It was as if they knew her, like there was some kind of intimate bond. I couldn't work out if it was all about her, or all about them, or all about a desire for a new way of doing things. Heaven knows what she would have made of it. She knew she touched people, but she can't ever have imagined this.

Meanwhile I had a meeting with Philip, Margaret McDonagh [deputy general secretary] and Peter H re conference and a few new ideas involving real people, co-ordination, and they bemoaned the lack of an overall strategy and felt I should do more in relation to overall co-ordination. I said that was meant to be Peter's job. TB had met GB and GB had asked for me to go and see him re overall strategy. He was in good form, relaxed and friendly. He said that August showed up personality and presentational weaknesses. Peter was exposed and weakened and there was no substance to what he'd done. 'You wouldn't put him up to deal with substance, would you?' There was no message or strategy, he said. He clearly wanted an alliance against Peter and wanted to take a more active role in strategy. He said TB had been wrong to make Peter Chancellor of the Duchy of Lancaster as it would keep him in the same role. He needed a real job. It was the first proper chat we'd had for a while but it was all too obvious. GB could always play a part in strategy if he wanted to. I didn't like the way he let problems build and then put himself forward as the solution, provided others were done in.

I did a 3pm lobby on TB and JP representing the government at the funeral, and Robin going in a 'personal capacity'. The press were really trying to push us into the story being the Royals remote and stiff, and I deflected all that, as did TB in his OK doorstep. He had a phone call with Charles and said afterwards he sounded really done in. One day I'll tell you the whole story, he said. He was still not clear if he was going to follow the coffin. He said it was really grim up there. Stuart Higgins called. He said I had to persuade TB to get Charles to persuade the Queen to put a half-mast flag up there. Also, Sandy Henney was OK in what she was saying, but it was not enough. There was a lot of pressure building against the Queen and the family. Given some of the things I've written about the Royals in the past, it is bizarre in a way, finding myself in the position of not only defending, but also thinking of ideas to build them up. TB said they could sense that there was real change among the public. They would have to respond to it. We could help only if they went for it and realised they had to respond. In a way, while some may have seen Diana as their problem, in some ways she had been like a shield. Now she's gone they are suddenly exposed to this harshness. In the media, the feeling was that we could do no wrong and they could do no right. Only Charles Moore was really speaking up for them.

Peter called from the US to try to get to the funeral 'as a personal friend'. He also called Mark Bolland and tried via him, saying he was setting up a phone call between TB and Charles. He just could not resist it. There was something pathetic about it. Fiona thought I should take up GB on his offer of building an alliance against him. Philip [Gould] called and said he felt TB should go to the crowds in the Mall.

Thursday, September 4

In an extraordinary week, this was in many ways the most extraordinary day yet. The mood was really turning against the Royals and they seemed helpless in the face of it. It wasn't just the media, but the mood out on the Mall was dreadful. I called Fellowes and Janvrin and said it was becoming dangerous and unpleasant. The press were now fuelling a general feeling that the Royals were not responding or even caring. They both sounded very down. The ugliness of the mood was growing. Today's media would make it worse and it had to be addressed. TB's intervention yesterday got good, straight coverage. The *Telegraph* had a line that Peter M was 'believed to be advising' on the issue when he had spent the whole time in the States. I said to Fellowes that there had to be more big announcements to fill the vacuum and also the Royals had to be more visible. In an ideal world, they would come back early to London and mix with people. I also suggested they invite some of the people queuing to sign the condolence books to come to the service itself. They were in a bit of a state though.

Geoff Crawford [press secretary to the Queen] was back from Australia, which was good news. Hilary C was now with me at the 10am meeting, as well as Anji and Angus, and she suggested another giant screen in Regent's Park. They liked the idea of tickets for some of the people signing condolence books. Anne from Diana's office was in a real fury about the fact so many tickets for the service were going to the media. And the Spencer family were livid at James Whitaker [*Daily Mirror* royal correspondent] claiming he had been invited in a personal capacity. We had already agreed to cut media from a hundred to fifty but they felt even that was too many. Anne said there should have been real consideration of this, and it had not happened. The Lord Chamberlain tried to close it down but it all got a bit steamy. In a very prim and proper way, without sounding offensive but clearly giving offence, Penny Russell-Smith said the problem was that the princess did have her links with the tabloids and Anne snapped back that was completely irrelevant, the family should have been consulted about which media came. We then discovered, to Fellowes' fury, that Charles Spencer had 'disinvited' the editors.

We discussed screens, disabled access and then the Lord Chamberlain asked me and my team to stay behind for a conference call with Robin in Balmoral. He came on and said he was with the Duke of Edinburgh. The Duke's voice sounded old and frail and he was clearly nervous. They had finally got the message that something had to give but they really didn't like it. He said he was letting us in on the latest thinking about whether the boys would walk behind the coffin. They were divided on it, which is what TB had picked up from his call with Charles yesterday. Robin said if William did not do it then Charles couldn't 'for obvious and understandable reasons'. So he was back to proposing cars for the princes but Charles S was against that. He was called off for a meeting with the Queen and William. They had agreed something of a 'fightback' plan, and Janvrin stayed on the line to go through it. They would issue a statement authorised by the Queen to explain why it was best to stay at Balmoral. Today and tomorrow members of the family would start to visit the Chapel Royal. The Duke of Edinburgh has suggested that they go to church this evening before the boys head south. The Prince of Wales comes down tomorrow and visits Kensington Palace, Buckingham Palace and the chapel. The Queen and Queen Mother would come back and also visit the Chapel Royal and the Queen would do a broadcast. Even as they told us what the plans were, I could feel tension dissipating a little. It would all help. I said it should be briefed out of the church visit that they are saying prayers for Diana, and Charles must at some point make a display of compassion. I also felt the various visits should involve seeing and talking to people in the crowds, particularly the Queen and the boys. And I felt that the broadcast should be more conversational than the usual Christmas broadcast. The LC seemed fine with all that and said she was keen to discuss it all with the prime minister. The Duke came back on, sounding tired, and it was clear they were hurting at this idea that they were just up there, uncaring. In the meantime, I said they had to get her statement briefed with a clear sense of her sharing the grief of people.

It was still not clear who among the princes would walk behind the coffin, and I suspected it would not be clear until the last minute. But what they were proposing would certainly help deal with the mood outside. They realised that if William doesn't go behind the coffin, they have a real problem because Charles would have to go behind the coffin with Charles Spencer. There is no way he can do this without the boys, he said. When I said to Fellowes it was possible to sell the idea of the boys going behind by car if they left from Kensington Palace, he said they were just against cars full stop. He said they had to keep pushing for it. Sandy Henney had been sent up to try to explain why he might do it. She was obviously saying it was what his mother would have wanted whilst there was also the fact it would avoid the risk of Charles being publicly attacked.

I had another discussion with Fellowes and said again it was a matter of mixing announcements with expressions of grief and feeling. TB was at the education summit at Number 10 and I filled him in later. I was also trying to sort the DTI briefing the Fairness at Work white paper. Mike Brunson [ITN] called and I said there were major changes to come. He called back and said they had picked up hints, via David English, re the broadcasts. I confirmed and explained some of the thinking, and his lunchtime two-way was fine. I was worried the Palace would think I was jumping the gun but it was important the first pitch on it was right. TB was not in an easy position. He was fully aware of the public mood, which he too believed was more than just a media thing. His role was to give advice, frankly, but in circumstances where the Queen was clearly feeling sorely treated, and that people were not being reasonable. They would be feeling terrible, and there can be few things more terrible than feeling like that but also having your motives questioned. TB, Jonathan and I had a chat before his call with the Queen. I'd given him a vague outline of what they planned and he felt that a stage-managed series of walkabouts and a grand statement might not work. He felt she had to expose a little vulnerability somewhere along the line. It was the first time I'd heard him one on one with the Queen and he really did the Ma'am stuff pretty well, but was also clear and firm too. He said the thing was Diana was a personality who made people feel they knew her when they didn't, so there were many people out there feeling loss and wanting to blame. As he told her, it was unfair that it was being directed at the Queen and the family. He saw his role as offering support for her and the family and doing what he could to unite the country in its support for her and the family. It was so important that the funeral service was healing. He said he felt she had to show that she was vulnerable and they really were feeling it. He said 'I really do feel for you. There can be nothing more miserable than feeling as you do and having your motives questioned.'

William was refusing to speak to anyone and he was consumed by a total hatred of the media. It was pretty clear that he really felt strongly about the role of the media vis-à-vis his mother, and would not want to be doing anything that he felt was for them. He was being strong and clear about what he wanted. But as TB said, they were just one of the things he would have to deal with as King, and he'd need help. He felt that if he loved Diana as she had wanted him to, there was the chance he would set his mind on becoming King but having nothing to do with the rest of them. I asked him where he thought we as a government needed to be at the end of this. He said

September '97: The Queen is hurt; William angry

1. people saying we handled it well and captured the national mood, 2. Diana still there as a symbol of modernity, and 3. the Royals modernising a little.

The Palace did their briefing at 3, which seemed a bit chaotic, and then the Met had theirs. I was constantly pushing the line that the Palace were very much in the driving seat and we were there with help and support. Yes, we had ideas but they were in the lead on it all. It may not have been strictly true but we were never that far away from an interference/politicisation/exploitation line, and we had to stay the right side of the line. It was complicated by the fact that the *Standard* second edition had a line that Peter had come back to help, and cancelled his holiday to do it. I showed it to TB as he and I were working on the Queen's broadcast for tomorrow. He was angry, bottom lip trembling angry, said he really intended to lay into him for this. It was damaging because it made it look like the whole thing was about presentation, and our presentation at that, rather than theirs. Up to now, they were fine with the help we were giving, and there was an understood mutual benefit, I guess. This took it to a different place. In briefings I specifically denied it. The main briefing problem was the press going too hard on the notion that Blair was saving the whole show. In truth, they had pretty much delegated a lot of the judgement on this to him, and he to me. He saw TB who claimed he gave him a real talking to, told him he was now on trial. He had four things he had to do: first, do his job and give advice without constantly getting publicity for doing so; second, rebuild his relationship with me; third, rebuild his relationship with Gordon; and fourth, show some humility. If he didn't he would have to take stock. But he was already taken in with the idea that Peter was nothing to do with the *Telegraph* and *Standard* stories.

The exact line-up behind the cortège was still not clear. Prince Charles spoke to TB again and it was clear that they were still hopeful that William would walk behind the coffin. This was probably because Charles Spencer would not go in the car with Charles. There was an idea the family should just stand together at the Palace as the coffin went by but that would look like they were separate from the event, just part of the crowd, which was absurd, and TB pretty much said so. We suggested that they follow from Kensington Palace, perhaps with Spencer, and then join the charity people. I sensed that the boys were holding firm, and they seemed to feel it was being done for the media and the public, not for their mother.

To make matters worse between me and Peter, Philip told me he had said my problem was that I was jealous of him. Fucking unbelievable.

He had learned nothing from the summer. PG said he had come up for the first time unprompted as a negative in the groups.

Friday, September 5

Things were definitely turning their way. There was huge interest in the fact she was doing a broadcast to the nation. They got a far better press than on any other day this week. There were a few pieces on the TB link and the general feeling was we pushed them into all this. Nobody believed us when we said we didn't. TB was still fretting about whether he'd become too involved and was now unsure re doing *Frost* on Sunday. I wanted him to do it because there was a job to be done settling the country down, give the message that there must be hope and confidence for the future. I think Peter was arguing against. There was a far better mood at Airlie's morning meeting. The details were falling into place though it was still not clear whether William was going to march behind the coffin. 'It will go to the wire,' said Airlie. We went over some of the logistical issues, like the fact there would be one million bunches of flowers to deal with. They read out a series of engagements and walkabouts the Queen and Charles would do, and it was clear they were really motoring. We went over the Crathie church[1] visit. There had to be some expression of emotion from Charles. The main picture was Harry reaching for his hand, though Charles took it away quickly and the effect was rather spoilt, not least by them wearing kilts, and also Philip virtually tearing off a note from the flowers.

The morning meeting was fairly quick and then Airlie thanked everyone for their contribution. He then asked me to stay behind for a smaller meeting. We agreed that things were better and the broadcast and walkabouts will improve things further. The mood was definitely turning a little against the media, a trend Charles Spencer had helped. There was still the vexed question of William and walking. It was clear they were still trying to get him to. TB said later they would be stupid to push it too far. He was also worried that people were saying the Queen was persuaded by Charles to do more than she wanted. This was doing the rounds and he feared it was Peter's work and would backfire on all of us. 'What on earth would she have made of all this?' he asked. She would not believe it, not this. Airlie was very relaxed, and very nice to me and my little team. He said he genuinely appreciated the work we had done. He was hopeful that all the princes would walk behind the coffin, alongside Charles Spencer. We discussed

[1] The Royal Family's place of worship when they are visiting Balmoral.

September '97: Things turn the Palace's way

the car situation again but it was not a runner. They were still thinking of them all watching from the side of the road but that would have the effect of them looking totally divorced from the event. Fine for some but not for all. We agreed there had to be involvement in the procession itself, that the idea of watching from the road was a non-starter. The mood had really improved, but it was important they got the broadcast right. We agreed it should be done in the room where we had been meeting, so that the shot would capture all the people in the background. Fellowes said he felt we had all worked well together and were getting there. We were a day off the pace but we recovered, he said. William was the key to it all now. He said he was in a better mood than yesterday when he came back from the moors. We walked back through the ever-growing crowds to Number 10 and there was no doubt the mood was improving, and the ugliness would melt away once they came back and did their stuff.

TB again spoke to Higgins and was too supplicatory for my liking. I did a Sunday lobby on background and further bolstering the Royals. They didn't much buy it. Richard Stott [*News of the World* columnist] called later, and said 'You guys have saved the monarchy. It was turning into a total disaster.' The afternoon could not have gone better for them. As the Queen walked around in front of the Palace, looking at flowers and talking to people, you could sense the pressure lifting, the mood changing. Anna Ford [TV journalist and newsreader] was doing the live stuff and said as much. William and Harry did well, so did the others, and the mood was changing totally. The broadcast script was fine. They sent it through and we made a few final changes. TB wanted her to say she was speaking from the heart. I persuaded Fellowes she should put in 'speaking as a grandmother'. I had a long meeting with TB and Peter to go over the reasons for and against *Frost* and sort out logistics and difficult questions. The press, Camilla, memorial, what it all meant. TB was getting into the black humour, said he should do the interview with two thumbs up as a way of seamlessly moving into the devolution campaign. TB had to leave for the abbey for a rehearsal and he met Charles Spencer, who was really fired up re the media. He said William wanted to become a recluse because he hated the media. Both William and Harry had done really well on the walkabout and my sense after the reaction they got was that they would want to walk behind the coffin. Piers Morgan called and asked me to do all that I could to stop Charles Spencer attacking the press. As if. I went to see Rory play football and then got the message Mother Teresa had died. I got home in time to see the scenes of the coffin being moved, which was very powerful. The combination of the

Queen's broadcast, William's walkabout and her walkabout had got things back on track.

I went back to Downing Street, having decided it made more sense to stay there overnight than fight through the crowds in the morning, so I borrowed Euan's room. TB and I sat down in the kitchen and went over everything for tomorrow. I was telling him about the Airlie meetings. He said Spencer had suggested TB see William. He also thought I should be seconded to the Royals. They must be grateful to you for what you've done for them this week, he said. I felt the people had moved the Royals, that it had been a genuine public response that they had been forced to respond to. I also felt privileged to have been part of events that would represent a moment in history. I watched the news and as the crowd surged towards the hearse along the extended route, which had been our idea, I couldn't resist saying to him 'I did that.'

Saturday, September 6

I was up early and the only other person up was Carole Caplin. We just about managed to make polite small talk. We were both wary of each other, and she knew I really didn't think she should be there, but we got by this morning. TB and CB came through and CB made a joke about whether Carole and I had spent the night together. At least I think it was a joke. TB was continuing to fret about *Frost*, feared we lacked a real message. We were back to the days of testing a line again and again. The basic message was that good must come out of bad, we must be able to build from this a more compassionate Britain. Part of the stress of the day was trying to persuade him it was the right thing to do. My feeling was that there would be a big down tomorrow and we had to lift things. There was a big crowd at the gates so before they left for the Abbey, just as the coffin was leaving Kensington Palace, we went to the bottom of the street and he said hello to a few people. There was a ripple of applause, which I felt was odd and I was worried people would say he was milking it.

Once they'd gone, it felt very odd watching it all on TV. It was all happening very close by, but as I wasn't there I felt very remote from it. Yet I also felt some sense of authorship. The longer route. Some of the details of the service and procession. The way the mood had softened to its current state. I watched mainly on TV but then went upstairs to watch it come across Horse Guards, then out to Whitehall as it came past Downing Street and there was more noise than I expected. There was a good mood in the crowd and several moments

I found particularly moving. The card from the kids. I thought Elton John was tremendous. TB's reading was OK. The main event though for me was Charles Spencer's tribute, in which he directed barbs both at the press and the Royal Family. TB was sure the attack on the press would be the main thing. As soon as he came back he asked me to go and see him, even though he had a stack of kings and queens and others coming for lunch. Hillary Clinton arrived and the three of us went into the duty clerk's office. He asked her how she thought we should respond to what Charles Spencer had said about the press. She didn't seem to think it was much of a problem, said we should play it long, say obviously there were issues to look at but we would not get rushed into anything. Fairly obvious stuff. She talked about how hard it was when photographers physically invaded your space. Jackie Kennedy [wife of former US President John F. Kennedy] hated it. But she was clear this was not a legislation thing.

TB asked me to speak to GB and Peter, which I did. They were more relaxed. GB felt, rightly in my view, that Spencer's attacks on the Royals would be far more newsworthy. Once lunch was over, we prepared for *Frost* full-time, first on message, which was about the legacy of a more compassionate Britain, then worked through the more tricky questions. He asked me to speak to Dominic Lawson [editor, *Sunday Telegraph*] and David English and ask if they would chair a committee of editors to look at the issues arising from this. Both were fine, though English pointed out that that was what the Press Complaints Commission was meant to be doing so we dropped it.

I got home at 6 and we went out for dinner. Fellowes called and said he wanted to say how grateful he was for the support and advice we had given. He said he didn't believe Spencer meant his speech as a great attack, he was just very emotional. On the royal train up to Althorp, he was struck by the camaraderie and the warmth. He was in an unusual position as he was both a royal employee but also, through his marriage to her sister [Lady Jane Fellowes], part of Diana's side. He said the burial was both sad and beautiful. It was one of the most beautiful places in England yet the event was so, so sad. He was clear the whole week would see the Royal Family change. This was echoed in a call later from Robin Janvrin, who said he felt a relationship had been forged in days that would normally have taken years. The barriers were broken down now, he said, and that meant they could push on for change. The fact that the Queen had said herself lessons must be learned meant that they really were intent on change. The funeral was absolutely wall-to-wall, every aspect of the service and the day. There were a few pieces on TB and the Royals and he didn't much like them but they were more or less drowned out. He particularly didn't like a story that he had been going to make her a kind of ambassador. This came from a Tina Brown piece in the *New Yorker*, based on a conversation with Diana, which Godric sort of confirmed and it went too far.

Sunday, September 7

The *Frost* interview went pretty well and the story they were most interested in re government was the committee with GB in the chair, to look at ideas to commemorate Diana. I was feeling stressed all day, but also feeling I had been part of a historic moment, and one which might lead the Royal Family to change. We had a Scotland visit tomorrow for the devo campaign and TB was able to go via Balmoral, and it meant the usual long stay was cut to a few hours. I flew up with Roz Preston. It was the first time I had used an airport without TB for ages, and what a difference. It was worrying how quickly I had got used to just being driven to airplane steps and never seeing a passport or ticket. I was picked up by Jack McConnell [general secretary, Scottish Labour Party] and we headed for the Caledonian [hotel]. TB arrived, did a quick doorstep, a photocall with Elizabeth Smith [widow of John Smith] and then we went upstairs for a drink with GB. He was in very good form, regaling us with stories of how [Kenneth] Kaunda and [Milton] Obote [Presidents of Zambia and Uganda respectively] had responded to a display of Scottish culture at a CHOGM [Commonwealth Heads of Government Meeting] during the last devolution campaign. 'Are you sure these people are ready for self-government?'

GB was a different person when he was open and relaxed, but I sensed it was all a bit of a show for Elizabeth, who would be appalled if she knew how he sometimes was with TB. CB said she had asked the Queen if the John Brown story of Queen Victoria having an affair with her gillie was true. She said it got a bit frosty after that. TB said the Royals were very pleased with the help we had given, but whenever he tried to raise any suggestions of future change, the blinds came down. He said they are very different people in a very different age. They don't know what to make of me, he said. They think I helped, but they also wonder whether my calling her the People's Princess didn't fuel the public feeling. They know I'm not left wing but they also know I'm Labour and want to change things. They believe things should pretty much stay the same, and they want them to stay the same.

Monday, September 8

The press was still massive on Di, and on TB allegedly discussing modernisation of the Royal Family. TB was pretty clear though that the Queen was having none of it. He sensed she had been pretty horrified at them turning up in trainers and jeans for the drive around the Balmoral grounds. He was up early for a round of very good interviews, pushing the line that the Scots should trust him, but above all trust themselves. He was in his stride at the moment, like at the height of the election campaign. We did a very good school visit, a couple of doorsteps and walkabouts in Glasgow and Edinburgh. He felt confident in the arguments, that DD had been too defensive and it had taken David Hill to sort them out up there. I felt no problem in the interviews and that we were strong on substance. We were leading the Scottish news all day, with Di still leading nationally. I didn't brief the TUC speech as we wanted the devolution visit to be the main thing. I managed to get some time to myself and went for a swim and sauna but then we had a rash of calls about [news presenter] Jon Snow's report on Channel 4 on big rows re the funeral. It was broadly crap and we put out a strong statement denying the bits re TB, e.g. he spoke to Charles on the flight deck to put pressure on the Queen for a proper funeral, and that he had negotiated between the Spencers and the Windsors. Piers Morgan said the buzz was that Peter was the source because he had had dinner with Snow on Saturday. I spoke to Peter after we landed. He said yes he had dinner with Snow but he had not discussed this. Fellowes found himself at the centre of the story and he called and said he was beginning to feel a bit paranoid. I said it would blow over. Geoff Crawford had been pretty robust. On the plane down we worked on the TUC speech, modernisation the main theme. I was annoyed at Donald D through the day. He believed the Diana response was 'just a London thing'.

Tuesday, September 9

The denials had just about killed off the Snow story, though *The Times*, *Guardian* and *Mirror* did it fairly big. Butler called me and asked me to see him. 'We have a right royal row,' he said. He had been speaking to Fellowes and he wanted help in establishing the source for the story. He said he felt it was likely that Peter was the source. I said I didn't believe that and Peter had said Snow would say definitively it was not him. Fellowes felt someone was out to get him, but as the story was wrong, and easily denied, this was an odd way to do it. I said my sense was that Charles' people were overzealous in promoting Charles' interests at the expense of others. Butler asked for my help in finding the source, which I said I would try to do. He said Fellowes was a personal friend and he wanted to help him. He said that the Palace made clear they were very grateful to me for the help I had given. He said Robin Janvrin had taken him to one side at the entrance to the abbey and said I had been a real help.

TB was working on his TUC speech. We had not done much but the basic message on the need to modernise was clear enough. Yesterday [John] Edmonds [general secretary of the GMB union] had said that when he heard a Labour government speaking Tory language on labour market flexibility, he shivered a little. I wrote in a line about it being warmer in the real world. We worked on the train on the way down, and were met by Brendan Barber, as ever worried that TB would take too tough a line. He agreed I should brief very hard the line about qualification for recognition next year. TB didn't go down well in the hall, where George Carey [Archbishop of Canterbury] got a far better reception earlier on. As two years ago, he was best when he went off script but the reception was pretty muted. Brendan told me afterwards that he felt it was another kick in the balls for [John] Monks [TUC general secretary] as there was no recognition from TB that the TUC were modernising at all. It was as if they were doing nothing to change and it confirmed their fears that basically we didn't want them around, didn't want the link at all. I said they got too emotional about this. The TUC speech was the third story on the news and came over fine. Though TB didn't get a great reception, it was a good enough speech to report and would be the splash in several papers. TB held meetings with several union leaders including Edmonds but I felt he didn't need me there and got the train home. TB called later and said he felt it had been OK, that they would rather he was there as prime minister than Leader of the Opposition. He didn't believe Jon Snow's source was Peter. GB called about a few ideas for his Diana Memorial committee. He was seeing Charles Spencer on Thursday and going over the kind of ideas they might be looking at. He was clearly beginning to move in on the Millennium. He said it's crap and nobody has thought it through.

Wednesday, September 10

Some of the columnists were continuing to see Diana's death as TB's Falklands, which was ridiculous. GB wanted TB to do more clips on devolution, so I arranged for that before taking Grace to school. I decided to take the day off because I felt tired yesterday. I went for a walk and visited John's grave.[1] Butler was chasing me re the Snow

[1] John Merritt, *Daily Mirror* and *Observer* journalist and AC's closest friend, died from leukaemia at the age of thirty-five in 1992. His grave became a place for contemplation.

story, and eventually I called Jon and said he'd been misled badly. He said he was called out of the blue by someone he had never met but who he knew was close to the royal circle. He said he then got a second source who said the same. I got the impression that we were talking about a peer. He also said Alan Clark called him to say Fellowes had attacked Lord Blake [political historian] for being critical, which Jon saw as a sign of Fellowes losing the plot. He did say that he was leaving the story now. I called Fellowes and he said maybe they just have a loose cannon somewhere. I told him re Blake and he said yes, he had spoken to him because he didn't like the line he saw in *The Times* on Blake leading criticism. I recalled last Friday when I asked at the end of the Lord Chamberlain's meeting whether there was a deliberate attempt to build up Charles. He said it was very timely because he had just had the biggest up-and-downer with Mark Bolland about the way that Charles had been briefed up at the expense of the Queen. Bolland was blind to anything but protecting his master's back, he said. He said he would not mind criticism for himself but the Queen herself came out very badly from the Snow story because it looked like she was uncaring and didn't grasp the mood. I said I felt he should drop it. Butler called again on the same thing. He also said he was asking Robin Mountfield [permanent secretary, Office of Public Service] to set up a group to look at GIS review. He agreed ministers were not happy and that we had to find ways of improving things. He felt this was the way forward. I agreed to sit on the committee. TB saw Trimble who agreed to stay on board, provided there were more confidence-building measures on their side. Tony Banks was in trouble again. He said England could not win the World Cup.

Thursday, September 11

I tried to take a day out of the hurly-burly to get a proper draft for the [Labour Party] conference speech. We were way behind and David M and I were both anxious. The devolution referendum was the big story of the day, plus GB seeing Charles Spencer to discuss memorials, though it was clear Spencer was also pushing his agenda on a privacy law. Philip had done a good note on conference, and the need to spell out what we meant by new Britain, try to make modernisation come alive again. 'The British people are the true modernisers' was classic Philip. It was pretty clear we would probably have to do something on Diana. It would be odd without it but we would have to avoid being mawkish or proprietorial. I also had the idea of using the concept of the contract to get through the policy sections, and all the boring bits and the buttons that have to be touched. TB was clearly having a messing-around day, not doing much and playing tennis, and I was trying desperately to get out of doing any day-to-day work but Northern Ireland intruded.

TB saw Trimble and we agreed to a media strategy that would involve one or two announcements of confidence-building measures, TB article in the [unionist Belfast] *News Letter* on Saturday stressing the principle of consent, then over the weekend a story on the BBC about new language on consent agreed by the two governments, which we would put out in part through Trimble on *Frost*. But *An Phoblacht*, the Republican newspaper, had a piece saying they had trouble with the Mitchell principles.[1] This struck me as a real problem but TB felt it could help Trimble, because they could say it was all the more important that they were there to hold Sinn Fein to what they were saying. It was tricky and TB asked me to speak to Trimble direct and make sure we were on the same page re the media plan. We spoke a couple of times. I got a call from Robin Mountfield about his committee on the GIS, which I said should be a no-holds-barred review. He told me in passing that the Treasury was a total mess. I was keeping in touch with the referendum through David Hill, who had done a great job up there and was getting more and more confident as the days wore on. We had a conference draft of sorts by the end of the day, the basic core script on modernisation, a strong message, and now we needed lines and announcements. I settled down to watch the referendum coverage. It was better than expected.

Friday, September 12

TB called very early re the referendum.[2] 'Quite a result,' he said, but we must get the message out loud and clear that there must be no pandering to nationalism, and we must stress that it's good for the UK, not just for Scotland. The papers were full of it. After the morning meeting, we left for the airport, TB and I as ever when en route to Scotland putting on our posh Jock accents. He was worried about

---

[1] The Mitchell principles called upon all partners to affirm total and absolute commitment to the peaceful resolution of political issues, total disarmament of paramilitary organisations, opposition to force that would influence negotiations, and effective steps to prevent punishment killings and beatings.

[2] In the historic referendum on September 11, 2,645,308 Scots voted – 60.4 per cent of the electorate. 74.3 per cent agreed that Scotland should have a Parliament, and 63.5 per cent agreed that a Scottish Parliament should have tax-varying powers. The Conservatives were the only significant party to campaign for a no to both referendum questions.

English nationalism, a worry exacerbated by the questioning from the London hacks when we got there, all on the lines of why should Scottish MPs now have a say re English health or schools when English MPs have no say in Scotland? On the plane, he went through the conference draft and thought it was OK, but we still had a long way to go. Then he said something very odd and interesting. 'Do you think a Scot can be prime minister now there is a Scottish Parliament?' I said yes. He said 'Gordon must marry Sarah and he must live in England.' Then he looked out of the window, and I thought how weird it was that a few months after his own election, and with another victorious campaign behind him, he was thinking about the succession.

We met Donald D at Holyrood Park then through to Parliament Square, where they both did little speeches. Neither went over the top. The mood was good, without being ridiculous and the rain and the odd crying baby helped ensure it didn't go too OTT. TB was enjoying it until the doorstep with all the questions about English nationalism. We then set off for Wales, using the momentum of the Scottish win and again the mood was good. We did the press in Ron Davies' office, alongside which was a little flat which had been horribly decorated by William Hague when he was there. There was something a bit weird about it, like going back several decades. We were fine on the arguments and there was definitely a sense of momentum provided by the Scottish vote. TB spoke to Trimble again to say he would go hard on consent, decommissioning and the links between IRA/SF. The interview was fine, stressing to the UUs the need to stay in the talks. We spoke to Trimble again and agreed he would go on *Frost* and call for further concessions and then be seen to get them. TB said fine. 'He is such a mercurial character.'

Saturday, September 13

TB called early. 'What will the English make of this Parliament?' The same scepticism you've got, I said. He said DD should be first minister and also that we should have a series of measures to deal with sleaze and the quality of candidates. His main worry today was Northern Ireland and Monday's resumed talks. I took the boys to York vs Burnley. On the way up Tim called to say there was a lot of interest in the Royals again with the heavies all pushing stories about various aspects of modernisation, including, in several cases, scrapping the civil list. I spoke to all the political editors of the heavies and they all said they were getting the same lines from the same people. I wondered whether it was Charlie or Peter but I think they would have given me a hint of that so I was left, as before, assuming it was friends of Charles. It followed a piece by Robert Hardman in the *Spectator*, which was very pro Charles. On Monday, when John Holmes said to TB and me that Stephen Lamport had assured him there was no such briefing going on with Charles' blessing, TB had said he was not so sure. 'He was saying some of this kind of thing to me.' We got back at half seven after a 3-1 defeat and Fiona and I went to Alan Haworth and Maggie Rae's for dinner. There were plenty of sad reflections about the last time we were there, with Diana. We moved quickly on to TB and CB. Alan regaled us with a few holiday stories like when he thought he was going to kill him when they went for a suicidal walk on a glacier, and he could see the cops getting more and more worried. He felt TB was in much better shape, but was worried about tension between him and CB who they both felt was changing. They felt TB was becoming ever more focused on work to the exclusion of all else, and she was getting a bit grand, which would soon become a big problem.

Sunday, September 14

As expected, the Sundays were full of Royals but we were quickly given a gift to get round the problems this caused because William Hague was doing *Frost* and had revealed to the *Sunday Express* that he was going to accuse us of hijacking Diana's legacy. He told Frost that we had been briefing up TB at the expense of the Queen and it was all very shabby. It was obviously an effort to get back on the radar after his dreadful initial response but it would clearly backfire. Tim called and we agreed to put up Alun Michael [Home Office minister], go low-key, more in sorrow than in anger, say it was inappropriate after we had worked so hard to make it a healing event. Robin Oakley called and said it was a silly thing to do. Hague's problem was that all the journalists knew that we had done no such briefings. Phil Webster said he was doing a first-person piece to this effect for *The Times*. Oakley also made clear we had if anything been playing down our role. Tim and I briefed pretty hard on it, and it was backfiring badly. This was all leading up to a potentially big problem for Hague pre-conference. I was hoping for a quiet day but had to deal with several calls on this, on which we were able to say that all our briefings had been done with their blessing and we had not talked up TB. I spoke to Geoff Crawford, who said they would endorse our version of events. He felt it was pretty pathetic of Hague.

TB called a couple of times, worried about pay. He felt there was trouble coming with a pay freeze allied to Cabinet ministers taking their full salaries. The other issue today was Northern Ireland, with talks due to start tomorrow. Part of the plan was that we put out a statement early tomorrow, agreed by the Irish and British governments, on consent and decommissioning. TB had persuaded Trimble we would present it as a concession to him, that we had forced Ahern into it because DT wanted it. TB had spoken to Bertie, who was such a good bloke that he was just about happy with going along with it. TB said the trouble with Trimble is that he is so bloody mercurial it was impossible to know what he was really up to. The statement was finally agreed at 9.30. I gave it embargoed to Oakley and Alison Little at PA. Oakley was excellent. I said we would really appreciate it if he made clear that we were bending over backwards to woo the Unionists, and he called to read me his script, which was nice of him. He said, I realise that sometimes the national interest is potentially affected by what we say, and I'm perfectly happy to go through it with you. There was definitely something about Northern Ireland that brought out the better side of the media.

Monday, September 15

Oakley's report was leading the news and Trimble came on to make broadly welcoming noises and later in the day he announced he would be joining the talks, which was seen as a real breakthrough. It had been balls-aching getting there but got there we had. Hague got a total caning in the press. At the morning meeting we went over the looming problem on pay. The combination of low pay-review offers and the Cabinet being offered huge pay rises. Peter M said we had to watch it like a hawk and he was right. He was also worried about JP in particular pushing for more for public service workers which would have big knock-on effects. The eleven o'clock was mainly Ireland, Royals, Lib-Labbery, Hague and the week ahead. But there was no doubt we were going to get a kicking over pay.

Butler called in me, Jonathan and John H for a meeting. Fellowes had sent over a rather defensive draft press line, rebutting some of the stories around in the last few days. I was opposed, feeling it was just Fellowes being stung, and wanting to get back at the Charles camp who appeared to be continuing to brief against him. I said there was no story in it and it could come over as being too defensive unless they made it clear it was part of a broader response, and we worked on that. TB was at Chequers and we chatted over the interview we were planning with Bevins for the relaunch of the

Independent. We thought about laying into Hague, maybe give a push on the single currency, but in the end settled on a general message re new Britain/era of confidence. The Palace statement went out and was leading the news pretty much the rest of the day. I had a session with Mike Granatt about some of the concerns among information heads and then MIO. I didn't really know what to do with some of them. They were clearly worried but what could I tell them other than what I had said – that they had to be more proactive, engage more with ministers and the centre and it would be fine. It wasn't exactly asking the earth but I wondered if some of them even had the basic skills. Granatt was also clearly not sure about the Mountfield review and was pretty defensive about the whole thing. He said people were up for change but they felt they needed more encouragement and support from the centre. I was also making clear we had to get a proper GOVERNMENT media-monitoring operation. I was still basically reliant on the party for knowing what was in the media. The *Sun* splashed today on the Queen not wanting Di stamps and someone had sent them correspondence on it, so clearly there was a lot of briefing and leaking going on. TB came back for a meeting on Montserrat.[1] I was keen for him to sack Clare now rather than later when she would be a hero again no doubt once she started slagging everyone off. TB felt it was not possible. RC called, said he could not understand Clare. She could not have made it plainer that she wants nothing to do with the people of Montserrat. RC said he had given her the rope on which to lead on this, but she had decided just to hang herself. Hague made a dreadful speech defending himself and attacking TB, but on *Newsnight* [Cecil] Parkinson could barely bring himself to back him but said it was a personal statement.

Tuesday, September 16

I had fucked up on [ministerial] pay. As TB said, for some reason my populist instincts had deserted me. I had been warning since last Sunday we had a potential problem but for some reason had not properly focused on it. So once it appeared in a couple of papers (that they would take the full salary) I said just confirm it, though both Tim and Godric were warning it could be a problem.[2] TB, I think for

---

[1] The people of Montserrat, a British territory in the Caribbean, would be granted residency rights in the United Kingdom in 1998, following devastating volcanic eruptions in the late 1990s.

[2] In fact the Cabinet would be heading for significant pay restraint, urged by Brown and agreed by Blair.

the first time I can remember, said I had fucked up. TB, Peter M, Jonathan and John Holmes and I discussed the situation and agreed it would be impossible for him [TB] to take it. GB was in Mauritius. Charlie and I spoke and said that GB should stay out of it for now. We were going to try to get away with the line that TB was different, and would not take it, but he believed other Cabinet ministers should. He broke the news to Cherie as we left the building. Peter was still there and she turned on him. 'It's OK for you, swanning around with friends who don't need to worry about money.' Peter, not surprisingly given that he had actually supported the decision, looked a bit taken aback. This would take to well over £100,000 what TB had given up.

I got in the car with TB and worked on a statement while he spoke to GB. GB said that there was no way he could or would take it. I said that would make it impossible to hold the line for the others. As the plane took off for Chester, I dictated the statement for Tim to give to PA. There was an inevitable element of U-turn but I said to Tim we should brief that the press people – me and him – fucked up, say the position was not agreed when we had indicated that it was. We landed, and Jonathan said JP was on the pay rampage. TB spoke to him, said there was no way he could take it, we would be crucified. JP said they had a deal from last year and now he was reneging on it. I was on the phone to Alistair Darling, and he was suggesting we get out the government advice on public sector pay, but asking what did he say if asked if he was planning to take the pay rise himself? By now the press were ringing round the whole Cabinet to ask if they would take it and we were saying nothing. TB did a doorstep, first on devolution and then on pay. After lunch, TB spoke to GB who promised not to brief that he would not take his rise, a promise broken by the time we got back to London. He was impossible when it was like this.

When we got back, Alistair Darling was waiting for us. Jonathan was getting the clear message that they all wanted to do the same thing, whatever it was. Peter and I both felt that the line would not hold, especially as JP had torn into Darling in front of his officials. When JP came in, he was not at all happy but TB talked him round. TB said this would haunt us the whole way through the pay round. JP said they would have to offer the Cabinet something. Eventually they agreed to carve up a ring-round of ministers. Apart from Donald, nobody was very happy with it, but only Margaret Beckett and Jack Straw were really violently opposed. I prepared a line which we eventually agreed in the flat with TB and JP, to the effect that Cabinet ministers had agreed they wanted to show restraint. It was a bit vague about what it meant but it was OK. I also played up JP's role. We had recovered reasonably well from a real fuck-up, largely I felt of my making, not getting on top of it when we obviously needed to. By the nine o'clock news it was OK and the papers were not as bad as they might have been. Peter M felt TB had panicked in a way that we shouldn't when under media attack.

Wednesday, September 17

We just about got away with the pay story. Today's main problem was Ireland, Trimble enjoying being the one needing to be courted and looking for excuses not to go to the talks. He was vitriolic about Hague. The Lib Dem committee was exactly as I thought it would be. If this is history in the making, forget it. It was pretty clear they felt much greater excitement on their side than we did on ours. They were wetting themselves with excitement. TB, RC, Jack Straw, Ann Taylor, DD, Peter, Pat McFadden as the main official in Number 10. On their side Paddy, Alan Beith, Robert Maclennan, Ming Campbell and Richard Holme, who made a classic opening intervention – 'Can I make a few pedantic administrative points?' TB started by saying it was an important test of whether co-operative politics could work. Paddy said we should concentrate on constitutional areas where we agree. TB went through the mechanics, which he had discussed with Butler: meet every two months, two weeks before every meeting agree an agenda, circulate a week before, emphasise the papers are confidential. Pat McFadden acting as a sherpa. TB said he had enjoyed the meeting because they went away very happy and we gave away precisely nothing.

He had a private meeting later with Charles Spencer. He said he was sharp and you got a clear impression he hated Prince Charles. TB said Spencer was worried about William and Harry and he [Spencer] would like to see them but he didn't think [Prince] Charles would like that. They were due to have lunch tomorrow and Charles had insisted it was at Highgrove with some friends. TB said if I was him I would move heaven and earth to have a proper meeting. They basically think it is going to go away after a while and it will all be fine. If they're not careful, they'll be forced into more change than they are contemplating. During the Lib Dem meeting, Peter M passed me a note saying that Prince Charles is making a speech in Manchester on Friday. Any thoughts? I gave him a few lines.

Thursday, September 18

I worked at home, and David M and Peter H came round to work on the conference speech. As ever the hardest thing was making mere words newsworthy, and policy not just one long boring list. We kept going all day, and eventually felt ourselves moving towards a proper draft. Apparently at Cabinet there was a bit of whingeing over pay, but nothing too much.

Friday, September 19

Yesterday had gone well, so I took another day off to work on the speech. I'd gone to bed last night with David Hill telling me that we were going to win [Welsh Assembly referendum] but it could be close. Just how close became clearer as the night went on. It was not clear until the last result, and we just scraped it. TB and I discussed the doorstep he was due to do later on. Prince Charles got excellent coverage for his speech in Manchester. I was amazed to see him deliver virtually line for line the stuff I had got typed up after Peter M asked me to help. No doubt he was taking credit from his royal friends for the fawning coverage Charles was getting on TV. TB called from Chequers to say should he cancel his tennis match in light of the [Southall] train crash? Earlier, JP had wanted him to go to the scene of the crash, but TB was worried it was on overreaction. JP went instead.

Saturday, September 20

The papers were pretty grim for Hague. TB called to say he'd made some progress on the speech, but we needed a powerful ending, and he wanted me to work on that, and on the theme of modernisation through the policy sections.

Monday, September 22

I worked at home all morning on the speech, and was feeling depressed and unable to lift myself. The best passage came when I went for a walk on Hampstead Heath and got a big number going on Diana and compassion. I typed it up when I got back and it may have been just the wrong side of the emotional divide, but it was OK. Stan Greenberg [US pollster and political adviser] called with the latest polling. TB's ratings were pretty much stratospheric. Ninety-three per cent positive job approval, twenty per cent higher than before. He was strong on leadership, direction and trust. The most important areas were public health, schools, and getting inflation and interest rates under control. There was a lot of doubt about whether we were delivering on the economy. I went in for a strategy meeting with heads of information. I said we really did need to see improvements. Tim drafted an article for Peter for *The Times*, at Tony's instigation, because he was fed up with the Lib Dems attacking us. I warned TB it would go too big, and it did.

Tuesday, September 23

The UUP going to talks with Sinn Fein in Belfast was the main story. Peter's *Times* article was second item. Cabinet pay was still a problem. On Sunday JP had said on TV that there was an agreement about pay, but did so in a way that suggested there was an ongoing negotiation. After the morning meeting, I spoke to him, and agreed we had to try to get a shared line on all this. The problem was the message that we were in negotiation. Also GB put a line in his speech in Hong Kong, which would be taken as a warning on pay restraint. I went to the first meeting with the Mountfield group re his inquiry. I did my usual line about the need for more strategic communications, proper co-ordination and a more modern approach. Mountfield said he wanted it wrapped up by the end of October. He felt recent problems were about personal chemistry in part, but accepted there were systems problems. He said there were clearly propriety questions that had to be addressed too. I got the sense that he was up for change but there would be pressures all round to pull it back.

Wednesday, September 24

We were not as well prepared as we normally are on the Wednesday before conference and above all I was worried we were not in the creative state that we normally are. Peter H and I had done an OK complete draft but we were now a bit hamstrung without TB's instructions. We felt a little that we were working blind. TB came back from Chequers last night for CB's birthday dinner, and we spoke to him before this morning's business breakfast. As ever, his worry was whether the argument was right, whether the lines were strong enough, and he was beginning, as he always does at this stage, to worry that we had no real jokes. His other worry was that Peter M was not going to get on the NEC. Sally was pretty sure that [Ken] Livingstone would be on and Peter not. I was pretty clear what we should say, that this was about Peter not TB, that in large part he had brought it on himself. TB said he would have to learn some humility. As JP said, 'There is no problem with Peter, apart from Peter.' He said TB had always exaggerated Peter's abilities, although not as much as

Mandelson does! TB was worried the basic message was 'Fuck off New Labour.' That was why it was so important this was seen as being about Peter not TB. The NEC has always been in part a personal beauty parade. Peter should say it was part of his attempts to come out of the shadows, be a proper politician, and he would learn from defeat.

Butler called a meeting on pay with Jonathan, Ann Taylor and a group of officials. It was a classic piece of Prescottery, the whole thing. We were trying to work out how to get out of the mess we had created. I had done a draft line we worked from. At one point Butler had suggested we say that the £16k rise was a 'catching up' award. Thereafter it was referred to by JP as 'the catchment area'. It was not clear whether at the end JP realised he had agreed to forego the rise for the second year running. He said that GB would rat on any deal anyway. Both he and DB described him as 'the real villain'. PH and I went home to work on the speech and tried to redo the policy section in three areas – creativity, compassion and outward-looking, and it worked better. It was always so hard to fit in all the policy areas that would be expected, without it becoming a bore. I felt the planned announcements were not as good as last year. PH and I kept going till just after midnight. TB was calling fairly regularly and I could sense he was getting more and more nervy. I was getting pissed off at the way people just faxed through ideas and thoughts without any reference to an overall framework or plan. Re Peter M, TB said we should have played safe, and put up Jack Straw. Peter had just put up too many backs, taken too much credit and messed up in August. We had a breakthrough in NI in that the UUs were staying at the talks. 'It really is an amazing achievement,' he said, 'I hope you know that.'

Thursday, September 25

We had another Peter M problem, an interview on Scotland which contradicted the Dewar line. TB said later 'He is becoming a liability.' He said he can rebuild himself but he has to start pretty quickly. TB was working on the speech at Chequers, PH and I at home. He was finally getting down to it and said he just wanted lines from us now, he would drive the argument through the speech. But the creative juices weren't flowing. I had a bath and then went in for a meeting with the office to tell them of the changes I wanted to make. They seemed more or less up for it. RC called from New York to fill me in on his trip and also to lay into GB re pay, and to go over conference. I took the boys and TB's boys to the Oasis concert at Earls Court. I enjoyed it a lot more than I thought I would. I wish we could bring some of that energy to our operation.

Friday, September 26

TB was in a foul mood because he felt we had scored a number of own goals. The *FT* had a story about a minister saying we were moving towards EMU. *The Times* had a Field/Harman split story and in the *Guardian* RC was blocking two arms sales for Indonesia. TB said 'He just can't resist pandering to the party. But watch him run for cover if jobs get lost. Ridiculous.' The Sundays were all chasing the *FT* story, as were the dailies, which we were trying to play down. I spoke to GB who was massively against TB doing an announcement on extra funding for health. He said it would look very Old Labour and it would also look like he had been pushed into it. I suspect his real reason was that he just didn't want TB to be making a major spending announcement. It was hard to know where he was coming from on it, but he just kept making the point it would look like an Old Labour move, damaging to TB. He said they should both be doing the themes of modernisation.

GB had done an interview with the *Guardian* and then went on to do much the same interview with the *Sunday Times* which really pissed off Andy Grice. GB was constantly asking about the NEC and whether I thought Peter M was going to make it. He was also pushing me to lean on TB to dump the Dome. I don't know why we agreed in the first place, he said. Butler sent me a note about a conference attended by Peter Riddell and Will Hutton at which both complained about the politicisation of the GIS. In theory Butler was supportive in that he knew ministers felt the service was poor. But he also felt we were a bit tricky and in truth, on this, we were a bit tricky because yes, I was trying to modernise the GIS because it needed modernising but I was also trying to make changes likely to benefit us. I assured Butler I was trying to bring people on, not do them in. There were people in Number 10 who were really responding well. David M, Peter H and I set off for Chequers and we did a run-through on the speech with TB. The opening was much better now. TB said he was panicking because he wasn't panicking. I said that meant the panic would come later, which was a screaming pain. We were honing the argument now, trying to strip it right down to a simple message. I briefed out the private polls – ninety-three per cent approval, Hague dying on his feet. Earlier both GB and CW had said they wanted to do 'no new royal yachts' as a way of signalling a tough line on public spending. TB said no way. I paged CW to say under no circumstances brief this. I had suggested earlier that if it happened it should come from the Royals and then lo and behold we started to get calls from political hacks saying the Palace had said they had reached agreement with the Treasury about it. CW denied being behind it. I spoke to Geoff Crawford who said he believed it was all coming from the Treasury. Geoff said he was simply saying that the Queen had always said she did not need one personally. We discussed whether we should get out the Peter M situation before it happened but agreed it was a bad idea because it would make it an even bigger thing when it happened.

Saturday, September 27

The press was quiet for a pre-conference Saturday. Grice called in a state about GB's interview so I gave him stuff on welfare from TB's speech. We went through the speech line by line and sharpened it. The key message, modernisation for a purpose, was coming through. TB was going through the phase where he thinks it is all going too easily. I called Peter and said it did not look good re the NEC. He said what do you mean? I said I don't think you're going to get on. I could tell he was crushed. TB said it was not the end of the world so long as he heeded the advice about how to deal with it. He had to learn from it, be strong, emerge stronger. He said he felt awful. He thought August was the reason and Peter had to accept it had not been great. Only he and GB had ever got on first time so on another level it was not such a shock. I gave Peter M ten minutes to take it in and think about it and said he should call me back. He did so, said he would just have to take it on the chin and learn from it. Ten out of ten.

On the drive down to Brighton, TB was worrying about whether we had too much on compassion at the end. He did a Q&A at Hove, where the audience was fine but a bit subdued. The worst thing was that TB was coming down with a cold. We got to the hotel and he and I just ploughed through it line by line, challenging every fact and assumption, making sure the clap lines worked, above all making sure the argument came through. He still wasn't convinced. The other argument was whether to talk about Di directly or not. I was keen. The other press problem was the *Sunday Telegraph* saying we were going for a referendum on EMU next year. At 11.30pm, after the switchboard had been trying to get GB for ages, he and TB finally spoke. TB said we had to kill this. His antennae were twitching on it and we had to kill it straight off. He said the Tories in the media were running the line the whole time to editors and owners that our plan was to bounce the country while we were so popular. But it wouldn't work. This is not something you can bounce. GB was still arguing that we should do extra spending for health in a fortnight's time, not now. TB said we are taking a hit on health for no reason.

Monday–Thursday, September 29–October 2

Writing this on Thursday, that makes it the longest period for ages when I have not recorded stuff day to day. The conference period has gone like a blur, most of it lived out in two hotel suites, his and mine, as we endured the worst part of the speechifying process. We came down on Saturday and though TB was having to do the usual round of receptions and meetings, I spent most of the time holed up in the hotel until we left for the speech. We had the argument right I think – that modernisation is the only route to Britain being a successful country. The rest flowed easily from that. The main last-minute struggle was a search for a phrase that brought it to life, the notion of Britain as a 21st-century model nation. I picked brains around the place and GB came up with the best – beacon, Britain as a beacon. His own speech had gone OK and he must have been in an OK mood to pass it on. As we arrived on the Saturday the beginning and ending of the speech were fine. But the middle bit centred on policy had become a long boring ramble and that was where we did most of the work. The breakthrough came, as it often does, when we called in an outside mind. I sent it to Joe Haines [former press secretary to Labour Prime Minister Harold Wilson] who quickly came back and said we had to decide whether we wanted an inspirational speech to rouse party and country, or a list of policy announcements. He had identified the central tension and TB and I agreed it was more important to inspire. The policy proposals had to serve that purpose and that meant cutting them down. We decided to do announcements very briefly, and inject more and better rhetoric.

The other breakthrough came when we had a conflab on Monday afternoon and we agreed, Jonathan I think having first pushed the idea, that we should tie everything under the theme of hard choices. It gave real backbone to the speech. So the theme was that modernisation was the route to Britain being a model nation and it required tough choices to be made. Though TB was having to do the rounds, and we were bashing away in his absence, he was doing a lot more on his own now. He would come back, go through it with us, scribble some thoughts which Liz [Lloyd] and I would blend in. We had the usual trouble of people just wandering in and out of the room. PH did some terrific stuff on Britain can be best. We also had the Giving Age stuff I had done on the heath, but the women in particular felt we should not mention Diana. TB and I went round in circles on that one and finally agreed, late on Monday night, to take it out. For some reason the end didn't work any more. The only time I went out from the hotel was to go spinning for Peter on the NEC elections. Peter had come round to the little office that had been set up for the speech team and he asked me to go and brief. I said I had the speech to do and if I went out I would get swamped by people wanting stuff on the speech. But he really feared it was going to get out of control if I didn't. So at 4pm I called a briefing on the speech but it was really so that I could try to shape the coverage on Peter. I didn't mind doing it because he had taken a big hit and we needed to use it to build him back up again.

Sunday had been fine with the Sundays quiet, all the usual pre-conference guff but nothing too awful for us. Monday was dominated by GB. He had briefed 'full employment' overnight which I thought was a mistake. It looked Old Labour and did not really fit with the theme of the conference. TB was worried about it and asked Gordon to come to his room to go over it. He asked him to set out the argument and GB gave him a big convoluted spiel that it was not full employment he was promising but full employment opportunities over time. TB said what was the headline then? He said Labour offer full employment opportunities – and between us we added 'over time'. Great headline, I said – but you'll be lucky. We were still trying to get him to agree that TB should announce we were going to give extra cash to the NHS for the winter. He was strongly against because he felt it was Old Labour and because it looked like we were caving in to pressure. In the end, whatever the suspicions people had, I agreed with him that it was the wrong signal to send at this time. It was not a modernisation or a tough-choice message. It was something we would be better getting out at a later stage when the Tories were in better shape. At the moment they were falling apart. The other mini drama was whether Pat McFadden should go for the Paisley South by-election. He was pretty keen and so were a number of us but GB was pushing very hard for Douglas Alexander [solicitor, former researcher for GB] and it was pretty clear TB did not want to pick a fight he might lose. He was not really seized of the agony it was causing Pat. It was out and about and he was being pushed this way and that and the problem was that he did not have a clear signal from TB. It took days of should he shouldn't he before on Thursday he finally told Pat he didn't want him to go for it. But the problem was he didn't really convey any sense that he was saying that because he wanted Pat to stay. It was much more that he didn't want a big argument over DA. We put together a briefing note making clear TB had begged him not to stand. I had very little sleep through the week, at most three hours. Liz and I were up till late working on the speech and when I finally knocked it on the head in the early hours of Tuesday morning, I felt close to collapse.

It was great having Fiona down and she was doing a great job with CB, who seemed a lot calmer than usual. I felt sorry for TB at having to traipse around so many receptions. His only respite was a tennis match on Sunday when JP had wanted him to go to his thing at the races. TB said he went for a shower and there were three guys there who practically collapsed when he suddenly walked into the shower area. There was a feeling around conference that TB was totally dominant. The *Indy on Sunday* reported the ninety-three per cent ratings and there was a general buzz that our position was so strong because of TB. GB didn't get a standing ovation which they spun as being because the speech was so tough. His problem was it was neither Old nor New Labour and people saw through it. TB didn't much like RC's or JP's speeches, feeling they were over-triumphalist. But by and large things were going well and there were certainly no disaster areas. Anji appeared to have been sidelined by CB so Fiona and Sally [Morgan] were doing most of the rounds accompanying TB. The day of the speech was the usual exhausted crack-of-dawn start and then the last-minute finish, changing the ending right up to the last minute, even after we had signed off the press and autocue version. We got it done and dusted by lunchtime and then walked over to the conference centre and up to the little room where he and I worked through it one last time. Even then he was still saying this could be a strong speech and he was finally happy the argument was right. I said do you ever think we will do a conference speech that doesn't require this exhausting and tortured process? He said the conference speech always had to be good and we had set ourselves high standards which had to be maintained.

We went down to the back of the stage waiting for the end of the video which was playing as a warm-up and cue. He went on to a fantastic reception. He didn't do the opening as well as he might have done but he got into his stride fairly quickly and the mood was warm. The reception at the end was terrific, not just in the hall but the press too gave it a near universal thumbs up. I was not sure though and was going through a sudden mini depression. I don't know whether it was tiredness or a weird kind of post-natal depression but I felt very down and couldn't wait to get out of the press centre and back to the hotel. I was in the bizarre position of hacks telling me how good they thought it was and me agreeing while feeling they were missing something. The reaction all around the place was good. Yet I felt it had not been what it might. I wondered whether there was actually a depressive element that came into play at these big moments, like the election night. Peter's defeat on the NEC had been the big story overnight into Tuesday's press and we did as well as we could to limit the sense of it being a blow to TB and New Labour rather than just Peter. I thought about writing to him but didn't get round to it. To be fair to him he did at least look and sound a bit humbled by it and genuinely looked like he was going to learn from it. But then he rather spoiled it all by saying he had done humility rather well.

Wednesday was difficult personally because of Nicola Pagett [actor]. I started to pick up rumours her publisher or someone was putting it around I was the guy she was stalking. I tipped off George Pascoe-Watson and did a deal on how it was projected with Higgins. He did it perfectly well and straight though too big. He spoke himself to Nicola Pagett's husband who neither confirmed nor denied it. She was on a tour promoting her book [*Diamonds Behind My Eyes*, an account of her manic depression and obsession with a man she called The Stranger] somewhere. George asked me if I felt threatened, worried or flattered. I said none of those things, it was just a bit weird, having this person out there who bombarded you with stuff and who at the time genuinely seemed to think not only that we knew each other but we were together. The other weird thing was how perceptive she often was about how I was feeling or what I was thinking of some of the key people and events. I warned Dacre and Piers it was coming. Piers took the piss mercilessly. It was a weird one though. I was a bit worried about it and felt Fiona and the kids would hate it.

The other story on the Wednesday was Tony Banks calling Hague a foetus, and saying Tory MPs thought he should have an abortion. It was over the top but it was so funny, and instantly connecting, that it was hard to bollock him too hard. There was the usual knee-jerk outcry, *Sun* and *Mirror* saying he should go. TB said we should just laugh it off. TB was beginning to worry we had made a mistake with Banks [as sports minister], that he was a character but not a very clever politician.

Thursday, October 2

We did a crime visit with Jack Straw and lots of the photographers were trying to get pictures of me with TB, to go with the Pagett story. I endured a fair amount of piss-taking. There was a very interesting divide of the sexes on it. Most of the men, including TB, thought it was basically funny, that it was flattering to have an actress wildly obsessed with you. But most of the women, especially Sally and CB, saw it differently, thought it must be horrible. CB in particular was really nice about it, said no matter how much people joked, it can't be nice to have your space constantly intruded into.

I was doing the rounds later while TB played tennis and the mood was pretty good. I had a session with Pat to try to cheer him up, TB having finally said he should not stand in Paisley. TB had been pretty pathetic about the whole thing, not wanting to go against GB who was dead set on Douglas. Pat was a bit down about it, although he had not said clearly enough that he really wanted to go for it. But he was very pissed off about it all. I went to the BBC dinner later but had to leave because I'd promised JP I would help on his speech and we had the usual mad processology on that, writing by committee, rehearsing at full pelt in his half-opened shirt with the wind blaring in off the sea front.

Friday, October 3

The main drama was JP telling me that Clare had had too much to drink last night and got into a row with a copper. I told TB who said he would have to see her. I did the media rounds with TB in between helping JP finish his speech, which went down well. I went back to Number 10, where Godric had put together a good note on the Moscow trip.

Saturday, October 4

TB called early on re the discussion we'd been having about whether Peter M should go on *Frost*. I felt not, that he should be keeping a low profile, but Barney [Jones, producer] at *Frost* had made it clear if it wasn't Peter they would go for Ken [Livingstone, elected to the NEC in preference to Mandelson]. Then Ben Wegg-Prosser [Mandelson aide] told me Peter didn't want to do it anyway, so we would leave it to Ken. It wasn't ideal, but I think we had just about got the message up OK through the week and TB in particular had had a good week. TB spoke to Murdoch to take forward something we'd discussed with Irwin Stelzer [US economist close to Murdoch] earlier in the week, re RM wanting to help put every school on the net. TB also spoke to

GB and told him he had to get a proper grip of Charlie W and Ed Balls. He felt they were too loose in the way they briefed around the place. GB said he accepted there was a problem. Whether he will do anything about it is doubtful. GB said who briefed Phil Stephens [FT] to say his speech had been too left wing? TB said why would he need anyone to brief him? He's not stupid and it was obvious. GB could never believe journalists could reach conclusions unaided. It rather gave the game away about how much he was constantly working at the columnists. The only other thing I was dealing with was the script for the Russian soap opera TB was going to be in, as part of a BBC cultural scheme. I asked to make sure he could get the line 'education, education, education' in Russian in there. It made several of the Sunday front pages when I got the translation back and gave it out – образование [pronounced 'obra-zovanie']. The papers were great for us, dreadful for the Tories. Several of the columnists ran on the line re Nicola Pagett that you'd have to be mad to fancy me.

Sunday, October 5

TB felt GB had a bit of a problem. His speech had gone down fairly badly and Ed and Charlie had played into the idea of him not being a government figure but a political figure only. Derek Scott had been telling me that the City no longer viewed the Treasury as being straight. On Moscow, TB said what's all this soap opera about? I said it was a good thing to do, that we would get good coverage there and here, and that it would also allow us to put out a domestic message, while abroad, namely education. The ambassador had been against it. TB said he'd been thinking over the weekend of three things. Single currency. Murdoch told him he was not theological about it but was not convinced it was in Britain's economic interests, to which TB said fine, as long as people accept it is economics not politics that will decide. Second, Lib Dems. He was now moving towards an April reshuffle in which he would like to bring two Liberals into the Cabinet, with some kind of full-scale merger after the next election, with an electoral commission on AV[1] for this time, 'proper' PR [proportional representation] afterwards, at which point the Tories would be wiped out. Third, family. It was not clear where this was going but he felt

---

[1] Alternative Vote. System where voters rank candidates 1, 2, 3, etc. in order of preference. The candidates with the fewest first preferences are eliminated and the subsequent preference votes on the ballot paper are redistributed to remaining candidates until a candidate with a majority is identified.

we had to get to a modern position on this. It was possible to be pro gay, but also pro traditional family. He felt we had to move, and fairly quickly.

At the airport, and again on the plane, the press lapped up every detail of the Russian soap-opera stuff. TB could not believe how much interest there was in it. We also pushed on the anti-crime agreement to deal with the Mafia, and BP, John Browne [BP chief executive] having been to see TB at Brighton to press for help in getting greater access to Russian markets. TB spent most of the flight reading through a stack of briefing papers. At one point he looked up and just said 'We can win on EMU if people accept it is economic not political.' At the embassy we did a pooled doorstep with Sky, and then a fascinating dinner with Anatoly Chubais and Boris Nemtsov, two key modernisers who were pushing economic reform inside the government. Chubais was formerly Yeltsin's chief of staff, Nemtsov first deputy PM to Viktor Chernomyrdin [Russian Prime Minister]. They were very bright, energetic and not at all Russian stereotypes. But they underlined how hard it was to make change happen. Chubais in particular was pretty unpopular. TB felt he was the hard nut whereas Nemtsov was more of a showman, but very bright nonetheless. TB said to them that they were brave, and that their work and commitment would help decide how future generations lived. Over dinner it was reasonably formal, and TB worked through an agenda – crime, G8, economic reform, energy, BP. But over coffee it got very political. It was clear Chubais didn't set much store by public opinion.

Monday, October 6

I was woken by a call from the ambassador who said TB's tennis had been cancelled because of the weather and he was looking for me. He had been impressed by Chubais and Nemtsov, particularly Chubais, but was worried they failed to understand the need to have a sense of strategy and the need to explain it properly. He was worried that Hague was well set for a good week because the run-up had been so bad for him, and the media were beginning to feel sorry for him. I said if sympathy was all he had, we didn't have to worry. He did a business breakfast, during which I briefed out the final soap-opera script. We were getting days' worth out of this thing. We set off for the Kremlin and once we had driven through the old parts, Yeltsin's working quarters were very different. All new, a bit nouveau kitsch, lots of high white walls and fake gold leafery on furniture that didn't quite do it. I couldn't work out whether it was meant to say grandeur or modernity or both. It didn't do it for me, added to which the floors squeaked terribly and there were so many hangers-on that at times all you could hear was squeak, squeak, squeak outside the meeting. Yeltsin was a huge physical presence and he did everything in an exaggerated way. Big, big handshake, big grin. Spoke loudly. When the cameras were in, he made sure to do a great warm tribute to TB. The one-on-one session went on a lot longer than the protocol people had planned. At the lunch, I had to lose the vodka so as not to attract attention during the toasts, at which Yeltsin got ever warmer and more ostentatious. 'To a young energetic leader who is so popular in his country.' He cited lines from TB's speech. 'Britain not the biggest, but can be the best – good, good. Good speech.' Tony Bishop, the interpreter, was wonderful to watch. He had done every Russian leader since Stalin and he seemed to take on some of the mannerisms of both sides as the conversation unfolded. At times it felt a bit stilted but TB and BY seemed to get on fine. TB said we were trying to leave the things Thatcher improved, and change the things she didn't, keep a spirit of enterprise, but invest more in education, infrastructure, technology. BY said he was going in the same direction. He said Russia had buried Communism for good, but China had not. TB said China uses the language but not the reality. BY said Thatcher had a quick mind and a quick wit. 'Talking to her, you must always be on your guard, or she will have you.'

We did a quick tour of the Kremlin, then Red Square, and then a new Moscow shopping centre, which all got a bit chaotic when TB was effectively hijacked by the mayor. We then had an equally chaotic ride on the metro. We got back for a meeting with Chernomyrdin and Chubais which was very heavy going. Seeing the two of them together it became clearer what the modernisers were up against. Chernomyrdin was dour, very little light or shade. He was wearing a very expensive suit. They went through all the areas of greater co-operation and TB was pressing on tax reform and BP, where the Russians seemed fairly warm, but it was all very stilted and Chernomyrdin was far less flexible and open than Yeltsin. We then recorded the soap, which had the watching press in near hysterics, as TB did his *'obrazovanie, obrazovanie, obrazovanie'* ['education, educa-tion, education'] line. Rarely has one translated sound bite had so much attention.

On the flight back, I persuaded TB there was no point seeing the media. They had had OK access and Major so often got into trouble by going back for a friendly chat when things felt OK, and giving himself a problem. TB was happy with that and they seemed fine about it. On EMU, which was slightly obsessing him at the moment, he felt we needed a few big players around Europe saying EMU without the UK would not be a real European EMU. He was also going on about getting Libs into a postponed reshuffle and a deal with them being the way to put out the Tories for a generation or more. In the car on the way in from the airport, Moira Wallace called, worried because they had heard Harriet was announcing tomorrow she was uprating child benefit and pensions which would beg the question whether the other benefits would be uprated too. I spoke to HH and got it pulled pending further discussions tomorrow.

Tuesday, October 7

I spoke to TB and GB first thing and we agreed to do pensions etc. today, but without interviews. I conveyed this to HH. We had a school visit on the back of [Microsoft chief executive] Bill Gates' visit. TB got a kind of pop star welcome at the school in Holland Park. There was nothing on the ITN lunchtime news so I complained and it was covered later. We had a very desultory strategy meeting, GB looking at papers, Peter M in a bit of a sulk, TB a bit tired. He trotted through a few areas he thought were problems, family, EMU in particular, but the discussion didn't really go anywhere. GB was pushing on how we would measure progress. Hague had decided to do two speeches to the Tory conference and his first today was quite effective. I had a meeting with David Wilkinson from the Cabinet Office to go over my take on the GIS review.

Wednesday, October 8

I was feeling very down, possibly depressed. It was in part tiredness but also I felt I was having to do too much and carry too much on my own. Peter M and I just weren't working together and though I felt it would work out, it was a strain because I felt I was picking up a lot of the load he should be carrying. I stayed at home and went for a long walk on the heath. TB called before his meeting at Chequers with Trimble and Donaldson. My letter to GIS heads leaked straight away, promoting another mini flurry about politicisation.

Thursday, October 9

I went in late and saw TB who wanted to discuss Anji. He said he had persuaded her to stay and hoped Fiona could help smooth things over with CB. I said I doubted it. I said Fiona wasn't keen either. I felt with Fiona the hostility was because she had felt excluded in opposition in particular, with CB it is because she senses you are a bit dependent. He said he had always got dependent on people. He

October '97: Personal stresses and strains

said he was dependent on me for certain things, but because I was a man that didn't bother her so much. He felt in his current position he needed different sorts of people with different sorts of skills around him and Anji added a huge amount. TB also saw David Hill who was finding life a bit dull at the party and, especially as he was not paid a fortune, not surprisingly looking into some of the other offers coming his way. I had suggested he stay on and we try to get him in to head up the new communications strategy unit I was keen on establishing. TB felt it should be under Peter M but I was not sure about that. The Tory conference was dominating. Michael Portillo's [former Conservative Cabinet minister defeated in the 1997 election] speech calling for more tolerant attitudes on families, sex etc. showed efforts by some to move on to our ground. Just before we left for the airport, Kenny Macintyre [BBC Scotland] called to warn me of the scale of the furore re Jason Campbell, a convicted Rangers thug who knifed a young Celtic fan to death. Campbell had been granted a transfer application from a Scottish to Northern Irish jail and the Scottish Office had said that the peace process – helping Protestants – had been part of the reasoning. This was viciously attacked in the press and Donald D and others wanted to reverse it. On the way to the airport, we couldn't raise DD so TB spoke to Henry McLeish, the minister responsible, who was unclear about the facts or even who made the decision. TB asked Butler to sort it out and Butler came back with the suggestion that we could change tack because a review had been set up to change procedures. But TB spoke to DD later who felt the only grounds to justify the decision were indeed that he had been told it would harm the peace process if the decision was not taken, and that was not a good enough reason. So we agreed he would go on the radio tomorrow and say he intended to review it, and we would brief he was likely to come to a different decision. It had been woefully handled. TB kept emphasising the only thing that mattered was whether the criteria had been properly applied, and that it was nothing to do with the peace process. The press were in full cry up there.

To Luxembourg, where we went straight to the dinner with Jean-Claude Juncker [Luxembourg Prime Minister and European Council president] which was mainly EMU, enlargement and the jobs summit. On beef, TB said he we had a tougher regime than anywhere else and we were worried the commercial interests of others would mean they kept looking for excuses to knock us back on getting the ban lifted. They did a brief doorstep at which I leant on the wall and accidentally put out the lights, and TB was close to cracking up laughing.

I woke up to one or two unexpected problems. Ann Taylor had visited drug cafes in Amsterdam, without us knowing, and that meant a great drugs splurge going. And *The Times* ran a story that we were planning to apologise over Bloody Sunday, which I played down. TB was anxious about the Tories, who did a big number on the new 'compassionate Conservatism' yesterday. On the short flight to Strasbourg, we discussed Hague, agreeing that the line should be that they buried Thatcher but didn't know what to put in her place. We arrived at the Council of Europe, and at the lunch Chirac pronounced 'Tony is a modern socialist. That means he is five miles to the right of me.' Everyone laughed. '*Et j'en suis fier*,' said TB ['And I'm proud of it']. He said Chirac remained very chilly, while Kohl and Yeltsin were all over him like a rash. After we left, Yeltsin announced three-way summits annually with France and Germany, which was needless to say reported as a snub, but we believed it was Chirac who was behind it, not BY. Chirac thinks we're too cocky. Cherie called to get the go-ahead for a brief advising the Liberal Democrats on how to get more women into Parliament. TB, no doubt because of the Anji staying decision, was being very nice to her, full of 'sweetheart' as they spoke. GB and Charlie were calling pretty regularly. There had been agreement to get more money to the NHS to deal with any winter crisis and we would announce it on Tuesday. GB wanted first to announce that we were fining the MoD for over-spending and getting more back from the DTI. TB felt it was all too clever by half. Far better that we announce it whilst saying we maintain a tough line on spending. Basically GB, having made sure TB had nothing to do with this at conference, wanted to control the whole spending picture. TB spoke to him on the drive to Chequers, and agreed to do it Monday for Tuesday. But I later did a Sunday briefing and gave a pretty clear steer that we were going to get more money to health. GB was adamant that a straight 'more money for health' story was a bad story. Of course, Charlie was just peddling the same line. How they could think more money for health was a bad story was beyond me. They just wanted to do it in a different way, only on their terms. I suppose I did them in a bit, first with the Sundays, then afterwards giving more to Grice and [Patrick] Wintour [*Guardian*].

Back in Number 10, I listened in to a conversation with DD, who had still not sorted out the Jason Campbell case. He'd done *Good Morning Scotland*, said there would be a review but he could not see the point that it had to be announced that it was going to be reversed, and also that we had to admit it had been badly handled and had not been related to the peace process. In the end, I had to go over to the Scottish Office and write the press release for him. I read it to TB and to Mo, who was fine about it, even though she was going to get a bit of stick.

Anji came to see me, having been offered a job by British Airways but TB had said no way could she go. I said she should stay but try to understand CB's insecurity about her, and just do the job he wanted her to do. Health was picking up, and I agreed to meet Frank Dobson to make sure we were all on the same line. GB and Charlie were going to Rome for the England-Italy [football] match. They were taking a party of press with them, which was pretty extraordinary behaviour.

Saturday, October 11

I did a ring-round pushing the health story into a better place. Mo called and we agreed it was best to say nothing about TB's visit [to Northern Ireland] yet. I gave pretty much the whole NHS story to Patrick [Wintour], telling him that there will be new money and it will come from MoD, DTI and European rebates. I called Charlie in Italy and said I had given the story to the *Observer*, because they had been planning a story about £1 billion extra for health. Wintour and Grice were now on £250 million. The England match dominated all day [England drew 0-0 with Italy in the World Cup qualifying match in Rome]. I called TB to agree words to put out after the match. I had to be careful not to go over the top because there had been crowd trouble.

Sunday, October 12

A typical awful Sunday. It started with Charlie calling just before 7 to say he was thinking of putting GB on *The World This Weekend*. I said the health story was not running massively and I thought we were better to wait till Tuesday. They obviously believed I had given the story to the *Observer* to make sure it was done as a pro-health story, rather than a tough Treasury story. We agreed we would put nobody up and I called Dobson and said he should keep his head down and we would get another hit on Tuesday. Then just before 1, Magi Cleaver called to say she'd spoken to the Treasury and Alistair Darling was going on the radio. I called Darling and Peter Curwen [deputy head of communications, Treasury] and exploded. Alistair said it was not appropriate to have a go at him, because GB called him and said he should go on. I said theirs was the only department that gave us this kind of problem. He did the interview and though he was a bit defensive, he was OK. I spoke to Charlie, now in Luxembourg, who asked me to believe it was all the work of Peter Curwen who had taken it upon himself to put AD up. Ridiculous. The idea that Peter would do it off his own bat, without any reference to GB or CW, is ridiculous. I said so. I spoke to Alistair who admitted he had done it on instruction directly from GB. I called Charlie and gave him a real mouthful. I mentioned it to TB who said it was an outrage. He is incapable of playing as part of the team. He said he was sending him a minute.

Problem two was Ireland. TB was due to go tomorrow and meet Adams and, again, the focus was on whether they would shake hands and whether we would see that. The NIO called to say SF were making clear it would be unacceptable if TB was photographed with the other leaders but not Adams. I spoke to TB, who said he wanted us to get it sorted as it would be bad if the meeting now didn't go ahead. Mo called to say that she feared if we got on to them it will become a story straight away, that we were promising another meeting. TB had been against a filmed handshake so the earlier plan of meeting Adams in a line of people fell. Now he was saying he would meet all the participants privately. There was massive interest in it and we had very little to say. Problem three was football [violence in Rome]. I offered a TB piece to the *Sun*, who also wanted one from Tony Banks, who didn't return calls. I pushed the line that the Italians were largely to blame though we did not condone any yobs.

Problem four was Anji. Michael Levy called from Israel. He had been negotiating the terms on which she stayed and he wanted my take on how it was going and how it would settle. I said I thought CB was livid. He asked how much I thought TB needed Anji around. I said she was very important to him but nobody was irreplaceable and his relationship with CB was more important. But we ought to be able to work it out. He said TB had said to him that I was the one person on whom he was dependent. 'You could make a fortune advising on the media in the open market,' he said. As ever, he was fishing to be told how important he was, and how much TB relied on him. He admitted he felt insecure about this and needed assurance he was a key figure.

Monday, October 13

I was up really early and in with Jonathan to Number 10 to pick up TB and head off to Northolt for the flight to Ulster. Football violence was still the main story, with some pick-up on the Adams handshake situation. On the plane, TB wrote a pretty stiff note to GB re the handling on health, in particular the breach of the agreement with us and Dobbo re no interviews. It was fairly tough and later CW called and said he was fed up of being blamed for everything and there was no reason why we should fall out. I said he had to start playing these things straight or there would be a major fallout. On the plane we went over how to handle the Sinn Fein meeting. As we arrived, it was still not clear it was definitely happening because SF were so pissed off there was to be no camera present. They were big on visuals these guys. We did a brief doorstep so TB could say why he was meeting Adams, the importance of trying to move from violence to dialogue.

We then had a short helicopter flight to Trimble territory. DT was his usual self, veering between smug and downtrodden, which was an odd combination. At the main meeting he sat on the sofa with TB and just whispered to him, making sure nobody else could hear, and he was clearly contemptuous of Mo, and was trying to signal that she didn't matter, that only TB did. She just looked over at me, smiled and shook her head as if to say it happened all the time. DT gave him a little lecture on the history of the handshake – it was to show you had no arms, which could not be said of Mr Adams and Co. 'I'm sure my hand will be tainted,' said TB. TB also had a couple of little speeches to do and we had to do some careful footwork to avoid a meeting with a group of SF councillors who were clearly trying to ambush us.

We flew to Stormont, where he had maybe ten meetings with different groupings. In most of them, we were just going through the motions and everyone knew that. He had a good session with [Senator George] Mitchell and his colleagues. He said they had one of the most difficult and thankless tasks and we were incredibly grateful to them. George M said that SF were skilful and articulate and worked the process well. The SDLP were hurt. DT was getting hit every day by Paisley. DT took TB to meet his staff. Seamus Mallon complained that TB was letting Trimble control the negotiations. He said every time DT went running to him for special favours, it undermined the whole process. We kept TB in there longer than planned because Adams was due to come down the corridor and for now we were avoiding him. As TB worked his way through all the parties, I could see they were impressed at his grasp but also the determination. He was basically saying he wouldn't stop till they sorted it. As Gary McMichael [leader of the loyalist Ulster Democratic Party] left and shook TB by the hand, he said 'Is this the one that will shake Gerry

Adams by the hand?' TB smiled at him and shrugged. TB was with the [non-sectarian] Women's Coalition and said it would all be fine if they were running it.

Then, after a brief interlude to go over what he would say, we went in to the talks administration office, Adams, McGuinness, Pat Doherty [vice president of Sinn Fein], Siobhán O'Hanlon [Sinn Fein negotiator], TB, Mo, Paul Murphy [Northern Ireland Office minister], John [Holmes], Jonathan, myself. They all shook hands with TB, who was steely but welcoming and warm at the same time. He said it was good they were in the process. He believed in equality of treatment. He knew there had to be change. The question was what kind of change? He emphasised there could be no return to violence and no change that does not carry the consent of the people. It will all require goodwill. 'I understand history better than you think. We have an opportunity which, if we do not seize it, will not come again in our lifetime. I feel a deep commitment to make it work. All the energy and dynamism I have will go into this if need be. It is a very rare thing for humanity to make sense of history but that is what we must try to do.' It was powerful stuff. They hung on every word, but very steely-eyed with it.

GA and McGuinness were both impressive in different ways, Adams more prone to philosophising, McG always sizing things up, with a smile that veered from charm to menace. He said to TB he [TB] was the only man who could take this forward but he had to understand they had taken more risks than anyone. TB said he wanted to make this happen but it meant he had to get inside their minds. GA gave him a gift of a small harp. He said he acknowledged we had moved the process forward. But it is hard to build peace when the playing field is not level. The biggest cause of conflict is British involvement in Ireland. 'I want you to be the last British prime minister in this jurisdiction. Do you have any idea what it is like to live in your own country without proper rights?' He said he was still stopped by police the whole time, and asked what his name was. I was trying to gauge their sense of TB. They were impressed. GA said he would like to meet him often and talk more. 'I think you can be the person that brings peace to Northern Ireland.' TB said both sides had to try to see the other side's perspective. It's pointless to go back to the old ways. You need to unlock the better side of humanity among your people. He made a joke about how he was attacked by the Orange Order for marrying a Catholic. These things don't stop you. There is no point just going into all the old feelings. McG put in a stack of complaints re the NIO, the RUC. Doherty spoke a little, O'Hanlon not at all. They felt John Major messed up because he listened too much to the Unionists. They still felt TB's statements were the statements of a British PM looking from a Unionist perspective. The security agenda has dominated for thirty years. We need a political agenda, said GA. TB asked if the ceasefire would hold. GA said as far as he was concerned the last one was genuine. McG stressed the risks they were taking, said he saw no reason why there should be any more lives lost. He struck me as more pragmatic than GA, which surprised me. 'I know we won't get everything we want.' They pushed on Bloody Sunday, said it needed an international investigation. It was a running sore. GA said, I know British people have died at the hands of the IRA and I regret it but we have people who were shot by Soldier A and Soldier B. TB said he could not stress enough how unique was the opportunity we now had. The political will is there from us, but it has to be matched.

TB exuded a sense of confidence and authority on this. Even some of the NIO sceptics were beginning to shift, I sensed, and think it might be doable. I did a press briefing then GA did an OK doorstep. They had to go through a few ritual attacks, but the overall sense was that they were engaging in a way they had not done before. Then I heard that TB had met a lot of trouble on a walkabout in a shopping centre. I called Anji who said I had better get down there. He had basically been set up by the DUP who had tipped off a few friends to get down there and hurl abuse at him, and the policing was a bit loose. He was a bit shaken up by it, but above all angry that he had been set up. It was a total pain in the arse. I half blamed myself because Trevor Butler [protection officer] said when we were at the RUC earlier that they were worried about it. My alarm bells were ringing and if I had followed my instincts I would have got it called off, but I didn't because all the focus and forethought was on Adams. I was really pissed off and so was TB. We laughed about it later, but it left a nasty taste.

Tuesday, October 14

There was an inquest going on into the shambles of the [Belfast] walkabout, and whether anyone from inside the RUC was involved in tipping off the protestors. 'The big PR disaster' was one of the Irish headlines. But the substance of the event cut through as well, and there was plenty of focus on GA etc. Derry had a big speech on legal aid on Saturday and he and I had a meeting to go through that. There was a fair bit going on today, with the drugs czar appointment and Piers Merchant quitting as an MP [the Conservative MP resigned over his affair with a seventeen-year-old girl] and [Neil] Hamilton at the [Standards and Privileges select] committee hearing. And on the single currency, I had to do a big briefing operation to get round the growing appearance of a rift between TB and GB after Bevins' piece yesterday. It meant restating the referendum pledge and emphasising the economics, but someone was stirring somewhere. GB was convinced we were behind it, especially as Macintyre [*Independent*] had done a piece saying TB always won the big arguments. I asked him what earthly point there would have been from our perspective, on the day we were trying to get up health, to have to do a big defensive operation on EMU? TB was livid about it. I suspected a minister down the chain. Fiona told me CB had made it clear to TB how unhappy she was at the new arrangements. I said he had to be allowed to choose his own team.

Wednesday, October 15

Boris Johnson [*Telegraph*] had a bizarre column saying basically that I would decide whether we went into EMU or not. Peter M was being more reasonable but was still very hoity-toity in the way he spoke to people, especially officials. He also missed no opportunity to make clear to Whelan he thought the fly-on-the-wall documentary on GB was a terrible mistake. But he was in better form overall. TB called on his way back from the dentist and sounded very low. He and CB had had a dreadful row last night because he had made clear Anji was staying, and he had to be allowed to employ whoever he wanted. Fiona and Roz both felt he had pushed her too far, and their respect for him had gone too. I was on his side, in that the demands of the job had become clearer and clearer, the Civil Service was limited in what it could do for him, and surely he could pick and choose the people around him. But it was complicated and difficult. Macintyre filled me in on the GB trip to Rome but was adamant the latest Euro stuff was not a GB/CW operation. We had a meeting about the Mountfield review and I sensed something of an ally in Michael Scholar [DTI permanent secretary]. I was trying to emphasise the difference between information and communication. Also wanting to know the process by which all those who were going would be replaced, and how we guarantee better quality. I said it would be hopeless if ministers lost people and then felt all they got was a replacement that was no better or even worse. There was a reception later and despite everything TB and CB were on good form. Melvyn Bragg [writer and broadcaster] and I spoke about the idea there had been for me and Alan Clark to do a TV thing together.

Fiona was pissed off that I had backed TB over Anji and she said she could not understand how he could see his wife upset and angry over something and do nothing about it. I said I couldn't stand the *Peyton Place*-ness [early TV soap opera] of it, and if he wanted someone to work with him, I would work with her. Jonathan was staying above the fray.

Thursday, October 16

India was our main problem early on, the Queen's visit being seen as a debacle, especially after it emerged the Indians had stopped her making a toast to Madras. RC was getting a bit depressed with it all and blamed a mix of the royals and [Sir David] Gore-Booth [high commissioner to India] who said on Radio 4 it was 'just a snafu' ['situation normal – all fucked up']! TB had a meeting with JP then with RC on environment, Kyoto planning and on India a fightback strategy based on RC articles and a lobby briefing. We put out a line from TB that the visit was far more successful than people imagined, not least in the eight big contracts being signed. RC briefed the Cabinet and put a brave face on it all. But he had been pretty well stitched up on Kashmir.[1] He said Pakistan was an overwhelming success but the Indians really went for him. TB ran through the political scene, felt we had won the battle of the conference season, that the Tories were still fundamentally divided on Europe and on whether truly to dump Thatcherism or not. He felt they were only in the first phase of opposition – causing trouble for us. The PLP was in a second phase – after the euphoria of victory, now the tough choices. They would find it hard but we had to give leadership, make the case for what we were doing. TB did a photocall with Sir Pat Neill [chairman, Committee on Standards in Public Life], the new Nolan, and they all went off on one re state funding [of political parties]. We had a big hoo-ha over whaling, Elliot Morley [fisheries minister] changing our approach in a letter to MPs, without even telling Jack Cunningham, who was going totally ape. There was a lot of pre-reshuffle pressure building, e.g. Robin Mountfield yesterday saying 'Please take [David] Clark away from me – he is hopeless.' I was also having a few meetings re planning for CHOGM, and trying to build an argument around the question – what is the Commonwealth for? Jack Straw came to see me in a complete fury,

[1] Indian accusations of a new British imperialism followed suggestions by Robin Cook that the UK could mediate in any negotiations over the disputed territory of Kashmir.

because the policy on hardcore porn videos had seemingly been changed without him knowing. Moira and David M said TB had been dreadful in the CSR [Comprehensive Spending Review] meeting with the Treasury. He looked awful for a start. He hadn't really read the brief and he didn't engage in the argument, with the result that GB did all the running. He was pretty hopeless in the *Time* magazine interview as well. This was the CB/Anji thing getting to him.

With the GIS review under way, there was a lot of guff being written about politicisation, as though we were threatening the crown jewels. Jonathan Haslam called to say he was leaving for the private sector. So another one was gone. I put out a statement saying he had done a fine job and he made clear he was leaving because he was offered a good job outside, not because of unhappiness with the new government. We had a 4pm strategy meeting, for which Peter M had produced a good paper to work from. We contrasted the way education and health were being handled. DB had managed to get up big messages and the policy detail flowed from that, and fitted a bigger picture. He was clearly being seen as a reformer. Dobbo was not. PG said people needed to know what targets we were to be judged by. GB said it would all lead to massive rises in public expenditure. TB was stressing we needed to work up a proper strategy for our EU presidency. GB saw nothing but problems there too. 'It will be EMU, EMU, EMU.' TB dropped in that he and I had been discussing a new strategy unit but nobody really picked up on it. He was hopeless today, really useless. Steve Evans [BBC] had a ghastly piece on the six o'clock news re the GIS review and union claims of politicisation. Also, though Haslam said he was making clear to me and others he had no complaints, *The Times* were leading on a story that he had had a row with [Stephen] Byers about being asked to put anti-Tory stuff into a government release. As I told John Lloyd [FT] when I briefed him on the GIS review, the press having spent years saying how useless the government press officers were, were now presenting them as great heroes as we were trying to change things. It was preposterous rubbish. I got home to a big piece about me on *Newsnight*, more of the same crap. It really was a ridiculous fuss about nothing, minor reforms presented as major events because they gave the hacks the chance to talk about themselves and wank themselves silly.

Friday, October 17

CB called Fiona while I was there and Fiona asked me to listen to what she was saying. TB had said she was being irrational about the whole thing, and that he had to have the team around him he wanted

and that included Anji. She said she found the whole thing humiliating. We agreed that the four of us would get together and talk it
through. I said she was overreacting. The truth was everyone was
having to adapt to government and the new pressures and there was
so little time to talk things through in a calm and rational way. I called
TB as he was about to leave for Chequers and said I was worried the
thing would spill out publicly and we would just have a gigantic
soap-opera splurge. I said that however irrational it may seem, she
was his wife and he had to deal with it, and try to see things from
her point of view. I was sure this was sortable but not if they didn't
talk to each other about it. This had the effect of him calling her and
asking why she had called me about it, which of course she hadn't
really. I said to Fiona I would just leave them to get on with it. Then
she took that as me saying I wasn't bothered and she and I had a row
about it too. I was sick of it all. The problem with the whole thing
was that it was becoming TB/AC vs CB/FM. They just felt Anji was
too close in, too influential on the diary and TB's time and modus
operandi. TB and I knew that she was an important part of the team,
and could not get why they were so against her. She helped him in
his role, and she helped me in mine.

I briefed on Derry's speech, which led to more crap re the GIS
review because it was me not his department doing it. But EMU was
our main problem of the day. Charlie Whelan and Ed Balls wanted
GB to do an interview 'clarifying' the situation, saying policy was
unchanged but making it clear we were clearly not going to be in
the first wave, and therefore it was unlikely for this parliament.
Jonathan called and said though TB was not sure of the need, GB
was trying to push him into agreeing to the interview. With all the
chatter there had been around, I agreed with CW it was probably
the right thing to do. It was not really an interview so much as a
form of words which would be given to Phil Webster. The Treasury
drafted the words and I made a couple of changes to tone down the
pro-Europeanism in a couple of places. I spoke to Webster and agreed
that the intro was that he was effectively ruling it out for this parliament while saying it would be folly to close options. God knows
how we had got to this, or to the headline at the end of the day,
'Blair rules out single currency for this parliament', because while
CW and I both believed we were doing what TB and GB wanted us
to, they having discussed it earlier, it seemed they had not really
gone over the line in any detail. GB was pushing where he wanted
to go, I'm afraid I was keen to push my instinctive anti-EMU feelings because I didn't want TB outflanked by an impression that GB

was keener on EMU. The words went to Webster, the spin was applied, and away we went.

It was all quiet until after 10, when TB called after he had seen the news and said what the hell is going on? 'We never agreed this,' he said. I said I thought they had. Peter M came on too, amazed. I said I couldn't understand, given this would run for days now, why GB wanted to do it like this. He said because he didn't like being seen to do things under pressure so it was a way of trying to do it on their terms. I suddenly realised that because I had not really checked and double-checked with TB, we had briefed an enormous story on the basis of a cock-up. TB sounded really, really pissed off and exasperated. It was so messy. He could not get hold of GB – 10.15pm – so he spoke to Charlie who professed himself 'gobsmacked' by the conversation. TB asked if we had ruled out EMU this parliament. Yes, said Charlie. 'Is that not what you want?' No, it is not, said TB. 'Oh,' said Charlie. GB was also now on the rampage, saying this had all gone too far, as if suddenly the headline he had been asking for was not what he had asked for at all. Even today, writing this one day after the event, I cannot piece together exactly how we reached the point we did.

Both CW and I felt we were driving the position to where they wanted it, now they were both saying that they didn't. They had agreed this was what they wanted, or at least so we thought. It was all a bit bizarre. CW and I both had a good moan about working for these guys, and how difficult they could be when they were not communicating properly with each other, but in truth we had ballsed up. Word got out early, CW having tipped off the *Sun*, and we then had to start a ring-round. *Newsnight* said it was a shambles because Ed Balls had confirmed the *Times* story, while the Treasury press office said the policy was unchanged. We said this had been done because there had been so much damaging and inaccurate stuff in the press, especially [Robert] Peston's story in the *FT*. But it was all very messy. I had several conversations with TB and he sounded more and more fed up as the evening wore on. I said we had ballsed up and we were going to have to put it right somehow. It was also clear that Ed Balls was now going to be saying this was all down to me spinning Webster. I thought it was doing what had been agreed and what had been wanted by them. How we had got to this was beyond me.

Saturday, October 18

Pretty much a weekend from hell, at the end of which I was totally unrested as we went into another week. I was beating myself up

October '97: TB and GB on rampage re EMU fiasco

too because I knew I had screwed up. We had all screwed up but I felt I hadn't done what I normally do, which is double-check every base. Writing this on Sunday, I still think Charlie and I were doing what we thought our respective bosses wanted us to. TB wanted GB in line, GB wanted to stop all the split stories by spelling out the logic of our position for the parliament. TB thought we could get by a while longer, GB felt we had to clear it up now. CW and I took those different positions and thought we were merging them to mutual benefit. Big mistake. TB called early, a bit more relaxed about things, because he felt we had reached the right position, even if we had done it at the wrong time and in the wrong way. 'What actually happened is that you and Charlie thought you had an instruction, after which GB and I were out of the loop about how you went about it.'

As the day went on, he started to laugh about it, asking when CW and I were planning the Budget, that kind of thing. He said there was no rowing back on it now, so it was simply a question of how best we handled a very messy situation. It meant the day was dominated by a series of conference calls to get things sorted out. I spent a lot of Saturday trying to persuade the Sundays it was not such a big deal, just a logical extension of what we had already said, and that if the story had said 'set to' or 'likely to' it would not have been so dramatic. It was the definitiveness that made it go so big. Some of them were trying to run the line that TB had overruled GB and made him do it. When I told TB he said 'I wasn't even aware of it. What the press are saying about this is bad enough – but the truth is even worse.' He knew I felt pretty sore about it and was pretty fair considering, but I knew he was really pissed off at the whole thing.

The other drama of the day was David Clark. Godric picked up a line that Clark had said he was being smeared – something to do with a few piddling little diary stories about rail travel. Peter Kilfoyle [junior Cabinet Office minister] called and said he was worried Clark was close to the edge, full of conspiracy theories and he could say anything if, as planned, he did *On the Record* on freedom of information tomorrow. I filed a memo to TB, explaining Clark had gone on the radio to say he was being smeared by his officials. Jonathan and I spoke to Clark on a conference call and he set out, in full detail, the background to this piddling story, which was something to do with his bags going missing, and costs of a flight. I said if John Humphrys [BBC *Today* programme] spent ten minutes on his missing bags, he would end up a laughing stock. He said there was a point of principle about ministers being supported by officials, but eventually I persuaded him it was crazy in these circumstances to do an interview about this. He had had a perforated eardrum, which was an easy way out. I said the other thing to remember about lots of stories is they just happen, and it may not be the case that an official put the story there deliberately. 'It could have been someone from British Airways,' I said. 'Aaaah, but it was a Qantas flight,' he said, missing the point. 'Why would an Australian want to brief against me?' I got the papers later and they were full of the EMU situation, mainly about how the decision was taken, a total spinola about meetings which took place, and many which didn't. TB knew we had screwed up but he felt the real problem was GB's modus operandi. 'It's a disaster area.'

Sunday, October 19

Dreadful day. Dobbo was the first call because he was due on *Frost* and wanted to know what to say re EMU. I said he should say we would not be in the first wave, and therefore it was unlikely this parliament, but we never say never. This is what we had agreed yesterday but GB went ballistic, said we were changing the line without consulting him, and I was beginning to wonder if I lived in a madhouse. Then Blunkett called re the same. It was a real nightmare. Nick Robinson [BBC] was reporting Dobbo as being at odds with GB though of course he was only at odds with the *Times* headline. TB called and said CW, Peter M and I should get a line agreed and put round to everyone, along the lines that we would not be in the first wave, that meant unlikely this parliament but there was no need formally to rule it out. But GB did not want to move at all, wanted to do a briefing and clips saying he would not be bounced, that we would take the decision in an orderly fashion based on the reports he had commissioned into the five areas of assessment for the workings of EMU. He was pretty insistent and got his way, which I think was right. TB was keen to move the story on. GB was keen to make a virtue of not moving, and we had an opportunity in his words to the Stock Exchange tomorrow.

TB said we should say there would be a statement next Monday, ruling out the first wave for economic reasons, and saying that makes entry this parliament unlikely. But there is no need formally to make a renunciation. GB said we should try to shut it down before Parliament returns. The danger was that in trying to end the confusion we create more confusion. He felt we should brief the outlines of what we would say next week, the five areas for assessment, then park on that. Anything that looks like a new line will just be another U-turn. We agreed to give out his Stock Exchange words today as a way of signalling the forward process to next week's statement. TB was happy with that, said we then say Parliament will have the full position set out next week. He did say, though, 'If the markets go haywire tomorrow, we are in deep shit on this. We will be subject to extreme and justified attack.' So after endless calls we agreed – we will not be bounced, and a full statement will be made to Parliament first, setting the issue in long-term national interest not short-term politics.

Catherine MacLeod [*Herald* journalist] said the problem for the government was Whelan. She said I should go totally on the record and be named so that people knew when a government spokesman was me rather than him talking some rubbish to his pals. TB said pretty much the same thing, and was now pretty sure we should get rid of the old lobby system and do proper on-the-record briefings. 'We get the worst of all worlds. The press make up anonymous quotes and say they are from us. We'd be better off if everything you said was on the record.' He said recently when he complained to Irwin [Stelzer] re a *Sunday Times* story about us going into EMU, Irwin's defence was that the source was Derek fucking Draper. GB sounded totally exasperated but strongly felt we should not be panicked into moving an inch. I said it was not movement we needed but clarity. He did a series of clips which were OK but they still sensed we were vulnerable on it. I hated the way one or two of them said it felt like the last lot. Charlie was getting a lot of the flak for it which for once wasn't totally fair. Peter M thought we should go up front and say the spin doctors fucked up, but TB/GB felt that could end up anywhere.

Monday, October 20

I got a rare queasy feeling in the morning re 'Brown Monday'. GB spoke at the Stock Exchange and had the ultimate horror backdrop, the screens behind him going red as he spoke. The press were all unanimous we'd had our worst weekend since the election. I spoke to TB as he waited for Kohl. 'What I can't stand is the incompetence. I don't mind if we are attacked for what we do or stand for. I can't stand the incompetence though.' Whelan was beyond repair, but I felt I should support him because we had both been involved. The one good thing to come out of it was that Peter M and I agreed it would probably not have happened if we had been working together properly. I wrote him a note saying it was vital we worked together and we should let bygones be bygones. He sent back a very nice note.

The morning meeting was full of black humour re CW's fate, but we agreed to let GB's words speak for themselves and put up the shutters. For the eleven o'clock briefing, I decided attack was the best form of defence, went at the *FT* for the stories that led us to need to clarify things, said I could not be held responsible for *Times* headlines, and then just referred them to GB's words. Webster said afterwards it was 'superhuman'. By the lunchtimes it was calmer though [Peter] Lilley was out calling for Whelan's resignation. Charlie was beginning to sound more worried but Tim believed he was enjoying his 'fame'.

Trevor Kavanagh came in with some lunch and it was clear he was going to be as much trouble as possible, especially on Europe. There was unfinished business there, I felt. He was not happy at having been told to back us in the *Sun* and would give us a hard time, no matter how polite in private. TB had five hours with Kohl, mainly one-on-one with interpreters and he said they got on well. They did EMU of course but a fair bit too on defence restructuring, which TB was keen to push, enlargement, G8. TB said he felt Kohl was much warmer than Chirac because he didn't mind having other big characters around.

Alex Ferguson came in for a cup of tea and a chat before the sports reception. Later he came round for dinner and was great with the boys, trying to persuade [Burnley fan] Calum to support Man U – and failing. Rory's face was a picture when Alex walked into his bedroom and gave him a couple of tickets for next week's European match as a birthday present. We had a nice evening though I was interrupted by several calls re EMU. Alex was full of his usual advice about staying focused.

Tuesday, October 21

TB felt we had just about saved the EMU situation from catastrophe. But he was determined we had to learn lessons, and called in GB for a very heavy session, just the two of them, telling him he needed to sort his operation out. Then he called in Peter M and told the two of them they had to work together, then me with the same message, then Charlie and Jonathan and Ed Balls. TB was very steely, in a real no-messing mode. He said we got away with it, just, but it was a fiasco. It happened because we had stopped working properly as a team. And though we saved it from being a catastrophe, two or three more like that and we will be dead. If we do not get back as a team, we will be beaten at the next election, and the people in this room will be responsible. We put the election strategy together and it worked. The party will expect us to deliver the next one too, and it will mean being a lot more united and professional than we've been recently. GB looked hurt and embarrassed, and clearly felt most of it was aimed at him, but it was a general message for the four of us, himself included.

TB saw it as a big warning. This is all about relationships and psychology, he said. 'When we worked together, we were unbeatable. We won the arguments because of the way we made the arguments. We terrified the Tories because we were so professional. And the party saw us as winners. We erode that at our peril. But at the moment all the key relationships are wrong. TB/GB, GB/Peter M, Peter M/AC. Unless we get back working together, we are dead. I mean dead. I mean a lost election, and the people in this room get the blame. I cannot make myself any clearer about this.' He then turned to GB and said 'Gordon, the key figure in this is you. If you do not face up to what I'm saying, you will ruin yourself and you'll ruin the government.' GB said fine, he was happy to work with others. TB said he wanted the Treasury properly integrated into the rest of the government. GB said fine. He said it was also important we had proper procedures for recording meetings etc. TB said you can have all the procedures you want but unless you have the psychology for this, to accept what I'm saying and work together, then we are finished.

He had to leave for a meeting, so the rest of us carried on. We agreed we had to be more open with the press, and push to on-the-record briefings from Number 10, and greater trust and co-operation amongst ourselves. TB was now convinced, for reasons I could not fathom, that GB had actually wanted all this to happen. TB's reasoning was that he didn't want to be seen to be bounced, so he went too far the other way. He had shifted his position in an exaggerated way to avoid people thinking TB had pushed him into a position he didn't want. TB said he didn't mind so long as we reached the right decisions but it was really worrying if true. But the mess had been so big that business feared we were making the decision for political not economic reasons and the Murdoch press thought we were just diddling them. There had been very little upside, beyond maybe the shock to the system getting people to get back working together. TB wanted the message to go to business that we were stepping up preparations for entry at a later date. The big worry was what all this said about the TB/GB relationship, and the difficulty GB had with the basic idea that TB was prime minister.

The other dynamic in this was the Civil Service who felt we had taken a hit and deserved it.

Wednesday, October 22

One of those days where TB was getting angrier and angrier. As we travelled to the Commonwealth Business Forum, he said 'I cannot believe what Gordon has done. He has damaged our credibility in a way that could take ages to restore – with business, with the media, and it will get through to the public too. And all over something where there is in fact no division, but he has to pretend that there is. It is absolutely mind-blowing.' GB was being very friendly and constructive in meetings, either because he had heeded TB's words or, if TB's theory was right, because he had created havoc and now needed to calm things. I thought it was the former but who knows? Charlie was very sheepish, and constantly looking for people to tell him it was not so bad after all.

I had a session with James Carville [US political consultant, former Clinton adviser], Philip and Peter Hyman. He was less in your face than the public image, and more reflective. I liked him. He had a face that combined toughness and warmth and he had a big laugh and was great at instant one-liners. He had some good thoughts on campaigning while in government, though he was clear he was not himself a government person. But he still spoke daily to George Stephanopoulos [fellow former Clinton adviser], which underlined how close they were at a time when our key people were getting more distant. As he left he said 'It's nice to meet someone with even more piss'n'vinegar than me in him.' I think it was a compliment.

Thursday, October 23

I had a session with RC to go over the 'outing' of Gaynor [Regan], who was due to go with him to CHOGM. He also wanted to take her to the Middle East. Cabinet was mainly on EMU and most of them were saying how important it was to keep the option open. It was striking how pro the majority were. GB was not saying much. TB set it in a political context, said there was a mood to change the climate, knock us more, and we had to be on our mettle. He said GB would go through the outlines of his statement and he did not want anyone discussing it outside. GB did a very chunky briefing on the background to the assessment and the five tests. On convergence, we were clearly in a different cycle. We were not convergent now and would not be in '99. On flexibility, and the ability to deal with shocks, he also felt there was more to be done on skills. He ran through investment, impact upon City and financial services, gave a fairly balanced picture but concluded we would not be joining in 1999 but we should be preparing to join later.

The changes we would need to make were right for the British economy anyway. Margaret [Beckett] said the business community were nervous about saying we would not go in this parliament. Jack C said it would be taken as a signal we are not going in this parliament so there needs to be a statement of principle that we are in favour. George R echoed that. GB had caught their mood about right though they were on balance more pro than he and TB were pitching it. Gavin Strang said he was reluctant to accept we could not join in '99 and said he thought we could win a referendum. The mood was for something a bit more positive but TB said he felt it was positive to be in principle in favour, say there were benefits and no constitutional barrier to joining, the economics would decide and the people would have the final say.

RC did a number on CHOGM, emphasising how we were trying to give it a bigger business and economic pitch. At 12.30 we had a two-hour meeting, the first of several planned, on GB's EMU statement for next Monday. TB had done a draft. So had GB. The test was to marry not going in in the near future with the stepping up of preparation for business etc. It was a difficult thing to pull off but we agreed that had to be the approach. We also agreed there should be a hint of apology for the way the thing had been handled up to now. GB was being far more friendly and constructive and said he wanted the ideas of others in the room on the way he was setting it out. Nigel Wicks [second permanent secretary, HM Treasury] and I both advised him against briefing business and others tomorrow. There had to be a real sense of this being a parliamentary occasion, added to which the last thing we needed was a row about whether market-sensitive announcements were being trailed selectively to business. GB liked the line – prepare now, decide later. The sense we would be giving was preparation for a referendum in the next parliament if the economics were right.

GB and Ed Balls went off to work on another draft and then came back for another meeting at 6, this time with Peter M also there. He was keen that we do not forcefully rule out the option. GB said we had to show the economic reasons why we were saying no to 1999. TB said if the City or business thinks we are doing this for anything other than economic reasons, we will pay a price for that. They would think we were just as bad as the Tories. In between times he had gone off to play tennis with Michael Levy and called on his way back, clearly wound up again. 'This is definitely beginning to hit us. I feel it. It still has the potential to be a disaster and we have to find a way through.'

He asked me to go and see him as he was heading up to the flat later and he was very down. I filled him in on a call a few moments earlier from Alex [Ferguson] who had called to ask how the boys enjoyed the match last night and who said re recent events, just remember that you guys are the biggest scalps so they will go at you the whole time, but you are doing more good than bad and this will blow over.

Friday, October 24
I was cheered up by the Shadow Cabinet having met and agreed to rule out the single currency for two terms, hardening up the policy in an effort to exploit our troubles. TB said we had to be pragmatic but positive and I fed that thought into the briefing note I was preparing for 4.30 to announce GB's statement. TB and I were both moving to the view that he should do the statement because it was in large part his credibility that had been hit, and he was better at nuance and tone. Peter M and Jonathan were both against, feeling it should be GB, but through the day we all mulled it over and moved around on it. By the time we landed at Edinburgh [for CHOGM], he was back to thinking GB should do it. I worked on a note on it on the plane and felt it was getting there, not ready for '99, so unrealistic this parliament but sensible to prepare for after that. The Tories helped because we could emphasise the economics at a time they were so obviously being political.

On arrival I took in GB's suggested changes to my briefing note and started to get going on it. We took out the note of apology over the handling, feeling it would be the only story out of it. Then just after 4, TB threw a spanner in the works. He came back from the opening ceremony and said he thought he should do the statement. I called GB, who had agreed the briefing note, and said if TB did it, we might as well put out a statement saying he had lost confidence in his Chancellor. I fed this to TB in the meeting and he said OK, though he said we could still change at the last moment if we thought it sensible.

[Robert] Mugabe, [President of Zimbabwe] arrived with a little posse of expensively dressed officials. He said in the past he used to get invites to Labour conferences in Scarborough, but it was so far to travel, and how Labour was always on their side against colonialism and imperialism. The Tories always looked at them as elements to be avoided. TB said our colonialism is something we now read about in history books, it does not define what we are. They ran around the main issues on the G8 agenda, talked on land distribution, during which we had another history lecture. He was pretty repulsive.

While TB was greeting the heads, Jonathan and I had a conference call with GB etc. to agree the final words. I met Nigel Wicks and we went to brief together. I ran through the bilaterals and then dropped in the EMU statement, which immediately became the main story. They all did it fairly straight though Jonty Bloom [journalist] on the Beeb said I had already breached the Treasury's 'no spinning' edict by saying what I did. Dickhead. One or two took it as a rebuke of Charlie which was a bit unfair. Back at the hotel I talked to Peter Temple-Morris. I assured him next week was the right time to defect. He said he was going to write to his constituency chairman to say he could not support the new [Conservative] policy on Europe, so that it was in the ether he was against what was going on. He said he was warming to the theme and also his wife was more comfortable with the idea, which was good news.

TB was in better mood and quite enjoying chairing the summit. I asked how the Queen had been with him and he went into his impersonation: 'Now Blair, no more of this People's Princess nonsense, because I am the People's Queen.' He said she was fine, and brilliant at the way she handled all these very different characters. She got terrific coverage on the news, though she looked a bit bemused at the modern rendition of the national anthem. The news was fine on EMU. TB spoke to GB a couple of times and drafts were now flying back and forth. Geoffrey Howe wrote to TB pleading with him not to rule out EMU.

Saturday, October 25

TB was chairing the summit, and packing in bilaterals as we went, whilst in truth he had nothing but EMU in his mind. The briefing went well, and we got stacks of fairly straight coverage. The Sundays were going big on it with big background pieces but I told them we would not be briefing at all beyond yesterday's statement – though I sensed from what they were saying that both CW and Peter M were getting their own versions out. I went to the conference centre to do a briefing, mainly CHOGM-related, but I used it to get out, as we had agreed, that Peter Temple-Morris was writing to his constituency chairman to say he could not support them on Europe, and that he wanted a meeting with their chief whip. I'd suggested it as a way of getting his discontent into the ether, and a sense that he was in contact with us, without it going too big. It worked.

I did a Sunday lobby, half of them in person, half on conference call, which seemed to go OK, though I spent most of it stonewalling on Europe and EMU. It was a good example of a briefing that could be reworked to get repeat coverage for the same lines and arguments. I worked on a note on the reform of the lobby system, with on-the-record briefings the main change. The draft for Monday was going backwards. It was clear GB and Ed were now having trouble seeing the wood for the trees and the argument was getting more and more convoluted. They persuade themselves that intellectual means complicated. The outline was now fairly clear: 1. no to '99, 2. no to this parliament though no need to say so explicitly, and 3. step up preparations as part of 'prepare then decide'. It was likely to be welcomed by business, whilst the contrast with the Tories was becoming clearer. TB was getting more and more fed up with GB. 'Why can't he just take what I say to him? We have agreed the structure, we have agreed the argument but he just keeps sending back the same draft, more complicated each time.'

The main story out of CHOGM was Mandela saying the Lockerbie bombers should not be tried in Scotland. After a visit to the NGO [non-governmental organisations] Centre, I went to the Queen's reception. I was hanging back just keeping an eye on things when Fellowes said I ought to meet the Queen. He took me to where she was listening to a gaggle of heads [of government], and as she turned from them, Fellowes said to her how much help I had been to them in the week after Diana's death. She looked deeply unimpressed, nodded a little and then said 'Do you always travel with the prime minister?' I said yes, usually and that was about it. Lady Hussey [lady-in-waiting] took up where she had left off and we ended up having quite a good natter.

Back at the hotel Fiona and I had another row about Anji, saying she couldn't understand how I didn't automatically take her side with CB. I said I thought everyone was being irrational to which she said she had supported me when I was irrational and I should support her now. She and Roz were livid that Anji had got yet another pay rise, and they were working harder for a lot less than most of the others. I said there was no reason for us to fall out about it. TB and CB had to sort it. I had to leave for another EMU meeting. TB had sent down a long note on the structure, with the nine steps to a clear argument, but GB kept murdering the argument, and the drafts were definitely going backwards.

Sunday, October 26

We had the grimmest set of papers since TB became leader. I still think it had been best to have a news blackout re EMU because it meant we could dismiss their stories as fiction, and the Mondays were willing to believe that. There was far too much on spin, loads on Charlie, a profile of me on Radio 5 today, lots of negative stuff. TB was late up and in a foul mood because he was late for church. He came back and found the latest GB draft unacceptable. He felt it was just too dense and lacked the light touch he would need in places to persuade that it was a thought-through position. As we left for the station to get on the Orient Express for the journey to the retreat [private weekend session for the heads of government], he looked really grim. I said for God's sake lighten up a bit. You look dreadful and people are beginning to notice. He said he was getting exasperated at what it took to manage GB. Any spare moment he was working on the statement, trying to get that balance right between assuring business we were still committed and preparing without sending the right-wing press into meltdown. We reached St Andrews and he had another conversation with GB, trying to impress on him the need to make the statement more penetrable, and clearer. I worked on a briefing note, with TB words, and political dividing lines, and making the point that TB always tries to turn disaster to opportunity. He had to chair the meeting on Nigeria and new criteria for members and then we had a bilateral with Mandela on Lockerbie which was tricky enough, but I could tell he was really just wanting to be working on that statement again.

We organised pictures of Mandela and TB going for a walk, then John H and I went to play a few holes of St Andrews. We played the first few holes, and I didn't do too badly, but then came back via the seventeenth and eighteenth and there was a big press contingent out just watching for the heads of government to screw up on the golf course. Little did I know I was about to give them what they had been waiting for. I have never hit so many bad golf shots in such a short space of time. Hacked off the tee, then in and out of the water, sliced towards the photographers. It was unbelievable and eventually I just packed it in. I was able to cheer up TB a bit when I described how I almost killed someone with the slice on the seventeenth. We went for a walk down to the beach. He said he was really frustrated having to spend so much time on CHOGM stuff when he ought to be sorting this damned statement. He said he could not fathom what GB was up to and why he was being so obtuse about it all. After twenty minutes or so, we were ambushed again by camera crews and headed back after doing some clips on Lockerbie, Mandela and EMU.

The only briefing I did was by video link back to all the hacks in Edinburgh. They liked the stuff on EMU but as I left the briefing room, Magi said I had committed a huge faux pas in full view of top guys from the Commonwealth secretariat. Apparently there should never be any briefing of the discussions themselves until the communiqué, and also I had briefed that Yemen and Rwanda were likely to have their applications rejected, after which the Commonwealth spokesman went out and said I had been badly briefed and got it wrong. On EMU I spoke to one or two after and they liked the TB words and felt it was turning our way a little. There was far too much interest in how crap at golf I was.

Back on the train we were back to working on EMU, TB finally getting more confident that it was in shape. Peter Temple-Morris called and he, Jonathan and I had a conference call. He said he wanted one more meeting with TB to assure himself on one or two points and then he would come over. I said to Jonathan you had a year to get him over: I did it in ten days. I recommended we do it through a Sunday newspaper followed by *Frost* and he was fine about that. It was great getting him over, and would really hit the Tories hard again.

Monday, October 27

The British press had pretty much left and were back in London waiting for the EMU statement. The last TB/GB argument was over whether we said something by way of apology for last week's fiasco. GB was against. TB felt there should be something at least. But GB persuaded him, with my, Derry's and [Treasury permanent secretary] Terry Burns' backing, that it would be wrong to play up an apology because it would not be clear what we were apologising for. Far better just to say that we were only focusing on substance. The big laugh for everyone was the coverage of my golfing. Nick Matthews [duty clerk] plastered the cuttings around the walls. I had a couple of calls with GB while TB was chairing the final CHOGM session and we finally settled on 'We do not propose to enter a single currency this parliament.'

The statement was now clear and there was no question that we had not thought through. CHOGM finished on time, TB telling us how brilliantly he had chaired it. TB was regaling us with a few stories from the receptions. One of the African leaders pinching Cherie's bum and asking her who she was, then him jumping a mile when she said she was Tony's wife. Mandela being difficult on a couple of issues and TB saying to him 'You are so revered you can come out with any old nonsense and nobody is allowed to say it's nonsense,' Mandela laughing. We got back and went through the final final version, which was fine. GB was excellent in the House. Lilley's response was hopeless and I could sense in the briefing afterwards that they felt it was turning towards us. TB spoke to Rupert Murdoch who said 'Let the debate kick off. Let the Little Englanders at it. Let the Europhiles at it and see where it ends.'

All in all, it was another big occasion which had gone well. We'd done exactly what the strategic briefing said we would – turned setback into opportunity, shown clarity, direction and leadership, wrongfooted the Tories. What they didn't know was that we had also laid the ground for another defection.

Tuesday, October 28

I had a session with Robin Butler before the select committee hearings on the transition, where he would be asked about politicisation, on which he was supportive, though he said he would have to dodge questions if asked about Charlie Whelan. I had found him pretty supportive of me and my efforts to improve the GIS. He knew it wasn't right. At the morning briefing, I really tore into them over Jon Hibbs' [*Telegraph*] report today, saying that I was being criticised by CHOGM leaders over having briefed on EMU at the summit. I said they had to decide whether they wanted me to brief or not, I didn't have to help them, and I certainly wouldn't if it meant getting this kind of crap.

It turned into a seminar on the lobby, and I was stressing that TB could not believe some of the stories attached to his name. Of course they loved talking about themselves, and it went on longer than usual, then the one o'clock news did an item on it, with pictures of me and TB and quoting me on the record. This led the papers to do the same. At 12, I had a meeting with Charles Moore and George Jones. They had written to complain that we were not giving the *Telegraph* fair treatment and George said he was not getting stories, and we were rude to him. Charles said we were obsessed with presentation to the exclusion of anything else. I pointed out the inconsistency of their complaints. I said they got the same treatment as everyone. They had to understand we were going to do things differently. I accepted I was aggressive but I felt I had to be, because we were dealing with a dreadful press. I had no illusions about them. I said I would take on board what they were saying but it was basically an unfriendly meeting.

Roger Liddle came to see me, upset by the letter I sent him, because he said it showed I did not trust him. I said he should just let me know when he was seeing journalists, and what they were saying. Jonathan saw him too and TB spoke to Peter M about him. I said it was no bad thing if he saw media people but he should be less blabby. I don't care how friendly he is with some of them, in the end they are journalists with a job to do, and we have to make sure we are all setting out the same narrative, and not feeding a different agenda.

Robin Butler came to see me after his appearance [answering allegations of Civil Service politicisation at the Commons Public Administration Select Committee] and thought it went OK. We discussed the lobby system again. He clearly felt we had to get sorted on the GIS review. I didn't feel he was against what I was trying to do. Peter Temple-Morris called to say he was feeling nervous. He'd seen the chief whip again, and knew they were going to come after him. I spoke to Alan Howarth [arts minister], who had lunch with him today. He said it brought back memories [Howarth had defected to Labour from the Conservatives in 1995]. He was able to tell him he had no regrets. I said it was important to keep in touch with him. The four o'clock turned into another seminar on the lobby. Charlie was worried that what I said earlier was being seen as a go at him, which to some extent it was. This whole spin thing was getting ridiculous. Philip felt that I emerged stronger from recent events. Maybe. I wasn't so sure.

Wednesday, October 29

It was the first PMQs for a while so we were doing more work than usual in planning it. TB had been asking for a new system of putting together the various files, where he wanted facts rather than argument, and then he worked on the argument himself. He was spending more time on his own preparing, using his own notes in the end as his main aide-memoires. The eleven o'clock was the shortest I can recall. I gave very clipped and uninformative answers, just let them know that if they wanted to go back to the kind of briefings they got under [Major's press secretary Jonathan] Haslam, they could.

Through the day, there were rumours that Ian Taylor [Europhile Conservative MP and Shadow spokesman on Northern Ireland] was going to resign from the Tory front bench. I spoke to Peter Temple-Morris again and told him I was going to brief Patrick Wintour on the background. Patrick was thrilled, but also clearly panicking that it wouldn't hold. I assured him that it would. I spoke to Temple-Morris again and could tell he was getting jumpy. We went over all the arguments again. I think his big worry was the Tories just opening all barrels on him. I said that was why it was so important that we made sure our people took to him straight away, and I was confident we had the plan to do that.

I had to leave early because Fiona had slipped on the stairs and was at the Royal Free getting an X-ray. We got back to see the kids and then we were out for dinner with TB, CB and the Levys. Michael had just taken his seat in the Lords, and was very chirpy. I sat next to CB, who was on good form, though she did say she was not going to let go re Anji. She was not going to let TB say she was irrational about it, because she knew Anji tried to exclude her. I talked to Michael about it and said TB was going to have to face up to the fact this wasn't going away.

CB said to me that he may not see this as she does, but if there was some impediment in your relationship with Fiona, you would get rid of it. She said the problem is Tony is not good at these emotional situations. Look at the Peter M/GB situation. He just cannot handle it. Both Michael and Derry were coming to the view that if she felt so strongly about it, he ought to concede this, but TB was if anything more stubborn not less. I said she was getting the whole thing out of proportion. Surely he had to be allowed to have the team he wanted and Anji did a lot of good for that team. Michael was very down on Peter, said he would just 'blow with the wind'. But once we had done our bit re Anji, we actually had a nice evening. Cherie was more relaxed than I'd seen her for ages, and TB was very funny about some of his CHOGM experiences.

Thursday, October 30

As I came out of the eleven o'clock briefing I got a message to call Peter Temple-Morris. He sounded pretty desperate. 'I can't do it, I can't do it. I can't go through with it.' I felt he was mainly worried about the charges of betrayal, and treachery, and I said we would do everything to guarantee he got a good welcome, and was made to feel he was where he belonged. Cabinet was mainly EMU, after which I briefed GB words and by now there was a bit of a flavour of meltdown re the Tories. GB did a long spiel re the background and the positioning and I could sense some of them thinking why hadn't we had this before? He said we had to show we are sincere in our preparations, and serious about informing the public, that the next few weeks were important for building up business and trade arguments.

I told TB re Temple-Morris' latest feeling about things, which was a blow, but at the worst we could say that he decided last minute to stay and fight, fuelling the sense of division. But I was still hopeful this was just a wobble and he would come over. Jonathan was very disappointed re Temple-Morris but I still felt it would be OK. At the four o'clock, amid all the rumours about defections, I was asked about PTM and just talked him up as a good thing, and did not hint one way or the other. I got back for the end of a meeting on privatisation where GB, [Geoffrey] Robinson [Paymaster General] and Balls were pushing hard re NATS [public/private ownership for National Air Traffic Services], Post Office (forty per cent) and the Tube. All very difficult politically but GB seemed to think we could make the argument. The strategy meeting was hopeless because TB was not terribly focused but we were ending the week in better shape than we started it. It had started with us in a hole. We got out. They got in and they haven't yet stopped digging.

Friday, October 31

Louise Woodward[1] verdict day so there was not much point competing with that, and I decided to take a day off. I got Derry up on TV in courts, against Peter M's wishes, re us being against the televising of courts.

Saturday, November 1

Work-wise it was really quiet, and I was just pushing the Tory turmoil along with the Sundays on the way up to Burnley vs Walsall. I had a really nice day out with the boys. TB called a couple of times re the Euro situation, which had calmed down. All the problems were theirs at the moment. Hillary Clinton was down at Chequers. The Sundays had quite a few pieces about how brilliantly CB was doing.

Sunday, November 2

Robin Butler called saying again could I help Robert Fellowes? There was another attack on him in the *Mail on Sunday*, which I hadn't noticed. Fellowes called too and sounded very down about it all. I said all I could do was continue to talk him up, which we did, but I didn't think this particular piece was worth worrying about. It was

[1] Woodward, a nineteen-year-old British nanny, was sentenced to life imprisonment by a court in Massachusetts for the murder of a baby, Matthew Eappen. On appeal, the judge reduced the second-degree murder verdict to manslaughter and sentenced Woodward to time served, equivalent to the 279 days she had already spent in jail.

just a Sunday columnist with nothing to say, who rehashed something someone else had been saying.

Monday, November 3

I felt properly rested for once, after a weekend in which Tory troubles was the main news, and there seemed to be minimal pressure on us. The Louise Woodward case was big news still and everyone was trying to get us into the story by suggesting TB must have talked to Hillary Clinton about it. Ridiculous. Alan Clark called, which was another sure sign of Tory turmoil, and we agreed to meet for lunch at Wilton's.

Derry called early about a story that Robert Fellowes was lobbying for a back-door privacy law through the European Court [of Human Rights]. Fellowes called to say it was rubbish. He said there was a lot of Charles image-building going on but what was bloody was that it would seem they had to do it at the expense of others. Allan Percival gave me a paper on Number 10 re the GIS review, and it was a very impressive piece of work.

I went to a meeting with TB, Butler, Jonathan, JH, at which Robin made a classic observation when they were discussing contenders for the next head of GCHQ – that Hayden Phillips [permanent secretary, Department for Culture, Media and Sport] might be a runner, having been overlooked for a couple of jobs recently, and he had just bought a farm in Wiltshire. TB did not look terribly impressed. TB said he was looking to do a reshuffle before Christmas, and that David Clark and Gavin Strang were obvious contenders to go. After the others left, he said I must get Fiona to persuade CB to be more rational re Anji. I said he and CB were both irrational. Michael Levy felt he was moving to let Anji go, because he could see how much Cherie was upset by it, but that was not the impression I got today. Far from it.

Alan Clark was on great form at lunch. He came in, swished through and said very loudly before he had even sat down 'You lot are just tooooo brilliant.' He was contemptuous of Hague. But he felt they should blow off Clarke and Hezza and be a bit more Little England, properly right wing. I said that was suicidal. 'I know, but we're dead anyway for God's sake. You bastards have killed us.' He was raving about TB – brilliant, storming. He said at the recent 'bonding session' someone said to Hague, I'm all in favour of more gays, women and ethnics, but why hasn't the leader's office hired any women or ethnics? He roared with laughter. He was longing for it to get out we were having lunch. 'Are there any journalists in here? Can't see any. Shit.'

Robert Fellowes and Tony O'Reilly [Irish businessman] were at the next table. 'O'Reilly will tell someone.'

I got back for a meeting of the GIS review which went on for ages. TB called me and said could I go up to the flat? He, CB and Fiona were there and the mood was dire. I later discovered Cherie had gone into his den, seen Anji there and stormed out. He stormed out after her and by the end of the evening he was so wound up he was talking about the job being impossible if he couldn't do it on his terms. He said to CB he had to have a balance of people around him and Anji added something to the mix. When Fiona and I left, CB followed us down and out into the street, thankfully free of media, and said he didn't understand how she felt. Fiona and I drove home rowing about it. I think I was the only one who could see both sides, but on balance I came down on his side, because he ought to be able to have who the hell he wants around. In the end, he is the one under the most pressure.

Tuesday, November 4

At the Lib-Lab committee meeting, Jack S sent me some very funny notes translating some of TB's words to the Libs e.g. 'Treat this confidentially = this has been in the *FT* for weeks.' 'Treat this as being between ourselves = I imagine you'll be straight on to the *Guardian* with this.' I think JS and I were the least enthusiastic about this exercise, though to be fair to Paddy he was on top of things policy-wise. Robin C did a number on where we could work together on Europe. Paddy said he greatly welcomed the commitment to step up preparation for EMU. TB focused on jobs, crime and the environment as the three areas we should be focusing on re Europe. He also felt we should be explaining better what the single market would mean for people, the advantages it would bring. We agreed a line and then I left early to pick up Calum and head for Luton 2, Burnley 3. TB called and said he needed Fiona to persuade CB re Anji. I said no chance, she feels just the same. It was a bloody nightmare this, and the whole *Peyton Place*-ness was wearing me down.

Wednesday, November 5

I awoke, as feared, to tobacco and Formula One climbdown leading the news.[1] TB called, pissed off and denying that he had agreed to the change. But in truth Max Mosley [president of the Fédération

---

[1] Formula One had originally been exempted from Labour's ban on sports being sponsored by tobacco manufacturers.

Internationale de l'Automobile] and Bernie Ecclestone [president and CEO of Formula One] had been lobbying and TB immediately sensed real danger because of course Ecclestone had given the party £1 million before the election. Whatever the rights and wrongs of the policy, which had been worked out by people unaware of the donation, it would look absolutely dreadful, and it was bound to come out. I felt confident in the arguments though, and we had to argue the policy case on merit. TB suggested we give the donation back to Ecclestone because if it came out it would look so awful, or get [Sir Gordon] Downey [Parliamentary Standards commissioner] to look at it, but Derry and I persuaded him that would be a mistake and would not help.

At PMQs, we assumed Hague would come at us over Formula One and broken promises, but didn't. Most of the day I was working on Mountfield's draft and said it was too defensive. Our 6.15 meeting with Jack Cunningham and his team confirmed my view that ministers just were not getting the kind of service they were entitled to expect. Bernard Donoughue [Labour peer] had the best anecdote so far, a press officer who said they didn't put out press-calling notices about ministerial visits 'because it tended to draw attention to them'. Jack was scathing. Not up to it. No urgency. No understanding of the need to mix policy and press people. No proactive approach. The comparison with Millbank could not be greater.

I then went to another extraordinary meeting on the honours list, at which John Holroyd [Secretary for Appointments, including honours] was defending the rather dull list they had put together and Jonathan was being snide about the whole thing. There was not much we could do in the limited time we had but I stressed they needed to do more for serving teachers. It was so hard to get these people to change anything. Any really radical suggestions were met with all manner of reasons why it was a bad idea. The list they had, they defended to the hilt, but in reality so many of the judgements were purely subjective, theirs and ours.

The TB/CB row was rumbling on and I'd decided both were being irrational – TB about how important it was to keep Anji even if it meant all this, CB about it being any real threat to her. CB said he could not accept the idea that she should be able to say who he hired. I said nor should he. You're his wife. She is a member of his staff, the same as I am. It's different, she said. It was impossible to reason on it. TB told me later he found the whole thing ridiculous, and a bit humiliating. He was tired and depressed about it. 'I've got Iraq, Formula One, PMQs, GB/Peter M, JP giving me grief and I've got to deal with all this too.' I said the problem was that, unlike us, CB and FM did not believe she was talented, so why was she there? 'It's ridiculous, the whole thing is ridiculous.' Maybe, but he had to acknowledge CB's feelings, however irrational.

Fiona and I had another row about it on the way home. It appeared to be the only thing that he and CB, or Fiona and I, fell out about. It was fucking ridiculous. I said she was sounding like a stuck record and I was fed up listening to any of it. Earlier, I gave Anji only a flavour of the kind of thing that was being said, and she seemed shocked, and said maybe she should just go. I said TB valued her and that had to be a factor. He valued her too much to see her go without really good reason.

Thursday, November 6

We were taking a big hit on tobacco. At Cabinet, Robin C ran through plans for the Anglo-French summit, and then did Iraq. He said it was dangerous and nobody should underestimate Saddam's determination to develop weapons of mass destruction. We were working to get the French and the Russians with us but it was hard. George R said the situation was more dangerous than before and every effort was being made to get him to back down. I had an unpleasant eleven o'clock, and they sensed they could get a lot of mileage out of this. What was worse, of course, was that I knew there was worse to come in the form of the discovery of the Ecclestone donation, which was inevitable. I was at the dinner for Chirac when Hilary paged me to say Jon Hibbs had called to say the *Telegraph* had had a tip on it, which led to me missing most of the dinner, leaving TB and Chirac to disagree noisily over Iraq. After the dinner, TB and I had a long chat about Ecclestone. It was going to be bad. The question was how bad, and what could we do to minimise the badness? My instinct was it would be really bad, and the best way to deal with it would be to get everything out in the open, soon. I felt for TB, because I knew this was the kind of issue he hated most of all. He hated anything to do with funding and though in truth there was nothing wrong about the way the decision was reached, people would not want to believe that. I was very robust at the four o'clock when they were going hard on David Mills[1], saying it was the kind of thing I used to kill the Tories for.

---

[1] Tessa Jowell's lawyer husband was later found guilty of accepting a bribe from Silvio Berlusconi, but he always denied the charge and on February 25, 2010 his conviction was quashed because the case ran out of time.

The Chirac dinner was fine on one level but they really disagreed fundamentally on Iraq. He was totally dismissive of the US and any suggestion of bombing. 'What does bombing achieve except it pleases the US Congress? Nothing.' TB was emphasising the UN inspectors had to be able to do the job properly. Chirac said there was no way he could support bombing. They were a long way apart. He said threatening force was not the way to treat Saddam. He said we had to persuade the US to be reasonable. 'We will explain and you will translate.' TB said the least we needed to do was agree he must hold to the UN resolutions. He was also scathing re the Yanks on the Middle East, and about [Binyamin] Netanyahu [Israeli Prime Minister]. Chirac was more supportive re our position on EMU as outlined by GB.

Friday, November 7

We set off for the Anglo-French summit [at Canary Wharf], and after the first exchanges TB and I had a conflab re Ecclestone. I felt we could not hold off much longer and I went off with Anne Stenson from the [Downing Street] Garden Rooms and drafted a briefing note, all the facts re the donation, making clear we have nothing to hide, that it would have been published in due course anyway, that the policy on banning was made after donation received, which blows the idea he bought a change, that the recent change was about making the policy workable without losing F1 [Formula One] from Britain. Anne let out a big whistle when I dictated the point about the million, but I felt totally comfortable in the argument, that it would be a rough ride but one we could tough out. We would also announce he planned to make future donations but TB felt in the light of all this, that might not be appropriate. I spoke to GB and Peter and at one point during the day, all four of us were agreed.

As the day wore on, doubts grew that the papers actually had the story. They had a tip but nobody seemed to know for sure. I didn't think it made much difference, because it was going to come out anyway. The argument in favour of waiting or stalling was that we were getting terrific coverage, words and pictures, out of the summit. Just before they did the press, Chirac asked me if there was anything I'd like him to say. I said it would be great if he talked of how impressed he was with *'jeune Angleterre'*, which he did. He had enormous charm when he wanted to, though he could also be overbearing and rude. Even I was impressed by the event, and how stylishly it was done. Chirac seemed very taken with it too, even the catering.

TB was becoming more and more worried. Then GB, up there for a bilateral, got him to agree that unless we were absolutely clear the press had the story itself, we should hold fire, and let it dribble out. One problem was that the circle of people who knew was widening. I had asked Tim to check out whether Dobson and Jowell had known, and they hadn't. 'Cor fuck me' was Dobbo's response and of course at some point he would be bound to talk to others as a way of getting his line out properly. GB came back with us to Number 10 where he, TB, Jonathan, Tim and I met and agreed that as neither David Hill nor I were coming under any pressure on Ecclestone, we could stall again, and see where it went. Both David and I felt it wasn't possible to hold out much longer. Philip thought GB was enjoying all these difficulties for TB. I was pretty sure that another weekend was about to bite the dust. Only the combination of luck and media laziness would see us through. We were also coming under pressure on the policy itself, even without the Ecclestone complication, and were not really fighting back. The news on the summit was terrific but this was a real worry hanging over us the whole time. I was losing sleep and so was TB. I said to TB the story was bound to break, that it was question of when not if, and it was as if we were just waiting around for a car crash to happen. One thing we did do was get a letter from Tom Sawyer sent to Pat Neill to set out the position re Ecclestone and ask for his advice, and also ask re the question of principle.

Saturday, November 8
We got terrific coverage out of the summit and there was nothing much in the press about Ecclestone. But the Department of Health got a rash of calls from the Sundays, inspired by the Tories, and we were again in the position of having to think how to get out of this. TB and GB still felt it was possible to stall but I felt sure it would come out and that we were just setting ourselves up with the slow build-up. I spoke to GB who said if it was imminent we should get it out but if not, we should hold fire. We had a few conference calls through the day. David said he was having to fob off a few people, but they were not pushing terribly hard. I was not getting media calls, so we agreed simply to say the listed donors will be published next year. I felt exhausted and low at the moment and couldn't really get on top of things. We were not doing well on strategy, being distracted by things like this the whole time. We were also below par on news management. TB went to play tennis. I was feeling real pressure which only lifted when I went to play football on the heath with Calum, and then went for a swim. The conclusion of the various calls through

November '97: GB persuades TB against openness

the day with TB, GB, Peter M etc. was that we should hold off for as long as we could. It was going to look bad.

Sunday, November 9

We had got a bad press because of U-turns etc., but both TB and I were amazed the papers were so light on Ecclestone. It was not a big story at all. Jonathan said Ecclestone was beginning to get jumpy. He wanted to put out a statement saying he had given us a fraction of what he had given the Tories. Peter felt we had the chance now to lay into the Tories and the *Sunday Times* over their stuff on David Mills, which was low. I wrote up a briefing on Iraq, trailing TB's speech tomorrow, which by the end of the day was leading the news. We left for the Arsenal/Man Utd game. I met Alex for a chat before the game in the marbled entrance. He was more nervous than I'd seen him for a while. It was a great game but they lost and Rory was upset as we walked home.

Monday, November 10

I slept really badly. I was dreading being grilled on the who knew what where when, and I knew this thing was going to hit us. The papers were low-key and there was not yet any real heat in this. I went to see TB and Jonathan. I was getting more worried not less. TB was sure though that the best course was to let it dribble out. I felt we were in danger of ending up with the worst of all worlds. I got Tim working on a briefing note for tonight's Mansion House speech and also TB's anger at the tatty upside-down Union Jack at the MoD for the Cenotaph ceremony. ITN led the news on it so it was a handy diversion. I met TB and Butler who were both moving against the lobby changes because they thought they would make me more vulnerable and more of a target.

Sally M told me that Neill had replied to Tom Sawyer's letter on Ecclestone and he was saying we should give the money back. I thought this was really odd. It meant very few donations were acceptable, because very few major donors would not be affected by a specific government policy at some point or another. And who the hell was he to decide? But decided he had, having been asked his view, and it was going to have real implications.

Then to a meeting with TB, Peter, Jonathan, Sally M, Robin Butler and, later, David Hill. We went through the tough questions, and drafted a briefing but we were still holding back re the size of the donation, which in the end was what made it the problem it was. Butler spoke to Neill to try to get a positive response to any decision to hand back. TB felt we had right on our side but that it was very unlikely to come out like that. GB felt we should give the money back straight away, but it meant state funding was inevitable. Through the evening the broadcasts were not as bad as we expected them to be. Indeed they were far better than we dared to hope. We now had to get the money back and get the thing dealt with finally. We got Blunkett to do interviews on it and he was fine. Also, the BBC still went on TB's speech as second item. With the Louise Woodward verdict wiping everything out, there was a chance the Ecclestone story would die. I doubted it though, and felt we were sleepwalking to a disaster.

Tuesday, November 11

I woke to the BBC saying the Labour Party was 'still refusing' to reveal the size of Ecclestone's donation. TB called a couple of times, angry that they were not even reporting Neill's view that we had done nothing wrong. He said we needed to get it on to the issue of party funding generally. My own view was we had no option but to get out that it was £1m but Ecclestone was opposed to that and Jonathan said we had to wait until he agreed. It was beginning to look and feel worse. TB first agreed we should get out the figure but changed his mind after speaking to Peter M. I felt we could only get on to the front foot once the air was cleared. I felt the whole strategy had failed, badly. TB rightly said this was bad for him and his reputation. I said there would obviously have to be a closer look at state funding if donations like this were not acceptable.

Donald [Dewar] was brilliant on the *Today* programme but hadn't wanted to do more, so we got Jack S up who was fine. At the 11, I also dropped hints that we had wanted to disclose the sum but Ecclestone didn't. As we left for the CBI, TB was still dithering and fretting about it. We were taking a big hit particularly in the *Sun*. Irwin Stelzer had done a big attack and TB wanted GB to respond to it. GB wanted TB to do it. Ridiculous. GB called and tried to get me to get TB to do it. Jonathan said GB had a big smile on his face over the F1 story. It was not that big on the lunchtimes again though *World at One* devoted half the programme to it. By the time we got back I said that we had to get Ecclestone to agree to announce the sum involved, and Jonathan did so. Then Peter M persuaded TB back in the wrong direction again. Then at 3.30 Jack Straw was told on Radio 5 Live that Ecclestone had confirmed it was a million, so I set off for the four o'clock and 'announced' it and again defended the policy. It wasn't easy. I could see on their faces they were thinking, God knows

November '97: TB dithers about disclosing donation

how they thought they would get away with this. David Hughes [*Mail*] was asking if it was credible GB didn't know the sum, as he claimed on the *Today* programme yesterday. I got back for a meeting on the tobacco policy itself. TB was looking tired. He was taking a real hit and there was a problem with his mindset, in that he was thinking he could do no wrong, and that people would therefore not assume he could do any wrong on issues like this. But in part because of the way we had handled it, it looked like he had done something wrong. We had made a big mistake in not going up-front, but he would not admit it. Dennis Skinner [veteran left-wing Labour MP] called and said we had to have something big to announce at PMQs tomorrow, or else it would all be funding. I got home for *Newsnight*, which was awful. His reputation was damaged by this. So was our reputation as effective managers of the news, and I was pissed off at that too. We had taken the wrong course and we were getting whacked.

Wednesday, November 12

Tobacco/F1 had been running for a week now. The £1m was big in the papers and we were looking shifty and shabby. We agreed the tough questions were: why didn't we refer to Neill until it was clear the media were looking into it, and what was the policymaking process? I'd got Bevins to do the story re Hague pushing for a knighthood for Ecclestone and that was running a bit.

TB felt Hague would go [at PMQs] on how the policy was made. It was clear Hague was terrified of going on the funding issue, and instead went on the other sports being excluded. This meant most people felt he had done badly, and you could sense the disappointment among the hacks afterwards. We also had put together the terms of reference for Neill's inquiry and he was clearly going to be trouble. This was a real fiasco unfolding now and it was all so avoidable.

PMQs was fine until Martin Bell [independent MP, former BBC journalist] got up and had a go, to pretty devastating effect. But at the 4, though the questions kept coming, I sensed interest among some of them beginning to wane. But I was really not enjoying this at all. I felt things were on the mend a little until on the way home I got a call from David H that Phil Webster had got hold of the Neill letter, presumably through a Tory MP, which made clear there was an offer of a second donation after the election. I told Jonathan and TB, who went straight into head-in-sand mode. 'How can that be a story, that there was not a donation? This is getting absurd.' He was blaming everyone – Michael [Levy] for getting Bernie in, Jonathan on the policy, Jonathan for having a baby – Jonathan and I fell about on that one – and GB for persuading him it was the wrong thing to get all the facts out early. I said I blamed him for being persuaded. TB had wanted to pay the money back straight off, but didn't follow his instinct. I had wanted to brief straight away, but he was talked out of it. GB had started off agreeing with me, then changed his mind and with Peter's help changed Tony's. Then day after day we were forced to reveal more and more, look like we had more and more to hide. It was a disaster and getting worse and worse as the days wore on.

The *Times* story guaranteed another horrible day tomorrow and another sleepless night thinking about it. I was also getting a bit alarmed that TB was becoming a bit remote from real life, couldn't really see that people would be shocked by this, and also a bit obsessed with himself. He said I wasn't sleeping because I was worried this was affecting him and his integrity. I said no, I'm not sleeping because I hate saying things I don't believe. I had overdosed on bullshit on this one and was totally fed up with it.

Thursday, November 13

Gallows humour was starting to come into the conversation. I was desperate to move things on, but this was the only story in town and we were handling it badly. At yet another meeting on it, I argued for openness. I also thought we should say we had made mistakes in the handling of it. Again, TB and GB were against on both fronts. He left the room and said to me and Jonathan 'Get it sorted out before Cabinet.' Unbelievable. Peter M came down. I wanted to do a mix of saying the second offer was not agreed, and a bit of an apology for not being more up-front. TB disagreed. Ditto GB. Then in Cabinet Jonathan sent me a note via TB, from Butler, suggesting how we might now handle it. This was useless. TB was just hearing what the last person said now, and it happened to be Robin sitting next to him. I re-read the paper I had done last week. It was right then and it was the right approach now. If we had done it, we would have taken a hit that day, a hit over the weekend, but we would have won on points on openness and been far better placed to defend the policy. Instead of which it was being dragged out of us and we looked awful.

Another dreadful eleven o'clock that went on and on and on. It all revolved around the second donation and I went on the attack, said it was one thing to be attacked for taking money, it was another to be attacked for giving it back, but it was quite something to be attacked for a donation we never took in the first place. But it was not fun. TB left for a memorial service and came back for lunch with Murdoch. We got him through the back door, where he ran into Mark Seddon [editor of the left-wing journal *Tribune*] of all people. I said to TB we had handled things badly and had to learn from it. He said the mistake was taking the donation. The rest had been fine. This was balls, total balls. He was blaming everyone but himself.

Then to a meeting with Peter M, Butler, Mountfield and Jan Polley [Butler's private secretary] re the new strategy unit. I thought it could be headed by a special adviser. They clearly wanted it in Downing St, working jointly to me and Peter M. Peter wanted it in the Cabinet Office. I set out why I thought we needed it and what I wanted it to do, while they gave me reasons why they thought it wouldn't work. It was crazy that we had no central co-ordinating unit like this, but I sensed the department could be tricky, and Peter would see it as a piece of possible empire-building. I was sure we had to have it, and it had to be in Number 10. Then Peter and I left for Derry's office to meet him and GB. TB had asked Derry to work up a strategy re donations. Derry knew the full background re me wanting to do it last week, and GB talking TB out of it. He said to GB, I don't know what you think Gordon, but I think the handling of all this has been idiotic. He had met Pat Neill earlier and agreed we had to come clean about the whole episode, and all aspects of it, including the figures of the second donation. These were in letters from Levy to David Ward [Ecclestone contact and former aide to John Smith]. There was a problem in that they contradicted what we had been saying to now. I felt sick. I said I would have to go up and say I had misled them because I had not been in full possession of the facts. I sensed this was the only way out of this now. I then spoke to Jonathan who said TB was against that course of action. What a fucking mess. I felt totally wretched about the whole thing, and felt strongly TB was to blame for this. Derry was also adamant we should be more open. 'How the fuck have we managed to bugger what is actually a good case?' he said. Then came the news that Ecclestone told the *Mirror* he never offered a second donation.

Friday, November 14

This nightmare would not go away. Every time we thought we were through it, something else would come up and hit us. It was one whole week since I wrote a memo that, if we had followed it, would have put things in better shape. TB called around 8 as he was heading north. I said what I thought of it all, and he said I should not get myself into such a state, as we would tough it through. I said I had done nothing else but tough it through. I said we were in a problem entirely of our own making and we had badly handled virtually every move to get out of it.

At various points through the day, I said to him I did not feel confident he was learning lessons from the mistakes we'd made. Nor did I feel GB could be trusted on this. I was still unconvinced he had followed his own judgement in persuading TB not to back his. I listened in to their call and it was nauseating. 'Oh I really feel for you on this, Tony, it must be awful to be attacked like this when you've done nothing wrong.' It all sounded so insincere. Added to which, to my amazement, there was a line in the *Guardian* today that GB had been 'out of the loop'! The same man who had been largely responsible for the mistake – both of not being open and of referring to Neill. Why the fuck did we listen to him? TB did not believe GB was being deliberately malign. I was not so sure.

GB said he was putting together a plan to get a line drawn under it but as far as I was concerned, he was busted on this. Derry called. He was still keen we publish all the facts, everything we know. He was worried TB was believing his own propaganda on this. I went over to his office to review the situation. We gave the right advice, he said, and he ignored it. Derry felt the problem was the way TB worked, the decision-making process, a lack of clarity. He could not believe how badly we had fucked it up. He wanted a proper meeting where we could go through the whole process and work out where mistakes were made and why.

Talking to Fiona later, I said I felt pretty disillusioned. I had been evasive too often on this, didn't feel comfortable with our version of events and all for what – so TB could not change and keep making the same kind of mistakes. I was close to the end of my tether on it. I was not getting enough time for the kids. I felt inside Number 10 that I was having to make too many decisions others should be making, and generally I had too much to do. I felt down, was not sure it was all worth it and I knew there was another weekend from hell ahead of us. Derry called again and said he intended to have a very heavy conversation with TB tomorrow. 'He thinks he's invincible. It happened to Thatcher after ten years. It's happened to Tony after six months!'

Saturday, November 15

It all started the minute I woke up. The papers were grim and the phones started early. It was now part of the legend that we were pro smoking, despite my efforts to avert that yesterday. TB said he felt we would only be able to draw a line if he went up on it. We talked about it several times over the next few hours, and agreed that was the thing to do. The question was what format and after some discussion, we settled on *On the Record*, live. I also put together a briefing for the Sundays, both to announce the interview but also indicate the tone – that we had made mistakes, now intended to try to turn to our advantage and get party funding sorted out.

Later TB called me and said 'I'm really sorry about all this. You have taken a lot of the heat on it and I really do apologise. It has been awful.' TB had the idea of saying we would publish all donors from the last five years if the other parties did the same. The problem was we were in government and they weren't and nobody really cared about the other parties. I said to TB I was really fed up. I had done nothing but deal with this, with precious little support, for days now and I was sick of it. He asked me to go down to Chequers and stay there overnight so we could talk it over and prepare for the interview. Calum was really upset at me leaving, probably in part because I had just told him Ellie [Merritt, daughter of John] was ill [with leukaemia]. TB apologised again for the misery of the past fortnight. We were up till half twelve going over the difficult questions. We had the answers but I was more worried he would not learn anything from this. Cherie said he would. He had obviously told her how pissed off I was because she came in and gave me a big kiss and said he knew he had handled it badly and should have listened to me and Derry last week, because the advice given by GB had been wrong.

Sunday, November 16

I got up just after 6 and went for a swim, then to breakfast with TB. Derry came down to help go through the tough questions again. He said TB's mistake was to think we could spin our way out of anything. This was a straightforward claim of malpractice, he said, for which we needed legal not media minds. He was at his most overbearing, but he was right, and had been from the start on this. The setting for *On the Record* looked fine, though his make-up was a bit odd. I said he had to reconnect on the basis of trust, make clear he was the same person they elected. TB did well on tone, and on fact. I watched it in the lounge with Cherie's mum. He was especially strong towards the end. The weakness for me was that we were apologising for the handling of it, rather than what we did, which made it seem like it was only about presentation. [John] Humphrys was full of himself and I was probably a bit too rude to him, but he was so up himself it was hard not to be. Over lunch, CB and I both emphasised to TB he had to change his modus operandi and learn lessons from this, get proper decision-making structures. TB said there had been a failure of decisiveness on his part, both on the policy and on handling. I said I was fed up with all of them and he said 'You love me really though,' and laughed. The problem had been lack of precision and lack of candour.

Monday, November 17

The papers were about as good as we could have hoped for. There was a feeling that a line was being drawn under it. Though the eleven o'clock was another seminar on the subject, I felt the heat had gone out of it. Jonathan and I were getting it in the neck a bit in the press, which pissed me off and I made sure one or two people knew we had been pressing for openness. There was another reference in the *Guardian* to GB not having been fully briefed. TB was pretty contrite and at a meeting with Robin Butler, Jonathan, JH and me, he said to Robin – what lessons do you think we should learn from this? It was a great opportunity for Robin to have a go at Jonathan, re his view that the same person cannot be doorkeeper for party and government. He said that if he was being frank, he felt that the meeting with Ecclestone should never have happened. And then, in a real dig at Jonathan, that if Alex Allan had been there, it would not have done. I'm not sure that was accurate but it was quite a dig.

I had lunch with Mike Brunson at the Oxford and Cambridge. Though I like Mike, I can't for the life of me understand why people like eating in these ghastly Pall Mall clubs. He was arguing in favour of keeping the lobby pretty much as is. I said that wasn't a runner. It had to change and it should benefit not hinder the broadcasters. I worked on the new GIS draft, which was a lot better now. At the MIO, I admitted the last week was a shambles, but let them know the press advice had been ignored.

I went to see Lindsay [Nicholson, widow of John Merritt] and Ellie at Great Ormond Street and the moment I saw Lindsay, I just burst into tears. You just cannot fathom cruelty like this. Ellie had the same leukaemia as John. When the doctors were talking, and trying to be reassuring, I picked up on some of the words they used to say to him. So did Ellie. She was a real mix of strength and vulnerability, the same as he had been. I don't know how Lindsay can cope with this, but she is doing fine. I said all the things I could think of saying, but you feel totally useless. I managed to sort out proper access to a phone for her, and then left for home. I walked all the way, crying most of the way, and getting angry.

Tuesday, November 18

The smoking story was just about dying away. The big story was rising [NHS] waiting lists. Dobson was on the radio and was asked three times if he supported the exemption of Formula One and three times refused to answer. I called him before his 10am press conference and said he had to support the policy. Peter M asked for advice on a speech he was making tomorrow and I suggested we use it for another 'lessons will be learned' message. TB was meeting Trimble and more focused on that now. We had the final meeting of the GIS review group before the report was sent to Butler and then to TB. It was in far better shape and I felt most of the major changes we needed were now in there. In truth though it would require a change of culture which would be a lot harder to bring about. I went home early to see Calum at football and then went with a school trip to Arsenal vs Coventry. It was really dull, Arsenal winning 1-0 after extra time.

Wednesday, November 19

There was a classic piece of GB-ery in the *Guardian*, leftist gesture bollocks about the need to fill the Bank of England with trade unionists and women. GB denied to TB he had anything to do with it. What was laughable was that he pumped this stuff into one paper, as if the other papers didn't notice, while he went round giving them a different kind of message. At the 9.30 meeting in the flat, TB was angry at Derry raising the future donations in front of everyone else, as he kept pressing for total disclosure. He said the longer we waited, the more damage was likely to be done when the Levy letters finally came out. TB said if he was asked direct, he would answer, but he felt we had taken enough hits on this. If Hague went on funding, the second-donation notion was the only worry we had. TB had now taken to staying up in the flat on Questions day, working on his own a lot, calling us up as and when.

The eleven o'clock was pretty good-natured and I did a big push on the jobs summit. Hilary did me a briefing note on the Queen/ Philip's fiftieth-anniversary banquet which was called 'the People's Banquet' once we went through the kind of 'ordinary people' going to it. The main focus at PMQs was the letter to Hague and Paddy suggesting donations back to 1992 were referred in confidence to Neill. Paddy wrote back straight away. Hague did not. TB was on better form than recently. Hague was useless.

At the four o'clock, I pushed hard on the need for Neill to get into the bigger funding picture, though he was apparently pissed off at the way it was coming over that we were making this proposal together. Peter M's speech was being seen as an attack on me, which was pretty amazing considering I had helped him write it. TB and I worked on the speech for the golden wedding tomorrow. His instinct was to make it quite personal and I spoke to Fellowes to check they were up for that, which they were. FM and I saw Cherie and we agreed that she should wear a hat. PG had said that she was being mentioned negatively in groups at the moment.

Thursday, November 20

I got in early and TB was already working on his speech on the Queen. He took these big Establishment events seriously, and also knew that he was always on the at-risk register with them, as people were always so ready to criticise the politicians by comparison with Her Maj. There was a lot of interest at the 11 in the people attending the banquet, and again they were probing on how much of the planning was ours and how much the Palace's. Cabinet had been brought forward to 9.30 and was mainly George Robertson reporting on Iraq and GB going over the general approach for the pre-Budget report. He did not like it when TB summed up the discussion.

TB went off to the Abbey, then back for a meeting on the jobs summit, then hanging around waiting for the Queen and the Duke to arrive. They got some nice pictures out in the street. As they came through the door, TB said he was surprised that even with the Queen, the photographers showed no respect at all, just yelling out at her like she was a singer or something. The staff had lined up and TB took the Queen on a little tour. She stopped for a chat with Alison [Blackshaw], who was beaming. The walkabout went well, though TB was maybe a bit too enthusiastic and should have hung back more. Also, Geoff Crawford and I were in the shot far too much when I watched the news later. I went back for an office meeting, then we set off for Luxembourg, getting TB fully briefed on the jobs stuff on the plane.

Friday, November 21

TB's dad had had a mild stroke and his speech was badly affected, so TB was a bit distracted about that. The by-election results were extraordinary. Winchester, Tories wiped out, and we almost won Beckenham. We had a working breakfast, then set off for the summit. As we arrived, and I was on my way to a briefing, Tim called to say Temple-Morris had had the whip removed. Jonathan and I both spoke to him, and said it was a bonkers message to give to the public. Temple-Morris said he intended to sit on our side, as an independent.

I said I'm sure he would be made welcome. I said there would be no problem if he went straight over, all the way, though I could see why he would be worried about that. 'They are doing my job for me,' he said, 'establishing the conditions to do that.' We agreed that we should both be briefing that Europe, constitutional reform and social policy were driving him out of the Tory Party.

I did a second desultory briefing later in the day, and then had a kip in the office. I got TB out to do a quick interview with Oakley but there was little news content in it, and they all looked bored with the whole summit. TB and Bertie Ahern had a bilateral, BA briefing on his meeting with Trimble, which he felt went well. He felt we should be removing more troops [from Northern Ireland]. TB said he was agitating on that the whole time but he had to listen to what the security people were saying. When the summit wound up, TB's press conference was attended by a fifth of what we normally get. We were all a bit tired at the moment and not firing. TB was being leant on by David M, Jonathan and others against the idea of extra money for fuel bills for pensioners, but TB and I were both keen. He said the problem was that such were the tensions between Number 10 and the Treasury that people assumed if it was their idea, it was a bad one, or at least being done for the wrong reasons. It was a good idea and we should support it.

Saturday, November 22
TB did his usual, telling me I really must have a quiet weekend, and then phoning the whole time, usually with something that would require me to do something else. He was worried about Robert Earl [restaurant entrepreneur], as we were announcing his £1m donation. We went to see Wimbledon vs Man Utd and had a good chat with Alex about things. He had been out of the country for part of it, but said he had no sense that people were talking about this funding business the same as the media were.

Sunday, November 23
It was quiet on the work front, a bit of mopping up on funding, discussing the idea of Ecclestone giving the money to a cancer charity, and the *Record* were chasing some line from *Scotland on Sunday* about drugs and a Cabinet minister. I went to see Lindsay and Ellie, and Tessa came. It was amazing, and a bit scary, how quickly people settled into the idea of being seriously ill. I suppose they had no choice but Lindsay seemed fairly on top of things and Ellie was incredible, very calm and just wanted me to read to her.

Monday, November 24

Virtually the whole day was taken up dealing with Humphrey the [Downing Street] cat, because it was being put around that because CB didn't like cats, we had done away with it. Alan Clark, knowing I hated cats too, also got stuck in. It was raised at the 11, and I could tell that Brunson wanted to go big on it, and it made the lunchtimes. 'Is Humphrey alive?' I asked Hilary to set up a photocall in Bromley, and we had the ludicrous situation of me and the Cabinet Secretary both having to spend a large part of our day dealing with it. The bloody thing was retired in Surrey, and a bit old now, and Robin B wanted to be sure we would not be bringing any undue stress or attention on his new owner.

In between times, I took the chance to make the case for the kind of strategy unit I wanted. TB discussed it with Robin B too, and made clear he wanted it in Number 10, reporting to me, not in the Cabinet Office under Peter M, because he did not want it to be seen as part of a fiefdom. I explained briefings would be on the record but not for filming and I didn't want to be named, but described as the official spokesman. There was a statement on the jobs summit and I organised for Temple-Morris to sit on our side. TB was saying we would have to get a new cat, because there would be a section of the public up in arms, some believing we had killed the damn thing, and others appalled we hadn't replaced him.

I had to go to another dreadful honours list meeting where Butler was adamant it was a good list and felt the popular side of things should be met because [Crewe Alexandra FC manager] Dario Gradi (about whom he seemed to know not much at all) had got one, and so had his local lollipop lady. The honours business brought out the worst in me, and in the people who defended it. I'd always thought it an absurd system, which just reinforced stereotypes, and I thought it even more now.

Tuesday, November 25

The main story from our world was Humphrey. Thankfully it was pre-Budget statement day and GB would take over pretty quickly. TB was meant to see reps from the sports affected by the tobacco advertising ban, and that was going to be the main focus media-wise for TB today. They were more reasonable than I thought they would be. In fact they were positively friendly, welcoming the fact we had said we would work with industry to get alternative sponsorship. The other problem, conveyed to TB in a letter from Neill, was the claim that Levy and Jonathan solicited cash and that TB said he would intervene to help them get other forms of sponsorship. The eleven o'clock was back to being all about this again and I was in a foul mood.

I went over to the House with TB. GB was excellent, did the big picture well and hit the right notes on pensioners, childcare, energy efficiency. It went really well. I did the briefing afterwards with Peter Curwen [Treasury] and Charlie W, and didn't feel they were on top of the detail sufficiently. PG called, said he was worried TB was becoming a bit disengaged. GB was too dominant on domestic policy. He had also got away from the F1 shambles scot-free, because we did not play dirty, even though he had been as responsible as anyone for making it go wrong. In the run-up to today, Ed Balls and CW had been fairly open, up to a point, but GB was pretty offhand with TB, who pretty much let him get on with it. The private office were getting pretty frustrated at the modus operandi though.

Harriet Harman called in a panic about the *Indy on Sunday* because they were reporting that she had threatened to injunct (though they didn't name her). She was now being chased by the *Record*, no doubt encouraged by the *IoS*. She said the story being put out – that she went to a party and bought cannabis – was untrue. She was writing to Rosie Boycott [*Independent on Sunday* editor] to say the story was not true but was not answering questions about whether she had ever taken cannabis – which she had.[1] She said her children were barely speaking to her because of it all.

Wednesday, November 26

GB got a good press and had been working hard at image-building, which had paid off. There were a number of pieces suggesting GB was the real radical, TB the presidential figure, GB the real power in the land. TB felt as long as we were doing the right things as a government, he could live with it. But Jonathan, David M and Sally M all felt it had moved to a different level. They were worried about Nick Brown too, that he was operating factionally, that he had been encouraging people to stir up the lone-parent issue [many Labour MPs revolted over cutbacks in lone-parent benefits], and giving out signs that fox hunting could yet be given a go by the government. TB was getting very pissed off that too many of us, but especially Jonathan, were gabbing too much about GB in front of civil servants, and fuelling a sense that GB was rolling TB over.

[1] In July 2007 Harman was one of ten Cabinet members who admitted to using cannabis in their youth. She told the BBC and the *Daily Mail* that she had used the drug when studying at York University.

TB said it was a good thing if the Chancellor got a good press, and we should all welcome it. Both Philip and Peter Hyman felt, however, that he was getting it at TB's expense, and deliberately so. TB was not persuaded. He said to me later he was aware GB was motoring but so what? It was good that we had big figures in the government, that we were not seen as a one-man band. I spoke to Charlie W at the *Spectator* Parliamentarian of the Year (which GB won) and said we had to get pieces done on the relationship being a strength for the government. We would have to work at it, because the press were attuned to the TB/GB wedge-driving story.

TB was on good form at PMQs, which he easily won, and said afterwards he felt he was getting the measure of Hague. I felt it was his best yet, and the troops were up afterwards. Hunting was picking up as a problem and Nick Brown was apparently suggesting it could be done as an amendment to the Criminal Justice Bill. I knew TB would not want it, and so did NB. There were a lot of issues with the potential to go wrong at the moment – coal, single parents, welfare reform. The press was still OK-ish but it could get quite rocky quite quickly.

Thursday, November 27

I was going down into a tired and depressed phase, feeling over-worked, and underperforming, and getting ratty with people around me. Mountfield was the main thing for me today. TB briefed the Cabinet on it, emphasising there should be proper interchange between policy and presentation. Clare Short piped up against a co-ordinating strategy unit, and when TB said Number 10 had the smallest press office in Whitehall, she made some crack about how the others were all extensions. On the changes re the briefings, TB said 'At least when it's Alastair, people will know it's Alastair,' and everyone fell about. 'I don't think we ever doubted it, Tony,' said Jack C.

Cabinet started with David Clark on the switch to a new millennium and the potential problems re computers etc. and the so-called millennium bug. There was a good post-Budget statement discussion which had a bit of politics in it. TB said the Tories looked shot yesterday. We had the opportunity for real economic definition, as well as modernisation and fairness. He said we were still in the period of post-euphoria, but pre-delivery of what people want. Clare S had another go, saying they did not discuss things collectively. She said she didn't feel involved in the big decisions. Thank God for that.

At the eleven o'clock, I was taking the piss out of them being more interested in stories about themselves – i.e. Mountfield – than they were in stories about their readers and viewers. It was true. There were a stack of crews outside filming the hacks arriving. In his 6.30 two-way on *Today*, John Pienaar said on the radio I was a 'cult figure' to people interested in government-media relations. It was fucking ridiculous. Nick Jones [BBC] went on and said, wrongly, that I would be identified by name doing the briefings. Even without it, as the prime minister's official spokesman I was going to have to be even more careful what I said and how I said it. I was actually quite nervous about it now that we had got the changes agreed.

I got back for a meeting on coal, which was becoming a big problem. We were going to get the blame for lost jobs. Then to a meeting on the tobacco directive. TB was impressed at the way Tessa was dealing with it. After the PQ [Parliamentary Question] on Mountfield was published, I went to the four o'clock and we put a tape and mike on the table. Mike White [*Guardian* political editor] was chairing and said he was not sure about it and we would need to discuss the implications. He made a joke about only speaking into microphones for money. We had an office meeting to go over lessons re EMU and Ecclestone. Both Anji and I emphasised the need not to play into the TB/GB wedge-driving. They had worked the way they did for some time, and though it could be frustrating, it had worked pretty well up to now. I made the point that any thinking time seemed to get driven out of the diary. There were too many meetings which were there as furniture rather than as part of a plan. If we were not careful, he and the rest of us would be run ragged. At the moment, the weekend was the only time he really got to think a little.

TB said later he was getting very pissed off at the obvious briefing from our end about GB. I said there were too many people talking to the press, often without even realising they were being used. We got select committee reports savaging us over tobacco. The Department of Health said Tessa should not go up. I called Tessa and said she should, and she should show balls of steel. To be fair, she did.

Friday, November 28

The Mountfield coverage was low-key and fine. I was up at 6 to leave for Number 10, then set off for Bosnia. Hunting [bill] was to be the main story of the day and nobody really suggested TB was avoiding the vote deliberately. But he was going through one of his 'not sure' moods as we drove to the airport. He told me that GB had suggested he, Tony, reply to the letter from MPs on benefit cuts. In other words, get TB more closely associated with the bad while he, GB, took the credit for anything good happening in the economy or public spending. I'd worked on Don Macintyre [*Independent*] re TB/GB and he did a good piece which would probably stop things for a while.

Both TB and GB felt Butler and [Terry] Burns were winding this up and they had to get the message that they had to get used to TB/GB's ways of working. CB was taking a hit for defending a rapist who wanted to sue a harassee for libel. On the flight, [General Sir] Charles Guthrie [Chief of the Defence Staff] briefed TB on the difficulties of going after indicted war criminals in Bosnia. I liked him. Of all the posh Establishment figures so far, he was the one with the most natural empathy and humour, and he was clearly a pretty hard bastard to boot. He told me later he thought TB was 'sound as a bell', that he liked George R, that [Lord] John Gilbert [minister for defence procurement] was 'more right wing than anyone I've ever met', and he said ministers went white whenever I paged them. He said it was an important part of TB's writ running, because ministers jumped to attention, and that meant their private offices did too.

He was ex-SAS, very witty. I suggested he do a toned-down version of the briefing for the press on the plane, which he did, and he did it well. There was no real story for the visit, other than the fact of it, and John Sergeant [BBC] decided straight away: 'War criminals – that's the story.' The media pressed all day for TB to do something on hunting, but he refused despite their blandishments. We'd had various options planned for the visit and because of the weather we had to go for the one with the least flying around. TB met Biljana Plavsic [President of the Serb Republic] at the airport, then we set off to a metal factory to meet the troops.

The broadcasters did their pieces to camera then we flew to Sarajevo. We met the SFOR [Stabilisation Force in Bosnia and Herzegovina] top brass, General [Sir Roddy] Cordy-Simpson and a US four-star general [Eric Shinseki]. They were clearly planning on staying beyond the July date for leaving. The place was very drab and dingy, with a post-Stalinist feel to it, though it was not hard to see how beautiful it might have looked if peaceful and prosperous. We visited the marketplace that had been hit by a mortar. The troops seemed to go down well with the public as we travelled about. There was some sullenness but a fair bit of warmth too. TB did a couple of little off-the-cuff speeches to the troops, which went fine. We visited the war cemetery, but it was all a bit of a scrum, then to a meeting with the three-man presidency, and you could feel the hatreds, particularly for the Serbs. It symbolised how difficult this was going to be.

On the flight back, I chatted to Guthrie about the way the government functioned. He was totally supportive re the GIS changes, said the place needed a shake-up. He said the MoD sensed they had an ally in TB. TB went to talk to the press and was there so long I left him to it, and when he came back we went through all the times he had inadvertently dropped stories to the press on planes. I drafted a briefing note on the latest Sinn Fein delegation coming on December 11, and went through it with Mo as soon as we landed. TB said I must have a rest this weekend. I said don't phone me then. I was feeling really stressed out at the moment and at home Fiona and I had a dreadful row. It started on hunting, but it could have been anything.

Saturday, November 29

Fiona and I weren't speaking. It was a quiet day work-wise, apart from briefing on the December 11 Adams meeting. I briefed my SF note in two separate conference calls, one for the press, one for the broadcasters. It was pretty rich and was leading the news within minutes. And that was without even getting reaction from the Unionists, which duly came – anger, fury, outrage etc. The Tories piled in as well, said it was provocative. But TB was clear we had to press on and maintain momentum, and that he did not want to be in a position, if the talks collapsed, where the IRA could say they were never given the chance to come in.

I had a bad cold but went out most of the afternoon with Calum on the heath. The phone went mainly re Ireland. Charlie called about an *Indy on Sunday* story re Geoffrey Robinson's offshore trust. The *Mail on Sunday* had a story re GB overruling TB on royal tax avoidance. I called CW and said it better not have come from him. He denied it as ever. It was all adding to the idea of GB the mover and groover and TB the figurehead.

Sunday, November 30

TB called from Chequers. He'd had dinner there last night with Elton John and others. Levy was there and he was interrupted by Tim [Allan], sending through questions put by *World in Action* for their investigation into funding. It threw Michael into a spin, and he duly threw TB into a spin. I said to TB he should speak to Hague because Andrew MacKay [Shadow Northern Ireland Secretary] was very anti the Adams meeting, and we should try to defuse the politics on it. He said he had to speak to him on a security matter anyway, so would also raise Adams.

He was unfazed re the GB stuff, and felt we were in better shape than I thought. GB called to say he had nothing to do with the *Mail* story, and also that I might have to defend Geoffrey. We went round to see Lindsay and try to cheer her up a bit before tomorrow, when Ellie was getting chemotherapy. She was amazing, considering, but God knows what she is feeling.

Monday, December 1

The Times splashed on suggestions that the government was thinking of a U-turn on single-parent benefit changes. Having spoken to TB, and then to CW travelling with GB in Brussels, we agreed to stick very robustly to the line, which I did at the eleven o'clock. There was also a lot of Geoffrey Robinson in the papers and I had to defend him pretty robustly too. Coal was also rumbling and I had to be pretty robust on that too, saying they should start asking questions of the [Sir Richard] Budge people and not just us [RJB Mining, owned by the Budge family, was poised to close mines and make thousands of miners redundant]. The *Guardian* splashed on the electoral commission [set up to study voting reform, chaired by Liberal Democrat Lord Jenkins] and all day we had the Libs on our back, wanting this pushed as the most exciting thing since the last most exciting thing. They wanted TB to make a statement on it. I told Sean O'Grady [Lib Dem press office] he would not be, and that we would be handling it very low-key. They were not happy. They were briefing that TB had an open mind on PR, and I told them not to brief what TB's mind was, because they didn't know.

Tessa came round for a meeting to plan how we handled Thursday's [European Commission] meeting on Formula One. We had to make sure nobody was surprised when we went for a derogation rather than an exception. She was holding up pretty well. A lot was going to depend on how the other countries felt and we put together a plan for who dealt with which. TB saw Peter Riddell and did a good job on the big picture, which I tried to push at the MIO meeting. Mountfield seemed to have gone down pretty well with them. But I emphasised you could have all the systems you wanted. People had to make them work, and they had to make sure they were properly integrated in the policy process. The press seemed to be adapting easily to the changes re briefing.

Fiona told me Cherie had submitted a bill to the Cabinet Office for a new bin, because she wanted to make them understand how ludicrous the rules were under which she was having to operate. She'd also sent a handwritten note to Butler saying he should look at Kathryn's mattress, and would see it needed replacing. We had a new Derry problem later on. He had given a speech to the Reform Club political committee in October which for some reason he had given to Frances Gibb of *The Times* to present as an interview. That was bizarre enough, but it had a line in it comparing himself to Cardinal Wolsey [Henry VIII's Lord Chancellor] which would set off the next rash of anti-Derry articles. GB was in Brussels, raising the stakes by saying we had to be in Euro X [committee to co-ordinate economic policy in the eurozone].

Tuesday, December 2

JP was doing his council tax statement and GB was launching ISAs.[1] The Treasury ignored our advice and Robinson launched it. The *Standard* splashed on 750,000 people to be hit by it. It was not dealt with quickly enough and it stuck. It led to another shouting match with Whelan because I had protested on Wednesday at the way they were handling the build-up to it. TB was getting more and more worried about it as the day wore on. They had not worked out a proper communications plan on it, and didn't want to be helped. They had a totally skewed idea of what constituted rich. Also Geoffrey Robinson was very loose in his language on it, talking about the well off doing well out of PEPs.

Wednesday, December 3

We got a dreadful press on ISAs. Nobody from the Treasury came to the morning meeting so I fired off a letter to CW and Peter Curwen. I sent an even angrier one to Charlie later when Brunson said he had been the source of the 750,000 figure in the *Standard*. Charlie admitted he had taken his eye off the ball and had to tighten up. I said the problem was they tried to operate in secrecy. They didn't trust us. Fine, but then don't expect us to clear up after them. Of course TB was going to have to do just that at PMQs. We got in Geoffrey Robinson and Ed Balls. It became clear that the £50k tax relief ceiling only applied to PEPs and ten per cent of three million was 300,000 not 750,000. The press were saying it was a retrospective tax and we were having to deal with that too. I was livid at the cack-handed way they had handled it and said so. I felt a bit sorry for Peter Curwen because he was obviously having to do what he was told. They had let things fall between Treasury and Inland Revenue stalls.

TB got the facts together pretty quickly, and did fine at PMQs. He finally used the 'longest pee in history' line re the Libs [promise to fund substantial additional programmes via a 1p tax rate], which went down well on our side. The other thing was a moratorium on

[1] Individual Savings Accounts with special tax rules, replacing PEPs (Personal Equity Plans) and TESSAs (Tax-Exempt Special Savings Accounts).

gas-fired power stations pending the energy policy review. It was a bit Old Labour but with the miners in London and with the DTI select committee doing Budge and John Battle [energy minister] and others, it was fine. The initial strategy to turn the heat on Budge had not gone well but it was beginning to turn.

ISAs took up a lot of time. TB was appalled at the handling of it, though GB was claiming to him Charlie had nothing to do with the 750,000 figure. Both my briefings were dominated by ISAs, and the feeling was there was something odd about it, that it had not been worked through, and more people would be hit than they were admitting. I found myself having to defend their handling, which I knew had been woeful.

But the big story was BSE, a leaked SEAC [Spongiform Encephalopathy Advisory Committee] inquiry saying there was a risk to bone marrow in meat sold 'on the bone' like T-bone steaks. I spoke to Jack C re doing lunchtimes before a statement, saying he would have to square the Speaker. We went over the basic messages. Jack was always terrific under pressure, and able to work out quickly what we should do. It started OK but by the end of the day it was running badly, farmers angry etc.

Fiona and I had dinner with Blunkett at Orso's [restaurant in Covent Garden]. He was OK, but a bit stressed and obsessed with GB. He came up every few minutes. He said Gordon didn't understand children. He said 'Please tell Tony not to fall under a bus because the conventional wisdom if he did is that GB would be prime minister and he would be a disaster.' His main beef was GB's inability to work with people unless they were disciples. I had told DB by letter – because he had been complaining at our handling of Ecclestone – that GB vetoed the openness plan. He was raving about that too. I had a bizarre comment from [Sir] Richard Wilson [incoming Cabinet Secretary, replacing Robin Butler] earlier. 'As you are an important and powerful person, I would like you to be an ally.' Maybe it wasn't odd, but it was so brazen.

Thursday, December 4

BSE was massive in the press.[1] It had been decisive public health policy, but led to a lot of alarmist coverage. TB was not too happy

---

[1] Tony Blair and Jack Cunningham had announced a UK ban on beef on the bone, because of potential infectivity in bone marrow and dorsal root ganglia in older cattle. The advice of SEAC had been followed but provoked media hysteria.

but Jack [Cunningham] felt that having had the advice he'd had from the Chief Medical Officer, we really had no option. ISAs was still getting bad coverage. I saw Derry and said we were not that thrilled re the *Guardian* story that Alison [Irvine], helped by Christopher Farr [carpet retailer], was helping to tart up Number 10. I said I had to deny it, and he needed to be more careful post the row about the cost of the wallpaper in the official quarters. He ranted at me for a while but later bollocked Farr.

TB was looking tired, and too thin. A bit of weight had fallen off his face and he looked too gaunt. Having taken a succession of hits, we were all a bit tired and we were definitely lacking firepower at the centre. Philip came in to see me and said TB looked like someone not in control at the moment. TB kept insisting he was in command, consulting colleagues, but in reality he was finding it hard to keep on top of everything at the moment. We lacked capacity when the unexpected came up and hit us. He lacked people he could turn to, and feel reliant upon and confident in.

Cabinet kicked off with Ireland, but the meeting was totally dominated by beef. Jack C said he had to act on the advice and was confident the ban would not devastate the industry. We were talking about beef on the bone. But he said farm incomes were low and this will make them even angrier. Ron Davies said farmers felt that the UK was being harshly treated compared to other EU countries and the mood was getting angry. The protests were getting pretty heavy. I briefed the 11 we would be going for a proper BSE inquiry, and I sent Robin Butler into a tizz because it was still being discussed and he was worried we would have a Betty [Boothroyd] problem as she was on the rampage re announcements being made outside Parliament. It ran on the lunchtime news and I was potentially in a bit of trouble. I told Butler I had said nothing more than we had said before. Of course he didn't really want an inquiry at all, because the whole episode was a pretty sorry one, particularly inside MAFF which everyone knew had been hopeless for years. TB was growing more and more suspicious that Butler might be behind some of the 'government not collective enough' briefing that was going out. Dobbo also said he did not want to trail anything from the health White Paper in case Betty got angry.

Richard Wilson called round. He was very odd-looking, with huge great ears and a face that didn't quite map together. He seemed quite nervous and gabbled quite a lot. He was obviously making friends around the place pre Butler's departure. He repeated the line about me having enormous power and influence because I was so clearly so close to TB. He felt the Cabinet Office was not giving TB enough support, also that we used him too much publicly. He didn't seem naturally on our wavelength. 'Opposition must have been such fun.' Mmm. He thought the SCU [new Strategic Communications Unit] was all about 'news management', and when I tried to explain strategic communications, I don't think he got it. TB was seeing a number of journalists and was OK. But I felt he looked a bit diminished. He was down at the moment. Both of us were and neither seemed capable of lifting the other, which normally we could do. I said we had agreed to try to get him back on the domestic agenda but he was pretty much the whole time on foreign affairs, defence, Ireland. We also had a problem in that the wisdom had settled that we reacted too quickly on beef. I worked late because Tessa's negotiation on tobacco was coming to an end and we needed to work to get it in the right place media-wise. We got ourselves a 2006 cut-off, which was easily spun as a success. I put out TB words saying we were delighted that all our objectives had been secured.

Friday, December 5

The [British] European presidency launch was overshadowed by the continuing protests by beef farmers. The launch was well planned and worked fine. TB did a couple of video clips and one for [Labour peer and eminent scientist] Robert Winston's *This Is Your Life* before we set out for Waterloo, having agreed to do the launch at the station. In the car there, as ever he was mulling over where we were. I sensed he was going through his lowest phase yet. Ecclestone/EMU/tobacco/coal/lone parents/museums/hunting – a number of things had come together and just made the situation tough at the moment. Also, with the Tories useless, the press had pretty much decided to be the Opposition. There was a new and not very nice mood in the media and we just had to guard against it overly infecting the public.

We had the pre-meeting on a train by the platform where we were due to do the press conference. RC was very full of it, and clearly relishing the idea of the presidency. TB and I both emphasised we had to come at this from the standpoint of being good for Britain, not what was good for Europe. TB wanted to set it up as a challenge and a test, not a piece of PR flummery. Robin was on very good form. Jon Snow told me he thought he had gone totally FCO-native. But I felt he in many ways carried the launch day because he was confident and chirpy.

We got OK coverage but TB was mainly on with his warning to farmers to uphold the law. I did the Sunday lobby on the [new] Social

Exclusion Unit and then all afternoon interviewing for the Strategic Communications Unit. Some of them were total no-nos. Alun Evans [senior civil servant] was the only one who really seemed instinctively to get what the unit was designed for, and I felt he was the right man for it. There were one or two others who could make deputies.

Saturday, December 6
TB called early from Chequers. He said he had written Derry a private note saying he had to watch himself. He said Derry was a great man but he had two weaknesses: 1. he was incapable of hiding his arrogance, and 2. he did not understand the media and the need to work it properly. He said he was sure the current media mood was cyclical. They just go through phases when they think they should be doing the government in. Ian McCartney [DTI minister] called, said the *Indy on Sunday* were doing a story that he had threatened to resign over the minimum wage. He said it was true he was pissed off at the way it was being handled, but he had never resigned from anything in his life. Farmers were still the main story, plus the build-up to the rebellion on single parents on Wednesday. I took Calum out and about in the afternoon and bumped into lots of people, most of whom felt we were going through a rough patch.

Sunday, December 7
JP was on from Kyoto before he did *Frost* but generally it was a quiet day. PG sent me a very funny fax – 'Can't TB see it now? There is even a GB/cat story in the papers!!' It was [GB's fiancée] Sarah Macaulay's cat, Felix.

Monday, December 8
We did well press-wise out of the Social Exclusion Unit, though all tied up with the build-up to the vote on single-parent benefit on Wednesday. Also we had more questions being asked about Geoffrey Robinson after yesterday's *Observer* and *Sunday Times* had stories on the offshore trust. Peter Riddell had another very sniffy piece on PR froth. The single-parents change could hardly be seen as that. The trouble we were having was explaining it as something that fitted the kind of issue on which people elected us. But while it was offending the interest groups and the chatterati, there was a sense coming through that we were serious about welfare reform.

TB was looking tired. Fiona thought he was ill, and CB told her he had a bit of a turn on the tennis court, and that he hadn't slept at all well. We were also preparing the way for [Gerry] Adams' visit, with TB on Thursday planning to table the UK Heads of Agreement, with the Irish doing it separately, despite their being opposed to doing it that way. I went with him on the visit to Stockwell. I don't know what it was about cars, but the minute we got in, he always asked 'Where do you think we are then?' I felt we were OK-ish. TB was also getting more and more anxious re GB. 'I hope he's right on his economic strategy.' Channel 4 pre-record was fine, strong on single parents, and the Social Exclusion Unit, but his defence of Robinson was going to be the story. TB had another GB meeting later and although he was more on top of things than before, I was getting worried at how he looked, very tired, a bit yellow. I ran into Alan Clark, who said [Nicholas] Soames would give up his seat if we could get him the Paris embassy. Couldn't tell if he was joking.

Tuesday, December 9

The main annoyance first thing was the *Today* programme leading on a leak of the Freedom of Information White Paper, which we assumed was [David] Clark or his special adviser. TB asked Jonathan to complain to Clark, as I did to Barry Sutlieff [Cabinet Office press office], but they all denied having anything to do with it. He said the same when he apologised to the Speaker for the leak. I was in early for TB's meeting with [Jean-Claude] Juncker, at the end of which we agreed a briefing line on Euro X which got things going at the eleven o'clock. TB was insisting that Ecofin [Economic and Financial Affairs Council] was the main economic policy body, and that Euro X must have a seat for Britain. He said it was a big test for Britain in Europe. Juncker, who smoked too much, said there was no question of supplanting Ecofin, but on a practical level, nobody could prevent the 'ins' (members of the euro) from meeting if they wanted to. TB said we had to be fully involved in that. We should be there unless there is a specific reason not to be. TB did a quick ring-round of a few other leaders to make sure we had the right support.

I had a meeting with Keith Hellawell, the [newly appointed] drugs czar, and his deputy Mike Trace. I emphasised the need for them to establish a regional profile, and to have a clear sense of strategy. Hellawell was an effective communicator, though I was a bit suspicious of just how well groomed he was, not a hair out of place, a bit too manicured for my liking. They were a bit of an odd couple but it ought to work. I played up Euro X at the four o'clock, leading to Brunson doing a big number saying it could be TB's first big defeat in Europe. [Sir] Leon Brittan [former Conservative cabinet minister, vice president of the European Commission] told TB he would be lucky to secure it.

I went to the BBC party, which was the usual mix of media and politics. I had a nice chat with Ken Baker [former Conservative Cabinet minister], who said he thought TB was impressive. [Michael] Heseltine said we were still in the extended honeymoon period but it would end and we would find it hard after that. He said 'Look at all these people desperate to talk to you. But one day you'll be history and nobody will want to know.' Jill Dando [TV presenter] and I went down memory lane a bit re the *Breakfast Time* days. The feeling was very hostile on single parents. I was called out to speak to JP re the state of negotiations in Kyoto. He was in full flow, and I wasn't sure what all the details were, but he seemed confident we were heading to a deal we could support, and we had played a central role getting it.

Wednesday, December 10

A deal was close to being done at Kyoto and I was starting to talk up JP as a pivotal figure. We had been hoping to publish the Heads of Agreement on the NI talks, but couldn't in the end because of various difficulties with the Irish and the UUP, but there was growing interest in Adams' visit. I had words with Ed B and CW re the *FT* story which suggested we were going to cut the Swedes out of the deal on Euro X, which we weren't. Balls had briefed [Robert] Peston at GB's request. I told Charlie to stay clear of briefing on Euro X. Add that to a major [back bench] rebellion on single parents, and we were heading for a bad week. TB actually believed the policy was wrong and could have been changed without overdoing things on the spending front, but as ever GB's inflexibility got in the way of doing the right thing.

TB said all we could salvage from this was strength – the sense that we saw difficult things through, that we were tough on spending, tough on sticking to decisions, tough on backbenchers. It was the best of a bad job and though the media were enjoying our troubles, we just had to keep going and focus on the big picture. So we did, though it was not easy. I got in Alun Evans to see TB and he seemed to think he was OK, so I got going on finalising the SCU team.

TB did fine at PMQs, though it was tough, with plenty of boots going in. He had mapped out the big messages of reform and got them over. The one area he looked vulnerable was when he was challenged over it being punitive to women who want to work, he agreed with that, but couldn't say without dumping GB in it. He did not look at ease. Afterwards, before I went up to do the briefing, he said again – all we can get out of this is strength, the bloke is not for turning kind of thing. Afterwards we had a meeting with Nick Brown to discuss various grades of punishment, from yellow cards up, for the rebels. I got home to watch Juventus vs Man U, and news came through the rebellion was far bigger than expected [forty-seven Labour MPs voted against, one hundred abstained]. Then to cap it all, there was an IRA breakout from the Maze [prison]. TB called to ask whether I thought it meant we should cancel the Adams visit. I said no, don't be daft.

Thursday, December 11

The press were loving it, the rebellion plus abstentions both bigger than they had expected. GB went on at 7.30 and was excellent – tough, clear and giving a proper explanation. He said we had always faced up to opposition and won our case by argument, e.g. Clause 4, tough spending limits. I was due to go to [TB's former driver who had been killed in a road accident] Sylvie's funeral so I drafted two statements to be read out at the 11, one on the vote, with a very determined New Labour message, saying every MP was elected on a New Labour platform, and we were not rewriting the manifesto once the going got tough, and one on the meeting with Adams, which was likely to take over as the main story later in the day, defending TB for seeing him despite the risks.

On the way to the funeral, TB called Jospin, and was really digging in over Euro X. Jospin said he had made it a manifesto commitment to have Euro X as a counterweight to the Bank. TB said Jospin was a tough negotiator, and could be a hard, stubborn bastard. 'But then again so can I,' and he laughed. TB spoke really nicely at the funeral, and you could tell everyone was really touched he had gone. It was a really sad do, and her grandson Jack was distraught. On the drive back, he said how bad a hit was last night? I said bad. He said again the only thing to salvage is toughness, sticking to our guns, seeing through the difficult things as well as the easy ones.

Adams and his team arrived fifteen minutes early, and he did a little number in the street, where the media numbers were huge. This was a big moment, potentially historic in the progress it could lead to. They came inside and we kept them waiting while we went over what TB was due to say. Mo and Paul Murphy were both there and Mo was pretty fed up, feeling she was getting shit from all sides. They were hovering around the lifts and were summoned down to the Cabinet Room. We had agreed TB should be positive but firm. He actually came over as friendly, welcoming them individually as they came in. I shook McGuinness by the hand, who as he sat down said, fairly loudly, 'So this is the room where all the damage was done.' It was a classic moment where the different histories played out. Everyone on our side thought he was referring to the mortar attack on Major, and we were shocked. Yet it became obvious from their surprise at our shock that he was referring to policymaking down the years, and Britain's involvement in Ireland. 'No, no, I meant 1921,' he said.

I found McGuinness more impressive than Adams, who did the big statesman bit, and talked in grand historical sweeps, but McGuinness just made a point and battered it, and forced you to take it on board. Martin Ferris [Sinn Fein negotiator] was the most cold-eyed of the lot. He really did emanate a sense of menace. Mo slipped me a note saying he had a very bad history. Of the women, I could not work out whether they really mattered, or whether they just took them round with them to look a bit less hard. They were tough as boots all three of them. TB was good in the use of language and captured well the sense of history and occasion. He said we faced a choice of history – violence and despair, or peace and progress. We were all taking risks, but they are risks worth taking. He said to Adams he wanted to be able to look him in the eye, hear him say he was committed to peaceful means, and he wanted to believe him. I was eyeing their reaction to TB the whole time, and both Adams and McG regularly let a little smile cross their lips. Ferris was the one who just stared. Mo got pissed off, volubly, when they said she wasn't doing enough. TB was maybe not as firm as we had planned, but he did ask – which I decided not to brief, and knew they wouldn't – whether they would be able to sign up to a settlement that did not explicitly commit to a united Ireland. Adams was OK, but McGuinness was not. Adams said the prize of a lasting peace justifies the risks. Lloyd George, Balfour, Gladstone, Cromwell, they all thought they had answers of sorts. We want our answers to be the endgame. A cobbled-together agreement will not stand the test of time. He pushed hard on prisoners being released, and the aim of total demilitarisation, and TB just listened.

TB said he would not be a persuader for a united Ireland. The principle of consent was central to the process. Adams said if TB could not be a persuader, he could be a facilitator. He said we would be dead in forty years, but in the meantime this was the biggest test of TB's time in office, how he deals with the displaced citizens in a divided territory. A lot of people believed the armed struggle was legitimate. They have to be shown a different route to the same goal. There are two blocks – British policy, and the Unionist veto. He gave a series of history lessons on the way, including the industrial carve-up against the nationalists. McG was the more aggressive of the two, inside and outside. He said this was the most important meeting in seventy-five years, but it would pass quickly. There were things in our power we could do now, if we stopped the securocrats from stopping us. He said the next meeting has to be with Trimble and TB must encourage it. Mo mentioned an escaped prisoner. Adams said 'Good luck to him.' Mo snapped back 'That is not a very helpful comment.' But there were flashes of humour. Mo slipped me a note saying she found GA sexier than MMcG.

On the way out GA took TB to one side, and clearly wanted to be able to brief they had had a one-on-one session. All he said was 'Merry Christmas.' I said we needed to agree a briefing line. He said why don't we say we've agreed to withdrawal of all troops by February and a united Ireland by spring? Fine, I said, I like a good clear line. TB roared with laughter. They were clearly trying to hang around and, added to their early arrival, exaggerate the length of the talks. I'd already learned how much these things mattered in relation to their impact on the other side. The three women went to the loo, and our security people were getting antsy at how long they were in there, while Jonathan and I chatted to GA and McG re holidays and Christmas and kids and stuff. Vera Doyle [Irish messenger at Number 10] was on duty and came over to chat to them, and within seconds McG was charm itself, checking out where she came from and where she went on holiday. Vera was clearly a fan, but said to them as they left 'Now you two just behave, and help out our man here.'

TB had gone back to his office, and I saw them off as they went out to see the press in the street. It had gone pretty well, and TB was pleased. I got the press in straight away and had to strike the right balance between being positive, and going over the top. They wanted as much detail as possible, seating plans, who spoke first, who said what. I could see them all scribbling when I did the line about TB looking him in the eye. They all sensed it had been a big moment, which of course it was. TB said later McG might have had a point when he said the 'securocrats' did not really want to bring about a settlement. TB did a series of clips on the SF meeting for UTV, BBC and RTE. He was a bit too pro SF on RTE so I arranged for UTV to be the pool. Meanwhile Adams was doing the Millbank rounds with a bodyguard. Some of our security people were clearly horrified that they were in here, and that we were being civil to them.

I travelled with TB to the airport, and he was still fussing about the office. He had just seen [Sir Richard] Wilson and thought he would make a difference. I had briefed a very tough line from him to Cabinet re what his message to the PLP would be, namely that they had to toughen up, and stop behaving like political amateurs. He said it was important they got the message that they were the ones out of touch on this, and that we would come down on them if rebellion became 'habit forming'. Robin had not looked happy but the rest were OK. On the flight to Luxembourg we were focusing on who had to be squared re Euro X. TB went straight off to the PES leaders' meeting, pushing our bottom line that we should be able to attend Euro X. He came back from the dinner more confident. His sense was that the French were angry that we not they had done well out of the jobs summit, not least in their own media. *Le Monde* had called it *'le sommet de Blair'* ['Blair's summit'].

Friday, December 12

The Adams coverage was OK. Papers you'd expect to be hostile were hostile, but the others were OK. It was also huge throughout Europe. The briefing I had done last night re Euro X had led to some pretty anti-French coverage. We were OK with that, because we had to build the story up through the day, hopefully to a successful conclusion. TB had come back from the dinner pretty confident that we would be able to attend the meeting of the 'ins', apart from a few narrowly defined areas, and in any event have the right to refer anything to Ecofin as a superior body.

GB travelled down to the summit with TB, having earlier taken me to one side and said 'I have to tell you, bluntly, that this will be very bad if it is seen as Tony succeeding where I failed.' Again, I was left with the impression he would rather we lost than have to face headlines saying Blair had saved the day. Surely we just wanted it sorted in our favour, I said. He said that during the presidency, if we were to provide economic leadership, then it was important he was calling the shots. Through the day, he was predicting failure and defeat, and I couldn't work out if it was wishful thinking.

In between briefings, I popped in and out of the meeting, and both TB and GB said the French were getting more and more difficult, that they were determined to add a political dimension to economic governance. I was getting big turnouts for the briefings. I attacked as a myth the Franco-German paper allegedly being tabled. It was becoming a very traditional Anglo-French bust-up. But by and large it was fine, though the French tried to spin it as a great triumph because the eleven 'ins' would be able to meet separately. The Germans had swung behind a deal early on, and only TB, Chirac and Jospin were really going at it later on.

RC was constantly asking me why we got into this, his answer being that GB had gone OTT and set the thing up badly out of the economic ministers' meeting. The FCO didn't like the way things were going, but again TB was of the mind that we would gain definition by sticking to our position. He was on a high as things wound up, said we had to get out briefing quickly, that we had secured every single one of our objectives. I did a briefing while he did a doorstep. I had been briefing the broadcasters pretty non-stop throughout, but I was worried about the press, some of whom were complaining I had been rude to them the whole time.

The French were briefing hard and we were going to have to put over a sense of real confidence, which we just about managed. The PA headline was 'Blair wins'. The other story developing was that TB/Chirac relations had taken another hit. We had to start building bridges. The briefing was the best so far, and I felt we were on top. TB was a lot happier. The early evening bulletins were word-perfect, but then C4 news got a leaked Department of Health document on cutting sickness and disability benefit, which got us back on the back foot. David Hill had written a letter to the BBC re John Humphrys which had leaked and led to a rash of Labour/BBC stories.

Saturday, December 13

The papers were mixed, the later editions better, because by then we had secured a better deal. Some of them suggested we started a fight we could not win, but TB was adamant that we had to, and he was endlessly going on about how we'd actually done well, and won people over to our arguments. The problem was the other countries had been briefing that TB had tried too hard and used up too much capital. He was late for the morning meeting, which was largely about enlargement and Turkey, then we pre-recorded the *GMTV* interview, where he was strong on welfare reform.

I got dropped off from the convoy on the way and went to the press centre to manage the fallout from yesterday. I was surrounded by foreign journalists wherever I went and was trying my best to explain why he went as hard as he did. I did a Sunday lobby by phone, focusing on his interviews, pushing hard on welfare reform. I went up to where the leaders were having lunch and watched the laying of flags for the photocall of the leaders of the former Communist countries wanting to come in. Things were running late, and I drafted a few lines for the press conference. On the way TB said Kohl had said to him he was 'Thatcher with charm'. Chirac was very fed up with him but TB said a majority believed he'd been right to fight over it.

There was a massive turnout for the press conference and he was in good form. There were so many people trying to get in that we had to be moved to the presidency briefing room. In the end very few of the questions were on Euro X, but he still wanted me to draft a piece for *The Times* on Monday. On the flight back, in between analysing what had gone on in Luxembourg, we talked about Geoffrey [Robinson]. Charlie was back in London and worried that the *Observer* and *Sunday Times* had more stuff they had dug up. GR had done a series of interviews and in one admitted he could influence the Orion Trust [Robinson family offshore trust]. That could be a problem.

We talked about a possible reshuffle. TB was thinking of doing it before Christmas, Clark and Strang, maybe [David] Simon and Mandelson in. TB said the Italians were genuinely upset at the logo for our presidency, which had a pizza as a symbol for Italy. I got the papers later, which were bad on welfare, and on Robinson and not brilliant on Europe. I briefed JP pre *Frost* tomorrow, and said he must defend Geoffrey.

Sunday, December 14

TB felt we had to fight back on Europe, so we worked on the *Times* article and he also wanted us to push hard to defend GR. JP was OK on *Frost*.

Monday, December 15

The papers were bad on Robinson, a David Hill row with the BBC, and on welfare reform. I took the kids to school, got in late, and TB was meeting Leon Brittan who said of GR 'I've been here before with John Major who fought to keep people but found that when the press really went for them, they tended to get them, because they went for the ones who could be got.' TB said he wanted to keep him because he had not seen evidence he had done wrong, and because he did not want to give the press a scalp. I said to TB later we had to establish beyond doubt what more there was to come and if there was a lot of it, to find him and ask him whether he shouldn't think about going. From the start, it had not been easy actually to establish fact on all this and he was so vague. The eleven o'clock was all about GR. I was pretty firm, said TB not the press decided who was in the government and smear upon smear did not amount to evidence.

Later Jeremy [Heywood, new economic affairs private secretary, former Treasury official] and Jonathan had a session with GR to try to establish whether there was more to come. I hadn't felt comfortable defending him so robustly because I'd had a feeling about the whole thing from the off. The problem was he had said he had no influence on the Trust and was now saying he had made suggestions. TB was clear that he did not want to concede to pressure. He asked me my gut feeling and I said if there were no new troubling facts, it was fine, but I was not holding my breath. Jeremy then established that the Orion Trust was set up on advice of GR's accountants in Guernsey. Meanwhile Jack C was banning European beef and that was the big story of the day.

Tuesday, December 16

TB was angry that he had allowed the ban on beef on the bone. Jack C was now at war with the EU after the unilateral ban on European beef. I drafted TB's speech to the PLP tomorrow. I was maybe a bit hard but given recent events he had to give them a pretty tough message about the realities of government. We could not afford to allow what he had called a habit of rebellion to grow. He also had to set welfare reform in a more positive framework. The eleven o'clock was all beef. TB did a health visit, which got zero coverage. Beef was the only show in town, and Robinson was fading away too. There was an interesting little old guard/new guard spat, and TB went with the old guard, with John Holmes speaking up for them, to have the Christmas carols in Number 10. There was a definite sense of there being two cultures, and somehow this had come to represent a clash.

I had lunch with David Frost at Le Caprice. Jeffrey Archer came over and was loudly telling me he was a friend of TB. Weird. The office party was dull, and everyone seemed tired. I did get the strong sense of the two office cultures, old Britain/new Britain, and the old culture had a strong grip at the moment. I shouldn't have bothered about the carols but, like some of the ludicrous honours, it was symbolic.

Wednesday, December 17

Predictably my letter to the *Guardian* re the *Today* programme was seen as an attack to stop Kevin Marsh [BBC producer] getting the editor's job. TB was fairly relaxed about the row David Hill's letter had caused. He felt the BBC was weak and did actually respond to pressure. The beef fiasco was becoming more and more of an issue. They had not fought on it or rebutted some of the worst coverage.

May 2, 1997. Campbell's son Calum and daughter Grace sit on the steps of Number 10, waiting for Tony Blair to arrive from Buckingham Palace, while the newspapers of the day record the landslide election victory.

Tony Blair greets the crowds gathered in Downing Street to celebrate Labour's return to power.

Tony Blair's first cabinet. Front row, left to right: Donald Dewar, Margaret
Beckett, Jack Straw, Robin Cook, John Prescott, Tony Blair, Gordon Brown,
Lord Irvine, David Blunkett, Jack Cunningham, George Robertson.
Back row, left to right: Nick Brown, Alistair Darling, David Clark, Clare Short,
Mo Mowlam, Chris Smith, Frank Dobson, Ann Taylor, Harriet Harman,
Ron Davies, Lord Richard, Gavin Strang, Sir Robin Butler.

The two Tony Blair said he could not do without: Anji Hunter and
Alastair Campbell – here looking tired and fed up in the US.

na, Cherie and the children; clockwise Nicky,
an, Calum, Kathryn, Rory and (head only) Grace.

Cherie and Humphrey: one of the PR moves
Downing Street made to halt Alan Clark's
rumour that the cat had been put down.

na and Alastair in his office
erlooking Downing Street.

Cherie and Fiona: tea at Chequers after
Fiona had formally joined the team.

John Prescott in good mood as he settles into his new job.

Tony Blair and Gordon Brown promote the Budget in a joint interview, but it was not always easy to get them to work together.

William Hague goes for Tony Blair at PMQs. Blair and Campbell developed the line of attack that he was good at jokes, bad at judgement.

Campbell's first select committee appearance, as MPs investigate his role, and he defends changes made to government communication.

Tony Blair welcomes
Bill Clinton to Downing Street.

Bill Clinton's first visit to Number 10
after the election, shortly before he
addressed the Cabinet; with Alastair
Campbell and his White House
'oppo' Mike McCurry.

President Clinton
explains a finer
point of policy
to Alastair Campbell
and David Miliband
at a White House
'wonkathon'.

Diana, the People's Princess.

The Queen and Prince Philip walk among the mass of floral tributes to Diana outside Buckingham Palace.

The young princes walk behind Diana's coffin, after days of agonising among the Royal Family.

Bernie Ecclestone: his pre-election donation to the Labour Party led to the first 'sleaze' problems for the new government, which Blair sought to bring under control with a TV interview.

The Number 10 party that came to be known as 'Cool Britannia'. Tony Blair greets Oasis star Noel Gallagher, whose brother Liam was not invited on the advice of the band's management.

Also at the Cool Britannia event, actors Kevin Spacey and Sinead Cusack.

Nelson Mandela brought a little magic to an otherwise fractious summit in Cardiff, as England football hooligans rampaged in France.

Hillary Clinton and Cherie Blair inspect Campbell's tie, emblazoned with the logos for the UK presidency of the EU. A pizza drawing upset the Italians. President Clinton and Number 10 private secretary Philip Barton are in the background.

'Leading in Europe, get it?' Campbell was keen for Blair to win the leaders' bike race at a summit in Amsterdam. Dutch PM Wim Kok is more intent on waving. Helmut Kohl refused to take part. The Italian foreign minister fell off his bike.

Liz Lloyd had been at some MAFF meetings and said she couldn't believe how useless they were. TB was getting angrier and angrier at the original decision to ban beef on the bone, which he had always felt was an overreaction. On the reshuffle front, Gavin and Clark were certainties but depending on his frame of mind, Harriet Harman, Margaret Beckett, Chris Smith, Ron Davies, Jack [Cunningham] and [Clare] Short moved in and out of the picture. He was not sure whether to do a limited move now and a big move later, or vice versa.

There was a lot of interest in his speech to the PLP, which I had redrafted early morning, toning down the very harsh message of yesterday, keeping the firmness of intent without going over the top. But I sensed the more sensible MPs were up for a tough message, and getting irritated by ill discipline. The PLP speech went fine and later DH and I hardened up the line, because some were saying that where TB said there was always room for dissent, he was signalling greater tolerance of it. Some had been critical, some had been very supportive. One had said all Old Labour MPs should go, prompting JP to throw a fit.

Pre-PMQs, we thought Hague would do Robinson, which he did. TB, at Betty's suggestion, had a nice line about Hague's marriage and Hague had a very good line on honeymoons. TB was becoming more and more self-reliant pre-PMQs, but liked Rob Read [new private secretary]. He still didn't quite have a handle on Hague, and was troubled by his apparent total coolness. I had a meeting with [Lord] Wakeham [former Conservative Cabinet minister, chairman of the Press Complaints Commission], and was as ever unable quite to work out where he was coming from. My sense was he didn't much like the press but nor did he want to change the way the PCC worked.

I then had another honours meeting. I still felt it was a crap list, and we would have to go on education honours as the main news pitch. On the flight to Belfast I worked on a briefing script to go with the honours list. The visit went fine, Waterfront, school Q&A which was quite emotive. We talked to the driver, who was a quiet, self-effacing kind of guy, but had a quiet authority about him, and said to TB there had never been a better chance of making peace happen. On the flight back we talked things over. I felt strategically we were weak at the moment, that Jonathan was slightly getting the runaround from the old guard, and that ministers were being captured by their departments and we lacked clarity on the big issues – economy, Europe, health and education. TB was more relaxed about things.

Thursday, December 18

There were some good letters on my side against Humphrys in the *Guardian* and a couple of ex-*World at One* journalists attacking Marsh as a Tory. Clive Soley [Labour MP, PLP chair] was leading the news, saying we had mishandled lone parents. We were back into a welfare reform debate without really knowing where it was going to end. There was a lively discussion at the Big Four, where RC was bristling at anything GB said. GB was emphasising the need for fundamental reform, RC arguing pretty much for benefits as they are. JP said we had to show what we were doing was rooted in Labour values. It was a fractured discussion. GB and RC could barely conceal their loathing for each other. JP was just loud. TB got more and more anxious-looking as it went on. RC said we were losing trust inside the party.

Irritatingly, as ever thinking things could only be sorted if he led the sorting, TB had decided to make a welfare reform speech on Saturday, so another weekend was going to bite the dust. To be fair to him, he had always said welfare reform would be one of the toughest areas for us, and we were not helped by the fact Harriet was fronting most of this for us. He did a big number on it at Cabinet. He praised Harriet and there was a half-hearted murmur of support.

He felt the party and public understood the need for reform. He felt there was greater support in the public than the party because they knew money was being wasted, vast sums, but the public did not like it if the party was divided on it. We had to hold our nerve on this. The more confidence we show in the arguments, the more we can show money being spent in better ways, the more the party will come round. The press will kick us on it because they think the Tories are useless and in a way they are becoming the Opposition, so we have to push them back in argument.

JP said they needed to know this was rooted in our beliefs. GB said there had to be greater focus on the attack on poverty. We should start from the argument that the welfare system is failing millions of people and our job is to reform it so it helps those who most need it. He said the welfare-to-work programme was central to this. DB wanted an awayday to talk it all through. Clare wittered on about lost trust in the party. I really pushed hard on the principles of reform at the 11.30 briefing, and asked Harriet to do clips for the lunchtimes. She told me how brilliantly she had done her earlier interviews.

I saw David Bradshaw [*Mirror*] and offered him an SCU job. I also confirmed with Alun Evans he would head the SCU. Phil Bassett [industrial journalist] looked like he was coming too, so that was coming together fine. PG did some dreadful focus groups last night

– non-delivery, betrayal and incompetence all coming through as problems. At the weekly strategy meeting, TB and GB just rowed about welfare reform. As so often they found areas where they actually agreed to disagree. What we didn't do was agree a forward strategy.

GB said we needed a welfare reform strategy unit, which was his way of saying he didn't think we needed a communications strategy unit co-ordinating for the whole of government. TB said if the party was getting jumpy at this, wait to see what happens if we face up to some of the difficult decisions on pensions and child benefit. GB said we had not made the case for welfare reform from first principles and therefore it looked like piecemeal attacks on individual groups. I said there was a case to be made but Harriet could not make it, and there was a sense of people running for cover when it got tough. He got the message, and looked livid. In truth he had been a common link to all the recent fiascos, from Ecclestone to Euro X to GR to this.

I went to Robin Butler's farewell, which was OK, and the duty clerks' Christmas do. They are a really good lot. Attacks on my style of briefing were picking up in Europe, with arrogance the main charge. Issues of presentation were becoming a bigger and bigger problem area. Jeremy Heywood came to see me with Jonathan and said Paul Foot [*Private Eye*] was asking if GR had recommended allowing owners of offshore trusts to get their money back to the UK without paying tax. This was bad news. True. This was grim and there were clearly enough people out there wanting to get him. I felt this was all heading in the same direction and we should ask him to resign. TB was adamant we should not.

Friday, December 19

Overnight I was sent the *Times* leader and a vicious report by Charles Bremner [*Times* Paris correspondent] about me and the European media. I felt I had to get it rebutted. The *Guardian* had finally published my letter denying an incident with a Swedish journalist on Saturday. I wrote a pretty heavy letter to *The Times* which, after a couple of changes, they agreed to use. Peter Stothard [editor] called and said they had had a lot of European media complaining. I was aware that to some extent I was being made an issue, but in handling it I did not want to stop doing things that needed to be done. Nobody batted an eyelid when the French were laying into TB. I found it a bit unsettling though and Peter M was right when he called and said it showed that collectively the Brussels press had decided to have a go.

I was working on TB's speech for tomorrow, him chairing a ministerial group on welfare reform to be the main news out of it. Plus ten facts on the failure of the welfare state. I sent it through to Chequers before he set off for Sedgefield. He was not sure whether it needed JP as well as himself. I felt he should, if only to avoid the story of exclusion and the inevitable reaction. I had Harriet on bleating at me that I should be briefing that she was the real architect of welfare reform. I said it was better to present her as part of a strong team with TB and GB centrally involved. I met Pat Dixon [new Number 10 house manager] and we had a very good and frank discussion about the sense of there being two cultures in Number 10 and knocked around a few ideas to bring them together. I felt that in parts of the operation, there was just no understanding that a change of government meant a lot of things changed. There were plenty of people who felt that nothing should change at all, but I felt it was the old ways of doing things, and the refusal to challenge them, that gave the last lot so many of their problems.

I had a meeting with Jack C, who was having a tough time. TB had pretty much bollocked him over the ban on beef on the bone and now GB was cutting up pretty rough about the extra money for farmers, due to be announced on Monday. I left at 5 to collect Calum and go to see Burnley at Fulham. We lost 1-0 and he was in tears at the end.

Saturday, December 20

The papers were full of Hague's wedding. I had been hoping for a quiet day, but a letter from Blunkett to GB, attacking a number of DSS [Department of Social Security] proposals in the CSR, was about to hit us hard. I didn't react quickly enough and it was not really till late in the day that I got a grip of it. Welfare reform was running away from us as an issue. TB's speech went OK, though for some bizarre reason unknown even to him, he didn't actually deliver the line on the new ministerial group, which I had been pointing the broadcasters to as the main news in it. It led the bulletins anyway but it would have helped if he had actually said it. JP called and said he had had Simon Walters [Mail on Sunday] on saying he understood JP had asked TB to sack Harriet. JP and I agreed he should see GB on Monday to go over recent events, not least the way GB was operating at the moment. JP wanted to tell him that the party was very suspicious of him because they didn't know where he wanted to end up on welfare reform.

We were travelling up to Mum and Dad's, and with the kids in the car I didn't really bother with the Blunkett business when I first heard of it. Godric was handling it and he called me several times through the day, sounding more and more alarmed. 'This is beginning to feel like the last government,' he said. That was the thing that shook me and got me motoring in trying to sort it out. 'Blunkett declares war on Brown' was the headline. I emphasised the commitment to reform, but GB called and said I had to dump on Blunkett, make clear that the entire Cabinet had signed up to welfare reform.

Then I had Robin C on, then Dobson, because they were getting called. GB said I should put out a statement saying the CSR was a collective decision and DB had to stick to it along with everyone else. He believed someone close to DB had leaked the letter to portray him as a hero, fighting against GB for the poor. He said 'You cannot let him get away with it.' He said neither he nor TB had seen the paper he seemed to be reacting against, and this was the kind of ill discipline we could not accept. It was a tough call, because of course any kind of attack on DB would just inflame it even more. I spoke to TB, who was livid. 'What is David playing at, writing in those terms, e.g. saying we would lose our right to be seen as the party of social inclusion? It is as if it was written to be leaked.' Maybe it was but what do we do? He agreed the line should not be intemperate but should come down clearly on the side of reform. I tracked down DB and he, TB and I had a conference call. TB had calmed down but DB was apologetic. We agreed he should do the radio tomorrow, reaffirming his commitment to welfare reform. He was adamant he was not behind the leak. Though apologetic, he said on industrial injuries, he felt very strongly and talked about the accident that killed his dad when he was twelve, and how we had always to be on the side of people who suffered like that. TB said afterwards he was not impressed.

We were facing a real problem of leaks in this area at the moment. Godric said the day had been a nightmare of Majoresque proportions. After setting up the broadcasts and doing the overnight briefings of ministers and hacks, I finally got to bed at 1. Another fucking day off gone.

Sunday, December 21

The papers were grim. I said to David [Blunkett] he had to go up and do a pro-reform interview and clips, which he did, though GB felt that he 'got off with it' because we didn't put him down. However, in the news reports, the Treasury anger was coming through pretty clearly. TB called saying we had to get two things out clearly, his iron determination, and his confidence in winning the argument. He was less exercised about David's letter than GB, now he had seen it in context.

The phone went all day and I was feeling pretty hopeless, both as a father and a son, spending hardly any time with the kids or with Mum and Dad. TB wanted to do a piece in the *Mail*, pushing ahead on reform messages, which I got Tim to draft. TB called several times and we agreed he should do clips as he arrived at the Newcastle vs Manchester United match. I told him I was tired and pretty fed up with life. David was excellent on *The World This Weekend*, didn't get stuck in detail, and put over the big-picture message well.

TB's doorstep, which I organised by remote control, went fine, and went straight to the top of the news, though his new haircut was awful and the backdrop was crap. I then called GB about him going on the *Today* programme. Last night, when he was incandescent, he said he would want to. Now he was not so sure, and wondered if it was best to put on someone more low-key. Eventually we settled on Patricia Hollis [Baroness Hollis, junior social security minister], and I briefed her. All in all, it was a pretty ghastly weekend, totally over-whelmed by work and, I felt, bad on the substance. TB felt it was fine, we had to have these arguments and come through them. GB kept saying to me that David had 'got off with it' and because we hadn't been firm, next it would be Dobson, Cook and Short. The *Observer* reprinted the article from *Die Presse*, saying I was the most unpopular man in Europe.

Monday, December 22

The press was not nearly as bad as it might have been. The *Mail* gave straight coverage to TB's article which was also leading the news this morning. The sense of TB's determination also came through, the feeling that it will be difficult but we were on the right path. TB was up north, and did another doorstep to keep it going. Pat Hollis was excellent and I phoned to tell her. We were getting some satis-faction out of having turned a problem into a potential opportunity. TB called and said again we must keep our nerve on welfare reform. What was crazy about Blunkett's letter was that it would frighten people who had no need to be frightened because it raised things we had no intention of doing.

JP called prior to meeting GB. He said he was going to see him 'as a friend' and tell him he was storing up trouble and he was damaging the leader, which the Labour Party would not tolerate. He said GB had a real problem about sharing information, because he saw it as power. He intended to say he was not the prime minister and should not think he could ever behave like he was. Meanwhile GB sent TB a note saying he was planning an interview and that he intended to make clear that the TB group on welfare was somehow subordinate to the Martin Taylor [chief executive, Barclays bank] tax and benefit review. I called Balls to find out more, then within minutes GB called to say it was important not to have different briefings going out, as we had over the single currency. This was paranoia. I said he could not possibly say a prime minister's group was inferior to some outside review. They were distinct operations but it was clear where authority lay.

The big story of the day was disabled protesters [against welfare reform] in the street, which was leading the news as they threw paint at the gates and rolled around all over the place in the paint. I really wanted to say that just because a Trot was in a wheelchair did not make them any less of a Trot, but it was very difficult to say anything that would be taken as an attack on people in wheelchairs. The main story of the day was meant to be beef, the compensation package and the BSE inquiry but it was delayed because of a computer problem.

Then, proving once again that just when you think things can't get worse they always do, Jack Straw called to say that Will, his seventeen-year-old son, had been set up selling drugs to a reporter. Two of his friends and a freelance had flogged a story to the *Mirror* that he dealt in drugs, and then sent a reporter to get confirmation. Jack sounded remarkably calm about the whole thing, so much so I was even wondering if he somehow thought it would help his street cred, which was harsh, but I couldn't believe how calm and matter-of-fact he was. He said Piers Morgan had said they would not run it as a set-up but would he do an interview? I said I thought he should take his son to the cops, get him cautioned and then do the interview and a short statement. Jack called later, as I was at the [Lord] Rothermere reception, to say that they had arrested and charged him and because he was seventeen, he could not be identified, and it was *sub judice*. I feared that would not be the end of that.

The other problem was the minimum wage. The Ministry of Defence had briefed that the Armed Forces would be exempt and Jon Cruddas was worried [Ian] McCartney would resign. Thatcher was pretty much centre stage at Rothermere's party. Welfare reform was the main talking point. I hated these parties at the best of times. I hated them even more when the right-to-left ratio was so high.

Tuesday, December 23

Predictably, the disabled protest got quite big coverage and the *Guardian* led with a line saying a statistic we had used on the share of disability benefits going to the rich was 'black propaganda'. This, allied to [former *Guardian* political editor] Ian Aitken's piece attacking us for writing in the *Mail*, prompted me to do another letter having a go at the *Guardian*. It was probably a mistake, but they made me so angry these people. If we had ever listened to them, we would never had been in power in the first place.

GB's *Times* interview went fine, as did his interview on *Today*. TB called from Sedgefield and while he was airborne, we fixed a number of interviews at the pub near Chequers. The aim was to continue to push hard on the welfare reform message, to go through some of the achievements so far, and also to curb the demand for him when he was away on holiday. I had arranged to travel down with GB, as he and TB were due to have a meeting. I had to chivvy him out of a meeting with Frank Field. GB finally came out and as soon as he got into the car started laying into Frank, said his ideas were very thin, he's not all he's cracked up to be, and more interested in his own profile than real policy solutions. He said much the same re Peter.

In the car, he went through some figures on disability benefit and teachers and as he read them out he said 'How can we put up with that?' He was clearly gunning for real cuts. He said there had to be more direction of resources towards what he called 'the real poor'. He was hugely disparaging about Frank, and said we had to rebuild Harriet as a tough woman who was really taking things on. I said I didn't think HH cut it, and she was not really taken seriously. I guessed he wanted her seen as the strong one because he could control her better. There's more to her than to Frank, he said.

In a relatively short journey, all the sides of GB were there. At times, he was really commanding and in charge, with a real and powerful analysis. Then he would get tetchy and paranoid and be worrying about things he shouldn't worry about, like who we were putting in the SCU. He did tell a couple of funny stories though, which reminded me a bit of how things used to be between us, like when Geoffrey Robinson's wife went to buy some booze, and the assistant wrapped her 'carry out' in pages from the *News of the World*, and there staring at her was some story about GR he had been trying to hide from her. But the overall impression he left was bad – the mangled fingernails, the mass of papers, the plastic folder with bulging files that kept falling out, the mad scribbling with his thick felt pen.

We arrived and the three of us went through for lunch. TB kicked things off straight away, suggested ending all tax reliefs and slashing the basic rate to 10p. GB said it would not help the poor as much as the rich. TB said why not? GB was even more tense than he had been in the car. He didn't like the formality of Chequers. Nor did I. He didn't take easily to having what were basically servants in uniform hanging around. TB had taken to it all too easily.

TB told GB he thought Charlie Whelan should go. Who would replace him? TB said I have no idea but while he is there, your colleagues won't trust you. I was called out to help deal with Jack Straw's problem. Things had got more complicated. Like me, Jack imagined that Will would have been cautioned, rather than arrested and charged. On one level, Jack was pleased because it meant the affair was *sub judice*. But Piers Morgan said he intended to run a story saying simply that 'the son of a Cabinet minister' had been arrested for drug dealing. That meant there would be a hunt for all of them, so Jack said he would put out a statement. I said that would prejudice Will's rights as a juvenile entitled to protection. He agreed when his lawyers advised the same.

Piers called me and said he understood Will was bailed not charged but Will and Jack were adamant. It was all very confusing. Piers called again and said if the Home Secretary's son is peddling drugs, it's hardly going to stay quiet. It was complicated by the fact that the *Mirror* had played a part in entrapping him, but I could see it becoming the unexpected Christmas story.

GB set off back for London. TB and I travelled to the Bernard Arms where he did Oakley, Brunson, and [Jeremy] Paxman [*Newsnight*]. He was pretty uncompromising and clear on welfare. The interview with Paxman was odd, and I said afterwards he was eccentric. Earlier he'd had a go at me about me having a go at Humphrys. I said you presenters have such big egos that they've lost all sense of self and humour. TB was probably a bit too tough on the disabled protests. He was better on the tough welfare message than in communicating achievement.

JP called after seeing the interviews and said he was too tough and would inflame the PLP. He was on good form at the moment, wanting to help, and worried about GB. We swapped notes on our different chats with him and agreed he just found it hard not to be in control. JP had told him he was at risk of alienating people. He had to involve his colleagues more, be more collegiate. I got JP to call TB who was busy avoiding Prodi [Italian Prime Minister] over the continuing row about the wretched fucking pizza logo. Madness. Late on I had a rash of calls about the *Mirror* and the Cabinet minister's son. There was still some confusion because Jack and Will said he had been charged and the police said not. Needless to say, the police were right.

Wednesday, December 24

With no papers tomorrow, it was quiet on the media front but I had several calls from Jack. He kept saying how awful it all was for Will, but there was part of me that thought he was enjoying being the centre of a big human interest story, even without being named, because he was so calm about it. I guess that was just his way of dealing with it. I would be scraping myself off the ceiling by now. The *Mirror* did five pages on it and it was a big broadcast story which would kick up another gear when the papers came back. They were helped by Paul Flynn [Labour MP] calling for Jack's resignation. What a fucking lowlife. TB said we should move to get Flynn out. My letter to the *Guardian* was headlined 'Campbell's column' and prompted another rash of letters criticising me. I took the kids to see *Home Alone 3* and fell asleep.

Thursday, December 25

Apart from a few calls re Jack, we managed to have a proper day off.

Friday, December 26

The minute we left for Chequers, TB was on the phone, worried about the Seychelles [the Blairs' holiday destination]. First, whether there was a political problem them being there at all. I felt only if something terrible happened back here. Second, would they get bothered out there? Probably. We arrived and it was a mix of family, old friends and new friends. It was sad to see TB's dad virtually unable to speak. I remembered some of the conversations we had just before we won, and how proud he was, and how moving when he talked about what TB's mum would have thought. Bill [TB's brother] made a point of coming over to me and saying that TB would not have won without me. He said you take a lot of the heat for him and it's important you understand that people really appreciate what you do for him. It was a nice thing to do. There were a few dozen people there and it was OK but I had grown quite quickly not to like the atmosphere at Chequers very much. TB really liked it but I found it was neither efficient enough to be a good working environment – like the fact the mobiles didn't work – but nor was it relaxing enough to be a place I found it easy to unwind. And I could tell from the fact he kept wanting to steal off to his study for little chats about political things that TB felt a bit on show the whole time.

Cherie on the other hand had really got into the hostess bit, learning the history, showing people around. Michael Levy was wearing a very funny wig and taking the piss out of TB's haircut which had got a lot of attention, not least because the hairdresser was going round to all and sundry saying he had done it. TB said he was really tired and desperately in need of a break. He felt we were in better shape on welfare but we had still not worked out a way of keeping him properly focused on the domestic big picture when so much time was taken up with foreign policy.

He felt the one thing that had left perhaps lasting damage was the Robinson business. He said if there is one thing I will do differently, it is to follow my instincts more on some of the key decisions. Most of our problems have come from when I have let others make decisions and it is a mistake I won't make again. It sounded arrogant, and to some extent it was. Yet there was some truth in it.

Saturday, December 27

We were having a bit of an argument about how to handle the Seychelles. I felt we should put something out shortly after they left. They were adamant that would just attract people to follow them there, and it was best to let it drift. I spoke to Jack S a few times because he was worried one of the Sundays would just name him re the drugs arrest. But on the ring-round, we found no sign of it. Nick Brown called and said he thought Paul Flynn had put himself beyond the pale with his attacks on Jack. The news was being dominated by Northern Ireland, Billy Wright having been murdered in the Maze.[1] There were a few ritual calls for Mo's resignation, easily dismissed, and between them Mo and Adam Ingram [junior Northern Ireland minister] were handling it fine.

Sunday, December 28

A bit of a nightmare day. I went with Calum to Oldham vs Burnley, which was postponed as we arrived. I called Alex to see if we could get tickets for Coventry vs Man U but by the time he called back we

[1] Wright, the imprisoned commander of the Loyalist Volunteer Force, had been killed by three nationalist prisoners, Christopher McWilliams, John Glennon and John Kennaway, members of the Irish National Liberation Army. The three issued a statement: 'Billy Wright was executed for one reason and one reason only, and that was for directing and waging his campaign of terror against the nationalist people from his prison cell.'

were heading for Leeds. Eventually we settled on Barnsley vs Derby. TB was due to leave and must have called four or five times, going over the same questions about how to handle the holiday. He was clearly bored. He also told me he had been talking to Paddy Ashdown, and had promised him that he would do an interview over the holiday suggesting that Lib Dems might come into the Cabinet. He seemed keener on this as time went on.

He said obviously as he was going away he couldn't do it now but maybe I could drop something into a column somewhere. I said I would do it with Don Macintyre, Monday for Tuesday. He had obviously oversold the whole thing to Paddy who came on to me with his contact numbers 'so he could be ready to react'. I said TB was due to leave for a holiday but I would let him know. I was pretty clear this had to be done softly softly, if at all. We had the key conversation while I was standing outside the ticket office at Oakwell [Barnsley FC ground] and there were a few people there clearly wondering what I was doing there. One of them, a Labour supporter, said she thought he was doing a great job, and I put her on to TB. She almost fainted.

Monday, December 29

AP broke the news that TB and family were in the Seychelles and the *Standard* quickly established it was near where *Emmanuelle* [1974 erotic film] was filmed, so we had a rash of calls about that. TB called as I was taking the boys to the heath and we had a good laugh about it. He said it was the nearest thing to paradise he had ever seen, and it would be a lot less like paradise if any reporters joined them. Dawn Alford, the *Mirror* reporter involved in the Will Straw story, was arrested, prompting fury from the *Mirror*, and signalling a change in their up till now sympathetic approach to Jack. They claimed we were trying to hide the embarrassment of a minister behind secrecy. I said that was self-serving balls, and that a teenage son of a minister was entitled to the same protection under the law as any other kid. Of course everyone in the media village knew about it and the argument was building that it was wrong that the so called elite knew about it whilst the public didn't, another piece of self-serving rubbish. I suggested to JS he call a number of sensible editors and make clear he would be happy to be named, if the law would let him. He said the whole thing had knocked him sideways. The Seychelles was being seen as a picture story, with not much political heat attached to it. I got hold of Don Macintyre on his day off and briefed him re Libs and Cabinet. Liz Drummond [former Scottish Office information director] had done a big inter-view attacking Donald Dewar and me.

Tuesday, December 30

I went in to do the honours list briefing, with John Holroyd alongside me. He muttered the whole way through, not in a hostile or unpleasant way, but as though I was talking to him not the press. I had probably been a bit harsh on him and his list, which having seen the process I realised must be a bit of a nightmare to put together, but the conser-vatism was strong, and the energy taken even to get minor change had been in excess of the outcome. In the pre-meeting, Tim Allan said 'Are you going to say that if you had your way, you'd get rid of the whole system?' I said I thought not. I pushed hard on the education names, to show they were honouring more people in the front line of public service, and there was some interest in the Diana-related names. Nick Jones [BBC] was pushing the line 'the People's Honours', which had been a *Sunday Times* headline, and I tried to kill it.

Macintyre delivered pretty much word-perfect on the Libs, though the headline was a bit overcooked. Paddy was thrilled. 'That should take things forward a few notches.' I said TB would no doubt take it forward on *Frost*. TB called and I said Paddy seemed pleased with Don's piece. 'That's all that really matters,' he said. He was enjoying ninety-degree heat and was loving it though Bill Lloyd [protection officer] said there were press at the local hotel. The *Sun* had got hold of a story that RC had bought an engagement ring for Gaynor as a Christmas present. RC did not want to comment and said 'I resent living in a country where this is considered to be a story.' He was very harrumphy about it and what with the other things taking up my time being TB's holiday arrangements and Jack's son, he had a point.

Jack called several times and said it was a bad scene getting worse. He would be far happier if he could be identified and if the *Mirror* reporter had not been arrested, and he could deal with it all out in the open. The Attorney General [John Morris, Labour MP] had not been very receptive, saying it was not a matter for him and it was the function of the law to defend the public interest and the rights of a child. We agreed the best thing to do when it was over was for him to do a press conference and make clear he wanted to be identified but could not be.

Wednesday, December 31

The honours briefing went fine. JP called from Dorneywood [official country residence] for a chat. He was in a good mood and felt things were OK but said we had to understand there was real anger in parts of the party and we had to claw it back. GB called to say he had done an interview with the *Guardian* on welfare to work, and that he wanted to do something for the Sundays pre the New Deal launch re jobs for the young unemployed. He was worried about the way the media was developing at the moment, and we had to get welfare to work going for us on our terms. It was an odd call, the chief purpose of which was probably to tell me, as a fait accompli, that he had done the *Guardian* and then pretend it was part of an agreed strategy.

Thursday, January 1, 1998

We had a fairly quiet New Year's Eve, then set off early for Paris. My New Year resolutions were to stop swearing, stop eating chocolate and try to go home earlier in the evenings. The first two bit the dust fairly early on. Tim did a good job of keeping most calls from me but even so I felt under stress and generally overworked. Tim called me for a line re the enquiries he was getting in follow-up to the Ashdown stuff. Also Jack S was finally named by the *Record*, *Scotsman* and *Mail* [re his son and cannabis]. I spoke to Jack from Disneyland, including at one point on one of the stomach-heaving rides, and he seemed relieved it was all out and he was able to handle it properly. He did a press conference and the general response seemed to be sympathetic and there was some anger at the way the *Mirror* had reported it. I managed a couple of days which were genuinely days off. But I had done very little thinking over the holiday period, unlike TB, as was clear when he came back, brimming with energy and ideas.

Monday, January 5

The weather was foul, which didn't help as I went in. I was pleased that both Alun Evans and Phil Bassett were there and the SCU was up and running and by and large making an OK impression internally. I had a long chat with PG who said the groups were consistently poor at the moment and we had a particular problem with women. There was no sense of progress or achievement, and even where there were genuine achievements we were getting precious little coverage for them. There had definitely been a shift in mood in media reporting. It was becoming a given we had not kept promises, as if six months in a whole programme would be delivered.

TB said he was rested, had had a great time and was really up for the battles ahead. He had read the Nick Timmins book on the welfare state [*The Five Giants: A Biography of the Welfare State*] and it had clearly made an impression on him. We had blundered our way through the pre-Christmas period but we still lacked a clear route map for the issue as a whole. He was keen to take the arguments around the country, really confront people with the need for change. We also needed a strategy for the party. 'It has always been the party that ends up buggering up a Labour government.' He was worried about whether Frank Field had the political skills needed for the welfare job.

Richard Wilson came to the first office meeting of the year, along with Alun Evans. TB had done a note while away and went through it line by line, starting with welfare. Richard Wilson's solution to everything was to have more ministerial meetings, and at one point he came over almost hippy-ish, like all we needed was to love each other a little more, be nicer to each other, more collegiate. My overall sense was he was generally more simpatico than Butler but overkeen to make an impression, and a bit naive about politicians. I had a few private sessions with TB through the day and I could tell he was more worried than he had let on. He was becoming more concerned about GB's modus operandi. He felt his own standing had taken a hit with the public and the idea of him as a bit of a toff was back, not helped of course by the Seychelles.

Ireland was a major problem with the talks in danger of collapse. TB agreed to see Trimble and John Taylor, hopefully privately but it leaked. TB was determined to get a Heads of Agreement tabled by Monday, preferably with the two governments, UUP and SDLP, but it looked pretty remote. Taylor went through the problem areas – the Billy Wright killing, documents being given late, prisoner release, and the feeling that the nationalists are getting too many concessions. TB was pretty strong on the idea that you cannot allow murderers to dictate the flow of the process. 'It would be crazy, if the extremists start to kill each other, for the moderates then to say the process is at an end. It gives them a permanent veto on progress.' When TB said that Sinn Fein had to be able to point to progress on their terms, Taylor raised his eyebrows very ostentatiously and coughed loudly. DT said it was impossible to engage [John] Hume in a serious discussion about an Assembly. TB said what would Hume do if you showed him a draft Heads of Agreement? 'He would certainly pick his nose,' said Taylor. 'No, he doesn't pick, he rubs it,' said Trimble and there followed a discussion between them about whether he was a nose picker or nose rubber. John [Holmes] and I exchanged looks of bewilderment. I could tell TB was avoiding looking at me in case he got the giggles. 'I'll speak to Hume,' he said. 'I'm determined to do this this week.' He was totally gobsmacked when Taylor said that Maze prison officers have to go through metal detectors but prison visitors don't. Taylor said it was good to see scales falling from eyes.

Tuesday, January 6

The Maze was the main focus of any news today, because UUs and others were going inside to see some of the paramilitary leaders, and came out having failed to persuade them it was the right thing to stay in the talks. TB was busy on the phone, to Ahern and Hume. Adams came out and said the whole thing was a ploy to stop any further engagement from the Unionists. We had real problems getting things up on our terms at the moment, and I was finding it hard to work out how to win that back. PG's view was that people were in a kind of post-euphoric letdown mood. The mood at the time of the election was so excited and so exuberant and yet they did not feel a massive difference in the reality of their own lives.

TB was disappointed at the way the mood was running, but saw it as an explanation rather than a reality problem. I feared this was the culmination of a period in which he had largely been seen either firefighting at home, or working abroad, and people could not easily see the connection between summiteering and their lives. He was still our greatest asset by far but of late had not been communicating to the reality of most people's lives. He had a meeting with GB today, and had a real downer on him, felt he was in a real troublemaking mood. RC was at the FCO select committee and definitively ruled out being a minister in the Scottish Executive. I met Geoff Martin of the European Commission who had a few ideas on improving our relations with the EU media. He said our problem was that the rest of Europe did not have a media like ours, so they could not understand why I was so aggressive with them. They were scared I was going to spend the next six months banging their heads in. He also wanted to pick my brains on how the Commission and other EU leaders might try to get a better deal media-wise out of the Murdoch and [Conrad] Black titles [Telegraph group]. I was working on a draft of the Tokyo speech which was important, and there was a lot of interest in it but at the minute we had a solid draft, nothing more, and certainly nothing to get the travelling press worked up.

I had a meeting with TB/CB in the flat at 6.30. They were horrified that they had been sent a Cabinet Office bill for private use of his car, e.g. going to play tennis or going to church. It was ridiculous, given that he HAD to use that car, and for security reasons could not go out on his own, and yet he was being charged for it. Cherie also felt the rules on holidays were far too stringent. TB and I discussed the plan for his meeting with the Commission on our presidency, which we wanted to put over as an opportunity for Britain, and an opportunity for Europe. We really had to watch this next period because TB was going to be so visible on foreign policy and there was a danger the public would not feel it had anything to do with them. Making Europe relevant is one of the toughest communications challenges we face. This was again confirmed by PG who said recent groups of Labour supporters were a bit pissed off, and two out of the group tonight said they would not be voting for us again. One or two others, however, who had not supported us last time, had come over.

Frank Field called, worried that Harriet's [welfare] document was going effectively to sideline him. He said he was fed up at being told not to go public in all this. The doubts about Frank were quickly coming to the surface, and his relationship with HH was not good, allied to which GB was at it the whole time with him, and he sounded very fed up with the whole thing. There was a little flurry late on re a *Times* diary story saying that TB, Jonathan and I had our own 'secret' focus groups being done through the campaign because we feared PG was always over-optimistic in his interpretations. PG was worried it would damage his business and I put out an on-the-record statement to calm it, and him, down.

Wednesday, January 7

It was a big foreign affairs day, with my Japan briefing and the 'elite' Brussels press corps coming in to see TB and other senior ministers, so I spent much of the day preparing for both. There was a [Franz] Beckenbauer [German football legend] story about a possible joint Anglo-German bid for the World Cup, which we talked up and they didn't much like. Ireland was still the main story but [Professor] Michael Barber's [head of standards, Department of Education] announcement on private companies going into failing schools was getting a bit of play. Peter M was back and we had a strategy premeeting which, as Alun Evans rightly pointed out, was shambolic. TB's note lacked its usual rigour and clarity and we were thrashing around a bit at the moment. Peter M was preoccupied with the Dome, and TB had passed on that I'd said I was worried about it and didn't feel it was being gripped, so he was edgy about that. But both of us seemed determined to get on better than before the break. TB saw

GB for a while, at the end of which Peter M, Jonathan, PG, Alun E and I went in. As soon as the discussion started GB went into his shell. PG gave a rather depressing analysis of the recent groups. He did say though that some of the men had said TB was far and away our main asset while one said GB was a problem. TB winced. As for GB, a rather faint and embarrassed smile crossed his face, one that said he was bothered while pretending to say he wasn't.

TB's focus was on these three areas: 1. a strategy for the party, 2. how to deal with what we had defined as 'post-euphoria pre-delivery', and 3. as ever, how to communicate properly an economic message. GB did not seem so bothered about the last of these, but my hunch was he would screw us over on it. We agreed Health and Education were not sufficiently focused on meeting the pledges. 'If we don't do it, we are fucked,' said GB. TB said he still felt we had more support than not but both PG and I stressed there was a corrosiveness we had to worry about.

The Japan briefing was fine, and even the tricky stuff on the Asian economic crisis I seemed to get through OK without always being terribly sure what I was talking about. TB refused to wear the EU presidency tie for the Brussels hacks briefing. They were a pretty pompous lot, clearly of the view that as people who lived there they knew more about the workings of Europe than the government did. TB struck a pretty pro-European tone but I could tell he was irritated by them. They either didn't, or didn't want to, understand the dynamic of the relationship between government, media and public on Europe. It was much more complex than there. I had a little chat afterwards with some of the more serious ones, including the guy from *Die Welt*, and asked them to understand we wanted our relations with them on a better footing, but we had to take a robust line with our own media because of the very different way they operated. They went off to a lunch with Peter M. I think it was worth getting them over, but it was going to be a tough job to persuade them we were serious about Europe, and just as tough to persuade people here we were not selling out.

TB saw Mo to assess where we were – not in a good place – and go over a few options to move it to a better place. None of the options included the one that was leading the news at six o'clock – namely that she was going to go to the Maze to talk to the Loyalist para-militaries. TB was totally unaware of it, and genuinely taken aback that she could just announce something like that without thinking and talking it through. I spoke to her and she said it was something Gary McMichael had suggested to her at her meeting with the UDA and she went straight out and announced it. 'Sorry,' she said. Actually, I felt OK about it. It was big and it was bold, though of course the Tory press would say she was pandering to criminals. I said I thought it was fine, but she should not have done it without getting TB's agreement. After we talked it through, he also saw the potential upside. I briefed very firmly that TB backed what she was doing, and didn't let on we didn't know.

Fresh from the row over TB having to pay for the use of his official car, Fiona was now embroiled in a row over whether CB could use Number 10 notepaper. Apparently she could if she signed them Cherie Blair, but not if she signed them Cherie Booth. It was antediluvian.

Thursday, January 8

Mo was just about getting away with the Maze idea. Only she could really have done it, though even so there was a lot of unease around the place. There was a tense mood at Cabinet. Just beforehand TB and I saw GB and said we were worried at the way ISAs were being handled, and didn't feel they had fully assessed the impact of the changes. Also JP was on the warpath over the way Education Action Zones were being presented, looking like privatisation, and we had to hose him down before everyone else arrived. Mo said her gut feeling was the ceasefires were holding. TB said it sometimes looked terrible when it wasn't and sometimes looked good when it was terrible. At the moment it didn't look good but he was still hopeful. He was fulsome re Mo. Robin did a number on the presidency. On welfare to work, RC asked when the special Cabinet on this would be. We had rather been hoping this would go away. JP said he had had more than 1,000 letters on it and we had to be careful to take the party with us.

TB was a bit down as we drove to Lancaster House for the meeting with the European Commission to launch our EU presidency formally. 'It is going to be tough this,' he said. 'They talk the language of being up for reform but they baulk when it happens and vested interests get upset.' The Commission meeting was the usual long-winded Euro-crap, pompous statements being made back and forth across the table, and as yesterday I was going out of my way to be nice to everyone. Stephen Wall [UK ambassador to the EU] commented that the Rottweiler had become a pussycat. We even got TB to wear the presidency tie. TB then had a meeting and a lunch with [Jacques] Santer, who I found less and less impressive every time we saw him. I guess it was a nightmare job trying to marry different positions, compromise the whole time, but he was so vague and indistinct. TB pushed hard on CAP. I was called out to see Donald Dewar who had told TB he was going for a seat in the Scottish Parliament and wanted to announce it today.

At the lunch I was next to Margaret B and it was nice to talk to her, about lots of stuff away from politics. She said she always knew TB would win in '94, but felt she had to try. She liked and respected him. Later TB was livid to learn she had turned down speaking to the British Retail Consortium, and was blocking massive BNFL [British Nuclear Fuels] contracts. TB was on great form at the press conference, and was firing on all cylinders afterwards. We sat down and agreed a series of strategies – for women, the left press, business, the arts. We were getting everything in place for his 'welfare tour'. On the way to the airport, Ben Wegg-Prosser called me to say that Paul Routledge's book on GB had found its way to the *Guardian* and they were splashing on a story about the TB/GB 'pact', claiming TB went back on his word. It was the usual stuff – also that TB was out campaigning when John Smith's body was still warm. I called Whelan and said he had to deny it was done with GB's co-operation, though the *Guardian* said otherwise. He also had to make clear GB knew there had never been a pact. If he WAS behind this stuff, it was ridiculous.

TB said the real pact was between GB and Smith. 'People talked about Neil going before '92 but they would not challenge him, so I was pushing GB to go against John when the time came, but he wouldn't do that. That was the only pact. It is desperate this stuff, it is tragic. He will never get over it, will he?' On the plane to Japan we worked flat out on the speech which was taking shape. I showed a couple of sections to some of the hacks and they were clear EMU would be the story. The main economic message was that we had to face up to tough reform and develop a new economy founded on education, welfare reform, skills. I had dinner with CB while TB was writing and she said of GB 'He is a sad, sad man. He will never, ever get over it. The truth is if there had been a contest he would have lost, and he knows it.' She was right. We arrived in Tokyo at 3pm local time.

Friday, January 9

Magi [Cleaver] called with the cuttings, including one in *The Times* saying that I had ordered [Robin C] to end his marriage. It came out of an interview with Margaret Cook. It was fairly buried in *The Times*, but I was the nose of the story and it was one of those that would stick. It was also totally untrue, as I made clear in a briefing later. What a cow – though I suppose there was the chance it is what RC said to her at the time, as a way of making his decision easier. I don't know. But the other problem was that she mentioned other women. Got a message to call RC urgently. I did so. There was not a word of apology that I was getting this in the neck, just irritation that it was up in lights again. I said to him I was not totally sure how we dealt with this. He was clear that if she carried on like this, it would be hard to reach any financial settlement with her. He was also clear she had the potential to do more damage to him. I said one of the names being mentioned and he didn't exactly demur. 'I'm well aware this has the potential to damage me,' he said. 'If I speak to her, I'll make sure she understands any settlement rather depends upon my career surviving.' He said Margaret had deliberately given the media 'gold dust' by hanging out the bait of 'other women'.

Trevor Kavanagh [*Sun*] had asked me what TB's view was of serial adultery and I did not really respond, but there was a danger that by the weekend, there would be a bit of a meltdown around this. RC sounded very fed up. He said he would speak to her. Later TB said to me and CB 'I'm surrounded by these weak vessels who can bring the rest of us down. If ever there was an argument for a presidential system . . .'. He was half joking. CB said if he was president, I could be his Goebbels. She was half joking too, I think.

Saturday, January 10

The time zones were playing a bit of havoc in Tokyo and having spent hours trying to sleep, I finally did and slept in. Fiona was furious at the way the Margaret Cook story was running at home. 'It's as if you are the immoral one for telling him to end the marriage, when he was the one who ended it. The next time one of the Cabinet gets into trouble and they and TB ask you to help them, tell them to get lost.' I was not overly bothered now, feeling we dealt with it OK yesterday, but she was really steamed up. The GB 'pact' story was also running fairly big and TB was livid about it. GB was of course denying having had anything to do with it. So though we were getting OK coverage for Japan, GB and RC were getting more of the wrong sort of coverage.

TB went off to the Keidanren [Japan Business Federation] and was way over the top in support of EMU which led to a totally over the top AFP [Agence France Press] report, saying he'd said we would definitely be going in in 2001. It meant I gave PA a 'quote' saying he said we would be 'in a position' to join. He was on good form though, and clearly really popular here, as shown on a pretty remarkable walkabout, on which one of our diplomats said he had never quite seen anything like this for anyone other than film stars or musicians.

The old temples were fabulous but the most moving part of the day was the visit to the war graves, walking slowly through the snow, with a lone piper playing. TB didn't stick to the poem we had been given but instead delivered words we had worked on in the car on the way over, which really caught the mood. I briefed, maybe overdoing it, that we were expecting something positive to say re FEPoWs on Monday.[1]

Ireland was a problem again. Someone had leaked to the *Telegraph* the details of the negotiations between Trimble, us and the Irish over the latest paper, which included proportional representation for Assembly elections and a new idea, the Council of the Isles. Worse, he had done it to the one paper more hostile than any other to what we were doing. They featured the idea of keeping Mo out of it because TB had to take over and they also said, rightly, that the SDLP and SF would be unhappy. This was all very irritating and John Holmes was deeply pissed off. TB was fairly calm about it. I feared Trimble was trying to scupper it. It meant that from 8am London time, with Jonathan negotiating there, and John H here, every spare minute was going into trying to fix it. If ever peace is secured in Northern Ireland, and a film is made, then one of the key scenes will see TB in a posh Japanese restaurant, cross-legged and barefoot, with our hosts serving course after course as he tried to talk to Mo, DT and others and get it back on track. Even now, he was very optimistic. John thought he was overly so. He did a doorstep on Ireland, FEPoWs, Japan generally. Siobhan [Kenny] in London said the pictures were fantastic. I had a meeting with the Japanese ambassador to London, and introduced him to some of our more serious journos to discuss how we could try to get better coverage for the emperor's visit to London, which did not just revolve around the usual old clichés.

I spoke to RC 7.30 UK time and he said the papers were pretty grim. He had spoken to Margaret who was full of chagrin and now wanted to close it down. I said provided the Sundays did not have any new women to plaster around, it would die away quickly. But when the cuttings came through, it was even bigger than he had suggested, a three-page tabloid job, with lots of 'Cock Robin' headlines. Fiona wanted me to dump on him and GB, saying 'these people made our lives a misery'. TB spoke to GB who again denied anything to do with the book. One of the themes being built up was TB being

[1] 'Far East Prisoners of War' and former civilian internees objected to the planned visit to London by Emperor Akihito, son of Hirohito, and demanded an apology for their treatment during World War Two.

a toff. Rather implausibly I thought, I was being put into the 'party set', along with Peter M and Harriet. I drafted a letter to GB saying I did not want Whelan at my morning meetings, but TB would not let me send it. I was now convinced Whelan was little more than a menace. TB, CB and I sat in their suite, CB saying to TB he had to understand that GB would never ever get over him being leader. She and I had no doubt GB was at least partly responsible for the whole book project. TB said it would do GB no good. 'What is so crazy is he knows it is not true. It's a post facto script born out of grievance.' He felt some of it, e.g. the Granita [restaurant meeting between Blair and Brown] stuff, could only have come from GB. Nobody on TB's team had spoken to him. TB said he was saddened by it but ultimately it was pathetic. He said of the Big Guns, JP was the only one not to have let him down so far.

Sunday, January 11

Anji sent me a note saying how the awful Routledge had been feted by GB at Ed Balls' wedding. There was stuff about Peter M in *Scotland on Sunday*. Peter and I were accused of a 'gay smear' on GB. This was all getting very silly and nasty at the same time. Having stopped me sending a note re Whelan, TB also stopped me sending a note to Margaret Cook pointing out that it was not true I had asked RC to end their marriage. TB did Japanese TV, who showed loads of pictures of him being mobbed, then he went to church, where annoyingly Sky turned up. I waited in the car and worked on lines for his *Frost* interview, including getting up the welfare tour. 'I'm going to the heart of the country to debate the heart of the matter.' Maybe.

The vicar made a big fuss of him during the service and as he came out, and then we set off for *Frost*. He was strong and clear and there were four or five good news lines out of it, Ireland, welfare, Lords reform, PFI [private finance initiative], RC. I took the tape back to play to the hacks and by the end of it they were pretty breathless, with Ireland and welfare the strongest lines. The general feeling was the trip was going well and so did the interview. After losing to John Holmes at tennis, TB made a stack of calls on Ireland, Mo, Bertie, Trimble and later, as a private call, to Adams.

Some great pictures at a superstore where he was mobbed again. He was milking it, pumping hands like it was an election. The Brits based in Japan said it was phenomenal, and our lot were picking up on it as a theme of the trip. I did a note to send back to departments post-*Frost* on the lines to push on welfare reform and to ensure Harriet did not over-brief. She was insisting on doing *World at One* and we also had

Frank Field's tantrum in the *Sunday Times* to contend with, saying his radical ideas were being watered down. I called home and Fiona was horrified at the GB book, and the way it was clearly being fanned by them. She said nobody thought it was anything other than ill-advised.

Monday, January 12

TB had been up till 3, arguing with various people in the Irish situation, the main stumbling block being the UUs on the wording for the cross-border bodies. As soon as he was up, in between the meetings in Tokyo, he was on the phone again, first with Ahern. The other distraction was RC who announced he and Gaynor were getting married as soon as his divorce came through, which led most of the tabloids. I sent him through a note saying I thought he was better to say nothing from now on. The nonsense about Peter M and I spreading rumours that GB was gay was still around and I had totally lost it with Whelan over the Routledge book. It was the denial of all knowledge that really got my goat. I phoned him 3am UK time and said I don't know what your strategy is re the book but it isn't working. Other than being bemused at being woken, he went into his all innocent, nothing we can do to stop people writing what they want mode. I said they were pumping this stuff out the whole time.

At the briefing I was asked if TB had spoken to Adams, and said no, and then had to go and correct myself because he just had. The Japan coverage was terrific. TB said of GB that on reflection he would not like the way it had all played. He would not like all these headlines. I said I would be surprised if you didn't end up having to sack him some time down the road. He looked sad about the whole thing, then said every Labour government has perished on division, tax and spend or ego. The worst thing about this situation is that it's ego. He was also annoyed at RC at the way he was handling things and felt recent events showed up flaws in both him and GB. Peter was all about ego too, he said. At least JP being difficult was usually about policy or direction.

We were still talking to the Japanese about how to generate better coverage for the emperor's visit. They were terrified of big protests, and of the press whipping them up. I'd suggested a policy-based strategy but they were not keen. Then Trevor Kavanagh had the idea of [Ryutaro] Hashimoto [Japanese Prime Minister] writing a piece for the *Sun*. It was a good idea. I drafted something, and we sent it through to the Japanese. By the time TB met Hashimoto, after his visit to the emperor, the Japanese delegation all seemed to have a copy of my article in front of them. Hashimoto explicitly asked for help in getting good coverage for the emperor's visit. He said he was aware of the strong feelings on PoWs and it was important the British people knew we were 'fully aware of the mistakes we had made in the past'. He repeated the 1995 statement expressing deep remorse. He said they were 'ready to bear the heavy burden of our past history'. The aim seemed to be to build up a sense of remorse that allowed us to tell the PoW families and survivors he had gone further than before.

The bilateral was a lot more productive than the EU-Japan summit at which TB did an OK presentation, and Santer read from notes. Re the *Sun*, Hashimoto said it was a very bold proposal, and he did not rule it out. They were aware, so far as we could tell, that the *Sun* would present what I had written as him saying sorry, which they were always loath to do, but the fact they had not ruled it out out of hand was interesting. He was very self-deprecating and even through interpreters you could pick up a sense of humour. On FEPoWs, he was very close to an apology, and that was how our media took my briefing. But then the Ministry of Foreign Affairs put out a much softer line and we were clearly heading for a dispute of interpretation, with us saying this was new and them saying it wasn't. They were clearly worried we were pushing the PoWs issue too hard and during the meeting I could see them pushing my article around, swapping notes and worried looks. Hashimoto being a right-winger, I felt we had secured a lot.

I then had a meeting with the Japanese to go over the *Sun* article and various possible formulations, and we settled on 'reaffirm' the position and make a formal statement to TB as prime minister. I stressed that for this to have the desired effect of changing perceptions pre the visit, there would have to be something new. They said they had been told they must just repeat the old formulation of the apology. There are groups who kill those who attack our war record, they said. They took it off to let Hashimoto see first thing in the morning. TB went off to bed, I did a final briefing. RC called and said he felt chastened by my note, but didn't sound it. He said he had decided not to take Gaynor to China and Hong Kong but he would take her to Washington and Canada. I advised against.

Tuesday, January 13
I barely slept again but the trip was going well and TB got good press overnight out of both Ireland and PoWs. TB saw a group of young entrepreneurs who said they would never be asked to such a meeting with Japanese politicians. Allan Percival rather clumsily announced at the London briefing that RC would not be taking Gaynor on his

trip which was bound to lead to 'Blair blocks Cook', which indeed it did. My main focus of the day, other than the press conference, was pinning down the Japanese on the *Sun* article. Their main worries were the apology going too far, and also that Hashimoto get to keep in his rather eccentric reminiscences of Britain. Graham Fry [FCO] was working at it the whole time. We did another draft which they took back to him and they came back with just a couple of changes, including a new reference to [Robert] Baden-Powell [founder of the Scout movement] and Hashimoto's days as a Scout! We had the press conference to sort and in the car, TB agreed a line on Ireland about taking the first steps from darkness into light.

The Japanese press liked TB, especially when we went way over time, and also the fact he was witty. All the British questions were Ireland, welfare or what TB called 'noises off', i.e. GB and RC. He was on good form at the moment but more and more worried about GB. He felt he was a deliberately destabilising force. He said he was sure GB would be feeling contrite now because ultimately he had sound political judgement. I said that was exactly what he said after the STV documentary as well. He said Whelan would definitely be out by Easter. I said I had heard that before too. All his instincts were to be supportive of GB but he was more and more worried. Fiona said last week she could see a situation developing where I found it impossible to stay while GB operated as he did. TB said GB may have fatally damaged himself, because this whole exercise had shown bad judgement. He said he planned to say to the Cabinet on Thursday that ego and division destroyed every Labour government and if the Tories got their act together, changed their leader and started landing blows, we would be in some trouble. In the car to the press conference he said 'Do you realise we are carrying the whole show, you, me, one or two others?'

We went back to the embassy to say thanks to the staff. I was still working on the *Sun* article. The ambassador and the foreign ministry man came to the residence with yet another draft. They had pages and pages of stuff and I thought oh God, this is going to be a night-mare. But it was fine. The apology part was exactly as we drafted it and the additions were all about his time with the Scouts. Then we had a nightmare getting the computer to accept changes. The convoy was waiting outside and I had the whole Garden Room and IT staff working on it. Eventually we had to re-type the whole thing and get it sent to the *Sun* in London. It was 3am UK time, so I dictated a note to [Stuart] Higgins for the morning, saying they had to present it in a positive way, or else we would have a major problem with them. On the plane, I told Trevor it was sorted and gave him a copy and he was pretty gobsmacked we had managed to get them to do it. When he read it, he was even more gobsmacked. 'This will be enormous,' he said.

Earlier CB and I had a bit of a flare-up at each other. She said I should not have kept the convoy waiting. I said I was doing something he wanted done, so it couldn't be helped. She said it can't have been that important. I thought it was half in jest and tried to respond half in jest and said if she didn't like these trips, she didn't have to come. TB said will you two stop it, and later I said sorry, that I thought she'd been joking etc. We made up on the plane, and she gave me three little presents for the kids. I had lunch with TB on the plane and he was really getting quite exercised by GB and RC. He was also agreed Harriet was not really up to the scale of the task.

I was worried Kavanagh was going to go over the top with the Hashimoto article so I called Higgins from the plane and said he had to understand the sensitivities. He was fine but when we landed it was, as I feared it would be, 'Japan says sorry to the *Sun*', though the piece inside was positive and would go down fine with them. The leader [column] was awful though, saying the emperor should come here and announce compensation and I persuaded Higgins it would undo all the work we had done, and he agreed to change it and we effectively rewrote it together.

Wednesday, January 14

The *Sun* piece led some of the bulletins. Graham Fry was ecstatic about it. Even [Arthur] Titherington [chairman of the Japanese Labour Camps Survivors' Association] was pretty good about it. And we got word back that the pick-up in Japan had been reasonably good. There was certainly a breakthrough with UK opinion, as the message came over that the Japanese really were making an effort.

One of the first things I did back in the office was speak to Whelan. I had totally lost it with him, and in between screaming abuse at him, I said we needed a written strategy paper on how he intended to get us out of the mess into which they had led us. I said I was not prepared to put up with his nonsense any more, that I knew he was in part responsible for the content of the [Routledge] book, that he had not been able to make the transition from opposition to government and his efforts to pursue a pure GB agenda were pathetic and doing GB more harm than good. He interrupted several times and I said if he had been in my line of vision in Japan I would have taken his head off.

Richard Wilson came to see me and said TB should be doing more to build alliances elsewhere. He felt Jack Straw and David Blunkett were impressive, basically loyal, but didn't feel so involved. He said I was 'the wiser counsel' in the operation and I should try to get TB to work harder at his relations with the others. It was true that he somewhat took them for granted. GB took up so much time and emotional energy. TB met Harriet and came out of it saying she was impossible. At one point he sent out officials so that he could give her some heartfelt advice. He said you are desperate to succeed but you are not thinking things through and so you're making mistakes. Mo called, wanting to push for a Bloody Sunday announcement and trying to deter TB from going to Ireland next week 'because it would be bandwagoning'.

PMQs was fine, Hague opportunistic, TB OK but afterwards he said again we didn't really have the mark of Hague yet. It was somewhere in the area that he was a debater not a leader. At the four o'clock I briefed on the speech in Dudley on welfare tomorrow but got a rash of questions on the SCU which was suddenly being seen as a way of doing in the Treasury. I went to see [Sir] John Kerr [FCO permanent secretary] to put my idea of having another policy-focused FCO press officer inside our press office. He was pretty keen. Re Gaynor, he was worried whether she was strong enough to cope with a lot of media pressure and felt RC allowed her moods to affect his morale too much.

Thursday, January 15

I was getting more and more irritated with the GB situation. Siôn Simon [journalist, later Labour MP] had a piece saying TB should sack him. TB kept saying Whelan would be gone by Easter and then things would improve. But I wondered if CW was really the problem. He was clearly programmed totally by GB. The GB situation was worse because a Routledge article in the *Scotsman* said it WAS an authorised book and also that Nick Brown was a key source. The other interesting development was the Tories (Iain Duncan Smith) signalling they would support us on welfare reform if they felt it was the right thing to do. David H went round saying this was mischief-making but TB wanted to welcome it, say it showed they recognised the failings of their policies.

I had a very good chat with Richard Wilson who advised me against legal action against *Scotland on Sunday* over the gay smear story. He had a pretty astute analysis of the government. He spent ninety minutes with GB last week and said he was energetic, lively and full of ideas but TB MUST start building other alliances. I said, so what you are saying to me is that spending so much time with GB is like marooning yourself on a desert island with someone who wants to kill you. He laughed.

RW said if TB really wanted to make progress with his idea of political realignment, Libs, Ken Clarke etc., he really had to start thinking about big changes in the Cabinet. He felt Peter M should go straight in, maybe [Alan] Milburn, [Stephen] Byers, [Tessa] Jowell. I said he should come to more internal meetings and he welcomed that. He said TB heard what he wanted to hear from what was being said by the others but actually they were subtly distancing themselves the whole time, and because TB lacked roots in the party, that could become a problem. He had clearly thought a lot about how the politics were affecting the government.

TB saw GB before Cabinet re the Budget but we were struggling to get real detail. I got hold of JP and we agreed we needed to make clear he would chair the welfare group in TB's absence. Cabinet was mainly welfare. TB did a pretty strong presentation. Work for those who can; help for those in genuine need. He also talked about the importance of solidarity within the Cabinet, which would be taken as a whack at GB, said Labour was always good at talking about solidarity, less good at practising it. Then Harriet cut her own throat when she came in with a burble saying how well we were winning the arguments. JP looked over at me, shook his head and was finding it hard not to laugh.

Then David Clark made an extraordinary presentation about the idea of an 'electronic red box', saying how it was all very James Bond. Again, I was caught in not just JP's but TB's eyeline and both of them were rolling their eyes and making it clear they thought he had totally lost the plot. God knows what a member of the public would have made of Clark's presentation. I didn't have a clue what he was talking about.[1]

We set off for the train. TB felt we were entering into a really difficult debate, but he was up for it. It was good to get out with real people again, and he was on top of the arguments. He felt we would almost certainly end with a compulsory second pension, taxation of child benefit maybe, big changes on disability benefits. The press on the train were mainly focused on the middle-class aspect of the situation. We

[1] The prototype of a hi-tech ministerial red box would, Clark was to say, 'draw people to thinking how government and government services are moving from paper-based to the transferral of electronic documents'.

arrived in Dudley, Fiona Gordon [Labour Party regional organiser] as ever having set everything up brilliantly. There was a good buzz in there and though there were some tough questions, he did fine. We had a meeting with farmers re BSE then headed down the motorway. TB was still feeling very jet-lagged.

Friday, January 16

I tried to have a day off, but the Sunday columnists were all into the TB/GB situation. I didn't hide my irritation with Whelan and how him being there reflected badly on GB. I probably went over the top, and said to [Andrew] Rawnsley [*Observer*] that it was all about them thinking GB was robbed of his rightful place as leader, but that anyone who seriously thought he would have beaten TB in a contest needed their head examined. I denied we had been behind any of the recent nonsense and GB had to realise the damage he was doing by letting his advisers operate like this, and how he would be judged by the party if he didn't stop it. I was pushing at an open door with Rawnsley, who was clearly of the same view. So was Simon Walters and while I did all the stuff about TB being a strong admirer, and this being a strong relationship which benefited the government as a whole, I made clear it was not on for them to behave the way they were.

I told TB I had reached the point where 1. he had to face up to this and deal with what was going on, 2. they had to realise they would not be allowed to carry on regardless, and 3. the revisionist theory of history had to be challenged. The downside was that these TB/GB stories would be part of the furniture now and we were losing moral high ground by responding. But it was surely time to fire a shot across their bows. Jonathan came up with the idea of an all-party committee on Europe, which I put to TB who was working at Chequers. He was fine about it. There was an element of mischief-making but it was a good idea, and we got it out in advance of Hague appearing on *Frost*.

Saturday, January 17

On the way down to Bristol Rovers vs Burnley I became alarmed to learn the *Observer* were splashing on my briefing to Rawnsley and the idea GB had 'psychological flaws'. I called Rawnsley and said when I'd talked about people needing their heads examined and exposing flaws I meant people who thought TB would have lost to GB. He had taken a background chat for his column, which would look very different presented as a news story. My worry was that it would be a problem tomorrow, allied to Simon Walters going over all the old ground. I tried to get him to row back but he said the paper was keen on it, because it went with the flow of what a lot of people were thinking and saying.

David [Miliband] and Louise [Shackelton] came round for dinner. DM said there was part of him that felt sorry for GB. The basic problem was that GB did nurse a grievance and he did bear a grudge and TB's way of dealing with it was to rely on him, cede a lot to him and hope that would deal with the sense of grievance. But it was getting worse not better. DM's worry was different, that GB did have roots in the party, and driving beliefs, whereas TB was too easily swayed by people on the right.

Sunday, January 18

Neil [Kinnock] on *Frost*, and he said that the Tories took years to get to this state of affairs. He said it was about the spin doctors, the spin doctors in Number 10 hating spin doctors in Number 11. Hague took it up too, saying Number 10 and 11 were at war. TB called from Chequers. 'So we are retaliating, are we?' He was not pleased, felt things had got out of hand. I told him that not all the attacks were mine, some of them were, and I was sorry if it went too far. I had made a basic error, in allowing my exasperation to spill out in a way that risked a real frenzy. He said he understood how exasperating it all was, but we had to calm it, be dismissive, make clear this would not disturb the basic strength of the TB/GB relationship. 'You must rely on my judgement on GB. It is not as good as it should be, but it is not as bad as it may be.' He knew that I knew I had gone too far, so he didn't need to be too heavy and he didn't sound as pissed off as I thought he would.

He then actually went and read the papers, having until now only relied on the review on the news. He said re Rawnsley, if you are going to do a briefing as heavy as that, you really must discuss it with me in advance. You cannot have this kind of stuff running around. I said even if I had not actually used the psychological flaw line, I did say anyone who thought GB would have won was off their heads, and this was all about nursing a grievance that was not justified. I couldn't deny I'd been pretty heavy. He said there was a tactical as well as strategic reason not to have done it – GB will now be able to get on a high horse and claim the moral high ground when he doesn't deserve it, and I don't want him there. 'If we are to persuade him to get rid of Charlie, we cannot allow him to use the line that we are all just as bad as each other.' I said fine but we were reaching the stage where they felt they could do whatever they wanted without any comeback whatever.

January '98: TB 'not best pleased' with AC

Peter M called and said while it was difficult, he felt it was the right thing to do and there was no harm if GB felt I was behind it, because the only language he understood was the language of force and we must not back down on this. He would be in a rage because the fundamental point was true. I don't know if he had also spoken to Rawnsley. He said GB fears you in a way he doesn't fear TB, and the occasional reminder is no bad thing. I said I didn't like the feel of this. Nobody was asking if I had been responsible for the briefing, and I was able to say the prime minister had nothing to do with these stories, but it would get tricky if we were really pushed. I got Anji to speak to Sue Nye to get their real view. Sue said as far as GB was concerned, this was a deliberate AC/Peter M operation, authorised by TB and it was therefore 'war'. She said CW had not spoken to me because he was threatened and upset by my last call. Anji and Sally Morgan both believed this was all getting a bit scary, that it might spiral out of control, but both also agreed we had had to do something to rein in GB.

Sue said the 'psychological flaw' headline was like a bullet. Peter M said we had to hold firm, and stick to our guns. GB only understood force. This would finally make him sit up and think, he said. It ran on the bulletins and was going to be big in the papers. Liz [Lloyd] said the GB camp still felt it was OK for them. They must be mad. At the moment it was just about manageable but for how long?

Monday, January 19

I had a real sense of foreboding about the week ahead. The *Mirror* and the *Mail* both splashed on the GB stuff. GB was not coming out of it well, but nor was anyone else. I knew TB was going to hate it and as soon as I got in I got a message he wanted to see me. He was upstairs in the flat and the mood was not the usual. He said if he wanted someone briefed against, he would say so. He could not have me acting independently like this. He knew how frustrating the whole thing had been, but this is not on. Even if I'd said the half of it, I had given them the licence. They knew I was the only one with his full authority, so they will have felt I was sending a signal that he wanted him done in. He said, again, that he knew how to deal with GB and we should leave it to him. But at a meeting later with TB, Peter M, Jonathan, SM and AH, I said that he had to face up to the fact there was a separate operation. We had tried everything and failed. He said yes, but it is his prerogative to work out how we deal with that. He said GB could now play the injured party. It made it harder to get rid of Whelan.

As I was preparing for the 11, I was dreading the straight question whether I had done the Rawnsley briefing. Though I could deny 'psychological flaws', if they then pushed on other parts of it, it would be hard. I'd used some heavy language and, as TB saw several times, I gave them licence. The lobby turned out not to be as bad as I feared. I made clear irritation at Balls and Whelan, stressed TB's admiration for GB and said that had not been changed by the events of the last few days. Ministers were calling in, both to say it had to be calmed down, but clearly some of them also thought it was about time he got a taste of his own methods. Mo said it was bad on one level, but it had to happen. His people did us in all the time, she said. There was a feeling Nick Brown should be sacked, that GB's network was a problem and he had to be reined in. Blunkett said TB had to reassert his authority but once that was done, it was GB who had to take a long hard look at himself.

GB was at Ecofin and didn't engage on it at all, but of course he was livid. When Nick Brown sauntered in to see TB later he said 'Hello, it's the wine waiter ... I have no psychological flaws.' Fiona was worried I was going to end up in an exposed position, once this went to the floor of the Commons. Anji said TB was not as pissed off with me as he was letting on. But in myself I knew I had let my anger get the better of me, and had made a mistake. I should not have gone over the top. It gave GB licence to get revenge and he would. Needless to say *World at One* did a big number, all pointing towards me. TB said the trouble with declaring war was that we could not be sure where it would end.

There was a meeting with Sinn Fein at 4, and Mo insisted it was in the Cabinet Room because that was where we met Trimble. TB gave her his agreement to a Bloody Sunday apology and the handing over of new evidence to the police. She was very happy with it. TB said the recent killings meant the situation was 'very grim indeed'. But we have to make progress despite that. Adams did most of the talking early on, then McGuinness with Pat Doherty chipping in from time to time. They all made the point that the Orange card was being played. They want to minimise change. We want to maximise change. Adams said nobody envisaged the Billy Wright killing but it was almost inevitable in this climate of destabilisation. Adams was not angry with TB, indeed kept saying he didn't blame him, but felt the 'gap' over Bloody Sunday and the way they were shafted by Trimble made it very difficult.

TB said he understood their situation. Nobody should have a veto. He said he had hoped that a single document, covering NI itself,

North-South and East-West, would be the way forward. As ever the one who got their story out first causes difficulties for the others. McGuinness said the document was a mistake. Trimble had gone out of the door and told the world 'I've got my Assembly', as if that was all there was. Presentationally it was a 'disaster' for SF. The bottom line was that the most reluctant participant in the talks was being allowed to dictate the pace. TB felt the killings were an attempt to derail the process.

Adams gave a detailed statistical picture of where the nationalists were and where they had majorities but said their political agenda was nowhere near being met. He said Trimble was 'playing a blinder internally', but he had created space for the LVF [Loyalist Volunteer Force] to operate. TB thanked them for the measured way they put the case. They were certainly calmer than usual though McG was seething away quietly. TB said the most important thing was they contribute positively to the detail on the North-South discussions. I know these guys get up to bad stuff but I found them nicer and more intelligent than the other side.

Tuesday, January 20

The papers were more low-key on the GB stuff. Some were saying I was behind the attacks on GB. Hugo Young [*Guardian*] was saying CW should go. Riddell was having a go at me and Charlie. The *Telegraph* leader was saying TB and GB were proxies in an AC/CW war. I called JP, who last night had seen TB, to get his take. He said nobody was in any doubt that I was behind the attacks, and he felt I was absolutely right to do it because for the first time they had sat up and taken notice. The GB people were getting out of hand. The way Nick Brown operated, the receptions every night of the week, the drip, drip undermining of TB, it was an outrage and it had to stop. TB and the government were damaged by it so he had to reassert his authority and even though TB was pissed off at me, JP felt I did the right thing. He said lots of people will be gunning for you, but I'm not one of them. He could not have been clearer and I was grateful. He said he had told TB that he had let GB get away with too much for too long.

He felt it was a guilty conscience at work, that they both assumed GB would be leader after John, but then things moved around the time of his death. He said the party was in disarray, membership was falling and the welfare debate was a nightmare because Harriet was useless. As for GB, he was clearly not going to challenge TB but he was getting a machine ready to roll and it was ridiculous. He felt TB was changing his view re GB but he did say again last night he didn't think GB was driven purely by leadership ambitions. He'd also said to TB yes, you cannot afford a piece of paper between you and GB, but you cannot afford it with me either. He was clearly going through one of his withdrawal phases but he said he would get more involved if TB made the decision to involve him more. He'd also said, much as [Sir Richard] Wilson had, that TB needed to build stronger relations with the Cabinet.

TB said GB had 'wanted peace' when they met last night. I asked how JP was. 'Mmmm,' he said. It was amazing what an 'mmmm' could communicate. He meant JP was happy GB's wings had been clipped. But it also meant don't think about doing it again. Also he sensed JP was using it to assert his own position. Which he was. Jack Straw called. He too said he was delighted GB had been done in. People could not work out what he was up to and he had to be exposed. It was now an opportunity for TB to reassert his authority and get the Cabinet more involved. I spoke to Neil [Kinnock] and suggested he have a word with GB, tell him to slow down, get a grip of himself, understand the damage he was doing. I was really worrying now about the issue of me briefing being raised directly on the floor of the House. It was amazing that I had not been pressed about it at the briefings. But I had not slept well.

Peter Hyman and I met TB re the speech and he wasn't happy with the top line, so we went away to work on that before we set off for the flight to The Hague. We worked on the speech on the plane and had it done by the time we got there. I got him to tone down the EMU bits. Peter H had done a strong section which I briefed and was running fine. After a meeting with [Wim] Kok, and a doorstep at the residence, we set off for the Ridderzaal [main building at the Binnenhof parliamentary complex]. I was sitting next to my opposite number who also doubled as the spokesman for the Queen. We had a good laugh talking about floating it as a new model for Britain. I was with a guy from the British Council who used to teach TB at Fettes. TB debriefed us later on his chat with Kok. They were really fed up with the French over Duisenberg/Trichet.[1] TB liked Kok and the Dutch though I wasn't keen on one of the civil servants. To my amazement the *Sun* were seeing the speech as anti EMU. TB said he didn't have a party problem on EMU, he had a media problem. He said the truth

---

[1] The Dutch politician and economist Wim Duisenberg was to become the first president of the European Central Bank, much to the chagrin of the French, who backed French civil servant Jean-Claude Trichet.

was if we were not in EMU, we would have less clout in Europe. What do we do about Murdoch? he asked. I said his papers' line would not change till he died.

Wednesday, January 21

The GB story had died in the press. Murdoch told Anji last night that it had been a quite brilliant operation to enflame it and extinguish it in two days. But I nonetheless spent most of the day worrying about how TB should respond to a direct question from Hague about whether I briefed Rawnsley. After the main meeting he asked me to stay back and said 'How do I answer it then?' I said either by saying you are not playing the tittle-tattle game, or say that I had assured him I did not say anything to justify the headlines. He was uncomfortable with it, and so was I, because although I may not have used the exact words, I had been pretty heavy.

We were helped by an idea I had out of the fact that TB took a hoax call from Steve Penk [presenter] of Capital Radio pretending to be Hague. TB had twigged straight away because the guy called him Tony, not prime minister, which is how Hague always spoke to him. But he guessed he was being recorded and chatted away. We got TB to list it during his engagements for the day and the plan was to come back and make a joke about it all if Hague came at him on the briefing. In the end he didn't, he went on welfare and I was relieved. The whole event was quite jokey and I was amazed the question of me and Rawnsley never came up.

I saw Kilfoyle who said it was brilliant that GB's operation had been exposed and we should get rid of Nick Brown. [Peter] Oborne [journalist] told PG that 'psychological flaws' was a killer phrase because it was true. The big political story for the TV was [Stephen] Byers getting his sums wrong [he had said 8×7 was 54 in a BBC interview promoting numeracy], plus Ireland, with more killings, and the IRA put out a statement saying the talks were in crisis and they rejected the blueprint. Mo and I met up to work out the best way to respond. I spoke to Siobhán O'Hanlon but she just recited the mantra at me. The four o'clock was partly about that but mainly about the hoax call.

Thursday, January 22

The peace process was looking in more trouble and all we could do was keep talking it up as best we could. But just before Cabinet Mo told me Ronnie Flanagan [chief constable, Royal Ulster Constabulary] was about to say that the recent killings involved the UFF [Ulster Freedom Fighters], linked to the UDA in the talks. It meant we were going to be under pressure to kick the UDA out of the talks. I was working on a post-Cabinet briefing script on the forward plans for the Cabinet, with a series of speeches across the board, starting with Jack S tomorrow. I built up Jack in the briefing which some inevitably took as a hit at GB but that was less important than us getting up the sense of being back on the front foot and focusing on the big picture. Cabinet itself was OK, Iraq, Bosnia, Ireland, with both TB and Mo pretty gloomy. Clare surpassed even her ludicrous self on interventions. 'It's very important we try to catch the killers.' JP just sat shaking his head.

Peter M said GB was suing for peace, even with him. He had said the only way to win again was to forget the past and work together. Peter said Charlie was a real impediment to that, and he would find it hard to work with GB while he was there. Peter sounded pleased though that GB had decided to make an effort. He said the attacks had really hit home, and he was sure it was the right thing to do. I was also having to deal with RC wanting to take Gaynor to Brussels. RC said he really wanted her to go, and she really wanted to go. I couldn't believe I was having to deal with this stuff. He said it would be a serious psychological blow if he keeps having to ground her. I said we must be able to say there is no cost to the taxpayer. He sounded very fed up about the whole thing. I agreed we had a ridiculous media but it was a reality, and there was no point giving yourself headaches you didn't need. But he was really anxious for her to be able to travel with him given how much time he would spend abroad.

Alison [Blackshaw] came in with a tape from last night on Channel 4, some comedian called Mark Thomas doing a ten-minute film on my 'Busking with Bagpipes' article in *Forum* [pornographic magazine AC wrote for as a student and busking in France] and stopping people in the street and asking if they knew who wrote it. It was quite a funny idea but I cringed watching it when they read out the words. Clinton was in a lot of trouble on the [Monica Lewinsky[1]] sex scandal cover-up front and I put out TB words of support at the four o'clock.

Friday, January 23

TB was in the car with GB on the way to Chequers and called Tim [Allan] to say we really must do more to talk up GB. It was getting ridiculous this stuff. Phil Stephens [*FT*] and Don Macintyre

---

[1] White House intern who had an affair with Clinton.

[*Independent*] both did columns, only in part helped by me, on the 'GB should grow up' theme. It happened to be their view but GB was incapable of imagining that they made up their own minds. Everything must have been briefed. I travelled down to Oxford with David Hill to the Nuffield College seminar on the BBC and political reporting. Tim had prepared me an excellent note and I went through it after [BBC director of news and current affairs] Tony Hall's rather vacuous and waffly introduction. My main points related to balance, packaging and the fact they were driven by the press. The serious-paper people – Peter Riddell [*Times*], Martin Kettle [*Guardian*] etc. – all made intelligent points, and so did some of the BBC people. They tend to talk a good game but in the end seem unable to stop the drive downmarket. I quite enjoyed it and couldn't resist making the point that as our ratings were rising and theirs were falling, maybe there was a case for them listening to some of what we were saying.

I spoke to TB a couple of times after his meeting at Chequers with GB, Jeremy Heywood, David Miliband and Sharon [White, policy adviser]. He said it was a real bonus not having Balls there whispering rubbish into GB's ear the whole time. Back at the office, the wives issue was becoming a bit of a disaster area. Trying to help Robin re Gaynor, Tim tried to get the FCO to say there had been public money involved in Ffion going with Hague to Hong Kong. He was told by them that was the case but it turned out to be wrong, so we ended up with a smear story and a backfiring. TB was not at all happy, and I had to bollock Tim.

Clinton's problems were getting worse. The problem was not his affairs so much as the fact he asked Monica Lewinsky to lie. Philip had spoken to George Stephanopoulos who said they all felt totally betrayed, that he had promised once he got to the White House, all this kind of stuff would stop. We were being pressed to say we were rethinking the visit, but on the contrary we were expressing strong support for him despite his difficulties. TB said he intended to be very supportive when we went there and maybe say he thought it was ridiculous to have this system where someone like Starr[1] was appointed at massive public expense to go fishing for dirt on the president. I went home, then to the *Mirror* party at Kettner's [Soho restaurant]. Charlie was there, pissed, and told Anji he knew he had fucked up and eventually would have to go.

[1] Kenneth Starr, American lawyer and former judge, appointed as Independent Counsel in 1994. His investigations led to the impeachment of President Clinton.

Saturday, January 24

Ireland and above all Clinton would dominate the weekend. TB had asked me to find a way of signalling TB/GB back together again. I said we should brief that GB and Peter were working together on specific areas and Peter M and I drew up a briefing note. GB didn't like it and did not want any reference to TB taking an interest in the Budget. He said it would produce 'Blair takes over' headlines. 'Do you want to undermine your Chancellor?' he said. I said no. He said that's the effect. I disagreed, felt it was just him wanting to present the economy solely as a GB issue. It felt like though he said he wanted a truce, he didn't want to do anything to signal there had been one. TB said it was not worth pushing but I should talk to the commentators and get them to reflect things were working better. GB didn't raise the weekend briefings at all, and though he seemed hurt, he was in some ways more consensual.

I went to see Lindsay and Ellie, who was not doing well. She was beginning to look a bit distant, and a bit scared. I don't know how Lindsay copes as well as she does. I feel like a basket case every time I go, and worse every time I leave. The Sundays had a fair bit on the idea of the war with GB going on, a few blaming me for the 'psychological flaws' line and saying I was full of regret. The Tories were cranking away on the fripperies and the wives stuff. They put out an 'indulgence index', including a section on 'trips for tottie'.

Sunday, January 25

Someone had briefed the *Sunday Times* on the BBC seminar, which they ran as all party spin doctors joining forces to attack the BBC. Work-wise it was fairly quiet, though they were all trying to get me to say something distancing TB from Clinton, which I resisted.

Monday, January 26

Clinton was mega in the press and it was looking pretty bad for him. Clinton, Hillary and Gore did a press event on childcare, at the end of which BC said he did not have an affair with Lewinsky. He did a pretty good job.

We were taking a hit on all the perks and fripperies attacks and TB said in his weekend note that we had to work out a proper strategy to grip it. TB was sufficiently concerned to get Wilson over for a meeting on it. We also had the problem of the story of RC getting rid of his diary secretary, and I knew he wanted to replace her with Gaynor. At TB's strategy meeting, so much for GB reining in CW. He turned up the same as ever, which meant half of the people there did not feel able to be open. We were just going through the motions. Peter M barely spoke. PG said disillusion was beginning to set in. TB made his usual plea for a proper economic narrative and speeches from GB aimed at the public, but it fell on the usual deaf ears. I went through all the costs of modernising the flat and TB was furious at how much it was costing, largely because there were a limited number of companies cleared for security. But the Tories were really going to go for it.

TB was seeing Prodi. The pizza row was still up there, ludicrously, and Prodi seemed genuinely hurt. I had a separate meeting with Prodi's press guy. The Italians were particularly pissed off because the FCO had said it was amusing and the Italians had been fully consulted, which they denied. Then the UDP walked out of the NI talks in London which were now in their latest stage of collapse. I spoke to Mo to get myself briefed before the four o'clock, but they were less interested than they were in the flat. I was not on good ground and must have come over as evasive and misleading. I said I didn't have all the facts yet. The Queen Mum broke her hip [in a fall after church] and that, allied to Clinton, was all that kept the costs of decorating from going even bigger. GB of course was presenting himself as the hair shirt non-spender on this kind of thing.

Tuesday, January 27

The *Mirror* ran a bogus 'through a friend' interview with Anne Bullen, RC's old diary secretary, which was becoming a big problem. RC called me from Brussels where he was due to do a press conference and I wrongly advised him to respond. He said he was confident of his case. I gave the eleven o'clock lots of TB at Lancaster House for the NI talks. I spent a lot of the day working on the speech for tomorrow, and wanted TB to go big on the minimum wage as part of the 'many not the few' agenda.

TB took a call from Clinton. He said he and CB were thinking of them and anything we could do to support him, we would. BC was straight on to Iraq and the need for firm action against Saddam because of his latest challenge to UNSCOM.[1] It was pretty clear to anyone listening that what Tam Dalyell [Labour MP] offensively was calling 'the war of Clinton's penis' was about to begin. He said I hope you can support us if it comes to military action. TB said the bottom line

---

[1] In December 1997, inspectors for the United Nations Special Commission, investigating Iraq's development of non-conventional weapons, were denied access to a number of presidential sites.

was that Saddam could not keep flouting international law. He said it would be better if we stayed together with a UN resolution. They talked over MEPP [Middle East peace process] and NI [Northern Ireland] but the purpose was clearly to get us focused on bombing of Iraq. He said it was vital we were together, got the French onside and the Chinese and Russians to abstain. TB said afterwards that the last time they spoke, BC was less hawkish than TB, but that had definitely shifted. They were preparing for an attack, no doubt, and we had to be out there setting the ground for that, because there is no doubt we were going to take a political hit on this.

I saw JP re Eurostar and asked him whether, as GB was saying, he had given the go-ahead for CW to stay. JP said no. Mo called re the North-South structures document. TB felt betrayed, that they had agreed the document with David Andrews [Irish foreign minister] and now squared Trimble, who was going mad because it put back in the framework document that the UUs hated. Trimble was screaming abuse at John Holmes as though it was all his handiwork. I had to meet TB at Lambeth Palace, where he was seeing the Archbishop [of Canterbury], before heading to Lancaster House for the NI talks, where TB had to have separate meetings with all the parties, large and small. It was clear from the mood in the SDLP team – upbeat and happy – that the document went way too far for the UUs, who were walking round with faces like thunder. They were incredibly rude to TB, who seemed to laugh it off, but I said at one point I was surprised they felt they could talk to the prime minister like he was a taxi driver who had taken them on a route they didn't much like.

Ken Maginnis said the NIO were treacherous and disloyal as well as totally incompetent. They just played the Irish game. David Ervine [PUP] was calmer and more sensible than a lot of them, but started by saying 'We are not happy campers' and told TB he should stop making it so obvious he has to give special treatment to Trimble. He said DT was like a big girl's blouse, constantly running to TB to whinge when the slightest thing went wrong. 'A good swift kick up the arse would do him no harm at all.' There was a similar black-humour feel to the SF meeting. TB said 'It's a great life. How is it for you?' 'The earth didn't move,' said Adams. He too felt Trimble was overreacting and losing the plot. They are not really negotiating. He said that if right-wing groups with links to the Tories were killing Hindus, you'd all be outraged and doing something about it. That is how Catholics feel at the moment. That people linked to a party in the process are killing them. I saw John Holmes raise an eyebrow and a smile and it was extraordinary how they could present themselves as innocents in the killing game when the killings were on the other side. McG told TB he had to stand up to Trimble and the Loyalist death squads. The nettle of Unionism must be grasped. TB said nobody was more frustrated than he was.

The SDLP said we needed a few days away on this, without the media. TB felt on Strand 1,[1] we were close, but the North-South issues were difficult. DT told him he had to get rid of Mo. TB said he would not, and told DT he had to understand how this was all perceived – that the UUs called the shots. He was pretty firm with them, and really fed up after taking all the rubbish being spouted at him all day but as we went to the reception he said he was furious with Mo. He felt we had been bounced into a position that wasn't sensible. She had to understand that DT needed the extra support because the SDLP have the Irish batting for them, and they need a sense of us batting for the Unionists because they feel isolated and beleaguered.

Wednesday, January 28

Clinton was still going strong but Cook was coming up on the rails. His press conference intervention attacking Anne Bullen was a bad move, and I was kicking myself for not advising him against doing it. Ditto his releasing of the letter from Diana to rebut Bullen's argument that he had kept Di waiting. I said at the morning meeting that there was no point going to war against a secretary. Richard Wilson came to see me, as near to being in a fury as I've seen him. He was clutching a cutting of yet another attack on Terry Burns, clearly put there by GB's people. He said he knew they didn't want him and he was trying to engineer a change but this all made it a lot harder. 'All he wants is dignity in going.' Sue Nye later complained to Anji because I had made clear my view these stories were coming from Ed [Balls] and Charlie.

RC was the only story in town, and we were going to struggle to get up TB's speech in Luton tonight, where I had wanted to get the focus on the minimum wage. RC had made a big error of judgement in even thinking he could sack a diary secretary and put Gaynor in there. It said arrogance. I was in a foul mood at the eleven o'clock, and was rude and aggressive. They took themselves so seriously, when in fact they were obsessed with the detritus and trivia and I

[1] The peace talks would focus on three 'strands': Strand 1 related to exclusively Northern Ireland matters; Strand 2 to relations between Northern Ireland and the Republic of Ireland (North/South); and Strand 3 to relations between Ireland and the UK (East/West).

just lost it a little bit. Even Tony Bevins said afterwards he thought I'd gone over the top. He thought they were a bunch of wankers, but why give them the satisfaction of letting them know they could wind you up? I briefed him on the Tory strategy which was basically to make people think we were as bad as they had been.

TB was excellent at PMQs and I prepared a tough, written script for my briefing at 4, went at Hague for being pathetic and playing the non-policy agenda, and laid into the media, said they were obsessed with trivia not substance. Mike White said 'Steady on, you do want to be here for four years, don't you?' I said we intended to be around a lot longer, and for that to happen the public needed to understand the reality of the government and its actions, not the rubbish in the media most days. It was twenty minutes pretty much head to head, maybe OTT but I felt it was time to do it. The Robin story was chugging on like a train.

We were working on the wording of the Bloody Sunday Inquiry announcement. We were going down the 'inquiry but no apology' route. TB was not totally convinced but the arguments from the NIO were fairly strong. It was a running sore. There were a lot of people we would have to tell, political and military, and TB was due to speak to [Sir Edward] Heath [Conservative Prime Minister when 'Bloody Sunday' happened in 1972] and Hague. I was keen to brief nothing overnight but as the circle widened, it started to leak out in all directions. Luton was OK, if a bit flat. His peroration on the need for welfare reform as a way of delivering on Labour objectives was terrific. By the time I was at home, I was into full Bloody Sunday mode. PA had put out a story based on an SDLP briefing which had a few serious inaccuracies – e.g. there would be an apology and an American judge – so I briefed them and Denis Murray [BBC] on the right lines. There were potential problems with Betty [Boothroyd] but it was one of those we had to get in the right place as it started. John H felt Mo would be offside. TB was growing a bit fed up with the NIO, felt they didn't handle the UUs well and lacked subtlety. In the car back, he said of the Big Three, JP was the only one operating properly at the moment. GB was self-obsessed, RC was losing sight of why we were here.

Thursday, January 29
I'd been up till 2 dealing with the Bloody Sunday briefings, and first thing I got a message to Betty explaining that I had had to brief in advance to stop adverse reaction which could have got out of control. For example, as soon as PA did their story on the SDLP line, Ian

Paisley Jr [DUP] was straight out of the traps saying there would be trouble. Denis M was great, checking the emphasis with me the whole time. If only there were a few more like him – knows the subject inside out, cares about it but always wants to get the balance right.

The papers were still going wild with Cook. The *Mirror* was becoming demented. They had a whack at me, saying we were the hunted now. The *Express* said RC was being moved so we had to get out a flat denial. They just made up what they liked once they were into frenzy mode. JP came to see me, angry that TB was planning to do a local government pamphlet. He said it would undercut his authority, and look like he was being sidelined as Old Labour. TB didn't think it worth pushing too hard, so we dropped it. Robert Hill and DM felt it was a bad move, that we needed a more modernising approach to local government. GB came to see me before Cabinet, worried we would come under pressure to soften the line on public sector pay. TB saw RC and assured him there was no question of moving him, the press were mad and he and he alone would decide who was in the government.

Cabinet was largely Iraq, which was all pretty worrying; Ireland, and a discussion on Bloody Sunday; pay and welfare reform. Mo thanked George R re agreeing to the Bloody Sunday Inquiry, said he would take a lot of flak in the military. Dobbo was pretty solid on pay, saying more money for pay meant less for services, and GB did quite a good number emphasising the long term over the short term. He said the settlements were relatively generous but phasing in was necessary to avoid wage inflation. I had another go at the trivialisation of the media at the 11, as the Robin C questions kept coming. You had Ireland, public sector pay, welfare, serious issues and they went on endlessly about his bloody secretary. I called McCurry and we agreed to float the idea of a joint radio address. I gave it to *The Times* and the *Sun*, *The Times* because they would do it properly, the *Sun* because I wanted to fuck the *Mirror* for the way they were doing in Cook. I went over with TB for the Bloody Sunday statement, which went fine, as did the briefing afterwards. Even though some of the Irish experts were in there, I felt on top of all the detail.

I had a long chat with Chris Meyer [UK ambassador to Washington] about the US trip. I went home to work on a piece for the *Observer* on John and Ellie [Merritt], appealing for bone marrow donations. I ended up weeping over the desk. I remember John saying how he wanted us to help Lindsay look after Ellie and Hope [the child Lindsay was expecting], and he hoped Ellie would always remember him for the days he was fit, not when he was ill and wasting away. Rory asked me the other day who my best friend was and in truth I didn't have one, not like John, and I wished he was here. I just don't know how Lindsay copes.

Friday, January 30

[Don] Macintyre and [Tony] Bevins did me proud on Cook and the media, saying as a story it just wasn't that significant. I trawled round the Sunday columnists on the train to Sheffield, emphasising TB would stick to his guns, and getting up the difference between the media world and the real world. Jeremy Heywood came up with us and was clearly making an impression on TB, who said he wished we had two or three like him. I wrote a clip for TB, taking his jacket off, and saying we were going the full monty[1] in the fight against poverty. As we arrived at the *Full Monty* job centre [a location for the film], there was a small Trot demo lobbing a few eggs but the visit went well. The mood inside the job centre was good and positive and even the hard cases took pretty well to him. We left for the Crucible [theatre] where he did a strong Q&A, which made it on to BBC and Sky but not ITN, so I complained to Nigel Dacre [editor]. On the whole though it was a good visit. But Iraq was boiling up, and as we left for a party meeting, there was a bigger and nastier protest, Trots' faces right up against the car windows screaming abuse.

Saturday, January 31

We'd decided yesterday that TB should do a little speech on Iraq, which led the bulletins all day. The Sundays were on all day for briefings on the Washington trip, which was really being built up as a huge thing. Burnley thrashed York 7-2 and David Mellor called asking me to do his radio sports programme, which I did.

Sunday, February 1

I went to see Ellie. Lindsay wasn't there and we had a really long chat about John. She said she missed his funny drawings. She used to say something and he would turn it into a drawing. She said she missed his cuddles. He always wanted to cuddle her and rub noses. He could always make her laugh, even when she was feeling a bit fed up. She remembered the day he died, and couldn't understand how she would never be able to see him again. She remembered being worried about Lindsay having the baby without John being there,

---

[1] A reference to *The Full Monty*, the award-winning 1997 film about unemployed Sheffield steelworkers who form themselves into a troupe of male strippers.

and how she would have to remember everything really hard so that she could tell Hope what he was like. I said I tried to do that too. We were both in tears by now and she asked me to read her a story. Then she asked me to tell her what John was like and I told her the stories of the Boy George night on the town we had, the royal carriage story, how he turned over the private ward when he was in hospital, the silly pranks in the office, how John could jump on to the desk from a standing start. I told her how he once doorstepped a group of terrorists and she suddenly had a look of panic on her face. 'Wasn't he scared?' I said probably but he was very brave. She looked so much like him when she laughed. She laughed the loudest when I told her about the pig-out in the South of France and she wanted to know everything he ate. She wanted to hear everything we did on holiday together. She was perkier than last week, and really sweet. It was the longest conversation we'd ever had, just the two of us, as usually there were other people there. She said I like talking to you about Daddy, because it makes it like he's here again and we were both blubbing in no time.

Monday, February 2

The Bill and Tony show was starting to hype up a lot. Iraq was the main focus with the French and Russians trying to get a diplomatic solution, but TB was pretty clear where it was heading. At the morning meeting, I said we needed less *Peyton Place* and more policy agenda. An Opposition defined by opportunism and a media consumed by trivia was getting through to the public to our disadvantage. At the main TB/GB strategy meeting, with Charlie still there, we were still not clear whether we were going to play on two tough years ahead, or that we were delivering. GB said he feared the Tories were getting the agenda on family and countryside and we were not clear in our messaging. I felt we had to be on something quite prosaic, that we were getting on with the job we were elected to do, that nobody said it would be easy but we were making progress. We agreed 'Making Britain better' was our overall slogan for the coming months, but we needed something added to this that said step by step, bit by bit. Philip and I discussed it and I preferred doing what it takes, doing what needs to be done to make Britain better.

At the office meeting, TB said he was determined to exempt the military from the minimum wage and also he was amazed that the Low Pay Commission was recommending from £3.50 to £3.75. He was off on one, ranting that they were all going native and not understanding the bigger picture and have they thought of the effect on business?

He said just because we have some superhumanly mad people running the unions does not mean we are obliged to meet them halfway in their madness. Sally M slipped me a note – 'Has he been seeing Thatcher again?' We had a brief meeting with the US ambassador [Philip Lader], who had a weird, and very American, over-firm and over-friendly handshake, a bit like Levy's. Then we started the rounds of US interviews, with Diane Sawyer [US broadcast journalist, former press aide to Richard Nixon]. I really didn't take to her. The worst type of TV blonde confection, gushing smile. She was obsessed with questions on marital fidelity, which TB non-answered. When they changed tapes, the producer started asking her to do more on Clinton/fidelity and I stepped in and said please stop wasting your time. They did Clinton, Iraq, Ireland, Diana. TB liked her a lot more than I did. As we left TB did a kind of swooning look and we had an argument about whether she was sexy or not. He had been worrying how best to express support for Clinton but in the end it was fairly easy. It was all about emphasising the big picture, the importance of the transatlantic relationship, the leadership BC had given to the centre left.

News came through the Russians had been invited by Iraq to inspect eight more sites and we said it was all game playing. Robin C was to go to Saudi Arabia on Wednesday, and we met and agreed we should use his speech on Wednesday to get up the message on Iraq. The ABC producer told me there was massive interest in TB's visit, more than he could remember for any leader.

Tuesday, February 3

I went to see TB and asked why Charlie was at yesterday's strategy meeting. Sally and Jonathan were there and could tell I was getting heavy about this. TB didn't answer. He shrugged. I went out, followed by Jonathan who suspected TB had done a deal with GB whereby either both or none of us attended these meetings. This was fucking ridiculous. Whelan added nothing by way of strategic thought, and Peter M and PG, who did have added value, felt they could not speak openly with the grinning clown sitting in the corner. I scribbled off a personal letter to TB, saying he had clearly done a deal with GB and it was pathetic that he could not even get GB to agree that Whelan did not come to a meeting.

He came round to see me, and could tell I was pissed off. He said I should not feel the need to send letters like that. I said he didn't respond when I asked him about it, because he was embarrassed. He is the prime minister and his Chancellor is telling him he won't come to strategy meetings unless he has an untrustworthy idiot at his side. Get a grip. I believed he had agreed with GB that we either both attended strategy meetings, or neither of us did. He said he had not taken any such decision and I said I didn't believe him. I said I was not going to work with people who work against us and that had to be understood. He came round twice during the afternoon to try to calm me down and appease me but I was pretty clear about this.

Later, I briefed on the US trip, and there was a real sense of excitement about it building. I discussed the Charlie situation with Fiona and Peter. Fiona thought it was pathetic that TB could not stand up to GB. Peter felt I just had to keep pressing on. Philip came in to see me re recent focus groups. He said they were grim. Women were disillusioned and men were moving in the same direction. TB as 'smarmy' was beginning to come back. He was not seen as the 'People's Prime Minister' any more. They felt we were not delivering. There was real trouble ahead unless we turned this round. TB was at his best when he was challenging people and taking risks, as was clear on welfare, which had broken through more positively within the public. I met David Mellor [former Conservative minister, Football Task Force chairman], Tony Banks and Co. to discuss the Football Task Force. I told David he must be careful not to be seen as a government spokesman. I was worried that Mellor and Banks would be keener on publicity than sorting the substance, though Mellor seemed pretty serious about it all.

Wednesday, February 4

The pre-US visit hype was really picking up, as was Iraq. I woke though to the *Today* programme trailing Michael Howard and Bruce George [Labour MP] to discuss RC/Anne Bullen. We turned the factual briefing into a paper for the media showing the extent of Saddam's capability and the damage he could do. Iraq dominated the 11. I chatted to Mike McCurry again and it was clear they were worried about how we would handle questions on Lewinsky. I said TB would be very supportive, but they were more worried about the direct questions to BC. On the school visit, for example, they were worried the press would get a child to ask him a question on Lewinsky. Mike had a nice turn of phrase and said this would be 'double parking in a no comment slot'. We agreed to a mixed pool as they came into the White House so that the questions were likely to be varied.

TB did a call with Yeltsin, who sounded a bit slurred and mentioned World War Three breaking out. He said we all wanted to avert a strike. Russia had influence on Iraq. We could get into their sites. TB was pretty hawkish, saying Saddam had to be stopped from developing these weapons. He [Yeltsin] said France, Germany and Russia favoured the same approach. If 'England' could come with us, you could persuade the Americans maybe and we could resolve diplomatically. On the way to the airport, I had a chat with Chris Meyer, who had done a round of TV clips on the visit. On the plane, we took TB through the detail on the trip, but he was worried about PG's recent groups. He kept asking me 'How much trouble do you think we're in?' I felt it was win-backable but we had to see it as a warning signal if we wandered off too much. We were on Concorde so taking TB up the back of the plane was a bit more crowded than usual. Some of them [the media] were a bit too excited for my taste and the feeling was more school trip than important visit. After our briefing I got back to find Jon Craig [reporter] talking to CB and Fiona down the front, with all sorts of papers on Iraq lying around. I told him to go back to the press bit and lost it a bit with Fiona for letting him stay down there in the first place when TB had just left his papers on his seat. Jack Straw was also up chatting to the press. Helen Liddell [Treasury minister] and Alan Milburn were with us. TB said GB was livid he was not coming with us, but that would have given us a JP problem. I had a chat with Gavyn Davies [chief UK economist at Goldman Sachs, husband of Sue Nye] about the IMF.

We arrived and there had been heavy rain, almost flood-like. We were driven to Blair House [official guest house], a stone's throw from the White House. It was like a very homely five-star hotel, but without too many flunkeys going round ringing bells. The shorter flight meant we still had a stack of work to do and after TB did *GMTV* – not pushed too hard on Lewinsky – he set off for the IMF dinner while I stayed back to work on the three speeches we had planned, one for the arrivals ceremony, then the others re Ireland, education at the centre of our politics. It was nice having Fiona on the trip but I was working till 4am UK time and was knackered but unable to sleep. They'd also put us in a room with single beds, which I hate.

Thursday, February 5

We'd fixed five US TV interviews for TB, mainly on Iraq, less on Clinton than we feared, and he just stuck to the line about the need to stay focused on the big picture. We had a slight problem from the *GMTV* interview which was being taken as him saying people had to decide whether they wanted good public service or perfection in people's private lives. This led to hostile exchanges at my first briefing, where they were trying to get me to say BC had not told the truth. Clinton had seen the FCO document on the facts on Iraq and liked it.

TB was really quite nervous as we left for the White House, wanting to go over every detail again. I was a bit pissed off to discover me, Jonathan etc. were meant to be part of the reception ceremony. I couldn't stand all that stuff, felt it should be down to the principals. Anne Edwards found me and took me away thank God. Bill and Hillary looked a little bit pinched and the body language between them was cool to non-existent, except when Bill tried to be warm, and she sort of responded because she knew she had to, for the sake of form, but there was none of the chemistry that was normally there. He seemed a bit diminished by it. He was still phenomenally charismatic and I could see the impact he was having on people who had met him for the first time, but I also sensed that slight diminution. The mood between the four of them was excellent. Bill was clearly grateful for the support. They went off for a private session, then came back and as we settled down in the Oval Office, the two pools came through. The American pool was half on Monica, half Iraq. The British were three-quarters Iraq and the rest Monica. Boris Johnson [*Telegraph*] annoyed TB with a question asking if he was jealous of Clinton. The news came in that Lewinsky was to get immunity. Clinton was starting to get a bit more steamed up. He, TB and I started talking about how we would deal with it all at the full press conference they were going to have to do. He was steamed up about some of the commentators, going on about stuff in *their* private lives. I said he was crazy to engage on the detail. He is so much bigger than them. Keep going on the big picture. He said there has to be a change in the way the media operates, that politics will become impossible if media trends carry on as they are, into this stuff the whole time. They went off for lunch, mainly Iraq, Iran, N Ireland. Mike and I did a joint briefing off camera in the White House press room. The hacks enjoyed it, felt the visit was producing strong copy, not least on the 'shoulder to shoulder' message.

The Yank media liked our Iraq document. I had prepared a line Educate, Diplomatise, Prepare, which we kept coming back to. These big long-running situations always needed that kind of strategic line. BC was definitely more relaxed when HC was off with CB and again that was totally understandable. I asked him what it was like having the whole world thinking and talking about your sex life. He said as long as he couldn't hear them all at the same time, he could get by. He said Hillary had been great, considering. There was still an awful lot that bound them together and she knew he was no saint, but somehow they kept going. I got the impression he was quite pleased to be talking about it in a very normal, human kind of way. His staff were close, and supportive, but I had picked up a lot of anger against him. Also, they were far more deferential to him as president, and I'm not sure any of them had the kind of really personal conversation that I could have with TB. I think TB was worried I was being a bit forward even raising it, but the fact BC kept coming over for little chats made me think he welcomed it. He said I can't tell you how good it is to have you guys in town right now. Then right at the end, I made the announcement about the Bob Hope [London-born Hollywood comedian] knighthood, which went down well.

Fiona came back from the Hillary/CB event and said Cherie had been brilliant at it. She had spoken really nicely about Hillary without undermining Bill, and some of the women there had been moved to tears. Mike McCurry and I were working really well together and I felt personally close to him, and we were able to watch each other's backs pretty well. He said they really appreciated what we were doing, but said it was important for TB that he tried to establish a good relationship with Gore. He was right to be supportive of the president, but he needed to be careful. The general view was that there had been some kind of physical relationship, certainly some kind of infatuation, and his worry was that this could still end in a bad place. Hell, he said, he's a fifty-year-old man and what is he doing chasing a girl like this? He said Monica had always been hanging around trying to be close, and Hillary had even got her moved to the other side of the building. They were all touched by the tribute from TB but be careful. We had a good chat on the nature of the job and the impact on family life.

The only time during the trip I felt Hillary was really looking at BC was when, during one of the wonkathon[1] sessions, he appeared to be nodding off, and she really stared into him. He opened his eyes, nodded forward, saw she was looking at him, and smiled weakly, then she just looked away. There was a real strength and dignity to her, but the hurt was there. After the dinner there was a glitzy event with Harrison Ford, Spielberg-type people. Elton John and Stevie Wonder did a double act, and again I found Fiona and me seated right behind the principals with the press all looking on as we arrived, and I felt uncomfortable. Bill and Hillary looked great as they arrived. He still had the ability to turn it on and sparkle. TB was looking a bit tired by now. I was desperate to get to bed, and felt a bit of a heel,

[1] Policy debates of policy thinkers known as 'policy wonks', hence 'wonkathons'.

thinking how many people would love to be sitting five yards from Stevie Wonder and Elton John doing a double act. I think Elton was meant to be a surprise but we had heard him rehearsing during a session, mainly on Turkey, with BC, Gore, [Madeleine] Albright [US Secretary of State] and Berger. BC did most of the talking, and I sensed a fairly strong rivalry between Berger and Albright. Gore was effusive about JP on the Kyoto front, said he had made a massive difference because of our leverage with the EU.

Friday, February 6

TB and I were going over how to handle the press conference. It was going to get massive coverage and we decided there was no way to finesse, we just had to be shoulder to shoulder. The tough question was whether he thought BC was telling the truth, and we agreed the best answer was to say Bill Clinton had always been a man he could trust and do business with. Clinton came down with Sandy Berger, Mike and one or two others and we started to go through difficult questions. The breaking story was about a secretary being told to lie. He said he would deal with it, no need to bother Tony on the detail. The others went away to take their seats with the press, leaving the four of us there for five minutes or so. BC was in a fairly vulnerable position. This had built up and up and up and he was more nervous than TB. TB took me to one side before they went through, as he often did, just to restate everything we had agreed, and get that final reassurance he was on the right lines. Total support. Big picture. Important relationship between our countries. I told TB which of our hacks to call, and in what order. BC took a few deep breaths, cracked a joke about asking how many of the press could claim hand on heart to be faithful, then off they went.

Mike and I went in on the side, and got there just as TB and BC got up to the lecterns. There was an explosion of camera clicks, then they waited till everyone was settled. Both did good introductory words and closed down the Monica stuff well. TB could not have been clearer, nor BC more grateful. There was the odd flash of humour, as when Phil Murphy asked whether Bill appreciated TB's support and he said no. TB was even more warm and supportive than we planned, and Bill really appreciated it. As theatre, it was virtuoso. As they came out, Bill said TB would increase his standing because of what he did and was effusive in his thanks. He and TB walked down the red carpet and met us in the room where we had done the briefing. BC took us to one side and said I'm going to make sure you will always be proud of what you did out there. 'It was a noble thing to do.' He was on a bit of an adrenaline rush, realised it had gone well, and was glad it was over. The others came through, Berger etc., and everyone was pleased. There had been a real sense of foreboding, that the whole thing was going to be humiliating for him, and it was fine, in fact better than fine, though the reality remained.

Afterwards Mike McC said he was worried still. We are not out of the woods, he said. The BC/TB wonkathon was, according to several of those in there, hugely exciting but I was pretty underwhelmed. TB and BC both did introductions. TB said the purpose was to define centre-left politics with clarity and force, work to a new settlement by which people accepted the pace of change but managed it for the many not the few. BC said the New Democrats and New Labour had broken down some of the traditional right/left thinking and barriers, but they still had a lot of the best tunes. Larry Summers [Clinton's Treasury Secretary] was fairly impressive, pitching what was basically a stakeholder economy argument. Gavyn Davies was rather listy and dull and BC was finding it harder and harder to stay awake. It was all wandering around a bit, Tony Giddens [sociologist and influential political thinker] on Europe/America, Gore on families, then BC and TB trying to bring it all back together under the Third Way banner. TB said the two great driving forces of change are globalisation and the information age. We believe in fiscal and monetary prudence. We believe in the ability of government to help people through change. We must construct the tax, benefit and welfare system around work. BC talked of a new social contract in which economy and equality came together. They had been pretty much quoting their speeches at each other, but it was fine. BC was also pretty keen on pushing the 'right-wing conspiracy' theory, that the left always had a fierce propaganda machine ranged against it.

As we left, I asked Clinton if he had any thoughts for the briefing I had to do, and he said what about Northern Ireland? Tell them I've told Tony I'll do whatever he wants to help, that I'm going to reopen all the channels, push them hard, including with Trimble, but say if there is any return to violence, that's it. I said what about you make a visit to NI at the time of G8. 'Say we're looking at it.' What a pro. Fiona had been up in their flat with Hillary and CB and said it was really nice compared with Number 10, very homely but really smart. Alison [Blackshaw] was hanging around waiting to give me some papers and BC spotted her. I introduced them and he really turned on the charm. She was a bit embarrassed but what was interesting was how he just could not help himself. The farewells were really warm, though again Mike had a little word with me, and said just keep a bit of space and don't forget about Al Gore. We regrouped at Blair House and TB felt he had done the right thing, that we had sealed good relations not just with Bill but with America. If Gore came in, we were in OK shape. If the Republicans came in, they would see that this was as much about America as the incumbent.

Saturday, February 7
The Sundays were doing tons on the trip. I wrote up a stack of background notes, on the visit, Iraq, Ireland, Lewinsky, so that they could share some of the briefing back there. Fiona and I went for a long walk around the back of the White House. We agreed BC was feeling really vulnerable, and that if he was anything but president, it's hard to see how Hillary would stay with him. She said Hillary was much softer and nicer when she was away from him, but in his presence he was softer, and she was harder. I had picked up from Mike and from Berger that they really didn't think he was through the worst yet.

We set out for Andrews air base and waited half an hour before TB/CB came in, absolutely full of it, what a great time etc. I had a session with Helen Liddell who was worried about ISAs and felt GB had not been on top of it. She said it was impossible to have a proper conversation with him. He always had Ed and Charlie there who chipped in the whole time, whilst Gordon didn't want to listen if you were saying something was not going quite right. She thought Clinton had been terrific at the policy session, really clear and compelling. I got TB back down to earth by reminding him we had a local government speech tomorrow [in Scarborough] and the draft was not up to it, so once we got settled on the plane, we had a go at knocking it into shape. TB saw the hacks, who were pretty upbeat about things. The visit could not have gone much better.

Sunday, February 8
TB's speech at Scarborough went fine. Enoch Powell[1] died and I organised TB's tribute. Peter M called me later and said he thought it was over the top.

Monday, February 9
Charlie appeared to have given half the Budget to Larry Elliott of the *Guardian*. TB asked why and GB said it was because the Fawcett

---

[1] Maverick former Conservative parliamentarian, whose 'Rivers of Blood' speech opposing mass immigration thirty years earlier had caused huge controversy.

Society [women's rights campaigning organisation] had been critical of him. TB laughed. So if the Fawcett Society criticises us we have to leak the Budget do we? This is an interesting new constitutional principle. GB was not amused. TB was also seeing Derry to bollock him for the looseness of his *New Statesman* interview. Derry was a fine man and a real character but he was not quite in the modern world and it showed whenever he came into contact with the modern media, which he loathed. At the weekly strategy meeting, we had finally got rid of Whelan so it was TB, GB, Peter M, PG, Jonathan, Alun Evans and me. But it was just as hopeless and depressing. GB was in a total non-communicative sulk. Even if asked a direct question, he was not engaging. Added to which PG gave a very downbeat assessment of the public mood. TB and I were convinced it was because we had not faced people up to the reality of difficult choices. Two tough years needed to become part of the landscape, but too many of our people still wanted to do an 'everything is fine' kind of approach.

TB's efforts to engage GB were almost comical. 'What do you think Gordon?' 'About what?' 'What we're talking about.' 'What about it?' 'What do you think about it?' 'Which bit?' 'About communicating a message for the government as a whole.' 'It's not happening.' 'Yes Gordon, I know it's not happening. That's why I'm asking you how we make it happen.' He said he didn't have the time needed to speak to opinion formers and asked GB if he explained the government case to the media at all. 'I make speeches all the time.' 'Yes, but do you see journalists and take them through the story of the government, not just the economy?' 'Mebbe.' I said to PG if the public could see this, they would vote for anyone else in the world. TB was exasperated and we just kicked a few ideas around, then it wound up and GB skulked off. 'What do you do with that?' said TB afterwards. He was also worried the Budget was going to be a hit on the middle classes, that GB basically saw anyone over £30k a year as being well off, when they were anything but. Derek Scott was pushing the line that we didn't need a Budget, which was radical I suppose.

TB was not motoring and he was angry with GB who was playing a really silly cat and mouse game over the Budget. For the four o'clock I put together a big number on the New Deal to coincide with the ads going out on Wednesday. I went home fairly early. It had been a bad day. After the success of the US trip, we were straight back into the grunge of trying to get some kind of cohesion and energy going. GB was impossible at the moment, just didn't want to know. At the strategy meeting he reminded me of the kids when they don't want to go somewhere.

Tuesday, February 10

TB was doing a business breakfast which I had briefed as part of the New Deal push, though their main thrust was ISAs and financial services, about which they were complaining loudly. TB was still pressing us to keep building the factual case on Iraq, but after the first hit last week, there was less interest now. We kept going though and at the 11 I did a big number on why we had to keep preparing for the possibility of military action. I had lunch with Kevin Maguire [*Mirror* political journalist] and said I could not understand why the *Mirror* was undermining its USP as the only pro-Labour paper. He said it would come back but not in the same way. I said I thought they were making a terrible mistake. TB did *Larry King Live* [US talk show] on Iraq and NI but we were still struggling to dominate the agenda. Roy Hattersley came to see me and stayed for a couple of hours. His theses were many and varied. He wanted to do an interview/profile of me, and his thesis was that I was more powerful than people realised and also more left wing and I had sold out more than TB who actually believed all this New Labour stuff. I gave him a real whacking on his attacks on us. He felt there was something in the charge that I was a bully. Mo came to see me, a bit upset because Maginnis had called her a liar. I said she had to understand their game was partly to undermine her the whole time so they could feel they could run to TB whenever they wanted.

Wednesday, February 11

The New Deal launch was excellent, and led ITN though after the morning rounds it fell off the BBC radar. The Budget leaks were still dribbling out, and I was gearing up to challenge CW over it publicly but he didn't show up at the morning meeting. We couldn't work out what Hague would go on at PMQs. We went round in circles trying to decide and ended up with TB spread too thin in his preparation. Hague did Derry and privacy, and was pretty useless. I was working on a TB class-sizes article for the [London] *Evening Standard*, all part of the getting back on domestic priorities plan. Nigel Sheinwald [Foreign Office press secretary] came to see me, worried that the Cabinet Office was trying to take over policy co-ordination on Iraq. Richard Wilson called, worried about the Clare Short BBC documentary.

Northern Ireland was getting trickier. [Ronnie] Flanagan had told Mo they believed the recent killings were the work of the IRA. If this was right, it meant SF would have to leave the talks. We agreed Mo should speak to Adams, and JH should speak to the US to get them to put pressure on to condemn. Flanagan did not give Mo all the intelligence that led him to the conclusion that Adams knew. TB said we had to know it was kosher. If we had to throw out SF we were pretty much dead, as the UUs were going to walk if we didn't kick them out anyway, so we were pretty much dead either way. He looked unbelievably fed up and angry. John Holmes was cautioning, saying that strange though it may sound, the IRA would not want to say something that was not true. TB had to leave for the New Deal reception, saying 'You guys work on it.' All we could really do was try to buy some time.

I talked to Piers Morgan who said he had seen GB with Kelvin [MacKenzie, journalist and former *Sun* editor] and thought they should see TB. I said I couldn't see much point. They had made a decision to go anti, and that was up to them. He said it was in nobody's interests to be adversarial. So they can pour bile upon our heads in print, but when we say that might condition the way we view them, we are being adversarial.

Thursday, February 12

The *Spectator* did a front-cover article about me, all the usual bollocks. As part of the effort to get back on the domestic agenda, we did a good school visit, which got good coverage on the lunchtimes. Cabinet was almost totally dominated by Iraq, and I later briefed the line about the 'presidential site' the size of Paris. TB warned them there would be the need for further savings re the Comprehensive Spending Review. He also warned them to get a grip on the perks within their departments, saying we were taking a hit for no reason at all. On Iraq, he briefed them on all the diplomatic comings and goings, and on the nature of the presidential sites. He felt the diplomacy was better placed than was commonly understood and ran through some of the countries on our side. He felt that if Saddam refused a reasonable offer re inspection, even the French might shift. Clare chipped in that she wasn't sure bombing was the answer. TB said that if Saddam invaded another country, the response was obvious, but this was more complicated. This was about diminishing his ability to develop capability. GR said doing nothing was not an option, but took a long time to say it. DB asked about the potential environmental impact of hitting these sites. Frank Dobson said that the British people would

February '98: Cabinet debates Iraq threat

judge it a failure if Saddam was there afterwards. The Foreign Office were getting very fed up at the Cabinet Office trying to take control of the media side of things on Iraq. The Clare film[1] arrived and was totally nauseating. It was trivial at one level but revealed an ego the size of an elephant's arse, and of course I had to go through all the bollocks of pretending we were relaxed about it. They could tell what I really thought, but she had engineered her profile so that the slightest hint of criticism was taken as a full-frontal assault on a saint. TB took a meeting on PIRA [Provisional IRA] with RW, Mo, Quentin Thomas, John Holmes, Jonathan, AC. Mo had seen the transcripts of the calls that showed beyond doubt the killings were the work of the IRA. She was now ninety-five per cent sure and felt we couldn't really do anything but go along with it. TB and I were arguing we didn't have to go so hard, and we needed more time. TB felt Irish and US opinion would push them back in if we could keep the temperature down a bit. John H, Mo and I worked on a statement but it was at best ambiguous and she said Flanagan would not wear it. TB was desperate to keep the thing going. He said there were times when you had to do things that might seem unprincipled to others, in order to give yourself the time you need to make positive change happen, and this was one of them. He was really fed up about the whole thing. Mo said Flanagan had been very tough with them and resented her wanting evidence to back up what he had said. The police believed that they were doing it first, as a warning to show they could always go back to it (as if anyone doubted it) and second, to push the UUs towards the exit door if the blame game had to be played. They didn't want to be caught out but they fucked up. It was going to be difficult to buy much time at all.

TB spoke to Bertie and Clinton, Bertie being helpful and Bill less so. Despite the pressures, Bertie was brilliant, said he was totally with us on it. TB felt that if the two governments stuck together Sinn Fein would then have to come back in through a ceasefire. He said there will be a lot of ups and downs and this was a big down. He felt let down by Adams and McGuinness. I spoke to George Robertson, then later Charles Guthrie, and said we needed cleverer material for coverage on Iraq because we were losing the media battle. The FCO and MoD briefings were useless. Guthrie said he would happily go up and do stuff. He was definitely a man to go into the jungle with.

[1] In the BBC documentary, Clare's New World, Short accused an unnamed colleague of maliciously and untruthfully leaking details of a Cabinet discussion in which she allegedly likened Ulster Unionists to the Ku Klux Klan.

Otherwise things were a bit grim, Ireland grim. Clare grim. NHS next week grim.

Friday, February 13

TB was seeing GB first thing on the Budget, but his big worry was NI. I briefed Denis Murray overnight on condition he waited till after 6.30am. As ever, he played straight and did the business. He was really good, totally on-message, put where we were in a proper context. It is an incredible help having someone you can actually level with, explain why certain things have to be said in a certain way, without them bleating about me trying to do their job. The thing about Denis is he understands the sensitivities he is dealing with.

The Clare story was effectively killed by the niceness of my briefing. I wrote a note to TB nonetheless saying he should rein her in. He said it was pointless because she will never change. One or two of the papers were starting to say that Harriet was for the chop. I prepared a strong line saying it was untrue and TB was not even thinking about a reshuffle. On Ireland, TB felt Bertie was fine but we needed more people coming in behind this, especially Bill Clinton. Sinn Fein were saying that they should not be pushed out and denying that there was incontrovertible evidence it was them. Godric put together an excellent briefing from Porton Down [government defence laboratory] on what chemical and biological weapons Saddam Hussein had, and what effect they could have. I got a letter from Jonathan Holborow [*Mail on Sunday* editor] saying that they had been told Saddam had developed nuclear capability, and thought we should know. TB laughed out loud when I told him. Both of us had Holborow fairly low down in the editors' league, and it was unlikely a newspaper would find out before we did that they had nukes. But it gave me the opportunity to get TB to chat generally and explain why we were concerned about chemical weapons, and I got an MoD official to brief on what they had. Holborow phoned me later and said 'I hope I didn't scare the prime minister. He sounded very taken aback.'

Peter M chaired a brainstorming session on the Dome, with Matthew Freud [public relations consultant], Alan Yentob [BBC], a few others. Peter seemed unsure of what the message was. Philip felt the only message was that it is Mandelson's Dome, and that is not a good message. It had to get more political backing, and it had to be part of a bigger sense that Britain was young and confident and coming together at an important time. Assuming we weren't involved in military action, the plan was for TB to relaunch it on the 24th.

Derry came on, wanting to do a right of reply to the *Sunday Times*.

February '98: Briefing on Saddam's weapons

I said they would simply use it to say it was another gratuitous attack on the press. He was also nagging me about a friend of his who wanted to do a piece for *Interiors* magazine on how good the redesign in his residence had been. I love Derry dearly but he does lead with his chin. I said the press would murder him, and for no gain at all. Phil Stephens told me GB had been into the *FT* for lunch and was totally relaxed and charming.

Saturday, February 14

What should have been a good weekend turned out pretty dreadful. I had a lie-in, the papers were quiet and we had the Sundays under control. Tim had worked up a briefing on TB's view that the Diana death industry was tacky, and too many people were cashing in. I sent a note to Major's office to make sure he was onside in case, as I feared, the papers tried to set up a split between them on Ireland. After the kids' football we left for Wycombe vs Burnley [Burnley lost 2-1] and on the way I was briefing on Iraq and Ireland. I had a dreadful cold and did not remotely feel like going out for dinner, let alone driving down to Chequers. Then Fiona and I had a dreadful row which started about nothing and escalated into a shouting match, so that when finally we left, we went down with me in silence. I was now in a foul mood. Salman Rushdie [novelist] was there, Mick Hucknall [singer] and his girlfriend, and we talked about football. GB and Sarah [Macaulay] were there and GB pretty much blanked me. He looked pretty tortured the whole evening. CB was doing her best to be nice to him but it was forced. I was next to Sarah and we had a very frank conversation, which got franker as the evening wore on. She said GB felt it deeply when TB was against him on something, and he currently felt he was against him on a lot. I said it would help if he was open about the Budget. She thought I was joking. She said he genuinely hadn't encouraged the Routledge book. He regretted the STV documentary. He really wanted things to work better but he felt it was difficult if I would not work with Charlie. I said if I had pushed I could have got rid of Charlie over the EMU fiasco but I held back because I was as much to blame as he was. But since then he had been an outrage. I said I was particularly angry at the 'gay smear' stuff, and asked how on earth anyone could think that was in our or GB's interests. I did not believe Charlie when he said he tried to get Routledge to be balanced. I had a lot of contacts in the media who said if Charlie briefed only for GB, not the government, whose interests are served? Not Gordon's. I could make a case that most of the government's problems, in media terms, have CW somewhere in the mix, and I'm not going to put up with it much longer. What's more, nor should Gordon, because it does his interests no good at all. And his colleagues hate him because he allows this briefing against them the whole time.

She didn't put up much by way of counter-argument, just said 'I didn't realise you felt so strongly' once or twice. I said Charlie's cons far outweighed the pros. What's more, I felt that Ed Balls was a problem for him too, because he might be clever on economics, but politically he is not fully grown up. CB took people on her tour, and TB and I had a long chat with Cameron Mackintosh [theatre producer] about the arts. He felt we were losing support in the arts and not doing simple things that would win people back. We left the first, and after a continuation of the row, drove home in silence. Crap night all round.

Sunday, February 15

It was largely a day of emotional torture between me and Fiona. We were pretty much in deep-freeze zone. She said I had created a form of tyranny under which we all had to live. We went in circles and we were losing it in front of Calum and Grace so I went upstairs and wrote it all down, which was probably a mistake. So the mood was pretty foul by the time Neil and Glenys [Kinnock], Philip, Gail and the kids came round. I barely spoke. PG asked what was wrong. I said I was feeling emotionally shot, professionally frustrated, fed up of all the egos, hating the press, feeling I had to take too much of the burden and not feeling supported.

Monday, February 16

The Northern Ireland talks in Dublin, and the possible expulsion of Sinn Fein, were the main thing for the day. The *Mail* ran some bollocks about Peter M and me trying to get Derry sacked. I said at the 11 it was all total balls, but Derry was largely seen as damaged goods, and there was a new rash of stuff about the spending on his official residence, getting up the perks row again. I was led to believe this was a decision of the Lords authorities, but it wasn't exactly so and became a problem as the day wore on.

TB chaired the first meeting on the Iraq media management group I had suggested, which would then be chaired by Derek Fatchett [Foreign Office minister]. TB was alarmed at how poor the FCO/MoD propaganda effort was, and I certainly felt we were not really ahead in the PR battle. Charles Guthrie and [Admiral] Alan West, the Chief of Defence Intelligence, were doing a briefing later today. At the strategy meeting, GB didn't show. Philip gave a gloomy assessment of the private polls and the real damage was losing the sense of being the people's government. TB said there was nothing much we could do about it, that it was one of those phases. The important thing was that we kept focused on the big issues and made the right decisions. I went to Guthrie's briefing, and he was good on the military object-ives. West was strong on the factual account of Iraq's capability, and on missing weapons post-UNSCOM. When he started saying that the presidential sites so-called would stretch from Greenwich to Streatham or Wapping to Hyde Park, they finally got some idea of what was going on. They ran though some of the WMD [weapons of mass destruction]. Charles looked at his most menacing when he said very quietly 'You wouldn't want to bomb a tank full of anthrax.' They were both impressive in different ways, Charles very soldierly, upper-crust-sounding but not remotely twerpish like some of them, while West had a very quiet authority. They both emphasised the aim was to get the inspectors in, and there was a diplomatic route. But if the Iraqis were watching, they'd have got a pretty heavy message put through to them.

I got back to read up on the Jack Straw statement on the press in relation to the ECHR [European Convention on Human Rights]. Jack had done a deal with [Lord] Wakeham, and it seemed OK-ish. I read it as a back-door privacy law but we put together an argument that it was even stronger protection than the PCC. I went into the end of TB meetings with the disability organisations [on welfare reform], which was grim. These were the professional lobbyists, who were not friendly at all, and they clearly irritated TB. There was a really sullen mood and a kind of uniform sanctimony about the way they put their case. It was very unsubtle moral blackmail, and showed how little they had thought about how to deal with him. He was interested in argument not the emotion on issues like this.

Tuesday, February 17

The Derry problem grew. A line in a December PQ appeared to contra-dict what I was saying, namely this was a decision by the Lords, rather than Derry, and now the knives were out. Ivor Richard [Leader of the House of Lords] called to say watch out. He said Derry had instigated these works and he was also the person who pushed it through. The Lords committee had voted for it but it was not as if this was their idea. It was a huge problem. I grilled Derry on it before the 11 and he said he would of course accept responsibility for it, but also, as if this was a defence, that Alison [Irvine] had been involved in all the decisions. I said that made it worse not better. This had the makings of a bit of a disaster. He said the residence was in a poor state of repair when he got the job and he was expected to live there. But there was no way they were living there the way that it was. He said two committees passed the refurbishment plans. Black Rod had been on top of the detail throughout. He was fairly bullish but it was going to be pretty hellish.

Derek Fatchett chaired the first Iraq media meeting, following TB's orders for a daily ministerial on it. John Reid [Armed Forces minister] was there from MoD but because he wasn't in the chair, Peter didn't come. The tensions between FCO and the MoD were clear with Reid trying to get in the whole time. He was impressive and good on detail but went on too long. He certainly got the point about the need to have an argument around which to persuade people of the threat. But even something like the size of the presidential sites being excluded by Saddam had not been adequately communicated. We went over the current P5 [China, France, Russia, UK and US, the five permanent member states on UN Security Council] discussions at the UN, and the sense from Kofi was that it was the last opportunity for diplomacy before a move to military action.

I was always struck at these meetings how much ministers looked to me for the ideas and the execution. It was one of the things that pissed me off, that I got seen as assuming 'power' and all the other bollocks, but I didn't actually ask for it. I'd love it if they took this stuff away and just did it. TB was worrying that there was not enough public support for action and also worried that we were overdoing diplomatic rather than military. He wanted the message toughening up. He had spoken to Clinton last night, who was clearly fairly set on a course. He said the Monica situation was better than before. I don't know if that meant the politics or the Hillary situation. Possibly both.

The day was really marred by Derry, and I was trying to get it sorted. Peter Hyman said this was defending the indefensible. Siobhan [Kenny] said it was like the old days when briefings were spent defending ministers who shouldn't be defended. We also had a spot of bother on Iraq because people were sensing a difference between what I was saying – that there was not really a need for a new UNSCR [UN Security Council resolution], though it would be helpful – while Robin was saying in the House that there was such a need.

TB was pretty fed up by the time we left for lunch at the *Guardian*. He said he had given Derry a real warning about this kind of thing, but he just ploughed on. He also spoke to Bertie in the car and things were rocky there. The *Guardian* was the usual conspiracy theorists and leftists, and one or two voices of sanity. TB did fine on Iraq, Ireland, welfare, but didn't really shine until the lunch itself. Peter Preston [editor] was obsessed with the idea that the security services were lying to us all the time, because that's what they did to Labour governments. It was reasonably friendly and TB probably overdid the attacks on the *Guardian* but Mike White thought it went fine. He'd been looking a bit fed up throughout.

Fiona and Cherie saw Lauren Booth [CB's half-sister] at Cherie's chambers. Lauren crumbled in tears when Fiona told her in terms that she was exploiting Cherie's name, and exploiting Number 10, and it had to stop. This led to her agent calling Fiona to complain she had ruined Lauren's confidence. Fiona suggested she change her name again, to stop so obviously cashing in. She was absolutely right about this but worried Cherie would relent. I'd been asking all day for mock-up aerial photos of London, with areas blacked out to show how big these presidential sites were, and we still didn't have it. I complained to John Reid at how slowly this was moving. Then Oona Muirhead [MoD director of information strategy and news] complained that I complained.

Wednesday, February 18

The Lords PQ on Derry did not get much coverage and it all seemed to be going away, until we heard the *Standard* was splashing on a story, 'Brown floors Irvine', some piece of nonsense about how he was not even replacing carpets at Number 11. It was all part of his hair-shirt image-building and people were generally appalled. TB assured me again that Whelan was leaving after the Budget. Kofi Annan getting agreement to go to Baghdad was the main focus. Bevins was causing us trouble at the briefings over the legitimacy of any military attack and suggesting a split. TB was worried the FCO were pushing too much diplomacy in the line. Later that again became clear when Nigel [Sheinwald] had another go at trying to get the line agreed that we needed, as opposed to wanted, a new [UN] resolution before possible action. At the Fatchett/Reid meeting, we agreed we should produce something on the secret sites, which we got done for the four o'clock, TB having referred to it at PMQs. Fatchett wanted to say that this was Saddam's last chance, which I didn't support. There was constant tension between him and Reid, and again I felt too much expectation on me to have the ideas.

I had another session with Derry on the background to the refurbishment. He admitted it was his idea that there should be major refurbishment if he was to live there but insisted it was all properly agreed by all the committees. He looked pretty hurt by the whole thing, and it must have been humiliating to have to go through all this just so I could answer questions from people basically out to do him in. I said he should get on with his job and try to avoid any publicity for this kind of thing. He was now certainly a target.

Eleven o'clock was almost exclusively on Iraq, a bit on GB carpet story, about which I was suitably dismissive and had to pretend I didn't think it had come from GB's clowns. Philip Barton [private secretary, foreign affairs] sent my line on a resolution to the FCO to say that this was the line, not what they had been saying. I had one or two unpleasant exchanges with Hattersley who, having first said he wanted an off-the-record chat, now was turning it into a full-scale interview but would not, as agreed, let me see more than a couple of the quotes he was using. I sent him a note saying I thought he had been disingenuous. TB came out after PMQs and had a meeting with Hague and [Michael] Howard [now Shadow Foreign Secretary] on Iraq. Last night he had seen Hague and [Andrew] MacKay on Ireland, where he sensed they were moving to ditch bipartisanship if we let Sinn Fein back into the talks. On Iraq, he said Howard was clearly basically of the view that if it worked they would support us, and if not they would kick us all over the place. He reminisced about some of their encounters when he was Howard's Home Office Shadow. He felt he was clever, but not as clever as he thought. A lawyer not a politician.

TB was seeing Kohl who was supporting our line on Iraq. I then heard Clare Short had done another interview, this time in the *New Statesman*, saying that the deal was that she told the truth in Cabinet, and that meant she could not tell 'my truth' outside. What a silly woman she is, this never-ending distancing and positioning as the great purveyor of truth. She was also critical of our approach to lone parents and benefit fraud. TB said to play down, which I did. I went to see Ellie [Merritt] in hospital. She was pretty weak and tired-looking. Word came back through Anji that Sarah Macaulay had fed back everything to GB that I said re Charlie, Ed and the whole GB operation. TB thought I had gone too far. I was not so sure. At a minimum Charlie had to go, but Balls was becoming a menace too, constantly feeding the sense of grievance.

Thursday, February 19

Hattersley wrote back 'Get your rebuttal tanks off my lawn.' Quite funny, and the piece turned out to be fine. NHS waiting lists was the main news, and Dobson did very well deploying our 'take responsibility as well as credit' line, and admitting we had to do better. The question of legality in relation to Iraq was getting difficult. Yesterday the FCO tried to have another go at changing the line, saying there would have to be a new resolution come what may, after Kofi Annan's visit, where he was calling for full, unfettered access by the inspectors. Michael Pakenham [Defence and Overseas Secretariat, Cabinet Office] called me early to say that I had used the right line and the FCO were playing silly buggers trying to move it. I told Nigel Sheinwald it was silly, pointless to do this when there was no need, and we just stuck to that and waited to see what happened with Kofi. Nigel looked very fed up and was clearly getting it in the neck from Robin.

The Iraq meeting was quite bad-tempered. Cabinet was mainly Iraq and Ireland. TB said the FCO had done a good job getting the P5 together on this. Robin seemed to take that as a signal to push the line again that we had to go back to the UN for a new resolution. This was getting ridiculous. The last thing we needed was publicity over a Cabinet split on it. RC was very full of how their diplomacy had brokered the way for a P5 agreement. Re Kofi, he said none of us knew if Saddam was ready to cut a deal. He said he was brutal and psychologically disturbed. Clare was irritating as ever, saying we could not let SH build up CW and BW but she was worried about military action. She cited some briefing she'd got from a professor somewhere. TB said it was not an option to do nothing. We either got the inspectors in or we had to take action. There was a comical moment when Mo suggested Clare do an article about it all. Yes, said TB, you could get some coverage if you were out batting for the government. TB said the fear was Saddam would pitch a response perfectly to Kofi to get the French and the Russians into a different position to the rest of us. After the 11, I went to the JIC [Joint Intelligence Committee] briefing room with TB, Jonathan and John H, joined by [Richard] Wilson, [Roger] Liddle, Edgar Buckley [senior defence policy adviser, MoD], Air Marshal John Day [Deputy Chief of the Defence Staff (Commitments)], Guthrie and a few others, and we got the presentation on targeting plans. Ninety-six missiles from B-52s, 300 from ships in the Gulf. They envisaged 1,500 to 2,500 casualties. What struck me was not just the detail in the aerial photos, and the quality, but the extent to which they calculated where the mosques or any historical sites were, and the lengths they went to to avoid them. They whizzed through with a very straightforward approach. It was an odd feeling to be shown all this, to know where bombs might be heading, and to know people were going to be killed. I wondered if you ever became immune to that thought, and suspected you did.

The plan was to use B-52s, cruise missiles, wave after wave over a relatively short period, but non-stop. The main targets would be the Iraqi Republican Guard, command and control, air defences in the south. The planning documents stretched to about four dense books the size of *Yellow Pages*. TB raised re-attack if not all targets were taken out and Guthrie said there were no re-attack plans because the US were worried about 'Hanoi baggage', and he laughed. I sensed he wasn't totally taken with the Yanks. TB said he would speak to Bill. He agreed with Charles Guthrie you may need a second wave. Guthrie was clearly keen to get going. Robin C was not. RC said if we did not get another UNSCR we would be politically and diplomatically isolated. He was a lone voice pretty much, but kept going.

Charles said it was not helpful to think we needed to go for another resolution because it could take up to two weeks. He also said he was clear about what they were going into. There was tension with Robin on this and TB sided with the MoD. Later, Guthrie, out of uniform and wearing a very smart suit and the shiniest shoes I had seen for yonks, came over for a cup of tea and a chat. He said he sensed a like mind and wanted me to know the MoD had a lot of time for TB, and for me, and he was happy to work closely with me on the media front. He knew the MoD had traditionally not done media well and if I needed help in changing attitudes, he would provide it. He invited me down to Hereford [SAS HQ]. TB was working mainly on Ireland. Bertie still wanted to be able to say that Sinn Fein could be back in by March 2, less than two weeks away. TB said it was not possible. He was worried both about the Tories and public opinion. March 9 was their next offer. He said, as he left for the theatre, that he felt between a rock and a hard place on this. He said, I don't suppose it's possible to get them in too soon, is it? I said no, not really. He had another long chat with Kofi.

Friday, February 20

TB was having a two-hour meeting with GB on the Budget. At the pre-meeting, he went through the various difficulties. He agreed with a lot of the specific things being planned, but GB was basically trying to position it as a Budget for the poor, whereas we felt it should be more broadly aimed, including at the people who helped us win. So he was pushing more on the ISAs U-turn, not taxing child benefit, enterprise. He felt enterprise and tough economic management should be central to the communications. While that was going on, we had real problems on Ireland. Bertie was still pushing for Sinn Fein to be back in the fold by March 2 as a condition for expulsion. TB said it was not possible and we finally settled on March 9. That in itself will be difficult, as was clear from a very difficult call with Trimble, though at least he did not say he was walking. He asked TB to start pushing for the talks to wrap up earlier than May, something I started to hint at to the Sunday lobby.

The Iraq meeting was better, but the tensions are still there, with the FCO pushing a much more concessionary and negotiating line. As he left for Chequers, TB said he was getting fed up at the way they kept picking away at an argument we had settled. Then more Derry problems in a *Scotsman* story about eighty-seven paintings he'd got from Scotland's art collection. We were really taking a hit on this now. Sinead Cusack [actress] came in for a cup of tea and said that the arts really were fed up with us. The Irish and Mo put out statements on the Sinn Fein expulsion.

Saturday, February 21

In media terms, Ireland was not nearly as bad as it might have been, but an overnight bombing made life difficult again. TB called to say that the early intelligence suggested it was some renegade Republican outfit. He was also concerned that we were seen as pivotal re Iraq, with Kofi Annan now in Baghdad. Kofi called him and briefed him on his conversations post-Tariq Aziz [Iraqi Deputy Prime Minister] and pre-Saddam. The main calls of the day were on whether TB would accept Adams' suggestion of a meeting before Sinn Fein came back to the talks. TB was more confident the Budget was going to be a success. He said yesterday's meeting went OK, and part of the story around it had to be TB and GB coming together again, and he wanted me to make another effort to work closely with GB and his people. I had probably gone a bit too far with Sarah and should never have said I thought Ed should go as well as Charlie. TB said that was not a very wise thing to say, because GB believed now I was doing him in on a daily basis, systematically. I said that was ridiculous, and showed how off-balance GB was. He said that was no longer the point. He also said the problem with 'psychological flaws' was its brutal truth, which is why it hurt him so much. Then he said 'But I'm worried, Ali.' He was the one person who called me Ali when he was being serious. He said there had to be a sense of the two of them coming together after a difficult phase. Brian Wilson called to tell me the *Mail on Sunday* had got hold of the story that Donald Dewar rejected a knighthood for Sean Connery.

Sunday, February 22

There were several reports on the difference in emphasis between TB and Robin Cook, or between us and the States. I sent TB a note saying he must speak to Robin. He said he was getting fed up with the FCO. TB said that also the talk of concessions must stop, because it will be harder to get a deal backed by the US if we are still talking about concessions. He felt the problem was that Robin was too loose with his language, for example on the radio today talking about it being OK, if Saddam felt the deal was wrapped up in 'bows and ribbons', which again was taken by some as the language of concession. TB wanted the sense clearly communicated that we were sticking to a tough line to get what we wanted. He was also keen for there to be a proper understanding of Britain's role in the diplomacy. I could gauge how fed up he was with Robin by the fact he must have called me half a dozen times to say the same thing, which got a bit irritating.

I took the kids skating and then got a message that I had to go to a landline to listen in on the TB/Clinton call. The only place I could find was the foyer at the Sobell [leisure] centre and it was a bit surreal, kids wandering around in skates, and at one point the cleaner mopping around my feet as I listened to TB and Bill C talking about military action. Both were deliberately sounding a bit vague, and all I could do, briefing-wise, was put out a line saying they had spoken and reiterating the basic position. The main thing was that they wanted to get a new resolution, which would allow a military attack for material breach of the resolutions. They were both worried that Kofi would get a deal that would split the big five, and allow Saddam to diddle around. The bottom line was still unfettered access.

Then Kofi called TB and gave him a not very satisfactory briefing. He said he had an agreement, hoped that we were happy with it, that he got all that he was asked to get and now he was very tired. He said he would be leaving tomorrow and would be back in New York on Tuesday. TB did not press on the detail, assuming Kofi would not be able or willing to speak freely. Kofi sounded exhausted, TB sounded nervous, as if he was hearing behind the words a bit of a problem which was looming. There followed another call with Clinton, and this time both of them sounded a bit nervous. Bill said I don't like this delay. One and a half days, not knowing the detail, and he says it's a deal. But the problem is Saddam does know the detail and he could outspin and outsmart us on this, and I don't like that one bit. TB said a lot of this now was about who got their line out first and Saddam had the upper hand. We had to keep the focus on repeat inspections, not just a one-off inspection regime. TB said he got very little out of Kofi, and Bill said he was worried. He again stressed it was important [Richard] Butler [head of UNSCOM inspection team] was happy. There seemed to be some kind of hybrid agreement, and hybrid agreements usually let two sides say and do different things. Kofi had used Chirac's plane and we were trying to work out if there was any way of getting to him in Paris when he took it back there. If we had the French on top of the detail before we were, that would add to the problem.

Neither Clinton nor TB liked being in this position where it was being said a deal was done, that Kofi had got everything he wanted, so we were meant to look and sound pleased, but we had no idea what the deal was. TB was worried we would get to Tuesday and then not be able to sign up to it, which would be incredibly embarrassing for the UN. The UN were briefing the deal being done before we had any detail at all. The news was fine in terms of TB's role, lots on his calls etc., but it would all look a bit silly if we ended up not signing up to it. The danger was clear, that we end up being isolated with the US, everyone else agreeing to a deal we are not sure about.

Monday, February 23

The Kofi agreement was the big thing all day. As I said to TB, it was incredible that we were all signing up to it without any of the P5 actually having seen it, yet that was the case. There was plenty of talk around of Saddam having climbed down and backed down, but there was still a danger that he would get his version in first and we would not have time to catch up. I wrote a briefing note that said in his call, though it was difficult to speak openly, TB asked Kofi three questions on the key points of principle that we had hoped to secure, and he got a yes to all of them. It all seemed a bit too easy, and I was worried it would unravel but, as we agreed at the morning meeting, we had to decide very quickly whether to go with it, in terms of our tone. We adopted a 'yes, if' strategy, making clear that if it showed clear concession on the points of principle, that was fine. If not, we had to push to change the fine print.

The TB strategy meeting was low-key, though at least GB was engaging a bit more than usual. He even looked up from his notes when others were speaking from time to time. TB was sure that we were OK on the things that mattered and getting some credit on the economy, but I felt we had a real problem on people/privilege, and on trust/promises. We had to get back on the people's agenda. We were also worrying about the coming countryside rally [pro-hunting Countryside Alliance rally to be held on February 28] and my weekly SCU meeting was largely about that. At the morning meeting, I introduced the idea of another UNSCR which would give the allies the chance to move in on him in the future without all the diplomatic rigmaroles, based upon past resolutions. I had lunch with Kelvin MacKenzie. I felt there was no doubt he was partly responsible for the shift at the *Mirror*. Murdoch was his real hero and he waxed lyrical about him. He also said if I wanted a big job when I left, I should call. I got back to discover that the US had got hold of the Kofi document. It was OK in the main but there were one or two areas that we had to sort out the detail, which could be seen as being quite difficult, better for him than us. I wanted to get out there briefing on it straight away. TB spoke to Clinton, after which we organised a doorstep in which again he could push the tough message that we would accept it if ... Also that we wanted the new resolution to make sure that we didn't have to go back again. There were a couple more calls with Clinton later, then Chirac, who said TB was being intransigent, though he did at least concede that this was a victory for diplomacy backed by force.

Tuesday, February 24

The big question for the morning meeting was whether to do an Iraq statement or wait until tomorrow. Our minds were made up for us when the text of Kofi's agreement leaked on Reuters, while we were at the Festival Hall for the Dome event. TB also had to talk to Yeltsin, and I put together a new briefing for the 11 on the need for a new resolution. The line that it was a win for diplomacy backed by force was easy to get through.

Peter Hyman had done a very good draft for TB for his speech at the big Dome event, which was aimed at winning financial support and turning some of the media. He delivered it brilliantly and you could feel minds being changed. He pitched it as good for Britain, and really managed to enthuse people with it. David English said the *Mail* would find it much harder to criticise blindly now. Hezza was there, looking a bit old I thought. Kofi got a fantastic welcome at the UN, and he singled out Bill C and TB, which would drive Chirac crazy. Donald D came to see me worried re the Connery story which was still running big in Scotland. I said just stick to the line that we never comment on individual honours, and eventually it will go away. Then one day, give him the knighthood.

Wednesday, February 25

There was a real sense that TB had turned things on the Dome. The main media issue for us overnight was Polly Toynbee in the *Guardian* suggesting a U-turn over single-parent cuts. GB insisted it had nothing to do with him, and was blaming Harriet, who also denied it. GB and I spoke to agree a tough 'no U-turn' line, and indicate other areas for pretty tough reform. TB was livid about it, but I felt on one level it was fine, we should push it, saying that there was no U-turn, but yes, we were going to be doing the working families tax credit and other welfare reforms. We could then do health spending some time after the Budget. [Michael] Meacher was doing his Green Paper on right to roam [legislation allowing freedom of access to rural areas, opposed by the Country Landowners Association], and was in real hot water because he gave it to four countryside groups. JP wanted to sack him but TB said no, he should just apologise for it. The Derry story was rumbling along, with *The Times* splashing on his letter to Black Rod. PMQs was fine if dull and at the briefing afterwards I really went for it on welfare, single parents, signalling no U-turn, possibly further change. Things were suddenly a lot quieter. There had been a steady march to what we thought was an inevitable war, and now it was gone and there was a real void.

Thursday, February 26

We had a real problem with the *Guardian* yesterday being followed up big time and a senior minister, described as 'he' but possibly Harriet, giving several of the papers details of the childcare package. GB called and said he was really fed up with it, his Budget strategy was being completely hijacked. Then she went on *Woman's Hour* and *World at One* without any consultation and ended up walking out when she was asked a question she didn't like. GB was in a fury all day. The way we were going, there would be nothing left from the Budget on the day. He was largely to blame. He had allowed a culture of leaking to surround the Budget, and it meant that the basic discipline that for years had been taken for granted had broken down. If it was her, she was just following that. Peter M came to see TB to say he was worried about the Budget strategy, he didn't feel involved either in the thinking or the implementation. TB had had dinner with Derry last night, and said he must do nothing with the media without first going through me or Peter and work on the big issues and get on with the job.

The UDP meeting was fairly positive despite all the difficulties. They raised several times the point TB must not see Adams and if he did they would have to review the position. Yet they were still giving us the impression it could be OK by May. TB had a fairly jokey JP bilateral, then Cabinet, which was Iraq followed by GB going through the outlines of the Budget. Robin said there were really worrying signs about what UNSCOM can do. We were pursuing a balanced twin-track approach – light at the end of the tunnel on sanctions, allied to clear warnings if Iraq breaks the agreement. TB said we can only tell if it is a good agreement by whether it holds or not. He said he was assured by Chirac he agrees the language makes clear military action will follow if Saddam breaks the agreement. JP did a number saying how well TB, George Robertson and RC had done. Clare piped up: 'Robin has played it beautifully.' On the Budget GB started by saying that we were into a stage where the press seemed to know more about the Budget than the Treasury. JP fell about and was chuckling away for ages, thinking like most of them that GB was the last person to complain about the Budget being briefed out in advance.

GB rattled through a stack of economic figures, did a number on welfare to work, set everything in the long term and gave as little detail as he could get away with. He went through the areas in which we would be looking for change, without really saying what the change was. What was clear was that it was going to be a fairly tough Budget, take away more than give, certainly not an electioneering Budget. Earlier GB had said to me we were in real danger and needed to get out a strong message that this is not a giveaway Budget. I briefed a very tough anti-public-spending line, and emphasised the Budget as part of the welfare reform programme.

Bertie Ahern arrived and Joe Lennon [Ahern's press secretary] and I had agreed there should be pooled statements by the two of them from armchairs, as if the cameras just wandered in and found them. It was a bit Saddamesque but it went OK. They were both determined that we can get there by May. It was a good meeting. TB said he feared if we did not keep working towards a deal, and get one by May, we were sunk. Bertie spoke of evil criminal elements who were trying to derail the whole thing. He said he had told Adams and McGuinness that TB had been generous with his time but could not wait around forever. We were at least back into real detail on the North-South council and the ministerial bodies. Bertie said the UUs believe you can leave all the North-South bodies in a grey area and you can't. We have to be specific.

TB and I left for Paddington and the train to Reading [for a welfare reform consultation]. In the car, as ever, he went over his various current angsts. He was not sure we had a proper grip on the Budget. Chirac was being difficult on Iraq. The Iraqis were making pretty clear they would not deliver. He was alarmed about Harriet. He thought Frank Field's White Paper was crap. He felt they were both proving to be useless. The Reading meeting was the best of the welfare tour so far. He spoke to a group of disabled people who were a lot more reasonable than the pressure group people. He told me he was thinking of a reshuffle before Easter. He was wondering whether to add Harriet to the list. I said I bet you don't. He was also disappointed with Chris Smith.

Friday, February 27

TB was seeing Trimble, otherwise it was a fairly quiet day. I went to the *What the Papers Say* lunch, which had all the Fleet Street great and good, so-called, and was fairly jolly. But it was at these kinds of media events that it always got home to me that I had left journalism for a very different world, and felt more comfortable in the new one than the old. It was nice to dip back in for an hour or two, but that was it.

Saturday, February 28

The story dominating the weekend was the countryside march, which was pretty big, and, whatever the focus on specific issues, indicated a sense of rebellion against change, and so against New Labour. We had had plenty of meetings on it, and in the end we may have gone over the top in terms of concessions, which suggested we accepted their somewhat apocalyptic view of their fate. We'd announced no closure of village schools without reference to the Secretary of State, which led the news.

Sunday, March 1

The march got huge and largely favourable coverage. We had basically taken the view not to be too provocative. On the contrary we had gone for broadly conciliatory messages and may even have gone over the top. Things were going fine until Jack C made some silly remarks in the *Sunday Express*. Jack had said on Thursday that Elliot Morley was going and then on Friday said he wasn't. This all got ridiculously huge coverage. We were struggling with the balance and tone on this.

On Friday a letter came out effectively showing the march as a front for hunting, which led some in the government to suggest we should not send a minister but again I felt we had to put the case for what we were doing.

Monday, March 2

There was huge coverage for the march, but you sensed it would go out of the picture fairly quickly. The line I used at the 11 was that we governed for the whole nation, and the policies we were pursuing were for the whole nation. At the political office meeting, TB said he felt we were losing our grip a little. On hunting, he said he wished we had never got into it, and we should never have let Mike Foster do his [anti-hunting] bill. He felt there was a general lack of focus. I felt a lot of that was about the ability of ministers, which was another reason why we needed a reshuffle fairly quickly.

Geoffrey Goodman [industrial journalist, former *Mirror* colleague] came to see me and said that at the TGWU dinner last night GB was doing his 'red Gordon' act, all focused on GCHQ, union recognition, poverty, the history of the unions in the party. Geoffrey said it was totally transparent and moderately effective. Peter M felt that the whole history of the government so far was that when ministers were integrated into the centre, things went well. When they weren't, things went badly. GB was easily the most guilty on this front.

We were planning to announce a 15p prescription rise, which would lead to another rash of 'honeymoon over' stories. At the SCU meeting, PG said that we had a problem with TB seeming to cave in to vested interests. I argued that the strategy on the march had been right, but he wasn't alone in thinking we should have been a bit tougher on them. I was called into a TB/GB meeting and said to GB he had created a problem in that we had lots of good stories from the Budget, all of them already out there, and as far as news was concerned on the day, only a few stories left. I stayed for the Treasury presentation of forecasts, which was not as good as we expected and then left for the four o'clock, which was all about prescriptions and the country-side march.

There was a bit of a growing anti-TB mood in Number 10, the political staff in particular feeling that he was now reacting instinct-ively against anything that might be deemed traditional Labour. TB was finally accepting he could not really treat GB the same way as before. Jonathan pointed out, for example, that GB was the only person TB had told about Roger Moore, like Connery, getting snubbed re a knighthood and it had since appeared in the *Mail on Sunday*. I had another call with Derry on how he should handle his appearance at the PASC tomorrow,[1] and any interviews on the legal aid plans he was doing on Wednesday. I said it was imperative he separated refurbishment from policy issues and showed a bit of humility, understanding why there was concern at this kind of thing. He felt if he dealt with it all factually it would be fine, added to which he had the backing of the Lords authorities. I was maybe too blunt with him, but I was worried he was heading for another disaster. I said he must understand that what we see as his humour and humanity, and his intellect, others see as arrogance and he must avoid anything that plays into this.

Tuesday, March 3

We took a big hit on prescriptions and I wrote first thing to Romola Christopherson [director of press and publicity, Department of Health] saying it had been a mistake not to field a minister. That, the march, Derry and the war pensions inaction to come, meant that we were in for a rough ride. There was a real sense we were losing our grip and another real problem developing, that we were in danger of being seen as a soap opera not a government. It was why the Budget and the welfare reform programme were even more important. The main story overnight was the new UNSCR on Iraq, which the BBC was saying was an isolation of the US and UK. We had to fight hard all day to get up the line that it was actually what we had asked for, but without much success. TB called me in on Iraq, and asked me to speak to the French and Russians to try to get them closer to saying what we and the Americans are saying. I gave it a go, but the truth was they were on a different page, and though Catherine [Colonna, Chirac's press secretary] was very nice about it, Chirac wanted to cause us problems over it. Incredibly, at the eleven o'clock, nearly all the questions were on trivia, not one on Iraq, and I had to raise Iraq myself.

The press were warming up for Derry at the select committee, which we finally managed to find on TV, and I settled down to plough through some paperwork while watching a PR disaster unfold. It was so bad that it was comic, and he seemed to have no sense whatever of how it would be seen. Yes, he conceded, it was a lot of money to spend on wallpaper [£59,000]. But that was the total extent to which

[1] Lord Irvine had been called to appear before the Commons Public Administration Select Committee to explain the £650,000 spent on refurbishing his official residence.

he followed the briefing. Then came a succession of extraordinary remarks, which would be panned all over the shop. He said the refurbishment was a 'noble cause'. The whole thing was a storm in a teacup, and he had this hysterical line that the wallpaper would last sixty years, because it was not like something from your local DIY shop. It also became very apparent that he didn't know what B&Q was. I love him dearly but even I found him arrogant, overbearing, pompous. Then Sheila Thompson from his department called to ask how I thought it went. She said that at the department they thought it was quite good. I told her it was a disaster area, awful, and he was going to get a total pasting in the press. I told Derry the same just before I went to the four o'clock briefing, and said he had fed all the preconceptions they wanted till they were stuffed with joy. He was having none of it. He said 'I am totally unrepentant. It was important to get the facts on the record, I have done so and I'm happy about it.' I said the tape will be played again and again, because the media felt they could have a field day with it. 'Well, be that as it may, I am absolutely convinced it was the right thing to do, and I'm glad I did.' I said we will have to agree to disagree. Indeed we will, he said, good day, and he put the phone down.

TB called Derry and was very firm with him. I sat opposite and so could only half hear Derry but it was a pretty tough conversation for TB to have. He said we have a problem and if you can't see it's a problem, then that means we have a bigger problem. It's not what you said in terms of the facts, it is the manner and the expressions used. DIY stores are used by millions of people, and what they will see out of that is a snob. It cuts right through to them. I thought we got the message through last week that if you are going to be in this game, you have to be political. Derry then said that his officials said he had done well. TB said in which case they are completely bonkers. It pains me to talk to you like this but you are being damaged and in turn that is damaging the government. Derry now sounded hurt. He said I can send you the transcripts. TB exploded, I'm not interested in the fucking transcripts. I am interested in what the public are saying, and the problem that poses to their understanding of the government. You may have right on your side, but how on earth can you call the refurbishment of an official residence a noble fucking cause? As he spoke, he was pulling faces at me, looks of ever greater exasperation. I couldn't remember the last time TB swore so much in one conversation. He said he hated going over the top but he felt it was the only way to get it through to him. Otherwise he would not take it seriously. He said what really worried him was that Derry didn't seem to realise it was a problem. He asked if I thought he was rescue-able. I said it was difficult. TB was thinking about doing a political Cabinet on Thursday and really going for them, repeating his analysis that Labour governments founder on egotism and division. There was too much briefing, too many special advisers talking without knowing what they were talking about. Later I had to deal with the leak of a document showing Derry blocked Donald D's plans to amend the Sex Discrimination Act to get more women Scots MPs. Someone was clearly doing in Derry now.

Wednesday, March 4

TB was incredibly rough with Derry, almost losing it at points. He swore several times, and said that he was in no doubt yesterday had lost us council seats. 'You are doing yourself and the government real damage. Maybe some people think it is good to tell the public to fuck off, but I am not sure it is entirely sensible. They think, we got rid of the Tories because they were out of touch, pompous, up themselves and couldn't care less about ordinary people, and then we have this and they think what's different?' He said the most worrying thing is that he couldn't see it was a problem. What he said about B&Q will leave people wondering whether he was on our planet, he said. You have to take it from us on this, about what the public will take. It pains me to say this but you can't take much more damage than you are. Derry asked him if he wanted him to leave the government and TB said no, but he had to be rebuilt, and that would only be done if he took advice. He must not do any media without talking to me. I advised him not to do any interviews for a while. He said it would lead to stories he had been gagged. I said that was preferable to more interviews on the wallpaper.

At the briefing after PMQs, all the press were interested in was the PA story that TB had been seen in Westminster Cathedral, on his own, and was he converting to Catholicism? I was pretty brutal, saying even prime ministers were entitled to some privacy. We ran around the block on that for ages. The other important thing today was a meeting with TB, GB, Peter M, AC, Jonathan, Jeremy, Ed and Charlie on the Budget. I said I was worried about expectations and that there were a lot of bad things to come. GB said he could handle that. He agreed there should be no more leaks. TB said it must be New Labour in every line, not just helping the poor through tax reform, health, childcare, but also big on enterprise. GB said ambition was to be the theme. We tried and failed to think of a way of renaming the working families tax credit. As these things go, it was reasonably good-natured. GB said we had to work together. In that spirit I suggested TB should label the Budget in his Scotland speech on Friday, but GB was very resistant, saying it would open up a new flank on Budget stories. We agreed we should do health spending, with a Dobson statement on reform the day after the Budget. We also needed a JP statement on the Tube and one on childcare. The childcare package was way above what they had originally put forward. Up from £250 million to £1.5 billion. TB said what was missing at the moment was New Labour. That was the main message and it had to infuse the Budget. I also felt we had to use it to get a sense of TB and GB coming together.

Thursday, March 5

I was working late last night dealing with *The Times* on discussions between us and the Tories on reforming the Lords. I worked up a holding line about initial soundings. The first call of the day was from Derry who was worried about it. He felt these meetings had been suspect from the start. His worry was that he gave the impression to the PASC that there were no discussions and had therefore been misleading. We agreed we could hold the line that these were initial soundings about Lords reform. What was not clear was whether the Tories were playing games. Cabinet was Ireland, agreeing to see Adams next week, Iraq, BSE and the Lords. TB mildly read the riot act with them all, said he was fed up with leaks and the like, that there was not enough discipline. MPs were complaining that ministers and special advisers were out of control so why should they be so well behaved? Ivor Richard said he could not work out if the Tories wanted a deal on the Lords or not, but they have accepted the hereditary peerage has to go. TB was not so sure, felt they were engaged in a stalling exercise. They were trying to get us into a box. I was dealing with Mo re Adams and also the various Lords competing forces.

Trevor Kavanagh called, clearly on a tip-off from the cops, about the incident with Euan being attacked, and Fulham police investigating.[1] Then ITN called about it and I spoke to Nigel Dacre and said it was not remotely in the public interest and totally unfair on Euan to report it. CB and I agreed we should cite the PCC code re children. TB urged caution.

[1] The prime minister's seventeen-year-old son and a teenage friend were confronted by a gang of youths and mugged when returning after an evening out in Swiss Cottage, London.

Some of the papers did Euan, but apart from a brief mention on *GMTV* there was no broadcast coverage. The BBC was leading on an extraordinary story about Gavin Strang who said on *The World Tonight* there may be a windfall tax on Railtrack fat cats, and was then slapped down by a DETR [Department of the Environment, Transport and the Regions] spokesman. In the car on the way to the airport, TB was worrying the speech wasn't strong enough. He wanted a message speech, New Labour, reform, tough on welfare, Labour the party of economic competence. There was an unbelievable cock-up on the way up to Scotland. As the plane neared the airport we realised the sea was in the wrong place, and the mountains were the wrong mountains. They had flown us to Edinburgh not Glasgow. It meant we were half an hour late getting there. TB said he had a very difficult meeting with Margaret [Beckett] and GB on trade union recognition. He said MB was pretty Old Labour on it and GB refusing to engage really. We did a good jobs visit in Glasgow.

The *Standard* splashed on Euan, until I told Max Hastings [editor] of all the discussions yesterday. They dropped it, helped by the Treasury PQ announcing a crackdown on offshore trusts which would turn out to be the main story of the day. It was clearly going to get TB's speech totally upstaged. We were finishing the speech at the station hotel in Perth, with TB locking himself away. Donald came up and wanted to take out the word entrepreneurship, feeling it would go down badly in the party. When I told TB he was gobsmacked. He was worried DD was losing his nerve a bit. He said he was worried what might happen to the Scottish party once the Parliament was up and running. 'There is a real rabbit in headlights feeling.' The speech was OK, but it wasn't terribly newsy. Briefing the Scots press afterwards, they were the usual whining lot, why didn't he say this, why didn't he say that, never asking about what he actually said. I emphasised he was PM of the UK, which includes Scotland. It was a UK speech.

I saw Charlie who insisted they had had no choice but to do the loophole trusts story today. Peter M was convinced that GB deliberately upstaged TB today. I called GB and said he had totally blown out Tony today. He said he hadn't meant to. They had to do this measure today otherwise risk losing money. He wanted to do it yesterday but couldn't because they could not get a question down. 'Why would I want to upstage Tony?' Fairly obvious. He said he thought it was a great speech, but also that the Scots were a pain at the moment and wouldn't necessarily buy it.

We spoke about current working operations and agreed we were not working well together, that the pre-Budget leaking had been bad, and we were not in the right shape. He wanted me to work with Charlie. I said that was difficult against this background. He asked me to meet him and talk over it. Then we had by our standards a fairly pleasant conversation about the Scottish party, Budget strategy. He tried out a few of his jokes on me. He was apologetic about the news, in which TB was just tagged on to the end of his story. He said Scotland had had a clear idea about the way forward but Donald was really only interested in steady as she goes, no real strategy for big change. We agreed to meet next week, and I said I was willing to get together on our operations but it would require mutual buy-in. TB was still thinking GB was basically a good thing. But he said his big weakness is that he has to dress up New Labour policies in Old Labour rhetoric, whereas TB says things as they are. He reckoned their first big argument had been over whether there was a need to expel Militant.[1] TB was absolutely clear about it, but said GB was equivocal. He wanted to build up membership instead, and felt that would do the trick.

Saturday, March 7

The only real work of the day came when Mike Prescott [political journalist] called to say the *Sunday Times* were doing a story on three Mossad agents being arrested trying to bug a prominent Arab's home. As [Binyamin] Netanyahu was due to see TB tomorrow, the timing was pretty bad. I spoke to John Holmes who said it was crap and we just about persuaded the *Sunday Times*. The royal story was running big all weekend and people were constantly claiming we were involved in it, which was total balls.[2] The one problem was JP being done in by the *Sunday Times* over a donation from the Rowntree Trust not being declared and a story in the *Observer* that his son benefited from a deal sanctioned by the DETR.[3] I spoke to JP, very pissed off, and agreed we should put out a statement with all the facts.

[1] The Militant Tendency, a Trotskyist organisation set up within the Labour Party in 1964, left the party following an annual conference decision in 1991, claiming Labour had become a wholly capitalist party.
[2] Following an internal memo, minor members of the Royal Family could lose their HRH titles in proposals to be presented to the Queen.
[3] A company secretary, Jonathan Prescott, son of the deputy prime minister (who was also Secretary of State for the Environment) had bought eighteen modernised council homes in Hull for £5,000 each. The Department of the Environment had given approval.

March '98: GB pleads with AC to work with Whelan

Sunday, March 8

The papers didn't do much with JP but the BBC ran it all day. JP called me from the train saying he thought he should do *The World This Weekend*, which was fine. I didn't go in for Netanyahu.

Monday, March 9

There was a lot more royal stuff around the place and we were constantly being put at the centre of it. I felt Peter M was becoming more and more detached from day-to-day events. At the office meeting TB went over what he wanted out of the welfare Green Paper. He felt the big areas were the state pension and means testing, but that we should at least be thinking of major reforms even if decades down the track. He also wanted a lot more work done on disability payments and incapacity benefits. He was also getting more and more agitated about fox hunting. 'I always knew this was a disaster. We should never have let Mike Foster do it.' He said he was convinced that when it came to it, people will not want the consequences of this, the criminalising of people who ride around the countryside chasing a fox. Bruce [Grocott] said that the gun lobby accepted the guns legislation. That was after Dunblane, said TB, when a lot of children had been shot. He seemed very fed up and had clearly had very little rest at the weekend.

Also, the Anji situation had flared up again. She told TB she wanted to leave. He was totally against, felt she added something to the whole operation and he resented the idea she should feel pushed out. I felt TB had never really explained Anji's role properly to CB, who only saw the flirty side of her, not someone who could do a job of work. There had developed a total lack of reason on either side, with CB seeing no good, and TB getting angry because he felt that she was trying to decide who worked for him. Meanwhile John Holmes asked me to start thinking about how we could best present delaying the May deadline on the NI talks. It was clear from his phone call with Trimble later that it was getting very difficult.

TB was very funny, joking about all the little gifts that he got. He said he loved Chirac's watch. He liked the pen from Germany, so Helmut was a top bloke. Japan gave him a kite. So he could still make us all laugh, but I was finding life a pain in the arse at the moment. I felt I was running around putting out fires, stopping fires, managing things OK, but that we were not really driving through a strategy. And despite the recent chats, I felt the GB situation getting worse not better.

Tuesday, March 10

The JP story was dying away when for some reason he gave a statement to *The Times* that there was a vendetta against him. Then both he and his agent went on the *Today* programme. On one level it was fine as he was a human being reacting very angrily to his family being unfairly attacked. But it also led to the Hull can of worms being opened up and by the end of the day was leading all the news. There was a bad poll in the [Glasgow] *Herald* in which we were just one point ahead of the Nats [Scottish National Party] and there was a big analysis of all the differences between TB and GB. The reality was getting 'out there'. There was a Cabinet on the forward legislative programme, and the eleven o'clock was mainly about that. Nick Brown was clear the programme was about as full as it could be. TB had a Clinton call then a welfare meeting, which he said ended with Frank Field attacking GB for always moving the goalposts just as a discussion ended. We announced the Adams meeting for Thursday, which went fine.

I said to TB that if the Anji situation didn't improve, he needed to think about an exit strategy for her. He said he didn't intend to let her go. She was staying. I spoke to JP and said he had to try to wind down the whole thing. He said he would ensure any inquiry was done very quickly. Most people thought he was barmy to keep going on it, but he was really angry, and adamant it had to be challenged.

Wednesday, March 11

JP was still bubbling away. I was promoting the TB dinner with European leaders. I met Brian Bender on CAP and structural funds. Then a pretty tough meeting with Donald, Murray [Elder] and Wendy Alexander [Dewar's special advisers]. They were complaining about lack of resources. I said the problem was lack of strategy, and the need to take on the press rather than let them feel they had you on the run. TB was looking really pained by the whole meeting, and had become extraordinarily defensive. He felt he'd tried to be tough, that there was only so much you could do. It was difficult. They believed if they got a couple of decent press people, they would be fine, but I felt the problem was much deeper than that.

PMQs was fine then I got back for the meetings with [John] Hume and [João] Havelange [FIFA president]. Hume was doing a doorstep in the street as Havelange arrived. He said he would back our bid [to host the 2006 World Cup]. On the way out I asked him if he would say that in the street and he said yes. He said the reason was that he had asked to see Helmut Kohl who was too busy, whereas TB had

March '98: Difficult meeting with Dewar re Scotland

replied straight away. These top sports administrators were a certain breed, over-dressed, terribly self-important and with a ludicrous entourage of people blowing them up the whole time.

Thursday, March 12

I was getting really tired and had to be up early to get in and prepare for the Adams meeting. McGuinness was away. The visit was leading the news all day. I was working on a Budget article but despite the conversation with GB last week, and the plan to meet and agree a communications plan tying TB and GB together, nothing had come of it, and he was clearly ploughing his own furrow. Inevitably, there was a lower media turnout for Adams, and a diminished sense of excitement or expectation, but in substance it was a good meeting, more positive than we had felt in advance. Adams was a good talker, maybe talked a bit too much, but he had a rich voice, usually stopped to think before speaking and didn't let up till his point was made. He struck me as less emotional than McGuinness, whose absence maybe took a bit of tension out of the meeting.

Adams said he did not have control of the IRA, but we have influence and we have tried to use it. He was adamant the crisis of confidence came before the killings, though he accepted they had not helped. But he felt there were double standards applying. We got down into some real detail and Adams sensed TB and Mo didn't exactly know the constitutional implications of some of this, and said he found it odd. TB said Jonathan [Stephens, NIO] could work it out with them afterwards. TB said if they could embrace consent, they would get greater US support. TB had to leave for the EU conference at Lancaster House. Adams and I had a little session at the end and agreed he would say he wanted back in the talks as soon as possible, which was good, and the press were picking up positive vibes.

Alex F came in for a cup of tea. He was due to meet Cathy [his wife] later and suddenly remembered it was his wedding anniversary. I got Alison to bring up some of the Number 10 items [official gifts made for 10 Downing Street]. I went to Lancaster House. TB's press conference went fine then we walked back through the park. He said he wanted Anji and Kate [Garvey] more central in the operation, getting a grip of the diary. He said he felt his key people were not working properly. 'Peter is preoccupied with the Dome. You and GB are not working together. CB and Anji can't get on so Anji is being frozen out. Jonathan is finding the pressure of work hard and sometimes his political judgement is weak.' He said we had done what Clinton warned us against – we had allowed the operation to become depoliticised. Ministers were not political. The party machine had been weakened.

Peter M called a meeting with Jonathan, Anji and Kate to try to work out a better way. CB was railing at Peter who then blamed Fiona and it was all getting silly. CB and Fiona felt Anji was exploiting TB's current vulnerability because he was admitting, for the first time really, that there might be a real problem with GB. He and Cherie had had a whole stack of rows about Anji now, and it was going nowhere. I was really getting worried this was going to get out publicly and *Peyton Place* really would take off. At Roz Preston's farewell, TB made a moving speech but lodged a couple of references to 'those who have been with me from the beginning', as a signal re Anji. Fiona and I had another great hoo-ha about it all. I said TB had to be able to have working for him the people he wanted. Yes, she said, but if that meant a woman that his wife felt was there in part for emotional support, he had to understand how wounding that was. I said we all have to give him emotional support at times.

Friday, March 13

The hunting bill finally got kicked out today. The CB/Anji situation was pretty bad, but frankly I could not be bothered. I drove in with Jonathan who seemed fed up, undermined and was really pissed off that he was at the centre of this nonsense. I called TB from the car. He was due to meet GB for another Budget discussion and I said that there had to be a presentation meeting too. I went to the TB/GB meeting, and we were later joined by Peter. Jeremy [Heywood] was already there. There was a constant tension though for once GB seemed more relaxed than TB, probably because he had greater knowledge of the contents and greater control. It was ludicrous that we were having to prise out details like teeth.

TB was absolutely sure that it had to be New Labour, while GB was clearly wanting the focus on helping the poor. There were a number of ideas we were still unclear about, child benefit, married couple's allowance, for example. GB had a draft of the speech with him and said we could go through it line by line, but TB was due to leave for Chequers. We flicked through it. I said I was not sure what the central message was yet. There were too many messages. We were also having trouble with the Treasury because I had circulated a note on the Budget, which I had sent to GB for clearance but he had not come back, so I just went with it. The tensions between the two offices were ridiculous. The *Sunday Times* were doing a profile of GB's team on the line they were preparing him for the top job, also that it was

March '98: TB wants Budget to feel more New Labour

a Budget for the poor, and the middle classes were going to have to pay. There was a real stupidity to what they were doing. They were feeding division. Nor was it sensible to piss off large numbers of people who elected you by saying this was not a Budget for them.

TB seemed tired. After he left for Chequers, GB and I had a chat in his Number 11 office. I said I wanted to have a briefing strategy that had them coming back together around the Budget. He said there was no point coming together just for that.

He was being friendly, but he veered from being fairly relaxed to being in a state of absolute torture, his hands held tight together, his leg going up and down, suddenly getting up and pacing. He was rubbing his hand through his hair again and again and looked a nervous wreck except in a few moments of calm. He seemed at the end of his tether but I knew him well enough to know some of it was acting to make the point he was making. I think his aim was to get me to work with Charlie, but as the conversation went on, it got a bit deeper than that. He was clearly testing out whether there was any way I would turn against TB. He asked why I couldn't work with Charlie. I said I was actually fairly easy-going and could work with anyone provided they were professional. But I didn't trust Charlie, and would never do so. He was constantly briefing against TB, me, and anyone to do with us. The final straw for me was the *Scotland on Sunday* story that I had said he was gay. He said, why on earth would I want that written? I said maybe you wouldn't, but you allowed these people to operate in a certain way, and they were forever putting it round that we did you in. It was bollocks. On the contrary we were always going out of our way to talk you up. That was the story – Peter and I in a plot against him.

He then picked up the pace and the volume, said 'You have enormous power in here and you shouldn't use it against me. I could go away and have a nice life but I believe in what we're doing. So do you, so that's what we should use any power for.' He said if you leave welfare to Harriet and Frank Field, you're dead. There is nobody in Number 10 who can do it. I laughed. 'What about TB for God's sake? He's the prime minister.' 'He's too busy and he's not focused. It can't be done. You have to work with me on it.' I said I can work with both of you. We were then back to imagined slights and plots. He said it was crazy if he had a few people in for drinks in Number 11 and this was written up as a plot to do in Tony. He said I really want you to work with Charlie. I said I can't work with someone when I can't be sure he's not using anything that is said against us the whole time. 'I feel the same about Peter,' he said. I said Peter is

Peter. I am me, I am not Peter, and I can't work with Charlie. I said at times Peter was a nightmare, but I can work with him because he is clever and for all his faults basically on the right side of the line. Charlie is a menace, with very few redeeming features that I can detect. We left it that we would just keep in touch on the Budget on an ongoing basis. It had been useful to clear the air but the overwhelming sense I was left with was the torture, and also the rather clumsy way he tried to set me against TB. He said that at one point TB was to the right of 'both of us' on a lot of issues, and that Peter – 'unlike you' – was motivated more by status and profile than using politics as a force for good.

Saturday, March 14

The Times did a big piece on GB planning for the leadership, again emphasising this was a Budget for the poor, which the middle classes would pay for. Work-wise it was a quiet weekend. I allowed myself to let David Wastell [Sunday Telegraph] talk me into a splash on TB taking over the Northern Ireland talks, which as a result went too big on the news, and with no real strategic gain. I should have just told him there was no story. These Sunday guys were so fucking desperate the whole time, whining that we had to feed them or they would have to write shit that would cause us trouble.

Fiona spoke to CB several times over the weekend, and apparently Anji had a session with TB on Friday to try to sort things out. I think they were both pissed off with me for not getting too involved, but I was at a loss to know what to do, added to which Fiona was so firmly supporting CB that it was impossible to talk about it at home without us flying off the handle at each other. I genuinely felt now only TB and CB could sort it. They had both locked themselves into ridiculous positions. He was angry because he felt he was the prime minister and being told who he could and couldn't hire on the basis of what he saw as irrational over-the-top feelings about her. She was angry because he didn't seem to understand why she felt it so deeply. She felt totally undermined by her presence.

Sunday, March 15

JP was on Frost, raging at the press, particularly the Sunday Times. We went to Philip and Gail's to discuss PG's book [The Unfinished Revolution: How the Modernisers Saved the Labour Party]. It was a good read and would be well received but he clearly pulled his punches. His thinking was that he had to work with most of the people in there. But I felt he needed to explain better why TB became leader, and that would mean analysing more up-to-date mistakes than just the years when the party went off the rails. But PG really didn't want to say anything that would be taken as undermining Neil, which was fair enough.

Jonathan and Sarah [Helm, partner] came round for a drink, in a real state. Jonathan looked tired, like he had not been sleeping. He felt badly undermined. Sarah was really angry that he could work so hard, and be so loyal, and be made to feel like trash. I said he shouldn't worry. TB was forever pushing us all harder, was not great at compliments or thanks, and could criticise all of us from time to time, but I had heard not the remotest hint he was thinking of getting rid of him. He should also ask TB what he actually wanted him to do. But also, let's not pretend that things were working very well, because they weren't. Anji was just one of the problems. The big one was GB. Peter M was another. I guess I was another, because TB's constant complaint to me was that his key people were just not working together, and he didn't think I made the effort I should with GB and Peter. Jonathan was very down, and very down on TB. He said he wasted so much time and energy, duplicated so much work. 'If he wants me to be a glorified diary secretary, then no thanks, I'm off.'

Monday, March 16

I picked up Jonathan on the way in and he was very subdued. I was wondering if he was tough enough, and I think he was too. The Budget was still being set up as a hit on the middle classes. Another problem was the *Independent* saying that TB had stopped GB taxing child benefit. This led to a pretty angry bilateral at 5.15. Jonathan and I were there at the start but it all got a bit heated and TB asked us to go out. They were then blaming each other. TB felt there was a deliberate strategy to use the Budget to position GB differently to TB and what we were elected on. GB felt we were deliberately running a strategy of TB binding him in. Peter M and I both felt GB was thinking more about party opinion than the public.

What was ridiculous was that the Budget, on the policy side, was in good shape. This was essentially at this stage an argument about presentation. We had the office meeting up in the flat and Cherie came through to see we were OK and did not for once react viscerally to seeing Anji there. TB was complaining his diary was a problem and that we never had time to think. TB said he didn't mind GB doing a bit of repositioning himself, so long as he was not pursuing a different policy agenda, and he didn't believe he was. At both [lobby] briefings

I was repeating the Sunday lobby stuff about them working together, but I was in a foul mood and snapping at everyone the whole time.

TB had come to the conclusion the Harriet was not up to it and that Frank [Field] was not much better but had authority in the area and we had to use it. We had a long discussion about the [welfare reform] Green Paper, whether we should stick to principles and success yardsticks, or whether it should be something more hard-edged. I felt it had to go beyond waffle, that 'where's the beef?' would be a hard question to answer as things stood. The message is pretty clear – work for those who can and security for those who can't. We have to be tough on work, soft on the disabled, but also see through change to incapacity benefit long term. And we had to start grappling pensions. At the welfare meeting later with Harriet, she struck me as being shot to pieces. The department was simply not being run and you sensed three zones on this – GB, HH and Frank and there was a dysfunction between them.

JP finally and reluctantly agreed to do his [post-Budget] statement on Friday, then Blunkett and I had a tussle about him doing his on Thursday. Then I discovered Dobson had not even been told he was meant to be doing one on Wednesday. Why on earth it was part of my job to be organising these fucking statements was beyond me. At the TB/GB meeting, GB was vile to TB, friendly to me. Later I learned why when they asked for help on the Budget TB statement. But he was not terribly happy with my briefings strategy. He said it looked like I was trying to communicate a sense of TB stopping him from doing what he wanted. I said I was trying to give the sense of them working as a team. 'What's wrong with that?' TB asked him. 'This is allowing them to say you are in charge.' TB said surely the prime minister and Chancellor working together is a good message. Depends, he said.

Tuesday, March 17
We got the Budget back on track in terms of expectations. It was up as New Labour and the briefings on TB/GB working together had a positive effect. TB was becoming very hands-on re the presentation. He said he wanted me to stress that this was enterprise and fairness combined. It had to become a turning point. I had a meeting with Whelan and David Hill to go through the operation post-Budget. The Cabinet on it was OK, GB rattling through it all as fast as he could, his hair smart for once I noticed, but their reaction was more muted than I imagined, probably because so much of it had been in the press. I used TB and GB words at the morning briefing to hammer out

more of the same message, then kept back the broadcasters who would be doing it live to go through some of the detail, and made clear there would be no hit on child benefit. I also briefed that TB was fine with GB having a sense of power and his desire to build a base. I stressed that TB was confident enough to deal with other big people in the government. The lunchtimes were excellent, lots of TB/GB in harmony, and no hit on the middle classes. GB said there was no way you could say this is not enterprise or New Labour. Although he didn't want to admit it, I think we had just about won him round to the briefing strategy of the last few days based on strong message rather than detail.

Meanwhile Fiona had a long session with TB to discuss the Anji/Cherie situation. He said he really felt he needed her working there, that there were things she did that nobody else did. He felt it would be bad all round if she was forced out. He said he would go crazy if I went. Nor did he want her to leave. He valued the team. Fiona felt he was in a pretty bad way. He felt I should have got more involved in sorting this but she explained I couldn't stand it.

We went over for the Budget and GB did a pretty good job. The MPs reacted pretty well, and so did the press afterwards. I went round the gallery, like the old days, and it was going down well. Making work pay, childcare, child benefit, it was all playing well. I sensed we were turning the corner after a pretty crap period. I still felt we could get the big events right, and it was hugely important we did. These were the big connecting moments that mattered. The *Nine O'Clock News* was absolutely brilliant. I even sent Whelan a pager message to say so. Team effort, he said. Perhaps. The press liked it. The party would be happy. The middle classes were fine. The Tory response was dire. Murdoch called TB re his efforts to get into the [Silvio] Berlusconi media empire, and wanted TB to speak to Prodi to say he shouldn't interfere.[1] We had a discussion about whether he should. TB said if it was BT or any other company with major British interests, there would be no question, but we should reflect.

Wednesday, March 18

GB got a fantastic press for his Budget, and I wrote him a note to say how brilliantly he had done. We had got up health overnight but the Dobson draft [Commons statement] was poor and we had to rework it to tie it in with the overall message. TB was getting right into the detail in preparation for PMQs which he was doing more and more

---

[1] Rupert Murdoch wanted to take over Berlusconi's Mediaset TV network.

on his own now, calling me in every now and then, but basically he just had Rob Read gathering all the info, and then he worked through it. Rob had made a real difference to the operation. TB was also talking about moving his office. He didn't like where he was and thought he should move to the White Room and have the study as an outer office for Anji, Jonathan, Kate and Sally. I said CB would go crazy. He said I had to help to try to get Fiona onside for her staying. Fiona and I had dinner at [chief executive of Mirror Group newspapers] David Montgomery's with Piers Morgan, Adair Turner [director general, CBI] and wives. Monty didn't have much to say so it was mainly me and Piers goading each other about the press in general and the *Mirror* in particular, which I felt was losing the plot. I said on May 1 the public rejected cynicism and they didn't want the whole press against us the whole time. Alex F called me earlier just for a chat and sounded nervous so it came as no surprise when news came through they had lost to Monaco. PG called and said the Budget groups were not as good as we hoped. It was still seen as a Budget for the poor not for hard-working people.

Thursday, March 19

I took the planning meeting on the welfare reform Green Paper. We agreed Frank [Field] would do the statement and no briefing of the press before on the detail. The argument was about whether we should try to get coverage on the principles or have a single policy with a hard edge to take the communications lead. TB saw Frank and Harriet before Cabinet and went through the last bits, while also bollocking them for talking to the press the whole time. For example, the *FT* today had a big story on compulsory second pensions. Cabinet was OK, but very general. First on Agenda 2000 [strategy for modernising and enlarging the EU and the basis for CAP reform], then Robin on Israel, who are asking us to play a greater part. RC was back and said his visit went well despite the obvious. Harriet went through the welfare stuff, and JP's eyes rolled straight away as she managed to get New Labour and the Third Way into the first sentence. Then she threw in rejecting Old Labour by simply putting up benefit levels for good measure. Actually the principles were fine. First, helping people into work. Second, public-private partnership. Third, greatest help to those in greatest need. Fourth, the role of public services of high quality. Fifth, strengthening families and tackling poverty. Sixth, openness and honesty. Seventh, streamlining services. She then set out the success measures we should judge ourselves by. TB said it was not a blueprint but signposting and setting direction. He stressed welfare to work, pensions and disability as the most important areas. Work for those who can, security for those who can't. Donald [Dewar] was a bit dubious, and asked where is the beef? TB and GB were better together than for ages. GB was on his best behaviour and even managed the odd joke without it looking too strained, and there was lots of good humour and banter between them. They even seemed happy. GB was being friendlier than usual. He had a very pretty private secretary with him, and seemed to want to make a point of introducing her to us, and generally being nice. We got back to do the interview with Piers Morgan and Kevin Maguire. It was meant to be serious post-Budget but turned out to be the usual crap about the Royals, Derry, Di, all the bollocks and the cheap spills. The *Mirror* was becoming a comic.

Friday, March 20

Despite my anger at the Piers Morgan interview being about anything other than the Budget, he did five pages and it was OK. TB said he was basically a slug but he was clever, and we shouldn't over-alienate or underestimate. Derry had had his first charity reception at the residence last night. He was still labouring under the illusion that his refurbishment of the residence had the potential to be a public relations success.

We took off for Germany in a tiny plane, so small it was virtually impossible to work. Every time the guy came down with food or drinks he looked like he was going to send it flying all over us. TB was working on his German brief while I read, with mounting horror, the latest draft of the welfare reform Green Paper. It was long on words and short on substance. It was unbelievably repetitive and full of waffle. We were moving towards making the main story in the disability field. Soft on the disabled, tough on rackets, suspend the benefits integrity project.

We landed and I called GB from the car and filled him in on the extra-ordinary German media response to the Budget. Some of the editorials were unbelievable. I asked the embassy to get them translated so we could give them to our press. It showed our agenda of economic reform was striking a chord, contrary to the normal perception that France and Germany didn't get it. GB was keen to get something up in the Sundays because he was doing *On the Record*, and he was hosting Ecofin, which was clearly a big deal for him. He was being incredibly co-operative at the moment, so I was trying to speak regularly and build on this. There was no point in continuing the war that had been developing. So long as GB was being co-operative, so would I be. He would not like the press coverage today on the Tony and Gordon show, which had TB firmly in charge. On the Green Paper GB was worried that we were giving the Tories too much ammunition to attack us. He was also worried about coal. The one thing I always noticed when we were on regular speaking terms was how much of the detail he was on top of.

We arrived at Kohl's office and after a brief photocall – he clearly found that side of things really irritating and always rushed them – they went straight into the meeting. I got the German press coverage to our hacks and also showed them how the SPD manifesto had clearly nicked loads of stuff from us, even including tough on crime, tough on the causes of crime, and the same messages on welfare to work. At the lunch, Kohl did most of the talking, through his extraordinary interpreter Dorothea, who was very flirty and pretty, pro UK and unbelievably clever. Her English was flawless, but more than that she managed to get Kohl's mannerisms and intonations translated too. She could indicate his mood and the balance of argument when it was a complex issue. It was an extraordinary skill.

Kohl clearly liked TB. There was the sense of the older man passing on wisdom that was being gratefully received. He regaled us with stories of [Ronald] Reagan's stupidity, and said America should just accept the French as they are. There's nothing you can do about them. He liked [the late French President François] Mitterrand not because of his politics but because of his interest in culture and books. He described some of the dinners with him and [Margaret] Thatcher. Once Mitterrand said let's finish early and he got the planes on standby for 9pm. Then just as it was breaking up Thatcher would say Britain was better than France at something or other, and it would kick off and they would be there for hours. TB said very little and was really in listening mode. Kohl talked loudly and expansively, and ate noisily too. He had an enormous napkin buttoned on to his shirt, a huge great thing which fell over his chest and over his belly. He was very warm and friendly though and seemed to see TB as the younger brother almost. I didn't detect the same constant manoeuvring or jealousy you got with Chirac. At the press conference John Sergeant asked what Germany could learn from the UK and whether Germany needed a TB. TB was diplomatic and made light of it but Kohl seemed a bit irritated and said Germany didn't have a Tony Blair, which was taken as a whack at [the SPD's Gerhard] Schroeder.

We then went back to the ambassador's residence, which was one of the nicer ones I had been in, partly because of the view but also because some of the rooms felt lived in rather than museum pieces.

We met Schroeder who was reasonably charismatic though I suspected he dyed his hair and he was a bit wooden compared to Tony. He clearly wanted to pick his brains. His people seemed a bit wooden and old-fashioned and lacking in drive. TB was careful not to overdo the closeness to Schroeder. He asked him to do a clip for his election video and TB said he would have to consult the protocol people. He was quite impressive but I felt there was something missing, though I couldn't put my finger on it. But I got the feeling Kohl was on the way out. He had done a great job for Europe, but what about Germany? That attack line was hurting. On the plane we started work on the Paris speech which was going to be a big number and get a lot of attention right round Europe. TB was scribbling away while I was rewriting the welfare Green Paper. TB was worried about it.

Saturday, March 21
I felt tired and depressed and we had an awful weekend. We were supposed to be going to a party and I just wanted to stay in, which set off a great row with Fiona. I was feeling very down. I briefed the Sundays and our only real problem was the *Sunday Telegraph* which led on housing benefit, which could be tricky because that was one of the areas where we were not going to deliver all we wanted.

Sunday, March 22
TB spent all weekend working on his French speech, trying to work up a 'new vision for Europe' and also on the Green Paper trying to make sense of the rubbish Frank and Harriet produced. Later he met GB with David [Miliband], Jeremy, Ed Miliband [special adviser to GB] and Sharon [White] to go through it. TB's new preface was a lot better but he admitted it was poor on substance and we were going to need a very good spinology operation. On the title, Frank wanted 'From welfare to well-being'. We ended up with the more prosaic 'New ambitions for our country: the new welfare contract'. David and Sharon were against it, but I felt we needed something with a bit of edge, which contract gave it.

I couldn't really work out why I was so depressed at home. The problem was the pressures on me were really growing, as TB became more and more reliant. There was no escape or release from it. I got home and wanted to find it but either because the phone never stopped, or because the pressures kept coming in, I never really felt that sense of relaxation and depressurising that I needed. And Fiona was putting me under a different sort of pressure, to be there more, to be there in mind as well as body. We took the kids skating, and

Charlie Falconer [Solicitor General and close friend of TB] was there and he said it must be great to be the one that TB calls his Colossus, the one on whom it is all built and I said no, that's what drives me crazy. I don't want power, or more pressure. Yet the more I try to devolve, the more things seem to accumulate towards me.

Monday, March 23

The welfare situation was spiralling out of control too much for my tastes, and later I chaired a meeting with Jeremy, Martin Sixsmith [DSS], half of Number 10, to agree a core script and go through how we wanted to communicate this. I was keen on defeating dependency culture, plus contract, plus success measures, plus what happens next. I thought Harriet should do a scene-setting speech on Wednesday, then Frank take it on. TB wanted me, Richard Wilson and Peter M to go to the DSS tomorrow, and sort out a strategy for them.

Frank still had a terrific profile with the media and chatterati but he had not really delivered as a minister. The doubts that were around at the time TB appointed him had if anything grown. And Harriet had a few political skills I suppose, but this required a different order of grasp and reach. Add in GB thinking not much of what they had come up with and TB getting frustrated, and this was not a good scene. TB felt we would need to take over the whole thing. And as if we didn't have enough to be going on with, we had his National Assembly speech right on us. There was a lot of interest building and though we had a draft of sorts, it was not where it needed to be and I wasn't sure where we were going to get the time we needed to sort it.

TB took me into his office for a forty-minute heart-to-heart. He was back to thinking that Anji should say and said Cherie was happy to live with it. They had been up till 3am on Friday talking about it and she had agreed that it was silly to be so hung up about it. It felt like wishful thinking to me. He said he wanted to put Anji, Kate, Sally and Jonathan in the study, and he would work out of the White Room. He was worried Jonathan's confidence was low. I said he needed to be clear about what he should be doing. He said he wanted me to shut down all the reshuffle stories, which I said was impossible. People just talked and if they didn't the hacks made it up anyway.

The main enlivening issue of the day came when John Holmes came in to say that there had been a running battle between the *Sun* and the Treasury Solicitor, Roland Phillips, over a sensitive piece of intelligence the *Sun* got hold of. It showed up an Iraqi plan to get anthrax into the UK. They had agreed to hold off publication over

March '98: Need to get control of welfare situation

the weekend but now said they intended to publish. Stuart Higgins was at the Oscars so I was dealing with Rebekah Wade [deputy editor]. I said we did not want to injunct but we were going in that direction, unless we can come to some arrangement.

I spoke to TB who said we should try to do some kind of deal. I spoke to Jan Polley [Cabinet Secretary's office] and got agreement to get the *Sun* in. So by 4.45, with a 5.15 court deadline, we were round my table, me, various intelligence and security folks, with some other people from the Foreign Office, Tom Crone, News International lawyer, Rebekah and Trevor Kavanagh, John Holmes and Roland Phillips. Our bottom line was that we wanted to avoid any reference to sensitive intelligence which might damage relations. I raised the option of doing it as an all-ports-warning story, i.e. something they could have got from a source at a port or in the security services here, rather than from intelligence. They went for it straight away, if reluctantly.

I gave them a PMOS [Prime Minister's Official Spokesman] quote and after to-ing and fro-ing they agreed not to refer to intelligence at all, other than to say it was intelligence from Baghdad. They were pretty reasonable. Trevor stayed and wrote the story at my desk, based on the *Sun* saying they had a source with access to intelligence in Baghdad.

In truth they had a better story than the one they came in with, in that it referred to a domestic warning. I said to Trevor that from now on, I will be able to state with conviction that I know he writes rubbish because I have seen him do it at my desk. Rebekah, as when she did the [Robin] Cook story, was as good as her word. I wrote a line to take while leaving the *Sun* to brief the broadcasters. It led the bulletins from 10.

As if that and welfare were not enough, the briefing on the Paris speech was going fairly big and we had a Murdoch problem re his call to TB last week asking him to take up [Murdoch's planned acquisition of] Mediaset with Prodi. Though TB had had no objection, he didn't take it up, but Prodi did call him. However, *La Stampa* ran a story saying TB lobbied Prodi on Murdoch's behalf. It was first raised by David Healy [political journalist] at the eleven o'clock, and I went into my 'Not so far as I'm aware but I will check' mode.

Tuesday, March 24

The main thing today was TB's speech to the National Assembly in Paris, and he was pretty hyper about it. But we were also moving to the final stages of planning on the welfare Green Paper. TB was getting more and more alarmed about Harriet and Frank and as well as asking me to take over the briefing completely, he wanted RW and Peter M to go over there and brief them on how to handle things. We were still having problems with the Murdoch story. We stuck to the line that we would not be briefing on his conversation with Prodi, that it was a private conversation but it was a total joke to say he 'intervened' on behalf of Murdoch. That ran on all day.

TB had been practising his French on and off all day and was nervous. On arrival we went straight to the British Council but he was irritated at having to do lots of stuff before the main event, which he really needed to psych himself up for. There was a big scrum in the street as we walked to the National Assembly, a band playing 'Land of Hope and Glory'. We were met by an army of flunkeys and lots of twittering. TB was more nervous than I've seen him for ages. As Jonathan, John Holmes, Brian Bender and I were taken away to the public gallery, TB was taken by Laurent Fabius [president of the French National Assembly] through a line of really loud drummers. 'They're going to execute you,' I said and he smiled a bit weakly. It was a fantastic building, very French, incredibly atmospheric. It was terrific to watch the way the members responded to different parts of the speech. The left went for the obviously left bits, but there were lines the French left would never say, and the right rose up in over-the-top cheering. At times it was comical, but the overall effect was strong. He was tired by the end. He got Brownie points from the French for doing the whole thing in French.

We had an hour with Chirac at the Elysée. He was in very second-hand car salesman mode. I scribbled a note to John H at one point: *'Est-ce que tu sais où je peux trouver un second-hand Citroën?'* ['Do you know where I can find a second-hand Citroën?'] He spoke in big sweeping statements and then looked for a reaction, and I think was annoyed because TB just smiled at him, and then smiled around the room. Without being rude, he conveyed the impression he was not terribly taken with JC's grand pronouncements. Re ECB [European Central Bank] president, Chirac said he would veto [Wim] Duisenberg. Kok would veto [Jean-Claude] Trichet, but a third man would be acceptable to Kohl. 'Or woman?' said TB. On Iraq, they were in very different places, TB claiming a success for diplomacy backed by force, Chirac basically saying we were killing children through sanctions.

JC was full of praise for Robin re the Middle East, said he had done a lot for Britain's standing, which was a subtle dig at TB again. We left for the Matignon where [Prime Minister Lionel] Jospin was friendlier than usual, and more relaxed. TB was laying the ground on political reform pre-Cardiff [EU summit]. He felt the Commission was useless and would have to be changed radically at the time of enlargement if it was going to work. It was all in all a good visit. On the plane we worked on the Green Paper.

Wednesday, March 25

We got good coverage out of France but we had a real problem re Blackpool, because the NEC had decided we would not go there [for conference] in the next three years, and someone had briefed it was because the hotels were tatty. It was a real problem and nobody had a grip on it at the party. TB was looking tired and I was feeling dreadful. I was working pretty much full-time on the Green Paper. Godric had done a good briefing note and after PMQs I did a briefing on it to try to get the advance coverage in a better place. The truth was a lot of this was going to be in the spin because on the substance Harriet and Frank had just not delivered, and didn't know how to handle this now.

After Questions, Peter M, Richard Wilson, David M, Robin Young [Cabinet Office] and I went to the DSS to sit down with Harriet and Frank and their people. It was like a start-from-scratch lesson. Relations between the two of them were poor, and they had lost confidence while also still coming over as arrogant. Frank's statement was all over the place and we agreed I should try to rewrite it and make the argument clearer. Again, he was a curious mix – grateful for the help, but hurt because we were making it pretty obvious he needed it. We flattered away about his credibility as a radical, etc., but that too was a piece of spin now, and I think he knew that's what everyone in the room thought.

As I worked on the statement, I felt myself getting angrier and angrier. Why the fuck was I having to do this on top of everything else? Why was I having to deal with Blackpool for heaven's sake? I was feeling under more pressure because so much was falling upon me, because there were so few people able or willing to take responsibility for sorting anything out. Most of them operated in a world of constant drift. I got TB to do a clip for BBC North West and also when I heard the *Blackpool Gazette* were delivering some rock and some copies of the paper with 'Blair betrayal' headlines, I got the reporter and photographer to come in and see TB. The reporter almost fainted. He was a young kid called Vincent and he was literally dumbstruck. The photographer ended up trying to help him ask the questions.

Thursday, March 26

I was still really depressed and knew there was a tough day ahead. I was making a stack of changes to the welfare statement. It was a lot better but still not right. TB called a meeting and you had him, me, Jeremy H, David M, Peter M, Peter H, Sharon White literally rewriting the statement, which Jeremy and Sharon took back to the DSS. After Cabinet, TB wanted more changes, and I called the DSS people over to my office and we got it finished by half two, then got it over to Frank Field. It was a joke that Frank had this great reputation. He had produced absolute rubbish, we had to rescue the paper and then literally write the statement and train them on how to deal with tough questions.

TB, GB, Donald, Pat [McFadden] and I met to discuss the party in Scotland. TB told Donald he needed a proper media operation and above all a modernising strategy and agenda exposing the SNP. GB seemed to be on for putting together a positive New Labour strategy. Cabinet was mainly welfare reform and also Blackpool, TB telling the story of Vincent from the *Gazette*. TB went through the key messages on welfare, said we had to emphasise radicalism whilst reassuring people we believed in security for those at risk. JP said that the Blackpool decision was more Blackpool's fault than the NEC. Frank was pretty useless in the House. It really was a triumph of spin over substance. Later, the only story to bother us was in *The Times*. Just as the Murdoch story was going away, Ray Snoddy [media commentator] was saying that on the back of information from TB, Murdoch pulled out of going for Mediaset. It kicked off the whole thing again, and led to more allegations that I had misled people.

Friday, March 27

I tried to have the day off, but in between had to deal with TB at Chequers re Murdoch. He was unfazed by it. However it was now being wound up with the PASC [Public Administration Select Committee] wanting to call me to discuss GIS politicisation so-called and then Rhodri Morgan [select committee chairman] said they would ask me about all this. I started to use the line that there are two things that always make the media and political classes neuralgic. One was spin doctors, the other was Murdoch and so this was bound to produce a real media fest. TB said they were always going to go at me because the politicians were jealous of my role, and the media and the Tories hated my effectiveness. Frank Field called to say thanks and said yes, it was all in the spin! The coverage was good, the *Sun* terrific, *Mirror* OK, *Express* not bad, *Mail* six out of ten, the heavies fine. It could certainly have been a lot worse. Mike White called to say Joan Lestor [Baroness Lestor of Eccles, former Labour MP] had died. I got hold of TB for a tribute and he remembered she was there when he first spoke at the Beaconsfield by-election.

Saturday, March 28

Hilary [Coffman] was dealing with the *Sunday Telegraph* on a fund-raising story. They had a document written by Labour's fund-raising team which advocated using Number 10 for fund-raising. It had been rejected but Tim [Allan] and Hilary made the mistake of sending them the final version to prove it, so they had a new and different story instead. I was also having to deal with the *Sunday Times* who had got hold of the security plans of TB's house in Sedgefield. On Murdoch, I briefed hard that it was balls. TB was more worried about Blackpool than he was about the Murdoch stuff. The main problem in the Sundays was the *Mail* getting hold of two letters from me bollocking Frank F and Harriet. They were a bit OTT and meant more bollocks about me in the Sundays. I was becoming the story again. Robin called to say the *Mail on Sunday* seemed to know he was going to get married at Chevening [Foreign Secretary's official country residence] on April 19. I said he should put out a short factual statement announcing the bare facts and making clear there will be no public expense. He couldn't resist also having in some words about how they had had some of their happiest moments there. Robin seemed to think the nation was ready to rejoice. He should get on and get married, and shut up about it.

Sunday, March 29

Again, I was trying to take a day off, clear my head, somehow chase this depression way. I was also trying to work out how to strengthen the operation. Tim, Allan Percival and David Hill were leaving me, Peter M was semi-detached, and the pressure was getting more and more intense. A lot of shit was going to be thrown at me, because they didn't particularly want to throw it all at Tony yet.

I felt gloomy all day. I called Tom Bostock [AC's GP] in Ireland. He said I had to heed the signals. I had been going without a proper break for four years and three times in my medical history I had three major upheavals because I ignored the signals when first they came. Acute asthma, a nervous breakdown and a serious stomach complaint. He felt all three were connected to anger. He said all the people you help will have their moments in the sun, but you have none. You get no credit for the election, even though people in the know know you deserve more than most who do get the credit. You get no credit for the success of the government. You get all of the shit, none of the glory, and you spend a lot of the time taking seriously people you despise. You would not be human if that did not make you angry.

I told him Frank Field seemed under pressure when I saw him yesterday, yet I was operating under that kind of pressure, times three or more, all of the time. Dealing with the press, making high-powered decisions, always being asked to decide things in Number 10. Frank was asked about the letters to him and Harriet on *On the Record* and said I was perfectly entitled to send them. But I was becoming the story again, and didn't much like it. Nor did Audrey [Fiona's mother] or Mum, who phoned and said what was this committee [Public Administration Select Committee] all about and I could tell she was worried. She also volunteered the same view as Bostock – you get all the blame and none of the credit, and I don't know why you do it for them. Bostock's view was that made me angry and that was where the medical side effects were coming from in part.

Monday, March 30

I was really having trouble sleeping again. There was another rash of AC articles in the press. At the morning meeting, TB was micro-managing, trying to find out whether there was a structural problem that made us fuck up so many small things. His latest was Robin's photocall at Chevening. That was partly my fault because I gave the go-ahead. Philip G felt that the collective effect of recent events was becoming a problem, because the impression being created was we were just the same as the Tories. We had to have a counter-strategy. TB also felt I needed to get a new deputy, but it wasn't so easy just to bring someone in who would have authority dealing with the Cabinet and the media.

Frank Field called to say he was very upset that the letters to him and Harriet were out there and had led to me being attacked. Harriet also called and said she always kept quiet when she was being attacked in the media, while Clare always hit back, and she was fighting for her life, and thought she would have to fight back. TB, Peter M and I had a chat in the garden. I said I was feeling the pressure, and the lack of practical support which meant I was taking on too much. TB said I had to get extra help because either I would go mad or I would make mistakes. That was right. Fraser Kemp [Labour MP] called to say he was going to be the parliamentary adviser to the 'Free Deirdre' campaign, the latest *Coronation Street* storyline, and I should get TB involved. It cheered me up, and I went for it.

March '98: Select committee moving to grill AC

Richard Wilson came to see me, said he was worried because everyone seemed so miserable. I went through why, all the usual stuff. I said we had to get better people into the GIS. He said Peter M and I had been brilliant dealing with Harriet and FF, but I said it was ridiculous that we had to get involved at that level. We discussed what to do re the PASC inquiry and my appearance.[1] Alan Clark called and said fuck the critics – you're doing the right thing, shaking things up, and everyone knows it.

Tuesday, March 31

I woke up, tired, and was running as the second story on the news. I was the big story all day and frankly too knackered to deal with it properly. I spoke to TB who had not really been aware of how it had built up in the preceding days. He said don't worry, just be calm about it. Understand that they are building up to knock you down, because they know you are an asset to me. That is all this is about.

At the eleven o'clock, I went through Northern Ireland and Brunson asked me about [Shadow Cabinet minister Francis] Maude's suggestion that I had lied. At Hilary's suggestion, I rather dramatically challenged them to say whether they thought I had lied, and they sat there and said nothing. I said come on, anyone who thinks I lied, just say so. I got Alan Clark and [fellow Conservative MP Peter] Temple-Morris to put out words supporting me, just to remind people it was not all one-sided over there either. *World at One* did twenty minutes on me, Kim Howells [education minister] doing a good job. Because he had nothing else to do, William Hague stepped in. I got a stack of calls of support, which meant it was out there big time. [Dennis] Skinner called and said it was absolutely right that I bollock ministers like Frank and Harriet where they were not up to the mark. He wasn't supportive over Murdoch though. Tam Dalyell called to say I should not have bollocked ministers in my own name. Max Hastings came to see me and said it was extraordinary the extent to which I had become big news. He knew it was crap but everyone felt obliged to cover it. The lunchtimes were bad, *World at One* a joke, and Bernard Ingham [former press secretary to Margaret Thatcher] was all over the place saying how awful I was telling ministers what to do. Philip said in the focus groups I was 'out there' with Peter as an issue. TV and radio were going mad, political journalists interviewing each

[1] Among the issues it was to consider were the 'boundary between effective presentation and party political advocacy', and the 'special treatment' of some journalists.

other about their feelings about me. Lots of people were saying keep your chin up, and I said there was no reason for it to fall. I was feeling better about it, felt there was an argument going on now, and one in which we could make a strategic point, namely the Tories had nothing to say about the big issues, so they ran on this rubbish the whole time.

Wednesday, April 1

Alan Clark, who always managed to cheer me up, was the first call of the day. He said he was really pissed off he hadn't got more coverage for his comments supporting me. He said the whips were giving him a hard time but fuck it, I was his friend, I was under attack and the Tories needed to know they would get nowhere with it. He later called again to say he was doing a piece defending me for the *Mirror*. The cartoonists were into me as well now. TB said he didn't fear them coming at him about me, but about the relationship with Murdoch. And he didn't fancy a sustained set of questions about whether Murdoch lobbied him.

Harriet called out of the blue, and said she wanted to know if she could help me. I took it at face value but then as she wittered on endlessly, I found it hard to see how her help would help. She was incapable of expressing herself briefly and it just became a torrent, how she never leaked memos and why would she have done this because it made her look like a victim, and it just meant more reshuffle stories, and so she didn't brief anyway, never been her style, and was sorry that I thought she had, and on and on. The problem was, vis-à-vis the story about me, that there was little real news around. TB was fine at PMQs, but stupidly said that the reason they hated me was because I did such a good job attacking the Tory Party. This opened a new flank, because as a civil servant I wasn't meant to be attacking the Tories at all. I said to him afterwards he had made it worse and he was non-plussed. He didn't actually realise I was not meant to be party political, that I could set government in a political context but I was not paid to go around laying into the Tories. We had got Katie Derham [TV journalist] in to do an interview with TB – everyone was flirting away madly with her.

Thursday, April 2

The main thing today was getting lines out from last night's dinner with Bertie Ahern, which had been three hours' pretty tough talking, then get my head round ASEM [Asia-Europe Meeting] and the China summit. Alun Evans did his presentation on the SCU to Cabinet and

TB was very nice about them, though I think some of the ministers thought it all a bit odd. JP led a discussion on the local elections and appealed to the Cabinet to get more involved in the campaign. I slipped a note to TB to mention Scotland so I could brief they had discussed Scotland and Wales and use it again to underline that we had put together a strategy for a bigger campaign. I also started to tear into the SNP.

The most interesting part of the day was the lunch and bilateral with the Chinese. Zhu Rongji [Chinese Prime Minister] was not your usual Chinese politician. He did more than read his brief and seemed inquisitive as well as wanting to set out his views. The scale of China's ambitions, particularly in education, was awesome. TB was really welcoming, said we wanted China to succeed and supported their reform programme. ZR knew TB inside out, said 'You became PM 320 days before I did, so I will learn from you.' He gave a strong presentation on how they had handled the Asian economic crisis, and not devalued, but kept going to their strategy. Eight per cent growth was still within reach. He was wanting more Chinese companies on the Stock Exchange. They were studying our banking systems. He said re UK companies in China, they were trying to open up markets but it was a different system and it would be step by step.

TB slipped in the obligatory mention re human rights, but in a pretty friendly way, saying we welcomed continuing dialogue. Zhu went straight on to the environment. Then on Hong Kong, both were pretty upbeat. One country, two systems was working well. TB said the Queen enjoyed meeting him, and we were now operating one country, three systems, post-devolution. Jacques Santer and Leon Brittan were at the lunch and Santer did a lot of the talking. There was something a bit grim, and very unconvincing, about him. I went off to the DTI to do the briefing, and was very upbeat re China. After Cabinet, both Frank Dobson and Robin Cook said they would go up to defend me any time I wanted. Unprompted, there were quite a few positive letters about me in the press.

Friday, April 3

I saw TB re Ireland first thing, just before he spoke to Trimble. He complained that the Irish were making it more difficult by briefing so hard. We left for the summit and I had a nice chat with Bertie [Ahern] as TB was meeting and greeting. He said he didn't know how we coped with our newspapers, both the number and the way they were. Chirac brightened things up a bit, singing happy birthday to Kohl. TB had to persuade the PM of Vietnam [Phan Van Khai] not to walk out in protest that all the speeches and opening ceremony were not being translated into all languages. There was worse to come, when it became clear Kohl did not have a headset, and he was clearly getting into a rage, with people flapping around. Then it emerged there was no German on the translation, which was ridiculous.

The conference centre looked good, very modern and minimalist, but I found these set-piece summits really annoying. Bertie told me during one of the breaks he hated them too, with everyone on show and very little business actually done, particularly one like this, ASEM, where most of the work was done bilaterally in the margins. TB's speech went OK but I made sure afterwards he sought out Kohl and apologised. He had not even been able to get translation of the statement on the economic crisis. He had to follow it all with his own interpreters rather than through the headsets. I did a briefing on the morning session while all the leaders went to Derry's residence for lunch. Kohl was very grumpy, probably in part because the chairs were quite small, and he then started raging at the air conditioning. But of all the set speeches in the summit, his was the only one I found inspiring, as he did a big number of his vision of the new Europe. He said no country needed to give up its national identity as Europe became one. But the euro would bring us closer. Chirac made similar points but let himself down with his sly attacks on Leon Brittan and his little digs at the US. He said the world was not trilateral but multilateral. Asia was a power, the US was a power, Europe was a power, South America would become a power. 'L'Union fait la force, une force politique, une force économique.' ['The Union is a force, a political force, an economic force.']

The enlargement discussion was fascinating though, as the different leaders put slightly different slants on what they were pretending were the same points. Kohl said German unity and European unity were two sides of the same coin. Hashimoto was the most dominant of the Asian leaders, some of whom I never heard speak once. TB said it had been fascinating. He said enlargement was an ambitious project but the history of Europe was the triumph of ambition over cynicism. We can do it because the world is opening up. I did a briefing at the end of the afternoon, mainly on the economic statement, the Japanese economy and dealing with currency speculators. I also did a number about how TB made a fuss of Kohl on his birthday, giving him a bottle of his favourite port. In between times we were working on getting an agreed statement with the Irish. John Holmes and Paddy Teahon [senior adviser to Ahern] had pretty much done the business, but [George] Mitchell wanted us to put it down at 8pm. But we felt TB would have to square Trimble first. He was worried it would not take much to push DT off the ship. Trimble called after the Channel 4 news and said this was all looking like a UK-Irish stitch-up and he was not happy. TB and BA agreed it would be better if they had a bit more time and tabled the text at Stormont not here. I got Mitchell to do a conference call with them, agreed that was the way forward and then did a joint statement to that effect, mentioning the Mitchell call, indicating progress without going too far. TB said on the way back to Number 10 that it was ridiculous he was expected to deal with complicated negotiations like this while he was meant to be chairing a summit.

Saturday, April 4

The *Guardian* and the *Mail* both did profiles of me, both of which could have been worse. TB came down to my office as I was going through the papers and we went off for a chat. He was totally consumed re Ireland, but he was still fretting about my set-up, and the need to get in a strong deputy to lift some of the load. Both of us wanted me to spend less time on day-to-day, and more on strategic thinking, but we hadn't found the right person to fill the gap on the briefing. We set off for the summit, and I filled in his interpreter on the coverage re Kohl, which was pretty good, but he was still very grumpy. The air conditioning had become a bit of an obsession.

As the meeting broke up, there was a piece of nonsense between Chirac and Santer, Chirac making clear yet again that he would have nothing to do with Leon Brittan's ideas on US trade and that he would use the French veto against them. *'Tony, tu as compris. Jacques, tu n'as pas compris.'* ['Tony, you understood. Jacques, you did not understand.'] He was really up himself today, and the Frenchness was in overdrive. Even I felt a bit sorry for Santer.

I drafted clips for TB and Bertie to do, just to keep the Ireland story freshened up on the bulletins, and fill what was becoming a vacuum. At the Sunday lobby, there was an insatiable demand for Irish stuff. All we could do was give the sense of incessant pressure. The summit closing ceremony went fine, and the press conference – TB, Santer, Hashimoto and the Vietnam PM – was pretty low-key. Back at Number 10, TB was telling us all how well he had chaired it all. Alex [Ferguson] called and said ignore the press – they're going for you because you're the best.

Sunday, April 5

Harriet was on *Frost* saying I was brilliant, which came as a bit of a shock.

Monday, April 6

Ireland was the big story again. There was a little bit of follow-up to the ridiculous story in the *Sunday Times* about me being the twenty-third member of the Cabinet. At the office meeting, Peter M was stressing that we had to be more challenging on our policy prospectus, and it just was not good enough the way we were e.g. on health and education. We lacked edge. TB was asking for symbolic changes, and announcements that dealt with our negatives. At times like this, he tended to go down to things that ultimately didn't matter much, like some nonsense to do with tickets for the World Cup. Jonathan was in TB's bad books still, and sensed he was on the lookout for someone else. Wrongly, I think. TB did an interview with Lynda Lee-Potter [*Mail*], but there were too many questions about me, Derry and Robin. They did it in the White Room and then he showed her the flat, stressing that he wished he had a real home. He did the usual stuff about family etc. I told him later I didn't think Derry could go to Cordoba, it would be a problem if the press found him there, and that they would not have a holiday at all. The *Sunday Times* knew that TB was going there and it would be no holiday at all if the press found Derry with him. TB felt it was too tough to tell him that.

TB called me into his meeting with Robin, talking over his wedding. TB was worried he was becoming a devalued figure because of the Gaynor stuff. We said it would be better if he could do it quietly. I told Robin that he was being panned in focus groups, because they felt he was vile to Margaret. He said they would like to get married privately but if you got a register office licence for a private residence there had to be unfettered access for the public. We suggested he get a quick marriage and do it privately and he agreed to do that but was clearly not sure he could do it. He looked very down. TB said all I care about is that we have a Foreign Secretary back and not some extra in a soap opera, which is what the press are trying to do with you. I couldn't agree more, said Robin.

Tuesday, April 7

Mitchell finally tabled his paper around midnight and though it didn't leak, it was clear there were going to be problems. TB was furious when he came down from the flat because he felt both Mitchell and the NIO had not handled the UUs properly. He said they didn't understand how, because the Irish government had such a close relationship to the SDLP, we had to give the UUs the sense that we were there for them, at least keeping an eye on things from their perspective, even when we were pushing them in a certain direction. By 10,

April '98: Robin plans his wedding to Gaynor

we had basically decided we were going to have to go there but TB had to chair the PES [Party of European Socialists] at the FCO, which was a pain. He was worried about being associated with failure, but I said he would be anyway and if he could make a difference by going, then we should go. By 3, we were set to go.

I was still having to deal with Robin and his bloody wedding. He had established that he could get it done this week but was still going on about photos, and some kind of photocall on Friday. He then called me about whether his bloody mother should go. His judgement on this was becoming awful.

We left around 3.30 and I briefed Denis Murray and John Irvine [ITV Ireland correspondent] from the car. On the plane we went through the paper in some detail and it was obvious what Trimble's problem was. The areas for co-operation were too numerous and too all-encompassing. TB was a bit fed up with it because he and Bertie had not actually negotiated all this, but Mitchell insisted it was all in there. He had been angry with DT before, but felt he had a point here. He discussed plans for a doorstep on arrival at Hillsborough [Castle, Northern Ireland Secretary's official residence], and I drafted a few lines. But he pretty much did his own thing. This is not a time for sound bites but I feel the hand of history upon my shoulder. Hell of a sound bite. The press loved it.

DT arrived at Hillsborough and was perfectly friendly but a bit detached, as though this was all happening around him but was not directly in his control or even relevant to him. It was his coping mechanism, one I had noticed before, that he was almost like a commentator, but then something would spark him into seeing the total absolute relevance to himself and his situation, and his temper would go, and the face would go puce. Tonight he was calm and lucid, and said simply – and repeatedly – that he could not do a deal on this basis. TB said effectively that he would negotiate for him. I organised the departure, TB in shirtsleeves, chatting at length to DT as he left, giving the sense he was in there and able to get his point across. A lot of this was just going to be about balancing the sense of treating the parties well, but at this stage DT better than the rest. Mitchell himself looked tired, as did Mo. We were not going to get the UUs signed up to this as it was. George [Mitchell] was less concerned, saying we would only get one bite of the cherry and they would not want to negotiate. TB said he feared they would want to negotiate every last point. He said DT was not grandstanding. He had genuine points of concern that had to be met, and we had to try to meet them.

Mo seemed a little peeved that TB and Bertie were taking it over, but this was inevitable. I went in to see TB as he was getting ready for bed. He said his gut feeling was very negative. He couldn't see how to fill the gaps. Adams had been pushing for another meeting. The SDLP had been on, saying we must not give in to blackmail. TB said if we were dealing with reasonable people, this would be fairly straightforward, but we're not, and the historical hatreds are just too deep.

Wednesday, April 8

I got a message to go and see TB before I was even up. He was in the bath, and said he was worried. I knew he was worried anyway because he was playing the fool the whole time, putting on a thick Irish accent, pretending he was a newsreader announcing that Cherie was going to become a Protestant and he was going to speak with an Irish accent as part of a deal to secure peace in NI. Bertie's mum had died and he was coming up for breakfast before then going back for the funeral. TB said what was important was to get Trimble pointing in a more positive direction. He said my task for the day was to get DT out there being more positive than the Neanderthals, by which I think he meant Maginnis and Taylor, who were doing most of the media and pushing the worst-case scenario for the UUs. Paddy Teahon said Trimble was asking for the Holy Trinity to be replaced by the Almighty God in the Irish Constitution. Even Bertie managed a laugh. Bertie said if he was exposed to either of them too much today, he would be worried he would end up thumping them.

We left by helicopter for Stormont and after a brief doorstep we were taken up to the office that had been picked as our base. It was not a nice building, and the room was too hot. The furniture was not nice either. A plain brown table, a dozen or so not very comfortable green-backed chairs, three easy chairs. We were going to be spending a lot of time in here and it was a depressing start. Then came meeting after meeting, with occasional pauses to take stock and indulge in black humour. The most important were with the UUs, and they were also the most difficult. Even Reg Empey [UUP vice president], who could normally be called upon to be reasonable, was being more Maginnis/Taylor than his usual self. Trimble was trying hard, but he just had too many people at him. He would say something, and then find the others translating it into something harder. Then Trimble would nod his agreement to the revised version. TB was getting frustrated and angry as the day wore on. He was emphasising the two main points – principle of consent at the heart of it, and proper recognition of different traditions.

TB was having to see all the parties regularly just to keep them on board but the focus was DT. He came in on his own just after lunch and this time TB really tried all the charm and the cajoling and DT was moving, but then moved right back again. [Jeffrey] Donaldson was being difficult, said it was all a charade being run by the Anglo-Irish secretariat. We were also a bit stuck without Bertie but he came back around 6.30, looking even more knackered than before. I felt really sorry for him. It was obvious the way he talked about her that he was close to his mother, and she was barely buried and he was back taking a whole load of grief from the UUs. They talked to him, and about him, with something close to contempt, and it was terrific the way he took it. TB was now getting very irritable and the surroundings were beginning to drive us all a bit crazy. The idea of being stuck in here for a day or two was not terribly appetising.

I did a reasonably optimistic briefing and then afterwards came the key meeting of the day, with TB, BA and the UUs, at which Trimble and, more implausibly, John Taylor suddenly signalled they were ready to do a deal. Bertie started, speaking very quietly, said it would be a great tragedy if we could not reach a deal now. Joe Lennon scribbled me a note saying DT had too many enemies for this to work, but the mood was fine. It was when Taylor suddenly piped up – 'There is room for manoeuvre here' – that we thought there was a sign of change. Bertie had said before he would walk out if he started up on his usual record. He said he couldn't be arsed listening to it all again. But this time Taylor was significantly different. It was the first time he had ever been anything remotely approaching positive. It was a big turnaround and they agreed to go away and sort it with their people. It cheered us up no end, because we had been half expecting the opposite, but something had clearly happened in their discussions to trigger a switch.

I still had RC on my case, desperately wanting to release pictures of his wedding tomorrow. He said he was worried it would look furtive. I said far better that than look like you want to draw attention to it, like it's some big official function, which will only result in Margaret wading in again. What is the point? He really seemed to think the public, and governments around the world, would want to see evidence of this great event that would gladden our hearts.

After the main trilateral, we had a long session with Adams and McGuinness and later with Adams alone. They were both very charming in their own way, also very clever, and always making points at various levels. I liked McG better of the two. Whatever he had done in the past, there was a directness to him that I liked and he was driven by a genuine sense of grievance about the way people were forced to live. I guess Adams is too, but he also strikes me as more interested in his own place in the firmament, more a politician than a people's person.

TB and I went for a walk out in the freezing cold. We didn't want to be seen so just found this little garden and walked round for a few minutes. 'This is like prison exercise,' said TB. But he had perked up. 'Do you think we can do this? It would be amazing if we pull this off. I think we can pull it off, I really do.' It was the Taylor shift that had put some fresh wind in our sails. The problem remained the implementation bodies. But as the evening wore on, Bertie was getting more and more depressed and felt it was all sliding back. Bertie met Trimble for hours, during which time we were either hanging around or seeing the other parties, who were spending more time hanging around than we were. The press pack was growing and I was doing fairly regular briefings just to keep them busy and stop them taking too many negative lines elsewhere. [Denis] Murray and [John] Irvine were terrific.

DT came to see us again, and said he had a UU solution that he thought would do the trick. We went down to the Irish office and TB tried it on Bertie, who was very gloomy. We bumped into Mitchell on the way back and he looked pretty fed up too. He said he felt we were living through a Greek tragedy. Maybe the UU shift had been bollocks. Also, TB was a bit spooked by Adams saying the shift on policing wasn't enough. TB said there was still the basis of a deal and he felt we should go through the night. Jonathan and I felt it was too early and the mood wasn't right. He was very pissed off. We had a last effort with BA and DT and the sticking point was the powers of the North-South bodies. 'They don't really want these implementation bodies at all,' said BA, who was really tired and gloomy by now. They want consent principle enshrined, an Assembly, the Irish constitutional claim on the North gone, and they want to give fuck all in return. TB said if we don't break it down tonight, we are in trouble, and suggested we get DT back in. He was getting tired too. 'I'll go fucking spare if he brings in Maginnis and the rest again.' DT was a bit more hopeful. TB said we should not leave the building until we have Strand 2 tied up and agreed. But we did, about 1am, exhausted and not there yet. On the helicopter back to Hillsborough TB just looked out of the window, his face tired and angry, occasionally shaking his head. We had been up and down all day, but were ending it very much down.

April '98: TB confident re peace deal; Ahern less so

Thursday, April 9

Writing this on Saturday, back at home, just random thoughts really, with the main notes done as the discussions happened, and a real sense I was recording history. It was an extraordinary time, and felt like it. It showed TB at his infuriating best. Once he got the bit between the teeth, and decided to go for it, he always knew best, there was no one else could put a counter-view, he was like a man possessed. He would ask to see someone and then ten seconds later shout out 'Where the fuck are they? I need them here NOW.' He would pace up and down, go over all the various parts of the analysis, work out who was likely to be saying what next, work out our own next move. We had room for the usual black humour in there. Jonathan was putting on weight and I christened him 'Five Bellies',[1] which stuck, and whenever TB was in need of a laugh he would put on a Geordie accent and ask 'Five Bellies' to get him a cup of tea and some pork scratchings. Nick Matthews [duty clerk] was fantastic, just kept the tea and the food and the laughs flowing. Claire [Harrington] and Lizzie [McCrossan] from the Garden Rooms were doing a brilliant job, having to record an endless succession of meetings, with poor old John Holmes having to take part, and record, and transcribe as we went. As the days wore on, he started to take on a grey-green tinge, and looked exhausted, but he was brilliant throughout. Thursday had started for me with a wrestle with a fucking bath. Not only was the plug stuck in, but the taps wouldn't turn off, and I had to get the cops up to sort it. Great start.

We had breakfast in the Throne Room, and started without Bertie who was on his way up. We agreed they should arrive together. Bertie was in OK mood considering and we had a load of small talk re Burnley and Man U. TB had been worried last night that BA was actually depressed but he seemed a lot better today. The plan on arrival was just for some nice clear pictures of TB and Bertie, with a few words, but David Andrews [Irish foreign minister] bounded in and buggered it up, interrupting the doorstep. TB did a couple of answers then cut it short and was livid when we got up to the office. I said DA ballsing it up wasn't worth bothering with. There would be a lot worse to come during the day.

It was the start of a long and emotional day. Mo did a great job keeping people's spirits up. She and I took it on ourselves to keep a bit of humour going through the proceedings. Even though it got on

[1] A reference to footballer Paul Gascoigne's rotund friend Jimmy 'Five Bellies' Gardner.

her nerves that she was largely kept out of the TB discussions with Trimble, because DT didn't really want her involved, she didn't allow it to get her down.

We had the benefit of a media who basically wanted this to work. One of the cameramen said he picked up Mo saying something she shouldn't – Maginnis and the Irish being in 'a paddy' – so he suggested we do it again and wiped the tape. He had also caught her belching on tape, something she did rather too often for most people's taste. I seem to have been taken up by SF as their point man, just as Jonathan was clearly seen by the UUs as their man in the Number 10 team. John Holmes and I were both finding the UUs very hard work. So was Bertie and at one of the joint meetings, I don't know how he didn't end up lamping one of them. They talked about him like he was a piece of dirt at times. I did three big briefings during the day, just really pushing the same basic messages and trying to give a sense of momentum. But by far the most important briefings were the one-on-ones with Denis Murray and Mike Brunson who did a fantastic job getting the balance right and reflecting a lot of the nuances. We all knew that whilst we were in the talks, the parties outside the talks were just watching the telly and following it that way, and by giving Murray and Brunson special treatment we definitely got the media as a whole in a better place.

The midnight deadline we had set just came and went without people really being bothered. Mo was sitting in our office, under the clock. It's gone past midnight, I said. Oh, she said. Oh well. TB said how bad is this if we fail? I did the 'better to have tried' bollocks, but truth be told it would be bad to come this far and fall at what now felt like the last. Come the early hours we started to feel that it was going to fall into place, but none of us quite knew how. There were lots of ups and downs but the mood most of the time felt doable. Nonetheless he asked me to sit down and work out an exit strategy. It would have to be based on the idea of returning for intensive talks. Mo came in and had us falling about with the story of Plum Smith [of the Progressive Unionist Party] asking whether he would get out in two years if he went in and wiped out Trimble. So the black humour was all around us.

TB at breakfast not very optimistic, and convinced maybe we should have kept going last night to get the thing done. When Bertie arrived we were straight back to could we get Strand 2 agreed or not. Trimble had said he was ready to compromise and do a deal but Bertie was pretty sceptical, said I'm not sure I trust these guys. North-South bodies, police and decommissioning were going to be the toughest areas.

1.05pm TB ranting and raving because he wanted to see BA, who was locked in discussions in the SDLP office. There is not one clever person outside this fucking room. His problem was he wanted everyone to work at our pace and to our agenda. E.g. there were times he was suspicious of Joe Lennon giving Bertie the wrong advice, but I pointed out the BBC ran a dire package for the Irish, full of vox pops saying they had to keep Articles 2 and 3 of the Constitution. When the Irish came in, I suggested to TB that he 'turn off the charm tap' and he start to get a bit heavier. The problem was they wanted clear Westminster legislation to set up implementation bodies; otherwise, said Paddy Teahon, it would be just like Sunningdale, built on sand, all too easily collapsible.[1] Bertie said on the one hand they are expected to change their Constitution – to give up the claim to the North effectively – and yet there is no 'on the other hand' of equal clarity. Bertie said he saw them last night and he knows they will use every trick in the book to stop the N-S bodies happening. We went round in circles. By prior arrangement, TB asked me what the reaction would be if we didn't do a deal. I said Bertie would be crucified. 'They think the other lot are mad anyway, but they think you guys are sane so it would be you that gets crucified if we fall apart over this.' Teahon laughed his head off, but Bertie nodded quietly, and got the point. TB said we had them in the right place on Articles 2 and 3.

Decommissioning was still a problem. Next meeting was DT and Taylor and we had an interminable discussion about N-S bodies, what areas, what they would actually do. TB called up Bertie for a meeting, during which Siobhán O'H came round for a chat. More gallows humour, Jonathan said we'd better get rid of the Taoiseach (meaning finish the meeting). SO'H: 'You don't need to get rid of him.' Jonathan: 'I didn't mean it in your sense of the word.' George Mitchell came in and said he had a document ready for tabling pretty quickly but now Trimble was away with his executive for two hours. Mitchell wanted to give them half an hour to read it and then have a plenary. He said to TB the difference he had made was in forcing the pace through deadlines. Major would never put a deadline, which meant they would keep us here for ten years if they could.

5.55 Adams, McGuinness, O'Hanlon. In to do some more chiselling. They were not happy. All the big concessions had gone to the Unionists.

[1] An agreement signed in 1973 at Sunningdale between the UK, the Republic of Ireland, the UUP, SDLP and Alliance Party of Northern Ireland to set up a Council of Ireland.

A changed Irish Constitution. NI Assembly. Right to veto implementation bodies. McGuinness said what can we point to? TB said changes to UK Constitution, nationalist identity recognised, implementation bodies, changes to policing, prisoners, equality agenda. And he said everything was protected by mutually assured destruction. If the Assembly failed, the whole thing failed. If the implementation bodies didn't happen, the Assembly falls. Adams said the UUs were the perceived winners and them the perceived losers. TB said they had to get over this thing with the spin on it, as if it was a zero-sum game. Everyone could win, but everyone had to compromise. He said 'I've got blood out of a stone from the Unionists, and the points you're making are not persuasive.' Paddy Teahon put his head round the door and said the SDLP were going wobbly. TB said in the past forty-eight hours I've been wondering whether I understand politics at all. Sinn Fein went away then came back, no doubt influenced by *Channel 4 News*, which had too much of the pro-UU spin, and said they would not be able to sell the document as it was. They could not accept the Unionist veto on the implementation bodies. Policing was also a problem. TB said 'I don't accept you can't sell this. This is a programme for change and a lot of the change is to the benefit of your community.' GA said he was a British prime minister speaking. Their audience didn't listen to British prime ministers. TB said this was the best framework for a united Ireland they had ever had – if people wanted it. His voice was rising as Adams' was getting softer. We have dealt with decommissioning on your terms. We did Bloody Sunday – Mo: 'And we applauded you.' TB: 'I appreciate the pressures on you, believe me I do, but this is fundamental change and you would be mad to turn away from it – N-S bodies, consent, new policing, prisoners, equality.' GA said we want to do the best for our people, to end the conflict with hope. TB: 'I cannot tell you how difficult this has been. If you pull out of this now, I don't know where that leaves us.' After they left, Jonathan, optimistic as ever, said it was just a good-cop-bad-cop routine to drag a bit more out of us. TB was downcast, said he felt they weren't able to get it through their heavies and they were going to fall off the end. 'You have to remember they are negotiating with at least a modicum of worry someone will come along and blow their brains out if they go too far.'

7.30 SDLP, Hume worried about the feasibility studies re N-S bodies. No, no, said TB, it means the six bodies will be set up by the time of the Assembly. He gave them the same line re mutually assured destruction but they were not convinced. TB asked me to get out a briefing for the later bulletins that there is a battle between an irresistible force and an immovable object. 'The irresistible force is the legacy and the baggage. The immovable object is me.' Seamus Mallon had a good line. 'Enough is never enough for those who think that enough is too little.' I said get Clinton engaged. TB – To say what? To tell them nobody will understand if they walk away over this. TB said we weren't cooked enough yet. 'They're deciding everything according to the spin of the others. It's pathetic. Yesterday the nationalists' tails were up. Why? Because the UUs were going round with long faces and saying everyone was against them. Today, one good headline in the *Belfast Telegraph* for Trimble and the other lot are going round like the world has ended. It's ludicrous.'

8pm I drafted an exit strategy, two notes, one from TB, one from Mitchell, saying how far we had come and how we would come back to it soon.

8.10 Trimble, Taylor, Reg Empey. They were in better mood, which John [Holmes] rightly took as a bad sign, because the other lot would be falling off the end. Rumours started of another DT triumph – Assembly to decide the implementation bodies, and it was running far too much in their favour. I got in Mike Brunson and Denis Murray and for the third time in a day did a very greenified briefing, stressing the implementation bodies could be up and running at the same time as the Assembly itself. I also reduced them to hysterics by saying, with a straight face, that they had to ignore the spin and just listen to me. All our problems today were really started by the headline in the *Belfast Telegraph*. The UUs reacted too positively and SF too negatively. It was just another fucking story in the end, I said to McGuinness. He said at one point to TB 'Believe me, this is not a threat, but they could return to violence.' Murray's reports were brilliant today, got the balance and the nuances and the little shifts. Bertie went off to a Mass, during which Paddy T came in with some more changes on Strand 2. 'No, no, I can't,' said TB. Bertie said he had to be sure SF were going to be on board. TB was worried Bertie was not getting enough out of the media stuff so I tried to correct it with Brunson, re the point about Westminster legislation, but he went OTT and said the UUs had made a massive concession to the Irish, so then we had a counter-problem with DT. I called Joe Lennon to make sure he had seen it, and make sure he understood we were trying to push the boat out for Bertie. He said SF were trying to persuade them the point about legislation was a concession TO the UUs, not by them. It was like walking a connecting web of tightropes. I called Siobhán O'H and said we were trying our best to get the spin in the right place for them to do what they had to do.

10.30 TB very down again because they were all off doing their own thing. John Holmes had come back with a whole load more Strand 2 changes from the Irish. He had a list of twenty implementation bodies they wanted. John lay down on the sofa, just shaking his head. TB: 'I've been wasting my time.' John said it has all been about keeping SF on board. TB said they will push the UUs off board again.

10.40 Bertie and Mo came in to go through the list. TB just listened, pretty stony-faced. Again, we had the odd light moment to help us through. An Irish official called Wally came in and said we should remove food safety from the list 'because the Irish government is not quite ready for it'. Bertie: 'We are going to poison everyone instead.' TB sat shaking his head with his arms folded as we went through them one by one. Arts. It's out. Language. They won't wear that. Paddy suddenly piped up. 'It's all quite simple. 1. Get Strand 1 sorted. 2. Do the deal with Trimble on Strand 2. 3. Get Clinton to force Sinn Fein into line.' TB just sighed and looked like he wanted to curl up into a ball. John H was almost asleep on the sofa. Jonathan was still smiling. Nick Matthews was in and out with food and drink. After they left, TB just said 'Fuck, fuck, fuck.'

11.28 DT came back. John Taylor was with him and rather cheerily announced there was a new death threat out against him. They had had a good meeting with the SDLP and felt we could make progress. Again we had to listen to the minutest detail of the smallest ideas for the bodies we were talking about. But at least the mood was better. They left at 11.50 and TB and I fell into hysterics again, putting on our best Irish accents and wondering what new bodies we could come up with – the waste-paper bin emptying body, the screwing tops off bottles body. They had been banging on about closing the Maryfield office block,[1] and I set TB off, saying why has Scotland's rugby ground suddenly become a crucial part of the negotiations? It was all designed just to keep us going through the low moments, of which we sensed there were more to come as we got tired. Mo's private secretary, Ken Lindsay, called me and Jonathan out to tell us [Ian] Paisley and 400 of his friends were in the grounds and marching to the press tent to be there at midnight. It would actually serve as a good media distraction for a while as the deadline passed. We called Clinton and asked him to be on standby to make calls to Adams and Hume and maybe DT.

[1] Maryfield, location of the Irish Secretariat in Belfast, became an issue in the talks. AC thereafter referred to it as Murrayfield, Scotland's rugby ground.

12.15 John H and Jonathan met with Dermot Gallagher [Irish diplomat] and Paddy Teahon and the Irish were saying they couldn't change a word of Strand 3. They were spooked by Sinn Fein. I said they could not possibly do a deal on prisoners if SF were not part of the deal. People just would not understand it. TB suggested a four-way meeting with Bertie, DT and Hume. He now believed SF were pulling the plug because they didn't want a deal at all. Nothing had changed on Strand 2, but they were holding the whole thing to ransom. Mo was trying to calm him down, but he was really aerated. GA has gone right down in my estimation.

12.30 TB spoke to Bertie. SF were stuck on three years for prisoner release. There was no way we could do a deal on prisoner release without SF being on board for the rest of it all. I suggested we make it clear prisoner release only applies to groups who are fully signed up to the deal.

1.10 DT and Taylor in to argue about the size of the Assembly.

1.45 Bertie plus his key officials, to discuss the weight of voting in Assembly. Mo said 18 x 6 plus a civic forum was fair and just. TB: 'We'd better reject it then.' Laughter. Joe Lennon: 'He's learning.' We were still arguing re Irish language.

2.15 Hume and Mallon re the size of the Assembly. I asked Hume to see DT and appeal directly re the Irish language. TB asked Hume what SF were up to. He said it was all about prisoners. They basically want them out in one year, and think they will end up with two. TB said this can only be sold as a meaningful agreement if they are signed up to all of it.

2.30 David Ervine [PUP] et al. UUP were saying voting weight 18 x 5, Ervine 18 x 6. TB was suddenly worried that we had told Hume we were prepared to offer one year for prisoners. When he told Bertie he had done it, he panicked a bit and got Hume back to say he was worried and, for now, forget he had said it. Mo was also of the view that we were giving away too much too soon. [Jeffrey] Donaldson was being pretty difficult about everything. TB asked me to go with him to see their people, and said I should interject at the right moment that they will be crucified if they suddenly throw in new problems now. George Mitchell said even for these guys, they were being ridiculous. I asked him if he intended to write a book about the talks. 'No, the truth would be too awful for words.'

3.10 TB finally said get Clinton.

3.15 UDP. Gary McMichael said they wanted 18 x 5 plus a top-up.

3.25 TB and DT, Trimble for once without his other people. TB had another go at getting the Irish-language promotion [body] in and equality of treatment out. We had a long lecture about the history of Ullans, the Ulster-Scots language.

3.37 TB spoke to Clinton. 'Where are we?' asked Bill. TB said we had been going non-stop for three days. We were close to a deal, and had been for some time. The problem is every time we get close to a bottom line, a new one comes up. SF have an issue on prisoners, and on language. They want their prisoners out in a year. They want to put together a long list, which they just want to throw in at the last minute. They are playing silly buggers. They have suddenly come up with a new list of amendments days and days into the negotiations. He said he was worried they were getting nervous about doing a deal at all. Nothing has changed except the UUs are on board and when they're on board, SF feel they can't be. BC asked about the [Irish] language issue and as TB tried to explain it to him, it was clear there was no way we could let this be a stumbling block. It was crazy. Bill asked if TB wanted him to call. TB suggested he call Bertie and emphasise the big changes they have won here. There is no way we can do the deal on prisoners unless SF sign up to the whole agreement. Our public opinion would rightly say what the hell is going on if we gave them that, and still they were not recommending the whole package. TB said the Irish and SDLP were happy. It was now about putting the pressure on SF. TB ran through the areas we had conceded on and it was a long list. But he still felt best to hold BC back from SF for now. Bill said there is nothing more important to me right now than this. Call me whenever, even if it means waking me up.

3.50 Clinton was ready to call Bertie. Paddy T was still pushing on language. For the first time, I detected Mo being pretty down, when she said she wasn't convinced they were serious. Adams was still holding out on some of the stuff they put in at the last minute. TB asked Mo to go and see him and tell GA he was 'staggered' at the way he was behaving. Paddy said there was no need, it was better we left the Taioseach to deal with him.

4.10 John H called Sandy Berger and briefed him for the Clinton calls. John was worried that if the side letter to DT on decommissioning was leaked we would be accused of playing the Orange card.

TB decided not to see Adams. Nick Matthews came in with a huge plateload of bacon sandwiches. Mo was doing the toing and froing between GA, who was clearly pissed off TB was not doing it himself. Mo had six issues they were still concerned with. They wanted a department of equality. TB was eating bacon sandwiches and bananas, and beginning to look a bit grey.

4.18 TB/BC. Bill had made some calls and said it was time to move for it. He said Adams was nervous about being blamed for collapse. He was trying to squeeze down to six months. TB said we were always at two years. BC said DT was 'really tight-assed'. He had slept so was rational. He had more energy. He was looking for something because he felt Adams had done better.

4.30 Another Clinton call: 'Hell, I'd rather be on holiday with Kenneth Starr than hanging out with these guys.' He said SF were moving to the deal, thought TB had done a great job, but we had to watch the UUs running away once GA said yes. TB called DT and said we have to do this now, otherwise it is going away. DT was in one of his distant modes, not really engaging. We had a problem when it seemed Donaldson was trying to engineer some kind of vote against DT but Trimble called and said he was going for it.

5am John Hume in for a chat. He makes TB nervous re prisoners. After he's left, TB says he's worried how DT and Alderdice will react. Mo, now looking exhausted, said her officials were saying the prisoners deal would be really hard to get.

5.35 We agreed BC should call Adams, and we briefed he should set out how difficult the prisoners issue was, unless they signed up to the whole deal. Bill got the point straight away and was on the phone to him immediately. It felt, finally, like it was falling into place. We were now working with Bertie on Adams and McGuinness with the officials kept out. They finally left at 7.30. Mitchel McLaughlin [general secretary of Sinn Fein] was being a bit more positive at the press briefing, and again the press got a sense we were going the right way. TB just about persuaded them on prisoners. Then Gerry read out another list of demands and TB laughed and said he was not prepared to negotiate any more. 'You are a compulsive negotiator, Gerry. This is a balanced package and you know it.' We then sat down to try and pin him down re his public reaction, which was going to be important. He was fine, if tricky. They said it was important I do my best to spin it positively for them, and said several times they would have to get it through their conference. McG was not saying much and I detected a little bit of anger directed at Bertie, but BA was brilliant at taking flak from the lot of them.

8.10 If you had to pin me down and ask me to explain how it suddenly came together, I couldn't, but by 8.10 I was in the press tent briefing that basically we had a done deal, that it was huge, historic, ginormous, all that stuff. I felt really quite emotional and had to hold myself together. I could see in some of the NI hacks too a real deep emotion, and a desire for this to be true. Even some of the real cynics from London who had managed to stay awake all night were almost wholly positive. Ted Oliver [ex-*Mirror* colleague] was there, Macintyre, Brunson seemed genuinely quite moved too. Jonathan paged me to say it had all gone through the plenary. Amazing, unbelievable. I actually felt like crying but held it together. The final TB, BA, GA, MMcG meetings were crucial and I did my best to spin for the Sinners without pushing the other lot too far off the other side. The whole thing nearly came unstuck over a fuck-up over the wretched implementation bodies, because by mistake the Irish-language promotion (Trimble's staff's fault) and export promotion (our fault) were back in the fucking list. We then had another history lesson from DT on the importance of Ullans. TB could not believe what he was hearing. I said why can't we just say it is promotion of Celtic languages? Because Ullans is not a Celtic tongue, said DT. We had effectively announced the deal was done, give or take a bit or two at the edges and here we were, with DT ready to unpick the whole thing over this. TB said at one point 'We are dealing with the Afrikaner mentality. They're tired, they're scared and they're panicking.'

We then had to sort out access for the ceremony at the end. I was so desperate for us to get away that I said no filming, but Denis Murray rightly persuaded me that would be a mistake, that something as big as this had to be on film. I said we would allow cameras in for the main speeches. We crafted a couple of strong sound bites for TB, though truth be told we were knackered and desperate to get away. TB and Bertie did the signing ceremony, and the closeness between them in their farewells was obvious. In the car out I asked TB if he was tired. He just shrugged and said he needed a break. He said Gale [mother-in-law] would probably have given away Gibraltar by now.[1]

As we got into the helicopter Jonathan said the Queen wanted to talk to TB but we couldn't make the call pre take-off. TB thanked his staff for once, said everyone had been terrific and should be proud of what we had done. He was on a bit of a high now. I worked on a briefing note for the Sundays which I'd just about done by the time we got dropped at Northolt and then TB headed on to Spain. He talked to the Queen from the tarmac. Brunson called me and said thanks for all the help I'd given him. He said we did a great job and he found the whole thing really quite moving. I got home, wired

---

[1] The Blair family were in Spain at the holiday home of the Spanish prime minister, José Maria Aznar.

April '98: Peace agreement signing ceremony

and exhausted, and still trying to remember how it all came together at the end.

Saturday, April 11

I felt totally shagged out, that awful mix of being completely wired whilst still having to work on to make sure the thing came out in the right place, so though I wanted just to be with the kids, it was hard because the phone never stopped. TB called just before 8, and sounded exhausted. He said we did something bloody good there, but we have to keep on the case. By which he meant I had to keep on the case. He said Aznar's place was fantastic, and the family were having a great time.

We felt the need to keep TB's voice in there today, so I got Peter Wilkinson [Downing Street press officer] to fix an interview with the local [Spain] BBC guy. There was a lot of scope for talking up the others, e.g. Bertie and the role BC played as it fell together. I said to TB, can you remember how it all fell into place? Not really, he said, but it did, I always felt it would. Bill came in at the right time, no doubt. I took one of the lines BC used in his phone calls for TB's words – time for the men of vision to defeat the men of history.

The Sundays were all after every spit and fart so I organised to do a conference call – seemed to go on for ages, but I could tell from their tone, even the total wankers, that they realised they were dealing with a pretty special story. They wanted loads of stuff – low points, high points, how we ate, who took notes, all the colour stuff. I did a bit extra with a couple of the broadsheets and wanted to give a real plug to John H and Jonathan. Jonathan was at his best in these types of situations. He never seemed to get down like TB and I did, and strangely the thing that people criticised him for – a lack of feel for politics – was sometimes what was needed, because he had a way of cutting through crap and when we said you can't do that, he would just say why not, and we would start thinking.

I took the boys to a birthday party where news came through the UUs had backed it two to one. Fantastic. The FCO sent through a digest of some of the coverage and reaction around the world, which was enormous and positive. PG called and said TB had moved up several notches on the world scene. I was starting to feel a bit more human but still exhausted. TB called before and after his interview, which went fine. He sounded revived already. His capacity to revive on a few hours' rest was a real asset, which I wish I had. He spoke to Bill C and also to Major, which helped stand up the line in my briefing that we didn't rule out TB and JM campaigning together to sell the deal.

I was so consumed with NI I had not quite realised how bad the floods in the Midlands were, and how the image of TB sunning himself in Spain contrasted with the misery there. I spoke to JP, who was having a weekend in Chester. I said I was worried this would move quickly to what was the government doing about it? He got the point straight away and got on to his office to get them to organise a visit tomorrow.

Sunday, April 12

The papers were good, still heavily focused on Ireland and the briefing of yesterday came out well. TB called from Cordoba, said there were a lot of photographers around and should he be pictured playing a guitar? No. He spoke to Kofi Annan and also to Hague, who did a pretty good interview. JP's visit went well and he was pleased he had done it.

Monday, April 13

Barely spoke to TB today. The only major work intrusion was JP who was livid at an interview [Michael] Meacher had given saying there would be a countryside White Paper as a result of the march. He bollocked Meacher rotten. He also warned me there were a few in the Cabinet wound up re Peter M at the Cabinet Office. He does himself no favours, he said.

Tuesday, April 14

TB called re whether he should do a doorstep in Madrid tomorrow. I wasn't convinced, but his constant refrain at the moment was how big he was out there, so he was bound to do it. I had a running battle with the FCO all day over advance briefing on the Middle East trip. They were really keen to start generating a lot of interest but TB and I were both worried they would push a different line. I got a message out that we didn't want anyone briefing on the trip but me. The press were starting to pick over the NI deal much more aggressively.

Wednesday, April 15

Paisley was dominating the news all day with the launch of his No campaign. He still has the capacity to put over a point with real force, and he was not to be underestimated. At the moment he was on big picture, but there was detail he would get into as we went along. Magi [Cleaver] called from Saudi to say that as things were currently planned, Michael Levy was in the motorcade and would be meeting us at the

April '98: Paisley launches the 'No' campaign

airport. The last thing we needed was a great Michael funding splurge so I raised it with TB when he called pre his doorstep in Madrid. David Kerr from Trimble's office called, said they were getting real grief re prisoner release. I got a note through to TB to address prisoners in his doorstep, to the effect that they would be out on licence, straight back in if they reoffend. We were watching the FCO very closely. TB wanted to play the Middle East trip right down the middle, and was worried they were going to push too hard on the anti-Israel side.

Thursday, April 16

TB back, and was doing a visit in Croydon. He called and said he was confident re NI. It actually helped that Adams was keeping his counsel, because it helped DT say to the Unionist community there was something here the other side didn't feel happy with. It was dreadful that was how we had to operate, but the reality. He was worried that the *Telegraph* and the *Mail* were straight on to what was undoubtedly the weak point of all this – decommissioning. We had danced around it for now but it would come back. Re the briefings I was doing, he wanted me to keep going with bolstering DT even if it meant pandering a little.

For most of the day, I was reading up on the Middle East, and getting an agreed briefing line written. TB was adamant we stay neutral and lower expectations of any great outcome. He was worried the FCO would fuck it up by getting the Israelis' backs up from the word go and we would not be able to move them at all. I did the briefing and felt OK on the substance. The breakthrough in NI was a great backdrop, though we had to watch 'Blair peacemaker' stuff, which was bound to set the bar too high. The Arab press were a bit down on us, so I emphasised we were there to support US efforts not cut across them. We could get easy headlines attacking whoever we wanted but would it actually help take the thing forward in the way we wanted?

We had an office meeting and argued about whether to make much of May 1, one year on. I was arguing for being low-key. TB felt we should use it to push substance over style, that we were doing the big things right. TB was still going on about how big he was in Spain. He was trying to make the point it was a potential benefit to the country and we had to use it better. But there was a bit too much vanity in there about it. I said being big in Spain does not strike me as a top-five strategic priority. No, he said, but Britain big on the world stage is. Correct. We agreed on that but had to agree proper definitions. Peter M was worried re Hugh Pym's book on GB [*Gordon Brown: The First Year in Power*, by Pym and Nick Kochan]. He felt they were deliberately pushing this line that GB was the real intellectual force in the government and TB just the frontman. GB called from Washington, wanted to use his speech tomorrow to say something re NI, which was fine and we trailed it.

I called Michael [Levy] and said we expected him to keep a low profile on the Middle East trip. He had done an enormous amount of work setting it up, and everyone respected his commitment and energy on this, but it would become a media negative if he became too big a part of the story. He said he and Gilda were made to feel like pariahs. There was no need to feel that, I said, but he had to understand the media would turn the story into something it wasn't.

Friday, April 17

I fixed up for TB to do three NI interviews, just to keep the pot boiling. TB was worried the see-saw was dipping too far the other way. But Donaldson was making reasonably encouraging noises and DT seemed OK. TB also spoke to Adams on the way to the airport, and he seemed OK, though Mo had told me that TB – or 'Blair' as she called him – had to be careful not to look like he was only worried about keeping the UUs on board, because GA was more vulnerable than he liked to admit. The Middle East briefing had gone fine, and the trip was fairly well set up. What I was trying to do was set expectations and lay down the idea that the success judgement was whether we could get some kind of formal EU role on economic and other issues alongside the US who were clearly in the lead on this. It wasn't exactly the highest we could reach for, as there was already a meeting planned for May 4 in London with US, Israel and PLO re the same.

Derek Plumbly [Middle East and North Africa director, FCO] was worried we would get very little back from the Palestinians because we were so timid in what we were saying re Israel. TB was clear there was no point him going there as though *parti pris*. This tension was there throughout the trip though to be fair most of the time the FCO guys played the game fine. We had a long session on the flight out going over the basic approach – be even-handed, aim for EU role, make progress on a few bilateral issues, get some kind of relationship with Netanyahu. The media were getting overexcited re the jailed nurses, and I did a briefing to try to calm them down.[1]

---

[1] Two British nurses had been jailed in Saudi Arabia after the murder of an Australian colleague at a Dhahran hospital in 1996. Blair won assurances from Crown Prince Abdullah that the case would be reviewed and the women, Lucille McLauchlan and Deborah Parry, were later pardoned by King Fahd.

April '98: TB should worry about SF as well as UUs, says Mo

We arrived in Cairo, CB in green, and in a good mood most of the way, though I always sensed she was never fully comfortable with her role on these trips which were so clearly working not ceremonial or showy, but he liked having her along most of the time. We were taken straight to the [former royal] Al Qubba Palace, which was extraordinarily grand, and had a meeting – another one – on the trip and what we wanted out of it. We assumed the place was bugged and were talking guardedly again. The ambassador [David Blatherwick] felt they would have questions on why the Americans were not doing more. They were promising to table land for peace proposals but were not doing so at the moment. In the end a lot depended on Netanyahu, or the armour-plated bullshitter as some of the FCO guys called him.

We left for [President of Egypt Hosni] Mubarak's palace, which was even grander. TB was taken off for a brief one-on-one, during which I learned that what we thought was going to be a brief doorstep was in fact a full-scale press conference. So we were in for a long haul. The dinner was an extension of the bilateral more than a discussion. I was between the ambassador and [Osama] El-Baz [presidential political adviser] who seemed like an elder statesman adviser type. The press event saw a succession of pretty much the same questions again and again re the MEPP. Mubarak buried one problem area, to the delight of the FCO lot, when he said they didn't see the UK 'housing Egyptian terrorists' as a major issue. He was lukewarm about an EU initiative but was fairly onside generally. TB was just pushing the same line as I had used in the briefing – never stop talking, never stop trying, do what you can – but was also trying to make progress on the interim economic issues. Plumbly was worried afterwards, said we risked being exposed as having no clothes and we should be staying very focused on the bigger picture.

We met to discuss back at the palace, but then news came through of a shooting in Belfast. The media were desperate for TB to react, but we refused. No point. I called Mo, who said it may have been a punishment beating that went wrong. A week on from NI, the reverberations were still being felt.

Saturday, April 18

We started the day behind schedule because TB was in the bath late, and kicked off with Egyptian TV. Derek Plumbly as ever was worried that we were not clear enough in restating commitments, which gave the sense we were tacking too close to the Israeli position. An overnight telegram was also making clear the Palestinians felt we were going too closely down the Israeli line. TB recalibrated a bit. TB had a speech, in which I inserted a couple of clips on Ireland, and then to a fantastic mosque to meet Sheikh [Muhammad] Tantawi [grand imam of al-Azhar Mosque]. TB was getting mad at the fact that the traffic was held up for him everywhere we went.

We went to see the press, TB mainly on MEPP, a bit on Cool Britannia,[1] while I was being vile to Rachel Sylvester about the *Telegraph*'s coverage of the Northern Ireland agreement. They were determined to do whatever they could to unpick it. They loved my Cool Britannia garbage, even though I freely said myself it was garbage purely designed to fill a hole in the Sundays.

TB did a doorstep on the UUP successful vote [David Trimble secured the critical support of his party], then back to the Palace to wait for a call to see the King [Fahd]. As we waited with John H, TB started musing about the Cabinet. He said he felt short of a couple of real heavyweights. He felt the FCO had good and bad in it but it really needed someone to go in and shake it up, and RC had been good on some fronts, but a disappointment on that one. He felt GB and JP were the only really big figures. Mo was OK but limited. DB was OK but it was not yet clear he would develop into a really big figure.

We got the call to set off for the King, who was much more frail and elderly than I imagined from the briefing. One or two people at the embassy said he was pretty near senile. We were ushered in, TB, John, the ambassador and I, opposite a huge line of Saudi princes. JH and I were both tired and committed a diplomatic faux pas in view of the Saudi camera – crossing our legs so the King could see the soles of our feet. The princes looked aghast, or one or two of them did. The King didn't seem to notice. He didn't seem to notice much at all. The conversation with TB was bizarre, mainly small talk. He asked at one point whether TB had a wife. TB said yes, and smiled. The King said he could always have helped with a young Saudi bride, and the princes laughed, though more in embarrassment than anything else. John and I were keeping our hands on our knees like a couple of footballers in a team photo so as not to cross our legs again. But I was so tired I did it again just before we left. Again he didn't seem to notice.

Then we were off and taken to another ludicrously sumptuous

[1] The media term adopted during the mid-1990s that was meant to presage the era of New Labour. First used in 1967 as a song title by the Bonzo Dog Doo Dah Band.

room to wait for the Crown Prince Abdullah. I sat next to his brother, who was hard work, but TB seemed OK and at least we were having a conversation of sorts. Again there were loads of them, all at a long table, and just a handful of us. They went over MEPP, trade, Ireland, defence. Abdullah was pretty feisty on terrorists using the UK as a haven, and TB was fairly robust in defence of what we were doing. On MEPP, TB was not as blatantly pro Israel as usual, but even so the feeling they gave out was that we were one-sided.

On Iraq, Abdullah said they loved the Iraqi people – they are our brothers. TB said we would not threaten the territorial integrity of Iraq. TB said there was always a danger that Saddam would exploit lack of progress in the Middle East. TB finally raised the case of the nurses, fairly gingerly it has to be said, but they got the point. The interior minister [Prince Nayef] made light of it, almost as if he didn't know what we were talking about. Then he went over to Abdullah and they talked quietly to each other. He said the families had sent a petition for mercy to the King and he and Abdullah would work it out. Abdullah said the British press did not help their cause. 'The press should bring people together – all they do is drive people apart.' TB pushed it and said what would he be able to say about the situation? 'Say you are optimistic,' said the minister, which was progress of sorts.

Back at our palace, where I was staying in quite the most over-the-top bedroom I had ever slept in, and with a gold jacuzzi thrown in, I worked up a fairly cautious line on it. The ambassador was clearly a bit worried about it. TB wanted me to play it fairly low-key whilst also getting the press to convey the impression we had a done deal. I watched the Saudi TV, which had edited out our shoes incident. The coverage of the meeting appeared to go on longer than the meeting had.

Sunday, April 19

On the plane to Jordan, TB said I had to make clear to Michael [Levy] that he should not come out to the airport. I spoke to him when he reached Amman and said he should come out but stay in the car. I had to be fairly blunt because anything else he would have taken as a green light. I totally understood why he was pissed off – he worked his rocks off to raise money for the party, and he was now meant to hide away.

The *Sunday Times* had run some of the Hugh Pym GB book, which I showed to TB on the plane. It was the usual total bollocks. TB said what he couldn't stand was the lies they peddled against us, like it was Jonathan who was responsible for the leaks on EMU. But the big line being run against us the whole time was GB was the brains and TB the frontman, and Peter M got the usual monstering all over the place. He said he would have harsh words with GB. I said I would believe it when I saw it. CB said GB is out there lying about Tony the whole time. 'I hate him.' Peter M called while we were visiting a Jordanian refugee camp. He was livid. 'What does it all say about their judgement for heaven's sake – first, they start a mini crisis for the government, and then they run away from it, and now they do a complete rerun. The whole thing is designed to lay me out to filth. TB has said he will deal with it, and hasn't, and in the meantime I am never allowed to put my case. Why should I be laid out and never allowed to fight back? Why should they be allowed to tell lie after lie?' He asked me to tell TB he did not intend to stay silent on it all.

We had a meeting with Crown Prince Hassan, then a refugee camp and then to the palace to see King Hussein. It was a big-deal welcoming ceremony. They had a fairly lengthy private session before the rest of us piled in. The King struck me as really intelligent and thoughtful, but was constantly interrupted by Crown Prince Hassan who was prone to make grand sweeping statements that he thought summed up what had been said but didn't quite do so. And he laughed far too much too. He did have one good line – people say the economic fundamentals are strong but you cannot eat fundamentals.

The King clearly didn't believe Saddam could be controlled, whereas he thought Gaddafi [Libyan leader] was improving. TB was dubious that Gaddafi could be rehabilitated. He was slightly less pessimistic than the others about the MEPP. On the plane we were joined by [Spanish diplomat] Miguel Moratinos, the EU envoy, who was a very jolly chap who seemed to like being up the front of the plane chewing the fat with TB. I got him to brief the press and he struck a fairly optimistic note. We arrived in Israel and I was taken to the car where Michael [Levy] was hidden away with some woman from the MFA [Israeli Ministry of Foreign Affairs]. It was so obvious Michael wanted to be seen, but to be fair he was making light of it all, saying he understood he would have to wear a veil for the rest of his life. 'I am the pariah,' he said. But at Yad Vashem [Holocaust memorial and museum] he got out and wandered around, clearly wanting to be seen, and said I had to understand what this place meant to him. Then when we went to [former Israeli Prime Minister Yitzhak] Rabin's grave, he suddenly pitched up just behind TB, virtually in every shot, and later claimed Leah Rabin [widow] had called him forward so he had no choice. Mmm. TB did a rather OTT speech at the memorial flame.

Then to Netanyahu's, where we were surprised by a full military welcome and then Netanyahu making a speech we had never expected, so TB had to respond. It was a bit pro Israel for my taste, and lacked the balance we had achieved so far. His basic message, public and private, was that he was pro Israel but there had to be compromise and the Israelis had to work for progress. He said there was a basic perception they did not want progress and they had to address it. They were a pretty heavy bunch, him, [foreign minister Ariel] Sharon, [defence minister Yitzhak] Mordechai and their advisers were hard. Mordechai hit the 'protect our security' buttons.

Sharon talked about how they were being asked to give up the cradle of the Jewish people. We are not being stubborn but these are matters of life and death. Nobody can be responsible for our security but ourselves. He said, one of the reasons it was hard to move ahead was because of the expectation we would move ahead under pressure. TB said 'With all due humility, I think you need to show that you are progressing.' Netanyahu said at least TB thought they were trying 'But you are in splendid isolation.' He said they knew about war, and did not want it. [Yasser] Arafat [President of the Palestinian National Authority] is basking in the glow of a sun shining on him, because the sense is all the pressure is on us. There must be dual compromises.

TB, Netanyahu, me and my opposite number went through to BN's inner office. TB was trying to pin him down re saying he would engage on the US proposals. We got him to agree he would say he would be willing to come to London within a month to discuss, but the mood we got was that he would not agree to them. So it was progress but only of sorts. They both did fine at the press conference, and certainly our lot felt it was a big story, but the experts knew better, including one who tried to wind me up at the briefing afterwards.

John H and I were standing together watching them. Netanyahu was getting TB to be nicer and nicer but not really coming up with the goods himself. The three of us travelled back together, TB doing his little finger-whirl to indicate the assumption the car was bugged so we did the usual how well it had all gone blah. He was worried the US would think we were cutting across their planned May 4 meeting, which was set date-wise but which Bill Clinton was apparently not very keen on. I called [Mike] McCurry and we agreed they would welcome the outcome of the TB/BN meeting but we would both emphasise none of it would matter unless the parties faced up to difficult decisions. We were getting good coverage out of today but I was worried it would unravel. We now needed Arafat to commit to May 4 tomorrow, with the Israelis now saying it would happen.

TB was back into superman mode. He said if I had three days with these people all in a room, I reckon I could crack this. John H and I both laughed. He also felt there was a lot more to Bibi [familiar name for Netanyahu] than met the eye. I failed to see it. I called home and Fiona said everyone seemed to be saying TB had solved the Middle East. It was going a bit too far all this, and I felt we were walking the high wire. The dinner was pretty dire, both the food and the conversation. I didn't find Netanyahu impressive, but he definitely had the best-looking secretary I had ever seen in a leader's office.

Monday, April 20

I was getting more worried about the high-wire act we were performing. We were dealing with some of the best bullshitters in the world in the Israelis and yet we were bullshitting our way to a media success, on which the substance was a bit flimsy, but which was at least keeping them busy and maybe helping build a bit of momentum. But it all felt a bit flaky to me. But for [wife of ex-Beatle Paul] Linda McCartney's death, the story would have gone even bigger, and certainly Netanyahu saying he would go anywhere was being seen as a big breakthrough, though both JH and I doubted it meant that much. Fiona said people back home were very sad about Linda.

I was called down to see TB, on his way back from church, to go over the next bit, and we agreed what was needed today was for Arafat to say yes to the meeting, and the US then to announce it for London May 4. But TB shared my nervousness about some of this – pissing off the Yanks by forcing the pace, and also that it would not actually add up to as much as was now being made of it. We were in the odd situation where a press that normally accuses us of over-spinning our own triumphs was having to be talked down, and told it was not as big a triumph as they were saying. But of course they just took that as a different form of spin, downspin to indicate confident upspin. You couldn't win.

We left for a meeting with the Israeli president [Ezer Weizman] and not only was Michael [Levy] there but he had managed to get himself put into the meeting, and was sitting there proud as punch as the media charged in to do the pictures at the top. I was livid, and though he didn't show it, so was TB. As ever, ML had an excuse, but it was pretty unbelievable stuff. At TB's behest I sent him a note, saying it was difficult to escape the conclusion he simply had a desire to be noticed, which was not what TB needed, and it might be better if he didn't go to Gaza. Philip Barton said ML was incandescent and took it out on him not me. I got the strong sense that Weizman did not like Netanyahu much and he kept urging TB to keep be nice to Arafat. 'Where there is a will, there is a way, and if there is something you can do, it is to firm up Netanyahu's will.' We had a meeting with [Ehud] Barak [Labor Party leader], who was OK but not everything he had been cracked up to be. He said he was pessimistic because Bibi was a total bullshitter.

We left for Gaza, and were driven up to the checkpoint then taken to the guest house to see Arafat. He looked old and frail and the lip-trembling was pretty severe at times. His hands were so white I looked closely to see if they were gloves. The conversation at times just came to a halt and we sat there in silence, in this small and rather shabby room, where he had a real feel of an emperor without clothes. CB and his wife were chatting away; the PLO London guy was trying to keep things kicking on, but it was hard. Then he would suddenly burst into conversation, TB would exchange and it was fine, but then he would lapse straight back again.

We then set off for the Palestine Authority HQ where we were met by an extraordinary welcoming party, including a pipe band playing the national anthems, badly. TB was taken round to shake hands interminably and as he came round he gave me a look that said he was finding it hard not to burst into hysterical laughter. I was chatting to the SIS guy about the EU security deal when Philip [Barton] told me TB had left his file on the occupied territories in the Israeli car we had been in. They were giving it back to us, no doubt after copying.

Arafat was not in great shape and so the others tried to over-compensate by being upbeat and loud, but the overall sense was very gloomy. At the end of the lunch I went to TB and said we had to be able to say YA had said yes to London and Arafat said he would say he looked favourably on the US proposals. They clearly wanted a four-way discussion. Armed with that, we went to the school for a Q&A, where TB got a terrific welcome from the kids, who were really warm and nice. Nabil Sha'ath [Palestinian International Co-operation minister] said he had never seen such a welcome for an overseas visitor. I briefed the press YA had said yes to the meeting and would say so afterwards. We left for the Beach refugee camp [al-Shati] which was not as bad as I remembered it when I went there with Neil [Kinnock] a few years back. Again, the kids were fantastic, really warm and friendly and with a dignity that was moving given the shit circumstances they lived in.

The press had totally bought into our strategy and now we were trying to hose them down a bit, and play down the significance of the whole thing. Derek Plumbly had discovered that the US were going to announce YA and Bibi had been invited to London on May 4. They had agreed to announce it at the same time as TB so again the sense of it being an important development was enhanced. As we got nearer the press conference, we had a session with TB to pin down words on Jerusalem, statehood, etc., and then when Arafat agreed he would say he welcomed the invitation and TB would thank him.

But Yasser did not stay on script, did not deliver as agreed and when TB mentioned the May 4 meeting, YA suddenly piped in with a line that it would be quadripartite with a clear role for the EU. I could tell TB was startled, and so could some of the hacks. He tried to row it back to supporting the US in taking the lead, while we would do whatever we could and would welcome an EU role in the interim economic issues. YA then really blasted into Netanyahu. After I briefed to try and get it back in the right place I was called to see TB and YA in the car as we were about to head off. My sense was Arafat knew exactly what he was doing. TB said I have clarified with the president and what we are saying is bilateral on the US proposals and possibly tri- and quadripartite on the economic issues. Thankfully that is what I had been saying to the press. I called Mike McCurry who said TB could come back to pick up his Nobel Peace Prize in Cyprus. He was happy enough for us to get some credit out of this.

TB spoke to Netanyahu on the way back and he said there was an edge to his voice that he found a bit alarming. Netanyahu clearly felt a bit bounced. The truth was we had bounced both the US and the Israelis, and there was still a chance of counter-reaction. We went back through the checkpoint, and again I was struck by the immediate difference – from poverty to affluence in a matter of feet. TB called from the car, anxious we had the story in the right place. I think we did but who knows. Back at the hotel, he said even he was feeling it was all a bit high wire.

TB called Levy and got him to come round for a drink because he was so upset about my note to him. No doubt TB was going to say I went over the top, and I left him to it, with ML looking really hurt. I did another Brits-only briefing and though they knew they were being spun all over the shop by all sides, they couldn't resist it and by and large felt we had done a good job here. Bevins said he thought TB was brilliant today. It was because he had pitched himself as a friend of Israel that he had been able to push the Palestinians to where they got to. He said he could think of no other politician in the world who could have done it so seamlessly. It was a good day but I couldn't help thinking Arafat would be dead within the year.

TB finally got to bed at 1.15 after soothing Michael Levy's battered ego. Michael said thanks for my second note, which he called an apology. I said it wasn't an apology. It was a statement that I did not want to upset Gilda [Levy's wife]. We were getting huge coverage still for yesterday, right round the world. TB was still in the bloody bath minutes before Netanyahu was due to arrive for breakfast. When they started Netanyahu was focusing on pretty small bilateral issues, presumably as a way of avoiding the main subject. TB let him for a while. But it was clear he was going to say yes to May 4 and at least give the impression of engagement.

We had agreed last night to no press conference but I thought people would think it odd. I worked on BN's chief of staff and his press secretary eventually turned up after failing to talk us out of it. It was fine. Netanyahu did a pretty grovelling piece on Tony who just banged away on the general substance. Re quadripartite we agreed with BN we would say it all depended what came out of the bilaterals but we didn't rule it out. It was all fine and now the press were into every last detail of how the thing was put together, blah blah. The travelling hacks said it had been a terrific trip for them. I was late arriving at the school where TB was doing a Q&A. He was in full flow and who should be the first person I see but [Dame] Shirley Porter [disgraced former Conservative leader of Westminster City Council, overseer of illegal 'homes for votes' policy], amazingly unnoticed by the hacks, and also there, needless to say, was Michael, hiding behind Plumbly and saying he was deliberately hiding. Then, as TB wound up, who should march straight up there and shake him by the hand and start making introductions but Michael. He was unbe-fucking-lievable.

We left for the residence where David Manning [UK ambassador to Israel] and his wife really looked after us. I had a swim and TB chilled out for a while. But he was adamant if he had a bit of time on it, he could crack the whole problem. CB was off having a Dead Sea massage, whatever that was, and was late back but eventually we left for the plane. TB saw the hacks on the plane, I did a briefing then slept the whole way back.

We got back to a domestic problem. The *New York Times* had been leaked a story that we were going to take 5.1kg of nuclear fuel from Georgia after doing a deal with the Americans. It was manageable

April '98: TB says with time he can crack peace in Middle East   369

but a pain to deal with. There was loads more foreign media coming through on TB the peacemaker.

Wednesday, April 22

Nuclear fuel was the main event story-wise but we got OK coverage for RC's Third Way speech, which was being seen – rightly – as part of his rehabilitation, with it looking like he was getting more firmly behind the project. Today was also his wedding party in Carlton Gardens. Earlier he told Jonathan TB must not say it was our idea to move the wedding forward because he had told Gaynor it was his idea and she would not be too happy if she found out it was all part of a spin doctor's plan to get the whole issue sorted sooner rather than later. 'If she finds out, I'll have a divorce on my hands.' He was also agitating that he needed a Charlie-type spin doctor to start fighting back a bit.

TB was of course failing to tackle the GB/Whelan problem. The morning meeting was mainly about trade union recognition, with [Jon] Cruddas warning us John Monks [general secretary, TUC] was in real trouble if TB didn't help him a bit. He felt we were far too close to Adair Turner [CBI] on this. The 11 was all going to be nuclear fuel though and I got an expert in to brief me on Dounreay[1] which was totally dominating the news. The briefing went fine. TB spoke to, and later wrote to, [Sir] Alistair Graham [chairman] of the Parades Commission [for Northern Ireland] to say he felt he should postpone their preliminary report of the Commission. Though technically we didn't know what it was going to say, in practice we did. We knew it was going to upset the Unionists, not least re Drumcree, and he didn't want that right now. I spoke to Graham and drafted a statement and we just about got it under control. Graham wanted to publish TB's letter and we could not really object to that.

Hague did beef on the bone and Ireland at PMQs. Nuclear fuel didn't come up till the end. TB was good, much calmer and less histrionic than of late. He went to the Tea Room afterwards and said the mood was pretty good. I was starting to work on a May 1 strategy, as there would be a lot of one-year-on focus. I was really tired today, and could feel myself dipping into a depression.

Thursday, April 23

I put together a speaking note for TB to the Cabinet, pointing to the one-year-on stuff, making clear we downplay any sense of celebration,

[1] UK Atomic Energy Authority site in Scotland, destination of the of uranium from Georgia.

talk up progress but most important focus on the future. I had a meeting with [Peter] Kilfoyle [Cabinet Office minister] who had an adjournment debate tomorrow which was basically going to be an attack by the Lib Dems on me and the press office. There was no real problem but I was becoming a bit worried about the way my profile was going up again what with this, the PASC appearance I had to do, and the [Rupert] Allason case[1] all coming together.

Cabinet was mainly Ireland and then a political discussion. TB was very nice re Mo, said it took a very special personality to absorb what she did from all the various parties and she had been heroic. Re the Agreement, he said we have a design for the building, but now we have to build it and there will be a lot of difficulties along the way. He said every time one side is on board, the other starts to get flaky. GB was doing an economic package for the province. Mo lavished praise on TB and, more surprisingly, on [David] Trimble, said he had finally shown real leadership. TB reported on his Middle East trip and said it was altogether more tricky. We should not get too ambitious re May 4 because it will not be the great breakthrough people are looking for. I got JP to agree he would do a one-year-on speech tomorrow, which I drafted. I interviewed for my new deputy and was keen on Godric [Smith], even though it would be a big promotion.

I went to the [Labour Party fund-raising] gala dinner at the Hilton. There were not that many ministers but there was a good turnout generally and TB spoke well. I chatted to [David] Montgomery re N Ireland. He thought we had made a mistake interfering in the parades but also felt media-wise we were getting away with it. TB was at the top table with [Lords] Sainsbury and Levy. ML told me he thought it best to stay low-profile! I spoke to [Mike] McCurry re Dounreay and said we were being hammered on the lack of openness angle and could he emphasise it was not possible to say in advance what these shipments were going to be.

Friday, April 24

I was feeling exhausted and a bit depressed and called in to say I was staying at home. I was having to deal with Dounreay which was still causing us problems. Mo called late. She said she was due to speak to TB in the morning and she wanted to alert me to what it was about as it could become a big problem. Someone had leaked to

---

[1] Litigious former Conservative MP Rupert Allason was continuing to sue (following a previous action) for malicious falsehood by AC and others in respect of a November 1992 *Mirror* article.

Peter Robinson the fact that Sinn Fein, after being tipped off, had discovered a bug inside [Sinn Fein negotiator for Good Friday Agreement] Gerry Kelly's home.

Saturday, April 25

TB and Mo spoke on a secure line and we agreed we should just say we didn't comment on intelligence matters, which everyone would basically take as confirmation. But there was not much else we could do. I took the boys to Bournemouth vs Burnley but had too many interruptions. Also, the Cherie/Anji thing was getting silly again. TB had gone to Chequers but after a conference in London with Derry, CB decided to stay up in London. By the time I got back from the match, Peter M was home talking to Fiona about the CB scene. She was still seething that Anji was there.

I'm afraid my state of mind was such I couldn't be bothered with it. I said they were grown-up people and had to sort it out themselves. As far as I was concerned, the PM should be able to hire the people he wants. There are enough people out there either second rate or trying to do him in without him also having to blow out anyone his wife, or anyone else in his midst, decides to take against. Peter M felt TB would eventually realise he could easily survive without Anji but for the moment he was being stubborn and CB had to live with it. Fiona was much more sympathetic to Cherie, felt both TB and I did not appreciate the pressures our positions put on them, and just expected them to go along with everything. He had to take CB's feelings into account more than he did. It was not just about Anji, and the fact CB did not want her there. It was also that she did not feel she was taken seriously. By the end of it, Fiona and I were barely speaking. 'You can be a total bastard sometimes,' she said. I said I couldn't be bothered with the soap-opera stuff any more.

I went to get the papers. The *Mail on Sunday* splashed on a story claiming TB had bollocked RC for his 'Labour in for twenty years' speech. Peter M was convinced it must have been Whelan. No such meeting or bollocking had taken place but it had been the tone of our comments at the morning meeting. The one-year-on features were OK, balancing out in the six or seven out of ten bracket. There was lots about the so-called dictatorial centre, nothing very original.

Sunday, April 26

Fiona and I picked up where we left off yesterday, with a bad row that ended with her saying the gaps between my down moods were getting too short. Her main complaint, which I guess had a lot to

April '98: CB/Anji provokes another AC/FM row

it, was that I was so focused on doing the job I had to do that I was not considerate enough of her. She said I was great with the kids but then after them and the job, I had no time for her. I said it wasn't so, but when I got down like this, it was impossible to describe how hard it was to stay up. I could just about manage it for the kids and at work, but the effort was such that when all that was gone, I just crashed.

Monday, April 27

I felt totally deadened. I'm writing this on Wednesday because I have had so little energy in the last few days. The only good thing today was when Rory came in [to Downing Street] at 6 and I took him to Crystal Palace o Man U 3. We saw Alex before and he picked up on my mood too, said I looked pressured and down. I said I was. I had barely spoken in the morning strategy meeting. PG was briefing us on the local elections polling. TB said the problem remained that we do not have a big-picture economic narrative that binds the government.

TB had a long meeting with Adams and McGuinness. The bugging row was a difficult backdrop but they didn't seem that bothered. We did schools, language, troop levels, 'signs of occupation' on the ground, plastic bullets, access to the House, prisoners. Mo, Adams and McGuinness came to my office afterwards to agree a line, which was easy enough and as ever they were a mix of charm, friendliness with the occasional hint of menace. McG and I talked about football. I found him more straightforward to deal with than Gerry.

Tuesday, April 28

I told TB that Fiona and I were having a bad time together, and I was really worried where it was heading. I said whether it was true or not, she felt the job was responsible and it was kind of hard to disagree with that. He said there was no greater priority than sorting it out. We were a great couple and I would be totally lost without her, he said. I said I was fully aware of that but it was really difficult just now. The *Telegraph* had the story of [Chris] Patten getting the policing commission job [chair of the Independent Commission on Policing for Northern Ireland]. The story was right but it was irritating it was out there. We had to confirm it without confirming it. TB saw a few hacks and did an interview with a very irritating Roy Hattersley, who seemed dreadfully upset that TB had said he was moved by [the Steven Spielberg film] *Schindler's List*. I'd long thought Hattersley was fairly superficial. I asked Godric to do the four o'clock, partly as a test for him, but in truth because I was feeling really depressed now. I struggled through the day then left early for home, and Fiona was pretty down too.

Wednesday, April 29

I was feeling better. I went in with Jonathan and felt myself coming back into gear. The main thing media-wise was David Frost's internet interview. TB was pissed off he was doing it for an hour but he did it fine. I primed David to ask TB re the Mary Bell story and by the end of the day it was leading the news.[1] PMQs was OK, but low-key. The briefing afterwards was fine. I got back to a meeting on EMU with [Brian] Bender and the Treasury people. I saw the referendum people and agreed we had to watch it did not seem to be totally a Labour thing. I told Godric he'd got the job as my deputy and called the disappointed.

Robin C wanted to see me re Nigel Sheinwald's successor [as FCO press secretary]. His pompous manner was getting worse and I was beginning to wonder if he even realised it was happening. On the one hand he affected to despise what a lot of the FCO stood for, but he was adopting their ways. He was not happy with the FCO list. He was convinced he needed a sharper and more strategic approach to the media and he didn't think the people being suggested could do it. He was also keen on David Hill but when I mentioned it to TB he felt it would be difficult. Tim [Allan] spoke very well at his farewell, said that Peter M was still a friend of his, which was quite something because Tim wasn't even a minor member of the Royal Family. John H called and said the IRA were putting out a statement which would sound worse than it was.

Thursday, April 30

I stayed home a bit late to be with Grace opening her presents. I was conscious of the fact I was home with her a lot less than when the boys were little. We were still trying to decode the IRA statement. It was coming over as very negative in the media, but those who know about these things reckoned it was possible they were trying to signal they would sign up to most of the Agreement. Mo came over and we drafted a line for her to put out as a press release and then a doorstep

---

[1] Bell had been released from prison with a new identity in 1980 after serving twelve years for killing two toddlers in 1968 at the age of eleven. A new book about her, *Cries Unheard: The Story of Mary Bell* by Gitta Sereny, provoked a tabloid newspaper frenzy and led to an injunction to protect the privacy of Bell and her fourteen-year-old child.

post-Cabinet. We presented it as a very clear message to the IRA they had to give up violence for good, but also making clear we should not link decommissioning directly to release of prisoners. TB was angry that GA had allowed decommissioning to become the issue for both sides and he was worried the Tories might start to pull the plug. He asked Mo to speak to Gerry A. She said she had already spoken to McG and when he said they had not been aware the IRA statement was coming, she just said 'Oh fuck off Martin.' Adams is in danger of fucking this up. TB was still pretty steamed up when we left for Northolt. On the plane I was just briefing myself furiously on all the ECB [European Central Bank] stuff. The one-year-on review pieces were fine, but spin was a problem issue. It was brought home to me when TB did a visit to Arndale shopping centre [Manchester] and people were asking me for my autograph. I was saying no. He did a crèche and a hospital visit and he got a really warm reception pretty much everywhere. It was a brilliantly organised visit. Good words, good pictures, in and out fairly quickly. TB was worrying about GB in relation to what he was doing in Scotland. He also felt Peter M's speech to the Institute of Directors was a mistake. JP was wound up about it. TB said it baffled him that Peter could have such sure touch but not about himself.

Friday, May 1

The one-year-on review pieces had if anything got better as the week went on. The *Express* did four pages, and pretty positive. Even the *Guardian* had a pretty good leader. We had done an article in there which we used as the basic message for his *GMTV* and IRN [Independent Radio News] interviews – lot of good progress, lots more to do, values. We went back to the flat and TB made some eggs on toast and we just sat about chewing the fat for a while. He was worried the ecomomy might tip. He was worried the NI situation was really unstable. The *Telegraph* was at it again, saying TB had said no decommissioning meant no seat in the Assembly, the very hook we did not want to get caught on. He was in a fretful mood and was now saying re EMU he wished we had not ruled out the option for this parliament. There was no way we could have gone in in this parliament though. He was not so sure, but what he didn't like was having shut off the option. We had a meeting with GB to go over the upcoming summit. The only show in town was going to be the ECB. TB was due to speak to Chirac, Jospin, Schroeder, Kok. GB was keen for me to set it up as us being confident we were going to get a deal but TB was very cautious. It was [Wim] Duisenberg or [Jean-Claude] Trichet [candidates to become the bank's first president], but it was all complex and ultimately political, and a pretty bad start. Kohl seemed OK with it all. Duisenberg was meant to be appointed for eight years but we would make it clear he would not stay beyond 2002 when notes and coins were in circulation. Chirac wanted it stated explicitly Duisenberg would be leaving January 2002. Kok felt we could not be so clear. This was the area for the deal TB had to strike and it was going to be tough.

I started to worry I was going to miss the Plymouth match which we had to win to stay up. It was a tough negotiation for TB. In the chair but not in EMU. Having to broker the deal but also, re the ECB seats, trying to make sure we were well protected whether we were in or out. Before we left, we had a one-year-on event for the readers of local papers and to my amazement David Burnley [fanatical Burnley supporter who changed his surname by deed poll] was there with the Stoke *Sentinel*. As ever, all he talked about was BFC, including with TB.

We set off for Holland, Kok having virtually begged TB to go and campaign for him. It was a risk in that it was a blatant intervention. The event was in a nightclub and very Dutch, relaxed and laid-back. TB did a brilliant speech. Kok seemed happy enough. TB and Kok had a couple of sessions re ECB and Kok was worried Chirac would force it all the way 'and we end up with a Finn for eight years rather than a Frenchman for four after a Dutchman'. They swapped stories on Chirac's ways. Though as TB said afterwards, Kok could have his moments. I liked him and felt he was straight but he could be unbelievably stubborn. TB said Chirac had ceased to be rational about it. It had become too important. He had set it up as a great national pride issue.

TB stayed till about 11 and was clearly not happy the way it was going. He did Sergeant for the *Today* programme which was almost all EMU. I couldn't believe I was going to miss the Plymouth match for this bollocks. They were like kids over this. Chirac would be unbearable tomorrow.

Saturday, May 2

TB spoke to Chirac, who was totally against Duisenberg, said he could not countenance him in that job without a specific date for his departure. TB said later he couldn't believe he would kibosh the whole thing over this. It sent a dreadful message to the markets around the world. Chirac's problem was that ultimately he wasn't that serious. He was a big character and a big showman but he was limited.

We set off for Brussels. TB wanted to see Kohl on his own, which he did, but at the price of deeply pissing off Chirac waiting outside, who then stormed off. It was going to be a fraught day. The issue was basically how long Duisenberg stayed in place. Kok had spoken to Duisenberg who seemed up to not staying the full eight years but felt it had to be his decision. But JC insisted it was clear he was gone by 2002 and Trichet gets it.

TB decided fairly early on this was not going to get sorted round a table. It developed into a series of running meetings and exchanges between TB, JC with Jospin around a bit, Kok and Kohl. It got bad-tempered quickly. E.g. when Chirac was not there, Kohl asked whether Jospin was coming and Kok said 'We don't bring our kings.' '*Jetzt bist du hochmutig*,' ['Now you are being arrogant'] said Kohl. Eventually we had all of them in the room, sitting on sofas. Chirac said he didn't trust Duisenberg. He would say he would not stay eight years but then he would, unless it was clear he had to go. He said it was non-negotiable, and if need be they would have to discuss a third person. Kok said it is totally illogical to say he is appointed for eight years but serves only three and a half. We would be a laughing stock. Kohl said if this was not resolved today, all of their reputations would be damaged, and he could not see where a third candidate would come from. He felt we should appoint for eight years, then say the successor would be French and the French name the name. TB said we must get clarity. There cannot be confusion. If we talk vaguely about a transitional period, we will be asked what it means, and we will need an answer.

Chirac was so contemptuous of Duisenberg. 'Who is this man who says we must waste all this time talking about a few weeks longer he stays in the job?' Kok said the bank's credibility depended on Duisenberg being able to set the time himself. He then turned on Chirac: 'You say who is this man? He is not someone who just turned up off the street, you know.' Chirac did one of his '*boeuf*' snorts. Kohl stepped in. 'I don't like the tone of this conversation. I'm assured this is a man of quality and honour. It is important we discuss this honourably.' He said we risk creating a terrible impression. Chirac did not change his demeanour. He said we learned about Duisenberg through the press and I will not be treated like that. He said they had already accepted the bank would be in Frankfurt. TB said 'This is not very productive.' Chirac said 'Nor dignified.' He said to TB 'You are a very clear and precise person. This is a not a clear and precise process.' Kok said we should say it is Duisenberg for eight years. It is odd to say the next one should be French but OK. Chirac said

Duisenberg must agree to 1.1.2002 'as a matter of dignity'. This was going in circles. The other leaders were getting pissed off fairly soon, there was a lot of hanging around for them, and every time I went out to brief I could feel it getting worse. The problem was that we had all thought the French and Germans had basically done a deal but they hadn't.

The morning meeting dragged on longer than expected, lunch was late and everyone was bad-tempered. I got upstairs to find TB locked in argument with Chirac, TB looking pained and exasperated, Chirac doing his best 'no way, and I told you so' kind of look. We were now into nine hours non-stop, mainly bilaterals with TB, Kok, Kohl and Chirac, and occasionally Duisenberg. TB had seen Duisenberg with Kok, who now had a permanent look of thunder. Kohl was basically saying it was our problem and we had to sort it out. Duisenberg was clear to TB he could not go along with the proposed deal. Chirac started to talk about the use of a veto.

TB: That is a very big thing to do Jacques.
JC: He cannot behave like this. We give him the job for three and a half years and he doesn't even say thank you.
TB: He refuses to be obligated to a date.
JC: We could move to March 1.
TB: You are getting a Frenchman for eight years.
JC: I do not want this man imposed on me. He is a man without dignity.
TB: He won't accept it. He will accept the process but not a date.
JC: So let's find a third man.

TB then saw Duisenberg on his own for twenty minutes. Chirac was getting more and more up himself. 'A mere civil servant is keeping fifteen heads of state and government waiting for hours and hours. This is a mad situation. Do you think Churchill or Queen Victoria would wait for someone like this?' By 6pm we thought we had a deal but the pro-Duisenbergers were briefing to great effect, giving a sense the bank's independence and authority would be undermined from the word go if this was stitched up as a political deal, and they had a point. Kohl's coalition partners were also busy at it, making clear they did not like a banker being told what to do by the politicians. Kohl seemed happy enough with a deal at first but then heard the German news were running on the idea it might be a violation of the treaty and his tone changed a bit. The deal was basically to be unstated but understood that Duisenberg would go after the introduction of

May '98: Duisenberg row drags on

notes and coins, as per the Madrid conclusions on the timescale for this. TB was now in the position of telling Chirac that Duisenberg would definitely be gone, while telling Duisenberg he was under no obligation. It was yet another bloody high wire, and one around which there was incessant briefing and counter-briefing to a media lapping it up as a problem going on far longer than anticipated.

Through the day, Duisenberg's position strengthened as Chirac's weakened but it was hard to persuade the press of that because they preferred it as a France vs UK situation, with the Germans torn all over the place. TB was worried. The non-involved leaders were getting more and more pissed off. [Jean-Claude] Juncker and [Jean-Luc] Dehaene [Prime Ministers of Luxembourg and Belgium respectively] were openly briefing that we had mishandled it, prompting TB to call in Dehaene and give him a – for him – pretty major bollocking. If you have nothing useful to say, say nothing. How are we helped by going out and saying this kind of thing? TB was getting tired. Kohl was looking more and more panicky between meetings, not at all his usual self. TB asked WD to speak to the leaders, and explain his case, and the mood was dire. He said he was honoured to be appointed, but added a man of his age would not want to serve the full term. It just about worked as a formula. TB emphasised it was our decision. WD said it was a decision made of his own free will. He summed up and they applauded but there was no small talk, no chat, but enmity between the big guns and the smaller countries feeling they had been excluded. Not a good start.

Some of them were clearly happy, though, that TB's gloss was wearing off. Chirac said Trichet would be the Frenchman, as if we didn't know. TB said it had been a long time but he felt we made the right decision. I felt we had to get our lines out pretty quickly so did an early briefing, which led to a row with the organisers because it practically caused a stampede. But I knew we were going to be briefed against all over the shop and needed to get our case out there first. The top line I pushed was that it was WD not the politicians who would decide his departure. Difficult discussions successfully concluded, and the Treaty upheld. I reckoned TB had had some twenty or so really tough meetings, the toughest and longest of which had been Kohl/Chirac, but we got there in the end. The best news of the day was Burnley winning 2-1 and staying up.

Sunday, May 3
We eventually took off from Brussels about 2am and I was in bed by half three. TB repeatedly compared it with the Good Friday

Agreement, saying that just when you thought you were there, someone came in with a new problem to fuck it up. He was worried the other leaders would get it established that we had mishandled it. I said there was no point going on about it. We had got a deal and that was that. The rest was for the birds. I did a briefing after getting up and talked up Duisenberg as having seen his position strengthen not weaken, but there was a lot of chatter of how the markets would respond badly tomorrow and the pound would fall. I felt that was probably bollocks and they would take it in their stride. I had to brief hard that the principal reason it took so long was the split in the German delegation. I wasn't having them joining in with the French in saying it was down to our mishandling or lack of preparation. The truth was Kohl had gone unprepared and unaware of how much it meant to Chirac, and unaware of what his own ministers and ministries thought or planned. The whole thing was pretty unedifying and it was definitely the end of the Blair walks on water in Europe phase.

Monday, May 4

Though we didn't get the predicted mayhem in the markets, we got a real kicking in the media. Kohl was getting panned too in Germany. Chirac, with his tame media, was getting away with it. I felt we just had to put it behind us but TB was all for a big counteroffensive. He had said to Kohl as we left that we had to make clear the bankers did better than the politicians but Kohl rightly said nobody would buy it, because the debate had been so bloody. It was Middle East summit day and we just had to move on. Before his meetings with Netanyahu and Arafat, TB was still more agitated re the ECB and at one point I lost it with him, and said for God's sake focus on this now. It was a shit weekend but it's gone. A few weeks ago, when we were in the Middle East, the summit was the big issue of that time. Now it was here, he was worrying about something else.

We met the Arafat delegation in the White Room, and Arafat's lip was trembling worse than ever. YA just didn't believe Netanyahu wanted to do a deal. TB thought he would, and we talked around the eleven to thirteen per cent land for peace area. TB said on both sides there were questions whether people were serious or playing games. The most important thing is the US makes a proper assessment of Israel's seriousness of intent. As they went over the issues, e.g. prisoners, land, policing, the parallels with NI were fairly striking, but if anything the two sides were even more entrenched.

Netanyahu was talking a good game but Jonathan and I thought it came over as bullshit. Only TB seemed to think there was something in it. He said his instinct about politicians was good and he really thought he wanted a deal. He said in their tête-à-tête BN had 'virtually confided he would be willing to go from twelve per cent to thirteen per cent land for peace'. TB was defending BN and provoked Arafat at one point when he said Netanyahu was clearly very intelligent. 'It is not very intelligent to have most of the world, and half of your own people, think you are wrong,' snapped YA. TB said 'I said he was intelligent. I didn't say he was wise.'

I did a briefing on MEPP and the ECB, pushing the line that the markets not the media got the right reaction, but we were definitely taking a hit. On MEPP I was playing everything down. The [US] State Department did a really gloomy briefing and TB said afterwards he was not sure we had made any progress at all. Levy saw BN as a result of which we agreed TB would have breakfast with Netanyahu tomorrow. He wanted to get a better sense of whether a deal really was possible or not. We were still getting hit on the ECB though nothing like as badly as Kohl was.

Tuesday, May 5

One of those days where you get to the end and wonder how you got through it and managed to keep juggling all the things we had on the go. God knows what it was like for TB. We had the MEPP talks, a Commons statement on the ECB, press conference on the local elections, lots of interviews and little bits and pieces getting in the way in between. I was out of the house before 6 to get in for the meeting with Netanyahu. TB had not really worked out how to play it. The meeting was largely one-on-one. TB said afterwards that BN told him that he would go to twelve per cent, and move on prisoners. He alone thought BN might mean it.

Netanyahu went off to see Albright, with whom TB spoke five or six times during the day, as they tried to play a bit more hardball and get BN to move in public as well as private. She was moving towards putting out a statement that Arafat said yes, Bibi said no, and they wanted to invite them for more talks in Washington next week – provided he said yes. TB spoke to Netanyahu while we were at Millbank for the local elections press conference, and by now we were moving to collapse. Netanyahu said he was being given an ultimatum, which was hopeless, and no way to proceed.

At the lobby, it was all ECB fallout and a bit of Middle East. I then spent God knows how long listening in to a succession of TB calls with the MEPP players. Albright really wanted to play hardball, said she was not prepared to put the president in a position where he just had to listen to Bibi's lines again. I also sensed she didn't much want us in the process either. TB, Bibi and I had a three-way call to agree the outlines of what he would live with in a statement. TB then asked me to join the US and Israeli delegations drafting it. We needed to indicate progress, more to do, and lead up to Washington as the next step.

When TB suggested to Albright I go over, she didn't bite. BN on the other hand jumped at it. I think he sensed TB was the only one who was willing to give him any benefit of the doubt. But TB said to Albright 'If he doesn't do the business next week, we all go for him, including me.' Albright bridled a bit at TB's role but BN would really only engage and open up with TB. He saw her as a glorified official. 'You are a politician,' he said to TB. 'You understand my interests, Clinton's interests, Arafat's interests.'

Around 12, Reuters reported a Palestinian source as saying the talks had collapsed. This was just as Arafat was due to come in to Number 10. I got Godric to ring round and just say the report was wrong. As Arafat arrived, Bibi called and wanted to speak to TB, so we had quickly to get Robin C out to greet Yasser. BN was going to be going home saying there had been progress but not enough, yet he would go to the US next week. It was largely now about managing the media. TB admitted to YA he could not be sure he was not being bullshitted but it was all we had to go on and we should not kick him in the face. He said YA had handled it well because all the pressure was now on Netanyahu. He was a little bit being all things to all men here – telling Madeleine there was no difference between them; praising YA for getting the pressure on to Bibi; giving Bibi the impression he was his only pal inside the tent.

BN had said he would welcome a quadrilateral meeting but again we were concerned he was just troublemaking, and finding a new way of avoiding commitment. YA sat there as TB and RC both praised his handling of the talks. TB said he felt the US were close to tabling the proposals, and BN was moving on quite a lot of things. He said there was no point going to Washington unless there was going to be agreement. Word came BN was pretty positive at his press conference. YA said he would try to be positive, but he said of BN 'He gives out promises very easily but does not carry them through.'

I slipped TB a note re what we wanted YA to say in the street and we just about got there. We were all pretty much saying the same thing – progress, not there yet, Washington the last chance. TB said 'No breakthrough but no breakdown.' Meanwhile we suddenly had

May '98: Madeleine Albright wary of TB role

the Euro summit statement upon us. TB had had virtually no time to prepare but did fine, though Hague did well and the press marked him up. We had been slow getting our case out, though TB still felt we could turn it. Bibi called again and asked TB to go to the Middle East again in the next few days. He said what is there to lose? But there was a danger the Yanks would get seriously pissed off. Bibi basically saw TB as a better way into Bill C than Madeleine. TB said he would think about it. John Holmes was totally opposed, said it would not be productive, we had done what we could and we were currently well out of it. TB was tempted though, and so was I.

I had a planning meeting on the EU summit in Cardiff. We had to work up a better narrative on the future of Europe. TB had his meeting with the Queen, and called on the way back to say he was worried the ECB fiasco was going to leave a lasting hit on us. We got the right result, he said, but the process was a disaster.

Wednesday, May 6

The press was not too bad re MEPP. A *Scotsman* poll was bad news, putting the SNP ahead of us. The main story of the day was going to be Ireland, with TB and John Major doing a joint Q&A tonight. TB was worrying re that, and re Sandline.[1] We had a discussion re Hague. TB's view was that he was a good debater but he had a judgement problem which would really hurt him over time. Netanyahu was back on, asking TB to go there [Israel], but TB had come to the same view as Jonathan, John H and I, namely that he was simply trying to erect barriers against the Americans. TB said he would only go if Clinton asked him to.

PMQs was largely local elections stuff, but Hague went on the decommissioning point re NI, and TB thanked him 'for his support'. He was furious afterwards, felt Hague was just dicking around under a bit of internal pressure. We left for Northolt and on the plane over did an interview with Des McCartan [*Belfast Telegraph*]. He felt the No campaign was stepping up and the Yes campaign going largely

---

[1] Sandline, a UK-based security/mercenary firm, had flown a shipment of arms into Sierra Leone, intended for forces allied to ousted president Ahmad Tejan Kabbah and to be used against a coalition of mutinous army officers and Revolutionary United Front rebels. Controversy ensued when, after initial denials, confirmation was given that Foreign Office officials had been in contact with the mercenaries and were aware of the shipment before it was delivered. Allegations that sanctions against Sierra Leone could have been broken by Sandline were refuted by the company, which insisted High Commissioner Peter Penfold had known it was going to import arms to help topple the junta.

by default. TB was good on the vision thing, had a good whack at Paisley and tried to send reassuring signals re consent, prisoners etc. Major was already at the Waterfront Hall and had earlier made a good speech. JM was a bit nervy, unfailingly polite as ever, though there was always an edge when I was around. 'He really hates you,' said TB. 'He prefers to blame you for doing him in than face the fact that we beat him fair and square.' But they both did well, and the interaction was pretty good with the kids. I could never take JM too seriously but he had a good manner, and was clearly on top of the issues. The sight of them together was a powerful one and I sensed it would have the desired effect in terms of impact.

TB met the Parades Commission and had to do a big number to reassure them of their independence. Then to the RUC where Ronnie Flanagan was very friendly in private but where TB walked in in total silence, and I sensed a bit of antagonism. It was a little better as we left, but warm it was not. Back at Mo's office, we had a meeting with [Jeffrey] Donaldson[1] and six young anti-Good Friday Agreement voters. TB was alarmed afterwards – they were clearly bright and reasonable and if we couldn't get people like them behind it, we had a problem. As they filed out, I asked Donaldson if there were any circumstances in which they might vote yes. He said maybe but it was hard to see what they were. I said would they not respond to leadership? He smiled.

On the way to the airport, TB was worried. He said he was worried the NIO and Mo found the Unionists such a pain in the arse they didn't show enough sensitivity to legitimate concerns. He had been shocked to be told more compensation went to prisoners than victims and he wanted a victims' fund launched. He was going to have to get more involved than we originally envisaged in the campaign. So was Clinton, even if the UUs said they were opposed. Idiotic. He was the best campaigner there was and would definitely shift votes towards us. TB felt we had to target people like the young people we met today. They were not bad people. They were also potential Assembly members. They were not unreasonable, yet they were intending to vote with Paisley. We had to win them round.

He said he would not be happy unless we had a majority of nationalists and a majority of Unionists. Their main beef was that they

---

[1] Donaldson was one of the Ulster Unionist negotiating team for the Good Friday Agreement, but was now part of the faction within the party campaigning against it, arguing there was no link between proposed Sinn Fein representation in government and IRA decommissioning.

didn't really believe the IRA would give up violence and they saw Adams and McGuinness as central to that. They could not stomach seeing them in government, no matter what they said. The prisoners issue was really tough and as TB tried to reassure them, I could tell he was recalling in his mind the phone call with Gerry A earlier, who reminded him he had said they would all be out within one year. Aaaargh. TB said they would never have got an agreement without a deal on prisoners but it was not easy to persuade them.

Donaldson said they had to say the war is over. Those words. And mean it. And be seen to mean it. He said the lines between violent and non-violent were too blurred. Prison officers, police officers, witnesses, magistrates, everyone who knew their ways felt physically sick at the thought of these people in power. TB said he had to show some leadership, take on the Paisleyites. He said it was the one thing he woke up in the night about, the thought that we get the Agreement passed but Paisley wins enough support to undo it.

Thursday, May 7

Today was the first of the daily conference calls with the key NIO people, me, John H and Jonathan to try to keep pushing on an agreed strategy to win the arguments and votes on the GFA [Good Friday Agreement]. Today, following the meeting with Donaldson, we were going to focus on the new government fund for victims. Sandline was becoming a problem. RC was not handling it well and [junior FCO minister] Tony Lloyd's poor showing at the FCO select committee meant the media smelled blood. Cabinet was fairly brief. Afterwards GB and I went through to Number 11 and agreed we had to move quickly re the economic package for Northern Ireland, and maybe do the Sundays on it. He also agreed I could go straight out and do the victims' package which I briefed directly as a response to the concerns of the Donaldson group last night. The DUP came out instantly, saying it was a bribe, which helped give it legs on the lunchtimes. The media bit straight away. We were going to have to make this a news-driven campaign. The overall narrative had to become about TB persuading and winning over the Unionists.

TB was seeing the Orange Order, who were difficult but I sensed even some of them were persuadable. He was very good at presenting the arguments and some left a lot less hostile than they arrived. The crunch point was coming around prisoners, decommissioning and the right to sit in the Assembly. They were looking for legislative expression of the links between them so that GA could not take a seat until it was clear there had been decommissioning and an end to violence, and that there could be no release of prisoners without it either. I kept thinking of, and shuddering about, GA's reminder on the phone of what TB said in the early hours of Good Friday – that they could be all out in a year.

Duisenberg suddenly re-emerged as an issue at the four o'clock because he had indicated to the European Parliament he might stay for the eight years and indicated he thought the compromise agreed was absurd. I did my best to say this vindicated the points we had been making, and strengthened the independence of the bank etc. but it was all a bit of a mess. RC called, claiming he was being briefed against. He was going to hire John Williams [*Mirror* political journalist] as Number 2 in the news department, and start to fight back a bit.

Friday, May 8

I tried to have a day off but the calls started just after 7, and carried on most of the day, mainly on the local elections. We did reasonably well and TB did a good doorstep. Out of the NI conference call, we agreed I would call Trimble and get up the line that Paisley was the man who would say no to anything that brought progress, which the media would pick up and run with as Dr No. I was also keen we start putting the US into the equation. I saw the [US] ambassador last night and explained the UUs were being resistant to Clinton being involved, but was confident we would win them round. Getting up the economic package was the best first start. We told the Treasury they had to improve the economic plan presented yesterday, and we asked NIO to plan for another TB visit next Thursday. I went to Calum's assembly, where he played Henry VIII's servant, and then out for another conference call with Peter M and Jonathan on whether to pull Michael L out of giving evidence to the [Lord] Neill committee on party funding next week. It was too awful to contemplate either way – either ML and funding up in lights and the press salivating on it, or accusations we had something to hide and were too embarrassed to put him up, and so were thwarting an important inquiry blah.

Later in the day I had a rash of calls on Sandline. Their solicitors had released letters showing the detailed contracts and RC was not responding well. He was adamant the problem was he was being briefed against. I felt the problem was we were not robust enough and looking defensive. TB called and asked why we were being so pathetic about it. We were also getting into trouble over the TB/Hague/Paddy Ashdown visit to NI. Everyone seemed to think it

May '98: Trying to get Trimble to take on Dr No

was a bad idea but we had no idea how to get out of it. The UUs felt Paddy might shift a bit of support but they didn't think Hague would. They worried the overall image was of Westminster telling them what to do.

Saturday, May 9

Sandline was a growing problem and RC was getting totally into the bunker on it. He was talking of it as another arms-to-Iraq situation, which was totally ridiculous. It was one of those stories that the media got excited about but had very little real substance or problem to it, provided we were robust and saw it off. I said we should emphasise Kabbah was a legitimate leader toppled by a coup though it would of course be wrong to flout the UN embargo.[1]

Neil Wallis [now editor of the *People*] called while I was taking the kids' football at school to say they were doing the Pauline Prescott secret child story.[2] As he started to spout a public interest defence, I went for him, said there was no public interest at all, it was lowlife stuff if he did it, that other papers had had the story and turned it down and if they did it we would go for them. I slammed the phone down. He called back twenty minutes later, said he had spoken to his wife, and now agreed there was no justification and they would not run it. Eventually I spoke to JP who was furious, said if they ever ran it, he would fight tooth and nail to get TB to do something about the press.

Once he calmed down, we talked about RC, and he too felt Robin had lost his judgement. 'Too busy worrying about his private life and the fallout, and not enough about his job.' Robin did a press conference today and it was OK, but he was far too defensive again. There was just no need. We had a perfectly good story to tell but he was

[1] A report by Permanent Secretary Sir Thomas Legg and banker Sir Robin Iggs into Sandline's 'logistical support' and allegations against ministers and officials criticised High Commissioner Penfold, commenting that he had 'given a degree of approval which he had no authority to do'. The report also criticised officials rather than ministers and made recommendations to combat the 'systemic and cultural factors' in the Foreign Office. The Foreign Secretary announced 'sweeping changes' at the FO and that no further action would be taken against any of the parties concerned. President Kabbah subsequently regained the presidency of Sierra Leone.

[2] The wife of the deputy prime minister had given birth to a son when a teenager and offered him for adoption by foster parents when he was three. Several newspapers became aware of the story but did not publish. It became public knowledge only when Pauline Prescott was reunited with her son, Paul, in 2003.

not telling it, and was looking like he had something to worry about. Also, the differences between him and his officials were beginning to seep out. It was not the big deal Robin seemed to think it was and he was falling into the trap. Sandline was the main story in the Sundays, though one or two did the story of me and Peter M stopping Routledge from getting the *Express* job.[1]

Sunday, May 10

GB was on *Frost*. I suggested he really push to get up the NI economic package as a broadcast story. GB said it would be more than £100m. He was also asked about the Routledge book and for the first time he said there was no deal and we reached the right decision when TB became leader. It was a good strong interview for all kinds of reasons – good on general message, good on personal, and he did the NI stuff really well. Re Sandline, RC was emphasising that Kabbah was the good guy but I put out a far less defensive line. Attack was the only form of defence here. TB was livid at the way Robin had handled it, and allowed a problem to become something worse. 'He has lost whatever judgement he ever had. Why do we have such weak vessels around us?' Sinn Fein had their special conference on the Agreement and the positive vote – ninety-five per cent – was even bigger than we anticipated. It made TB more determined than ever that we had to get a majority of the Unionist population. I wanted to get Clinton's response to be that SF would never be welcome again if there was a return to violence, but could not track down McCurry. The vote was so big it was likely to set us back with the Unionists for a while. In our reaction, we were cautious but emphasised they had now signed up to the principle of consent.

The Irish government had let out the Balcombe Street Gang[2] for forty-eight hours and they got a heroes' welcome, while Mo had let out four as well, including the IRA leader in the Maze. The sight of Adams and McGuinness out with the Balcombe St Gang [Adams

---

[1] Some journalists reported that Express editor Rosie Boycott's withdrawal of an offer of the job of political editor to the *Independent on Sunday*'s Paul Routledge was because of the intervention of AC and Peter Mandelson after Routledge had published a book on Gordon Brown that was critical of Tony Blair.
[2] Eddie Butler, Hugh Doherty, Harry Duggan and Joe O'Connell had terrorised London for two years in the mid-1970s. After a six-day siege in Balcombe Street, Marylebone, the four released their two hostages, surrendered and were imprisoned in 1977.

described the four as 'our Nelson Mandelas'] was awful, even if the overall effect was 'The war is over'. But their refusal to say the words clearly was a continuing problem. I went round to PG's. Peter M came over too. PG said that I was a lot less popular with the press than a year ago, that a lot of them thought I was arrogant and dismissive. I suppose the problem was I found it hard to hide contempt.

Monday, May 11

The press today was even worse than the Sundays. We were taking a big hit because we had been so pathetic and unrobust on Sandline. Peter M and I discussed at the morning meeting and then went to TB to say we were going to have to take control of this before it became a real problem. We felt that far from dumping on the officials involved we should be praising them, including [Peter] Penfold the [UK] high commissioner under investigation, accept any deliberate breach of embargo would be wrong, but also point out the circumstances of the coup.

Ireland was a disaster area. A combination of the Balcombe Street Gang plus the IRA leaders out of the Maze was about as bad as it could get for the strategy we were trying to pursue. Mo had let the Maze guys out without us knowing, which was ridiculous. It was a side favour Mo did for Adams, I suspect, but it was disasterville for the Unionist votes we were after. David Kerr called from Trimble's office. Even though DT could be very old-womany, he had a point when he said this was as bad a move as we could have made. It had prisoners, past outrages, SF confidence and two fingers to the rest of you all wrapped up in one. Mo was not nearly sensitive enough to the UU side of things, because she found DT irritating. But this showed a lack of judgement, also evident on the *Today* programme when she made a crack about how people were let out if their granny died, and that this had been necessary to get the vote up for the Agreement. TB was livid all round.

He asked John H to do a note to the NIO both on the substance but also why we had not been properly consulted. I said we had to be careful about leaks, and people would be appalled at the fact we had not even known this was happening. Mo had gone up to the North-East with TB on the train on Friday and had not even mentioned it – unbelievable.

The morning TB meeting was mainly about trade union recognition. Margaret Beckett had written a note to TB, which he suspected had been written with leaking it in mind, saying why she objected to a forty per cent threshold [a minimum 40 per cent 'yes' vote in union recognition ballots]. It included the line that Derry was backing thirty-five per cent. TB said he did not want to undermine [the TUC's John] Monks but if he backed down on forty per cent he would be weakened, and seen as having caved in to vested-interest pressure. 'I will lose part of the coalition.' Peter M and PG were adamant he could not back down. Sally and I were much more alert to the dangers of a summer of problems ahead if we got this wrong and upset relations too much.

We did our conference call with the NIO, and were pushing the economic package. I finally got hold of Mike McCurry and Jim Steinberg to get out the line that Clinton was making clear that he saw this as an irreversible moment, that there could be no going back to violence and if they did, he was through with them. Mike got Steinberg out of a meeting and as ever he wanted to tone down what I was saying but we got pretty much what we wanted. Godric was doing the 11 and I drafted lines on NI and also to back Peter Penfold and start to shift the ground on Sandline. TB was more convinced than ever we had to be far tougher about this. The shift in message worked, and it led the news, not a great story but at least a sense of perspective that had been lacking in recent days. Richard Wilson's view was very much that we should support Penfold, and really weigh in behind him.[1] This was echoed, though to a slightly lesser extent, by John Kerr and the top FCO lawyer, who I bumped into in the street coming back from a Cabinet Office meeting. TB had a [Belfast] Downtown Radio phone-in, which Eamonn Mallie [journalist] did very well. There was a good balance of tough but fair questions and TB hit all the right Unionist buttons. Definitely worth doing. He was very reassuring on prisoners, decommissioning and seats in the Assembly. It wouldn't take long for the other lot to complain, but TB felt we really had to push the boat out at the moment. The four o'clock was hard work. I did Northern Ireland up front, which went fine, but got into really heavy pounding on Sierra Leone. They could not work out why we had so aggressively changed tack and of course I couldn't dump on RC and the FCO, but it was not easy to present it as seamless and consistent because it wasn't. I was robust, but felt a bit slippery when trying to make out there was no great inconsistency. They still smelled a bit of blood on this but I think I pretty much saw them off.

[1] Penfold, as high commissioner, had taken a very high-profile role in the Sierra Leone dispute.

May '98: Press smell blood on Sandline

RC had allowed the whole thing to become more serious than it ever should have been. RC came over for a meeting and I worked up a new and tougher script. He was very down about it all. I was feeling a bit beleaguered and overworked, but managed to leave for home at 6.15. Then Jonathan called Richard Wilson to say Hague might be putting in an SO20 [Commons standing order calling for an emergency debate] which meant TB would have to do a Commons statement on it tomorrow. It was a pain on one level but could be the opportunity we needed to turn it. I was pretty sure the public couldn't give a flying fuck about it. TB said did we make a mistake in going out so hard on it? Maybe, I said, but there was no way we could leave it to Robin in his current state of mind. The problem of course flowed from RC's bloody ethical foreign policy statement after the election, which set him up for criticism at the slightest hint of trouble. We had two big problems at the moment, both exacerbated by the poor handling of Cabinet ministers who let their departments take the wrong tack. I said to Fiona what depressed me was having to work my arse off to cover for weak vessels.

Tuesday, May 12

As well as Sierra Leone running pretty rampant, we had a problem on trade union recognition. It couldn't have come at a worse time, with Monks in to see TB today. To make it worse, Murdoch was due in and nobody thought to get him in through 70 Whitehall, with the result he was spotted by a snapper on the way in. JP called me in a real fury about the trade union recognition story, which he assumed came from us. I didn't but he said it would have been one of the teenage scribblers, as he had taken to calling some of our people. I agreed with JP I would put out a line saying no final decision had been taken and discussions went on etc.

TB called me up to the flat. He was in a far better mood than yesterday, felt things were turning back our way, particularly on Sandline, which he had decided was just a lot of nonsense and should never ever have become a problem. Going through my in tray there was a letter from President Kabbah to TB which totally vindicated the story we had been putting over. I called RC and said I was going to release it at the 11. I said he had to break out of the defensive mindset he had on this. He was signalling a lack of confidence and they sensed it and were coming at us because of it. If we just told them to fuck off on it, eventually they would. The story had to become how we turned it around, turned a problem into an opportunity. Kabbah was an important part of that.

At the 11, the press liked his letter and I sensed it turning our way. I called Piers Morgan and asked if he would take a Kabbah article. He agreed. I got Godric to fix and he asked Switch [Downing Street switchboard] to get Kabbah's press guy and Kabbah himself answered the phone and agreed straight away to do it, so we got Bradders [David Bradshaw] to draft. Kabbah said his wife [Patricia] was being buried tomorrow so he didn't have much time! But he gave enough time for a decent piece. Godric called him to read the piece to him. 'I hope it draws a line in the sand for you,' said Kabbah, laughing at his own joke. I went home with David Blunkett who was coming for dinner. He was trying to get me to tell him where TB was on a reshuffle, and as ever raging at GB. Robin was thought to have done well in the Commons, with a totally different tone and there was a feeling Sandline was blowing out.

Wednesday, May 13

I started the day in a foul mood and it got worse as the day went on. Though Sierra Leone was fading, the lobby worked themselves into a mini frenzy re a story in *The Times* that Prince Philip had opposed the Order of the Garter for the emperor of Japan. I spoke to Robert Fellowes and agreed a robust denial. At the 11, I gave the line and they kept coming at me on it and I got totally fed up with it and started really going at them. I could see Godric and Hilary out of the corner of my eye trying to get me to slow down but I was in total 'fuck it' mode. I went for Liam Halligan [*FT*], totally over the top, was horrible to Patrick Wintour [*Guardian*] over Sandline – so horrible I later apologised – then took a pop at George Jones [*Telegraph*]. Robin Oakley said on a point of order that I was there to answer questions. I said I was there to answer questions as I saw fit and if they didn't like the answers, tough. One or two tried to talk to me as I left but I couldn't be bothered with them.

Ireland was still a real problem as we were trying to get off the decommissioning hook while trying to give the UUs the legislative expression they wanted. I was working on TB's Ireland speech with John H, and every word had to be weighed carefully now. I was getting more tired and irritable and although everyone in the office told me not to lose it at the 4, I gave them another whack.

Don Macintyre took me for a cup of tea and said I had to calm down. I said I was sick of dealing with wankers. Why should I pretend to respect them when I didn't? There were only half a dozen I would give the time of day to if I didn't have to see them every day. I told him the politicians were getting on my nerves too, and

I was thinking of quitting. It was the first time I had articulated that. I had a cup of tea with Betty Boothroyd [Speaker of the House of Commons] up in her residence. She was really nice, said she was very pro me, and not to worry about all the MPs who were having a go, they were basically doing it because I was good at my job. She advised me to play a very straight bat when I appeared at the PASC. Her Yorkshire accent was back in full flow as she went over some of the MPs on the committee. Her general take on the Opposition was that they were useless, but TB would be wise not to under-estimate Hague. I said he thought he was a good debater, and clever, but he had a judgement problem and he was listening to too many of the wrong people.

I couldn't really get a feel for her take on TB. I got the sense she was being as nice to me as she was because she basically thought I was more Old Labour than TB. It was a really nice meeting though, and I felt my batteries a bit recharged. She had been very nice about what she saw as my role in getting us elected and I suppose I should always hang on to that when the press and the politicians were getting me down. We were still doing good things, and TB was still the only show in town.

Thursday, May 14

I woke up tired and fed up, and wishing I could just stay in bed and tell the whole lot of them to fuck off. I knew I had screwed up yesterday. I had gone totally over the top and was now beating myself up. I did real damage to my own relations with the media yesterday. Most of them I didn't care about, but I actually lost it with some of the good guys too, which was just daft. I knew I could recover it, but it would take time and it would take energy I could be putting else-where. I hated making daft mistakes like that, and letting my mood drive me to make them. I went to see TB in the flat. He said he was worried I was exhausted and I would make mistakes and I had to get more support, and have the odd day off. I said every time I tried to take a day off, he created a stack of work.

He spent some of the morning squaring JP, Mo, Clare, RC and Dobbo re trade union recognition. After the NIO conference call, I put together a briefing note starting to trail the outlines of TB's Ireland speech, indicating a shift on legislative expression to make clear what had to be done re prisoners, decommissioning etc. John H was really worried Sinn Fein would go off board if we went too far, and empha-sised I had to be really careful on the balancing act. I was getting used to it. We didn't want SF to be happy with what we were saying.

But nor did we want them to be too unhappy. 'What are you saying, we want them mildly pissed off?' Yes, he said.

TB spoke to Bertie who was more relaxed than we thought he would be, said provided we were not reopening the Agreement, it was fine. He said the Balcombe St pictures were too much, and they were made worse today by the temporary release of Michael Stone, the cemetery killer.[1] Mo said it couldn't have been avoided, it just happened to be the time for it to happen.

TB and I met with Margaret B and I said we had to be able to say there was a final decision on [trade union] recognition next week, or else people would think there was a major disagreement going on. She did a proper presentation on the whole issue and did it well, getting the nuances and balance in the right place. She is a total pro is Margaret. She had argued her corner but without the histrionics some of them employ. The mood in the lobby was bad, the overhang from my ranting at them yesterday. Some didn't turn up. For half a second, I thought about apologising, but then imagined the satisfaction it would give them, and instead just decided to be less unpleasant than yesterday. I didn't speak to [Robin] Oakley. He and Patrick [Wintour] were the ones I had gone way OTT with, and I would probably have to apologise eventually but I couldn't face it for now. Later George Jones called about something and I did apologise, whilst emphasising I thought they were all take and no give.

John H did a fantastic rewrite of the speech. Of all the civil servants, he was top drawer, real quality. Sandline was suddenly back up big on the news because John Kerr [FCO permanent secretary] appeared to contradict RC. TB was livid. So was RC. It led the lunchtimes and sparked off another little frenzy. TB spoke to Donaldson from the car on the way to the airport. John had read him a few relevant extracts from the speech and he was quite positive. He was pretty nervy about the next twenty four hours. We took Mo with us, as well as Adam Ingram [NIO minister] and Kate Hoey [Belfast-born Labour MP], who was seen as one of theirs by the Unionists. Mo said she understood that Kate had to be in the picture.

On arrival we went straight to the Balmoral Show [agricultural show in Belfast] and as we walked in front of the stand, you could feel the coolness. This was real UU country. After talking around a bit, I reckoned sixty-forty against, but these were maybe more the activist

[1] Stone, killer of three mourners at an IRA funeral, was sentenced to thirty years, but released after serving twelve under the terms of the Good Friday Agreement.

May '98: TB nervy re vote on NI Agreement

end of the market. We did a meeting with prison officers, and then victims of violence, which was really moving. There were some dreadful stories of brutality and hatred and with effects that would outlive the victims. TB left more confident than I was that we could win the majority of Unionists we wanted. He was certainly the key to that, because the UU politicians were not shifting the arguments hard enough.

I complained to the BBC and ITN about them putting Michael Stone ahead of TB's speech and we got better coverage later on. On the plane home, I was tired and stressed, but TB was more up about things and said he was sure we could do it. I said we would need to take the campaign over even more. They were not capable of driving a strategic message and their continuing opposition to Clinton getting involved just underlined they didn't understand campaigning.

Friday, May 15

The Irish coverage was totally dominated by Michael Stone so the impact of TB's speech was pretty limited. Several times during the day, TB, me, Jonathan and John H variously said we could kill the NIO sometimes. They really had fucked up and we had to work extra hard to rein it in. It was going to be hard to keep on top of this while he had the G8 to chair as well. On the train up to Birmingham TB was trying to work out how to sustain momentum. We agreed we should go for the prison service medal idea,[1] as mooted by the prison people yesterday, but ran into one of those infuriating blocks straight away as it was a matter of the ceremonials committee and Buckingham Palace who would need time to look into it. TB, Jonathan and I also spoke at various points of the day to Donaldson, whose support we had to keep going for. He knew what he was up to, and we were happy to play along, provided he came out for it clearly in the end. But when TB spoke to him from the hotel he ended the call pessimistic. Donaldson said the speech didn't go far enough, which was code for no. TB asked me to call him and ask him direct. I said Jeffrey, we have to think about the PM's authority here, and how much time and energy he can expend on this, and I did not want him with egg all over his face. We need to know, in your gut, is it yes or no? He said I'm afraid I think it's no. I dropped in a hint that the press were beginning to see this as being about him and Trimble, rather than yes or no, to indicate we could move it into that if he milked it, but he didn't really budge.

[1] A medal was to be issued to recognise the services of the officers of the Northern Ireland Prison Service.

Meanwhile we were having to work out a response to India's nuclear tests and get fully briefed pre G7-8, though all TB was really focused on was NI. He said it was criminal the way they had let the Balcombe St Gang and Stone do what they did. On arrival in Birmingham, he did a doorstep on India and Ireland, and a clip about Frank Sinatra's death. It was a beautiful sunny day and Birmingham had put on a good face for the whole event. TB's first bilateral was Hashimoto, with all the *Sun* article crew there. Boris Yeltsin arrived for the EU-Russia summit. He looked and sounded awful, very blotchy and occasionally looking like he was nodding off. He veered from loud statements of seeming great import, to jokes that the interpreters seemed incapable of translating. Yeltsin's laughter drowned them out anyway.

Jeffrey Donaldson sent through his words and although they tried a bit of fence-sitting, I said to him they would basically be seen as a no. I said I needed to know if he was going to make clear it was a no in briefings and interviews. He said he would probably, that it was better to do it now than have it drag out over a few days. The wretched Sandline came back. [Sir John] Kerr told me he was worried RC DID mislead the House.

When Bill C arrived, he was full of the usual bonhomie. He asked if he could do anything to help on Ireland. I said a doorstep pushing the general line, and being a bit more pro Unionist and raising the pressure on SF would be good. Let's do it, he said. I got Anji to organise but of course the Secret Service made such a palaver of it that within a few minutes, Sandy Berger came panting in, clearly pissed off we were getting Bill to do stuff without his own people around him. He said they would have a riot if they did not get the US pool in too, which made it an altogether bigger event. I had another go at trying to persuade McCurry to change their pooling arrangements but he said they were all too set in their ways.

After the first G7 meeting wound up, we had a brief huddle then Bill went out to do it. Berger and Steinberg were not happy, but I couldn't establish if it was the process or the message they didn't like. Mike [McCurry] was a bit more relaxed but even he did a barbed 'Mr President, I wonder if you shouldn't speak to your own foreign policy team before making major public statements.' BC made light of it and said he was doing what I told him to do, because that guaranteed a quiet life. He asked what the line was – I said it was the best chance of peace for a generation; he sided with those who sided with peace; and if any of the protagonists went back to violence, they would get no welcome in the US. He did it brilliantly and it would go straight to the top of the news in NI and probably here too, after [Frank] Sinatra's death probably. He was a total pro. Later he did a photocall drinking a pint on the balcony of a pub by the canal, which would make big time. TB was happier now but still felt we needed more time to turn things round. The next story was the LVF issuing a cease-fire and a No vote call.

I had another briefing to do, both on Ireland and the summit, then back for the Heads' dinner. The row over dinner was whether to 'deplore' or 'condemn' the nuclear tests. Yeltsin and Chirac – the latter loudly, and the former barely making sense – were arguing for a softer line. Clinton's people were worried he would take a big hit if they were too soft. The dinner was almost comic though. Chirac was at his most Chiracian, grand gestures, saying *'la France'* when he meant 'I', generally huffy if anyone disagreed. Boris was laughing loudly when nothing had been said, making loud gestures to the waitresses. Bill was laughing at the pair of them. TB looked over at one point and mouthed the word 'madhouse'. TB and Bill hung round at the end and we ended up chatting about which world leaders were fanciable. Benazir Bhutto [former Pakistani Prime Minister] was probably tops. Tansu Çiller [former Turkish Prime Minister] got fairly high marks all round. One of the advance people told me that some poor sod had removed the stamens out of two and a half tons of flowers because of Clinton's allergy. I told Bill, who said it was bullshit. 'Everywhere I go this happens and it's bullshit. It's got into one of those State Department notes and it's wrong.'

TB was totally obsessing re Ireland, said we had to have story after story after story to keep the momentum going our way. I asked BC if he would do *Frost* with TB. He said he would do anything we thought would help. I said it would. 'You decide,' he said, 'I'll do whatever you want.' Jim Steinberg again looked a bit antsy at my just asking BC straight up to do stuff, but I said a big joint inter-view on Ireland would help ease his worry about BC being whacked too hard on India [nuclear tests]. I called to tell [David] Frost and Barney Jones [editor, *Breakfast with Frost*], who were orgasmic at the thought. Back at the hotel I put together a briefing note on India, Indonesia, MEPP and Kosovo, taking in the main points out of the dinner. I suddenly felt tired, deflated and depressed again. It was probably just overwork. Clinton cheered me up a lot, because he was such a laugh just to chat with, and a real pro to work with. Mo threw a wobbly because we were pursuing the prison medal from Number 10 not NIO.

Saturday, May 16

TB's main concern was Ireland again. We'd agreed to get a summit statement, which John and I drafted, purely to keep NI at the top of the news agenda over there, and on our terms. The aim was to get over the message that the world was watching, and willing them to embrace change. We did a *GMTV* pre-record where again he was mainly hitting the reassurance buttons for the UUs. TB was having to chair all the summit meetings, manage the outcome, as well as deal with NI and fairness at work, which was going a bit wobbly because the unions had finally woken up to the idea they could spin it as being good for them.

We set off for Weston Park, which was a lovely house in a beautiful setting, and just right for the more relaxed atmosphere we were trying to get. The Japanese were in a bit of a state over the *Mail* story which said the emperor would express regret over the PoWs issue. [Mutsuyoshi] Nishimura [senior Japanese official] said this was for the emperor alone to say and it would cause problems if this kind of media coverage gathered pace. I drafted a line with Philip Barton which we gave out to PA. We were talking to [Ryutaro] Hashimoto about it as TB was writing a good-luck letter to Newcastle [United] for the Cup Final and, bizarrely, Hashimoto said he would like to do one too. So I was sitting there with the Japanese prime minister translating his hieroglyphics on a Number 10-headed piece of paper to send to the Newcastle dressing room. God knows what Kenny Dalglish [Newcastle United manager] would make of it. In the break, TB regaled us with stories from last night. He said at one point it was like being in bedlam, with interpreters getting more and more unable to cope. Yeltsin was shouting and yet had a quietly spoken interpreter. Chirac had an interpreter who was louder than Yeltsin. Clinton just giggled and Kohl looked pained. TB said Clinton was intellectually streets ahead of all of them, with the possible exception of Kohl. TB was now worrying the Hashimoto letter would look like a stunt by us and piss off Londoners. Jim Steinberg said it showed the Japs were trying hard to please but couldn't quite pull it off, which was nearer the mark. We then heard there was a panic on because Clinton and [Jean] Chrétien [Canadian Prime Minister] had escaped the Secret Service and gone off somewhere and been spotted climbing a fence together.

TB and I were working up a script for *Frost* and settled on fear and emotion vs hope and reason, which was the kind of thing BC would do well. I saw Bill when he got back and we had a chat about it. He wanted to say it was time for a leap of faith, and that the risks of a

No vote are greater than the risks of a Yes vote. It was a good line. He was worrying that Frost would ask about his personal life and I pinned David down to an absolute assurance. We did it as a pre-record in the gardens. It looked great and Frost helped us get the message up. We had agreed he would ask straight out what could you do to reassure the Unionists and TB just went through the points one by one. BC was awesomely on-message. His use of a pause, his hand movements, the cadence of his voice, he was a remarkable communicator in so many ways. He was particularly strong at the end. After it ended he said how was that? I said awesome. We had agreed in advance he should push the message on US inward invest-ment, and also that any return to violence meant no welcome in the US, and he did both really powerfully. We agreed Mike King of CNN could piggyback on the end for a special he was doing on Ireland, but it led to a huge row later when they decided they were going to use some of it as news footage in advance of *Frost*. McCurry complained. Bill had been true to his word in helping but was now worrying whether he was too involved. It was odd how even people like him worried, maybe especially people like him, so needed re-assurance the whole time. As he left, he came over again and said was it helpful, because this situation really mattered to him and he really wanted to help. I said it had been a masterful performance, which it had, and if I knew anything about anything, I was sure he would swing votes on the back of it. I said I wished to God we had sent him to NI to campaign because I am convinced it would have shifted votes galore. But the UUs had been adamant. I said we were in his debt. Not at all, he said.

A hell of a lot of people had come out to wave at the convoys on the road into Birmingham, and although there was a big demo in town, the mood generally was great. Fiona and I went out for dinner with Mike McCurry and some of his media favourites. Mike had them rolling about when he told the story of how we got BC to do media without any of his people knowing. He had a friendlier rela-tionship with his media but when we discussed it later, he said the difference was that the press basically saw me as a politician not a spokesman. That was what gave me authority, but it also made me fairer game in a way maybe he wasn't. He also felt he benefited from being quoted by name because he could then be more dismissive of anonymous stuff.

I got back to see the late news, including the fantastic pictures of huge pro-Penfold demos in Sierra Leone, which confirmed me in the view RC had been woefully off the ball in his handling of this. I said to Fiona how can you have a situation where the people in the country we helped are out demonstrating in favour of a UK diplomat whose bosses were running around as if he had dropped them in boiling water? Ludicrous.

Sunday, May 17

It was interesting to watch BC around the place. Of all of them, he was the one with the most natural empathy with e.g. the stewards and waiters etc., and it was that basic human touch allied to his intellect and communications skills that made him the ultimate modern politician in many ways. I started to wind up TB about how much better BC was as a communicator. The big drama of the day concerned whether Pakistan had tested a nuclear bomb. The Pakistanis denied it. Yeltsin suddenly piped up, with his great booming voice, that at 11.41 precisely Pakistan had detonated a nuclear bomb. The US said it was total crap.

They did a bit on the Millennium Bug, then Indonesia, then Boris suddenly made a passionate plea for it [the G7] to be renamed the G8 in 2000 'as a personal favour to me'. Nobody seemed to know how to react, but TB made positive noises then wound everything up. The farewells were fascinating. Yeltsin was going round doing great bear hugs. Chirac told TB that the food had been better than any of the summits he had been at, which I suspect he said at the end of every summit, and he said he thought Birmingham was a beautiful place to hold it. Bill C was saying how he would like to go up in a hot-air balloon fuelled by all the discussions at summits. 'Hey, we could stay up there for days.'

We had a meeting with Colin Parry [father of twelve-year-old IRA bomb victim Tim] who was a lot nicer than I thought he would be. I don't know why but I had formed a bit of a negative view, but his genuineness came through in person in a way that was maybe diluted by TV and I ended up feeling bad at having thought ill of him. God knows what I would be like if anything happened to the kids. He was due to go to Belfast to campaign for the Yes vote which had the potential to make a strong impact. Parry gave me a couple of his books, one for TB, one for Clinton who seemed genuinely moved by it when I showed it to him later, just before they left.

On the way out of the hotel one of the hotel staff had asked if I could help her to meet Clinton. I arranged for her to be in the lift. She was a little old West Indian woman and by the time we hit the ground floor, he had her whole life story out of her. She practically collapsed as he left the lift and later we heard she had been in tears

May '98: BC a 'better communicator' than TB

for hours, moved to bits. Back in London, TB and BC headed off for their Chequers wonkathon. I was tired and hot but felt things had gone as well as they might have done.

Monday, May 18

The BBC were leading on Ireland, last week pre-campaign etc. On the NIO morning call we agreed TB should go on Wednesday and try to drive up support. TB was late back from Chequers where he had been with Bill who had been swimming and bike riding with the kids. He had also gone to play golf and TB, who had never played, went along for the ride and apparently hit the ball really well, so would be unbearable for a while. It also meant he was underprepared for the EU-US summit which actually had a lot of tricky stuff attached to it and he had basically spent the weekend schmoozing with Bill. We ran through the things he had to get on top of.

Both BC and TB had been worrying re Ireland and BC said he felt the problem was Trimble's failure to rise to the occasion. He exudes problem not opportunity. [Jacques] Santer arrived for the summit and again I had a sense of the absurdity of the position where the US president was meant to think a rotating prime minister from one of the smallest countries in the world [Luxembourg] was the person you deal with in Europe. It just wasn't serious and nor was Santer. TB was yawning the whole way through so clearly Bill had kept him up yacking.

I briefed at 11 – mainly Ireland, the summit, also golf. John Hipwood [*Wolverhampton Express and Star*] asked why Peter M had been at Chequers. 'He's the caddy,' said Oakley. For the press conference with Bill, trade was going to be the difficult issue. We got an FCO official in to brief TB and he was like a gibbering wreck. He had a two-page note which we thought was for public consumption, but then as we went through it, he would say 'Oh no, can't say that,' till eventually TB said what can I say? Finally, he realised the guy was falling apart, said OK, I think I know what to say, and off he went. It was almost comic.

Santer came in then we went up to the White Room where Bill was preparing with his guys. The trade stuff is fine, he said. Very fine, said Santer. I had one more thing I wanted BC to do. The *Mirror* had asked for an article on Ireland, which was a good idea. I asked them to draft something, and after I reordered it a bit, I showed it to Bill who thought it was fine. Jim Steinberg went ape though. He had not liked me dealing direct with BC, and he didn't like the doorstep operation we did in Birmingham. He said 'We will write the president's words, not you.' I said he seemed fine with it. Jim said they would have to look at it.

The press conference was fine and they were both strong on Ireland which would hopefully carry. Afterwards they did a joint call to the Pakistan PM [Nawaz Sharif] re nuclear tests. Bill didn't want much said publicly, simply that the call took place and we were urging restraint. In the call they had both been clear re the economic benefits of restraint for Pakistan. Jim [Steinberg] had another go re the *Mirror*. He was really pissed off with me now.

Tuesday, May 19

The golf got the biggest coverage out of yesterday, but Ireland was ticking over media-wise but there was a feeling on the ground that the Unionist vote was slipping away from us a bit. We were sending PG to do some groups to help sharpen the last few days' message, but without DT really motoring, we were going to struggle a bit. I said to TB we were going to have to try to use his visit as the big shifter, and we began to build it up as an event.

Geneva, for the WTO [World Trade Organisation] meeting when Stuart Higgins [*Sun*] called and reminded me they had asked for a Clinton piece. It had gone completely out of my mind and I said so, and added he was doing something for the *Mirror*. I had to weigh up quickly which one to piss off most. The revised BC version had come through and as I was unable to reach Jim [Steinberg] or Mike [McCurry], I took it upon myself to give it to the *Sun*, with my earlier revisions, on condition they splash it. The *Mirror* would go mental but I would just have to deal with it. In the Unionist context we were going to get more out of the *Sun*. TB did a phone-in before we left which was OK but he was worried about the slippage. I told Piers Morgan about the *Sun* and not surprisingly he went berserk, and I just let him sound off and needs must. But it would do lasting damage to our relations with the *Mirror*.

PG called after his first group. He didn't know that much re NI politics but he got a pretty good grasp quickly. He said that they were worried the IRA would use politics to get into power, then TB would leave them to their fate. They needed a lot of reassurance. Even though it didn't really fit the conference theme, we put in a section re NI and organised applause after directing the broadcasters to it. TB had a good meeting with [President of Brazil, Fernando] Cardoso, who was a very bright and like-minded guy and who had a really good feel for our politics. We also had the briefest of meetings with [Cuban leader, Fidel] Castro. TB just bumped into him, literally, and they found themselves standing toe to toe, shaking hands, and not a photographer in sight. He was taller than I imagined, also looked older but had a wicked smile. He said he admired TB and he had read all the Third Way speeches.

On the plane back, I read the *Times* leader attacking me over the [President] Kabbah article. As we landed, PG called again and said we really had to get a strong TB message out there. As things stood we were not going to get a majority among the Protestants and he was the only one who could turn that round. It would be hard but this was urgent. Then we heard the Saudi nurses [Deborah Parry and Lucille McLauchlan] would be let out on Friday which would be big. Piers called a couple of times to vent his spleen, said he had wound up Kelvin [MacKenzie] and Monty [David Montgomery] and they agreed we always favoured the *Sun* and they were all fed up with it. Higgins called and said it was the right thing to do, for the peace process. But I hated the double-dealing I had to do at times like this.

Wednesday, May 20

The Saudi nurses being freed was the big story of the day, especially as they were doing deals with the *Mirror* and the *Express*, which made me feel less bad re the Clinton piece. I didn't particularly want us to get into the nurses story at all. We had helped get them out, but in circumstances where most people were suspicious of them. I went up to the flat where TB was preparing for PMQs. He was tired and irritable and worrying re the vote. He was also livid that Sandline had reared again because RC had made yet another contradictory statement. PG had done a note which was pretty relentlessly negative re where the Unionist community was. But he did say that TB, trust, connection, conviction, still had the capacity to turn things.

I had the idea of a series of handwritten pledges which we would put up as a poster backdrop when he spoke in Northern Ireland. I called the NIO to get an ad van and agency on standby while John [Holmes] and I worked on the wordings. TB was not totally sure about it, and said the wordings had to be very, very careful. I said it was the best way of doing what we had to do – link him explicitly to reassurance. Charles Moore [editor, *Telegraph*] came in for a chat. He was impossibly hostile on Ireland and wouldn't listen to another side, but he was more friendly than before. He said I was doing a very good job and the reason I was becoming the story was because of that. People know that you are behind a lot of the things that happen, he said. You are not a press officer, you are a politician effectively so the media will treat you as such.

PMQs was fine, with the Tories attacking on waiting lists, and TB dealt with it fine. At the briefing I started to talk up the NI pledges and the poster and they latched straight on. I could always tell when a story was going to work, because [Phil] Webster and [Michael] White would both have a little smile, then scribble earnestly. TB sat with Hague on the plane and they mainly talked Ireland, Europe, Chirac. Hague was very proper in these circumstances, always called him Prime Minister, didn't push too hard, listened and then spoke briefly. TB thought he was likeable enough and a very good debater, but he felt he lacked judgement on the big-picture stuff. John H warned me there was a chance of more NI prisoner day releases. I said we had to make sure there were none before Saturday.

We landed and were flown to Coleraine. The backdrop looked good though as ever TB was a bit awkward. I don't know why he found posters so difficult. It looked good, there was substance to it and it would connect big time. He did a really strong emotional speech, without notes, and did a strong tribute to Trimble who was a lot more relaxed and malleable than usual. We did some strong pictures during which a little guy came up to me and said 'All he needs to say is "Trust me and trust yourselves."' It was a terrific line and we used it later in the day.

We left for dinner at Stormont and after I watched the news I felt things were better than before, and Mo said she felt things were turning a bit. The NIO officials were advising us not to do too much because they felt it would look like TB lecturing them. I called PG and we agreed that was balls, that we needed more not less. I got the news extended to get more time to keep the momentum going. We did a visit at Knock Golf Club then to the BBC for a fairly tough panel but again he hit the right buttons. There was a good *Irish Times* poll out so finally, at the right time, we had a sense of momentum. TB was knackered by the time we got to Hillsborough.

Thursday, May 21

Bill C said to me the other day that we wake up every day with fear and hope, and one is always heavier than the other. Today it was hope, and we all sensed things were turning our way. I don't know why but we did. Everyone's instincts were saying yes. Maybe it was the weather but things just felt better. The pledge poster had certainly worked and in Antrim TB met a guy who said he had seen him on the TV panel last night and he had swung him from no to yes, so again that cheered us up a bit. We had limited time in which to pack in as many interviews as we could. First up was Eamonn Mallie on

Downtown Radio, and it was tough because he focused totally on decommissioning and TB went further than ever in linking to prisoner release. Both John H and I winced a little, worrying he was making too many promises.

The next four interviews were better and as he got into his stride I felt we were back on a roll again. We were taken up by helicopter to Dunadry [Country Antrim], to a hotel. Trimble was again more relaxed and confident. He was due to take on [Bob] McCartney [leader, UK Unionist Party] and I gave him a few lines he might deploy. He was dismissive of [Jeffrey] Donaldson. But TB said my advice would be to be magnanimous in public but never forget. We did more pictures, then the poster signing and the media were taking it all in. We left for the Royal Irish Regiment, who were not exactly warm. But TB's walkabout went fine and among some of them there was genuine warmth. There was a bit of abuse from some of them, but not much and when McCartney had a go at TB at the end, members of the crowd turned on him. When he called them 'rentamob' they got angry with him and the stunt backfired.

TB did an emotional little speech, again using the line trust me, trust yourselves. I got a joint article placed in the *Newsletter* and the *Irish News*, and both editors were happy to go with it. We had had a good run-up to the voting and TB said he was not sure we could have done much more. Our lines were running strong and even DT was getting good coverage. We did an economic meeting in Antrim and that part of the message had definitely got through. TB said he was beginning to hope as high as seventy-seven per cent, no lower than sixty-eight. I felt it would be better still, that we were peaking at the right time.

. As ever we were having to keep tabs on things at home. TB spoke to JP to ask him to make sure Fairness at Work did not go the wrong way. He wanted it stated explicitly that there was no going back to the 70s, and Margaret [Beckett] didn't like it when Jeremy Heywood sent that message through. Both TB and I spoke to her and said we had to pre-empt the Tory attack and defuse it before they could get it off the ground. She felt it gave the wrong impression and set the balance in the wrong place. Wrong on both counts I would say. TB said he would have to tell the Cabinet next week that he did not expect to have to call ministers himself to get things done he had asked officials to get done.

On the plane home TB was really tired. He, Anji and I talked over the political operation in the office. He was down on Jonathan at the moment but that was because he was expecting him to do things he was never expected to. He was not the solution to a problem re politics, but he did a lot of other good things. TB was also thinking of a small reshuffle next week. Back at Number 10 I had to decide who to give the spare press job to and went for Lucie McNeil who was bright and had a bit of drive. I was feeling confident about the vote now. Today felt better than last time which felt better than the time before that.

Friday, May 22
Referendum day and with most of the media just waiting for that, I had a quiet day.

Saturday, May 23
The referendum results [71.1 per cent in favour of Belfast Agreement] came through earlier than expected and I spoke to TB from Wembley where I was watching England vs Saudi Arabia. I sent Hilary Coffman to Chequers to help organise his doorstep. The line was fairly straightforward – the beginning not the end, now make it work etc. It pretty much ran itself. We were also starting early on talking up voting not just in the referendum but the elections when they came on June 25. I didn't do much briefing because it was a big story pretty much on autopilot. The football was dire [0-0]. TB did his doorstep and statements came flooding in from overseas.

Sunday, May 24
Clive Hollick [Labour peer, special adviser at DTI, chief executive of United News and Media], called, alarmed at the *Mirror* situation. He felt things were moving in a really bad direction. Ireland was running fine though as ever after a big moment the media were wanting something to move it on.

Monday, May 25
It was a fairly quiet day. I put together a briefing re the Japanese emperor's visit. I said TB wanted him given a warm welcome, that we had to look to the future not the past, added to all the stuff re economic ties etc. Nishimura called me to say the emperor and the Japanese government would be very happy with it. It would almost certainly mean a good kicking from the tabs, especially maybe the *Mirror* who would be on the lookout for revenge re the Clinton article. TB was fine with it though and felt we had to push a positive line through the whole trip. I went to see Ellie in hospital then took the kids to the fair in Hampstead. The story in NI was focusing too much on decommissioning.

Tuesday, May 26

The briefing I wrote yesterday went big, splashed in several papers, and with some fairly heavy criticism too. But the Japanese were at least aware of the efforts we were making, Nishimura calling from his travels with the emperor to say thanks. Our ambassador in Tokyo sent a telegram saying that the combined effect, including TB's *Sun* article, was to take a lot of heat out of the right-wing attacks on the emperor's visit. The thing they most feared though was some kind of physical incident, which just wouldn't be understood back there and would be a humiliation.

TB was due to do a Japanese TV interview and I suggested he did a pooled clip with the BBC too, as it would be odd if the only media we did on this was for them. He was pissed off to be under attack on this but felt strongly we were in the right place on it. People would find it odd that we had this great protest over their behaviour in the war now, but not during the last emperor's visit in the 70s. The *Mirror* was particularly violent but that was probably as much to do with the Clinton fallout as the issue.

I got a personal letter from Peter Stothard over the [*Times*] leader attacking me over the Kabbah article last week. It was an apology and he said he owed me one. TB decided we should postpone the publication of the [government] annual report to July so that it took into account the outcome of the CSR. He was worried where we were on the health and education pledges and that we had not made enough progress, and needed the CSR to show direction and momentum. He said the reason he couldn't do a reshuffle at the moment was because he wanted Alistair Darling to go to DSS but he was running the CSR. Peter M felt we were making a mistake, that we should go ahead with the annual report now, but that was more because it had been his creation. There was no real argument against waiting a little longer. TB felt if he waited a bit longer, he could do a more radical reshuffle. He had decided on Clark, Strang, probably Harriet and he had reached the view that Frank [Dobson] didn't have the intellectual nous to run health. He was also worried that GB was focusing resources too much on pet projects and not enough on core areas like health and education.

The briefings today were almost exclusively about Japan, where I was very future not past, and they picked up on how co-ordinated the whole thing was when I trailed the emperor's speech, which Nishimura called unprecedented and which he had said to me to give 'the big spin to it'. TB came back from the NEC and we went up to the flat to get ready for the Japanese interviews. He came very close to saying the Emperor had apologised, which he hadn't. The veterans turned their backs on the emperor as planned but it was not as awful as it might have been. The broadcasts were not too bad but the press were driving it for all it was worth, and of course the vets had some pretty horrific stories to tell.

Wednesday, May 27

There was massive coverage of the PoWs and TB was taking a real hit. Intellectually he was in the right place but politically we were getting whacked. The one mistake I made was when I said TB wanted him given a warm welcome. 'Courteous' would have been better. 'Warm' infuriated and gave the PoWs an easy in to the *Mail* and the *Mirror*, who were the two most heavily determined to push it against us. The Japanese were pathetically grateful for all the efforts we were making to make the trip a success, and to talk it up, and I think they began to see the political price we were paying.

The main media event, going from sublime to ridiculous or vice versa, was recording the Des O'Connor [comedian and talk-show host] interview at Teddington [Studios]. He was worried the stories we had planned weren't funny enough, but it all worked fine. The feeling from the audience, where Hilary and I watched from, was strong and warm. It was a fairly old audience but there was not even a ripple re Japan, and it made me think we were on the right line – never forgive or forget but focus on future not past. TB was relaxed and on form and afterwards had a chat with Elton John who was going to Belfast for a concert and was interested in the whole NI thing.

Phil Bassett [special adviser] had done another draft of the CBI speech but TB didn't like it and ended up pretty much doing it himself after a pretty extraordinary ministerial meeting. Geoffrey Robinson had been talking the worst kind of bar-room nonsense about coal. Peter M said it was all part of a calculated GB effort to show contempt for TB from the Treasury. I was more of the view that Geoffrey R was incapable of explaining things even when he understood them.

The CSR process was not going well though. Jonathan lacked the authority to penetrate the Treasury and though TB said he was getting enough out of his bilaterals with GB it was a ridiculous way to go on. I was having to do far too much by way of liaison and decision-making and I was getting down again. We finally got the CBI speech in shape though it went out too late. Then, just as I was leaving the office, the Japs called again to say they had heard *The Times* were doing a story that the emperor said something different in Japanese to the English translation released to the press. He did not actually say 'sorrow' but 'pain of the heart'. 'Deep heart hurt feel I do' – the literal – was translated as 'our hearts are filled with sorrow and pain'. They wanted me to get on to *The Times* and say don't run it. I said I couldn't do that but we could explain to them we felt ours was an OK translation. I got Graham Fry [FCO] on the case. In his view it was fine and he found a professor of Japanese.

We went out for dinner with Philip [Gould], Gail [Rebuck] and Lindsay [Nicholson], ostensibly for my birthday, but I was definitely going into another dip. I felt overworked, felt I was firefighting too much, and doing too much that others ought to be doing. The office meeting earlier was hopeless, TB at his worst, meandering, unfocused, moaning.

Thursday, May 28

A bilious attack on me and TB in the *Mirror*, who had hired [Paul] Routledge. The Japanese situation was calming down but we still had to tread carefully in writing the toast to the emperor. We were nicer about the PoWs but basically stuck to the same line. A group of former PoWs came into the street at 12. I got Philip Barton and Magi Cleaver to ask them in and to tell them TB would see them in a week or two. It seemed to calm the situation a little, but they were angry. Just as the emperor arrived, Pakistan announced they had carried out five nuclear tests, which would dominate the agenda for a while.

While TB saw GB on his own re the CSR, Peter M and I had a mournful discussion about how fed up we were. Peter M said he thought I was fed up because I had a proper job and was being pulled in all directions because, as one of the few people capable of making decisions, I was being leaned on by everyone. He said he was fed up because he didn't have a proper job and as one of the few people capable of making decisions, he was not being asked to make any. He also felt GB was now effectively running a campaign against TB who did not seem to realise what was going on.

TB was very nice to the Japanese at the lunch and he felt the story was turning our way. That was, I felt, only on the bang your head against a wall principle. I.e. it was not quite as bad today as it was yesterday but it still wasn't great. He didn't want to get overly involved in the Pakistan situation. RC had put out some words and TB said leave it to Clinton and Cook. He said is it bad for the government? I said it's bad for the world. He said oh, as long as it's not bad for the government. I couldn't work out if it was a joke or not.

TB had to go to his seminar on Europe which was still going on when I got back. He was pretty clear he wanted us in the euro and he wanted to bring about huge change to the institutions of Europe, which would be easier said than done (this on the day MEPs were voting against our presidency). Richard Wilson had seen the GIS people. He said they were a sad little bunch but he had told them I was straight and if they engaged with me they could learn and improve. He said he was worried TB was tired and apt to lose perspective. He saw the four priorities for the next few weeks as reshuffle, [EU] presidency, Ireland and CSR. I had to keep TB focused on those four things and stop him being distracted. I chaired a long diary meeting, where it was blindingly obvious we were operating without a proper thought-through and agreed strategy. People were making ludicrous bids for TB's time.

Friday, May 29

TB was having a Policy Unit awayday at Chequers so I tried to take a day off. I worked on a couple of articles for the Sundays but otherwise it was quiet. We went to [*Sun* deputy editor] Rebekah Wade's party at Belvedere's in Holland Park. It was an odd corporate type of event, where you felt Stuart [Higgins, editor] was being prepared for departure and her for his job. The News Corp lot didn't like the Fairness at Work White Paper.

The *Mirror* launched Routledge on page 1 and page 11 as 'off-message' and then at the bottom of the page 'Achtung, Alastair, he's coming your way'. They were now deciding editorial strategy according to Piers' fits of pique. I told him the mention of my name merely served to remind their readers they no longer had anyone writing for them who knew the first thing about politics. The speeches were a bit grim. [Film director and *Sunday Times* food critic] Michael Winner's was truly awful. Piers shouted the whole way through Stuart's, which sounded like a valedictory.

Saturday, May 30

JP called, livid at the stories briefed overnight, which suggested more GM [grant-maintained] schools, and less power for LEAs [local education authorities]. He said it was typical Blunkett. He said he had called him, told him it was an outrage, that there had been no proper discussion and either DB put out a correcting statement, or he would do it. When I spoke to DB, he said it would have been a lot worse if he had gone as far as TB wanted him to.

I also took the opportunity for a chat with JP re GB/CW, to see where he was on getting rid of Whelan. Godric was pretty sure that

Whelan was responsible for tipping off papers out of yesterday's morning meeting that we were pissed off at Chris Smith going a bit off-message on PoWs on *Question Time*. I said to JP if we can't have frank discussions in those meetings, when can we? JP was unsympathetic to Whelan, couldn't really understand why GB kept him, because he thought he was bad for his image. I later saw TB and said I was pretty sure Whelan was at it all the time.

TB spoke to GB about it and later Whelan called me. 'What's all this crap about?' 'What crap?' 'The crap about me, you winding up Tony to complain to Gordon.' 'How do I know it's crap?' 'Because I say so.' 'There's your problem. I don't trust you, people don't trust you. I have private conversations with you and I read about them in Hugh Pym's book [on GB]. I say things at meetings and they end up as page leads written by your mates.' I said he had to change his modus operandi, or else there was no way he can stay inside the operation. I said I assumed he had been responsible for [Kevin] Maguire's [*Mirror*] story that TB was blocking a rise in the NMW [national minimum wage], when the truth was the opposite. TB had said to me if he really felt GB was at it, he would force him to change. I said even if Whelan freelanced a bit, there was no way he could operate like he did without GB knowing, but TB didn't really want to hear it. He said he had to be absolutely sure of his ground, because he could not be totally certain that getting rid of Whelan would make GB threaten to resign. I said don't be ridiculous. He said it would be like me being forced to get rid of you. Whelan sounded apoplectic, but I said to him he was damaging GB and once GB saw that, he would be dispensable.

TB called a couple of times from Chequers. He felt [Robert, Viscount] Cranborne [Conservative Leader of the Lords] was up to no good on decommissioning in the Lords. He was also alarmed re the presidency, and felt we were going to get hit on it. He was having one of his Chequers dinners, with RC and Gaynor. Robin's office had called Fiona to ask who else was going. When she said John Mortimer [barrister and writer] and Gerry Robinson [businessman and new chairman of the Arts Council], someone called back and said RC wanted to know why wives weren't mentioned. 'Are their marriages in trouble?' PG and Gail were there, and Philip called on the way back, said TB was in sparkling form, whilst Robin looked broken. The only thing in the Sundays I got bothered about was a story that GB had asked TB to be his best man. 'Nice idea, total invention,' TB said when I mentioned it to him.

Sunday, May 31

Mo was on *Frost*, and was a bit ropy re decommissioning, and why Adams and McGuinness were invited to the Hillsborough garden party with Prince Charles. She lacked the finesse needed for tricky questions.

Monday, June 1

Roy Greenslade [*Guardian* media commentator] did a very helpful piece re me and the *Mirror*. Maguire had a piece on GB defying TB re going to the World Cup. The *Independent* splashed on a GB report on the poor, which was actually the product of a committee chaired by TB. Gazza [Paul Gascoigne] being dropped by [England football manager] Glenn Hoddle was a big story and we were being pressed all day to get into it, and managed to resist. Decommissioning was rearing up again, probably being stirred by the Tories.

TB was installed in his new office which was bigger and better and lighter. The office meeting was largely about Scotland, PR and the presidency. I did the eleven o'clock early and it was mainly Ireland and Prince Charles. I denied outright the claim reportedly being made by Charles' people that they had not been consulted [about garden party invitations]. TB said later he felt they could have been more sympathetic to the idea of Adams being there. He felt we were going to have running problems with Charles because on many issues he was more traditional than the Queen.

We left for Northolt and the flight to Spain for the start of the pre-summit tour of capitals. [José Maria] Aznar, like [Bertie] Ahern later when we arrived in Dublin, was totally opposed to some big initiative on the future of Europe, and was worried we were going to be bounced by the French and Germans. The Tories did a reshuffle which we had to get portrayed as a shift to the right. We managed to do so, but I could tell TB was worried about it. He was also fretting about Jonathan, felt he was feeling insecure and his response was to keep [Richard] Wilson out of things, but TB needed him bound in. He also wanted Peter M more integrally involved to strengthen the centre.

TB was starting to plot out the reshuffle and was scribbling names seemingly randomly – Peter M, [John] Reid, [Helen] Liddell, [John] Denham, [Stephen] Byers, [Alan] Milburn, Tessa [Jowell]. He wanted to sack [David] Clark, [Gavin] Strang, Harriet and one other. He wanted to move Margaret B, put Ann Taylor in MAFF, Jack [Cunningham] to DTI, Peter at the centre. He said Wilson had suggested Jack could be Chancellor, but TB said he was not in the same league as GB. None of them were.

The meeting with Aznar was in the newish purpose-built PM's offices, which were stunning. Christ knows how much they cost. It was when I saw the tennis courts I thought maybe they didn't quite have the media and Opposition we do. The main focus of discussion was economic reform, TB wanting progress on employment, product, capital and labour market reform, single market, and entrepreneurship. Aznar said the two countries that talked the most about the single market, France and Germany, were the ones who did most to raise barriers to it. TB liked Aznar, liked his toughness and his directness. Chirac wanted a committee of wise men to do another blue-skies look at Europe. He said I don't need a wise man. They would be better off asking dead poets. TB said I think your words are the words of a wise man. They were also on the same pitch re Turkey, and equally pessimistic re enlargement being taken too far forward at Cardiff. There was a brief press conference, during which the interpreter translated Third Way as Third World, which went down well.

We arrived half an hour late in Dublin. We'd been working on a new statement to relaunch Anglo-Irish relations. Bertie asked TB to address a joint session of the Parliament. They did Ireland mainly tête-à-tête then over dinner, where they served quite the best meat I had ever tasted, they did the European summit stuff. As they went through it, I was worrying that we didn't have enough of substance to make Cardiff a success. There was a danger Mandela would be seen as the only big thing, and it would be seen as a distraction unless there was something else genuinely going on. TB was confident we could make economic reform fly, but I felt it was all a bit too dry and technical.

I liked Bertie a lot, and I think he shared my general unease about European summitry. He and Aznar were both adamant that we could not be signalling a big shift or another grand design for Europe. It was interesting to see how many of them lived in fear of the French and Germans getting together to produce a surprise and Aznar in particular basically said TB was the one who had to lead Europe in a different way, and there would be a lot of support if he did. Bertie said the public would not thank us if we came out with a stack of more institutional reform. He supported Europe but he felt the remoteness of it all was becoming a problem.

Tuesday, June 2

We were staying at the Westbury [Hotel, Dublin] and I had breakfast with TB in his suite, where he was wound up re Sinn Fein and decommissioning. He said we had to watch Cranborne like a hawk; when it came to NI politics he could do a lot of damage inside the Tory Party. We left for Belfast in the smallest and most uncomfortable plane the RAF could provide, the 146 having been taken off us to take Prince Charles somewhere. It was noisy, both of us did our necks trying to get in and drinking without spilling was virtually impossible. We headed for Parliament Buildings, did a big doorstep, where it became apparent there was no clear narrative for the day. As the meetings went on, the marching season was the main concern for most of them. Sinn Fein turned up with a couple we had not seen before, introduced by Adams as from a residents' association. One of the security guys told me they were in fact fairly high up the IRA ladder, so do not be taken in by the label.

TB seemed to have the measure of them early on. John Hume had made the point SF could pretty much turn the violence on and off like a tap, and Adams virtually admitted as much when he said he thought they could calm it if TB managed to get them a meeting with Trimble. They also reminded TB of his exact words on one year and prisoners, and he had to dissemble on it. DT was much more confident. He had Donaldson with him but was not deferring at all. He said the Parades Commission was damaged goods. Ian Paisley was missing from the DUP line-up because he was in Scotland, and there was a very funny moment when the fire alarm went off as TB was trying to persuade them re the principle of consent. 'It's a lie detector,' said Peter Robinson. TB laughed, glad to be able to stop talking under pressure when they clearly weren't buying it. [Sir Bernard] Ingham was at the select committee inquiry into the GIS and really laid into me but he was so over the top it got very little coverage. The nine o'clock news had GB on spending, TB on NI, JP on the Channel Tunnel rail link, DB on schools, Jack Straw on football violence so it was no wonder the Tories were getting frustrated.

Wednesday, June 3

Peter M was in a sulk about not yet being in the Cabinet and didn't come to the morning meeting. The *Guardian* ran a story re Terry Burns [Treasury permanent secretary] leaving so Whelan was pressing for us to get it all sorted today, so presumably he had put the story there in the first place. I got it sorted with Wilson and also spoke to Burns to agree a statement before the PMQs meeting. I had meetings with Wilson re GIS, where he seemed moderately on board but I could never quite tell; with RC re Sandline where the initial mishandling was still hurting us; and a clear-the-air chat with Whelan.

I said unless we sorted out the trust issue, we had a real problem. It was soon going to be untenable unless we sorted it. I said if he wanted to boost GB through the media, fine, but let us do it in an agreed fashion without others constantly being done down. He said he was down and fed up of being blamed for everything; he didn't do half the things he was accused of. I said while people thought he did, it was a problem, and it arose because he did enough of the things he shouldn't for people not to give him the benefit of the doubt.

At PMQs TB went a bit beyond the line on the two guardsmen and whether they could be released.[1] I had to calm it down a bit afterwards when I was huddled. The problem with the guardsmen was that it wasn't clear whether Mo was reviewing the sentence or the case as a whole. I had the first of my pared down heads of information meetings, a smaller group of the people from key departments, which was a lot better but the real problem was one of quality. Some of them seemed not to know what their departments were doing, and some appeared to have no relationship with ministers at all. I think they were intimidated by me but in fact I was trying to involve them more not less. Stuart Higgins announced he was standing down at the *Sun* and I put out a few TB words

Thursday, June 4

The day got off to a bad start, [Peter] Kilfoyle calling to complain that David Clark was stopping him from trying to do his briefing on older people, then Harriet on at 8 burbling about pensions. At Cabinet, TB and George Robertson were making it pretty clear that intervention in Kosovo was an option. He said it was a classic Bosnia situation and we could not let it deteriorate. Cabinet was a pretty desultory affair. I walked in through TB's office and nobody apart from Gavin Strang was in the room, the rest all milling around outside. There was something shambolic about the way they all filed in so slowly, chatting outside, pouring tea and coffee, never quite sure if TB was there or not. Gavin looked positively tragic, sitting all on his own, looking out towards the window, probably knowing in himself he would not be there for long.

TB had a meeting with GB, Margaret B and Ian McCartney [DTI

---

[1] Blair raised hopes that Scots Guardsmen James Fisher and Mark Wright, serving life sentences for shooting dead a teenager in Northern Ireland in 1995, could soon be freed. They would be released under the terms of the Good Friday Agreement in September 1998.

minister] re the minimum wage. TB and GB were both arguing for the lower rate for younger people, and GB was also wanting to bury the announcement in the CSR, which was odd. I said we should make a huge thing of it. He said 'Once Tony and I get our way, Margaret won't be that keen to get lots of publicity for it.' I couldn't work out whether actually what he was trying to do was get it more associated with him, or whether genuinely he thought there were more problems attached to it. TB was really wound up about interest rates going up. GB said it was better now than after the NMW announcement because people would link the two. TB nonetheless wanted me really to hammer the line that we were going to make sure boom and bust economics were at an end. We got a pretty hostile reaction because there had been no preparing the ground. We put Alistair D up after I spoke to Whelan, who was going through the motions of being more co-operative.

We set off for Holland for the latest pre-summit round. Along with Bertie, I'd say [Wim] Kok was the most likeable of the leaders, but he could also be very tough in negotiation and we had a lot on the Dutch contribution. Jaap van der Ploeg [Dutch government communications director] told me that every Friday the Dutch Cabinet did fitness training together! Christ knows what would happen if we tried the same. Both in the meeting and at the little doorstep afterwards, TB was very strong on Kosovo. There was still a lot of interest too in the Third Way agenda every time we went to mainland Europe, but our media were losing interest with it. On the plane back we worked on the Cardiff agenda, where he really wanted economic reform to take off. On Kosovo, it was clear we had to start preparing the ground and I wrote a briefing note stepping up the possibility of military action. The FCO, in the form of Emyr Jones Parry [deputy political director], were not keen. Several of the papers were claiming TB changed his accent [to a form of 'Estuary English'] for his Des O'Connor interview. What were they on?

Friday, June 5

We took the expected hammering on interest rates, and TB was keen to set out some of the deeper argument and wrote a piece himself for the *Sunday Telegraph* before we set off for Rome. We were basically back to the message of tough choices for the long term. He said on the plane that though we will get hit on one level, there are points to be won for seeing difficult change through.

Kosovo was definitely moving fast, and I adapted the briefing note I drafted last night with the view to giving to the Sundays, drawing on what TB had said to the Cabinet, warning troops may have to be used. Jones Parry said we were going for a new UNSCR, which the Russians would block, and we would end with the threat of air strikes, possibly strikes for real. Kok had been strong on it last night, and so were [Romano] Prodi and [Viktor] Klima [Austrian Chancellor] today. TB was worrying re NI again. Far from moving to decommission, SF-IRA were looking for new arms the whole time. Publication of the Prisoners Bill went fine, with both Trimble and Adams onside, DT because it contained the Balmoral pledges, Adams because there were no preconditions. So far so good.

The meeting with Prodi went fine, though he was hard to follow at times. There was a broad measure of agreement on the main agenda, and he seemed sound on Kosovo. Prodi went as far as saying he thought military action may now be inevitable. Klima was in pretty much the same place on Kosovo when we landed in Vienna later, but the Austrians were clearly not keen on giving any help to Turkey. He said they were still torturing and locking up political prisoners. TB was strong on Kosovo at both doorsteps, and did a good clip on his 'iron determination' to build a strong economy.

In Vienna we finally received the Franco-German pre-summit letter. TB's reaction was that it was fascinating because it was anti-integrationist, very defensive and written by two governments who clearly think they have a public opinion problem on Europe. On the plane back we were working on the reshuffle again.

Sunday, June 7

The papers were not too bad, though there were reports of Brown/Beckett at war over the minimum wage. Charlie W came on early to say GB was spitting mad about it, but that just made me think they had put the stories there as a way of forcing TB to side with GB. The *Sunday Telegraph* had a story saying GB wanted to stop Peter M moving into the Cabinet which was also either their handiwork or fiction. JP called, and said the TB/GB camps story was gaining ground and was doing damage. He said the party was disintegrating in Scotland and Wales. Donald wasn't up to it, and Ron Davies was constantly working against the government line.

JP said he valued the way he and TB worked but he was aware that TB had been friendly to him as a way of using him to win a few battles. 'I'm being drawn into a spider's web, where I end up having to side with him, and I know the game but it could be dangerous.' I raised Whelan with him again. He said the problem was TB really didn't like to think GB was a problem, but he had to wise up. CW called late to say *The Times* were splashing on the [Rolling] Stones calling off their tour because of one of GB's Budget tax changes. My instinct was to go for rock star tax exiles but both TB and Peter M were against.

Monday, June 8

The Stones were leading the news in the morning though it went down as the day wore on, the calming not helped by Whelan going with my line, that we were not going to be lectured to by tax exiles. The day was taken up with EU travel taking in Sweden, Finland, Denmark and Brussels. TB was mainly focused on the CSR, said GB had become more secretive again and he was worried there were going to be a few last minute bounces. But the top lines were fairly clear – new controls, money for modernisation, public/private. When he cheered up on one of the flights, TB was thinking up a few Rolling Stones lyrics to go with the new story – 'I can't get no . . . tax deduction . . . I used to love you, but it's all over now.'

The Europe agenda was becoming clearer because there was a lot of agreement on the economic reform package, and a sense that the future of Europe debate should be taking stock rather than setting off a new group of wise men to think great thoughts. As the day wore on, it was clear the Franco-German letter was going to leak, focusing on their desire for greater subsidiarity, so I put together a briefing line for overnight, pushing the pro-Europe, pro-reform line.

At the various doorsteps today, Kosovo was the main focus of the non-summit questions. After yesterday's calls to Clinton and Yeltsin, TB was continuing to push a tough line. Stockholm was fine, and they were all pretty laid-back about things. They had an interesting discussion on welfare, with Hans Göran Persson [Swedish Prime Minister] more on the workfare line than outsiders might think. He was worrying about bigger influx of refugees. He was totally against the wise-men approach on the future of Europe, which was a theme of the day. Helsinki (president and PM) was fine, and the scenery stunning, then we reached Copenhagen for dinner, and we were in Brussels by 11pm. TB joked about eating our way round Europe, and we agreed that Denmark had served the best food so far. We were up late working on the CSR statement with faxes going back and forth to GB.

Tuesday, June 9

I had a dreadful night, barely slept and worst of all, I wasn't really sure what I was losing sleep over. There was nothing in particular, just various things running endlessly round my head, home, work, kids, Fiona, health, just round and round in circles until eventually I thought fuck it, I'm not going to sleep, I'll get up and do some work. TB was up not long after and before long was on the phone to GB re the CSR, trying to sort more money for defence and also arguing about why we needed big surpluses at all. He was also agitated re the *Telegraph* splash on some nonsense about [Michael] Meacher wanting to put a tax on rubbish. I got Meacher to get up on the *Today* programme and deny it. The Franco-German letter had finally leaked and was seen by the Brussels press corps as a shift in their position towards subsidiarity. Our press were far more sceptical about the French and German strength for once, and were saying it was clearly a French or German source trying to angle it their way.

The [Jean-Luc] Dehaene meeting was long and dull and I became mesmerised by how often he said 'er'. At times he was doing it between every single word. The longest he went without a single 'er' was nine words. There was no love lost between them. TB didn't like his manner, and of course Dehaene never forgave the Brits for blocking him for the top Europe job. But even he was on our page re economic reform, and TB was strong, with the sense growing that economic reform, and the nature of the future of Europe debate, were moving in our direction. Lionel Barber [*Financial Times* Brussels bureau chief] said TB was definitely staking out a better position for the UK. The French were still talking about his speech to the National Assembly.

We then headed for Luxembourg, which was an altogether more low-key affair. I reckon the Luxembourgers were also the biggest smokers of the various delegations. [Jean-Claude] Juncker positively reeked of fags. But again, on the economic reform substance, we were OK. On to Bonn, where Kohl said to TB he was coming more and more to the British view of Europe, but we couldn't really work out how much he meant it. But as the day wore on, the initial anti-us reaction to the Franco-German letter was receding, and there was a feeling it showed them to be more defensive than before. He said the Commission was useless, there should be more not less subsidiarity and the national governments had to be in control of direction. TB left the meeting a lot more confident that we could make Cardiff a success. He detected Kohl being irritated with the French and wanting a more prosaic approach.

We headed to Paris, stopping by to see the Scotland World Cup squad. They were more nervous than I imagined at meeting him, and pretty psyched up generally. Craig Brown [manager] seemed to think it went well and was worth doing, though he said he reckoned a fair few voted SNP. We flew over the new World Cup stadium [Stade de France] which was impressive from the air, then landed before being driven to the Elysée. Chirac was in major Chirac mode, full of noise and wind and mad ideas, like wanting Russia to be part of any NATO operation in Kosovo. He was really pushing his wise-men idea and TB took delight in telling him how many of the others were against it. He said he didn't want a Canadian involved in the India-Pakistan dispute because Canada had criticised French tests. He was in pretty patronising mode the whole way through. *'Je ne sais pas si tu as apprécié ma lettre, mais elle mérite d'être appréciée, Tonee.'* ['I don't know if you appreciated my letter, but it deserves to be appreciated, Tony.'] He said Europe was becoming unwieldy, and needed leadership, which meant Germany, France and Britain. If we all had the same dynamism, Europe is strong. TB said afterwards he could not help liking him. He was at times a rogue and could be full of bullshit but he had such natural charm and beneath it all there was a part of him laughing at the whole thing.

We finally had the best meal of the pre-summit tour, which was a bit predictable and annoying. TB tried to maintain Denmark was better for a while but finally gave in. The French just did this stuff better than anyone. TB saw [Lionel] Jospin later who told him he intended to go for the presidency. He said he didn't really understand the importance of TB's discussions with Clinton, but said he would like to be part of them. Dinner over, we set off for the airport. Not only had they served the best meal of the tour, but their cops had easily the best escort too, just three bikes getting us to the airport in no time at all. The Austrians had been the worst, whole streets shut down and blocked off so we could leisurely make our way through empty main roads.

Wednesday, June 10

The media was beginning to be dominated by the World Cup. I stayed home to go to Rory's class assembly and got in for a meeting on the honours. It was like walking back in time. I went over with TB for PMQs where he did Japanese PoWs, but the World Cup expectation was changing the atmospherics.

Thursday, June 11

Some silly story about the minimum wage and tips was leading the news. I got in and was working on a couple of briefings, one on post-Cabinet CSR, another pre-Cardiff, when Alison put a call through. She said Terry Tavener [friend] is on the line, and I don't know why but the second she said it, I felt sure it was about Ellie.

'It's Ellie,' she said, and she was crying. 'She's dead.' It is so weird how people can sense these things. Alison had put through God knows how many calls but she knew as well, and came in and said are you all right, and I just collapsed in tears. At the hospital, I bumped into Terry in the corridor and we just collapsed again. There were a few kids running around, but around the main desk nurses were crying. A nurse stopped me and said she had just haemorrhaged and it was awful. I walked on and there was Lindsay, looking all cried out, but she started again, and as I hugged her she talked over the last bit in the minutest detail, and said she felt guilty she wasn't there when she finally went. She had gone home last night because she was finally to get a bed at last, and got a call at 9 to say come in because Ellie was ill. She got in to learn she was dead. Now she was worrying about Hope [her younger daughter] who was on her way to Cornwall and she had no way of contacting her. She wanted us to see the body, and I steeled myself. Fiona cracked though and then so did I. I so wanted John to be there now, because I had always had this feeling when he died that she changed and something dreadful was going to happen. She looked a little pained even now, the poor little darling. Her eyes were closed, her mouth a little bit open, her skin so fair but a bit puffy. Lindsay just sat there, stroking her hand and her hair, occasionally talking to her as though she could hear, then remembering, and crying again. I don't know how on earth she could cope this time. The hospital's priest was there, and really nice, and Father Anthony came in. The psychologist who was there to help Lindsay cope was a friend of Jonathan's. After a while we more or less managed to have a conversation, but by then I had that pain that follows crying, throat, eyes, chest, and also the feeling you were doing nothing useful. Lindsay decided she had to get to Hope and the only way to do it was to go there herself. We organised trains while I spoke to Geoff Lakeman [long-serving West Country reporter for the *Mirror*], asked him to meet her and look after her and try to find the place where Hope was staying. He was a real trouper, straight into it, dropped everything else. It was odd how someone like him, who had played a part in that period of our lives when we all met, should suddenly be involved like this. Then as we left the hospital, we bumped into David Hill of all people.

People were really nice back at the office but of course life goes on and all that had happened after several hours out was that a stack more work had piled up. And of course suddenly you felt none of it mattered. I went over for GB's CSR statement, which went fine, and afterwards Ed Balls and I did a lower gallery briefing and I let him take the lead and just wanted to disappear now. One or two of them knew John, lots knew of him, but in the end what was it all? – another story they had to file, another briefing we had to do, and it all felt like total bollocks really. I was home by 8 and talked to the boys, who couldn't really take it all in. Calum asked question upon question. Rory was just a bit quiet.

Friday, June 12

We were feeling pretty wretched. There were little pieces about Ellie in some of the papers, and the *Guardian* asked me to do an obituary, which I thought through while I was in the dentist's chair for ninety minutes. Lindsay said Geoff had been fantastic yesterday, found the place in no time, near Liskeard and when they arrived Hope was looking out of the window. She knew straight away and was crying even before Lindsay got in to see her.

Meacher called me, in full Meacher mode, saying he was really worried TB would side with [Jacques] Santer in thinking there was no need for a zoos directive. I could not believe I was having to deal with Michael Meacher and his passion for a fucking zoos directive. I then had the honours briefing, and the Geoff Hurst [footballer] knighthood, which we had inserted late on, got a lot of the attention. They knew it was pretty naff manipulation related to the World Cup, but they couldn't really knock it. We also had some really good NHS honours in there which we were trying to push along with the education honours, and at least keep some kind of public services theme. John Holroyd said a couple of daft things, first hinting that David English's widow [English had died on June 10] could take his award [a peerage] when I had said not. I pushed the line that there was change and modernisation, but truth was we had only begun to touch it at the margins.

The big problem of the day was the minimum wage. Margaret [Beckett] was holding out against GB trying to lower the youth rate. TB met them together. GB said there were very strong economic reasons why this had to be done like this. MB said the arguments did not stack up, that the difference to the economy between £3.20 and £3.00 was minimal, and that the Low Pay Commission had to be taken as a whole or its members would walk. Afterwards she said to me this was all about saving GB's face because he set up these arguments in the press and then had to be seen to win them. She said Balls and Whelan had been allowed to destabilise the debate. TB said to me she was only just realising what GB could be like.

GB called me and did his injured thing, saying MB was respon-

June '98: Beckett and GB argue re minimum wage

sible for all the briefings against him, which I found very hard to believe. Again, he was protesting too much. When I said I had to go because Margaret was on the other phone (these calls coming through while I was at Calum's class tea surrounded by shouting kids) he said 'She'll want to accuse me of being responsible for stories that she is responsible for.' I said to both that I thought it should be possible to get through the weekend without any briefing and counter-briefing which was doing nobody any good. GB was adamant that to do it her way would lead to job losses galore. She said he was scaremongering to justify a position he should never have become attached to.

Saturday, June 13
I was having to keep tabs on the NMW and stop the GB camp over-briefing what was already seen as a bad split story. TB was growing a bit concerned at the tone of the end-of-presidency reports. Maybe there was nothing we could do about it. For different reasons, the pro-Europeans and the antis wanted to give us a bit of a kicking. We had to deal with a piece of crap in the *Mail on Sunday* that we had blocked a knighthood for [businessman Richard] Branson. The Tories were stirring it and this, allied to them attacking us over the presidency, and saying they might vote against us on Northern Ireland, got TB really irate. He said Hague just wasn't serious when it came to it. I went to get the papers with Calum and we went round to Lindsay's. Calum was really sweet with Hope.

Sunday, June 14
TB spoke to Lionel Barber and Peter Riddell to get up our lines pre-Cardiff [European Council], but while he was reasonably convincing, they remained sceptical we were really running the show here. The Tories were being quite successful at getting up the 'bad presidency' theme, but I think we had the chance to turn it around. TB felt most of the criticism was coming from Brussels, Commission and media, but that the Heads [of government] felt we had done fine. We left for the train to Cardiff at 1, and I got his agreement to brief that Peter M was to be his rep on the PES economic reform group. Robin C's face was an absolute picture when he heard. He joined us on the train, where TB was ploughing through the massive briefs for the summit.

TB was also having to deal with the NMW, where he was going to back GB yet again, and with coal, which was a mess. I would be expected to do a big briefing for all the Euro hacks on arrival so worked on a script re economic reform, general summit messages. TB did a doorstep on Kosovo, EMU and beef but the big story emerging was England football fans on the rampage in Marseilles, which was getting blanket live coverage, with these idiots treated like stars. I wondered if the media just totally ignored them whether they might calm down. We even had reporters saying 'as we await the next confrontation'.

The mood at my briefing was good, and I felt more confident we could deal with the bad presidency attacks. The Germans were saying we did not need a new UNSCR for military action in Kosovo. On Tuesday Milosevic was seeing Yeltsin so again the heat on Kosovo was rising. I went out for dinner with some of the hacks but was called out for a call with Jack Straw and our Consul General in Marseilles, Ian Davies. We agreed to a line of total backing for the French police, and that Ian should do media pre-TB tomorrow. Jack was very calm and clear about it. Tony Banks called, said these people were morons, and we had to go for them. He felt it would kibosh our [2006] World Cup bid.

Monday, June 15

TB said he was ashamed to be English when he saw these tossers rampaging around in our flag. He was really fretting that the leaders would pick up on some of the negative UK comment on our presidency. He decided his best card was his ability to cut straight to public opinion in all their countries and we decided he should try to do TV interviews with stations from every EU country during the summit, which I got Magi [Cleaver] to fix. The morning discussion was economic reform, which went fine, though both Chirac and Jospin were in a very different place to TB. They did the future of Europe over lunch, and again Kohl was much less optimistic than expected, feeling there was a bit of a tide against now. TB announced that [Alan] Shearer had put England one up [against Tunisia, in Marseilles].

There was also a discussion on MEPs fiddling their expenses. Some were keen on doing a big number but Kohl was against. He said there was a wave of envy and it would lead to disproportionate hostility. The general feeling was that yes it was a problem but to blow it up as a big thing now would lead to all EU institutions being unfairly attacked. At the briefing I gave out TB words on EMU, which were really just emphasising our desire for it to be a strong currency, and also that the EU and US were pillars of stability. This fairly prosaic and straightforward statement was seen as something terribly important and made several splashes. This was because we were having to wean them off the usual diet of 14 vs 1 [member states] stories. They could not really cope with summits where the story was not some great bust-up.

We also got agreement for an informal council on political reform in October to take forward some of the political ideas. But it was an uphill struggle briefing-wise. I was briefing endlessly on Turkey but again had not much to say beyond a repackaging of what had been agreed at Luxembourg so all I could do was try to push TB's words as being positive, but that was uphill with the Turk-obsessives. There was a lot on interest in Kohl and whether he would demand his rebate but when it came to it he was very muted and didn't really seem to understand the arguments. The way Germany operated at these summits confirmed TB in his opposition to coalition governments. Kohl was constantly second-guessing and worrying about his coalition partners. It made it much harder for him to shape negotiations in a dynamic and flexible way.

The press had started to notice that I was being far less aggressive and argumentative to the European media. Robert Peston [FT] ran a piece saying we were starting to win battles. TB said that at one point, he reckoned five of the fifteen leaders were reading the FT, that we underestimated its importance to the European debate. In between trying to sort out coal and the continuing NMW row, TB did a doorstep which was dominated by football violence and Kosovo, but where he also did a good clip on what the summit was about.

England won 2-0 which cut down the chances of further riots, though there was more trouble on the beaches. TB loved his Austrian TV interview where the interviewer asked what advice he had for the others as he was clearly Europe's most popular and successful leader. TB went off for dinner with the Queen et al. at Cardiff Castle. Fiona and I went out on our own for once, which was nice, and talked mainly about Lindsay and the funeral which was set for Friday.

Tuesday, June 16

We were up early for a rash of interviews. TB apologised for the football thugs in French on French TV, otherwise all OK. The *Mirror* had another big whack at him, this time over not doing enough to stop the yobs. The morning session to agree the conclusions was awful, real nit-picking and narky, and rarely on big points of substance. Santer, Chirac and Dehaene were the worst offenders and TB was getting more and more irritated with it all. I did a mid-morning briefing and stressed there were three outstanding difficulties – Turkey, future financing, Agenda 2000. But I was basically using it to start laying a few end-of-presidency lines. There was more interest however in the stuff on fiddled expenses where we were taking a hard line whilst trying to stay within the parameters of the discussion yesterday.

By the time I got back TB had got the Turkey text sorted but was still ploughing through the conclusions. I told him Nelson Mandela had arrived and was waiting so he said that he felt they could leave foreign ministers to resolve some of the outstanding text. He said RC would come and report to the lunch on any problems. The lunch was a walk away, in the museum, and Mandela's presence always added something, and concentrated minds. Chirac was not quite his usual self in Mandela's presence. RC came through and reported everything sorted and set out where there had been one or two wrinkles which were now resolved. TB took Mandela out into the street for a bit of glad-handing. Then it was in for a quick final meeting and then the press conference.

Santer had grown on us both this time. He was a lot better than the last time we saw him. TB said he was even taking to Juncker and Dehaene which I thought was pushing it a bit. 'I like all of them,' he said. Chirac had been a pretty big pain throughout, and his small-point stuff in the morning was a bit alarming. TB was worried Kohl was rather losing the plot, and he certainly had seemed lost on the detail on a few occasions. Bertie was easily the best to deal with, no bullshit and hated these events almost as much as I did.

At the Mandela bilateral, TB let slip we were talking to the Dutch about the possibility of a third-country trial re Lockerbie. Mandela was wearing a fairly thick white vest under his colourful shirt. He had hearing aids in both ears, and his voice was also weakening. I think he thought John Holmes was Foreign Secretary. I caught a bit of Scotland vs Norway before we had to leave for the train. We worked on TB's Commons statement and also the speech to the European Parliament. TB was speaking to GB re the NMW, GB having leaked to the *FT* the details, because he was worried about the Eddie George [Governor, Bank of England] inflation warning today. I called Alex [Ferguson] who was at a restaurant in Bordeaux. He was happy enough re Scotland [1-1 draw], felt [footballer David] Beckham would not be able to cope without Posh [Spice, aka Victoria Adams, Beckham's future wife] – 'The boy's lovesick' – and was backing Argentina to win.

Wednesday, June 17

We got low-key coverage for Cardiff, but it certainly wasn't a disaster and Julian Braithwaite [press officer, foreign affairs] collated some very good coverage from around EU capitals which we were able to use in the statement to the House. Margaret B was livid at GB's briefing to the *FT*. GB had a strong intellectual case but as ever he was going about it in the way designed to antagonise most people. Margaret was not easily angered but she was really mad on this. He has no need to make me an enemy, she said, but somehow he does it. TB had checked out with Eddie George that he was happy with the lower youth rate and he was clearly going to side with GB now. We had had inflation up yesterday, and bad jobs and wages figures today, so GB was making the argument at the right time.

We were clearly going to get pressed on hooligans and we brainstormed a few ideas, the best of which was saying the RAF guy who had been arrested would face dismissal if found guilty. TB gave a strong hint, and I briefed hard afterwards that we would also be encouraging private sector firms to do the same.

Richard Wilson was giving evidence to the Public Administration Select Committee inquiry into the GIS and he was fine. The only stuff making the news was hinting he was keeping an eye on me. He came to see me afterwards and I said what he had said was fine. He said he was trying to present a different image of me, make clear I'd done nothing wrong but obviously as head of the Civil Service he would keep an eye on me. He said when I went there [GIS inquiry] I should charm them and put on a performance. On Northern Ireland, it was becoming clear Andrew MacKay was pushing to break bipartisanship. He is a total idiot that man. I spoke to [Peter] Temple-Morris [now sitting as an 'Independent One-Nation Conservative'] and said he might do his final step to defection [joining the Labour Party] on *Frost* on Sunday, and say MacKay doing this was the final straw in the way he was behaving on the Prisoners Bill.

As we left for Strasbourg, TB was still dealing with GB re the minimum wage. I'd seen GB earlier and he said he had to win because the argument was one hundred per cent right. [Jon] Sopel [BBC] came on the trip because he was doing a TV profile on me pre-GIS inquiry which would be watched by about three people because it was going out at the same time as the England match. Re TB's speech to the European Parliament I wanted him to go for the MEPs after everything that had come out about their fiddles and he was minded to do it but everyone else was totally against it.

Thursday, June 18

We were up around 6 to finish the speech, which was reasonably Euro-friendly. He added in more fairly general Third Way stuff. Sopel was filming with us all day and his best moment was filming me arguing with a Spanish reporter who wanted TB to play his plastic guitar. His first speech was to the Socialist Group which was fine. He did a very general political speech saying the left could stay in power if we stayed financially prudent, Third Way, and internationalist. He did a very strong Q&A and then to the Parliament itself where he got a much better response than we expected.

On the flight back I put together a briefing note on Temple-Morris, twisting the knife on Ireland as they were about to vote against us on the third reading of the Prisoners Bill. When I got back I called Barney Jones to get Temple-Morris on *Frost*. Back at the office I ploughed through a big briefing on the GIS inquiry with Mike Granatt [head of the GICS] and Robin Mountfield [permanent secretary, Office of Public Service]. The four o'clock was more NI than NMW, which is what I had been expecting. It was partly because Margaret had done so well, and had been a real pro about it all, as I said to her. By now I knew TB was planning to move her to Leader of the House, which I hoped she wouldn't see as a big demotion.

GB as ever had got his way but TB strongly believed we had made the right decision, regardless of how he had dealt with it. TB was not buying the GB separate-agenda argument. I felt GB had not decided whether he was New Labour or 'real' Labour and the tensions came out all the time. He was between stools. I went home then round to Lindsay's where the sadness was close to unbearable.

Friday, June 19

I took Grace to school then went for a haircut. The hairdresser had read about Ellie and asked if it was the funeral today. I wrote a little speech about Ellie for the service and then practised the reading I had to do. I cracked up several times and eventually got myself some tranquillisers to help me through it. Then walking into the church carrying the coffin I caught sight of the kids and that set me off. I just about held it together during the speaking bit but I was conscious my voice wasn't carrying as strongly as usual. The school choir was really moving. I noticed CB singing very loudly.

Terry [Tavener] did a really nice speech, and Father Anthony was very comforting. It was not nearly as bad as it might have been. We walked through Waterlow Park with Philip and Tessa and over to the cemetery for the burial, threw a few flowers in on top of the coffin, and there was something so ghastly about her being buried just a few yards away from John. Back at Terry's people's spirits started to lift a little. Lindsay was unbelievably strong but I guess it was going to hit harder once all the fuss was over and everyone else had gone back to their lives.

Saturday, June 20

Philip sent me a draft of his book [*The Unfinished Revolution*], which was excellent. He had successfully managed to write something that was insightful and insiderish without giving away too much and without trashing people's reputations. Peter M called and said he was worried about the book [Paul] Routledge was writing on him. He was apparently getting £100,000 for the serialisation from the *Sunday Times* and they were bound to want to focus on Peter being gay. My first instinct was maybe to pre-empt, but both TB and Fiona thought the best thing to do was stay above it, for Peter to be dignified and not respond in any way at all. The *Sunday Times* had a piece on JP saying spin doctors were out of control, which Joe Irvin [special adviser to JP] said he had intended as a whack at Whelan over the NMW stuff, but needless to say it ended up being about me.

Sunday, June 21

Temple-Morris did the business on *Frost* and was leading the news by lunchtime. There was a bit too much build-up to my select committee appearance on Tuesday. The *Sunday Times* had a story that they were going to ask for tapes of my briefings. There was a long profile piece on Sky. I decided against letting Sopel film a briefing. Joe Haines called and said when he was there [as press secretary to Harold Wilson] he didn't let ministers appear on *Any Questions* at all. So this idea that telling ministers what they could or could not do in the media was new was a nonsense.

We went in for a dinner with TB and CB for [Les] Hinton, [David] Yelland [new editor of the *Sun*] and Rebekah Wade. Before they arrived we discussed whether they [the Blairs] should go to Geoffrey Robinson's place for a holiday. Peter M, RW and I had all advised very strongly against. It would become an issue it just wasn't worth having to deal with. And it wasn't good to be in hock like that. The dinner itself was OK if a bit forced. Yelland was very quiet, to the point of seeming standoffish, but he may just have been shy. CB had a real go at the media and I joined in before TB moved the subject on.

Monday, June 22

All the bollocks about my appearance at the PASC was really starting to crank up. At the 11, I could sense how excited some of them were about it. I spent a lot of the day just reading through all the briefing and the previous evidence. Peter M came over and said no bravura, just be very polite and charming and answer their questions thoughtfully. Bruce [Grocott] said just be yourself. Hilary [Coffman] said do not lose your temper. That was my only real worry, that one of the Tories really got under my skin and I lost it. I was also worried I might go over the top re the BBC. Sopel's piece on me for the Beeb was fine. He was a bit pissed off because I had stopped Bernard Ingham from coming into the street to be interviewed. Petty maybe, but why should I help the silly old fucker land one on me?

Tuesday, June 23

GIS select committee day and some of the Tories had successfully got up the notion that I should hand over tapes of my briefings. There was a news piece running on the broadcasts overnight, a Sopel two-way, [Tony] Bevins and [Robert] Peston discussion, David Hill then Rhodri Morgan at 8.10 on *Today*, all helping to build my point that this was a story about a media obsessed with me because they were obsessed with themselves. The build-up had been pretty steady and clearly the media were hoping for some big explosion. I had a lot of good-luck messages, including from David Davis [Conservative MP] who said his advice as a select committee chairman was just to stay cool. They will try to rile you, and you mustn't let them. You are cleverer than they are and the only hope they have is you either show contempt for them or you lose your rag.

TB called me up to the flat. He said he hadn't realised how big this thing was being built up. He had much the same advice. Just stay calm, and be polite at all times. Be as greasy as you like. He said they would be more scared of me than I was of them because having built it up as an event they will want to have something out of it media-wise, whereas you do these kinds of events every day, just without cameras in. I called Richard Wilson to say I wanted to be able to do some politics, namely say the reason the Tories were obsessed with me was because they were in a state of denial about how they lost. I felt I needed at least something to be able to divide them politically and also hit back when the nasty boys started. RW was fine. Alison had put together a big folder for me, whittling down all the official briefing, but I was by now clear about the main lines, and memorising some of the big points I intended to put over. Bizarrely, just as I was really getting in the zone, Harriet H called again and said she wanted to explain she didn't like my memo. This was the one I had sent her and Frank [Field] telling them to stop briefing. She said she didn't like it but she hadn't leaked it. She didn't respond at the time because she didn't want a row. I assumed she thought I was going to be asked about it. I said I stood by the content of the memo and she had to understand it was done with TB's authority and knowledge but if it came up, I would not go into detail. I said I was perfectly capable of dealing with it without causing a fuss but she burbled on endlessly until eventually I said 'What on earth is the point of calling me at this exact minute, as I'm trying to get my head round everything else, to tell me you don't like a memo I sent way back when, especially when I kind of knew that anyway?' I was probably OTT but she was so incapable of thinking from someone else's perspective.

I avoided the press on the way out, got driven over and then up to the committee corridor. There was a big crowd outside, loads of hacks, researchers, students, all the sketch writers who en masse always looked a sad little bunch, Routledge muttering something about me meeting my match. I said Christ, if you're here it's even more trivial than I thought. Tosser. The little shit [Matthew] Parris [*Times* sketch writer] was to my left with that perma-smirk on his face. Brunson was the other one out of the corner of my eye which I didn't mind. I made a mental note to block them all out. There was a strong element of it being showbiz and Rhodri [Morgan] was loving the fact his committee was getting all this attention. Quite a few non-committee MPs came in. RM announced that there was a World Cup-style screen in an overflow room for those who had not been able to get in here.

After a slow start I got into my stride quickly. I got all the points out I wanted to make and I didn't feel the Tories had worked through their questions rigorously. They were looking to get coverage for their questions rather than probe properly on the answers. They started up on 'psychological flaws' but then it fizzled. I was worried they would go at me re TB saying I attacked the Tories but I got round it with a joke about 'Campbell attacks Blair headline' and it went. They had one or two specifics I thought they would go on, but they didn't sustain a line of questioning and I was always able to bring it back to bigger points. Added to which I was thrown the odd full toss by our side. I was conscious of getting tired as it went on, but felt on a winning run. I damned Ingham with faint praise. It ended with an exchange about whether I supported England or Scotland. [David]

Ruffley [Conservative MP] was the one they had expected to land a blow and he didn't really get near. I shafted him by pointing out the inconsistency in his argument – at one point my sin was doing too much with ministers, at another not enough. I was followed back to Number 10 by camera crews and photographers. The reaction back at the office was really positive, that I had done better than most ministers and mandarins do, but I was glad it was over.

TB came back from his audience with the Queen and watched the C4 news coverage, which he felt was fine. I called him during the Scotland vs Morocco match [Scotland lost 3-0] to say the *Sun* were doing a big attack on him over EMU, and he seemed pretty unfazed about it. I said I was unclear where he wanted to end up on it and until we knew it was hard to manage a media strategy around it.

Wednesday, June 24

I got a good press out of yesterday, both news and sketch-wise, with a general feeling I had won it hands down. Now the 'media obsessed with itself' line was made flesh with the *Sun*'s attack on TB as 'the most dangerous man in Britain' running as the second news item on the BBC. These people were never happier than when talking about themselves. Newspaper attacks politician because he disagrees with their line on Europe – so fucking what? Of course what the *Sun* wanted was to be noticed and the rest of the media were helping. I gave the PA a statement saying the fuss caused by this underlined the point I made at the select committee – that the media is obsessed with itself and not the important issues facing the country. TB was not too worried re the *Sun*, felt it was just them trying to get noticed, rather than a piece of Murdoch repositioning.

I bumped into Alan Clark, who was in mega-mischief mode, stirring against Hague. His other insight for the day was that I should use my select committee appearance as the basis for a pitch for the top job. 'Get yourself a safe seat now and you're the next man. Blair is the only one who could get near you.' And with that he roared off. Alex Ferguson called, said he had seen bits on TV and it was clear I was in control of it. He said you got a good press today but they will keep coming at you because they know you not they are in charge of the agenda. Fiona and I went to Peter Stothard's party which had the usual crowd of London mediaworld partygoers which always reminded me why I didn't like parties. John Birt [BBC director general] said he had watched my appearance and I could have my own BBC show whenever I wanted. Even among my enemies the feedback from yesterday was pretty positive.

Thursday, June 25

My main worry this morning was landmines. In the car on the way in I said to Jonathan this had the potential to be a real problem. Sally [Morgan] and I had been banging on about it for ages but it had just not been taken seriously through the system. Jonathan shrugged off any responsibility, but now we had the *Sun* and the *Express* doing campaigns on it. Why, when we were on the case on this before them, do we then allow them to give the impression we are being forced into doing things we don't want to? Peter M seemed oblivious at the morning meeting. I drafted a line for TB to deliver to Cabinet, making clear we would find parliamentary time, and that we will simply have to explain the problem of 'inter-operability' – those countries who have ratified working alongside those who haven't. I took the note to TB who was in with JP. I said this was the kind of thing that would become a problem at conference if we didn't grip it so they agreed we should go for it. I said there were systemic issues we had to look at that were illustrated by how this had come about. It should not be down to me to pick it up and grip it as a result of a couple of newspapers running opportunistic campaigns. We were doing the right thing so although I got hit with a bit of 'U-turn' at the briefing, I felt we were in a better place on it. RC had made much the same point at Cabinet – that as we had been in the lead on this, it was odd we deny ourselves the credit.

Donald Dewar came to see me and said he was worried, as was I, that the *Daily Record* under the ghastly Martin Clarke, were building up [Alex] Salmond [leader of the Scottish National Party] as an attractive figure and a man of judgement. I called Montgomery who said we needed to give Clarke a bit more cuddling time, which was a pretty revolting thought. I called Clarke who had developed the irritating habit of dropping Scottishisms into his otherwise very English diction. Stooshie. A wee bit of bother. I had no time for him at all but we did not want the *Record* going offside. He said he felt we were in trouble up there.

GB was not at Cabinet but TB went through some of the CSR arguments. Seemingly GB wasn't there because he was doing *Richard and Judy* [TV talk show] as well as a profile for ITN tonight. I briefed on landmines after the Cabinet and it was leading the news. We had a meeting to discuss whether Margaret McDonagh should be general secretary of the party. Peter M, Anji and I were in favour because for all her faults, she was a deliverer. Sally was strongly opposed, feeling she was incapable of taking people with her.

GB called me over for a meeting with him, Balls and Whelan,

ostensibly re CSR but first he went over [Geoffrey] Robinson. He also wanted us to decide when to do the planned £7m ad campaign on the euro. He said Peter M was winding up Seumas Milne [*Guardian*] to expect it soon. GB's instincts were to do it whenever the economy was next big in the news. He said the policy was not changing but every time anyone said anything, it was taken as news. It was his way of saying I should ask Peter M to shut up. On the CSR his main concern was to get it focused on health and education. We agreed we would start concerted TB/GB briefing around the Sundays. We had to get up health stories that were not just about bidding wars with the Treasury.

I was due to do a briefing with Dobson on the plans for the NHS fiftieth anniversary. GB was worried Dobson couldn't carry a message other than on spending. There was no clear vision for a new NHS. GB himself was more relaxed than usual but the three of them were all protesting too much about being leaked against. They were without a doubt the biggest users of the press to get arguments and divisions going so it was a bit much. At Cabinet earlier when TB had said there was too much leaking going on, both RC and Clare had blamed the Treasury direct. GB was also worried re departmentalitis, as was I. It was an odd meeting and I was not totally sure what its purpose had been, but with GB there usually was one.

Friday, June 26

TB was heading to Sedgefield via a Berlin airlift [fiftieth anniversary] event. There was a bit of gloom re the NI elections. As the first results came in, Trimble was not doing as well as expected. TB was blaming himself and the NIO, feeling that he should have followed his instincts to be more involved, but the NIO were insisting Trimble's position would be fine. He was very down about the government as a whole. If only people knew, he said, that we have to do virtually every significant thing this government does. Look at coal yesterday – why did that have to be resolved by us? What does the DTI do? Now this – the minute we take our foot off the accelerator, everyone else does. It just goes wrong.

I was working with GB to try to get up the NHS. We had a TB *News of the World* article and a minute to ministers that we were turning into something for public consumption. I agreed with Dobbo we would stay focused for now on an investment message. The [NHS] fiftieth anniversary, properly handled, was a big opportunity for us to harden up the dividing lines on health.

Saturday, June 27

Lots of the usual irritating crap in the Sundays to deal with. Andy Grice said he had a story that GB had submitted his own reshuffle plan. When I told TB he said he wondered if that came from Peter M. He sounded a bit dispirited by the NI elections and was worrying that Drumcree [planned Orange march] was just a week away. He was cursing the Tories and MacKay, feeling their diddling had done a fair bit of damage. The Sundays didn't follow through very hard on the select committee stuff, though [Bernard] Ingham had a piece whacking me in the *Mail on Sunday*.

Sunday, June 28

TB spent much of the morning on the phone to NI politicians – Trimble, Hume, Adams, [Lord] Alderdice. We briefed on the calls with the message that he was confident the future was strong, and was pleased more than seventy-five per cent of the votes went to pro-GFA parties. We had a conference call, TB, AC, John Holmes, and agreed it would be odd to exclude Paisley so he should try to speak to him too. When he did so, it was a very difficult call and TB sensed Paisley was feeling emboldened to go harder against.

Paisley accused TB of going back on his word when he hadn't, but it was becoming a given that he had said there would be no seat on the executive without actual decommissioning. TB never actually said it but of course for us to do a big number saying he never said it would look like a retreat. Keeping the balance right on these connecting issues was bloody difficult at the best of times, but harder than ever if Paisley was able to drive public opinion. TB sounded really fed up after the call and said he felt we would probably have to go there this week. We went to [daughter of Neil and Glenys] Rachel Kinnock's for lunch and Neil was a lot more relaxed than usual and we had a good time.

Monday, June 29

Health rumbled on. Geoffrey R rumbled on in the *Express*. I suggested to TB that we send him a covering note demanding an explanation to some specifics. I was also of the view, and said so several times, that Hollick's position as a special adviser at the DTI was untenable. He could not be advising the DTI whilst having so many business interests. At the moment he was circling round the *Mirror*.

At the office meeting, TB said he wanted to be able to say that there would be a three per cent real-terms increase in NHS spending for ten years. It was if anything more minimal than what the last lot had been saying, so I was not sure what it would give us. He said the CSR was very tight and we had to get over the fact that there were tough choices to be made, and that prudence was for a purpose, as GB said. But he was worried, I could tell. He said if we were spending any less, it would be a strategy to underspend our way out of power. He backed Dobson's plans for monthly waiting lists, though heaven knows what effort has to go into collating all these figures the whole time.

Peter M was constantly putting an anti-GB slant on things, e.g. saying we were developing a reputation as a 'spend, spend, spend' government, which was bollocks, or on Europe, saying that we were changing our tack, the unspoken point – though articulated many times elsewhere – that GB was trying to face both ways, pro European for the *Guardian/Mirror* lot, anti for Murdoch and the *Mail*. TB was getting exasperated with both of them. He called me in at 12 and said he was in no doubt they were both briefing against each other the whole time. He actually felt his working relationship with GB was fine at the moment. The latest rash followed a *Sunday Times* story – which Peter claimed to have got moved from page 1 to 2 – that GB was trying to block Peter at the Cabinet Office because Peter wanted to use it to build a rival power base. Peston followed it up in the *FT*, as did the *Evening Standard* today. Both Peter and Charlie W swore innocence. TB said he was thinking of moving Peter to DTI, and making Charlie [Falconer] Cabinet Office. I said to be careful of the private school situation, and the Tony crony charge, but he was confident Charlie F would easily see off both because people basically liked him. At the office meeting we also had another hand-wringing conversation about Scotland. Donald D was being savaged daily in the press and was not handling it well, because it was beginning to get to him. But to move him would be to risk a big backlash. The same people savaging him now would suddenly elevate him to the status of Great Scot done in by trendy London Labour.

TB had a meeting with [General Sir Charles] Guthrie re the defence review. Guthrie was said not to be happy with the way it was going and I knew he would find a sympathetic ear in TB. In fact he thought George [Robertson] was doing fine, and just wanted to make a few strategic points himself. GR would be a bit jumpy at the direct access and TB asked me to make sure GR got a good press for the work he had been doing on the review. Oona Muirhead [Director of Information Strategy and News, MoD] called and said George wanted to cancel his planned lunch with journalists to lay the ground tomorrow. I said no, he must, and set the thing out positively as his. This was actually an opportunity to take the modernisation message to the military.

The 11 was all about Drumcree and EMU. The moment I said TB was making a speech tomorrow, it was obvious they were going to overwrite. I told them not to get overexcited but I could tell they would. There was an ongoing debate about whether to hand over any of the tapes of the briefings. Peter Wilkinson felt we had no choice. RW wanted to ask around before taking a view. I was strongly of the view we should not. They were not broadcast quality and they would make hay where none needed or deserved to be made. Lord Alderdice quit [as leader of the Northern Ireland Alliance Party] to become Speaker of the Assembly. I went home to watch Holland vs Yugoslavia [2-1 win for Holland].

Tuesday, June 30

I was up early to get out to go to Frankfurt. The *Guardian* trailed their 'Neighbours at War' piece for tomorrow, so I talked to Seumas Milne to put the positive, creative side to the TB/GB relationship, but it was a struggle to persuade him. They had decided this was the story, and were probably getting plenty of encouragement. There were too many people, and some of them senior, who just talked and gossiped the whole time, and this kind of shit was the result. There was no doubt we were moving to another phase of TB/GB division as the government backdrop. GB was complaining to TB that it was all down to Peter and as things stood, Tony was minded to believe him. But Whelan was at it the whole time, as several of the hacks kept telling me. However, today ended with TB virtually accusing Peter of starting this whole episode off, and Peter exploding, later calling both me and then Anji to say he was sick with the whole thing and was having nothing to do with it. TB said he was getting exasperated with both of them.

In the car to Northolt, TB spoke again to Guthrie while I worked on the ECB speech. We had decided to try to make it a non-story, and used the exact same words as GB used in his last outing on the subject. We had Andrew Turnbull [Treasury permanent secretary], Giles Radice [Labour MP and chairman, Treasury Select Committee] and Helen Liddell on the plane. Turnbull said that even though they had their moments, he thought the TB/GB was the best and most productive PM/Chancellor relationship he had witnessed. Giles said he wanted to be there for the history of the moment, seeing the ECB launched. He could be a bit pompous in manner, but he was basically a decent man and we had a good chat on the plane. Usefully, after we chatted about the subject, he said he would write an article saying the FCO select committee brought the whole select committee system into disrepute.

The launch was not even at the ECB itself but at the opera house where a choir sang fifteen national anthems. They so overdid these things, and every time I saw the Brussels flunkeys wandering around with their little drinks and biscuits and all the rest of the gubbins, I felt this was a project in danger of disappearing up its own arse. I mean, it was a big moment, but they never do these things in a way that might connect with people. Wim [Kok] was even more white-haired than the last time we saw him [two weeks previously]. His wife [Rita] was there, looking a bit fussy. Kohl made what sounded like a valedictory speech.

TB's speech was fine and he had a useful meeting with Bertie Ahern. TB felt we had to pull off something dramatic re Drumcree. He felt Trimble, to his credit, had crossed a Rubicon and was now fatalistic. TB said it was Unionism though, not nationalism, that was in crisis. We were back in London in good time and TB went off to make the party broadcast on the NHS. I did the four o'clock which was pretty desultory because really people were only interested in the football.

I got home to watch England vs Argentina. TB and I spoke several times during the match. He was watching it on his own and as well as us having to prepare a response because of the demand there would be, I think he also just wanted someone to watch it with. At the end we agreed words based on how well they played, and how the courage of their game did not deserve the cruelty of their exit.[1] Rory was not as upset as he might have been. I tried to explain how stupid Beckham's kick had been, how he had let down the whole team, and all the supporters, and how [Michael] Owen was a better role model for aspiring sportsmen.

Wednesday, July 1
Got a nice letter from Betty [Boothroyd] re my select committee appearance. I organised for TB to speak to Glenn Hoddle at 10.50. Hoddle sounded absolutely dreadful. TB was really nice to him, said the whole country was proud of them and the reason people felt so disappointed today was because they deserved to win. Hoddle said they all really had the feeling they could do it. TB said he knew what it was like when you had to back your own judgement against everyone else's, and he picked the right team in the end, they just had bad luck, and Beckham did something silly.

TB saw GB who was still protesting Peter was behind the latest

[1] England lost to Argentina on penalties in the World Cup second-round match after a 2-2 draw. David Beckham had been sent off after one minute of the second half.

rash of articles setting them at odds. TB said to him that he would only ever see one side of this, would not acknowledge that his own people were at it the whole time. GB said why would he do that, how would it help him? I said it helped nobody because it was creating a faultline for the government. GB had his mega-pained expression on, like he was a victim not an aggressor. I said we had to show this relationship working well, and it could not be contrived. The general feeling was the shots of them watching soccer on TV together was a mistake. David Miliband said that the Treasury people were pretty vicious about TB now. GB no longer ever calls him 'Tony' in private, but 'Blair' or, the polite version, 'Tony Blair'.

I was asked about it all at the 11 and the 4 and did my best, but they were not buying it. This was where it became a problem for our and my credibility with the hacks. They were being fed this shit and then I was having to sit there and say they were working together well, most productive team ever, creative force, blah di bloody blah. I was trying to get up the NHS, with a big speech from Dobbo today and TB tomorrow, and this was the other poison of the current situation re TB/GB and the briefing game, that our own agenda got squeezed out.

Today was the first day of the NI Assembly, which was a fantastic achievement, but with a tough backdrop now. Trimble became first minister, [Seamus] Mallon Number 2. TB then did two interviews on England going out of the World Cup, BBC then Sky, and came out with one of the worst sound bites in history – 'a mountain of courage and a molehill of luck'. Yuk. I was almost tempted to start a coughing fit in the hope they would have to do it again. We went over for PMQs, did landmines, Kosovo, bits and bobs. Hague was still away and it was a bit of a non-event.

I had a meeting with Richard W and we agreed to refuse the select committee demand for tapes of the briefings. He said the rest of the Cabinet were growing more restless re the CSR because the Number 10/Number 11 process was holding everything up and taking power from departments. He said he was determined to protect me 'from walking blindfold over a cliff' re the Civil Service. I had to be more careful about the ways of Whitehall, and he would help me. He said I had more authority in Number 10 than anyone but TB but I had to be careful how I used that. I could never tell whether he was being genuinely helpful or currying favour or warning me off things, maybe a mix of all of them. But on balance his advice was worth heeding.

His two big current worries were the economy and Scotland. He felt Scotland was potentially a disaster area for us. I left early for

Rory's football prize-giving at Canonbury. I had a long chat on the way with Martin Clarke at the *Record*. The *Scotsman* had done a leader saying Donald D should be replaced by [Robin] Cook. Clarke said he wanted to get behind Donald, so clearly the call to Montgomery had had some effect. Clarke sounded unbelievably smarmy, called me mate, yuk.

Thursday, July 2

TB's NHS speech was running big and bold overnight. I got in early to go up to the flat and we did the usual last-minute rewrite. He had settled it on being a basic modernisation message. We were discussing again whether he should go to Northern Ireland or not. He spoke to Mo on the phone. She was not keen, but then she always resented the notion only he could sort things. Bertie was really keen for him to go and it was obvious he would. What was extraordinary re Mo was her inability to make a series of points simply, so by the end of the conversation he sort of knew she didn't want him to go but he was hard pressed to explain why.

Cabinet was fairly busy, what with GB going through CSR – or some of it – and then TB and GR setting out the Strategic Defence Review [SDR]. GB went through the numbers, but also said the message was as much modernisation and reform as it was extra spending. So there were targets and standards to be set. It was interesting how those who had been telling me how awfully GB had handled the CSR process said absolutely nothing now. He set out the settlement pretty well, and warned it would require their drive too to take it forward with some real momentum.

Jeremy Paxman had written a letter to *The Times* having a go at my latest whack at the media, and revealed a pretty thin skin. The problem was every time I had a go, the media loved it because it was another excuse to wank on about themselves and how important they were, especially the big-name guys. TB told me to watch I didn't end up fighting too many fights on too many fronts. He said I was in a different position to him. He had protection, not least through people like me, but above all of course because of his position. But I was in a way more exposed and there were a lot of people desperate for me to fall, and people who would help to push if the fall began. I said I understood that but you had to engage with these people, otherwise they would roll you over.

After Cabinet I had a meeting with Harriet to plan the briefing on the CSA [Child Support Agency] plans for Monday. She was clearly keen to present it as an anti-dad thing and TB asked me to keep close tabs on it, and make sure there was an understanding of the dads who could gain. It all became totally academic later when someone leaked what appeared to be the entire fucking contents. I also met the MoD people again to make sure we presented the SDR as a defence story, not a Treasury story. We left at 3 for Northolt, TB not exactly sure what he would do when he got there. Mo and I were both worried he would get trapped into negotiation and never get out of there.

We arrived at Aldergrove and were driven to a burnt-out church [there had been overnight arson attacks on ten Catholic churches]. Fairly big crowds had gathered and they were reserved. There was a real feeling of sadness, and a muteness that went with it. They were not disrespectful, just distant and sad and, when they did get close, clearly longing that he could do something for them. He did a strong doorstep saying this was exactly why we had to choose the path of democracy and dialogue. This was the past and we had to embrace the future.

We left for Castle Buildings. The last time we were there TB and Bertie hailed a great success. Now we were back with another great drama on our hands. Trimble and Mallon seemed to be getting on fine but were both very gloomy. Drumcree was a disaster area. The Orange Order were adamant they would march. The nationalists were adamant the Parades Commission decision should stand. [Brendan] McKenna of the [Garvaghy Road] Residents' Association was milking it for all it was worth. Adams was not contactable, probably because he was seeing IRA people and he would not want his mobile being tracked. We left for Parliament Buildings to see the churchmen, who were frankly pretty useless, really disappointing, lots of hand-wringing and rather needy looks in their eyes. They said they would support us if we had a plan, and they were praying for TB, but they lacked any sense of leadership quality. [Ronnie] Flanagan was full of foreboding. He feared the Loyalists would indiscriminately kill Catholics if the march was stopped. When you heard him say that, you just thought will these people ever ever be able to get on? Were we wasting our bloody time? Adams came up at 8.45 and TB wanted to see him on his own. GA was clearly ready to work towards some kind of compromise. TB felt maybe the march could go down, but with a commission to review re future routes, or a civic forum idea. Then John Hume who was very rambling and repetitive, and said he was anxious.

After the meetings ended, we had a stocktake and agreed it was a risk for TB to get trapped into being an active negotiator, and that we should get back. John Hume felt TB's presence hyped it too much as it was. Mo was really pissed off at the idea she could not just be left to do it on her own. She also feared Flanagan lacked balls. TB had a couple of Scotches and unwound on the flight home a bit. He told a very funny story about a guy at the NHS reception who said that when Thatcher was PM, most Alzheimer's patients could name her as PM, and most still did.

Friday, July 3

TB sent Jonathan to Belfast, and Mo was even more pissed off. Major was on the *Today* programme, and proving yet again what a silly little man he is. How he ever became PM is one of the great mysteries. He had done a speech attacking TB for doing interviews on football and being more interested in the Spice Girls than serious issues. It was an odd thing to say on the day TB did a major speech re the future of the NHS, which got very good coverage today, and was also dealing with Northern Ireland, but it didn't stop him.

After Paxman's go at me yesterday, today [John] Humphrys was at it in the *Mail*, confirming that the risk of me going at these tossers was just giving them a platform. TB said he totally agreed with my argument and my analysis of the media, but I just need to understand how much they will kill me if they can, and whilst that would be a problem for me, it would also be a problem for him. I said I was not going to stop saying what I thought, but I accepted we had to be careful when and how. Fiona thought I should pipe down for a while and stop provoking them. One or two of the friendlier hacks called too and said they thought I should slow down a bit.

I had a stack of meetings – Donald [Dewar], Brian Wilson and Henry McLeish re Scotland, with them wanting help in dealing with the rampant Scottish media. Harriet re CSA. David Clark re the spate of Freedom of Information leaks. I did the Sunday lobby, mainly on rough sleepers, the SDR and CSA, which was a pretty rich meal for them and went fine. I owed George Robertson big time after he managed to find me a really good set of pipes from London Scottish [Territorial Army unit] when I realised I was supposed to be playing at the international evening at school, and my pipes were not seasoned. The media picked up on Jonathan being in Belfast. It was an irritant but of course the real downside was it would send Mo into a mini meltdown. Trouble was TB just didn't think she had the skills needed to hold all the different sides of this together. He felt she just didn't understand how you had to deal with the UUs, and that to call the NIO civil servants 'a bunch of clods' – in front of some of them – was not very clever.

Saturday, July 4

We had absolutely no chance of a quiet weekend with the Drumcree march tomorrow, and a whole new load of Blair/Brown rubbish in the Sundays. TB, Jonathan, John Holmes and I had eight conference calls at various points in the day, most of which led to us then having to do something we had agreed, so we might as well have been in the office. Neither the Irish nor Adams seemed to have any control of [Brendan] McKenna at all, and he was very good at looking and sounding reasonable as he stirred away. TB believed the only way out was to allow a symbolic march, officials only, but John H was sure it would not be possible while McKenna was part of the equation. Jonathan had done a good job talking to the Unionists, and laying the ground, so that we did not have the feared backlash as the reinforcements went in to block the road and make clear the march was not going down. There had to be a real effort to get this sorted for next year. Our basic line was it had to be sorted, and only local entrenchment was stopping us from doing so.

Sunday, July 5

The Sundays were full of even more shite than usual, most of it TB/GB related. Reshuffle, Geoffrey R, Peter M, endlessly stories about the government that were all personality driven. TB said he was actually getting on better with GB than for ages, but the rift was in danger of becoming the driving theme for the whole government. TB was on the whole time, trying to push for local accommodation [re Drumcree] but every time Jonathan came on, even he sounded pessimistic. TB felt if we could get it sorted by the national leaders and churchmen we could do it, but locally it was proving the hatreds were so deep it was impossible. The only story that really bothered me out of the Sundays was the *Observer*, which had claims of their influence by [Derek] Draper, [Ben] Lucas, [Neal] Lawson [lobbyists, former Labour advisers].[1] Also it was reported that Roger Liddle [Downing Street policy adviser] had told the journo who had posed as a businessman that he would help get access. It was probably bollocks but was one of those stories that would fly a bit.

We had three situations on the go – Drumcree, which had the potential to be an absolute disaster area; the *Observer* stuff on lobbying,

---

[1] Claims of favoured access to ministers and advisers by lobbyists Draper, Lucas and Lawson had been reported in the *Observer*. One comment from Draper would come to sum up 'Lobbygate': 'There are seventeen people who count, and to say I am intimate with every one of them is the understatement of the century.'

which we had to grip quickly; TB/GB, which was running through the whole of the Sundays, and after speaking to TB, GB and CW we put out a statement simply saying it was the usual summer party, Sunday made-up nonsense. Peter M called re Derek Draper, said he was a young impressionable working-class boy who felt he had money and influence and didn't know how to handle it. TB, Jonathan, John Holmes and I had a series of calls through the day just trying to keep the Drumcree show on the road, but it was really difficult. There were so few rational people seemingly able to get into the situation and exert influence for the good.

Jonathan was speaking to the Orange Order, John Holmes to the SDLP, and we were just trying to work round McKenna. McKenna had next to nothing to do with the area yet had got in there and was now spoiling for a fight. I watched the start of the march on Sky. They came out of the church, walked peacefully down to the barricades, then back again. It was perfectly good-natured, then up popped McKenna to say that the government and the RUC were not doing enough to stop the march. I called TB and said it was time really to go for him. I called Joe Lennon and we agreed a joint TB/Bertie line welcoming the peaceful nature of the protest, and condemning the provocative and inflammatory language, wherever it came from. We named no names but I briefed PA it was aimed at McKenna.

TB wanted Jonathan to get even more deeply involved in the negotiations which pissed Mo off even more. TB was getting really fed up with her. She was more worried about how she was seen in the equation than actually solving the fucking problem. Lance [Price, special adviser, press office] was dealing with the *Observer* [lobbyists] story and said he felt a head of steam building on it. I was so consumed re Drumcree all weekend that I had probably let my eye wander off the ball on that one.

Monday, July 6

The Roger Liddle stuff was running pretty hard. Liddle called me around 7. He had said to Lance yesterday he did not say the things attributed to him and certainly did not claim to be able to effect introductions. Today he sounded not so sure. I put together a line that there were three serious issues here: 1. select committee leaking (a matter for them), 2. Mansion House speech leaking (nothing proved), and 3. Liddle. I suggested RW should interview him. TB was fine with that, Wilson less so. TB was clear he did not want anything heavy done because there had been no proof of any wrongdoing and his basic instinct was this was just a got up by the press thing. I guessed he had been a bit silly, a bit show-offy and boastful, but it was hardly a sacking offence. But I felt we had handled both Ecclestone and Robinson badly, so we had to get this right. I did not like the feel of Roger's detailed statement on the background.

The eleven o'clock was all about Derek Draper and Liddle. I took them through Roger's version of events, was as calm and moderate as I could be, and then took their questions endlessly. It was hard going. They were determined to present us as being 'as bad as the Tories'. It was obvious we were going to have to put up a minister to deal with it. I briefed Ann Taylor who did extremely well. Draper, because of his lobbying boasts, was in trouble with his company and sacked from his column by the *Express*, so the focus was moving to him. He was not someone I liked overly, or rated, but I did not think he was remotely corrupt, just a bit daft, and I was beginning to feel sorry for him.

I was now into a discussion on the reshuffle – TB, Jonathan, RW, AH, Sally. It was to be Clark, Strang, Harman out, and ten lower down. I didn't think it was enough change. TB felt he could not do Nick Brown because GB would be on the rampage. Some of them were suggesting Margaret B or Jack C but TB felt they had done fine, and it would be too harsh. I was pleased they were staying. Trevor Kavanagh [*Sun*] brought in my lunch and said Whelan told [David] Yelland he ought to get rid of TK and get [Kevin] Maguire or [Patrick] Hennessy [*Evening Standard*]. Talk about winning friends and influencing people. He said Whelan and one or two others were doing real damage to the government's credibility with the media. On EMU, his obsession, Kavanagh said he had heard TB was really angry at the 'Most Dangerous Man in Britain' front page. I assured him it was not the case. I had a meeting with Ed Balls, Whelan and Peter Curwen re the media strategy of the CSR. I was keen to have around it a strategy for dealing with TB/GB as a negative, but their basic line was that as it wasn't a problem, it would look like an overreaction. Ridiculous.

The four o'clock was a re-run of the 11, only worse. The whole session was pretty tough, because they were basically trying to pin Derek Draper on to us, and we just about dealt with it OK. It was going to be *grandes pommes de terre* [literally 'big potatoes'] tomorrow though. The news was really grim. It had slow-burned its way to the top. TB called me and Anji round and said he did not like the feel of it. We had got Jonathan to write to Will Hutton to ask for a copy of the tape from Greg Palast, the reporter from the *Observer*. TB was worried about Liddle and also that Peter M checked Draper's column, which he felt was pretty close in.

I briefed [Clive] Soley who did well on the media, basically saying if Palast could not produce a tape proving Liddle said these things, he should shut up. RW sent TB a note suggesting he issue a warning to Liddle but not sack him. TB was loath to take any real serious action. He said you are talking about ruining a guy's life because of what may turn out to be a crock of shit. It had a bad feel though, and was having an impact on people around the office. I said we would have to tough it out but, if the words attributed to him turned out to be accurate, we would have to sack him. Even that, TB felt, was harsh, but he accepted that was the best way to deal with it.

He came round to my office at 8.15 on his way up to the flat. 'Is this what politics has come to? Some piece of crap in a newspaper creating a frenzy and then saying someone has to go.' He said the media had shifted and even the *Observer* was part of a general desire to do us in now. The more he thought about it, the more he felt we should tough it out. They were trying to get us on division – TB/GB, and on 'sleaze' – [Geoffrey] Robinson, now this – and say we were just as bad as the Tories. It was part of the general degradation of politics. Just as he was going on about it, Alison came in to clear away my trays for the night. 'It's just like the old days,' she said. A French mag said TB was their most popular choice as president. I hoped Chirac saw it.

Tuesday, July 7

I gave a very a strong statement to PA challenging the *Observer* to produce a tape by 11am, or we would assume none existed. [Jon] Sopel called me to say their deputy editor [Jocelyn Targett] had admitted there was no tape. It was still leading the news at lunchtime, but much more on our terms. The papers were absolutely grim, putting this stuff into the same bag as [Jonathan] Aitken and [Neil] Hamilton [disgraced former Conservative MPs]. If we did not halt it pretty soon, there could be lasting damage. PG called to say the same. Once Jocelyn Targett had said there was no tape, we went on the offensive. I got media monitoring to dig up the quote where Palast appeared clearly to suggest there was. We got Peter Kilfoyle out on the media and he did fine. Jonathan and I went up to see TB in the flat and we agreed the line that they had proved nothing in the three areas but because we were a new government we had to be careful, and [Richard] Wilson would draw up new guidelines for those new to government.

I said to TB we were kidding ourselves if we didn't realise there were people who used to work for us who were now in companies pushing on government the whole time, and abusing the circumstances. I was worried TB was just getting into a blame-the-press mode, and maybe blinding himself to some of the things we needed to do, or certainly keep an eye out for. Draper was back in town from Italy and was going to do a statement and interviews. Liddle was in Germany. We were able to push things hard back at the *Observer*. Ed Balls denied their claims. Peter M denied vetting Draper's column.

TB had a rough sleepers' visit, where one or two of them called him a prat, at the end of which he did a doorstep on Ireland, sleaze and trailed the new guidelines. I was really robust at the 11, did all I could to make it about the *Observer* and not us. It was hard going, forty minutes of it, and they were fairly sceptical. Though TB was right it was all being overblown, he was wrong not to take it seriously. They got their facts wrong in the particular, but I reckoned there would be a general situation we should be careful of.

I had lunch with Robert Fellowes and Robin Janvrin. They thanked me again re the Diana week, said I had made a real difference and they were grateful. We talked mainly small talk, a lot of it about Diana. Robert told a hilarious story of a meeting about royal modernisation, so-called, and an idea they should travel on buses. Charles was opposed. We agreed that there was a potential problem with [Deputy Private Secretary to the Prince of Wales] Mark Bolland's ways of working and they should use the Simon Lewis arrival [as communications secretary] to lay down the law and get a grip. They denied anyone there was pushing out the message of disharmony between TB and the Queen.

They were keen for us to do some joint thinking on the [Queen's Golden] Jubilee, and also asked me for my views on how to protect William as he got older. They were clearly worried about the next few years. Their questions were those of people not totally sure of the ground they were standing on. There was a neediness in it all, a sense that there was change happening all around them, and they knew it made for a new world, and they did not quite know what to make of it. They were certainly not brimful of confidence. My sense was they felt strong and secure while the Queen was going strong, but there were tough long-term problems ahead once she had gone. They pretty much shared my analysis of the press.

At the 4, I stayed on the attack re the *Observer* and sensed the heat going out of it. JP called me from Shanghai and said his strong view was Liddle should go. I got home to watch the football [World Cup semi-final, Brazil vs Holland]. [Robert] Peston called at 10 to say he and several others had got hold of the defence White Paper. Oh my

God. How the fuck, after all the leaks last week as well? I got on to George [Robertson] and we worked up a handling plan but I was pissed off with it.

Wednesday, July 8

We were still getting a ferocious hammering in the press, though several did at least concede we had mounted an effective fightback. Draper was now doing too much. He was clearly loving the attention, and making mistakes. He had been far too belligerent on *Newsnight*. Several editorials were saying that my line on the tape issue was a threat to journalism. Oh fuck off. I wrote to them all to point out that it was the *Observer* who made an issue of the tape, not me. I was sure the problem was this nexus of the political and the social, people once fairly close in now trying to trade on it. I had several chats with TB and Jonathan who both thought I was being too puritanical. TB said he accepted there was a problem but you could not stop lobbyists from existing, or attending parties attended by people close to us. I disagreed, and said our people should be under no illusions – I said I believed Liddle did see Draper too often, and did probably say things that would be useful. There was no such thing as harmless gossip.

The Tories were doing quite a good job of getting it up and the hacks seemed to think Hague had his best day in the House yet. TB was fairly calm and measured and I had given him a pretty good rap on the Tories, but Hague was on good form – 'Even with my sinuses I can smell the stench out of these revelations.' TB also fucked up by saying all of the *Observer* allegations were untrue, and I had to clear it up, make clear he meant all of the allegations against the government were untrue.

I went to see RW to tell him of my somewhat Stalinist view, and I would say he was closer to mine than TB's view. TB was more nervous than usual before PMQs, so maybe he did see something wrong here but did not want to admit it too much. The 11 was dominated by the leak of the defence White Paper, which the numpties seemed to think we had leaked ourselves, though how we benefited was beyond me. It later transpired the Tories had been given one at 6pm last night, so the question was whether they got it from a disaffected MoD source or a journalist. Either way, the very good job we had done in planning the publication was now pretty well holed.

I had a meeting with the staff to explain we needed to make sure we were getting TB into situations where he was with people, engaging, being clear we understood the dangers of becoming remote in power, and making sure it didn't happen. George R called at 11.45, saying he had seen the papers and they were terrible re the leak.

Thursday, July 9

Hague got a ludicrously good press and TB a disproportionately bad one. Peter M was also being badly hit by it all. TB and I were again arguing over how serious it was. He tended to see it as a lot of nonsense got up by the press. I felt that though the detail may be wrong, there was enough in the general point for us to be worried about. TB later wrote me a note, which was a rare thing to do, preferring as he normally does just to call me round for a chat. He said he accepted the point, and he did realise it was a problem, but we must not let the press think they can push us around.

Bruce [Grocott] and I had another go at him later to do something more. TB said if Roger had clearly done wrong, he would deal with it, but he was not going to sacrifice someone just because the press was in a frenzy. I agreed with the principle but felt the politics were being ignored. He feared it would look like panic in the face of hysteria and he was having none of it. We were both right in a way. The last thing I wanted was to give a scalp but regardless of the PR problems I thought real problems existed here.

TB had a meeting with the Orange Order, which was particularly difficult. When TB said we could not possibly break our own law, [Revd William] Bingham [Orange Order chaplain] said it was a bad law that said you cannot protest and then started to compare it to a Hitler and the Jews situation. TB took it, but I could tell he was getting angry beneath it all. TB pushed hard to get them to reroute, or wait till September, or limit the numbers. But we were dealing with a very thick brick wall. It was bloody hard work. He emphasised how much he supported their right to march, but they did not share his reasonableness.

Cabinet was mainly Northern Ireland, CSR and a desultory conversation re the lobbying row. TB said the press basically believe we have had too easy a time and are trying to go for us and test us. They cannot do us on policy and so will go for us on the scandal and gossip. The morning briefing was mainly me trying to say we will get on with the things that matter, and them going on about Liddle and whether TB was depressed about PMQs yesterday.

I had a one-hour session with GB re the CSR, then another one with Charlie and Ed. On form, as he was in part of the meeting as he set out the big-purpose stuff, money for modernisation, tough choices, GB was as impressive as ever. But he could also be a night-mare, picking on a small point of argument and obsessing. He was pushing a bit re Liddle, but in general seemed keen to repair TB relations, and to get out tough messages on pay. The health and education numbers were OK, plus he had the free eye tests for pensioners and the science investment, strong stuff on public sector pay, tough efficiency targets, more for pensioners, child benefit reform. It was a pretty strong package, and covered a big sweep of things. He also wanted a new committee to monitor all this and keep the focus on targets being met.

The Tories were on to a story about Liddle having a blind trust handled by his neighbour. Jonathan seemed to think it didn't matter, which suggested a judgement lapse. Wilson was less sanguine. In atmospheric terms, this was getting sleazy. TB didn't like the sound of the blind trust. But he said we must not let the media set the agenda. I had been meant to be working on Drumcree and instead spent most of the day dealing with this stuff. It was a real drain on energy. Peter M came round and I said I thought this was worse than Formula One. F1 was perception whereas this was real. Peter looked fed up but said I was just too puritanical and it was not as bad as all that. Roger looked ridiculous on the news.

Friday, July 10

A genius piece of spin by Whelan on the front page of the *Mirror*, a story that the [Hugh] Pym book was saying I threatened to quit if CW was sacked over the EMU debacle. It wasn't true but it was not worth denying, because I had always said it would have been wrong for him to have carried the can. Why it was effective was that it played into TB/GB riftology in a subtle and different way, it stuffed the *Sunday Times* serialisation and it boosted Whelan. There had been some bad violence against the police in NI overnight and we got TB to do a clip with [Robin] Oakley which led the news at lunchtime.

I did a very long CSR briefing for the Sundays, which went fine and which made me think when we were focused on the stuff that mattered, we were fine. I felt the steam going out of the lobbying stuff. Jonathan and John Holmes were working flat out trying to get a plan for indirect contact talks between the Orange Order and the Garvaghy Road Residents' Association. Eventually we were in a state to send letters to both. We thought we had real progress; the sign of engagement, a venue etc. I called a 4.30 briefing to go through it and it was leading the news straight away. It was a case of taking the initiative and going with it. It was high risk though because it was so capable of being rejected. It became more and more clear that McKenna was the problem. He just didn't want to be co-operative. He said a venue for a meeting had to be Portadown as he would not be safe in their areas. He was basically giving us the runaround. I lined up [Clinton's Mike] McCurry and [Ahern's Joe] Lennon to be positive in response to what we were doing.

I was knackered by the end of the day. I hated Fridays because I had the going into the weekend feeling but knew the weekend would probably be consumed with work too. I was enjoying the NI stuff but was juggling too many things at once. I felt we could use the CSR to get the TB/GB show back on track. We went round for dinner at Philip [Gould] and Gail's. Peter was also there, full of his usual paranoid obsessiveness re GB. He basically presented GB as the root of all evil, with no redeeming features. I said it had to stop, that until one of them took the lead in just stopping it, it would be permanently destabilising. Peter defended Roger and Derek too much, perhaps because I was pretty tough on them.

Saturday, July 11

And so to one of those dreadful weekends that drive me mad. The Sundays were resisting our efforts to get them interested in the CSR, which actually involved things that would affect every single person in the country, instead continuing to obsess with lobbying. But Drumcree was again dominating our lives, a never-ending round of calls that led pretty much nowhere. Jonathan was there and was trying to get the talks moving. McKenna was a total pain in the neck, but eventually we got things under way. TB, Jonathan, John Holmes and I had a series of conference calls to work out at every stage where to take it. It was really tough. Anyone landing from Mars would wonder how on earth we could be arguing about this so intensely but it was about as hard as anything we had to deal with. You were dealing with something that looked simple but beneath the surface was really complex. Jonathan said the Orange Order were happy to talk up to midnight but then we would be into the Sabbath and they would have to stop. Then it would be on to the march on Monday. TB was getting really worried we would be into major violence and political crisis fairly soon. The best we could say was that we were pleased dialogue had opened.

McKenna was pretty much driving the media agenda, with the Orange Order making their usual noises. I listened in to a couple of TB calls where he was being pushed for the march to go down, but stood firm. Jonathan was doing a good job keeping things ticking over but it was hard there. I wanted to go on the attack against McKenna who was a nasty piece of work but TB was keen to keep the pressure on the Orange Order, which we did. The last call I took was just after midnight and meanwhile I was dealing with the Sundays over the wretched lobbying stuff too.

Sunday, July 12

Jonathan called to tell me three young children had been killed in Ballymoney [County Antrim]. It was a terrible thing to think, but it was true, that this would turn the mood, and the reality was we had to help it in that direction. People would think this had all gone too far and hopefully want to pull back. I spoke to TB and we agreed he would do words of condemnation. Then Jonathan called again and said the Revd Bingham, the Orange Order chaplain, was going to say in his sermon that people should get off the hill and go to their homes. It was crazy that it took these deaths to move people.

I called [Mike] McCurry to get another Clinton statement out. TB called and said we should put out fresh words saying people really needed to look at themselves and the consequences of their words and actions. The four of us had half a dozen conference calls through the day. Jonathan said Trimble and Mallon were meeting the Orange Order and were going to go up there to try to persuade people off the hill. The death of three children had become the catalyst for a major change of mood. Flanagan was excellent, in private and in his public statements.

TB was thinking he might need to go there tomorrow. He felt we had to move to build on this change of mood. He was worried some of them were so mad that they would go back fairly quickly. He spoke to DT, Adams and Mo, and took soundings. Bingham's words were excellent, Trimble did well and we had to keep the momentum now. The media had totally changed tack. The Unionists were spreading a rumour that the murders were domestic, not sectarian. What a jerk. In between it all I tried to watch the World Cup Final [France beat Brazil 3-0]. Chirac was milking it for all it was worth.

Monday, July 13

The day Margaret Beckett had a £1.1 billion allocation for science to announce – and it did not make a single bulletin. There was a rare nice piece about me in the *Mail*, by Lord Hanson [Conservative-supporting businessman]. I'd only met him once for a proper chat but it seemed to be enough for him to want to defend me in print, which was nice of him. Peter M was taking a big hit in the press and looked very subdued at the morning meeting. I still felt TB had his head in the sand re sleaze issues. TB was kicking Peter a bit while he was down, saying at the office meeting that his briefing war with GB had to stop, that it was doing real damage to the government and he no longer believed any of their protestations that it was all the other one. When Peter M tried to make a coded attack on GB at one point, TB snapped 'Peter – enough. I am not having this.'

At the end of the meeting he asked Peter to stay back, and gave him a real talking to, which wound Peter up even more, and he was trying to get me and Anji back on his side against GB again. I was sick of it, but Anji and Peter Hyman were more sympathetic to his claim. Philip and I tried to persuade TB again that he had a real as opposed to perceived problem with some of these sleaze issues and we needed to show we were different, and do more. He said it was important we did not sacrifice strength. There would be times when people in the media created these storms and the best we could get out of it all was strength. I agreed in principle but was worried he had a bit of a blind spot about people close to us doing things he and the people really close to him would never dream of doing. I had a meeting with Jan Polley [Cabinet Secretary's office] checking out the claim in the [Hugh] Pym book that [David] Butler asked TB to investigate the claim that Ed Balls briefed the Budget in advance.

GB and TB were working together on the CSR statement, and seemed to be going fine. GB was also working better with me at the moment, presumably because he realised Peter was out of favour at the moment. Philip sent me a note saying that I should become more public not less, as was being urged by some, and that Peter should move out of the centre. The statement was looking good but TB was a bit worried the Treasury would spin it too much in the spend, spend, spend direction.

Tuesday, July 14

CSR day. TB and I were both still worried about spend spend spend, especially as Whelan was planning to accumulate the spending figures. TB met GB early for a long meeting to finalise the statement. They were definitely working better at the moment. Both TB and I made suggested changes to the text which he accepted straight away, without the usual angst. He even asked before Cabinet if I could look at the final draft and write in any changes. I faxed them over and he called to say he had got them. It could be he was just looking to get me in the right frame of mind to push for him after the event.

At Cabinet GB rattled through it all at pace, good figures on the surplus, debt/GDP ratio improving, interest rates by the end of the parliament £15bn lower than we inherited. He said the main themes were investment for reform, money for modernisation. He said AD would be setting out an internal process of continuous scrutiny of spending. There would be tough efficiency targets. There would be an expansion of public-private partnerships. He set out the tough package on welfare reform, the new deal for communities, a pilot of Educational Maintenance Allowances, Sure Start. More money for the key public services but it had to be tied to reform. TB thanked them all for the co-operative approach, at which some of them – especially those who felt bounced – had a little look at each other or a shake of the head. He reiterated the key messages, especially money for modernisation. He said the Tories have opted out of the policy debate, but we still have to take on the difficult choices and explain them. He said we had to be emphasising the long term. We were being tough for these two years, laying the foundations, and we had to set out that narrative clearly, be clear where it was all leading. There were strong political dividing lines that had to be laid out. Public spending can be good not bad. But people need to know where money is being spent, what it is delivering. We have to get definition out of this. After Cabinet I briefed some of the best lines out of it, and they were beginning finally to get a feel for the scale of what he was planning to announce. If anything, there was as much as in a Budget but because it was a new process, they were not quite on to the scale or the breadth yet. The official Treasury background papers, as ever, were detailed and impressive. So was GB in the House. He had real reach, and the thing hung together well. Our side liked it and the Tories did not respond well. They were totally wrong-footed by the sheer scale of it, the numbers, the number of issues covered, the changes being made.

Ed Balls and I did a briefing in the lower gallery but it had been well set up and news-wise was pretty much taking care of itself. The only thing I found difficult, which I had spotted in advance and agreed the line with GB, was the fact that social security spending would rise in the third year. We had to work up an argument about spending on waste and investing in the fight vs poverty. The day had taken care of itself pretty much, and gone well. GB spoke to lots of the editors and leader writers, most of whom were buying the package. I was even able to leave around 8, feeling we had had a good day.

Wednesday, July 15

We got a great press for the CSR, mainly on health and education but the big-picture narrative was there too. I was in early and into the flat to prepare with TB for his round of interviews. He was still worried about spend, spend, spend, and also that the welfare package wasn't tough enough. I had warned TB/GB yesterday that I was worried the headline social security figures would be a problem, unless we really made an effort to explain. I felt GB and Ed were a bit blasé about it, they said it would not be noticed, but were wrong. The *Mail* was straight on to it. Others were following up today.

TB did half a dozen interviews, all of which were fine. We did a school visit, then a phone-in, and he warmed up as it went on. A nurse and a teacher gave him a really hard time and I felt he was a bit defensive and non-empathetic, but it was OK. We reckoned Hague would do welfare at PMQs, and he did. TB had all the figures, but it all ended up a bit statty and yah-boo and we didn't get the big message booming through. It was a score draw, though TB did a very enjoyable splattering of Michael Fabricant [Conservative MP]. TB and GB wanted me to push the line that there was bad welfare spending and good welfare spending, we were dealing with one and expanding the other. TB was fretting, as he always does after these big events, using that nervous energy to keep us focused and our eyes on the ball. There was a fair bit of TB/GB-ology in the papers, but TB seemed fine about it. He said, I don't care if these people say he is a powerful Chancellor. I don't want anyone thinking he is an Old Labour Chancellor. We were definitely back in charge of the agenda for a while.

Thursday, July 16

I spent most of the day trying to sort the visit to Scotland tomorrow, including a pretty chunky advance briefing. Donald D called in and was clearly a bit panicky, worried we would totally upstage him on health and Nat-bashing. I did my best to assure him that one of the prime aims was to build him. Cabinet was mainly post-CSR and NI. TB said he felt the modernisation message needed to be pushed harder. He said we have a broad coalition of support that will stay with us provided they feel money is well spent. We will be subject to two attacks – if the economy goes down, what then? And we have gone soft on modernisation because we just believe in spending per se. We need to deal with both. He said our right-wing opponents want to try to separate Labour from modernisation – say that you can only modernise if you betray, or if you destroy the Labour Party. That is a convenient argument for them because it has kept them in power most of our lives. We have to be clear that modernisation is the route to the fulfilment of our social justice and other Labour objectives.

TB felt the Tories were in deep shit though – [David] Willetts [Shadow Education and Employment Secretary] was basically saying he wanted MORE spent. They do not know which way they are going. [Francis] Maude [now Shadow Chancellor] is saying spend less, spending ministers are saying spend more. GB said we had achieved something we had not done with a Budget – got the agenda framed totally as planned, on our terms, and we had to capitalise on that. People want to say you can either be prudent or invest in public services. We are showing you can do both. We have to keep empha- sising reform and modernisation – if we don't, the Tories will make the debate all about the size of the state. Chris Smith said at one point 'Do the public like the word modernisation?' and before he could answer his own question, TB just said 'Yes' and moved on.

I had to do a speech to the top civil servants at the Civil Service College, where I did my usual spiel, which went OK, but I felt only some of them really got what I was on about. I was mainly focusing on the Scotland trip at the four o'clock. As I went up the little spiral staircase to the lobby room in the House, Tony Benn was there filming something about Parliament, and he wanted to come in – or said he did and probably hoped I would say no. I said I was absolutely fine about it, it was the traditionalists in the lobby who would probably baulk. He said he had not been in there since he was a minister himself. I had a pretty spiky set of exchanges with the Scottish press because TB had yesterday talked about 'middle Scotland' and Catherine MacLeod [*Herald*] was saying we were playing to the Nats' agenda by talking about what it meant to be Scottish. It was very hard to have a rational debate with them.

The draft speech was a mish-mash and Pat [McFadden] and I had a session to try to knock it into shape before showing it to him. TB wanted a tough message. He said we had to face the Scots up to the reality of the choice – separation or partnership. DD and Pat both wanted something more cautious, that just set out what we aimed to deliver, but TB said there was no point. He felt we had to have a big argument rooted in substance not spasm and emotion. The best way to challenge the Nats' agenda was to expose it for the policy-free zone it was, and force people to face the consequences of supporting them. Peter Hyman and Douglas Alexander both thought the draft was too Old Labour, but TB thought the balance was fine. He did not mind the trad grace notes provided the main tune coming through was clearly New Labour, and challenging.

TB, Peter M and I had a meeting to discuss the 'spin' problem. There was no doubt it was hurting and the focus on the spin side of things was growing. I was getting a bit alarmed just how much focus there was on me personally. It would help when Peter M moved to a department, but I said we had to get rid of Charlie [Whelan] who I felt was the one that gave the media licence to tar us all. We had to persuade GB he was being damaged by this. Pat and I worked till late on the speech and then we set off for the sleeper train. Even though the bed was too short, I slept reasonably well.

Friday, July 17

We arrived at half six, straight to the hotel to work on the speech. Alex Salmond was wall-to-wall on the media, saying two rather inconsistent things: 1. that TB had been forced to come up to save the Labour Party, and 2. he was a total liability. He was a very good message deliverer, but sometimes too good. There was something too obvious when you heard him say literally the same thing, with exactly the same force and intonation every time. We agreed we had to take on the arguments about separatism head-on, so we inserted far tougher language, including the line that we had to smoke out the SNP on their policy of separatism. TB felt confident if people felt their real agenda was separatism, only the emotionalists would really stay with them.

TB did some radio where he started to use the argument, as he did at a more than usually friendly breakfast with the Scottish editors. When TB started to put the fundamental point – separation or devolution – I could sense them all pretty much agreeing with them, and the more Nat-orientated among them feeling edgy as they saw an argument it was hard to defeat. Their questions were not rooted in substance but polls, presentation, a few local council issues, and TB was able to say that on the big argument involved here, there was no coming back at him. That was why we were confident as the argument was taken forward. Afterwards he said we should come back in the near future, but maybe for three days, and really take the argument on and force the SNP to respond with more than sound bites. At the moment their line was that TB had come up from London – they made it sound like Mars – because his party in Scotland was hopeless. They were able to avoid the debate being about them because it was all about us.

I was working on a script for the Sundays as we left for Dundee. Lorraine Davidson [Scottish Labour communications director] was getting a bit exasperated with Donald. She said she had tried to get him to use the same kind of messages TB was doing, but he always held back and made it all a bit cerebral. He didn't really like going for the SNP hard. At a press event yesterday he said he was not reading a script she had done because it was too tough on the SNP. She said he also took his shirt tail out to clean his glasses. We went back to Edinburgh for a meeting with Alex Rowley [Labour general secretary in Scotland]. Pat and I had substantially redrafted as a result of the morning mood, and the way the central message went through well, and the speech went well. Both [Scottish Parliament] candidates and media liked it. It was a substantial serious speech with a strong and clear message.

The message we were getting from the Scottish party was we needed to be more traditional and play to the Jock agenda etc. But Philip G said the groups he did showed the opposite – they liked TB and wanted us to be more New Labour not less. He said the SNP were worried about TB as a weapon up there. On the plane down, I was reading the transcripts of the [Rupert] Allason case. What a shit. I was really angry that I was having to go through this again. Harriet was leading all the bulletins so we had had another post-CSR hit. It showed that when we worked well with GB, and we planned properly, we could do it easily. The Tories were nowhere.

Saturday, July 18

Jonathan called from Belfast and said the talks were back on. We agreed a statement which I put out straight away. Otherwise it was a fairly quiet day. I had a row with Andy Grice because he said unless I told him definitively who was getting the Cabinet Office job, he was going to do a story that JP, DB and JS had complained to TB re the GB control-freakery. The Sundays had bought far too much into the 'spend, spend, spend' line and I was having to row back some of the commentators. The problem had been Frank [Dobson] and to a lesser extent DB's statements, the tone of which was just a bit more spend-y and less modernisation than GB's or TB's interviews.

Sunday, July 19

Jonathan was on a few times re Drumcree, which he seemed to think was in a better place. I sifted through the papers – too much TB/GB, too much spend, spend, spend, and too much pre-reshuffle bollocks. I told TB that I reckoned a good share of the reshuffle stories came from Whelan. The problem was sometimes less what he said, but the fact they saw him as a rival source who on all this personality stuff was far more forthcoming than I was. Tessa [Jowell] told me she would rather stay at Health in the job she was doing than be promoted to the Cabinet in a different department. *Sunday Times* had a big page 3 number of Cherie wearing a pendant that was supposed to ward off evil spirits and harmful rays, which was the kind of thing that would be picked up by everyone and connect big time. I said to Fiona she had to get a hold of all this madder stuff but she said Cherie never raised it with her because she knew she would disapprove. TB said they had to be slightly mad to cope. He was very sympathetic to Cherie doing this alternative bollocks because he thought it was her way of coping.

Monday, July 20

Philip G told TB at the office meeting that he felt New Labour took a bit of a hit last week. We had lost some of the New Labour part of the coalition. We had to now get Hague pinned into a corner where he was 'all spending, bad spending', to win an argument about investment and good spending. PG frightened TB a bit and he came back to it several times during the day, the point being that spend, spend, TB/GB simmering tensions, and worries re the economy meant that while in political media terms we had got back momentum, we might have done so at the expense of New Labour definition, which was damaging for TB.

Re the reshuffle, TB was now thinking Jack Cunningham at the Cabinet Office, with Charlie F below him. He said if he pushed out four, with the prospect of another five next year, that was a pretty big reshuffle. I sensed he was getting cold feet re getting rid of Nick Brown, because of GB, and also because he didn't want Nick's organisational skills being run against him. He didn't really know what to do with Frank Dobson, but hadn't been impressed with how he had handled Health. He was thinking he should leave Steve Byers and Alan Milburn where they are. He wanted to give Field some kind of all-party welfare fraud job. Philip had also said he was worried we were going a bit cold on welfare reform, which people really wanted to see. PG had done another poll in Scotland, which confirmed that TB and New Labour were what we needed there. Clinton announced his NI visit which ran pretty big. TB popped round on his way up to the flat and ran through his current concerns – economy, GB/Peter M, reshuffle, CSR fallout, conference. He said conference had to be effectively a relaunch of New Labour. That was how we should be thinking over the holiday.

Tuesday, July 21

JP got a pretty grim press for the transport White Paper and as I said to him when he called to complain about it, it was in part because they had not really devised and shared a communications plan. TB was not happy with it and called JP to say so, said we had not really been kept in the loop on either the overall strategy or the statement, and this was the result. There had even been some last-minute changes to the document itself. JP was upset, as he always was when he got a direct bollocking from TB. The other story was Lockerbie. Some idiot had briefed the *Guardian* that we were moving the line and would be willing to go for a trial in The Hague. Jonathan, John H and I had a conversation and agreed it was untenable to say nothing, so we agreed to push the line on and say now this was likely. There were US, UK and Dutch officials meeting on it in The Hague today so we had to go with it. But it would have been a lot better to get the detail sorted first. It was a classic piece of show-off leaking which didn't actually achieve anything.

I called Mike McCurry just after 5am US time and we agreed we didn't need to push too hard, just go with 'exploring all options' but not specifically confirm or deny. Meanwhile Madeleine Albright was speaking to US relatives of victims who were far less happy than ours about a third-country trial. TB was still mulling the reshuffle, and also post-CSR definition. He had written a long piece for the *Telegraph* which I had to cut while he went off to see the Azerbaijan president re some new oil contract.

I left with [David] Bradshaw for a meeting with Charles Gray [QC] and the lawyers re [Rupert] Allason, with the case starting tomorrow. We went through all the evidence and also some of the lines of attack he would try. Gray thought he would basically try to get me to lose my temper, and also to range more widely than the evidence, e.g. he had briefed *The Times* he was going to ask me re me and GB. Gray said he would step in at the first sign, but judges did tend to let people conducting their own case have a bit more leeway.

Bradders [David Bradshaw] was really worried about the whole thing but I felt he would be a totally credible witness. Gray felt Allason did not have much of a case and if he really went for me politically, he felt confident the judge would step in. Jonathan was off to Drumcree again. I went to collect Calum who had been up to Manchester with [friend] Jan and his mum and had taken it upon himself to call on Alex [Ferguson].

Wednesday, July 22
A combination of PMQs and the *Telegraph* article allowed us finally to get up a proper argument about the Tories and spending. Alex F called after yesterday's surprise visit from Calum, who he said had

been very good. Nigel Griffiths [DTI minister and ally of GB] in the
Edinburgh Evening News saying Michael Scholar [permanent secretary,
DTI] was doing him in, even though he was a good minister. I sensed
people needed a holiday. I didn't push the boat out in defending him.
I briefed the Scots on the plan for a longer visit and then chaired a
meeting on the annual report, which could still be good.

Thursday, July 23

The big story was the overnight House of Lords vote on gay sex last
night.[1] Thanks to a hostile media and opportunistic Tories we were
being pinned as though it was a government measure. We had a
hostile media coming at us from one angle and the gay community
on the rampage and vile about it too. TB and I had a conference call
with Jack Straw and agreed that the best outcome was that the PLP
agreed we drop the amendment and let the Crime and Disorder Bill
go through. JS, who had a close friend at school who was gay and
killed himself because of the persecution, was keen to get it back but
TB was clear this was not doing us any good at all.

I chaired the 9am meeting and asked CW for lines on Rover, which
was shedding 1500 jobs, for the 11.30 briefing but they never came.
I sent over a pretty vicious note to Whelan saying he and Peter Curwen
should be at the morning meeting. I was keen to do both briefings
today despite being in court. Cabinet kicked off with a discussion of
the gay-sex vote. TB said the bottom line must be we do not lose the
bill. We must not even delay the date of royal assent. George
[Robertson] said special forces had picked up two indicted war criminals in Prijedor [Bosnia]. They were identical twins claiming not to
be who we thought they were. RC diddled around on Lockerbie, and
then GB had another little go on the economic argument, which I felt
we still did not have clear.

Martin Cruddace [*Mirror* lawyer] came down to talk the [Allason]
case over, and then we heard there was a delay. We went up there later
and hung around Court 13. It was not one of the main courtrooms,
which no doubt annoyed Allason who would have been expecting a
grand stage. There were a lot of press there and I just avoided talking
to any of them, even the ones I knew well. And I managed to stay out
of Allason's way most of the time. I was getting psyched up, going
over all the possible questions and though I was nervous I felt confident at the same time. By the time I went in, I was pretty calm.

[1] The Lords rejected, by 290 votes to 122, government plans to lower the homosexual age of consent from eighteen to sixteen.

Allason was poor. I read out my statement and in the questions Allason signalled his intentions too obviously and was slapped down. I was sitting on a chair that was too high, and very close to the judge and I could feel his eyes bearing down on me when I was answering Allason. The problem with this case was that it would in many respects be our word against his and [maverick Labour MP George] Galloway's. He tried to stray off course e.g. asking me what Bradshaw thought, or about a recent *Spectator* article, but he didn't get far. At the end though I felt it might have been better if he had gone at me harder, because I didn't really feel I got my case across properly. I had a slight moment of panic when he thought he spotted a contradiction in my previous evidence from the last trial. But I got out fine and I could feel on leaving the court that the press felt cheated. Neither from him nor from me did they get the fireworks or the story they were hoping for.

I got straight out, briefed myself for the four o'clock on the way back and went straight into the briefing. It was mainly all gays again, Nigel Griffiths again, then back to Number 10 for a long, rambling and inconclusive meeting with Richard Wilson, Jonathan, David M, Jeremy Heywood, Geoff Mulgan and Andrew Adonis [policy adviser] on Wilson's report on the centre. It was a bit of a mush. Truth be told they were not really up for much change at all, and they couldn't decide if they wanted a stronger centre or not. So it was neither one thing nor the other, and RW looked hurt when I pretty much said as much.

We then had a reshuffle meeting, where Anji was pressing for a much bigger reshuffle, but TB felt it was big enough already. He had settled on Harman out, Field out, though he was still thinking about giving him something outside government, which we were all against. The real discussion was how GB would take it, particularly the move on Nick Brown. We were pressing him to be bold but he said 'I'm just telling you there is a case to be cautious if it all ends up with GB offside.' What would be any different, I asked?

TB said you have to remember we are co-creators of New Labour, and I do not want him offside. We have come this far together in part because of his nous and political skills and I want to keep them inside the operation. With Peter M and others in, and four out, you are talking a big reshuffle and I do not want a war with GB out of it. If we lose Geoffrey Robinson, Nigel Griffiths, Tom Clarke, Harriet H, and Nick Brown moved, the PLP will see it as a bit of a hit on GB. I do not want them to see it as an all-out attack. He was clearly dreading the day. I hate reshuffles, he said. You just have to steel yourself but they are horrible.

Only *The Times* and the *Indy* did much with the Allason case. Most saw it for the nonsense it was. Gray thought my evidence went well. The media had a lot around the place re economic problems, not just Rover, and later on the train back from Sedgefield a couple of guys gave me a really hard time re manufacturing. I was working on trying to take yesterday's meeting on the centre plus the annual report and turn it into a briefing note for the Sundays. TB had heard GB on the radio this morning and wasn't impressed. He felt he [TB] explained our message on the economy far more clearly and in a way people could understand. GB had a propensity to complicate.

We flew up north with [Lionel] Jospin. We had worked up a football initiative which Jospin liked. He was actually quite well informed re football in England. They talked defence restructuring on the way up and also had a chat re Germany. TB sensed the French and the Germans were not getting on great at the moment. They talked about whether to have a trilateral summit before the German elections, and went over what they thought of Schroeder. I tried to get him going re the way Chirac milked the World Cup Final, almost wrenching the trophy out of the players' hands, but Jospin was very diplomatic.

We did a number of visits and I think it worked taking visiting leaders out of London like this because people outside London were more interested in seeing them. They did a doorstep on football, and TB did a strong clip on the economy. He fucked up his French at one point, when he seemed to suggest he fancied Jospin. Later at the restaurant Jospin said 'the cook was delicious'. There were around forty French hacks there and they seemed to be enjoying it. I briefed them down at the [Trimdon] Labour club. I said they got on well and could not understand why everyone reported the opposite. The atmospherics were pretty good. They both had a pint at the Dun Cow [Inn, Sedgefield], salmon then Toulouse sausages, then down to business – future of Europe, need to change the Commission, Schroeder's chances, EMU.

Most of our press had stayed in London so I did a briefing by phone into the lobby room. They were all pressing me on who would get the Cabinet Office job, which after my briefing was being built up as a big thing. They assumed it would be JP, Peter M or Mo. I got Godric to drop in Jack Cunningham, Jack Straw and Frank Dobson so that we could at least get Jack C's name into the mix so it would not be a total shock. It was interesting to watch the French operation today. They didn't really manage their media and Jospin was allowed to do the press conference without really being briefed about where they might be coming from. On the train back I heard the Allason case result was being reserved. Reshuffle speculation was going crazy. Robert Harris in the *Standard* said GB/Peter M were behaving like children.

Saturday, July 25
It was going to be a difficult weekend because of all the reshuffle stuff. I guess I had broken 'no comment, never comment on reshuffles' by talking up the beefed-up Cabinet Office and a new minister. I wanted Jack C at least to be in the mix, so we were putting out a number of different names that it might be. I was talking up JC's handling of BSE and the [EU] presidency, in which agriculture was one of the hardest areas to chair. The other angle being run was that GB and Peter M were not really being consulted, that Jonathan and I were the only ones who really knew what was in his mind.

TB called me around lunchtime to say his current plan was Ann Taylor to chief whip, Margaret Beckett to Leader of the House, Nick Brown to MAFF, Byers to chief secretary, Jack C to CO, Peter M to DTI, Margaret Jay to be Leader of the Lords, with [Alan] Milburn, [John] Denham or [John] Reid to Transport. The *Telegraph*, one of Frank Field's fanzines, had a story saying he would quit if he wasn't given the top job and that he was constantly blocked from being radical. It was the exit strategy he had warned me of. It was the usual balls and I wished we could get out the story that he had wimped out on welfare reform, but TB felt it was probably too late. He would be martyred if we just kicked him out and dumped on him.

TB spoke to both GB and Peter M about the recent coverage. He said re Harris' article that it was like he was inside his mind – it was absolutely right that if they did not get their act together, one or both of them would have to go. GB was worried about the economy at the moment so was leaning on TB a bit more, looking for support. TB said there are only two ways to go – enemies or together, at one or not there at all. He also wanted me to push the idea of him, GB and Byers as a force for modernisation where the spending decisions are being made, driving through the key decisions from the CSR, and matching money for modernisation.

TB was really starting to focus on the reshuffle, the practicalities. He said the history of Labour's problems in power was one of egotism and division. He felt at the moment we had no real political differences but we had massive egotism. He was horrified when I told him re Frank Field in the *Telegraph*. TB said the truth was FF was nowhere near as radical as GB. GB was now pushing for Alistair D to go to

DTI instead of Peter. We were also discussing whether Margaret B could double as party spokesperson. She could certainly do a lot of cross-cutting media from Leader of the House. JP called and asked for a meeting. He was in a foul mood re TB's 'for your eyes only' letter complaining about the handling of the White Paper. He said he was always happy to co-operate with me, but now he would just do his departmental job and none of the other stuff e.g. campaigning, deputising. I said he shouldn't overreact to TB's letter. It had been a bit of a dog's dinner and he himself had admitted that. All TB was saying was we did better when we were working together properly.

Sunday, July 26

The general response from the hacks re Jack C at the Cabinet Office was very positive. TB asked me to call Ann Taylor and ask her to be down by 4.30 to see him. I had done a detailed note on logistics and also on key messages, e.g. re women, TB strong centre, New Labour. It was a strong reshuffle and would be seen positively for TB but he was worried re GB's reaction, particularly the move for Nick Brown. JP called and asked if it was true re JC. I said yes. He said 'You're not expecting him to do much work, are you?' I felt with JC, Charlie [Falconer] as Minister without Portfolio, and Peter Kilfoyle [Defence], it was a pretty strong team. Anji and I were due to be in by 4 and we had a session to steel him re Harriet and re Nick. He said the thing with Nick in the end was not just his closeness to GB but his quirks and prejudices, e.g. dislike of women and hatred of some MPs.

Ann Taylor arrived and was in with TB for a short while, after which he called in me, Jonathan, Sally M, Anji, Jeremy Heywood and Bruce Grocott. We had the list now and we started to motor. Ann thought MB would be fine with the move, but would hate being replaced by Peter. TB was not looking forward to the sackings. We agreed that [Charles] Clarke and [Patricia] Hewitt were the only ones from the new intake who might go straight in. We spent maybe three hours going through the list. TB settled on [John] Reid at Transport as an arch moderniser under JP.

TB went to see GB at 8. I was called up at 8.45. TB was in the kitchen getting a drink so GB was sitting alone in the falling darkness in the study. He looked really gloomy, and said nothing. I tried a few pleasantries but he was not engaging. TB had just told him – Nick B moved, Geoffrey [Robinson], [Nigel] Griffiths, Tom Clarke out, Ann Taylor chief whip. TB said how do we stop this reshuffle being seen as a blow to GB? I said it needn't be because there were enough big stories in here. The problem was less the reshuffle than the backdrop of the GB/Peter stuff. I said Charlie [Whelan] had made it worse by getting so involved in the pre-briefing, saying what GB did or did not want. TB said he and GB were getting on better but it still didn't come over like that. Again I said Charlie was the problem. GB didn't argue, but he was clearly worried the reshuffle would be portrayed as a big negative for him. It was clear TB was trying to keep him totally onside, and was currently very much siding with him vs Peter, to whom he had not spoken for days.

We agreed TB should see Nick tonight and GB said he would work on him to accept it as a good move. He wasn't really arguing with the decisions, and even said he had reached pretty much the same conclusions, but he was worrying re his own place in this. He was pacing around the room, and picked up a bit as we went on, because he could at least see TB and I did not want to use it to do him down. TB also spoke to Peter M and said he wanted him to meet GB tonight and sort a few things out. He said if they did not work together he would have to take drastic action, because he was not prepared to let them bring the whole show down. He said it was all about egotism and it had to stop. He also agreed I could brief that he had told Peter he had to knuckle down and do a proper job properly. JP came in and we went through the junior ranks all over again. TB was now having a wobble re Harriet, said that it would seem really cruel given she had been basically loyal the whole way through. He wanted me to indicate she still maybe had a future. Likewise he wanted to be nice to Frank [Field] and try to avoid him attacking us in the *Mail* and the *Telegraph* every day. We were thinking of some grand think tank on fraud that he might be able to run.

Jonathan was calling round the Cabinet and drawing up a timetable. He had to speak to David Clark several times because David was trying to delay what he knew was the inevitable. He said he had a dental appointment and would rather do it by phone. I suggested we do the sackings in the House to prevent them being filmed walking up and down Downing Street. We could go back to Number 10 for the appointments. I left for home at 11, with TB still there talking to Nick Brown.

Monday, July 27

The papers were OK, Jack C going pretty big. There was also a lot of interest in Peter M. My briefing of Phil Webster didn't go too well and came out as not great for GB. This led to a series of difficult conversations with GB who thought I had done it deliberately. I said the problem was the hacks wouldn't buy it because they had been fed all the bullshit by Charlie W. I said he could not deny that his people were at it the whole time and until they stopped he would get into these situations. Charlie had been busy briefing the press about the reshuffle without the first knowledge, and he not we was responsible for the idea of there being TB people and GB people.

I told GB I could not trust Charlie at all and he had to understand that and make a judgement about whether that mattered. He said the press liked him. I said that was because he was a rival source operating against the centre, so of course they liked him. I said even if Peter was at it, we weren't, and I wasn't, despite a lot of provocation. I said I protected him as much as anyone. He said Nick Brown was a victim of a phalanx of people telling TB he was a problem when in fact he had a lot of ability. NB had described himself as a 'victim of war', which was a bit dramatic. I said he was also a combatant. TB had been talking to Nick till 1am. He said he was hurt and disappointed that he was being moved from chief whip. He said he had stayed loyal and had not indulged in Gordon's games.

We went over to the House and managed to avoid the media. First in was Gavin [Strang], short and sweet, and he left with a smile which failed to hide the hurt. We then couldn't get hold of David Clark, which held things up. When finally we did, he was reasonably fine about it. Then Harriet, and TB thought it best I stay out of sight so I went into GB's Commons office till she was gone. He told her he liked and respected her but felt she needed a breather from the front line. She asked only two things – 1. that I didn't brief her down, and 2. that TB wrote to her kids to say she had done a good job. I respected her for that, but I couldn't pretend to feel we had lost a huge welfare reform talent. Then Ivor Richard, who left quickly and without looking at anyone. Trouble ahead, said Jonathan.

The papers had effectively written off Margaret B. I discussed it with Bruce and agreed I would call her and say the reports were not true, she was not being sacked. She said she was really grateful for the call, but was she being moved? I said she would have to see Tony for that, so she should come down. She said it would affect both her demeanour and 'my decision'. So she was clearly minded to move on if she was downgraded. Richard Wilson, Sally M and Bruce were all sure she would not quit. TB decided against calling her and said she needed to come down and see him.

We got back to Number 10. Amazingly none of them [the media] had known we were there, let alone that the main sackings had been done. It had been a very good operation and a good idea to minimise the pain. TB said on the way back he was worried about political balance if he ended up with GB, NB and MB all disaffected.

Jack C was absolutely loving the attention. We agreed he should go wall-to-wall today. He said I want you to know I owe nothing to JP or GB, my loyalty is one hundred per cent to Tony, and nobody else. GB came in for a basic moan, telling TB if he was not careful it would be seen as vindictive and there would be a backlash. I said his people had overplayed their hand and he had to live with that. The overall picture was shaping up as very Blairite and New Labour. TB got Richard W to see Frank F to sound him out re one or two non-ministerial positions but FF was clear he only wanted the top DSS job or none at all. Byers was brief, then Peter M, and we agreed he would not do any massive photocalls or major interviews and he would drop the president of the Board [of Trade] title. He said his meeting with GB last night had been OK. Peter Hyman suggested we get GB and Peter M to do pictures together. GB was very reluctant but eventually we managed to persuade him, though he insisted Darling and Byers were also there. I said we had to be seen to be making an effort, no matter how ridiculous the insiders thought it was.

Margaret B was putting a very brave face on things as she came out but Anji took her downstairs and she said she felt she had finally cracked the DTI and now it was all being handed over to Peter. Field was a real problem of course, and limbering up for a real prima donna response. He had been shown up for what he was – egotistical and ultimately useless, good at getting intellectual brownie points for bold ideas, hopeless at making them happen. Somehow, we had it all done by 1.30. I had put together a really detailed briefing note, five or six pages maybe, with the key message that we were moving from the processes of opposition to the proper processes of government. There would be more formality. I took a swipe at the personality spats. It was clearly seen as both interesting and Blairite.

The big fight for GB was Geoffrey Robinson. TB had pretty much reached the view he was a liability, despite his plus points, but GB was desperate to keep him. There had been another very bad article, this time in *Business Age*, which I faxed over to GB. TB's bottom line was that he was worried about what else there might be to come out and the drip, drip was damaging the government. He felt GR should offer his resignation. He sent RW to see first GB and then GR with that message. He came back to say we had two very angry men there. But Geoffrey was going to think about it. Several hours and a number of meetings later we were no further forward. TB was thinking of asking him to chair a task force on public-private partnerships. All in all though, TB had shown some real steel.

Tuesday, July 28

In terms of getting it done, the reshuffle went fine, but the press was awful for GB, saying he had been shafted, TB showed steel, got a grip etc., which was fine on one level but TB was not happy that the whole thing was seen in terms of division rather than momentum. GB was catatonic in his rage, in to see TB early and back to his absolute worst, real paranoia, with a sense from him that the whole thing had been deliberate, that we had briefed it as a wholesale shafting of him. I tried my best to say once more that this was all the result of Whelan setting something up without the first clue where it would end, but GB was having none of it.

Jack C was out and about doing interviews and saying he had spin doctors in his sights and though some of the media took that as a general whack, including at me, those in the know knew it was taking aim at Whelan. The drama of the moment was Geoffrey R. Wilson had been to see him and put to him the notion that he was damaging the government and should go. Both Geoffrey and GB were adamant that this was just caving in to media pressure when we said we would not. They were really fearful now. TB saw GR while the rest of us met to discuss the junior ranks. TB told GR he thought he should go. GR said he did not want to go under a cloud. They agreed that he would go in September as he was then due to have hospital treatment anyway. I said to TB that was an argument for him going now not later. I said they would spin this as a GB win. TB said even they could not be mad enough for that. Yet at the four o'clock, Tony Bevins asked me whether I would accept 'GB had won'.

Jack C chaired the morning meeting and didn't chair it well. He treated it like a Cabinet committee, rather than a quick run-through of the day ahead, and also gave a little lecture about how he only wanted people there who were going to be part of the team and work as a team etc. The sentiment was fine but I think people left the room thinking he would have to change his way of chairing it if he intended to keep doing it. It would probably end up with me taking it over soon, was the general feeling. I called a meeting for 12 with some of my people and some of Jack's and said I thought it better if I did the news management meetings, which was all the morning meeting was. Jack should be concentrating on proper Cabinet committee work and leave the media management department to me. I spoke to Jack about it and though he sounded a bit down about it, said he didn't want to double up or cut across.

TB had to do the NEC then the Lambeth conference [Anglican Communion] speech, then back to do the Ministers of State. There was a conveyer belt through my office as TB sent them round on the way out to talk about their media. [Helen] Liddell, [Brian] Wilson, [Joyce] Quin, [Estelle] Morris, [Patricia] Hewitt, [John] Denham, [Charles] Clarke, good people and the makings of strong middle ranks. Darling was up and about on welfare reform, and doing really well. So apart from the GB situation, it was going pretty well. I had a meeting with the press office and strategic communications staff, which was excellent, though it was still clear we were not getting the support we needed from the departments. I had a chat with Nick Brown [now Agriculture Secretary] to see if we could get him up and around on BSE tomorrow but dealing with MAFF was not easy. We had a meeting on the launch of the [government's new] annual report and agreed to go for a speech in the garden. TB was really opposed to doing it as a statement in the House until we had established it. People were winding down to the holiday, which had TB in his usual who-will-be-working panic. He went to see the Queen and filled her in on what was perhaps one of the bloodier reshuffles of her reign.

I was getting tired again. Alison was working brilliantly for me now. God knows what I would do without her now. When I briefed on the junior ranks, I said Robinson would continue to be unpaid. Bevins said 'Worth every penny.' Both Charlie Falconer and Kilfoyle told me Jack C was rather believing his own publicity and behaving rather grandly and ludicrously and suggested I have another word. He had already asked for a bigger office and a bigger car and told Kilfoyle it was important to have good food and wine there.

Wednesday, July 29

I travelled in with Jonathan and I told him re the Jack C meeting yesterday. Today's went better, but he still basically misunderstood the purpose, so that it went on too long and with insufficient outcome. We had written round departments re planning for August and the response was woeful. We were really not getting the service we were entitled to at all. They were rebelling against centralisation and professionalism and citing politicisation out of the side of their mouths. Joyce Quin's appointment as a very pro-Europe Europe minister was getting a fair bit of comment so we got her to do the *PM* programme [BBC radio] and she was excellent. I had a long chat with Derry who

July '98: Bringing fresh talent into the middle ranks

felt it had been important TB establish proper authority over the Cabinet and junior ranks.

TB had a bad cold and was losing his voice, which was a big problem. People hate politicians with colds, there is no sympathy at all, so we had to see what we could do to cut his diary down. Then Joe Lockhart, who was to be McCurry's successor [as Clinton's spokesman], came in for a chat. He was a nice guy but different to Mike, a bit more static maybe, but I could easily imagine working with him. I had a meeting with Whelan, told him again I thought he was a real problem for the whole operation. If GB had a different agenda fine, we needed to know. If it was freelanced by him, it was totally unacceptable. Either way we had to sort something out. I said if he was trying to present GB as a rival boss, he was mad, because history shows that in those battles, there is only ever one winner, and that is the prime minister. He said 'I agree' to virtually everything I said.

Then came the message that Frank Field had put in a bid to make a personal statement in the House. TB did not think Betty [Boothroyd] would grant it but she did. I called Frank who said he intended to be supportive, in that he would say TB did not hinder him, but GB did. I said that didn't sound very helpful. I made clear we had decided to go easy on him but we would have to respond if he went over the top re GB. I got it out that he had basically insisted on being in the Cabinet, and had talked about getting the Cabinet Office job. I agreed lines with Darling and Denham and Denham did well on the media as response to FF.

We had been close at one point to pulling TB out of PMQs because his voice was so weak, but he did it and it was just about OK. Hague was in rant mode and not very effective. After the Field statement, I was very robust on the line that GB was the radical and Frank the non-deliverer. TB felt a better strategy was to talk him up, and make him look small.

Thursday, July 30

TB's voice had recovered enough to do the *Today* programme, but it was a crap interview, Humphrys just trying to pin him down on pensions and TB basically going into shutdown mode early on so it was dull and pointless. TB got a bit of a bad press for not staying in for the Field statement but he was really pissed off with him. Jack C chaired the meeting a lot better. I also had a good response to the round robin I sent yesterday complaining at departments' response re August [media plans]. Jack said he really didn't want to cut across anything I did. We had the first meeting of the new Cabinet and there was a good mood. The main focus was a political discussion. Derry led a discussion on the future legislative programme. Margaret B set out the progress of bills etc. and truth be told a huge amount had been done already, and a lot of it big stuff. Derry warned there would be real pressure on space in the programme and people had to get bids in now not later. He said there would have to be a bill on [lowering the] age of consent for homosexuals. A London bill, two local government bills, Lords reform, fairness at work, disability rights commission, asylum, justice system reform. He was also still pushing re Freedom of Information.

The weather was nice and so we decided to hold the annual report event in the garden, Peter Hyman and I had written TB's speech, with modernisation the main message, a bit of Third Way, a sense we had done OK but there was a lot more to do. There was an awful moment a third of the way through when it felt like the skies were about to open but we got through it. It didn't quite work as an event. To have government ranks there and without being quizzed was all a bit old Soviet-style and although I enjoyed the fact the media felt compelled to report it, it didn't work and we would have to rethink for next year. One or two of the hacks were muttering about Stalinism and Ceauşescu [former Romanian dictator] as they left. The document itself though was quite good and we got perfectly good coverage for the lunchtimes.

Then we set off for Worcester for a public Q&A. On the train we were talking about Sally M who was really upset that TB had suggested she go to work for Margaret Jay, and now TB was annoyed with himself for upsetting her. He was hopeless at these micro personnel issues. He clearly wanted Anji more directly involved in the political operation, but there was surely a way of making sure Sally had a proper role within that. We were trying to work out new structures that would keep people motivated and involved. I was worried that if we lost Sally the balance within the operation would be wrong. Anji was talking about being the third person [after AC and Powell] for whom there was the room for executive status re the Civil Service, but I felt if there was something that so graphically showed her to be above the others, then not only would CB be hit but Sally would feel the need to walk. The Allason judgment came through.[1] I spoke to Frank Field again and said TB was really unimpressed by his attacks on GB and we would not be able to hold them back if he kept going.

[1] The judgment was that Allason should be awarded £1,050 damages and seventy-five per cent of his costs.

The Worcester Q&A was OK but again didn't quite work. As we left Worcester Peter M called and asked if TB could speak to the boss of Siemens [electronics company] who were about to announce 1,000 job losses tomorrow. TB spoke to him, established it was not going to change and asked them to emphasise this was to do with the Asian economy not ours, or the nature of the workforce.

Friday, July 31

I was working on a welfare briefing for the Sundays, which were bound to focus big time on the fallout from Field and which we had to use to get on the front foot again. We had a meeting first re Jack's new department – TB, JC, RW, Ann Taylor, AC – TB made clear he thought it better I stay in charge of day-to-day, and so chair the morning meeting, with Jack bound in at the strategic and policy level. He felt also that both Jack C and Charlie F should be members of the main Cabinet committees. He basically wanted them to sort the problems that would otherwise take up too much of his time. JC was a lot happier about his role, and would set off for Barbados feeling much better about things. He said as we left I want to work with you closely so just tell me what we need to do.

I did the Sundays who as ever were trying to probe for every piece of colour and bollocks, but I stuck to pushing a strong line on welfare, which I think worked. As I was leaving for home, Michael Levy came in having just had a heart-to-heart with TB and now wanted one with me. He said he hated his role in the Lords and he felt Fiona and I were always trying to cut him out of things. I said I just felt he should beware his profile because a bit like me he was one of those people who would always be portrayed negatively. He should accept that as part of the baggage that went with what he did.

Tuesday, August 11 (holiday, Flassan)

I was able to relax fairly quickly. Fiona and I were getting on a lot better, though the kids seemed a bit tense at times. Work-wise things were reasonably quiet, though the first Sunday we were there the papers were full of anti-Field briefing which was stupid. The best way to deal with Frank was talk up his thinking but say we needed change. It was counterproductive and ran totally contrary to the line I had used in the Sunday lobby and would just give FF more ammo, especially as one of his lines of attack was going to be GB and spin doctors.

The next irritant and intrusion was a great big row about the select committee report into the GIS. The Tories and the Lib Dems were now saying they would disown it, and there was a great hoo-ha running on it for days. I told Godric to say nothing and stay right out of it but in the absence of much else around, it was getting too much coverage. For days, everyone who came up to the house with UK papers, there was something in them about it. But, as Tom Bostock [AC's GP] said when he came over – in all these attacks on you, nobody ever says they don't respect or admire you. They do it because you're strong. I had a similar view from an Irish lorry driver we met at a pub in Marseilles when we went to the football. He said I love the way you stick it to the media. 'They're by and large a bunch of self-important twats and more power to your elbow.'

We had a nice day with Bostock who came up with his thirteen-year-old son James. Tom didn't believe me when I said that one day I would walk away from all this and it wouldn't be a problem for me. He said I would find it very hard to give it up. The other problem running through the month was a sense the economy wasn't in great shape and DB didn't help by saying it was on a knife-edge. TB called a few times, mainly to complain that Bruce Johnston from the *Telegraph* was pretty much following them everywhere they went [in Tuscany, as guests of Prince Girolamo Strozzi]. The twin themes they kept trying to run were freebies and ordinary people having their holidays ruined by security. I said I felt they would just have to grin and bear it. There was not much we could do to stop someone talking to people they had met, or digging into the background of people they were with.

I had a few chats with Alex Ferguson, who was having a difficult summer. They had been dire in the Charity Shield against Arsenal and he was having problems with [Martin] Edwards [Manchester United chairman] and the board. They were worried about the Matt Busby [legendary Manchester United manager] syndrome where the manager becomes the real power in the club. He was also still getting flak re his political profile. He said after the election he had said to the board now we can start having a decent country again – but it hadn't gone down that well. He had worked out he worked twenty-four seven-day weeks last year, but he had been picked up over one occasion when he didn't travel with the team.

Saturday, August 15

I was on the phone to Peter M in the States when Wendy Abbs [Downing Street duty clerk] came through on the other line to say there had been a huge explosion in Omagh [County Tyrone], twelve thought to be dead, the PM was just being told, having just arrived at the house in France. I asked her to fix a conference call with him and Philip Barton, who was manning the office as duty private secretary. PB had already done the basics you'd expect, but the details were all a bit patchy. As we spoke, reports were coming in that the death toll may be higher and all the holiday ease that had been in TB's voice at the start was gone. I said he would have to do TV straight away. There was a problem in that he had arrived ahead of his clothes and he was scruffily dressed. I asked which cops were with him, and he ended up using Bill Lloyd's suit and a shirt borrowed from one of the neighbours. We also had a conference call with John McFall, newly appointed NI minister, who was on duty. 'What a baptism,' said TB. It was clear John was nervous and I was worried he would hit the wrong note in extended interviews. For example, when I said what do you say if they ask if it harms the peace process, he said it's too early to say. I said we had to get over that the peace process is bigger than a group of fanatics who want to derail it. TB weighed in, saying we had to be making clear every peace process always faced disruption from people who wanted to destroy it. TB said this was the last resistance, and if we saw it off with public opinion there totally on our side, it could be another turning point. But how we react now will dictate that. It was pretty clear if the death toll was as bad as feared, he would have to break his holiday at some point, but I suggested for today JP went there. I spoke to JP, who said he would do whatever we thought was required, and we fixed it for the afternoon. I said the line we wanted to push was that we would not let a small bunch of psychopaths disrupt the will of the majority. We also had to get SF up on the right side of the argument. I called [Mike] McCurry, who was playing golf with his son, and said BC would be key in making the kind of noises SF would want to echo. PB called [Sandy] Berger and [Jim] Steinberg to brief them and try to get Clinton engaged early. We had to pull out all the stops to make sure SF said the right thing. Adams was on holiday in Italy but announced he was coming back. McGuinness put out a very strong statement. TB said that what we had to engineer was a situation where people felt the IRA were isolated from these people, that they were seen as a rump, that there was now an internal battle between the democratic process and renegades. TB did his clips which PB watched, and said he was quite emotional. When I saw it on French TV later, it looked fine. It could have been anywhere and the tone was good. In a later conference call we had a longer discussion about whether he should go. It was pretty much inevitable he would have to, the only question was when.

I barely slept and I guessed that TB wouldn't and phoned him early. I found it hard to understand how people can be so psychopathic, so dumb, to think this will work. Unless there was a strategy so deep and so sophisticated that it was beyond the comprehension of mere mortals, I couldn't see it. It was hard not to feel emotional about it after the real sense of progress there had been.

TB said there will be obstacles along the way but the forces of good have to prevail. He had got over the initial shock and was now working on next steps. He said he felt if he went he should go today but PB said there was a problem getting a plane. I said it was important he didn't just go in and come out but did something only he could do – like get DT and GA together to say the same thing, or get Adams to make clear in the tone of his denunciation that so far as he was concerned, the war was over. PB finally tracked down John Holmes who had been travelling and had been oblivious to what had happened. He too counselled caution, but TB sounded like he had made his mind up. He said if you go, you go today, you steady people, you give momentum to the process and you spell out a message of hope. It was obvious to me TB had decided to go so I said to PB and John we should just plan for it because it is going to happen.

After church TB got ready to go back and called from the car to go over the basic line – peace process can prevail, we can be stronger than these evil people, etc. Godric and PB had flown to Hull to met up with JP. I spoke to John as they landed and said he could say that TB was cutting into his holiday to come over. JP wanted to go over all the difficult questions and we had a long briefing session – he was worried about getting the tone right on decommissioning. I said best to avoid difficult interviews until TB got there. This was about empathy and about making clear the extent of both our condemnation and our determination to prevail. TB's feeling was that the debate would move quickly to what kind of security measures were being put in place. As he flew I put together a long briefing note for a phone lobby. TB had asked me to keep control of the briefing which meant the only way to do it was do it myself in a series of conference calls, which was pretty irritating for Fiona and the kids so I tried to do one before they were up and out and another when they were just chilling out in the afternoon. He called me after his meeting with Ronnie Flanagan who was clear it was [Michael] McKevitt and the Real IRA [RIRA]. TB said I could announce Flanagan was going to meet the Garda and together they would make recommendations to the two governments. It had definitely been the right thing for him to go today and given how much time I spent on the phone it might have been easier to go with him.

TB asked me to speak to McGuinness to agree what they were going to be saying and keep them in the place we wanted them to be. It then emerged Mary McAleese [President of Ireland] was going to Omagh and TB was to meet Bertie at Stormont tomorrow. I said they should do a joint doorstep. TB went to the hospital and then met Trimble at Hillsborough. The scale of it was becoming clearer now and it had definitely been the right thing to go. Indeed I was worried Mo was going to take a hammering for still not being there, with the world waking up to the enormity of it. There was also the fear TB would look a bit cruel ducking out after a day or so. Prince Charles was due to go on Tuesday. At the moment the main focus was on the carnage.

Monday, August 17

Again, I didn't sleep too well. I was just dozing when TB called around 1am. He had been up till 12 with Trimble but the real reason for the call was he said he was deeply affected by the visit to the Belfast Royal [Royal Victoria Hospital]. He described some of the scenes he saw, the wounds and the scars and the mutilated bodies, and all the human suffering around them. But basically they were all giving him the same message – keep going, don't give up, work for peace harder than ever. He said it was really humbling. He felt it had been right to go but it was also OK to leave. He had seen victims and families, met the politicians, talked to the police.

TB felt what we really needed was something strong from [Ronnie] Flanagan on the security front out of his talks with [Garda Commissioner Patrick] Byrne. Flanagan told TB he was sure the IRA had nothing to do with this. I said it was important he make that clear today because we were still getting reports implicating the IRA. TB did another round of calls before heading back to France. I did another lobby briefing from the house in Flassan on to the squawk box in the lobby room. The questions were much the same as yesterday – worries about decommissioning, about prisoner release, interest in arrests and any planned new security moves.

TB said it was vital that we came up, whatever the legal hurdles, with a security package that gave people confidence we were on top of things. TB was worried that Mo would find herself surrounded by the usual NIO dynamics and we would lose grip. But Tom Kelly [NIO official] was doing well on the media front and Bill Jeffrey [political director, NIO] seemed OK. Add to which a combination of Prince

Charles' visit and then the funerals would be the main focus for the next bit. There was a lot being done that people did not know about. The problem with some of the new ideas was the requirement of primary legislation.

TB said he was not convinced these people had intended to do quite as much damage as they did, but I doubted that. They had totally set the agenda on their terms and in different ways made life difficult for every part of the political debate with the possible exception of Paisley. On the flight back he wrote a very emotional reflection on what he had seen. It showed he felt it very deeply. What was amazing was that even before I had told Fiona or anyone about the new security measures, Rory said to me 'Why don't you just pick up the top man on phone-tap material, then the other top people, and find excuses to keep them inside until you find all their weapons, then break the organisation?' Not bad.

In one of the briefings I did, I pushed out the boat for Adams and McGuinness. I said TB was totally convinced of their sincerity, which again was the right thing to say for now, but a potential hostage. At 5pm I listened in to a TB/Mo call. Mo read through the joint statement she planned with the Irish justice minister [John O'Donoghue]. It was wordy and woolly and with no specifics to drive things forward. There was no reference to the things we had instructed yesterday, e.g. changing the balance on evidence, ending the right to silence, proscription, use of phone-tap material. I said that if she read out the statement she had just gone through with TB, she would be panned.

TB said he wanted to see the police chiefs' ideas and then take half an hour to redraft and get back. I said to Mo the press can wait. Mo sounded like she always did when we were involved – pissed off and sullen, but the truth was it was a second-rate piece of work. As TB was redrafting, she called me back to say the police were pissed off hanging about and so were the press. I said neither were good reasons to do it half-cock. Every time I tried to push back she said she was surrounded by officials shaking their heads. I said look, there is no need for anyone to get antsy about this. It is not unreasonable for this to take a bit of time. It is not surprising that the PM would want to be involved, and consult Bertie. She didn't like that at all.

Then another extraordinary conference call with him and Mo. The police chiefs [Flanagan and Byrne] want to leave, the justice minister wants to leave and they cannot renegotiate because Bertie is in a meeting in Dublin. TB was pretty firm with her. He said 'I'm very sorry, Mo, but I am going to have to press you and you are going to have to press them because the statement is not adequate. It needs a strong intro and it needs three specific areas that have to be addressed. 1. Proscription and a specific criminal offence. 2. Measures to make it easier to secure convictions. We do not need to go into detail here but people will know this is phone-tap material. 3. Specific operational measures, where there has to be a sense of detail.' We then had the ludicrous situation of TB having to ask Mo for her fax number, and her shouting out 'Anyone out there who knows the fax number?' and then saying the officials had disappeared. It was the Mo manner that was fine when things didn't matter, but deeply irritating when they did. She sounded more and more exasperated. 'I'll say whatever you want, Tony,' she said, at which point TB exploded at her: 'It is not a case of saying what I want. It is a case of doing the right thing and then explaining it to the public, who may have cause to be concerned about recent events.' She then lost the plot completely. 'You cannot do this to me. I'm sick of the long-distance control. You are making it impossible for me. I can't do it any more.' Well, you're going to have to, he said. Just calm down, Mo, we have to do this properly. Ronnie Flanagan came on the line and was like a voice of reason and sanity. He did not sound like a man trying to charge out of the door. TB took him through some of the changes and he sounded fine. But Mo was getting near hysterical. TB said to her if you went out and read that statement as you read it to us earlier, you will be dead. I mean dead, totally out of the game. Nobody would take you seriously. She said 'I'd rather be dead than carrying on like this. I don't care any more.' TB said 'Yes you do, and that is why we do the extra bit to get it right.'

Tuesday, August 18

I listened by phone to Mo's doorstep, which was pretty grim stuff. She got the three areas for action mixed up and had to be rescued by O'Donoghue and she got muddled with the Irish on internment. She was clearly in a bit of a state. Then I learned she wanted to resume her holiday tomorrow which would be a disaster area for her locally. TB called, having been told by Mo that her statement went fine. 'It was tough but I did it.' I told him what actually happened, that she had got things in the wrong order and did not even get out the line that PIRA [Provisional IRA] were not involved. He said 'You are going to have to take charge of this, and do a lot of one-on-one briefings.' I was genuinely worried about Mo, and what she might be saying. She said she wanted to go back to Greece because it was a waste of time constantly being second-guessed by remote control. The TB article [about his visit, in *Newsletter* and *Irish News*] went down a storm and was picked up by several of the nationals. It was the emotion that drew them in but it also included the main political points. In between dealing with NI, trying to spend time with Fiona and the kids, we also now had Don Macintyre up with us for a couple of days because I had promised I would help with his book [a Mandelson biography]. Peter was helping him, and Don was trying to be fair, but I sensed that his real interest was TB/GB or certainly GB/Peter M.

TB was less pissed off than I thought he would be about the *Sun* leader attacking him for going back to France. We were not making much progress on the Trimble/Adams meeting and we were not getting far on the security measures either, with NIO in a state of shambles from what I could glean from my various phone calls. Then news came through that the Irish president and Bertie were going to a service in Omagh on Sunday, which would put pressure on TB to go, so we had another round of circular conversations about that. TB said he desperately needed a rest but was getting none. It didn't help that he was worrying re Mo and the NIO the whole time. Prince Charles' visit and the Real IRA claiming responsibility was the big news. Re the church service TB felt it was OK for JP to represent the government and he would go to a memorial later.

Wednesday, August 19

The right-wing press was starting to be difficult, trying to link RIRA and IRA as pretty much the same thing. Their desire to fuck us over on this was pretty powerful. The GA/DT situation was going backwards, SF rejecting the language we had tried on them. It was making the UUs uneasy again. The RIRA called a ceasefire which we rejected in contemptuous tones, saying it was an insult to the dead and an attempt simply to stall the new security measures. The RIRA were intimating it had been intended as a big commercial hit, not heavy loss of life. That had been TB's view, that it caused more damage than intended. Mo was still intending to stay only until tomorrow, which was worrying me.

Thursday, August 20

TB called early, and we had a circular conversation re who should attend the service on Friday, what kind of memorial there should be, and what if any legislation we should be bringing in as a response. He felt we would probably end up recalling Parliament so it was probably as well to say so and set the terms ourselves. We were due to go with the Senes [a French family] down to the river so I wanted

August '98: TB back to France but cannot rest

to get today sorted before we went. I organised for TB to do a pooled clip responding to Bertie's new measures, with an appropriately tough line. I told him of some of the right-wing articles being run and we agreed I should ask Geoff Martin [*Newsletter*] to take an article warning these armchair generals risked provoking a Loyalist backlash. The basic points had to be rooted in what the peace process was for, and why people wanted to disrupt it.

We were effectively briefing that TB's holiday was over, though he was spotted up a mountain by photographers. Fiona and the kids were getting a bit fed up with me being on the phone, several hours a day, with today around nine calls with TB alone. We were doing OK re the message on legislation but going backwards re the war being over. I recalled the time I saw Bertie at Newcastle vs Man U last year and him saying he would come down like a ton of bricks on anyone who went back to violence and he had been as good as his word.

Friday, August 21
The last week of the holiday had been pretty much wiped out. Today was the last full day I had and most of it was spent working. We had to agree representation for the Omagh service tomorrow. In the end we opted for JP who did it perfectly well. I put together a briefing for the Sundays, TB to go there Tuesday and also decision to be made re recall of Parliament. I stressed that this could be the final such act in this particular chapter of Irish history. That was probably pushing it but there was a sense that people were longing for that to be so. I did the briefing by squawk box, and they were clearly desperate for a Diana [first] anniversary story. Mike Prescott [*Sunday Times*] said at one point 'Alastair, can I level with you – we are desperate for anything re Diana.' I said we would be doing nothing, apart from half-mast flags and TB at Crathie [church at Balmoral].

We were out at lunch when TB called after the doorstep, said it went fine and he had pushed again the line re new measures post Omagh. We talked about the conference speech. He was thinking of a theme on the lines that the right tolerated him because they thought he was a Thatcherite but in truth New Labour was a rejection of Thatcherism in that it kept those things that were now generally accepted but was addressing the failings and the negative impact, e.g. to jobs, economic strength, social justice. He sounded like he was up for the taking on the right for once. He felt that on e.g. Europe, the family, welfare, they [the Conservatives] had moved so far to the right as to be extreme. At its core a lot of Thatcherism had been rejected.

He kept asking if I had been able to have a rest because he needed me to be on form for the conference speech. In fact the first two weeks we had been able to rest and relax but the third week was a total write-off. Fiona had done a brilliant job keeping the show on the road while I was busy, and I think understood I felt there was no choice. People had said when I first started that NI would get to me, and it had.

Saturday, August 22
We set off at 6. TB was on the phone at 8. We got home in around fifteen hours.

Sunday, August 23
For the first time in three weeks I slept past 9. TB woke me at 9.30 to have a natter and go through where we were. He was really starting to focus on the conference speech and so we were into long circular-conversation mode as we started to develop and hone the main arguments. The Sundays were generally OK re our handling of Omagh. TB had been thinking about PR and had grown more persuaded against and regretted getting into the argument for reasons of Lib-Demery. TB feared Bill [Clinton] was getting really damaged by the Lewinsky affair now.[1] He said he should really try to engage in the Middle East, one because it was right and he could do it, but also because he needed something major to focus on to get away from the US obsession with his sex life.

Monday, August 24
First full day back in the office, and it wasn't too bad. The main focus of the day was to decide whether to recall Parliament. There was a school of thought that we did not actually need to for the measures we wanted to get through. But equally I felt we needed to send the signal of the importance of it, and the added legitimacy it would give if we had a full vote of the HoC. TB had read the various different pieces of advice and his basic judgement was that it was probably the right thing to do. Lockerbie and NI were the main focus for the eleven o'clock. We were pushing the line that if we did recall Parliament we were also looking at measures to allow terrorist offences committed abroad to be tried here. I spent most of the day with Mark Bennett

[1] Following allegations of impropriety, in January 1998 Clinton had claimed: 'I did not have sexual relations with that woman' – i.e. former White House intern Lewinsky. But the resulting investigation led to the instigation of the impeachment proceedings by the US House of Representatives.

[AC's researcher] briefing myself back in. At 7pm we had a final conference call and TB gave the green light for a recall [of Parliament].

Tuesday, August 25

I was picked up at 6.40 to head to Northolt to get a plane to Toulouse to meet TB. The news was leading with TB recalling Parliament. Toulouse was a bit of a bore, the tour of the factory too long and the press conference hijacked by a lecture from France's Communist transport minister. On the flight back, TB and CB were waxing re the holiday even with all the pressures on TB's time and the interruptions. TB felt Bill C was in some genuine trouble but the only option for us was to stand by him. I asked CB if she would stand by TB if he got involved with a Monica Lewinsky. She said probably, but she would make his life hell. TB said he was confident she would kick him straight out, and Fiona would do the same to me. CB was also complaining again that they were in real debt and it was ludicrous the things they had to spend money on without any official help. TB had a different kind of concern re the Parliament recall, namely that we would face a lot of opposition from the judiciary. We dropped CB and family off at Northolt and then headed for Belfast.

TB drafted his own press statement, which was strong. He focused on the emotions aroused, the recall as agreed by the Speaker and the general thinking behind it. He was worried though that the political situation was fragile. Trimble and Mallon were barely speaking, DT was vile about the service he was getting from the Civil Service, Sinn Fein were attacking everything we did and saying Trimble's sole aim was to ensure the GFA was not implemented. DT was a very difficult personality to deal with. When he was good, he was very good, but at times he could become very distant and disengaged and not focus.

Mo and Tom Kelly were both worried that Mallon would quit if things did not improve. We were flown by helicopter to Omagh, where the atmosphere was very subdued, as expected. TB did a meeting with local leaders and then groups of emergency services in little knots, all very friendly but some of them clearly shaken up. He talked to some of the locals in the street and though there were one or two difficult questions, he handled it all well. He was saying the measures we planned were tough but I thought he was wrong to say draconian. We had an unbelievably awful helicopter flight to Belfast, foul weather, low flying, dodging pylons, etc.

We arrived for the talks, first Trimble, who was clearly under pressure and not very friendly. Several of the UUs were making clear they would not sit on the executive with SF. They were also – in part fuelled by the Tories and the *Telegraph* – driving decommissioning up the agenda again. TB was seething afterwards, felt that whenever we took our eye off the ball, things slipped, and that DT was failing to offer leadership. We had an equally difficult meeting with McGuinness, Doherty and Bairbre de Brún [Sinn Fein's policing and justice spokesperson], who felt Trimble was stalling while they were constantly being asked for more. TB felt if we did not get progress going soon, the thing was in danger of collapse, and he was worried about the attitude shift on both sides.

Over dinner at Hillsborough, TB agreed he should do a statement on Omagh on the day Parliament came back, both to set the tone and give a broader context. DT came back for another meeting and TB decided to do it mainly tête-à-tête to try to get him to get a grip. It was a better meeting and TB had bought the line that Trimble was not trying to screw things for SF for the sake of it, but taking a tough public line to try to win more of his own people round behind him. They agreed to work towards a series of steps, e.g. 1. SF say something indicating the war is over, 2. DT calls a meeting of all parties, including SF, 3. McGuinness agrees to speak to the decommissioning body, 4. Trimble/Adams bilateral. Over a massive bowl of raspberries and strawberries, TB said he felt DT was a curious mix – he wants to lead but is needy about how to do it. It was as if he needed lessons – for example, he should bind in Donaldson and then every time Donaldson slips outside the net he diminishes himself not DT. He felt Donaldson was the one person who could really damage DT.

Wednesday, August 26

Over breakfast TB said he felt DT could get SF on to the executive but if he did it without decommissioning he was pretty much finished. He told Adams as much later. We left by helicopter then flew to Knock airport, which was a pretty extraordinary place, a huge runway in a small airport taking a few planes a day to get people to the shrine nearby. The Irish had laid on a helicopter to get us to Ashford Castle hotel, a fabulous building, part of it twelfth century, set in beautiful grounds. We were met by Bertie and Paddy Teahon, Bertie being positive and constructive and helpful as ever. We agreed the same first four steps plus then, 5. real decommissioning, and then 6. SF on to the executive. Bertie believed it was doable. TB thought DT wanted to move but he thought it would be very hard to have an executive with SF on it by September 14. BA felt Adams was almost irrelevant to the decommissioning argument. McGuinness was the key.

We agreed it would be good to get one of the big steps taken while Bill C was here, to use his presence but also help him. The Clinton people advance team were giving us the usual headaches. They wanted a speech opportunity in Omagh which we thought might not be appropriate. They wanted a visit to the new university site in West Belfast. TB was opposed and John Holmes and I had a difficult discussion with Steinberg later.

Lunch was pretty relaxed, fabulous food and Bertie on cracking form. On the flight back, TB was more confident we could do something to push forward politically. He said it was like playing multi-dimensional chess. We got back for a long meeting with Mo, Jack S, RC et al. re the planned bill. Jack was excellent on the detail. We agreed not to go down the road of phone taps being used as evidence partly because most were not transcribed but also so that we were not pushed into detail of who and how.

We then had a meeting, including with TB, re the Clinton visit. TB was keen this was a good visit for Bill, who he felt was looking pretty close to being knackered. We had to stand by him and show we stood alongside people through bad times as well as good. There were a number of joint things planned but we decided it would not be a good thing for TB to be driven around in Bill's presidential limo. The palaver preceding the visit was appalling. They had too many people and a lack of clarity about who could actually make decisions on BC's behalf. Christ knows in how many countries his advance teams were currently causing chaos.

Friday, August 28

The Russian economic crisis was dominating pretty much everything. We had already fixed in advance to do Kenny Macintyre [BBC Scotland reporter] at 7.30 and the main focus was Russia, and TB pushed the reform angle. For once, we were the ones pressing the media to quiz us on the SNP because we had the sense the tide was turning our way, even though we did not do brilliantly in a local by-election last night. TB pushed the economic impacts of separation really hard but there was limited interest. I had got the Scottish *Mirror* to do a big number on SNP hypocrisy which seemingly did serve to wind them up and unsettle them. Jack C was on the defensive re a story about an expensive mahogany table.[1] It was classic Jack. I spoke to him and then

[1] Cunningham had bought a conference table and chairs made from unsustainably sourced Brazilian timber, contrary to the government's ethical hardwood policy.

wrote to him privately warning that the media sensed he had a taste for the high life at taxpayers' expense and he needed to be careful they did not portray him as an extravagant wanker. I also suggested that he send it back.

We left for Edinburgh and then Stornaway. The weather wasn't great but TB got a great welcome. Lots of the kids from around the island [Scalpay] were out to greet us. We were flown over the island by helicopter, fantastic scenery, and then to Harris. We were eaten alive by midges and it was all a bit rainy too, but the atmosphere was good and TB was enjoying it. He did a good little speech at the makeshift marquee before he officially opened the new bridge. You felt the slower pace the whole time, and also the heavy weight of religion, as with the long prayer before the opening of the bridge, but also in the conversation. There was also a blessing for the Queen and a call for moral rectitude. Catherine MacLeod [*Herald*] was really excited he was there and thought he was absolutely brilliant. We had something to eat at the community centre, then TB did a doorstep on the visit and also re Russia. Back by helicopter to Stornaway then to Glasgow.

On the flight he was musing again about PR. Could we say we would wait to see how it worked in Wales and Scotland and that the Cabinet was basically opposed? By the time we landed around 7, David North [Downing Street private secretary] was on saying Jack agreed he should send the table back but he was worried anything would appear in the press that we forced him to do so. I assured him it wouldn't.

Saturday, August 29

TB called and said he felt that with Clinton disabled because of Monica, and Yeltsin now hit sideways by the Russian economic crisis, there was a bit of a vacuum in world leadership and we had to do something. He instigated a series of calls to different world leaders in his capacity as chair of G7, starting today with Chirac and Prodi, tomorrow [Keizo] Obuchi [new Japanese Prime Minister], Kohl and Chrétien and a further conversation with Clinton, who was keeping a brave face on things but sounded down when you listened closely. The main message TB was driving was that we were willing to help Russia but any help must be tied to economic reform. In most of the conversations, there was a concern that Yeltsin had pretty much lost it and didn't really know how to handle what was happening.

TB said there would be a lot of anxiety everywhere about Russia and we had to build an agenda to move forward from it. TB was also pushing us to keep the momentum going forward re NI. He believed after the talk with Bertie that we could get Adams close to saying the war is over and DT to agree to chair a meeting of party leaders including SF. I had to deal with a *Sunday Times* story that Prince Charles wanted to meet Salmond, which was a piece of SNP spin to try to embarrass TB at Balmoral. I spoke to [Sir Robert] Fellowes who put out a line that this was routine and low-key but needless to say the Scottish press were really going for it.

Sunday, August 30

Another fairly quiet day. The Sundays were trying to build a sense of rebellion over the new NI legislation and Mo had sent a letter to the *Observer* promising an annual review as a sop to the civil liberties people. TB spoke to more of the G7 leaders and he and Clinton did a bit of NI. We really needed some movement pretty quickly. TB called after church and I warned him some Dundee freelance was flogging a story that he and CB left a paltry tip after an expensive meal in some fancy restaurant they went to. It was exactly the kind of silly story that could dominate the whole holiday weekend. CB was vague, but what a lot of bollocks to have to deal with. I was talking to TB about it when Switch came on and said Clinton was on the line. It underlined how ridiculous it was we were having to deal with this, but these little things could sometimes define you in a really detrimental way.

The Royals seemed to be facing both ways on the SNP, telling us they were killing it, but actually not really doing it. TB felt his relationship with the Queen was good but he felt Charles had people spreading stuff against us a fair bit of the time.

Monday, August 31

I was trying to have a lie-in but TB called early, worrying whether we were in the right place re Russia. He felt there had to be more done by the G7 and people were looking closely at how we handled this. John Holmes was urging caution, saying there was no point signalling momentum if ultimately it went nowhere and the reaction of the others was not yet clear. The other thing I was dealing with was the media making something out of the shortage of time the NI bill would get. I called Jack S who said it was being sent to Opposition leaders today and MPs tomorrow. In addition we agreed we should brief the new element of forfeiture, seizing the homes of people involved in the Real IRA, which was the one thing people were seizing on as being a bit draconian. We were also still hopeful of some movement on 'the war is over' scenario we had discussed with Trimble and Adams. We had a pretty relaxing weekend. I listened in to TB's Yeltsin call and briefed a line on that, though it was not clear yet what exactly we would be doing.

Tuesday, September 1

Over the weekend TB and John Holmes had been toing and froing between Adams and Trimble trying to agree some form of words that would allow DT to react positively and convene a meeting of party leaders. Today it seemed to be coming right. Apart from Clinton in Russia, NI was the only big story around and we put together a briefing for the 11 on the bill which was being published in draft today. TB was down at Chequers, first for a meeting on welfare reform, then a bilateral with GB. GB called me as he was travelling down and said we needed to announce movement re Russia. He clearly wanted to be seen running the show and suggested Nigel Wicks going round G7 capitals. Jeremy said the mood at the bilateral was pretty grim.

Clive Hollick called to say ITN was moving *News at Ten* to 11, and the 5.40 to 6.30 and he hoped TB would not object as Major had done. I said my own view was opposed, and I could not commit on TB's behalf without talking to him. I presented it to TB neutrally and was pleased to hear his immediate response, that he thought it was a bad move. Equally he was not sure how much we could actually do to stop it. I felt it could be part of a broader anti-dumbing down sub-message for his conference speech.

After the eleven o'clock, it was pretty much all Northern Ireland. The feeling was growing Adams would do something significant today. I spoke to Joe Lennon, Richard Macauley [Sinn Fein spokesman] and David Kerr [UUP] and we agreed similar responses from different perspectives. We were still slightly operating in the dark because we didn't yet know exactly what Adams would say. TB had to speak to him again to try to pin him down. John said the problem was every time we suggested the slightest hardening of their position, Adams and McGuinness had to take it away and re-sell and it was not easy for them. But the key was to get Adams to say something Trimble could cautiously welcome, and then DT convene an all-party meeting. It took another round of calls before finally we pressed the button.[1]

It quickly replaced Bill [Clinton] and Boris [Yeltsin] as the main

---

[1] Adams announced in a statement that 'Sinn Fein believe the violence we have seen must be for all of us now a thing of the past, over, done with and gone.' Trimble then invited Adams to a round-table meeting.

story of the day. Though Trimble's words were not strong, I got Kerr to put 'cautious welcome' in the headline. Kerr then came on and said DT didn't like the statement, felt it was full of coded threats, it didn't go as far as they wanted and there would be nothing more positive from DT tonight. I said that TB had an agreement from DT that if words about violence being over were in there, he would respond as agreed. I said he could not possibly go back on that. He said DT had shut up shop for the day and they had real political problems. I got TB to call DT who actually sounded a lot better about it than Kerr indicated. He said it was welcome but he didn't want to make too much of the convening of a meeting. TB didn't want to keep him on the line too long in case he went into textual analysis and instead asked me to call DT back straight away and persuade him that he should announce the all-party meeting rather than have it dribble out on someone else's terms. DT said he didn't want it all to look choreographed. I said he was in danger of letting GA take the initiative. He said only for the short term. He said he had always planned this meeting of leaders so it was no big deal. In which case why had we taken so long to get here? Because they refused to say the war was over. But Adams WAS saying he would bring forward the date announcing McGuinness was to liaise with [General John] de Chastelaine [head of International Commission on Decommissioning]. So it was all going well, if only Trimble could seize the moment.

News-wise it was running fine, everyone saying this was a significant moment but there was a residual concern DT would cock it up. TB, Jonathan and John Holmes had done bloody well to get things to where they were today, and the media operation had got it in the right place so there was a sense of progress. TB and Bertie did most of the heavy lifting but Clinton was also getting credit because it was done to coincide with his visit. Joe Lennon called and said there was no substance to Clinton's Dublin visit.

I got home to Calum having fallen off his bike and Rory and Fiona fighting about something he wanted to watch on the telly, and I felt myself getting depressed again at the lack of time I had spent with them.

Wednesday, September 2

TB called early on, saying he was worried re Trimble. It was so obvious what they had to do but they were terrified of Sinn Fein stealing the show. He spoke to him later and DT was at his disconcerting worst, humming while listening, humming when he should have been speaking, and making clear the only people whose views he considered were his Assembly members. TB also called GA to try to get a better fix on where decommissioning was going. We had to get a response re ITN and the moving of *News at Ten*.

Hollick was pressing and so were some of the papers. After some persuasion TB, and after equal persuasion Peter M, agreed we were best to make clear our opposition, on the grounds it was further dumbing down, but also make clear these were personal views and this was not ultimately our decision. Hollick called, a bit antsy 'So he changed his mind?' I said he hadn't made up his mind till now because it is one of those issues on which you kind of have to have a view. I didn't like the assumption in his voice that we should just have gone along with it. Another diversion was JP sending a postcard to the *Sun* from the Mediterranean attacking their coverage at home on transport. I advised Joe Irvin to take out the most insulting bits. JP came on saying it was pathetic we couldn't attack them. I said I was just trying to get it so that it was publishable. He said he would rather they didn't and he could say they refused to publish it. It was perfectly good-humoured but he said he was going to go for them.

I drafted a couple of strong sound bites for the NI statement, of TB speaking direct to the bombers, which made all the bulletins. Then came news re McGuinness being appointed [by Sinn Fein] to deal with de Chastelaine [on decommissioning], another big hit, and they [the media] were starting to say it was all being choreographed to coincide with the Clinton visit. BC was clearly having a terrible time [over Lewinsky], as was clear from my various calls with [Mike] McCurry. Even he was a bit more tense than usual. It also took me ages to persuade [Jim] Steinberg we should have a pool camera in the meeting with the Assembly. Their worry was that Paisley would give him a big lecture on morals. I vowed they would not be there long enough and we would keep them off Paisley's lot when they met him. I spoke to [David] Kerr several times to make sure DT was responding OK [to Sinn Fein]. He was, though you had to read between the lines to get there. Kerr asked me to 'leave it to me', but I was worried at the pace and so got several of the Westminster political editors to call and ask for confirmation this was leading to a Trimble/Adams meeting.

TB's statement in the House went fine. Kerr then briefed Irish journalists that there would be no decision [on a meeting] until a meeting of the UUP executive on Saturday. [Richard] Macauley and Joe Lennon both called, worried. I tried to assure them this was just DT's way and we would get there. But TB and John Holmes were both worried. I had Brunson and others saying this all basically meant a Trimble/Adams meeting on the cards, but the Belfast media were not really going for it. TB was very down on DT at the moment, said he found it hard to imagine him actually running the place.

Thursday, September 3

I was up just after 5 to get to Number 10 for the convoy to Northolt. It was pouring with rain. Some of the broadsheets were clear re a DT/GA meeting but there was still no confirmation it was going to happen. TB and John H were getting anxious Trimble may stall right through. On the way to the airport, TB and I were discussing how he should handle Bill [Clinton]. I said there was no mileage in any distance and he should be close. The speech should be a mix of where we are in the peace process, but also talk up BC's role. Trimble was waiting for us on the plane. TB was working on the speech for the Waterfront Hall [Belfast], while DT read the papers. I made sure he didn't see the *Independent*, which was the most firm re a meeting with Adams. We then had a discussion about what DT might say. Trimble said he didn't intend it to be a big deal, as both TB and Clinton were around and bound to take the headlines. We persuaded him there was an opportunity here and TB asked me to draft a few lines for him. I did, including a further clear hint that he would meet Adams. I never imagined he would deliver them, especially when he just folded the paper and put it in his pocket without comment, but later he did deliver them, as drafted. He told us he was having problems with Ken Maginnis and also with his executive but he believed it could be done. We got TB's speech finished, arrived and waited for Bill C to arrive. There was the usual over-the-top security getting on everyone's nerves. I told the advance guy he should get hold of a copy of the *Independent* for Bill to see. They took it a step further, gave it to Sandy Berger as he landed and he had it under his arm as he walked across the tarmac. But they were clearly desperate for a success story with all the other stuff going on back home.

We left for Stormont, good pictures of TB, BC, Trimble and Mallon on arrival, then upstairs for a meeting. Bill asked a great question – 'What can I do to help?' TB said 1. show the three governments working together, 2. put pressure on SF re weapons decommissioning, 3. isolate pro-violence opinion in the US, and 4. economic help. DT was pretty churlish throughout and afterwards BC said to me 'Someone should tell him that part of the art of politics is smiling when you feel like you're swallowing a turd.' He also used that great line from Mario Cuomo [former governor of New York]: 'You campaign in poetry. You govern in prose.' It's about who clears the drains, he said. The Yanks were keen to be seen to be doing something for Adams.

Trimble said we were aiming for transfer of functions by February. Anji had a tight control on the cameras and we got our pictures of BC in the Assembly before he could be harangued by the UUs let alone the DUP. But now the US and SF wanted more – they wanted GA on the platform, claiming that is exactly what would happen with a constituency visit, and he should speak for a minute. John Holmes and Jonathan seemed surprisingly relaxed but TB and I were both worried that would wipe everything else out and send real bad waves through the Unionist community. But the Americans were really pushing, and Adams was pressurising Mo. It was a classic last-minute SF bounce and I felt we had to resist as we had not thought through the consequences. Jim Steinberg came to our offices but after ten minutes of toing and froing we couldn't agree so I went to see Bill. I explained why we thought it was a bad move and said instead it would be better that TB said some warm words re GA and his role when he was making his remarks introducing Margaret Gibney.[1] Bill, who was a bit distracted as he was working on his speech, was fine with that.

He was very friendly with all of us, but Hillary was pretty icy, and the more he tried to bring her in, the more rigid and fixed the smile became. She was clearly finding the whole Monica thing hard to bear and he was clearly still being punished. The speeches went fine. TB got a good reception. His words on Bill got the balance right. DT said what we had suggested for him and though it was never enough for SF, it was what was needed. He was an odd speaker. He waved his hands around at the wrong times, and he couldn't work out whether to hold the lectern or not, but it was OK. John [Holmes] and I had written a kind of tribute to GA from TB which we showed to Steinberg. We set off for Springvale [new education campus], the crowds getting bigger as we went through West Belfast. A huge tent had been erected where the new university was going to be. TB, BC, Cherie and Hillary travelled together. Mo did a little speech, then a young boy, then TB, who went off the cuff and called Adams 'Gerry', I think for the first

---

[1] As a twelve-year-old in 1997, she wrote to Blair asking him to continue the search for peace, and imploring terrorists to give up violence. After Blair read out her letter on American TV, she caught the imagination of many in the United States, including Hillary Clinton. Subsequently she became a UNICEF Young Ambassador.

time in public, which John H hoped nobody would notice. Berger said to me I looked pained when he said it. I said we were always pained when we saw and heard things which we knew would see the other end of the see-saw tip over again. Adams looked pissed off though. He said that unless Trimble confirmed a meeting officially, this was all meaningless. I said it would be fine because Trimble had given his clear commitment to TB. He shrugged at that.

Bill had a little catnap in the holding room, and looked pretty shattered when he woke up. Hillary looked tired too and there was nothing between them when they were together. He did his best, and chatted to her and what have you, but she was having none of it. Icy does not do it justice. This was the deep freeze but he was bearing it well. TB was pressing Adams on decommissioning. He said whatever the GFA said, the reality was without decommissioning it was hard to see how they took seats on an executive. Adams said how difficult it was.

We were taken by helicopter to Omagh. We went straight to the local leisure centre to meet families of the victims. There was a little boy there, wearing a Leeds [United] shirt, who was the double of Calum. It was very quiet, a few sobs around the place, but as BC and TB toured the tables, the noise levels picked up a bit and people started to pour out their stories. But it was pretty harrowing. I chatted to a policewoman who was helping some of them through it and she said she had never known anything as bad as this. There was no media at all, just a sound feed for TB's and Bill's little speeches. Then they went round every single table and by the end people were mobbing Bill asking for photos and autographs. The atmosphere lifted as time wore on, but you knew it would fall back soon after they left. We were briefed by one of Clinton's people on the walkabout and he referred to how we were meeting 'some of the fathers' of Omagh. Hillary cut in, 'And mothers,' cutting the guy right down.

They set off to the scene of the bombing, laid flowers and then walked slowly down the street. The crowds were warm and friendly, and Bill was clearly getting a lift from the crowds and their reaction to him. TB said to me later he felt Bill was very down, but hiding it well, and also feeling very damaged. A role in the peace process meant a lot to him, for lots of different reasons. We flew to Armagh over some stunning scenery. There was a big crowd – up to 11,000 – waiting for them and the US team had told Bill he had been a bit down in his earlier speech and this was the one to get pumped up for. He did, and got the best reception yet. [Seamus] Mallon spoke really well.

Trimble was flat and unyielding as ever. TB said later he had the worst personal skills of any top politician he had met. He just couldn't rise to these big occasions. DT looked gobsmacked for example when TB said he should try to develop a good relationship with Adams. He was still avoiding any official acknowledgement of a meeting. Both TB and BC felt today had gone well. We saw him off, then set off for home ourselves. It was getting massive and positive coverage here but a lot less so in the US, which is where he needed it. TB was anxious for him. He said if things were that bad with Hillary in public, heaven knows what it's like in private.

Friday, September 4

For the first time in weeks, Bill C had a good press, and a sense that he had rediscovered his old magic touch. However, it didn't last long as by the time he got to Dublin, a Democrat senator [Joe Lieberman, Connecticut] was stealing the show with an attack on Clinton as immoral, and though he later said sorry, the damage was done. TB having agreed with Clinton that there should be a G7 deputies group to look at the Russian crisis, I put together a briefing note prior to a conference call with GB and Ed [Balls]. GB was opposed to trailing a summit because he worried it would overinflate expectations. I briefed up Mo's visit to the US. The Belfast *Newsletter* was critical of Trimble's speech yesterday. Simon Lewis called, worried about the Demos [think tank] report on the monarchy. I assured him we would distance from it. Helen Liddell called to say Jack McConnell had done a piece for *Scotland on Sunday* saying the whips were responsible for Gordon McMaster's death.[1] I got a few calls, including from relatives saying they hated seeing TB call Adams by his first name.

Saturday, September 5

Joe Lieberman's attack on Clinton was going big and TB was more and more supportive. The bottom line is he is a good president but we have a 24-hour media fuelling constant denigration of anyone in public life who dares to make a difference. The whole thing was now totally out of perspective. He said we should be totally supportive. He had watched a bit about it on CNN last night and they were totally

---

[1] McMaster, 37-year-old Labour MP for Paisley South, had committed suicide in 1997, leaving a note in which he accused fellow MPs of bullying him and smearing him. After an investigation, Tommy Graham was suspended from the Labour Party and became an independent 'Scottish Labour' MP. Former chief whip Don Dixon was also named in McMaster's note as having made his life difficult.

hysterical. I took the boys to Luton vs Burnley and at half-time got a message from David Kerr – 'We are winning' – which meant the UUP executive were about to give their backing to a DT meeting with Adams. Clinton drew massive crowds in Limerick but the good vibes from there were being drowned by the bad vibes in the States.

Sunday, September 6

I was having a lie-in and was woken up by Tony Banks. The *Sunday Telegraph*, which hadn't been delivered last night, had led on [Rupert] Murdoch buying Man Utd. Banks said he had just done *Frost* and said there were obvious major implications and it would become a matter for Peter M and the DTI. It was the first I knew about it. I spoke to Peter in Hartlepool and he had known nothing either. Tim Allan [now director of communications, BSkyB] called him while we were speaking and later called me and said it was definitely on, but there had been a premature leak, that it was a done deal, Alex would be 'very well taken care of', the board would stay in charge but answerable to the BSkyB board. It would go to OFT [Office of Fair Trading], MMC [Monopolies and Mergers Commission] if needed and Peter M as last resort. I called Alex, left a message and he called back at half ten. He said he had been to the gym, then played nine holes of golf and hadn't taken his phone. He had two messages – one from me saying had I read the papers, one from Martin Edwards saying they needed to talk, so he assumed something was up.

He said he had been struggling to get a new contract sorted. He was totally unaware of the Sky bid. He called Edwards who said they wanted him to stay, that he would stay as chairman. He asked what my advice was. I said I thought he was in a strong position. Edwards was worried about building him up too much because he didn't want another 'Busby syndrome' but on the other hand it was Alex, not Edwards, the fans would look to. He should play it long, let them make the running, let them worry that he could turn the fans against this. I said these people believe everyone has their price and if he gives them the impression his only concern is his own position, they will think they have him, so he should be talking to them about broader issues – e.g. super-league, TV expansion, rights. I agreed a line with Peter M and Banks that normal procedures would be followed, any competition issues carefully considered and we couldn't comment further.

The confirmation of the DT/Adams meeting was going fine but Trimble was briefing there would be no handshake because a handshake was a signal that you had no arms in your hands, which could not be said for SF/IRA. There was also a lot of interest in tomorrow's TUC, with a growing sense the economy was in trouble. TB was at Chequers and I called him at 7 after hearing the *Guardian* had learned about the Cabinet meeting there later this week. He said play it down but they were clearly going to make it into a big thing. On Man U/ Murdoch, he said just emphasise the quasi-judicial role. On PR, he said he was moving closer and closer to knocking it on the head, arguing it was not worth yet more constitutional aggro, and that there was no real case for it. He said the only thing really holding him back was his relationship with Paddy [Ashdown].

Alex called after his meeting. He said Edwards had been nervous, [Mark] Booth [BSkyB chief executive] a bit wary and had said he mustn't talk about it. Alex said he wanted a separate meeting just the two of them, because he wanted to establish whether they were serious about making the club bigger. He was in a real dilemma. It was obvious they wanted him and would give him a good deal, that even Edwards had been full of niceness and platitudes, saying they had had words before but it was all in the past now. He said it was dreadful timing because last week he had learned they were giving him a testimonial and he didn't want the fans to think it was all part of a deal for offering support. He said he had been trying to get a new contract for three months and now learned these talks had been going on for five. I said he was in a strong position and he should hold out and be seen to be pressing for the club as a whole, and the fans, not just for himself. If he did stay and was able to say he was getting a lot more money for top players, the fans would be fine. If they felt it was just about him getting a good deal, they would crucify him. He sounded a bit edgy, said he wanted four more years at the top at least. He reckoned that Man U was the biggest brand name after Disney!

Monday, September 7

The Man U story was massive and mainly hostile. Alex called and said the fans were overwhelmingly opposed. There was also a growing political opposition. Tony Lloyd [Labour MP for Manchester Central, junior FCO minister] was up saying Peter M had asked for an OFT investigation when in fact he hadn't. He had described himself as a government minister speaking in a personal capacity and after the lunchtimes I called him to say there was no such thing when it potentially involved a government decision and he should stop doing interviews. Peter M came to see me and was clearly not yet up to speed on all the politics of it but with fans and MPs getting more agitato and the expectation of an OFT inquiry, he would have to get on top of it soon.

Another problem was a new BSE scare with a SEAC member saying there was BSE in sheep and it could be worse than cows. I had a meeting with Margaret [McDonagh] and Anji re conference which was going to be difficult, because RW had sent me a note virtually saying I could do next to nothing while I was there, certainly nothing deemed party political. PG's latest stuff showed Hague was beginning to make inroads, and we were losing it a bit. PG felt he should stop worrying about being unpopular and focus very much on the long term. Peter Hyman wanted TB to do a nationwide tour on the road to conference and gather insights and stories from people he met. It was a nice idea but unrealistic given how much time we always needed pre-conference. Hague announced his ballot on EMU, which was a good move for him, at least in the short term. I went to the end of TB's TUC meeting, with Rodney [Bickerstaffe, UNISON general secretary] in full flight re interest rates, PFI, public sector pay, but all in all the mood wasn't that bad. There was no real meeting of minds though and they always seemed very downtrodden and depressed. TB and Bertie had a phone conversation, in which BA said the Real IRA were about to disband and would we still go for them?

Tuesday, September 8

The Man Utd story was still running big. Peter M clips overnight were making clear he would take whatever action was necessary. Hague got a big press and though it was mixed, I felt he got a fair bit out of it, and it showed him leading. I could see a way for him to get the *Sun* back on their side. But TB was scathing because he said it gave more power to the [Francis] Maude [right-wing Tory MP John]/Redwood faction which was a stupid thing to do. He would make militants out of moderates. It also played into our basic insight re Hague that he was a good debater and a good tactician but a hopeless strategist. I had a meeting with TB and Peter M re the DTI but we ended up mainly discussing Hague. Peter was not too worried but PG's groups showed Hague was picking up a bit and I felt there was a danger we were being complacent. Alan Clark called and said he felt Hague's plan would backfire because it would further raise the saliency of Europe which he never felt was good for them. He said he had really enjoyed attacking TB over the recall of Parliament but hoped he didn't take it personally.

The Real IRA ceasefire statement came through and we got TB

out to do a doorstep. He also went to [Lord] Rothermere's funeral and the nurses awards lunch. Clinton's position was looking ropy and people seemed to be deserting him. We had another conference-speech meeting and agreed DM, PH and I should get something down on paper to start focusing TB's mind. As ever, he was searching for a big argument, and as ever we came back to modernisation. Tim [Allan] called to say the Man U deal was done. I assumed from one of Alex's calls earlier that he was going to go along with it, presumably for a better contract and more money for players. Tim said he hated this kind of work but it was better to be page 1 than page 30.

Wednesday, September 9

I chaired the 9am meeting where the main items were Man U and Clinton. JP called, wondering whether the Cabinet should go to Chequers by train and minibus. I spoke to one or two who felt it wouldn't work. On and off through the day I was trying to get going on the conference speech. I was due to have lunch at the *Express* but accidentally learned Elisabeth Murdoch [daughter of Rupert] had also been invited. With all the Man U/Sky stuff going on, I thought it could be misinterpreted and called her to explain, then pulled out of the lunch. Rosie Boycott should have told me she was going to be there. As it happens, EM was also intending to pull out.

TB, Charlie [Falconer], James Purnell [policy adviser], Angus [Lapsley] and I met re Man U and agreed it was hard not to refer to MMC. The potential conflict of interest was the same company being on both sides of the TV negotiating table. Alex called before his 4.30 meeting with Sky and was clearly in a quandary. He wanted to stay but he wanted to know he would get the time and the money to build a great side. He said Juventus and Tottenham had both been making moves for him.

TB, GB and AD had a meeting on welfare reform. GB had had his front teeth capped and the smiles were even scarier than usual. Phil Webster told me *The Times* were doing a leader on the *FT* story that there would be no welfare reform in the Queen's Speech. I briefed very hard the opposite, that there would be, focused on pensions and disability. I was struggling with the conference draft because we were not getting much direction. I had a meeting with Charlie Falconer and told him I was interested in doing something different. He said there was no way I could move from where I was, because I kept TB on the road. TB was getting more concerned re Clinton and wondering whether the New York visit was a good idea. Blunkett came round for dinner. He was worried TB was getting a bit remote from people who only ever see him getting on and off RAF planes, or hear about him being at Chequers or Balmoral. As ever he was going on endlessly about GB. He said he would stand, as would JP and JS, if TB fell under a bus. But GB would win.

Thursday, September 10

Pressure on Clinton was now really intense, with a lot of new voices saying he should go. The NEC results were trailed in the *Indy* which led to a bit of an up-and-downer with Tom Sawyer [outgoing Labour Party general secretary] who was suggesting I briefed them. I left early and headed for the Cabinet awayday at Chequers with Jonathan, Peter H and David M. We had to deal with a problem on the way down, a US agency having put out a story that TB told congressmen we would demilitarise in exchange for decommissioning. We put out a line making clear there were no such trade-offs. We got there by 9 for a pre-meeting with TB, who agreed there was a danger we were drifting.

He had dinner with Ashdown last night and said he could see a way out of the PR argument – not doing a referendum this parliament because of constitutional overload, but there were other things we could look at, tactical voting, standing down in some seats. He felt Hague's EMU move was silly, not least because it would make it impossible for the Libs to stay equidistant. The meeting itself started with a PG presentation, the numbers OK, doing well on values, TB strong though worries about arrogance, doing better on delivery but not getting the message on social disintegration. Hague was picking up a bit.

TB was on OK form, did the usual thing about how few of them we ever heard putting out a broader government message, stressed modernisation for conference, but with fairness as the purpose. He said he had a letter the other day which began 'Now you have been in government for a few years . . .'. Expectations were still very high. Economic strength has to be the focus, and it requires tough decisions for the long term. Modernisation of schools, hospitals, welfare, fight against crime. There is no point us just being the party of more money for public services. We have to be the modernisers too. The values come through in messages about fairness – New Deal, tax credits. He said ministers had to drive their departments harder, force them to be more innovative. And we all need to have greater ownership and use of a big picture. The pressures are all to go down the departmental road. Resist them.

JP kept talking about the CRS when he meant the CSR. Margaret Beckett said the Tories and the media were redefining the promises we made so they could say we had broken them. GB was good on basic message. JC waffled. Ann Taylor said some people were scared of change and we had to be careful modernisation did not become a concept people were fearful of. Peter M said he felt we had to be more challenging to the public about the need for the country to raise its sights higher. Clare [Short] did her Mother Teresa bit, said we had to stop all the briefings against each other. 'We actually all like each other so why all the stabbing in the back?' Chris Smith warned not to underestimate Hague. John Reid was excellent, really got the big picture and put it over. Ron Davies warned of farmers rioting. Dobbo said we had to present ourselves more as a team. Sitting there listening, you had no real sense of a discussion leading to a conclusion, more a group of people who felt they had to speak and who made essentially random points that wouldn't actually lead anywhere. At one point it was almost like listening to a studio discussion. After lunch, GB did a presentation on the economy (MPC[1] left interest rates unchanged) and did a number on his productivity spiel. He said we had to develop national policies for a global economy. We had to build a national economic purpose, become a rock of stability in an uncertain world. TB summed up rather differently – focus on macro-stability, micro-dynamism, welfare reform, skills, education, transport. We were clearly moving towards a conference more workmanlike than visionary. But the mood was OK. Anji called to say GB's lot were saying Whelan would go if we could help get him a decent job, e.g. the Football Association.

Friday, September 11

With the [Kenneth] Starr Report due for publication, pressure was really mounting on Clinton, and there was a lot of interest in how TB would handle it. I spoke to him at Chequers and he said though we should keep out of it as best we could in relation to the detail, basically we had to stand by him. There was no merit in distancing ourselves at all. Yet he then told John H he wanted to fix a call with Clinton later to discuss NI and Russia, with [Yevgeny] Primakov being confirmed as [Russian] PM today.

The Starr Report was published, and was grim for BC. It was wall-to-wall on the media all over the world. At 9.30, with the world just digesting the whole damn mess, TB's call with Clinton went ahead.

[1] The Bank of England's Monetary Policy Committee.

Considering what was happening around him, he was amazing. It was as if nothing was going on. 'Tony, hi.' If he was acting nonchalant, he did a great job. TB said we were thinking of him. He said he was confident, people were rooting for him, Starr was just a politically motivated rumour-monger. Then they were on to Northern Ireland and Russia. The DT/GA meeting had gone better than anyone expected, forty-five minutes instead of ten, and with at least some engagement. TB stressed again how important decommissioning was going to be, but it was difficult for Adams. BC suggested token decommissioning plus – as it was assumed SF knew who was responsible – an Omagh arrest with briefing that SF were helping with the tip-offs. Then Russia. 'The good news is they have a new government, the bad news is they have put troglodytes in the economic portfolios,' said BC. He said Primakov was smart but knew jack all about the economy. TB was straight on after the call ended – what a guy, that was not someone who was going down. He believed the process would start to turn in his favour, that people had heard all the reasons why he should go and would now be looking for reasons why he should stay. I spoke to McCurry, who was literally counting down [to leaving his job] 'x briefings to go'. Mike said BC was more confident than he had been, felt Starr had overplayed his hand.

Saturday, September 12

Fairly quiet workwise which was just as well, because I was becoming very depressed. I did very little all day, took Calum swimming and then played football but apart from the kids, there was nothing that could lift me. We were due to go out to [*Observer* journalist] Bill Keegan's sixtieth birthday party at the Garrick [Club], and I was just dreading having to talk about the same bollocks the whole time. I went to lie down in the hope the mood would pass but it got worse and worse. The Sundays ticked over, but got overexcited when the White House put out a far more positive line from the call, saying TB had expressed support and understanding. I chatted to Gus O'Donnell at Keegan's do. He said GB seemed to be moving towards acceptance that his modus operandi harmed him as much as anyone. I never quite knew if Gus was just saying what he thought I wanted to hear, but he clearly felt there was a problem there that GB knew had to be addressed but wasn't yet clear how.

Sunday, September 13

TB said re Bill C, of course he can deal with these things but the question is whether this is what politics has now become. He said if you looked at any sexual relationship in the context of a report like that, it could be made to look terrible. Likewise, he said, if every conversation you and I ever had was published, we would be dead – the lewd comments, the impersonations, the rudeness about other leaders and Cabinet members. Every leader had to be able to let go a little. TB called again later to say he had informed [Paddy] Ashdown, by letter, that he did not feel able to deliver on PR before the general election, that there was so much constitutional change going through we had to watch out for overload, added to which we needed to see how it worked elsewhere. Paddy wrote back to say he was virtually finished if he could not deliver PR. TB was not convinced and in any case could not get it through Cabinet.

Jeremy [Heywood] called and said the Treasury had picked up Clinton was doing a big number on the world economy tomorrow. TB decided we had to get a move on with this, e.g. a special G7 or G22 summit convened by us. Jeremy and I were cautious but he was adamant we had to be out there in front on it. I got hold of Robin Oakley, on his way to the TUC, and briefed him on some of the possible ideas. I spoke to Alex F about his TUC visit tomorrow, doing a pensioners' group. The Man U story had gone quiet again.

Monday, September 14
Having done exactly what TB wanted – got Oakley reporting that TB may call a G7 summit on the world economy – TB called and said we needed to haul it down a bit, not least because GB, as ever, did not want any economic initiative that did not come from him. He told TB on the one hand that he did not think we should be planning any great initiative; and on the other that he had his own ideas for an initiative to take on this. Typical. Jeremy said their conversation was a classic of its kind. Peter M had clearly briefed Seumas Milne on his gloomy contribution to Cabinet last week which was page 1 of the *Guardian* and bound to be taken up by others. I spoke to Peter in South Africa. He was fairly relaxed about it. He was more worried re JP at the TUC. TB had made clear to Peter he wanted him to row back on some of the Fairness at Work White Paper, and JP may not know and may commit to the whole package.

The eleven o'clock was mainly about tomorrow's report from the Social Exclusion Unit on the worst [housing] estates, world economy and Clinton. I said it would be wrong for a foreign leader to intervene, but people should understand TB was no fair-weather friend. We would act in the UK national interest which meant maintaining good, strong relations. We had a meeting on the Scottish party. There had been very little progress. We had to get up more attacks on the SNP before their conference. TB and GB felt we should concentrate on their pledge to cut corporation tax because it gave us economic illiteracy.

I had a meeting with Robin [Cook] to discuss his ex-wife's book [*A Slight and Delicate Creature*] which was due for publication in January but which he was worried the *Sunday Times* would run pre-conference. He looked even more diminished than before the holiday, and he sounded even more pompous. His accent was definitely changing. The office was too grand and the officials too obsequious for someone like Robin. He needed people to keep him on the ground, not give him excuses to float upwards. The officials left as I arrived and we sat down. He did one of his big sighs and said things were not good. He showed me two stories from the *Record* and the *Sunday Mail* about the new man in her life. The stories were neither very big nor terribly damaging and nobody had followed them up so far as I was aware, and yet he was doing the big victim thing. He said if he was asked about it, he would say he was happy for them. I said don't get asked and if you can't avoid it, you can always avoid answering. Just say it's nobody's business, and nothing to do with his job.

There was still a part of me that felt a part of him enjoyed being part of the soap. He said he worried she would do very personal inside stuff on their break-up, allege other women and possibly suggest names. Asked whether she might disclose what he said about colleagues, RC said he really only ever went on about GB and everyone knew what he thought of him. He said 'I do not recall saying anything too derogatory re TB though everyone knows I was not an early convert to New Labour and am basically Old Labour trying to come to terms with the new world.' Coincidentally he was expecting a call from TB which came halfway through the meeting. The pomposity rose to a new level as he strolled around his desk, chatting about his holiday, books he had read, then the odd policy issue, then Bill C, saying the US had extra obligations to the world and they would be mad to do this to their president. But what was really striking was how utterly self-regarding he was. Whatever the subject, he took it to a call he made, a minister he knew, something someone had said about him. I couldn't recall if he was always like this. I know it was worse than before but maybe he had always been like this and the FCO just made it a lot worse.

On the book, I advised that unless it was absolutely nuclear, and full of stuff he could not leave unanswered, it would be best to say nothing at all. She and her publisher will want a response to fuel publicity and we will be best to avoid helping them. I said he had to live with the fact she was always going to be seen as the wronged party. I strongly recommended a blanket silence, publicly and, as much as possible, privately too. I thought Robin had got it eventually but then he said he thought he should say he and Gaynor were happy, he hoped Margaret and her new man were happy but it was all in the past, and I said no, no, no, it all plays into the idea of government as soap opera. I said he was in danger of not being taken seriously if he went down that route.

What was obvious was that his instincts were all wrong because basically he hated her and she hated him and they couldn't leave it alone. By the end of the meeting, I couldn't see how he could survive very long in a top job when it came to this stuff. He was self-pitying and self-obsessed. His judgement was poor. He clearly felt this was an issue central to the government, and it wasn't.

Tuesday, September 15

A line in the article Bradders [David Bradshaw] had done for TB in the *Express*, re some estates being so bad they would be shut down, was picked up and was running fairly big. Inflation figures were good, and the timing excellent with Eddie George speaking at the TUC. TB was worrying re New York and in particular how they were trying to line him up so close to Clinton we got hit by it too. He wanted us to plan for as much other coverage as possible, Third Way, UN, [mayor of New York City, Rudolph] Giuliani, NY Stock Exchange meeting. He came round to my office first thing and said it was right to stay close and there should be no distancing but he thought my line 'One report on the Internet won't change his view of the president' was a bit close to saying whatever the facts, we would support him. It was right to stay close but we should not go over the top. He felt Bill would survive, and be an even bigger star on the global stage, but he wasn't out of it yet and we did not want to be exposed. He was also worried about the format for the Third Way event in New York – 'Me and the prime ministers of Sweden and Bulgaria sitting around gassing on comfy chairs' – but Hillary was very keen. I had a sharp written exchange with Piers Morgan re the *Mirror's* ludicrous line on it – the idea you dump Clinton because of this was absurd.

We got Jon Snow in to do an interview, a bit on Clinton, a lot on the economy, TB saying afterwards he felt he explained it a lot more clearly than GB who made everything sound so complicated. Of course it is complicated but you still have to explain it all in terms most people will understand. TB had lunch with Crown Prince Abdullah [of Saudi Arabia]. The FCO had warned he was likely to take a very moral view re Bill but in fact said he felt he was being treated very badly. On the plane north we worked on the speech for tomorrow. On arrival at Blackpool, he did a quick doorstep on the economy and then into the usual TUC rounds. The mood was a lot better than last time. Eddie George had gone down well.

We wanted a clean shot of TB, [John] Monks and Eddie George and used CB to keep [GMB general secretary] John Edmonds out of the way while we got the pictures done. He really was cutting an absurd figure at the moment. Also, I could not believe how patronising he was when introducing speakers at the dinner. TB did a good little speech from a few notes, a mix of warm words and policy substance, and drawing attention to where the unions were modernising. I had a nice chat with Jack Jones [former general secretary of the TGWU] who was always very warm when we met, and it meant I could avoid dealing with Clare [Short] who was at the same table. We left for the airport and then took a call re job losses at Ionica [ailing domestic telecoms provider], which were being announced tomorrow. Oh God. TB said he too had found it incredible how Edmonds had managed to patronise everyone he mentioned.

Wednesday, September 16

TB was annoyed at the fact today's broadcast media was so dominated by his visit to Fujitsu [electronics company]. It was in the end a local constituency issue but which was generating massive coverage of the national economy when the company had made clear that was not the reason for the losses. Added to which we had met the inflation target, unemployment was down again today, and yet that was barely being mentioned. He was also being nagged by John Burton [constituency agent] about not spending enough time in the constituency. We flew down from Newcastle to [RAF] Lyneham, working on the conference draft I had shown him earlier. We were trying to give a sense of edge and hardness to the concept of community. TB and CB were meeting Prince Charles for lunch, which meant Lizzie McCrossan [secretary, Garden Rooms] and I were separated off as the cars hit the driveway at Highgrove, TB taken to the front, us to the back. Then, it seemed, I was supposed to eat in one room, Lizzie in another. I suggested we ate together. We had wild pasta, salad and vegetables served by someone with a real smell under nose problem. I had asked the cops earlier to check out whether there was a pool I could use and they had said there was a pool, but not for use (except by PC) so I had another go when I got there. A man in uniform came through with two towels, gave one to me and one to Lizzie, who politely pointed out she wouldn't be swimming. It was a journey so far back in time it felt extra-planetary. Not only were Lizzie and I expected to eat in different places, but the drivers and cops were even further down the table, out in the barn according to Terry, with a sandwich. The cops were in different rooms according to rank. The rooms were comfortable without being over the top, but totally unwelcoming, though Charles' watercolours brightened things up a little. I swam for twenty-odd minutes and the pool was warm and a bit manky with too many leaves floating around. It didn't feel like it was swum in very often. TB was heading off to Coventry and I was due to come back with CB. We met up at the shop, where I had a brief glimpse of Charles who was showing them some of his organic produce. She said organic farming had taken up most of their conversation at lunch. The rest had been a meandering around foreign affairs. TB was always pretty discreet about his royal dealings, CB less so. She said when she first met Princess Anne, Anne had called her 'Mrs Blair', to which CB said 'Call me Cherie.' 'I'd rather not, Mrs Blair,' said Anne. She said she didn't bother to protest when Charles called her Mrs Blair today.

Fiona called and said we were close to another major *Peyton Place* saga, because TB wanted Anji to go to New York and Fiona was worried CB would go crazy. I said to TB and Jonathan that this time it was not worth the aggro and we would be fine without her because the planning for the trip was pretty well done. CB was interesting re Hillary. She said she clearly found the whole Lewinsky thing 'yucky', but there was no question she was going to dump him. She had decided her marriage was a compromise some time ago and there was no going back on it now, despite the humiliation. She felt there were three possibilities: 1. she was religious and her marriage was a religious union, 2. she was besotted, could not believe she was married to Bill Clinton – I don't think so, she added, or 3. it was a power partnership. CB tended to the third of these, that Hillary knew what he was like but lived with it for the access to power, and the feeling of power, and occasionally the reality of power.

Thursday, September 17

I spent a lot of the day tramping around the heath looking for inspiration [for the Conference speech]. I did a couple of OK passages, one on cynicism, another on NI. Peter H came round later and felt we

September '98: CB on why Hillary stands by her man

could make more of NI, suffuse the speech with the spirit that says problems people say are insurmountable can be dealt with if there is the will to do it. Yesterday didn't go brilliantly media-wise and there was a sense the economy was becoming a problem, and little sense of our response. TB was at Chequers all day, working on his boxes and trying to get going on the [conference speech] draft. Clinton was in deep shit again, the judiciary committee discussing whether to release the video of his evidence, which would just be another great global gorging on his sex life. Magi [Cleaver] called from NY and I told her I wanted to avoid any doorsteps if possible. I was putting together a welter of stories to try to minimise the 'Tony and Bill show' element of things.

Friday, September 18

Clinton was the big running story. TB was at Chequers and called a few times, ostensibly to talk about the speech, but I could tell he was worrying about New York. I said it was going to be a bit of a nightmare but we just had to get through it. Richard Wilson came to see me, worried about his profile, and how he was seen to be clearing everything we put forward. On GB, he agreed we had to get Whelan out. He said Peter M was a 'star – he will transform DTI'. He then raised what was probably the reason for the call in the first place. He said Major had called him and claimed that the story about his legal bills [as guardian] for Wills and Harry was leaked by Mark Bolland to Peter M and that Peter or I leaked it to the *Guardian*. This was paranoid nonsense but he was adamant, said RW, and had been 'ranting on at me about it'.

Saturday, September 19

I was working on the conference speech with PH. TB sent through some dreadful scribbles, then called me and asked what I thought. I said I was struggling to see what his point was. He said he was trying to make the long term interesting. I had dinner with Alex F at their [Manchester United's] hotel at Cockfosters. He was still playing a long game re Murdoch. He had still not committed himself to a new deal but they were clear he wanted a major new contract. He said he was finding it harder and harder to work with Edwards though. He was pretty relaxed about things and said Juventus were still sniffing around. He did a lot of reminiscing re his St Mirren and Aberdeen days, and said Cathy [his wife] kept reminding him how they once never had money so he should not worry about getting more! Re Beckham, he said he loved the attention but he was re-inventing what it meant to be a footballer. Re the sarong [worn by Beckham], he told him 'The last thing I need is you out with your missus wearing a dress.'

Sunday, September 20

TB called and said we needed to be far more positive re the NY visit. I pointed out I had been saying so for days, and he was the one sending out the negative vibes. He said we needed to show why we were going – to give leadership. He wanted to do a piece for *The Times* about why he was going. I talked him out of that, thinking it was far too defensive, but he called three or four times on the same theme. TB said this could be the last time we see Bill as president, but that does not mean we have to be totally paralysed by it.

I kept pushing the positives in the briefings I did, saying we kept focused on the things that mattered. Jeremy was working on the NYSE [New York Stock Exchange] speech, which GB was trying to neuter because he didn't really want TB launching a big economic initiative. TB was never off the phone, constantly pressing for new storylines and ideas to carry us through the visit without the only story being him and Bill. Magi [Cleaver] called and said the NYSE did not expect a speech so we had to get that changed. TB said it was important the US felt we were doing right by them, and standing by friends, but we also needed people to see we had our own agenda being driven forward.

Monday, September 21

And so to what, in a note to TB yesterday, Jeremy Heywood called 'the day trip from hell'. In fact the briefing overnight had gone pretty much word-perfect, several broadsheet splashes, with all the main points we put out yesterday and a lot of interest in the IFI [international financial institution] reform. There was only a little bit of 'why is he still going?' and TB was strongly of the view now that strong support for BC would stand us in good stead for the long term, not just with Clinton but with the US more generally. Needless to say the *Today* programme was less focused on anything we were saying, instead resorting to the old 'will be overshadowed' [by Clinton's situation] cliché. But he was dreading the [Third Way] seminar. 'How did we get into this? We have lost control of it.' He was exaggerating how bad it would be and from Clinton's perspective, there was something to be said for just keeping on keeping on. The original plan was Clinton, TB, [Romano] Prodi, [Hans Göran] Persson and the Bulgarian president [Petar Stoyanov]. Persson dropped out late because of his

[Swedish general] election result. By the time we got there, the organisers were still arguing about what kind of chairs to use! BC was said to be keen on a dialogue of the leaders followed by a Q&A.

On the plane out we worked on the NY speeches plus also managed to get some work done on the conference draft. David M was trying desperately to be serious about the Third Way seminar, but TB and I were in messing around mode. We called it *'le sommet surréaliste'*, ['the surreal summit'] with the world watching BC's videotaped evidence whilst he and we were locked in a policy-wonk discussion about the future of the world with Romano Prodi and the president of Bulgaria. TB started off embarrassed about the seminar. By the time we reached NY he was obsessed with the idea that we now turn it into a big positive thing about the rebirth of progressive politics. By now, they were one hour into the BC tapes and the initial judgement was that they didn't add much. At the UN we had bilaterals with the Pakistanis and the Japanese, mainly on the economy. Both had copies of the *FT* with my briefing of yesterday on the front and were keen on the IFI reform ideas. Doug Senior [Clinton staff] told me they were totally confident he would get through OK, that the worst had been thrown and he was still standing and there was a backlash in his favour. The public totally got why he lied about it, and didn't think it meant he was a liar in his political life.

The discussion over lunch [at the New York Stock Exchange] was mainly Northern Ireland, plus EU regulation. Nobody mentioned Bill. It was the same at the [Rudolph] Giuliani meeting. Giuliani was impressive, particularly on community and crime and he gave us a fascinating presentation of how he had worked with the police area by area to try to tackle it.

Bill and Hillary arrived, and he was in pretty upbeat form. 'Hey buddy, we just had a good day,' he said to me. Sandy Berger said it would be very good if TB could at some point make a reference to the importance of BC's leadership, which I passed on to TB. Sidney Blumenthal [former journalist, adviser to Clinton] said it would be 'appropriate' for TB to talk up BC's leadership! Whilst they were all being briefed on the format, Bill was again trying to get some kind of contact going with HC, without success. She was icy cold, literally froze when he touched her, and avoided any eye contact at all. With everyone else she was perfectly nice and friendly. I dread to think what the mood is like when they're on their own.

Then in they went and *le surréalisme* began. Prodi was just Prodi, meandering away, Bill and TB were fine but it was all a bit samey and heard it all before, though TB did his progressive rebirth line perfectly well. But there were no hostages and it didn't feel as bad as it might have done. Afterwards Hillary led him through to meet some students. Bill C arrived a short time later and got a terrific response, which seemed to cheer him up. HC froze again. We then had the TB/BC bilateral – NI, economy, G7-8, Kosovo – then to the reception. BC told him that Prodi had done a big number for him yesterday and it would be good if TB did the same, which he did with the students. Jim Steinberg felt he was still in difficulty. On the way out, Clinton asked me how it all felt and I said I thought he was through the worst and he needed to keep doing what he was doing. In the airport, TB was beginning to unwind. The whole day had indeed been a bit surreal, he said, but it could have been a lot worse. TB was by now on his world-celeb high, felt the day had gone a lot better than it might have done.

Tuesday, September 22

I took a sleeping pill for the flight and it saw me through to 7.20am. I was up for a chat with TB re the conference speech. We were making progress, but slowly. The coverage from yesterday was pretty much wall-to-wall. Clinton's people had got the expectations re the video evidence well set, and so he came out of it fine. We had an office meeting later to go over conference planning. The problem was TB was not yet clear what he wanted from it so we were working a little bit in the dark.

Wednesday, September 23

I worked at home all day with Peter H and we were pretty close to having a complete draft. Then TB called and said he had started on a separate draft which would be complete by tomorrow. So we were heading into the usual madness of separate drafts, and him flitting between them. PH and I now felt we were working in a vacuum because he had not really communicated what kind of speech he wanted, or what basic message. I was beginning to feel we were way behind. I had a mounting sense of panic. TB felt he had the basic argument clear – we had to modernise for the purpose of building a fairer Britain based upon our values. We were in tune with the electorate, which is why we were able to do it. I said it lacked edge. He said the policy would give it edge. We then had a series of circular conversations which didn't go very far.

Thursday, September 24

After the morning meeting I saw Jack C who was doing *Question Time* tonight. The *Guardian* had run a story about Margaret B being campaign co-ordinator and Jack was angling for it himself. He also said that at Chequers TB had asked him to take charge of negotiations with the Lib Dems. I went to Chequers where TB was working out in the garden. He had been working on the central argument, writing it out in various forms, and had then also done a couple of long sections for the conference speech itself. He said getting the argument right was the most important thing and he was not quite there yet. He wanted us to work on the theme of The Challenge, plus wanted me to do something on NI. He also needed something that said no U-turn without saying no U-turn. We settled on backbone not backdown. I stayed down for dinner with TB. He wanted to discuss the office. He said he liked Jonathan and rated him but he lacked politics. He was also insecure and that made him a bit silly re his relations with [Richard] Wilson, which he should build. He said he was fond of JP but both he and RC owed their Cabinet positions to the status they had developed in the party. They were not good at driving policy.

Although Chequers was not my cup of tea, I could see why he liked it on days like this. He spent most of the day just sitting out in the garden, surrounded by papers, taking an occasional phone call, the Wrens who work there serving him tea whenever he wanted it. The food was good and the atmosphere relaxed, and he did at least get a lot of work done on the speech today. He was a bit worried that he was not in his usual panic. Panicking about not panicking, I said, is hardly leadership. In any event, he has the Sunday Q&A to panic about instead. We watched Man U vs Liverpool, and he looked hurt when I told him Cathy [Ferguson] thought he was basically a Tory.

Friday, September 25

I had breakfast with TB, going over the speech pretty much line by line, then I worked on a Sunday briefing before Andy Grice and Don Macintyre arrived to do an interview. TB was on good form, strong on tax, economy – no U-turn – PR – very cautious – and the party – forward as New Labour. He was at his best when he was knocking back the most common chattering-class complaints – e.g. corporate power over policy, him being a departure from Labour. We had a kickabout a couple of times and over lunch and dinner got the speech pretty much in shape.

We discussed Bill C again. He said he totally understood how it happens. He likes women. He needs release from the pressures of the job. He wants to be a normal person. He said he still found it hard to deal with the fact that everyone has a view about him, that people talk about him as though they know him. Though I didn't much like Chequers, I felt that today we broke the back of the speech. We still had two drafts but they were merging into one. I fought hard for my version on Ireland because I felt it captured more both the emotion and the importance of what had been achieved, and how it related to politics.

Saturday, September 26

Rory seemed fine about both Fiona and I going to Blackpool, but Calum was really upset, so I was feeling down most of the day. I did a phone briefing at 9, fairly tough general message and for the heavies a robust line on the Lib Dems, saying there would be no commitments on PR. I went into the office to clear my desk before heading out to the airport. On the flight up I was working on the passages on the Libs, the Lords, and cynicism. But we were still missing the real purple passage he had asked me to produce. In the next twenty-four hours, whilst TB did the rounds, I tightened it, and also softened it, using the tough message of legislation to mix with a stronger theme of partnership, the sense the government could make laws, but actually achieve a lot more if people engaged with the big challenges. Once we got there, I was pretty much stuck in the room where we were working, our bedroom, and TB's room, except for twenty minutes when I went down to join Fiona for dinner with Neil and Glenys [Kinnock].

It was all a bit tense. It was also pretty clear the press were hoping to do us in, with some of the Sundays doing numbers on Anji/Margaret McD [incoming general secretary] vs Sally [Morgan], which upset all three of them. It also set Anji up for another bout of grief with CB who, when she saw her sitting there briefing TB about the Q&A, couldn't resist asking her when she was leaving. Anji just sat there as though nothing was happening. TB asked me to redo the section on community, which wasn't right yet, and we did a strong section based on the idea of looking at the world through the eyes of a child, which had the potential to be the purple patch he kept asking for. PG thought we were getting there. Peter H was still very down on it and I lost my rag with him because he was basically arguing for a speech which we all knew TB was not going to deliver. We did not have enough time to rerun arguments that had been lost.

Sunday, September 27

I was up early working on the community and challenge sections and took a revised version to TB, who felt we had just about cracked it.

September '98: AC and Peter H argue over speech

The problem was he kept taking out anything that was really personal or emotional, and so we lost a lot of the power. He maintained the strength of the argument mattered more, but if the argument was clear, you could have both. One would illustrate the other. TB said he was getting nervous about not being nervous. I said I preferred it that way, but predicted we would nonetheless have the last-minute panic leading to rewrite on Monday night. We had agreed to get the NEC results out early so that they didn't dominate the whole week. The *Guardian* were salivating at the prospect of the week starting with a 'bloody nose' from the NEC. I went round the press making clear we were unconcerned about the results and they would not change the direction of the party.

The Q&A was fine, with a few strong lines, been there, done that, got the T-shirt, re the party in the past, and also a whack at the *Guardian*. I thought he did fine, but he wasn't happy with it. He was now at that phase where he really couldn't see things in perspective until we got Tuesday out of the way. Although the papers were a mix of bored and troublesome, I felt they were overhyping the potential problems so that at the end of the week, they would be saying the week went well. The mood around the place was pretty good. As the German results [victory for Gerhard Schroeder] came through, TB did a doorstep for British and then German TV, including a tribute to Kohl.

PG told me Peter M had tried to get him to change his book [*The Unfinished Revolution*] because although it was clear Peter was the main figure outside of TB early on, I became the more significant figure as the campaign went on, and he hated that impression. Peter was doing his first conference speech tomorrow and was clearly worried. He knew that oratory was not his strong point and there was a risk he would overreach himself. As expected, the later bulletins were dire, with Mark Seddon and Liz Davies ['grass roots' left-wingers elected to the NEC] being filmed hearing the results, though our lines were in there fairly strongly. PG loved the latest draft but for some reason TB thought it had gone backwards.

Monday, September 28

The final haul, and the aim now was to keep the speech pretty much as is, try to stop a total rewrite, hone and polish, and get the media in the right place on it. The papers were crap, going way overboard with the NEC, though beneath it it was clear they did not see it as being that significant. TB had to go round to the conference for GB's speech, which I had on in the background as we worked through another line-by-line session. He was a bit flat and for some reason Charlie had briefed that GB didn't really want TB's job which was silly because it meant the main economic message didn't really get up at all.

Peter M did fine. He did the right thing and made a speech more suited to his speaking skills – workmanlike not flash – and by the end of it he had won a bit of respect I thought. When TB came back, he made a few more changes, the effect of which was to make community rather than challenge the clearly dominant theme. I had another go at the purple passages and both of us were happy now.

CB was now tearing into the *Mirror* because Tina Weaver [deputy editor] had refused to accept a denial from Fiona about a story that she had taken two carloads of Burberry clothes. She said they may have said they would send clothes but she only bought a bag and a coat. But Tina was obviously being told a very different story. I put together a briefing note with the top-line messages on the economy, modernisation of public services, New Labour the key, and went round to the Winter Gardens to brief the political editors. There were a lot of policy stories in there and I felt it would go well. They all went for zero tolerance; heads to be sacked for the *Mirror*; family for the *Mail*; lottery money/cancer for the *Sun*. I went back for another meeting with TB before he went out on his round of receptions etc. By the time he came back he had worked himself unconvincingly into a lather about the need to start from first principles again. But he didn't really mean it and after another session going through it, he went to bed around half one. Philip's notes had been excellent in shaping us towards the final product and he felt we had a real speech now.

Tuesday, September 29

TB was up around 6 and when I went in at half past, I was pleased to see he was reading through it calmly, rather than slashing out great swathes or scribbling madly. He made a few changes, and some good cuts, but by and large we were in shape. We ran the final fact and policy checks with the office and departments, then did the autocue rehearsal. TB was very happy with it now, said he felt, on going through it, it was the best exposition of the Third Way he had done. We made only tiny changes as we went through it. He was much calmer than at this stage in previous years.

I briefed the evenings and the broadcasters and as I was going through it I felt them latching on to the values and the community messages and there was enough policy in it to give it the edge we needed. It was also interesting to gauge their reaction to one or two of the lines we had been worrying about. They clearly didn't like the reference to 'zeitgeist' so we took it out. We headed for the Winter Gardens, with the usual live coverage all the way, and into the little office upstairs for a final read-through. There was a fantastic buzz around the place and I felt it was well set up. It was ninety per cent there and the last ten per cent would all be in the delivery. He looked very calm just before going on. Accidentally, though no doubt some would say it was planned, his tie almost exactly matched the set. He looked and sounded very prime ministerial, very in control.

The audience took to it pretty much from the off. I watched from the back of the hall, next to Roger Berry and Maria Fyfe [Labour MPs], and even they were very warm about it. It was very much the argument he had set out in his draft note coming through, and the redrafting process had definitely turned a strong argument into a good speech. He delivered it brilliantly. There was an extraordinary standing ovation for Mo when he paid tribute to her in the middle of the speech, which added to the sense of occasion. He got a good response re Stephen Lawrence,[1] women and children, Lords.

I did the post-event briefing but felt they were just going through the motions. The speech spoke for itself. Then Ben Wegg-Prosser [Mandelson adviser] warned me that Tom Baldwin [*Times*] was on to the difficulties between CB and AH. Anji had been pretty much out of the picture the last few days because every time she and CB were around each other, Cherie would have a go, sometimes subtly, sometimes not. Anji was partly blaming me for allowing it to develop, saying I could have stepped in earlier and got TB to face up to it and deal with it. It is true I had pretty much opted out. It was doing my head in, especially with Fiona basically on CB's side. Anji said she couldn't stand it any longer and she was going to leave. But it was perfectly clear he didn't want her to.

I saw Fiona and said she had to get CB to see sense and realise TB had to be able to hire the people he wanted and trusted. I said everyone was making things worse rather than trying to resolve. I then went to see CB on her own. She said she knew that part of this was irrational, but she was not going to apologise. She did not like having Anji around and she could not understand why her husband

[1] Black teenager whose murder in South-East London in 1993 was racially motivated. An inquiry into the way the murder investigation was conducted began in March 1998.

could not see that. Even if it was not entirely rational, she said it had reached the point where it hurt her that he took no notice of how she felt about it. I said he did, but surely he had to be able to build the team around him that he wanted? It was an odd, interesting conversation.

I basically liked Cherie. She was a mix of very strong and very vulnerable; very bright but in some ways unable to see the obvious. At these high-pressure moments like conference speeches, a lot of pressure was put on a lot of these relationships. I said we had to get through this period and see what happened. Jonathan said he could not understand why TB didn't just lance the boil. TB told CB she was being ridiculous, which only made things worse. He then said she had the potential to do a lot of damage to the government, and she looked hurt. Then he said it was amazing the papers weren't full of it and he would be livid if it carried on like this. I had pretty much had enough of it. Later, I couldn't face going out so I just stayed in my room, cheered only by the fact the cop on the door was a Burnley fan and we nattered a bit about that. I watched the main bulletins and the speech coverage was fantastic.

Wednesday, September 30

Apart from the *Mirror* and the *Telegraph*, we got fantastic coverage, probably the best yet. The best thing was the acceptance we had a clear and strong argument for the country. TB did the morning media rounds and was on great form. The main task was spelling out how this was not imitating Thatcher but explaining why her philosophy's day was done.

At the Winter Gardens, TB had a very difficult forty-minute meeting with Gerry Adams. He had been pretty provocative at the *Tribune* rally, talking about the need to take the united Ireland campaign forward, and a veiled threat when he said if you kicked the dog too hard, it would bite, which was seen as hinting about going back to violence. TB felt both sides wanted to make progress. But GA was clear how near impossible it was to get the IRA to decommission, and DT was saying he could not get the executive up and running without it. Worryingly, GA was saying that it may reach the point where people felt they would rather have a different leader. GA agreed to be reasonably upbeat afterwards at his press conference, while I just stuck to the line that we were determined and would get there in the end.

Kosovo was blowing up again, with evidence of a fresh massacre, but RC did not want to go up. He was worried there were too many questions he couldn't answer. First I and then TB spoke to him to say he had to go up and make clear we were pressing for a tougher response.

Cherie and Fiona were already at the dreaded *Mirror* lunch when we arrived. Monty [David Montgomery] put a shot right across his own people's bows saying he wanted a debate about the papers and how they covered the country. He said he felt this was a government with a real project for the country but he didn't feel that came over in the [Mirror Group] papers. He felt they were looking tired and cynical. Piers [Morgan] had a smirk on his face, but not one that hid his hurt. It was a pretty brutal assault on Piers and the other editors and at the end of it, Piers said 'Bloody hell, Alastair could have written that.' TB said he felt there was a time-warp mentality going through the media. They still saw politics through the prism of Thatcher, so everything had to be set by comparison with her, not a new and different agenda. He said he felt the *Mirror* ought to be a place for lively debate and intelligent criticism, not knee-jerk criticism set in an outdated agenda.

Then on Scotland, when Jim Cassidy [*Sunday Mail* editor] said he was worried about [Alex] Salmond's growing appeal to which TB replied 'Do something about it.' [*Daily Record* editor Martin] Clarke, as English as they come, said there was a real anti-English feeling. I said challenge it instead of pandering to it. Then on Clinton, TB said he felt they were totally out of touch. People had a gut instinct on these things, and they felt if the Republicans wanted Clinton out, they should do it at an election, not by this kind of stuff. It all became pretty aggressive and Piers was handling it badly. He had a lot of front and he could talk, but he only had one tune and when you had the prime minister and your boss there having this kind of discussion, it wasn't the right tune to play.

Montgomery said why couldn't the papers take the same approach as they did to Northern Ireland – be critical if necessary but basically supportive and wanting things to succeed? To pile on the pressure, I asked Monty if he wanted a lift to the conference to hear the NI debate, so he travelled with TB and said that had been a warning to the editors that if they kept on with the totally cynical approach, they would be out. By mid-afternoon, there was a lot of talk about it. I got Anji to call Piers and tell him we had not been involved in orchestrating that, but he was clearly suspicious. The question was whether Monty had the power to deliver. TB met Trimble and Mallon. 'Well how do we get out of this, because I'm buggered if I know,' said TB. I went briefly to the Women in Journalism event, where Piers was making a big drama out of the lunch, and Rebekah [Wade] was having to calm him down.

Thursday, October 1

The papers were quiet apart from Kosovo and Ireland. I was getting focused on the briefing for China. I did the briefing later and was pushed pretty hard re human rights. Coverage re conference was winding down a bit and the briefing went fine, with a bit of take-up on the need for a new and better relationship with the Chinese. I went down to listen to a couple of the debates and schmooze around a bit. The general feeling was the week had gone well. TB did a very good school visit, and a doorstep on Kosovo. He was indicating pretty clearly we were moving to a tougher response. He was seeing a few journos, and pointing down the military route. He was very sceptical re PR but also very pro Paddy. [Labour MP Dennis] Skinner having been put off the NEC, I arranged for him to see TB for a cup of tea.

CB had a really bad cold, so TB asked me to go with him instead to his dinner with Jim Naughtie [BBC] and Martin Kettle [*Guardian*]. Re PR, I liked the line [*Sun* editor David] Yelland had used about a voting system being able to give a country the chance to kick a government out. TB said it was tricky. We would probably have to accept a referendum this parliament. He told Kettle we may at some point have to go for the *Guardian* because their basic approach was one of cynicism and disillusionment-spreading. They both felt we would be in danger of looking Stalinist. Back at the hotel, I got a really warm reception from the delegates in the bar, then went upstairs to help JP with his speech. It was pretty well advanced but he needed a few decent jokes and a bit more political rah-rah.

Friday, October 2

TB's upsum interviews were OK, with a lot on Kosovo, where he managed to sound tough without being hit hard for prior positions he clearly felt had been weak. He pushed the line that this was the week the party had matured. JP's speech was fine, if a bit near the mark from time to time, e.g. saying it was a joke TB was a socialist, and GB should dump prudence[1] and marry Sarah [Macaulay], one I had given him last night but didn't expect him to use. TB grimaced once or twice and said afterwards he thought it was only just the

[1] A reference to 'prudence with a purpose', Brown's economic management mantra.

right side of the line, in its basic left-wingery. Jonathan called as we were on the way to Preston, saying Paddy was in a paddy because of the *Telegraph* story that said effectively TB would decide his fate. TB/CB went off for [CB's father] Tony Booth's wedding, which TB said was a bit weird.

Saturday, October 3

It was an incredibly quiet day considering conference had just finished. People were moving on to China, and the Tories. I took Calum to Man City vs Burnley. 2-2. The Sundays were fairly low-key re conference. [*Observer* journalist Andrew] Rawnsley said in his column that I would block PR. But the general low-key approach meant there had been no big dramas, and things had gone pretty much according to plan.

Sunday, October 4

[Kenneth] Clarke and [Michael] Heseltine were out and about causing trouble for Hague, and I felt we had set the Tories up pretty well for a bad week. GB was apparently livid re JP's jokes at his expense.

Monday, October 5

Out of my conversation with Ewen MacAskill [*Guardian*] on the train, when I told him of the Clinton photo and the job swap with McCurry suggestion,[1] the *Guardian* did something on the front, which was followed up by several of the others. It was harmless but embarrassing. Then the explanation about the picture was used as confirmation rather than denial. I sent a note to Joe Lockhart to explain it away.

Kosovo was the main event. TB was ten minutes late for a meeting with RC and George R. Both spoke to their notes, both sets of which were heading in the military direction. There was clearly a problem ahead though, and a big difference of opinion with the US who were willing to do air strikes but would not countenance ground troops afterwards because Congress would be wary of another Bosnia. TB was keen that we were in a position where we were very much in the driving seat of the argument, at the robust end of the build-up, and that if it did not happen it was because we could not get others to go with us.

Charles Guthrie [Chief of the Defence Staff] said he was worried

---

[1] Clinton had sent AC a signed photograph on which he jokingly suggested AC and White House spokesman Mike McCurry should swap jobs.

that though there was plenty of planning for war, there was insufficient planning for peace. He briefed in so far as he could on the NATO planning, but as all the options seemed to depend mainly on US air strikes, there was a limit to what he knew. RC and George R went off to meetings and Guthrie took the chance to take TB to one side and tell him that air strikes should not be seen as an easy option, and there would certainly be UK casualties. Ann Taylor put forward her concerns about Parliament not being recalled – only the Lords was sitting – but TB wasn't keen. We agreed that we would simply say military options were advanced.

The eleven o'clock was all foreign, Kosovo and China. We had finally got the [Chinese] *People's Daily* to take the TB piece. It included the bit on human rights, though they took out the reference to the environment, and the reference to [Chinese Prime Minister] Zhu Rongji modernising – clearly seen as being de trop by the Communist Party. By and large it was OK and we were able to generate a lot of interest in it as the first ever article by a foreign leader in the *People's Daily*. However, human rights was going to be a running sore and [Michael] Howard the opportunist was up on it today.

TB said he had had a heavy session with CB, and told her he was done pandering re Anji, and she just had to accept she was staying. He was not putting up with any nonsense about it any longer. She was a member of his team because he valued what she did for him and that was that and she had to live with it. He said CB had accepted it, but I would believe that when I saw it. On the way to the airport, John Holmes spoke to [Jim] Steinberg and it was pretty clear we [UK and US] were in very different positions re Kosovo. On the plane TB was going through all the China briefs. John Simpson [BBC world affairs editor] was on board so no doubt human rights would be their theme whatever. TB as ever was not that keen to push too hard on human rights, wanting me to emphasise it should not define the relationship. The plane people cleared out an area for a little reception for the press and the business guys. They swarmed CB every bit as much as TB and she handled it fine. TB did a little airborne doorstep and the stories taken out of it were 1. interest-rate cut likely, 2. tougher message on human rights than I had been giving, and 3. tough line on Kosovo and sense of impatience at inaction.

Some of the hacks thought the whole trip was aimed at taking attention away from the Tories but with Clarke and Hezza [Heseltine] on the rampage, it was no bad thing to have the focus on them. TB felt Hague was making a big mistake going for them. He was sure Hague was signing his own death warrant. But he scoffed at the idea

Hezza might one day come to us. 'He is a rank Tory. He hates Labour and he especially hates us in power.' I didn't think TB was as focused on China as he should have been, because Ireland and Kosovo were taking up so much of his time. We had lined up Heseltine as chairman of an Anglo-Chinese group which the press would go for as a story with the timing of the Tory conference, but I wasn't confident we had enough to stay on top of things throughout. I tried to sleep but failed, and feared a bad dose of jet lag.

Tuesday, October 6

Beijing. We landed 7.30am local time, 12.30 body-clock time and I was exhausted. We were taken to the Diaoyutai State Guest House, which was sumptuous, about as luxurious as any we had been to. Magi [Cleaver] had got me booked into the number two VIP suite just over from TB, thick, thick carpets, lounge area leading to an enormous double bed, a huge bathroom with jacuzzi. If I went into the bathroom, leaving a trail of clothes in the bedroom, by the time I came out the clothes were hung up. And I never saw anyone inside the room. We set off for Tiananmen Square for the welcoming ceremony, which was really hot and muggy. But they had put on the full works. TB looked the part, and the media were commenting he looked the part. I was irritated that I was expected to be part of the official delegation standing there through it all. I didn't feel comfortable doing all that stuff, though I sensed my irritation was a lot less than the irritation of some of the hacks seeing me there.

TB was much more comfortable raising human rights than the last time with the Chinese. There was clearly post-Clinton a greater degree of willingness to engage. TB liked Zhu [Rongji] and warmed to him as the meeting went on. He liked the way Zhu said he had a reform programme and then just took him through it, state enterprise by state enterprise. He said he would probably lose his job if he went too far but he felt he had to go forward with change. They both talked about the need for a new era in relations. Zhu said he felt he could trust TB. There was much more engagement on specific issues, rather than just two men going through speaking notes.

TB raised Tibet in the same spirit as human rights, certainly sufficient for us to say he had pressed them on it, and they said there were now channels of communication. We then had the extended session, with cameras in for the start, and Zhu was fulsome re TB. Then he asked TB to speak and said he should say anything he liked, mentioning human rights, which TB touched on, though with less impact than during the meeting. I was worried he didn't go far enough for our own domestic audience. He was worried he had gone too far for the Chinese but Zhu seemed fine. I briefed the media and needless to say they loved the Heseltine story, which they saw as a scam to undermine the Tories. I tried to play down its significance, but then they saw that as a scam to highlight the scam. On human rights, I said he had raised it and was not pushed too hard.

The Chinese let us down badly on specific business contracts we had been hoping for, but TB was gracious enough to put it down to the state of the world economy. TB was doing an interview with CCTV in the Forbidden City which turned out to be something the whole media could watch being done, but not listen to. Weird. So Charles Reiss [*Evening Standard*] was bundled away for getting too close. Nor did they like TB going walkabout. The interviewer was very small with a Donny Osmond haircut, but the interview totally straightforward. TB's *New Britain* book of speeches had been translated into Chinese so we gave the guy a signed copy as we left. John Simpson wanted a clip re China being more open, which we fixed.

TB and I both felt we lacked any real oomph in the main Chinese speech. TB wanted a specific China story. I wanted something more general that would resonate more at home. John H and I both felt his ideas on the world economy were not substantial enough to make the speech fly, but he and GB both felt they were on to something. We set off for the banquet at the Great Hall. TB said over dinner he had another session on human rights with Zhu, who said he felt much more open to discussion about it. We got back to the Guest House for a series of calls – RC re Kosovo, Clinton re Kosovo and international economy, and GB re the latter. TB told GB Bill had said Gordon had done a great job chairing the G7 on this. GB was thrilled but then said why are the US blocking all the difficult stuff then? TB wanted the speech to be seen as an international explanation of Blairism. If we were to make anything of the international financial changes we were proposing, we had to build him up. He said remember the reaction in the shopping centre in Japan.

Wednesday, October 7

The main story, as I feared, was TB pulling his punches on human rights, based on what he said when Zhu asked him to speak in front of the cameras. TB was irritated but his general view was this human rights stuff was overblown in terms of its significance at home. The news was dominated by GB in the States revising growth forecasts downwards, which was getting a grim response – jobs blow, GB in the shit etc. TB wasn't sure about the timing, during the Tory

Outgoing Hong Kong governor Chris Patten hands over a British flag as the former colony is handed back to the Chinese.

Tony Blair on the campaign trail in Scotland, making and winning the argument against separation from the UK.

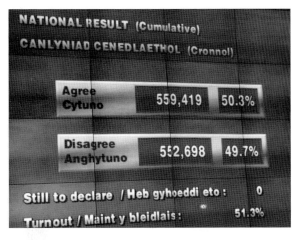

The referendum on devolution in Scotland led by Donald Dewar was easily won; less so in Wales.

Tony Blair with Mo Mowlam, who did not always like being in the background of the key Northern Ireland talks.

On a flight back from Northern Ireland Campbell dons Mo Mowlam's discarded wig. The colourful Northern Ireland Secretary had a habit of removing her wig in meetings.

Denver. To the mild consternation of White House press secretary Mike McCurry (standing, far right), Clinton (seated, right) is being briefed on Northern Ireland by Tony Blair (seated, left) and team. Left to right, standing: Jonathan Powell, John Holmes and Alastair Campbell.

Российская Федерация United

Nobody thought it could be done, but after days of negotiations, Tony Blair and Bertie Ahern sign the Belfast Agreement. April 10, 1998.

From the high of the Good Friday Agreement to the low of the Omagh bombing, with the Clintons as ever on hand to support.

Monica Lewinsky greets Bill Clinton – this was a picture that would haunt Clinton through his presidency.

Tony Blair serving Alastair Campbell for once – in the White House at the height of Clinton's Monica problems.

Bill Clinton's jokey job swap offer: his handwritten caption suggests Campbell goes to the White House, and Mike McCurry to Number 10.

To Alastair — I've cleared it with Tony. An ominibus trade just like professional sports. I get you for McCurry and two draft picks as yet unnamed — poor Tony! Bill Clinton.

Robin Cook with Gaynor
at Clevening, where they
married once his divorce from
Margaret came though.

Campbell did his pipe-playing party piece
at the wedding of David Miliband and
Louise Shackelton.

Alastair Campbell water-fighting with
Philip Gould on holiday. Tony Blair could
never understand why 'political families'
would go on holiday together.

AC and AC: despite being
poles apart politically,
Alastair Campbell and
Alan Clark were good friends
as well as fellow diarists.

Tony Blair (2nd left) chairs the G8 with, clockwise from left, Boris Yeltsin, Romano Prodi, Ryutaro Hashimoto, Jean Chrétien, Helmut Kohl, Jacques Chirac and Bill Clinton.

Campbell with Clinton at the G8 summit, Weston Park, shortly before the US President and the Canadian PM, Jean Chrétien, went missing.

A ragged photocall at the end of a bad-tempered summit to agree on the new boss of the European Central Bank. Front row, left to right: Tony Blair, Romano Prodi, Jacques Chirac, Helmut Kohl, Antonio Guterres.

Ron Davies reflects on the 'moment of madness' that cost him his Cabinet career.

Peter Mandelson leaves the home he bought with a loan from Geoffrey Robinson, which ultimately led to his first resignation from government.

Amid the Mandelson fallout, Tony Blair was dealing with a bigger crisis – Iraq – here chairing a meeting at the MoD, flanked by George Robertson and General Sir Charles Guthrie.

General Wesley Clark, who led the military campaign on Kosovo, and agreed to Clinton and Blair's request that Campbell oversee NATO communications.

For Blair, Kosovo became a moral crusade, particularly after visits to refugees.

But the military/ political divide was never easy – General Clark (right) with NATO General Secretary Javier Solano.

conference, because it gave them an easy hit, but I was sure it was right to do it abroad, because the context was more easily established as the world economy.

Philip Barton and I tramped round with TB to a succession of commercial events, seminars, scholarships, contract signings. TB felt we had to recalibrate the message on human rights, so we arranged for him to say a few words when awarding the scholarships to students who were going to be studying human rights at Nottingham University. We also fixed an interview with [John] Simpson at Beijing Observatory. We got there and, lo and behold, a dissident, Xu Wenli, had been arrested. He had been on *Newsnight* last night being only mildly critical, suggesting he was not convinced they would ratify a new convention. It coloured the interview but TB got the balance about right, that we should acknowledge progress made whilst still pressing for more.

The speech was coming together, with human rights, Kosovo and world economy all separate stories under one umbrella message. TB had a surreal call with Yeltsin. Listening in, I guessed Yeltsin was pretty much out of it. The interpreters seemed to give up at one point. TB was lying on the bed in underpants and a T-shirt rolling his eyes, trying hard not to laugh, then going into diplo-mode whenever he spoke. God knows what the Chinese made of that one, I said to John H, whose note of the call was a masterpiece. Anyone reading it would have imagined they had had a serious conversation. TB said he thought I was a bit disengaged at the moment. I said the visit was taking care of itself. He said he saw me like a star striker who occasionally went AWOL for a week or two and needed a spell in Barbados to get re-energised. He was right to sense I wasn't firing on all cylinders this week but I always had a bit of a lull post-conference.

Talks with [Chinese President] Jiang Zemin, which were a lot more formal, and a lot more small-talky than with Zhu. He told TB he was jealous of his youth. He also treated us to a lecture on Tibet. He was pretty scathing about the Dalai Lama, suggested he was influenced by young people in his entourage and said things he wasn't sure of. TB was a lot less nervy about raising things than he had been at that awful meeting in Hong Kong. TB said he understood because of Northern Ireland how they felt about irritating outside interference. Jiang told a few bizarre anecdotes, and the meeting overran by twenty minutes, which excited our increasingly excitable ambassador [Sir Anthony Galsworthy]. The press were doing a great u-turn on the dissident. His arrest having been denounced as a failure of our softly-softly approach, now his release was being seen as a success for it. TB had a cold by now but got through the speech fine.

Zhu came up to the Guest House to do a personal farewell which was meant to be a fairly significant gesture, designed to mean a lot. It had fifteen minutes in the diary but extended to forty-five. TB said he felt it was in their own best interests that they moved faster and further on human rights. Zhu invited the family out for a holiday there. CB was getting on fine with his wife too and we organised some pictures of the four of them in a little side room where they were going through an album of the trip. We went up to TB's room for a debrief after they left, TB sitting in the vibrating chair pretending to be Chinese. Ironically, the only serious point he made from the chair was that we had to build the message we were serious on the world stage again. I said all well and good but wasn't it time he tore into the Tories over Europe.

Thursday, October 8
TB was at me again first thing, saying I wasn't firing on all cylinders, though he did at least say me at half pace was better than others at full pelt. I said I was hardly on half pace, but I knew what he meant. We needed a new story and on the flight to Shanghai I put together a briefing which shamelessly played into the Tories' continuing troubles on Europe, which were dominating their conference. TB toned it down a bit but was otherwise fine about it. TB's cold had got worse and he was slightly dreading the day. We did clips for [Jon] Sopel and [Richard] Bestic [Sky] on the plane both on Kosovo and on the importance of an improving relationship with China. They ended up leading the news.

TB had a session with the business group and the media and was very relaxed and hitting all the right buttons. I was working on some of the broadsheets to do more considered pieces on the relationship. Some of the business guys were helping push the line that TB was an important asset in these kinds of business relationships in a changing market. TB was enjoying the leadership role and spotlight. We arrived in Shanghai and were taken straight off on a series of commercial events including the opening of the new Sun Alliance building, the first British insurance offices in China. There was a fantastic energy to the place, so different to polluted and slow Beijing. New and beautiful buildings were going up everywhere. He did a commercialisation seminar at the new stock exchange and then on to the floor, which was all a bit different to the London version, polite ladies sitting at

October '98: Politics going well; now to business

desks and screens rather than blokes in coloured suits screaming at each other.

We had a good meeting with the mayor [Xu Kuangdi], an interesting and charismatic guy and very different to your archetypal Chinese politician [Xu would be demoted in 2001]. He was fascinated by the red box, having seen John H carrying it behind TB on the TV news last night. Nice lunch, seven or eight courses, and the energy around the place was like a different planet to Beijing. We had a stack of business events back at the hotel, TB being taken round one by one by the ambassador. The whole UK staff seemed never to know where we were going or what we were supposed to be doing.

The UK photographers were suggesting an intimate TB/CB chopsticks picture to get Hague off the front pages tomorrow. TB wasn't keen but went for it later and it worked OK if a bit cheesy. I did my Europe briefing, then to the Britain in China food exhibition, then TB did a few general clips on China. Then Whelan called and said GB didn't want us to respond on interest rates [Bank of England cut of 0.25 per cent to 7.25 per cent] because he thought we had to link it all to the world scene. I said, and TB later said to GB, that we couldn't just take free hits or give up opportunities to relate the basic long-term message. The truth was GB hated TB doing anything on the economy, and yet in terms of explaining it in ways people understood, he did it better.

Hague's speech – 'The British Way' – came through and was poor, and the briefing I was working up on TB's next speech re Europe played well into that mood. It was a total piece of positioning and TB felt afterwards I had gone too far. Combined with the chopsticks picture, he thought I had gone from inertia to hyperactivity. Re CB, we made the mistake of sending John Deans [*Mail*] with her as a pool to the cancer event, where she got into the whole area of alternative medicines which ran the risk of getting her into an issues profile. She was doing some great pictures though, and was a much more natural photographee than TB. But the visit as a whole was picking up.

Friday, October 9

Godric called at 7am, midnight UK time, to tell me Clare Short had said on *Question Time* that Clinton was not fit to be president because he lied. My instinct, as so often with Short, was that TB should sack her. His argument was always that she would become a martyr and cause more trouble outside. But I wasn't convinced she actually had a following. She had got herself into a position where the press lauded her publicly, because she gave us a headache, but in truth did not see her as a very credible figure. Of course Clinton had done things that were hard to defend, which is why it was best to be in the position of defending in general while avoiding the specific. When I told him about it, he just said what a silly woman she is – does she have any redeeming features? Then he added 'I'm probably asking the wrong person.'

We were getting OK coverage out of the trip, and doing well on pictures, but the *Mirror* had the first of Piers' response to last week – Blair knifes our nurses – re pay. TB worked on the speech on the plane [to Hong Kong] and made it much more about IFIs, anti-protectionism, hedge funds. He felt we should be getting more mileage out of the Chinese relationship per se but I felt that was the one area where we were hitting above average, particularly with the broadcasters. We had [Sir] Andrew Burns [Consul General] looking after us in Hong Kong, which was a big improvement. The speech venue was the same place as the handover ceremony. The air conditioning was on full blast and very loud, which meant people at the back were straining to hear. I briefed hard on IFIs and hedge funds then went back for the lunch, next to a Swede and an oil executive, mainly small talk. I hated doing these sit-down lunches and dinners. The bilateral with C. H. Tung [chief executive, Hong Kong special administrative region] was OK, fairly low-key and he didn't really push him hard on democracy etc. When Martin Lee [chairman, Hong Kong Democratic Party] came in for his meeting, having already attacked us in *The Times*, TB was not really in a mood to hear him. He struck me as a real whine merchant who had really not thought out how to work on TB. He complained TB had not pressed hard enough on human rights but then admitted he was relying on press reports and had not actually read the speech. He made a big deal about the Chinese provisional legislature but Andrew Burns said that when last week they had asked him what he thought we should raise with the Chinese, he hadn't even mentioned it. He was clearly someone, a bit like the Lib Dems at home, who got easy coverage by being a convenient voice of attack, and was not used to being criticised, so TB gave him a bit of a going over.

Later he did a doorstep where, after the questions on Hong Kong, he was asked – by [Trevor] Kavanagh [*Sun*], [Phil] Webster [*Times*] and [Jon] Hibbs [*Telegraph*] – about Clare and he dealt with it by saying he had dealt with it earlier, and then by saying he had already dealt with it. They knew what the game was and the way he dealt with it told its own story. Mike White said we were applying A-level spin. We knew what the press wanted and we also knew that if we supplied it, the story would go bigger than we wanted so we were not responding at all. I said it had taken up fully one minute of our time, which was what it merited. We went to the C. H. Tung banquet.

I was sitting with [Sir] Dick Evans [chairman, British Aerospace] who said Kenny Dalglish [football manager, former player] was interested in buying Burnley and he was helping him. I was not sure how many more banquets and toasts I could take. C. H. Tung was fulsome in his tribute to TB and the UK. Katie Blair [sister-in-law of TB] had joined us. TB and CB were both knackered.

Saturday, October 10

The coverage was low-key and I was beginning to think we needed to plan these visits differently. A lot of the traditional elements just didn't seem to have the weight. TB did a *Sunday Business* interview where he pushed the line about a national credit rating as part of the new IFI reform plans. At the round table with the Hong Kong politicians he was pushed by two women on democracy and human rights but again emphasised that the relationship should not be defined by these issues alone. Then to the Buddhist nunnery, which was very peaceful and beautiful in the rain. Good pictures. Tom Bradby on ITN said that the visit was being covered almost like a royal visit, with coverage for pictures now almost regardless of the politics. He met a 111-year-old woman, then did a doorstep on Kosovo and Japan. The general feeling among the hacks was that though the trip was not a total disaster, nor was it a total triumph.

TB did another commercial visit which got very good crowds and pictures. I got some of the business guys out to say how these prime-ministerial visits helped them and helped Britain. Trip basically over, on balance OK. TB did a couple of interviews on the plane, and also had a chat with the hacks, who were looking even more ludicrous than usual in their white BA pyjamas. Over dinner, Magi [Cleaver] was gobsmacked when I said we needed someone full-time doing advance of these visits, and TB said 'What we need on these visits is Anji.' Magi felt she was too office political for some of the FCO lot. I took a pill and slept for nine hours.

Sunday, October 11

I was pretty knackered and had a total day off which was probably a bit of a mistake because it meant I didn't get on top of the *Independent on Sunday*'s story about scrapping widows' benefit. Kosovo was still the main event with Richard Holbrooke [US special envoy to the Balkans] seeing Milosevic. GB, after telling TB and me he thought we should go low-profile on the economy, did *Frost*. I bumped into Adam

Boulton [Sky] at the Sobell [leisure] centre. He said however bad the Tories looked from afar, in fact they were a lot worse.

Monday, October 12

The morning office meeting was the first attended by Charlie F, who always adds a sense of fun to proceedings, and also has pretty good judgement and isn't afraid to say what he thinks, so I was glad he was now part of that regular forum. PG said there was now real anxiety about the state of the economy. He felt it was affecting how people felt about their own lives and how they felt about Britain and its future. TB was angry at the way GB had allowed Whelan to let the interest-rates briefing get out of hand last week, and also felt GB was focusing too much on day-to-day rather than a big message of economic moderni-sation which is what the country needed to hear. They needed to know where all this fitted. He had done one of his weekend notes listing all the areas for discussion. So point three was 'Kosovo'. He looked at Jonathan and then me, said 'So – are we going in then?' We both said it all depended, and that was the sum total of the discussion. PR was on the list – 'We have to find a way of kicking this into touch without doing in Paddy.' There were mixed in-house reviews of the China visit. Anji hated the chopsticks picture. We then had a meeting with Darling and Byers to work through a strategy for the welfare reform Green Paper, which had to show we were back on track. The widows' benefit changes were difficult, and we were flagging up other changes too, and had to communicate that there would be winners as well as losers. TB was keen to use the argument that an EC court ruling was part forcing this more aggressively. We agreed to brief today that we were going to reform not abolish it, and that we were not going to resist the EC court ruling.

The problem we had in media terms was shown clearly today. When we argued for welfare reform in general, there was a lot of support. When you argued to make changes to specific benefits, it was too easy a hit to wheel out people affected and say Blair was taking on the people who elected him. TB felt we had to combine emollience of tone with the clear drive and direction of continuing reform. AD was up for that and wanted to do a big thing next Thursday – an overview document and two consultation papers on specific areas – incapacity benefit and widows' benefit; plus the general uprating, so it was going to be a big day for him.

A meeting on Kosovo, where I had to tune out regularly when Clare was piping up. It was important to get up the message that if Holbrooke got a deal it was because we stood firm. Nobody was sure yet what he was going to get out of Milosevic. I wanted RC to go up on it but he felt we didn't know yet what we were playing into. The worry was a deal that would let Milosevic off the hook, and all the time the ground troops issue was in the background.

Tuesday, October 13

The Holbrooke deal was just about gettable awayable with though it was not great. TB did a pooled clip after having a pretty difficult meeting with GB who was still against the world summit idea. He was also still making clear his intention to hang on to Charlie who had been causing more EU problems yesterday. The inflation target was hit, crime figures were down. The Neill committee went much further than we were wanting on referendum rules.

I had a busy day on the internal communication front, following TB at Richard Wilson's shambolically organised senior Civil Service conference. It ran late and so the timings were all out and we didn't have enough time for Q&A. I told them how in opposition we analysed their weaknesses and exploited them and yet were finding it hard to change them. I gave much the same message later to a COI [Central Office of Information] scholarship group. I also had a meeting with government heads of information. Eleven of them were new since the election, and some were a big improvement, but I still felt I was sometimes speaking a foreign language. I said we had turned a corner, but there now had to be a gear change in performance. We had a drinks do in the White Room for them afterwards, which was definitely worth doing. Mark Bennett felt I needed to get out with the younger ones more. Nicola Pagett cancelled her appearance in the play she was due in, so was clearly in a bad way, which explained the sudden increase in letters.

Wednesday, October 14

We were on the back foot on the Neill report,[1] which came over as being about us not the Tories, and on the Lords debate,[2] though Margaret Jay was excellent. There was barely any coverage of inflation,

---

[1] Committee on Standards in Public Life report on party funding. Amongst other things, the report proposed a £20 million cap on party funding for elections, that blind trusts should be 'prohibited as a mechanism for funding political parties, party leaders or their offices, Members of Parliament or parliamentary candidates' and that government should take a neutral stance on referendums.
[2] On House of Lords reform, ending the right of hereditary peers to sit in the Lords and moving towards political balance between parties in the Upper House.

jobs figures or crime figures. At 9.30 we had a meeting with GB, and a cast of thousands from the Treasury, led by Nigel Wicks, Gus [O'Donnell] and Ed Balls, about the international financial crisis. Wicks said it was a crisis that would have a real effect on the domestic economy, but it would take some time to come through. GB was worried about protectionist instincts in the States, and he was worried Brazil would be next. It was all about GB trying to resist attempts for a leaders' summit. We to-ed and fro-ed for ages until TB just said let's come back to it later in the week.

GB wanted a Commons statement on Monday re IFI reform, which I was worried would just give the Tories a free economic hit to start the week. [Viktor] Klima [Austrian Chancellor] was in for a pre-EU summit meeting and TB was pushing on defence, talking about the humiliation for Europe for the US having to take the lead in sorting European problems like Kosovo. He said Europe had to face up to more of its own responsibilities. At the pre-meeting with RC, he said GB had pissed off everyone in Europe with his handling of the economic situation.

Murdo Maclean [private secretary to the chief whip] and Nigel Wicks both said my speech to the top civil servants went well. Wicks said what they saw for the first time was that you are substance not spin, that you deal with the media because you have to, but that you do the job for other and better reasons. [Paul] Dacre [*Mail* editor] called to say he didn't think TB should accede to Lady Rothermere's request to TB to speak at the memorial service [for her late husband]. I totally agreed with him, but for totally different reasons.

Thursday, October 15

Despite Margaret Jay being terrific in the debate, we were very much on the back foot on the Lords. TB and I both felt we needed to be far more political, make more of the totally unrepresentative nature of the Lords – no blacks, no Asians, Old Etonians galore. We agreed Jack C should do a speech on it tomorrow. Cabinet went over the Lords, Neill committee, Kosovo, GB on IFI reform, on which the Yanks were cutting up rough a bit. Clare was at her most interrupting worst, chipping in with her views on everything. Jack C and Margaret B were both clear we had to reject Neill on referendums [neutrality]. Jack in particular was scathing about it. 'The line about the government not taking a view is bonkers.'

On Kosovo, George R set out where we were. TB said we should have been able to deal with this six months ago without grief or cost and it had shown up Europe's complete uselessness at dealing with problems on its own doorstep. President [Ernesto] Zedillo [of Mexico] was in for lunch, and I was pretty impressed by his media guy. We were launching the Britain-Mexico business network so Tristan Garel-Jones [Conservative peer, former MP] was in making a bit of mischief.

I had a meeting with Stuart Higgins [former *Sun* editor, now PR consultant] and a woman producer re a programme about [Prince] Charles at fifty. The more they went on about it, the more down-market it felt, so I was pretty clear we wouldn't help them with it. I wrote Robert Fellowes a note about it. It felt like a Charles the moderniser film probably being pushed by [Mark] Bolland.

We had a meeting with GB re welfare and it was clear both of them were a bit worried where this was all going. It was one of those areas where reform was obvious in principle but hard when you got into the detail of taking benefits from people who thought they were entitled to them. The work-related stuff was hard enough, but this was really diffi-cult. PG's book was being serialised in *The Times* from Monday and he was doing an interview today. He came in to see me and I advised he play down the 'friend of TB/GB' and instead play up the role of strategy and defend the process of constantly listening to the public. It was an opportunity for him to become an authoritative voice on New Labour.

I went to Tom Sawyer's farewell [as Labour general secretary] where both TB and NK made nice speeches. Neil was a bit senti-mental at times, but very warm and occasionally very funny. TB used it to remind people how awful things were in the 80s.

Friday, October 16

[Stephen] Byers did the 8.10 [*Today* programme] slot on the economy and was excellent. TB was in for the Nobel Peace Prize [for Northern Ireland] and we put out words and then did a pooled interview at Chequers. I was a bit nervous re PG's book after hearing *The Times* were leading their coverage on the chapter about the leadership election. Robert Fellowes called to say he, [Robin] Janvrin and [Geoff] Crawford were seeing the Higgins programme people on Monday. He had no doubt Bolland was behind it and the subtext was that Charles had been the saviour post-Diana's death. He sounded pretty fed up about it, though of course he was leaving soon and sounded glad to be doing so. Hollick called to complain about CB helping James Hughes-Onslow.[1]

---

[1] *Express* editor Rosie Boycott had sacked diarist Hughes-Onslow, who subse-quently allegedly visited her home as a potential buyer and allegedly secreted fish fingers in the bathroom. The resulting scandal became known in newspaper circles as 'Findusgate'. Hughes-Onslow later denied he was the culprit, claiming that he was 'an innocent prawn in the game'.

I didn't like his tone. He always spoke as though it was inevitable we had the same interest, and it wasn't always so, as re the *Mirror*. Nobel Prize was a massive story all day. I left for home early, and headed north to see Mum and Dad.

Saturday, October 17

I was hoping for a quiet day work-wise, seeing Mum and Dad then over to watch Burnley, but then it emerged [Augusto] Pinochet [former army general and junta President of Chile] had been arrested at a London hospital after a request for extradition by Spain for his murderous activities. It was one of those events that came out of the blue, and the media knew not long after we did, and we were scrabbling a bit to catch up. I said to the office we had to be in a position of saying this was not a political decision but that complex legal processes were being followed. The Chileans would be furious and we had to be in a position of briefing 1. that we had an agreement that we would not arrest him, 2. SIS had helped out with a security assessment before he came, 3. he had been here for treatment before and we had ignored him, and 4. he helped out during the Falklands war. We agreed to emphasise that it was not a political decision, but it was complicated because Jack Straw would make the final decision once we had the case put to us by Spain. He would do so not as a politician but in a quasi-judicial capacity. But it was not going to be an easy line to stand on.

The football was terrific, and we should have won [against Notts County], but conceded a late equaliser [1–1]. By the time we were home the Sundays had arrived, and there were a couple of difficult stories about the planned [Argentine President Carlos] Menem wreath-laying [at a memorial service for Britain's Falklands war dead during his forthcoming state visit]. Someone had been getting retaliation in first and running the line that Thatcher and Simon Weston [injured Falklands hero] were being snubbed. I could see a big problem looming. My briefing on Jack Straw's pitch for more black police was running OK but low-key, but it was picked up third or fourth on the broadcasts.

Sunday, October 18

I watched Peter M on *Frost* and then paged him to say he had gone OTT re Pinochet. We had been bending over backwards to keep it as judicial and he had been so hostile about Pinochet's record it would fuel the charge it was all political. He was also a bit high-handedly dismissive re Neill [Report] and referendums. Hague wrote to TB demanding that he make a statement on the economy – yet another reason for GB not to make one in my view. TB and GB had been discussing again what to do and the current thinking was TB do a conference call with the G7 leaders and we put out a statement on the back of that. Most of the day was taken up with Argentina. As I feared, the *Sun* and the *Mail* in particular were going mental about the Menem wreath-laying and the snub to Thatcher, Simon Weston and others. I called a conference call with me, John H, Peter Westmacott [FCO director, Americas] plus our and FCO press officers and agreed we should stick to the line this was a small service, Menem's idea, to be attended by government, Armed Forces and veterans, the last of these to be decided by the veterans' association. We should make clear that if it was broadened further, other problems would arise. So if Thatcher was invited, would the Argentines not feel duty bound to invite representatives from that era of their own government too?

I got Westmacott to speak to Charles Powell [former private secretary and foreign policy adviser to Margaret Thatcher, brother of Jonathan] who felt that though Thatcher wouldn't want to go, she would need careful handling. Westmacott spoke to Crawfie [Cynthia Crawford] her 'dresser', and then to Thatch herself, in New Orleans. She was ballistic. She said it was not possible to have reconciliation with these awful people, and she should have been consulted. Eventually she calmed down and said we could say she would not have been able to attend because of prior commitments, and she would not attack the event publicly, though I was not so sure about that. People were sensing that we were making it up as we went along, and to some extent we were, but it was better to have one day of chaos and recrimination than have it all build up and up and ruin the visit.

TB thought the whole event was a bit silly and wondered if it was too late to cancel. He thought it was ridiculous to have an event like that and not invite Thatcher but he felt the whole thing was a bit misguided. But he agreed we should not reopen the issue of the size or nature of the event. He was also wondering about some of the welfare reforms.

Monday, October 19

We managed to keep the Menem/Thatcher row pretty much confined to the *Mail* and the *Sun*, and the broadcasts were not touching it. Pinochet was taking care of itself, though Peter M's comments hadn't helped. The main story for us today was Northern Ireland with McGuinness in in the morning, and Trimble in the afternoon. We placed expectations very low and by the end of the day it was clear that we were right to. McG told TB they would decommission but not right now. TB said that wasn't good enough. DT was trying to get SF on to the executive and he needed better cover than that.

McG had someone called Jim with him who asked TB to sign a good-luck card for someone called John. As TB signed, I said it's not for someone who has a contract out on Paisley is it? Jim said it's for a good Republican friend. McG did his doorstep outside and was very aggressive – it's all about Trimble (he had a wonderful way of pronouncing his name to make it sound like a really unpleasant illness). It also made it easier for DT when he came in, not harder. He didn't have much new to offer. Both he and Taylor were pretty clear they could not move without actual decommissioning. I said to TB afterwards 'Your one great triumph and it's going up in smoke.'

Jonathan, Anji and I went for an honours meeting, which was the usual ghastly short walk into an entirely different culture. Jimmy Shand [accordionist whose 'Bluebell Polka' hit the mid-charts in 1955] was their number one Scot for example. I had nothing against Jimmy Shand, but the way we were meant to be impressed that this was showing a grasp of modern culture was comic. TB and I had a meeting with Victor Blank [new Mirror Group chairman] who was clearly a lot keener on Piers than he was on Montgomery.

Tuesday, October 20

Hague was on *Today* calling for a statement on the economy, but he was all over the place on spending, tax, borrowing. It was a classic case of thinking the wicket was easy and not thinking through your own position. I got hold of Jack C and got him to go straight on and make Hague's credibility the issue. He did well. He is excellent at taking two or three points, going up and making them without sounding like he is just reading a script. TB felt the line we should be developing on Hague is that he gets the small things right and the big things wrong.

The Pinochet situation was unravelling. The right-wing press were attacking us for not helping an 'ally' from the Falklands, while the Guardianistas were going down their usual route of cock-up and conspiracy. TB was wishing we had never got involved, but the legalities were complex. He was due to do a round table with six European journalists. We wanted to get up the line about a new role for European defence but within the context of NATO. It was a tricky area but we sat down in advance and worked through a line that would carry

October '98: TB's 'good luck' message to mystery Republican

clearly. The thing was to spell out the facts about our position without provoking a whole load of nonsense about a European Army. It wasn't a very satisfactory forum though, half a dozen people who all had their own ideas for a story so things just bounced around. There was a lot of interest in Third Way ideas and I was struck again by how mainland European journalists are much more at ease with discussing political ideas and philosophy, not just 'stories'. TB was worried afterwards at how several of their questions related to Britain lacking power in Europe if we were not in the euro. The woman from *El Mundo* was the liveliest and afterwards said I was becoming very famous in Spain for being rude to journalists.

We had a meeting afterwards on forward planning for speeches. I was trying to get a process going that improved forward planning so we were not always scrabbling around at the last minute. We should look at speeches much as we look at visits – pre-plan, immediate advance, and then the event, and the more time we have the better. But it will only work if TB buys into it, and my sense of his demeanour at the meeting is that we will never stop the last-minute-itis. But at least we now have a process for getting early drafts, even without his input.

Wednesday, October 21

It was the first PMQs since the summer and all the focus was on the economy. Rover planning cuts at Longbridge was the background to it. TB was convinced that over time we could win the argument though. Today was about laying down bigger arguments that would play out over time and PMQs was fine on that basis, even if on one level Hague had a fairly easy hit. He easily had the best lines and did well on the bulletins, but that could over time become his weakness. As TB said afterwards, he is basically a politician's politician, so he can score the points well when they are there to be scored. But he is not a strategist and when he is required to make strategic decisions, he tends to make the wrong call.

I was working with the Argentine Embassy back and forth re Menem's article [for the *Sun*] and they took all the changes we put through. It went through to Menem's office, who were fine about it. Fiona and I went for dinner with the Levys [Michael and Gilda] at Odin's, but he was clearly not right and I spent half an hour or so with him walking round the block being sick at various points. When we did manage to sit down and eat, he spent a lot of time saying he was worried about the Blair finances. I watched Philip G on *Newsnight* and he was clearly not comfortable. It wasn't a good interview.

Thatcher waded into the Pinochet row, saying he should be released. I put out a line simply saying it was a judicial not a political process, but the right wing were really gearing up on this now. TB was a bit distracted pre-Cabinet and as a result it was an odd meeting, just a run round the block on the economy. He shut down any discussion on Pinochet before anyone tried it. GB did quite a big presentation on where we were and he was impressive. People had real concerns but he gave the clear sense of a strategy being taken forward.

TB warned we were in for a period where a bored media would make as much out of any economic problems as they could. We just had to use this time to see through a strategy and emphasise the long term. 'We have to gird up our loins!' [Richard] Wilson winced when TB said 'We must always be thinking where are we going to be at the next election? The economy is central to that.' I slipped TB a note saying at least mention NI and the EU summit so that I can at least say something else was discussed. Otherwise they would have billed it as an economic crisis Cabinet.

TB did an Argentine interview and it was fairly obvious it was going to be hard to avoid the Falklands being the main story. The journalist told him the Third Way was going down big in Latin America and all the rising politicians were modelling themselves on Blair. I did a briefing on Argentina and the EU summit which was fine. I'd got myself properly immersed in the policy, listening to TB's round table had got me sorted on the tone, and there was no question there I feared. The main problem was the distraction of the woman from AFP who is absolutely gorgeous. Every time she asks a question, I can feel virtually the whole room going weak at the knees, and I can sense them realising I reply much more politely to her than them. On Pinochet Jack Straw told me he was likely to reject the case for extradition. He believed the FCO were 'up to their necks in it – Sandline times ten'. TB also said he felt we were not getting the full truth about the background for this.

On the Menem article, [David] Yelland wanted to build up the line about the apology and focus on that but I explained this had all been negotiated and there was no point me going back for more. It was a big property and they should go big with it. They went to get reaction from veterans, then Hague, Ashdown and later, through me, from TB. They tipped off [Michael] Brunson and ITN ran it as second item. I got on to the Argentine Embassy to make sure they understood it was going to go big and they seemed fine. I sensed of all our various foreign-leader articles with the *Sun* this was going to be the biggest yet, bigger even than Hashimoto and Clinton, and I was worried the

Sun were overcooking, especially when I saw the silly line in their press release that Downing Street would be putting out a response to the article.

Friday, October 23

I woke up to a potential nightmare. The *Sun* had splashed on Menem's article, focusing on the apology, and had the line in the press release referring to the Number 10 press office. But while we were asleep Menem did a briefing and denied that it was an apology. He felt it didn't go as far as that so we now had e.g. the *Standard* 'I'm not sorry' and lots of dancing on pinheads about what was or was not an apology. Yelland was on *Today* and didn't do it well. Irritatingly, and this not helped by their press release, a lot of the interview was about me, Sopel talking about the Hashimoto [Japanese PoW apology] 'template'. Ambassador [Rogelio] Pfirter [of Argentina] was excellent, not getting drawn in and simply saying it was an important gesture and should be accepted as such. I called him and suggested he did as much of the media as possible because he had a good touch on nuance. Menem was actually doing fine but at this stage it was better the ambassador set it up in the right place.

I had a dental appointment so Godric did the 11, which was all the usual process bollocks and what role did I play blah. It got rockier when Lance [Price] said they were saying in Buenos Aires that I inserted the words 'deep regret', which was not true. It had been a good idea to get Menem to do the piece but I was unprepared for the backlash, and I guess the comparison with Hashimoto was too obvious. It meant I was going to be going through another phase of being in the news again. The Menem article was the subject of a question of *Any Questions*, and a gag on *Have I Got News For You*, which meant it had connected, and probably for the wrong reasons. TB was worrying about how to handle the [Lord] Jenkins report on PR, on which he was pretty clear about the outcome, but conscious of different people he had to satisfy in different ways along the way. I was briefing some of the Sundays that Jenkins himself would make clear that the new system could not be brought in before the next election. I got a note from [Richard] Wilson saying that he did not think I could attend PLP meetings. Ridiculous. I would end up having to brief on them without being there.

Saturday, October 24

I couldn't think of many worse ways to spend a weekend than at a summit hosted by Viktor Klima, but here we were in Austria

[Pörtschach]. Very annoying. The Menem coverage wasn't great, and the general view that it was a mistake. TB was pretty relaxed about it on the flight out, the Argentine ambassador was still fine and said that so was Menem, but I was annoyed with myself that I hadn't ensured better atmospherics around it. TB said we are just going through one of those phases where the press are keen to give us a kicking and we just have to see it through.

TB was sketching out a few thoughts for us to float at the summit on defence. He was determined to push this on e.g. WEU [Western European Union] merger with EU and split the planning and political roles into NATO and EU respectively. John H and Stephen Wall [UK Ambassador to the EU] thought he was going too far. I went with TB to the PES lunch, where he said they were all pretty relaxed about some kind of G7 event. We had a bilateral with Bertie [Ahern] back at the hotel, up on the third floor. I think Bertie and I rivalled each other for who found all the palaver and protocol of these summits the most irritating. Bertie said his people thought the Real IRA were planning something, and it might be a hit on McGuinness. McGuinness meanwhile had told Bertie, with a view to him telling TB, that Trimble was at risk and needed to up his security. He seemed pretty serious. He wanted to push on and get the implementation bodies agreed by October 31. TB said he couldn't understand why they could not do some symbolic decommissioning.

As Arafat arrived, I did a briefing, mainly pushing on defence, Bertie, Menem, and a hint re a G7 summit. I went back for the main session, where TB really laid it on re Kosovo being a failure for Europe, said we had been hesitant and disunited and unable to act without the US. He said whatever military structures were agreed – and he went through a few possibles – we had to develop capability – strategic lift in particular. And there had to be greater political will. Chirac said the planned new EU Common Foreign and Security Policy supremo must be a politician who can make a difference. Re defence, he said he could envisage a European pillar in NATO, separable but not separate.

TB said during the break it was interesting how close Schroeder was trying to get, and he sensed the French were paranoid about it. When they discussed defence, Chirac was virtually alone in not welcoming what he said. The message was clear – defence was their subject not ours and we should stay out of it. TB asked both me and John H to speak to our counterparts and make sure Chirac got the message that he had clocked the attitude, and thought it bizarre. He said we had to stake out positions and see them through, and it was important that other countries had gone straight to us on this rather than the French. At the dinner, there was another row with Chirac, who suddenly cut up rough about the G7 summit idea on the economy. He said the Americans were too pessimistic about Asia. There was no chance of China devaluing. TB thought JC was trying to stall and hold over till the German presidency which follows us. TB said if GB had not dallied on this, it could have been done by now.

Sunday, October 25

The Pinochet background pieces were a bit grim; Menem follow-ups not as bad as I expected. I spoke to Robin before he did *Frost* and he was fine, though there was a fair amount of the usual 'Cook not happy' diddling around the place. TB went off to church and had been expecting a quiet time but the Austrians had turned out the whole village council in traditional uniforms bearing gifts etc. Klima said it was fantastic because none of the other leaders would be seen by the public, but Paddy Teahon was pissed off because he had been trying to get to the same church and the Austrians wouldn't let him through.

The main discussion was the actual substance of the summit, and the future of Europe debate. I put together a briefing note based on TB's speaking notes and a few lines from his contribution at last night's dinner, pushing the line on subsidiarity. There was a lot of interest in whether there was a new left/right divide opening. [Massimo] D'Alema [new Italian Prime Minister] told TB he would be pursuing centrist policies, and TB sensed from Schroeder that he would be far more business-friendly than [German finance minister Oskar] Lafontaine. TB found Schroeder fairly impressive, and he seemed keen to be close. The French were very iffy about it and we suspected they were behind some of the briefing against us in the press, so TB asked me to have another word with them. He said he could sense their fear and it was important they knew we sensed it. When the Tories were in, and isolated in Europe, Chirac could always hold out the hand of friendship but the last thing he wanted was us in a position of power or influence or strong with Germany. Their history with Germany, whatever the outward signs, made them very jumpy, and they feared our closeness to the US whilst simultaneously portraying it as an irrelevance. He said he was happy for them to be jumpy if Chirac was going to mess around the whole time and it was important we kept on building alliances around them.

Geoff Crawford called. Penny Junor's book on Charles was the big domestic story saying Diana was first to commit adultery and the

Queen was vile during the week of the funeral. Why anyone took these books any more seriously than the papers that published them I don't know but Geoff sounded worried. He indicated they might want us at some stage to say publicly 'Does anyone care about the boys when regurgitating all this stuff?' TB came out of the final session looking very bored. We then had a thirty-minute boat ride followed by a ten-minute bus ride to get to the bloody press centre. He was lobbying madly re BSE as we went. It was cold and rainy but as ever TB had refused a coat. Chirac asked him why he didn't wear a coat and then answered himself: *'C'est parce que tu es jeune et Chirac est vieux.'* ['That's because you are young and Chirac is old.'] One of [Jacques] Santer's people said he had read in *Izvestia* that I was going to work for Clinton!

On the flight home, TB was talking through the French situation. He felt it was possible to get better relations with them but Chirac was very suspicious and ultimately talking a double game most of the time. We needed to freak them out a little by building new alliances for the future, and that included with the small countries and with those coming in down the track.

Monday, October 26

To our surprise, the UK press was full of the line that TB was moving to the left on Europe, e.g. re the expansion plan. It showed once again that the UK press is only capable of seeing Europe in terms of Britain isolated and forced to do something we don't want to. By contrast the European media was broadly positive, in some cases very, re TB's contribution at the summit. The Menem article thing was dragging on, with the *Mirror* running a piece by an 'expert' saying the same person wrote the Menem and Hashimoto articles. Pinochet was big again with the plane due at [RAF] Brize Norton to take him home to Chile. At the office meeting, Charlie [Falconer] had to put up with a fair bit of piss-taking re the many profiles that appeared at the weekend.[1] They were by and large positive, though laced with the obvious stuff re Tony crony, etc. Charlie will in the end get by because it is so hard to dislike him, and he brings wit and warmth to the proceedings, as well as intelligence.

TB was still thinking away re Europe alliances. He felt we really had to work on the Germans and wanted me, Jonathan and John to go out there later in the week to plan their next meeting in real depth. TB felt Schroeder was looking to us for help. In Austria, when D'Alema

---

[1] As a result of Falconer's appointment to various Cabinet committees as Blair's 'eyes and ears' as the *Independent* put it, with the headline 'Charlie is my darling'.

had made a joke about having three former leaders in his Cabinet, Schroeder cracked the line 'You try having the current one,' and there was no doubt the Lafontaine relationship [Lafontaine was also still chairman of the SPD] was difficult. TB felt he wanted to take his party more to the centre, but he needed help. Michael Hoffman [German official] told me Schroeder was trying to pursue a more business-friendly approach, but Lafontaine was basically dealing with the economy.

I had a chat with Richard Wilson re the Royals. He was seeing Janvrin for lunch and reported back that they were still thinking they may need us to weigh in behind the kids [William and Harry]. They were convinced Bolland had to go but RW advised them to make sure he had something to go to. I was still trying to get TB to agree the response to Jenkins. Paddy was desperate for something and TB was still toying with the idea he could be more positive than Jack S but I was not so sure.

We had a meeting with Sepp Blatter [FIFA president] re the [2006] World Cup bid. These guys were full of themselves and had to be treated like heads of state which was all a bit irritating but had to be done I guess. TB set out the case, which Tony Banks echoed and then Blatter was pretty positive, though he made clear he was worried about our supporters and felt any serious trouble in the near future would be disastrous for us. He explained the voting system. He said it would be a calamity for us if Scotland did not support the FA bid. 'Otherwise why should anyone else?' UEFA was pro Germany but there were other votes to play for. He was clear that he wanted person-ally for South Africa to get 2006 [Germany would be the eventual hosts] but he agreed to be warm re England and to be fair, in the street afterwards, he was, but my overall feeling was that we were in a bad place on it.

We had a pretty gloomy meeting on the economy, with GDP fore-casts not looking great, plus there was the CBI optimism survey, out tomorrow, which would show it was the worst since 1980. TB felt we needed to do more to inject confidence into the system, and we did not have a clear economic narrative. GB was clear that he did not want us signalling any sense of upturn for a while yet. This was a difficult period and we had to get through it. I had a row with Peter M later because he made a speech up in the North-West that was very pro euro, or would certainly be seen as such. He told Jonathan it was time we started making the case properly for it. I said it was the kind of thing we should only do when we thought it through properly. He said the danger was we never did.

Jonathan came into my office and shut the door, which usually meant there was a problem. There was. He said Jack Straw had just called. He had had a call from John Stevens, deputy commissioner at the Yard, who said Ron Davies had been cruising on Clapham Common last night and had been picked up by a black male prostitute who later robbed him. This turned out to be an OTT account of what happened, but clearly something had and we had a real problem. Jonathan and I went to see TB who was up in the White Room being photographed by Anthony Crickmay [distinguished portrait photographer]. We took him into the dining room and told him what we knew. He looked surprised but not shocked and then, as I had, laughed. Bloody hell, he said. We have to get to the facts and not do anything before we have established in our own minds what has gone on.

We arranged for him to come in around 11. I did the eleven o'clock, dealing with economy, Pinochet, one or two other bits and bobs, knowing for certain that by the four o'clock there would be a different mood and a very different set of questions. By the time I got back upstairs, Ron had arrived and was in with TB and Jonathan who was taking a note rather more completely than usual. Ron looked absolutely shattered. He ran through the story, how he had been driving back to London from Wales, wanted some fresh air, stopped at Clapham Common, went for a walk, met a guy, got talking, agreed to go for a drink, met up with some of his mates, agreed to go for a curry, got into a car, got robbed of cash, wallet, car phone, went to police, and here he was. He set it out in a very matter-of-fact way, as though every step was in its own way logical, but clearly TB, Jonathan and I all felt exactly the same thing – what on earth was he doing there, how on earth did he get involved with a group of complete strangers, and how the hell do we explain this one? Ron was in a bad way and he could offer no real explanation as to why he got involved, just kept repeating the few facts he felt comfortable with. I could tell looking at TB's face that he had pretty much decided this was a no-hope situation for Ron, and that the only way for him to salvage anything from this was to get ahead of the curve, resign before anyone knew the first thing about it, and maybe get some sympathy and understanding. He said it might then be possible that he could still go for a seat in the [Welsh] Assembly. I started to play devil's advocate, said to TB that if there was genuinely no more to it than this, then we had to be aware we may end up in a situation where the charge is he is sacking someone for getting robbed. TB flashed me a look that basically said he had decided, and he did not need me to be offering Ron a lifeline.

TB then put to Ron what Jack S had been told by the cops and he looked absolutely horrified. Richard Wilson came in, having been asked by TB to look into it, and said the police were saying Ron had confessed to having gay sex with this man. Ron said that simply was not true. RW said you said it to the police and Ron said no I didn't. He went through the whole story again, the rest of us using RW's presence to get another reaction. As Ron went through it, Richard was flashing looks at Tony, me, then Jonathan, and all said the same thing – what on earth am I listening to? When he had finished, TB was in clear and decisive mode. Right, he said, the more I hear of this, the more convinced I am that as soon as people hear of this, they will think it all very odd and it will be very hard to explain away. The press would drag out every detail and he didn't like the sound of it. He went out for a pee, said he would be back in a minute, and while he was away Ron said this was the wrong decision and he didn't deserve it. He had been foolish, but did he really deserve to hang for it? But TB was clear. We agreed I would go back to the Welsh Office with Ron and draft an exchange of letters.

We drove over together and in the car he was 'business as usual', as if nothing had happened. When we got there, there was a sullen, uncomfortable atmosphere. The staff knew something was up and I could tell my presence was arousing some interest. He called in June Milligan, his private secretary, and told her he was probably going to resign. It was perfectly clear to me that she was pleased to hear it. I asked if he had spoken to his wife, Chris. He hadn't. He called her and told her, in the most perfunctory way imaginable, that he had seen Tony who had been 'very nice', and he was probably going to resign and something might be on the news. 'All right, love?' And that was pretty much it. I sat down with him and started writing his, and then TB's letter. Dealing with the incident itself was the hardest bit. He didn't like the draft. He said it looked like we were accepting the gay-sex allegation from the cops. Earlier, TB had said to Ron 'I am not going to ask you about your sexuality,' which of course was a way of asking about it, because if Ron had wanted to come back at him, he would have. He didn't. I was doing it long-hand and getting it typed up outside. We sent over the drafts to Number 10, via Mark Bennett. TB made a couple of changes including reference to 'foolish error'. Ron then said he wanted to wait until he saw the police, who had said they wanted to see him again and were coming over.

They came in just after lunch, two of them, clearly fairly experienced but I think shocked to be in a Cabinet minister's office, with me there too, talking about a mugging. They said their job was to catch criminals, whatever the circumstances or political implications, so they did need to talk to him thoroughly again. RW came in for part of the discussion, and was echoing my line to Ron that there was no way this was not going to get out and become a big news event, so we had to work out how best to handle. Ron said what if I decide not to press charges, and the cops said they had a duty to investigate the crime anyway. There was a farcical moment when I dictated TB's letter to Anne Stenson in the Garden Room over the phone and she brought it over to the Welsh Office, thinking TB was with us, for him to sign. Jonathan was meanwhile helping TB sort everything for the aftermath. We wanted Alun Michael in here as soon as Ron had gone. Ron then started telling me that someone called Mr Black had called him this morning and said he could have his car back for £100 if he went to a certain place. He did, but his car wasn't there. RW came over again having secured the police report which suggested Ron had not been totally honest in his first account of it all, that he had changed his story, which was all a bit murky, that he took the guy to Battersea Park, then to meet friends, have a meal, a drink, watch a video, then the robbery. It was all odder even than before and the fact that he changed his story along the way wasn't helping. I asked Godric to find [Robin] Oakley. He couldn't track him down so I said find [John] Sergeant and tell him we wanted him to come in and do a clip with TB on the economy. When John arrived with his crew, Godric and Mark B brought them over to the Welsh Office, briefed him on the letters and held them in the waiting room.

Ron got in his senior staff and told them what was happening. I didn't sense any warmth there either way, no real sympathy, and he struck me as being lonely in his private and public lives. He was trying to be matter-of-fact but must have known he was about to have his reputation shredded, and I felt in the room people who would help do it. TB saw the Queen for the weekly audience later. I went down to see Sergeant, who annoyingly filmed me as I went in. Ron did the interview and was very calm and dignified. I thought Sergeant did a good job too, given it was such an odd tale to land on you coming back from lunch.

We arranged for Ron to head off as soon as the interview was done, as the story would be around the BBC in no time, while I went back to Number 10 to brief on it. It was not easy. As I knew they would, they got straight to the point – what had he done wrong? – and I didn't particularly want to dump all over him, so I was avoiding a lot of questions. They were also straight on to the point that if he is not fit to be in the Cabinet, how can he be fit to be first minister of Wales? I spoke to Lance and Mark B – the gay angle was also going to lead to a free-for-all. I sent Hilary C to Wiltshire to meet up with Ron's wife in advance of Ron arriving. I felt sorry for him. He had always had a political reputation built on his infighting and his deviousness I suppose, but not much support, and he looked a diminished and friendless figure. Richard Wilson left a note and a Twix bar on my desk, said I had handled it brilliantly, which was kind of him. It was a bit worrying how these crisis moments were in a sense the challenges I enjoyed most.

TB called me in. He was with Paddy Ashdown discussing Jenkins and PR. Paddy was worried he would not be able to take his party forward without an explicit commitment from TB to a referendum in support for a change in the electoral system. I said TB's problem was isolation in the Cabinet, which shouldn't and couldn't be overlooked. Also, the media basically thought we were going to kick it out, so if TB was warm, and the rest neutral, he ought to be able to hold the show together. Paddy was unconvinced, looked positively agitated, said we were making it all very difficult for him.

Wednesday, October 28

Ron called to get a read-out of the papers. I gave him as neutral an account as possible, though did read him some of the gay-sex headlines. He did not sound angry or agitated and was still at the stage of wanting my advice and judgement and by and large following it. I said he should stay where he was and we would simply say he had gone away for a few days with his family. We would do our best to make sure people didn't track him down there. Hilary was confident they could stay low-profile there. I spoke to Ron through the day, three or four times maybe, his position hardened with each call. By the end he was saying he was a victim of a crime and he was being made to pay with his political life. He said we had always underestimated Wales and often misunderstood it, that his office was being inundated with messages of support and people wanted him to stay. I said that always happened at times like this but I had to tell him I didn't detect much support at Westminster. Mark B sent Hilary the media brief as we had made sure his family didn't see the papers. She said she had shown it to Ron and he was taken aback by the scale and the ferocity. Later, Ron broke down crying and Hilary thought she should leave them together as a family. When she went back it was clear they had all been crying.

October '98: Davies hiding away and calls AC to hear press

I wanted TB to speak to Ron, but he was holding back. Anji was of the view that nobody would understand if he stayed and we may have to go for him. TB eventually spoke to him and it was a difficult conversation. There was a hint of menace in Ron's voice now. He said he felt the wrong decision was taken. He had gone along with 'your' strategy but the Welsh party will not dance to the London media tune. He was not going to be kicked out by a kangaroo court. TB held pretty firm, said in a way the easier thing would be to leave him, and let events take their course but we needed to know 1. that there would be no other stories coming out about his private life, and 2. that the Welsh party genuinely wanted him to stay.

TB said there should be a special executive of the Welsh party. Ron said fine, let's go for Monday. TB said Friday, to avoid days of chatter about it that would damage the party. Ron said he had to have time to prepare his case and there had to be justice. 'If we stand for anything, we stand for justice and fairness. The Welsh party elected me and London cannot force me out.' Ron had totally changed his mindset during the course of the day. I spoke to him again after his call with TB and he was adamant – 'I am the victim of a crime yet it is me being punished.' The whips were taking soundings and whatever Ron said re support, it didn't look great. I think TB was wishing we had gone the whole hog yesterday. Ron watched the ten o'clock news and didn't like the tone re where Number 10 was on it, and I had to calm him down on that. He was digging in. Someone was briefing on his behalf that he was going to fight.

Nobody raised Ron at PMQs though Hague had one question on it at a press conference earlier. TB called as I was going to bed, and said he had a feeling Ron would end up staying. Hilary said she was trying to get him to see sense but he was becoming more and more intransigent.

Thursday, October 29

Another day from hell – Ron Davies, Jenkins [Report] and [Argentine President] Menem – every one of them enough for a full day's work, but somehow we were trying to manage all three together. Jonathan and I were both anxious about the inconsistencies emerging, not least in me saying we knew nothing else [re Ron Davies] and that the police had not been in contact. Ron said he was now thinking of stepping down. He hadn't slept again, he had thought about it all night and he was sure it was the best thing. He said he would probably just give a letter to his chairman. TB saw JP and Jack to finalise the agreed line in response to Jenkins, which was OK. At Cabinet, TB mentioned

Ron briefly, then on to PR and Jenkins. He said there was no point saying we all agreed because we didn't but we had to handle it in an agreed and collegiate way. When I briefed the agreed line at the morning lobby, though one or two saw where we were trying to help Paddy, basically they knew it [PR] was for the long grass.

I helped Ron draft his letter over the phone before going for the Menem lunch. He had a bit of an ageing Spanish pop star feel to him, but the talks went fine. He invited TB to the Welsh-speaking part of Argentina. 'Wales is very much on my mind at the moment, as you may have read in our papers,' said TB. Menem laughed, too loud. The Falklands discussion was really just going through motions, though TB was good on the improving mood music. We went a lot further on the arms embargo than they expected. We got Menem to wear an England World Cup bid badge which would go down well. I briefed the Argentine media in the street and found myself banjaxed by a Jeremy Beadle-type character for one of the comedy news shows out there, yelling and shouting about [David] Beckham and [Diego] Maradona. The *Guardian* were in seeing GB and as they came out I grabbed Mike White and introduced him to this guy as the Chancellor and got him to do an interview and get the guy off my back.

Ron was now at Devizes [Wiltshire] nick doing his statement and had to leave at 6.30 for an identity parade at Brixton. At the afternoon briefing, the take on PR was very negative so I found myself trying to talk up the possibility and get the balance TB would want for Paddy, though I was instinctively opposed, an insight which laced the tone of their questions. We couldn't get the Ron letters sorted so we needed a statement to make clear what was happening. I persuaded Ron that the sooner this was done the better. TB spoke to Ron again, then I went through the statement with him and he was fine. 'OK, let it go,' he said. I called Jon Smith [Press Association] and said he should describe me as a spokesman for Ron. I also gave him a reaction from me. Endgame. I felt totally drained and I felt incredibly sorry for Ron. He said to me just before we did the statement 'I'm not sure I can take much more of this.' Hilary, who had never been a fan of his, said she too ended up feeling very sorry for him. He was a tragic and lonely figure.

Friday, October 30

The press on Jenkins was OK, with some saying our response was pro PR. The Libs were pissed off with Jack Straw because of his *Newsnight* interview where he had let a day's frustration at having to pretend to be OK about PR shine through. The statement I did with Mark B for Ron took a lot of the sting but it was still tricky. Ron was due to do a couple of interviews today, for BBC Wales and HTV. Dennis Wise [Chelsea footballer] played a part in his response, having described a tackle he did earlier in the week as a 'moment of madness', and I advised Ron not to get into detail re Clapham Common but just say it was a 'moment of madness for which I have paid a heavy price'.

GB was due – finally – to publish the G7 statement aimed at helping the world economy back on track but we were still arguing re timing. He wanted to do it today rather than Monday when we would get a big bang for it, and TB could be tied in with Schroeder. I got back to do the Sundays and totally lost it with them. The basic inhumanity re Ron was revolting. I knew I should stay cool but I lost it with them, said they would really like it if the story could end in a nice convenient way, to suit their deadlines, with Ron topping himself. I then heard later they were writing that I had 'expressed fears' Ron would kill himself. I despise these people. They stand for nothing, care about nothing other than filling the acres they have to fill with shit. Matthew Parris' interview [the gay former Conservative MP turned columnist told BBC's *Newsnight* that Mandelson was 'certainly' gay] had sparked off a whole load of new stuff re Peter being gay. Ron's TV interviews were OK though in one he was asked four times if he was gay and didn't answer. Murdoch attacked the Man U referral as 'politically motivated'. Mo called in a real rage because of a BBC memo – from Anne Sloman [BBC chief political adviser] – that decreed there should be no mention of Peter M's sexuality.

Saturday, October 31

It never fucking stops. The *News of the Screws* were on, followed by others, with some angle about Ron and the security services. They said Ron had received a police caution and TB must have been informed by the spooks. Peter M called in a state because the *Sunday Express* had contacted Reinaldo [da Silva, Mandelson's partner] in Tokyo and how should he handle it? TB was in a total tirade re the press – 'scum' – when I told him re the Sunday briefing.

It was Rory's birthday party today and halfway through Huw Roberts [former special adviser to Ron Davies] called and said he was really worried re Ron. 'He is going under fast.' He asked me to arrange for a member of the Cabinet to call and just be friendly. I got Jack S to do it. Jack agreed RD was close to the end of his tether. Ron put out a very strong statement attacking the press. The Welsh Sundays were not as bad as the nationals, but all in all it was grim for him. I told him to make sure his family didn't see the tabs. Burnley beat Wrexham 2-1.

Sunday, November 1

I had a fairly quiet day, mainly working up the Schroeder visit tomorrow. Then Huw Roberts called and said Ron wanted to make a resignation statement in the House on Wednesday. Then he called again and said now he wanted to do it tomorrow. I knew TB would be instinctively against. He was. 'Oh God, it will just keep it running for another day when it is calming down.' He spoke to Ron, sounding less sympathetic than the last time they spoke, and said he agreed the press were scum but if he used a statement just to slag them off, it would just keep them going for him when it looked like it might pass. So clearly the Ron fallout was going to dominate for a while more.

Monday, November 2

I woke up to GB/EMU leading the news. Whelan/Peter Curwen had briefed that we were setting up the all-party national changeover plan, and stepping up preparations for the euro. TB had urged GB not to be too forward on this, but it went big and was likely to form the backdrop to the Schroeder visit.

Betty Boothroyd's office had indicated it was by no means certain she would grant Ron a resignation statement, but he was heading to London pretty determined to do it. His draft was basically a long attack on the media, with nothing to add on the detail of events, and both Bruce and I spoke to him to say as it stood it would harm not help his case. TB was still very unkeen for him to make a statement at all. GB was also not keen as he had his CBI speech and his G7 statement on the economy. At the office meeting, TB said he thought we had handled Ron about as well as we could.

TB also felt that there was insufficient sign of school improvements. He was worried that David B was talking a New Labour game but stymied by Old Labour thinking in the system. I said I felt the problem was teachers felt lots of pressure but not enough support, and the message they were getting from DB's rhetoric was that teachers were holding back change and advance. We had to make the messages much more basic – we had a shared vested interest in improving standards. We put in the resources and the direction, and trust the teachers more. And we had to maintain education as the top priority and be seen to be building up from the bottom. We then got into one of our usual discussions and I said to both Charlie and Anji that I would happily outlaw all private education, as whilst more and more people went private, so the pressure to improve schools for the many abated. TB was also feeling we were not going forward sufficiently quickly on welfare and we were going to take a hit on saying costs might actually go up, because we had not properly made the distinction between welfare spending we welcomed and welfare spending we didn't.

The GB G7 statement, as I feared, went off half-cock. We should have had tons of publicity from it worldwide but they had not really planned it. At the eleven o'clock I got into tricky waters on the Falklands. Menem had given an interview suggesting we might be in negotiation within two to three years. I was adamant there would be no negotiations on sovereignty. But it begged the question – what had been said that might have led him to say that? The honest answer was that RC had given that very impression when Guido Di Tella [Argentine foreign minister] raised it at the lunch.

I was suggesting Ron should be left in peace but by the time I got upstairs, he had been granted the statement. Schroeder arrived, and was keen to emphasise that he saw his *'Neue Mitte'* ['New Middle'] approach as being close to TB's Third Way. He was clearly keen to get on, politically and personally. He had a fairly strong aura about him, but I also sensed he got easily distracted and had a bit of a concentration problem. He by all accounts had a fair temper on him. He was pleased with the development on EMU and making clear, in private and in his CBI speech, that they hoped we went in. While he and TB were one-on-one, I had a good chat with his spokesman, Uwe-Karsten Heye, who was fairly dour and downbeat but clearly close in with Schroeder, having been with him for eight years.

We went straight into Iraq, where they were closer to us than we had imagined from the briefing, and then Kosovo and Agenda 2000. They got into more of the European detail over lunch. There were good vibes between them and whereas TB felt very keenly that the French did not want a strong UK, he felt the Germans were far less paranoid about us. They were as nonplussed as we were about the reaction to the Austrian summit. Before the press conference, I explained to Schroeder the politics of the GB euro statement and said it was important he did not overdo his reaction. The best thing that could come from the press conference was a warm body language and the sense of a developing political relationship. He was very assured and fluent at the press conference, and nodded along at the right bits when TB spoke. There were no ultra tough questions and he seemed to think it went fine. He was at first blush very likeable.

November '98: Good vibes from Schroeder visit

He relaxed enough to make a joke about [Oskar] Lafontaine's wife being involved in economic policy.

Ron's statement was in some ways quite powerful but it was hard to get away from the unanswered questions. The press basically took it as an admission he was gay. He called me later and said he was going away for a few days.

Tuesday, November 3

As expected, Ron got a fair old kicking from the press. Peter M came in to see me early on, and we just had a friendly chat. Only later did I learn TB had just bollocked him for raising the temperature on EMU, telling him that he (TB) would decide when to turn up the Bunsen burner. GB's statement [pre-Budget report] and the idea of extending share ownership was the splash in the *Mail*. Borrowing was set to be the story. I met Charlie W early to go through the main lines. I was worried that the whole picture was a bit too upbeat, not realistic enough. The agreed strategy had been to go for a long-term stability message, but with a £250 million rabbit on health, the notion of £40 billion for health and education, which were cumulative totals, and the forecasts in danger of being seen as too rosy, I thought we might end up with a problem.

At the special Cabinet, GB was fairly dour about things, though he kept saying we were well placed to come through the difficulties. He said inflation was on target, public sector finances strong, a long-term framework for monetary and fiscal policy being established. He raced through the figures, and I'm not sure everyone clocked it all. By and large most of them seemed to buy into the general approach and thought he was playing a difficult hand well. He stressed three parts to the report – 1. stress the importance of stability in difficult times, 2. push ahead with long-term reform, 3. the need for a continuing programme of extending opportunity and social inclusion. TB and I were pressing GB to make the obvious sound bites less upbeat, more realistic, more focused on the long term and an admission of short-term difficulties.

In the House, it came over fine, though I felt some of the hacks afterwards were scratching their heads and wondering how he did it. Ed B came up to do the briefing with me and was OK, though he had this habit of starting by literally repeating what GB had just said. The thing lacking, as so often, was a clear and compelling economic strategic narrative. I was working on a couple of TB articles on the family, and TB was worrying about his clear commitment on marriage because so many of his key people and our MPs were not married.

Wednesday, November 4

I was looking forward to being a normal person with a normal life today, having got Rory tickets for Man U vs Brondby [Danish Superliga side]. I did the eleven o'clock, with Ron still bubbling away but low-key, did the PMQs meeting, where we prepared most on the economy and Jenkins, and then headed to collect Rory from school. On the way up to Manchester I listened to PMQs on the radio. It was the first one I had missed since Tony became leader, and I got a very different perspective not being in the chamber. It sounded and felt different, and in many ways awful. So many of the rituals and the stuff we took for granted were pretty awful when you were confronted with them in a different way. I was knackered by the time I got home but Rory had a great time [Manchester Utd won 5-0]. Any chance of him ever being a Burnley fan again had pretty much gone I think.

Thursday, November 5

Interest rates down 0.5 per cent. But it was a bad day on the Ron front, with the story unravelling and people determined to draw us into it. *The Times* had a story, part right, part wrong, about the background but they were pressing that we knew more than we were letting on. I sensed real trouble on this. Part of the problem was that I had not been aware Jonathan had also spoken to [John] Stevens at the Met Police. It didn't matter on one level but they so loved to take us into these areas where we get a fact wrong and they build around it a great conspiracy. The lobby briefing was ghastly. The full note of it shows how grim. Some of the papers said they would publish partial transcripts. They were determined to say I had misled them. It all became pretty unpleasant and they don't take any account of how difficult these fast-moving, human stories are to handle when you have the media in your face all day and night.

I was refusing to give an inch and it became really nasty. I had been trying to make clear the differentiation between TB's role as PM in charge of his Cabinet, and a separate police investigation that had to take place totally divorced from us. But the fact of Jonathan speaking to Stevens changed their perceptions of that and they were hellbent on making a meal of it. Afterwards I spoke to Stevens to make sure we were on the same page, but that went wrong because Brian Butler [Home Office] said to PA that Stevens had spoken directly to Number 10. At the briefing, for the first time I think, I got a feel of what it means to say you feel the ground shifting beneath you. I didn't like the feel of it at all.

I spoke to Jack S to make sure we were all agreed on the Ron D chronology. Jack now said there was no mention of gay sex in his calls with Stevens. Jonathan said that wasn't true. Godric thought Jack should put out a full chronology. Jack wasn't keen, feeling we did not have to brief every detail in answer to every question. I heard *The Times* were doing a leader saying I had not been truthful and I spent half an hour trying to talk them into a better position. Hindsight was such an easy tool for a hack to use to build a conspiracy theory. What these people rarely did was imagine themselves in the position we were in. I had been clear at the very first briefing there were parts of this whole episode it was hard to explain fully. Did they really expect me to sit there and say it was all about gay sex, no matter how many times they asked me? We had a political interest in how we handled these situations. With something like the Ron incident, there was a personal interest too – I had not wanted to make it any worse for him. But their interest was purely what the story was. It was just calming down when RW and Jonathan came into my office and I could tell by the looks on their faces – Richard worried, Jonathan that smile-cum-grimace that he always has when we were about to have shit-hit-fan time.

The *News of the World* had apparently entrapped Nick Brown with rent boys – pictures, tapes, etc. As TB said later, with a touch of black humour, we could get away with Ron as a one-off aberration, but if the public start to think the whole Cabinet is indulging in gay sex, we might have a bit of a political problem. I could feel another weekend going away.

I drove with TB to the *Guardian* for lunch. We had a chat about pressure. He said the fact of being at the interface with the media was a pressure in itself, added to which they were always looking to have a go at me. He said I was a buffer for pressure on him, but ultimately the real pressure was on him. Take Iraq, he said. You have to help me communicate decisions. I have to take a decision that may lead to people losing their lives.

I was feeling a bit beleaguered and fed up at having to spend so much time and energy digging people out of shit they should never have been into. Wilson said he felt sorry for me, the way I seemed to cop so much of this, but it was because the politicians and the press knew I was a real force in the building, and likely to be the one sorting these things out. It is a cross you have to bear, he said. I was feeling the job was currently all shit, with little upside, and too little time for Fiona and the kids. Having just got through one gay-sex fandango caused by a weak vessel in the government, I was pissed off I was being plunged straight into another. TB said we should do nothing re Nick until tomorrow.

The papers were pretty grim re Ron D, especially the heavies, and though it was only running fourth on the news, TB was pissed off we were still dealing with it. There was also a silly little flurry re the *FT* story, totally untrue, that TB was going cold on the World Cup bid. I spoke to Neil [Kinnock] after TB called him to ask him to support Alun Michael plus Rhodri [Morgan] plus Wayne David [Labour MEP]. NK agreed to be supportive but made clear he thought we could lose. I was trying to have a day off and cancelled the lunch at the Chinese Embassy, deep down because I knew I would get caught up in the Nick Brown saga.

Richard W called him late morning. Apparently Nick's response was 'If you are asking could this be true, the answer is possibly yes.' He explained that this was a two-year relationship from the mid-90s, that the guy had been chased by the press, resisted them, but then when Nick ended the relationship – apparently when the guy asked for money for a holiday – he started to pressure him. RW said he was very calm, matter-of-fact, had been expecting a call like this, said he would go if TB wanted him to. TB told me he had once asked Nick if he was gay and Nick said no. Nick's explanation to that now was that TB actually asked him if he was part of a gay-sex scandal. Wilson said we needed rules on which to decide. Being gay or bisexual is OK. Having relationships with people that he and I might not consort with is OK. What is not OK is anything criminal, anything that might expose you to blackmail, anything which might call into serious doubt your judgement.

TB was in Sedgefield and he, Richard and I did a conference call as Nick headed back from Madrid. We agreed RW and Lance Price should see him on his return. They had a ninety-minute meeting in which NB was seemingly very frank. RW said it was as if he had been expecting this for a long time and he was very measured. He said he had known this guy for some time. They met every couple of weeks or so over three or four months. He did on occasion give him money. The most ever was £80, more usually ten quid for a cab. It was not, he insisted, a 'commercial relationship'. At the end of their relationship he asked for money for a holiday in Florida and said he was under pressure from the press. NB said he did not co-operate. NB denied cruising, cottaging, gay clubs, sadomasochism.

TB called into another conference call from the train south. There was not enough to dismiss him, he felt. He needed to see NB to make his own judgement. The options were 1. he resigns. 2. we engage with the *News of the World* as best we can and make the best of a bad job, 3. we pre-empt by getting the story elsewhere. But there was the slim chance the *NoW* would not do the story. If we pre-empted we would guarantee publication everywhere, and provoke the *NoW*, who would then spill all the dirt they could. I felt option 2 was best if he did not resign. Also, if it was true this pre-dated the election, then it may be they were worried about it themselves and didn't feel capable of running it. I called Phil Hall [editor] on a pretext and did not sense any major thing up his sleeve. I gave what I thought was good news to everyone else. NB saw TB with Lance and Richard W at 7.30 in the flat. TB came to the view that Nick was 'probably' telling the truth. We all had a hunch this one would go away.

Saturday, November 7

NB went to Lance's house in Chiswick and told him the *News of the World* had called. I got Lance to call the *NoW* on Nick's behalf. They said they had the confession of a self-confessed rent boy who had been paid £100 a time to beat up Nick and kick him around a room. I spoke to Nick who was in a real state. He said it was bad enough having to own up to something that was true – namely being gay – without being forced to admit things that were not true. He denied the money and the beating-up claims. We had a TB, AC, NB, LP conference call. TB heard the full story as put to us by the *Screws*. I could tell that his mind had gone into 'whirring' mode. He was listening and making up his mind. He said he was saddened Nick was being forced to 'come out', when clearly he had not wanted to. But the key to this was being honest, honest with us now so that we can best judge how to handle it.

He, JP and I then had a call. JP said the problem was if more came out on top of this. Nick had assured us that would not be the case. TB and JP agreed that without any other knowledge, if it came to a rent boy against a minister, we would have to back the word of the minister. JP said fine but if anything comes out to contradict what we have been told, his feet should not touch the ground. I drafted a statement for Nick. The dilemma was whether to include any reference to money at all. Anji and Sally favoured total disclosure. So did RW. GB was cautious. I called GB for his judgement. He was in the bath. He said he had never talked to Nick about his private life but his instinct was that if he was in a difficult situation, he would tell the truth. He thought my statement was fine but it would be better to show this was a normal open relationship. I said the problem with that is it wasn't.

I had another difficult conversation with Nick, said I had to ask him one more time whether there were any others who might tout themselves to newspapers on the back of this: whether he had ever paid for sex; indulged in anything criminal or perverted. He was adamant there was nothing else. He had been very calm and self-assured but he now sounded very low. He said before I finally gave them the statement, he needed a bit of time to speak to his family. 'My mother is ill, and frail, and she knows nothing about this.' He spoke to his sister, who was very supportive, but his mother was already in bed. When I said it was likely the press would find his mum and try to doorstep her, he cracked for the first time. I felt sorry for him, but especially coming after the Ron episode, what on earth were people going to think about us?

I spoke to Phil Hall and could tell he was worried about this one rebounding on them if they didn't handle it right. It meant I was able to negotiate headlines and some of the text, and de-luridise a bit. He agreed to remove any reference to the sadomasochism claims, and indeed volunteered to say they were unable to substantiate some of the claims. I was trying to steer this to being a story about a minister coming out by telling the PM, rather than the confessions of an alleged rent boy, and I gave them a supportive line from TB. I said I was worried the guy might go elsewhere to get another hit. Phil said he was not very strong and he thought he would run a mile once the paper was out. Then he came back, after a conversation with Les Hinton, and said they had decided not to name him, which meant the story would focus totally on Nick. We had missed the first edition, but agreed a last round of changes and that was that.

TB had to go to the Festival of Remembrance, and by the time he got back I had the *NoW*. I read him the headlines and the opening paragraphs. Phil Hall OBE. I called Nick and said it was about the best we could have hoped for, and there was the chance of him getting some support. The most important thing was to carry on with his job. He said he had a Q&A session with farmers in the West Country on Monday. I said it was best to get on and do it, and not be fazed. He was due to meet Prince Charles on Tuesday. Nick said he was grateful for the help I had given him. I was pissed off that another weekend was so eaten into by another weak vessel. Once the later edition dropped, the phone started and Christ knows what time it was when the last call came.

Sunday, November 8

TB said we had to watch the *Mail*, as they would be desperate to build the line that we were not normal family people. On the specific

NB story, we were ahead on points, but there was a danger of it un-ravelling. Emma Udwin [political journalist] was doing it for the BBC and was word-perfect, but the papers were likely to be another kettle of *poisson*. I agreed with Nick that he should do a pooled interview with Emma which though it would piss off ITN was definitely the right way to get decent coverage for him today. I gave Hilary [Coffman] another short straw and asked her to go to Devon with him. 'What am I, some kind of hand-holder to the gays in the Cabinet?' she said. I said we may as well turn his event with the farmers tomorrow into a big event, showing him just getting on with his job. It would also be a very powerful thing if a bunch of farmers were basically supportive and friendly.

The press were desperate to get into the process again and we decided to starve them, no background, no colour, no who knew when, just let them have the words as they stood, and build up tomorrow. He wanted to go by train but I persuaded him he should be driven and avoid messy pictures being chased on a train. He was coming over fine, and most comment was supportive. GB did *On the Record*, mainly on the economy. TB was on a couple of times re Jenkins [Report], saying Paddy [Ashdown] was still pushing for a more sympathetic line somewhere. I had tried a couple of times with the *Guardian* but they knew what the game was, and were not really buying it.

Monday, November 9

We could hardly have asked for a better landing for Nick, who got good coverage pretty much everywhere apart from the *Sun* who did a page 1 editorial on a 'gay mafia' running the country, which would get a lot of pick-up today. Hilary did a brilliant job with Nick down in Devon, good mood and pictures, but the 'business as usual' strategy was undermined by Clive Soley [PLP chairman] and JP on *Today*, who condemned the press as 'judge, jury and executioner'. I called Clive, explained the background to some of the deals we had done to help Nick, and he agreed to wind down. JP had gone OTT and TB was a bit irritated with that.

The Welsh party were meeting, with Rhodri [Morgan] refusing to back down and insisting he would go ahead for the leadership. *The Times* ran in full my letter attacking their coverage of the Ron Davies story. At the office meeting, TB said we had slightly lost our sense of direction because of the extraneous events we had been forced to deal with, and he asked us to work up a plan to get back on to the funda-mentals. On the Libs, he was still pressing me to get some coverage for the possibility of a PR referendum and I had a meeting with [David] Yelland re the *Sun* in Scotland to try to get him to rein them in, and gave him a stack of ideas to run against the Nats.

TB had a one-on-one with Gerry Adams and called me in at the end. The mood wasn't great and it was clear they had made no progress. 'So what do we say to our friends outside?' asked Gerry. I said we should say you had confessed to being gay and therefore TB was putting you straight into the Cabinet as Northern Ireland Secretary.

Tuesday, November 10

Massive coverage of NB and not that bad. Only the *Record* had much of a go at me about the handling of it. The *Sun*, milking the whole gay mafia thing, was ridiculous, but needless to say they made all the reviews of the papers, which is partly what it is all about. I asked the office to pull together a column-inch comparison on NB and [NHS] waiting lists – thousands vs next to none. Hurricane Mitch [Nicaragua and Honduras] was huge and Clare had been slow off the mark and we looked disengaged and uncaring. I said at the morning meeting we had to get moving on it. CW said GB had tried to press Clare to do more and at 5, GB did a doorstep in the street to announce a new trust fund and debt relief initiative. We were leading the later bulletins with it.

Martin McGuinness gave us a problem on the *Today* programme when he said that the reason they couldn't get the IRA to decommission was because the IRA 'won't do it'. I replied as best I could on it but then PA ran my quotes as indicating we were no longer saying SF/IRA were part of the same thing. Trimble complained and I had to square him and then clarify at the four o'clock, they were two sides of the same coin etc. What I didn't want to do was lay into McG at this stage. But we had to put the pressure on. With 200 prisoners now out, it was very hard that there was no decommissioning. The morning briefing was better-humoured than last week.

I went with TB to lunch with *The Times* at a private room in some trendy restaurant. TB was on great form, and [Phil] Webster was picking up stories left right and centre – party reform, Iraq, Queen's Speech, FSA. They were an odd bunch. Webster is just a great guy and a terrific reporter, [Peter] Riddell a bit set in his ways, Mary Ann Sieghart adores Tony and herself in equal measure, but the rest are so right wing I found myself biting my tongue and let TB patronise them as he listened to their gibberish. Neil called and said he thought if he came out for Alun M it would backfire. We got back for a 3pm meeting on Scotland. DD was hollow-cheeked and looked almost broken, with all the problems of the world on his shoulders.

JP called from Buenos Aires, said he had seen John H's note of the lunch with Menem, and me saying there should be no reference to what Robin had said [on Falkland Islands sovereignty], and what was he meant to say? We ran through the tricky questions and the lines to take, which took for ages and in the end he did fine. TB spoke to Bill C re Iraq on the secure hotline, with Iraq to be bombed on Saturday. TB was worried, but we had to go for it. He also spoke to Chirac re the same.

Wednesday, November 11

We were getting hit over the London mayor procedures and with Rhodri Morgan [contesting for leadership of the Welsh Assembly] and now Dennis Canavan [Labour MP] threatening to stand as an independent [for Scottish Parliament], we were in for a big 'control-freakery' phase. TB was worrying about Iraq now that it was clear there would be military action on Saturday. On Ken [Livingstone, Labour MP for Brent East, standing for mayor of London], he reckoned we needed a six- to nine-month campaign, making the argument that Ken did not want to fight for Londoners but against the Labour leadership; that his record was poor and he did not even believe in the job in the first place. He wanted Labour MPs up on it now. I tried to get Oona King [Labour MP for Bethnal Green and Bow] who said she would not do it. At the 11, Trevor Kavanagh came in with a new guy from the *Sun*. 'Are you gay?' I asked him. I then tore into Adam Boulton, who was getting knickers twisted because Jim Fitzpatrick [Labour MP for Poplar and Canning Town], a Scot, was speaking about London.

After yesterday's depressing meeting with DD re Scotland, with Donald worried we should not be attacking too hard, TB and GB agreed we had to push more aggressively the line that the SNP would lead to separatism. TB did a briefing for the Scottish media and really hit the line hard and you could sense them not only buying the line but relieved it was being put. TB was much better at PMQs, a lot calmer, a lot more measured and on the detail. Afterwards, after all the wittering and ear-bending from Paddy, I released the statement on the next steps for the great Lib-Lab project. It went big straight away, but they knew that my heart wasn't in it and as a result there was maybe more cynicism than there otherwise would have been. No matter how many times TB took me through it, whilst I could see that it was better to have them closer to us than the Tories, I could not see why we would want to take it much further than that.

We had a big Iraq meeting at TB's Commons office with Robin C, George R, Jonathan, John H and Charles Guthrie. TB said it was clear we were on for Saturday and we should be totally supportive. Equally, he had told BC he must accept the offer of support from others and we should be continuing to build support. Guthrie said that in the fifty-two hours of planned attack, it was possible 2,500 people would die, and UK planes and bombs would be responsible for about 250 of them. TB nodded, but looked nervous. Charles also said he could not rule out casualties among our Tornado teams. He took us through the plan of action from midnight Saturday. TB was clearly on for it, but worried, and felt we needed to keep building the diplomatic cover. Charles, who is a top man, and absolutely clear in the way he spells things out, said we would be responsible for twenty per cent of the flying, while the US would be doing most of the hits from elsewhere. He circulated secret papers on it which he took back at the end.

TB was doing a *Today* programme pre-record with Jim Naughtie which was meant to be about Scotland but he also did Iraq and Libs. TB was alarmed how big the Lib-Lab story was going. I resisted the temptation to say I told you so. Even with my scepticism covering, the press had taken it as pretty significant and of course it was right up Naughtie's street. Sally M said there was a lot of unease in the party about what exactly he was up to with the Libs. I said at the moment he seems to share it. He took me up to the flat after the interview, and said how do we calm it? I said you need to call JP to stop him going off on one when he hears the interview and sees the papers tomorrow.

Thursday, November 12
On Iraq, the main message at Cabinet was that air strikes were looking likelier, sooner rather than later. TB said Saddam was not moving. GR described it as the gravest crisis since the end of the Gulf War. Saddam had broken the ceasefire agreement, broken his word to Kofi [Annan], and was rebuilding chemical and biological weapons programmes. He was weaponising nerve agents. These are 'ferocious weapons' and his neighbours believe there is intent. TB made clear this was the US demanding and us complying, but that our own independent judgement was that he must be forced to comply. He said there was a real breach, not a technical breach. GR talked through the British likely involvement – twelve Tornado teams and 600 troops based in Saudi.

After the morning meeting, I went to Room 215 at the JIC [Joint

Intelligence Committee, Cabinet Office], which was chaired by Doug Henderson [now Armed Forces minister]. David Fisher and Edgar Buckley [officials] and I did most of the talking. We agreed to put out the WMD document and get a TB tabloid and RC broadsheet article. We had to keep stressing this was about getting compliance and stopping Saddam's capability at this stage.

Pre-Cabinet I saw George R and agreed he should do media in the street afterwards. Both he and TB set things out to the Cabinet, and it was clear the direction we were heading in. I briefed to that effect, that we were getting closer to military action. I said we didn't see much point in Kofi Annan going back to Iraq. There was no sign at all that Saddam was getting into line. Afterwards I went in for TB's meeting where Guthrie was seeking explicit authority for the targets UK forces were designated to hit. He was in uniform today whereas at the last couple of meetings he had been wearing a suit. He admitted we did not yet know the exact time it – Operation Desert Viper – would be launched. Later we learned it would be 3pm Saturday. TB again was looking nervous. When they went through the targets one by one, it brought home to you the certainty that people were going to get killed. I could tell TB was more worried about this than any of the other myriad of concerns he had been dealing with. In the car to Northolt, he spoke to Schroeder who said he would support.

On the plane we settled down to work on the Scotland speech. We had to frame the debate as a battle between the politics of social justice and the politics of separation. We also had to do it in a way that DD and Co. were able to pick up the cudgels after we left, but they were a demoralised and unimpressive bunch. TB and I were doing our usual messing around in Scottish accents, him posh Jock, me West of Scotland boozer, the real Scots rolling their eyes at us. Douglas had done an OK draft and we got it sorted by the time we landed. It went down well both with the audience and the media. Then to a *Sunday Mail* readers' meeting which was excellent. TB was far more popular with real people up here than the party either understood or liked to admit. TB and DD were both speaking at the dinner and both did well. I think TB's visit, and the response we were getting, had given Donald a bit of confidence. John H called to say there was another change to the time of launch of air strikes.

Friday, November 13

Scotland. At the breakfast meeting, there was a much better mood than on the last visit and I think we were showing again that if you take arguments on, rather than just sit back, you can make the weather not be driven by it as the party in Scotland had been for a while. TB had a couple of media events which again he used to crank up pressure on the SNP, at one point setting out a few questions for them on policy, and saying it was amazing the media were not pressing them to explain how these policies – e.g. a self-financing corporation tax cut – would work. I did a Sunday lobby briefing by conference call, lots of background re Iraq. On the flight home, TB said again that we had to keep Anji on board and he wanted her more not less involved in the planning visits. He said if the two of us left, he wasn't sure what he'd do.

Saturday, November 14

Jonathan and I got in at 9 to see TB, then the first main meeting at 10, TB, RC, GR, CDS [Chief of the Defence Staff – Guthrie], RW, Jonathan, John H, AC. The operation was being launched at 4pm, air strikes plus cruise missiles. I drafted a full statement, which TB then rewrote while I fixed for him to speak to Group Captain Alan Vincent [commander of the RAF's Tornado force] in Kuwait. Joe Lockhart [new White House press secretary] and I had agreed Clinton would go up around 4.45 our time, so TB should aim to do something around that time. We put together a list of the world leaders and foreign ministers TB and RC would call. We agreed TB would do a statement in the street and then lie low till tomorrow.

Then John Holmes came through and said Clinton was putting a pause on it. Iraq was sending a letter making clear they were ready to have the UN inspectors back in. The military were still keen to go but BC felt he had to order the pause at least until we had seen the letter. When it came, it was full of holes and at the end there was an annexe that was basically a list of THEIR conditions. But Saddam had managed to sow doubt and confusion and division and over the next few hours there were a few difficult calls with Bill C and Sandy Berger in particular. Clinton wanted a 24-hour delay. I immediately redrafted the statement to say TB had authorised use of force; that SH only climbed down because he feared attack; that the forces would now stay there until this was all tested and bolted down, and compliance clear. But the US did not want to refer to the authorisation of force because they did not want it known the operation had been about to begin even though we said – rightly as it turned out – that it was bound to leak in the US where they had a much leakier system, and where the military were likely to be annoyed at the delay. TB said he understood why Bill did it, but our general view was that we should have gone ahead without the pause but that now the pause was ordered, we would have to test the letter until a further breach. Our strong view was we had to be out there saying this attempted backdown was only the result of him thinking he was about to get hit – which he was. That was the only cover we had to the charge of dithering. We should now be setting clear conditions and if they were not met in full, immediately, we hit him. But the US – particularly Gore, Berger and Bill Cohen [US Defense Secretary] – felt we had to hit him anyway but instead of doing it Saturday, let's do it Sunday. We sensed Bill felt he had taken the wrong decision re the pause and was now looking for a way round that. It was a bit messy. They seemed now to be making the argument there was no way to do a deal with him. So why pause in the first place? we asked. TB was worried we would end up diluting the support we had. Clear breach would get us support. If we were signalling we weren't sure, or it didn't matter, we would dissipate it. That was his game. Why were we letting him play it?

In all TB had eight calls with Clinton over an eighteen-hour period up to Sunday 4.30am when he finally went to bed. He felt BC had taken the pause decision alone and was now under pressure from everyone else to go for it. TB felt Bill had slightly lost faith in himself. On one of the calls, around 5-6pm, Gore and Berger did most of the talking. TB was getting exasperated. If the pause was to test the sincerity of intent, but now we were going ahead anyway, but twenty-four hours later, what was the pause in the end for? GR and Guthrie came over to get a face-to-face briefing on what was going on, and were appalled. Charles said we should have gone ahead, and said the letter came too late. But now the decision was taken to pause, it was sensible surely to wait, till SH broke any aspect of the deal, and then hit him straight away. That seemed obvious to everyone at our end, but in the States there was obviously a big argument going on. I couldn't understand why they didn't see the one thing they seemed most worried about – a charge of weakness – was best addressed by promoting the fact he had responded to our strength.

We got our media into the street for around 6.30. They hung around while we had another round with the US team who were still very clear they did not want it said we were almost at war. In the end we put together words that made clear we did not think the Iraqi climb-down was enough, that they had to be clear and there could be no conditions. He looked and sounded good and it was generally accepted SH had climbed down, which gave us a bit of time. But TB and I were both worried it would before long be seen as a clever SH ploy that had split the world community and averted military strikes. I was exhausted by the time I left for home, having spent all day briefing, drafting and redrafting and trying with TB to get the Yanks into a more sensible place.

TB was clear we should have gone the whole way. The truth is they unilaterally reversed the decision to go and now they were trying to wind back the reel. It was a nightmare, but TB did say we should keep close with them, and was clear we did not want any hint of division spilling out. Guthrie was speaking to General [Hugh] Shelton [chairman, Joint Chiefs of Staff], his opposite number, and was telling them for heaven's sake stop winding yourselves up. He was proudly showing me his cufflinks which were a gift from the sultan of Oman for some act of derring-do he had carried out. He had a real glint in his eye at the moment. GR was also speaking to Cohen, and RC to [Madeleine] Albright. RC told TB that he could not see anyone supporting military action. That was the first sign of a consequence to the dithering. RC had been fine earlier. TB said whatever we thought of their handling of it, we should not peel off from the US.

Sunday, November 15

I got to bed at 12.30 and at 4.30 TB called again, wanting me to get briefing again re the Iraqis making further concessions at the UN and making clear we were worried our conditions were not in fact being met. He called again at 8. By now it was already out there that B-52 bombers had been in the air when BC withdrew the order, so a day late I started to brief that TB had given the authority for military action, and that he had spoken to commanders in Kuwait. TB was now worried the whole thing would seem like a backdown by us not SH. The answer was that we were prepared to hit him, and had authorised the action to do so – that was the difference with February. We were also making clear that in the event of any further breach, there would be no warning at all. I went in and TB was up in the flat. He said we had got the assurances from Iraq – whether meaningless or not they had been given – but the US were still talking about going in today. This was a nightmare, he said. Having taken the wrong decision, they think they can put it right by taking the decision they should have taken in the first place. But the circumstances have changed and they may be making the wrong decision again. Then word came through from the MoD that the US were preparing plans based on the assumption that the UK would not take part.

Jonathan and I went back up to tell TB. We cannot let that happen, he said. Whether we think they are in the right place or not, it would be disastrous for the transatlantic relationship if we pulled out on this. George Robertson, Robin, Charles Guthrie and officials arrived. GR and Charles were totally sound, and absolutely of our view. RC clearly felt there were no circumstances in which we could support, let alone take part in, military action. When I said later I would be very pissed off if the Americans briefed that we had talked them out of action, Robin said 'It would go down very well on the Continent.' In fact, one of the last calls of the night had been a three-way call between Bill, TB and Chirac and Chirac basically said that only the US view mattered, but indicated if there was a further breach, he would accept we had to go in. So we actually had quite a strong position but RC was being very weaselly, saying if we went in after the events of recent days, we would be isolated and it would take at least a year to recover our European relations. TB said he did not accept that. But if we pulled the plug on the Yanks, it would take a lot longer to recover. He said we still needed to persuade the Americans to get going with a public line that a combination of diplomacy and the threat of force had forced a climb-down and we had to maintain that pressure with a real threat of force at any breach. I did a briefing to push that line, gave out loads of detail on all the calls etc., but a lot of them were starting to see it as a win for SH because he averted the strikes and split the inter-national community again. Berger told us BC was intending to go out at 3pm our time to say we had the assurances and now they would be tested. In other words, as John H had suspected, they would not go ahead with it. We agreed Guthrie should underline that if any military operation was being launched, we would be part of it. TB was adamant they had to understand there would be no messing about from us. We agreed TB should do another stand-up in the street at 12.45. He wrote the script himself, basic message that there had been developments and we needed to test the assur-ances. Again he looked and sounded right and was on form.

There was now a bit of a lull and I went out for a couple of hours to meet Fiona and the kids at Pizza Express, then got back to watch Clinton's badly delayed press conference at the White House. I called Lockhart to say we needed to emphasise the big difference with last time – that this time use of force had been authorised. He sounded a bit panicky. Clinton put in a, for him, very unimpressive perform-ance. He gave the impression, as did Berger and Cohen, that they were not happy or confident, and people would pick up the sense that we didn't really think we had won, that there was a credibility problem having been in this exact same position before. They had clearly gone without sleep and had been overly worrying how the US media would respond. I briefed TB who felt I needed to brief again, emphasise that we had spun a web for SH and he was trapped in it.

TB was pretty exasperated at the way the US had handled things in the last couple of days. Their media operation had not been effective, and they had allowed the obvious division and dithering to get out on the public radar. Their body language had also been dreadful, especially as we were now getting pictures from Baghdad of the 'celebrations' of yet another triumph for SH. John H called me later to say Chirac was intending to say Iraq must now understand the threat of force will be there if they breach again. I spun it as Chirac being part of a united international response to an attempt to divide. We were just about in an OK place but the Americans had not been impressive. Bill seemed to swing between the various arguments. Gore wanted to be tough. Cohen was hawkish. Berger was difficult. RC had been very tricksy all weekend.

Monday, November 16

The press here wasn't bad. A lot better than the States, where there was a lot of scepticism and the feeling SH had diddled and won. At DOP [Defence and Overseas Policy Cabinet Committee] GR and Charles [Guthrie] made clear we could not keep troops there indefinitely, that it was fine to say we were maintaining the pressure, but it was a very expensive option. We could be there for weeks if not months. TB was fed up with the French. Chirac had said to him before that Saddam 'wanted to be hit' and he had been proved wrong. Now we had a proper diplomatic platform from which to launch a military strike next time. Though I was briefing that the French were more onside than before, TB said they were hopeless. Chirac could barely conceal his distaste for the UK. There was no mention of the UK in his statement. Some in the American system were beginning to claim that the French tipped off the Iraqis that the strikes were imminent. We fixed for TB to speak to Schroeder and then briefed the Germans had been very supportive.

TB spoke to Kofi and Bill later. BC sounded a bit fed up but did keep saying – so often he was protesting too much – that he thought he made the right decision. The main message vehicle on Iraq was TB's Commons statement, which went fine, but he murdered the clips – no warnings, no wrangling – and as a result the news was a bit muddled.

Tuesday, November 17

We got OK coverage on Iraq and not as bad as it might have been on special advisers' pay, with me taking the big hit on it, needless to say. We had a bit of a problem on last night's economy speech [at the Guildhall]. The TV coverage had not been great and the press wasn't much better. The *Telegraph*, and [Robert] Peston in the *FT*, took it as being a criticism of GB. The problem was compounded by the fact TB didn't actually deliver the lines on stability as in the text, and due to a cock-up in the office, two different versions went out. So *World at One* had an orgasmic pinhead dance fest, all the usual wank from the usual wankers, but bloody irritating.

We had another unexpected problem with Estelle Morris [education minister] saying it wasn't always right to expel children for having drugs, which set off a few front-page frenzies and was now leading the news. I called TB who said calm it down. I called Estelle, who was due on the *Today* programme re grammar schools, and we agreed she should say that usually there would and should be expulsion but all she was saying was heads should have flexibility. She was perfectly grown up about it and handled it fine. We hit the inflation target again but OECD [Organisation for Economic Co-operation and Development] forecasts on growth coming down the track were not great – 0.8 per cent. At the four o'clock, I really went for Peston and *World at One*. We were defeated in the Lords on the European Elections Bill [seeking to change the electoral system for MEPs] and I very quickly put together a very aggressive and political line – an affront to democracy that unelected hereditary peers could do this. I spoke to TB, then Straw who was clearly hoping we would end up with first past the post, not PR, which meant more seats for us, and more division for the Tories. I had the second of my GIS staff meetings – Home Office, Treasury, NIO – it was a bit better than last time but not much. Some of them just didn't get it.

Wednesday, November 18

The battle between the Commons and the Lords was the main story again during the morning and I put together a far more robust argument. We had to get far more aggressive re the hereditaries, who had the strategic vision of a bat if they could not see the folly of this one. The press preferred the line that this was a bloody nose for us, so it was a bit of a struggle to get it up on our terms. Paddy was back on to TB, saying the Lib-Lab game was dead if he could not get PR for the European elections. He was in a real panic. The Tories thought they were on to something. Hague did all six [PMQs] questions on it and TB was not on great form. Widows' benefit reform was going fine, and all the advance work, especially with the *Sun* and the Beeb, had paid off. AD and I did a joint briefing and he was totally on top of it and did well.

The *Sun* ran a piece saying I was worth 250,000 quid a year and could expect £500k for my memoirs. After PMQs, TB saw [Ken] Livingstone and afterwards said he may end up having to do a deal with him. 'The guy is an egomaniac. What he really wants is a job and what he really really wants is to be in the Cabinet.' He [KL] ended by saying he was not in the business of being Tony's enemy. We then waited for the next Lords defeat and when it came put out another tough line. Then there was the [Geoffrey] Robinson apology [a 54-second statement to the Commons over undeclared financial interests] which was another bad scene for us. I went briefly to [*Mail* columnist] Simon Heffer's launch party for his book on Enoch Powell, whose widow was for some reason keen to meet me. Michael Howard was there and said, apropos of nothing, that we were totally lacking in principle. I gave back suitably.

Thursday, November 19
Last night John Williams [FCO press office] came to see me with extracts from Margaret Cook's book, due for serialisation in January. It was pretty bitter stuff. RC an egomaniac, lots of other affairs, she had an affair, suggestions of impotence and drink problems, also vile about me and TB re our handling of the *News of the World*. RC came to see me after Cabinet and I advised non-reaction. I felt if he engaged at all, it would simply fuel interest. If he did nothing, then most people would reach the conclusion this was a very bitter woman. It would, however, underline the notion that he was a victim rather than master of events. Lords/closed lists was still the main story with the argument beginning to turn against the Tories, e.g. Peter Riddell. Bradders [David Bradshaw] and I were working on a TB piece for the *Indy* denying the control-freak charge when TB decided he wanted to do one for the *Telegraph* on Hague and how his handling of the Lords issue showed he was all tactics and no strategy. We had a Cabinet photo-stunt to show the fifty-three Acts passed into law since we were elected, which made TV but was in the end a bit naff. Cabinet was mainly discussing the Lords and the Parliament Act, then Iraq and the Queen's Speech. TB said there was nothing new in the Tories losing an election and then using their bias in the Lords to pretend they hadn't. He said this was a crazy issue for the Tories to go on,

and showed Hague was useless at strategy. Jack C had been hopeless on *Today*, totally bogged down in detail and not explaining comprehensibly at all.

I went home to get the kids from school, took the boys to football and then back into Number 10 with Fiona for dinner with TB/CB, Charlie and Marianna [Hildyard, Falconer's wife] and Jonathan and Claudia Harmsworth [*Mail* chairman Lord Rothermere and wife]. She seemed a lot brighter than him, and was also very attractive, if too thin. He constantly gave the impression that he was worried he was out of his depth. I couldn't see him reining in [Paul] Dacre like [David] English did from time to time. He was overly keen to impress but he lacked force in the way he made an argument. He said there was not much that the government was doing wrong, but that a lot of people 'out there' were very worried, if not paranoid. Charlie and I tried to tell him that it was the press who by and large spread the paranoia. There was little sense in the media of the government being a success, and zero sense of it in the *Mail*.

Claudia was very into process questions re me – what role did I have in the Menem article? Did I tell TB to say stability is sexy? [the phrase had been inserted by AC into the recent Guildhall economic speech to ensure coverage]. I hadn't seen the *FT* but she said they had said Hague was desperate to get someone like me and offering £150,000. She was also quizzing a lot re Diana. Fiona and I were badgering her to say she wouldn't send her kids (aged two and four) to private school. No chance. TB was very relaxed and chatty but left it to me and Charlie to do the heavy stuff. I felt we were not dealing with the power at the *Mail*.

Friday, November 20

I took pretty much a day off and slept for most of the afternoon. Re Ron D, charges were dropped by the Crown Prosecution Service, so that became the main story of the day. [Don] Macintyre did me proud on the Chirac briefing, including the doubt that he was '*un homme sérieux*' ['a serious man'].

Saturday, November 21

UNSCOM inspectors were having difficulty getting the documents they wanted. We agreed to keep a line between firmness and *casus belli* [justification for acts of war] but it was clearly a bad sign. I spoke to TB as I left for Bournemouth – Burnley lost 5-0 – and he said we had to keep a close eye on it over the weekend.

Sunday, November 22

The papers were dull. TB wanted to take action – possibly even legal – re the *Mail on Sunday* story saying he had ordered new beds for the VC10 at a cost of fifty-odd thousand to the taxpayer. It turned out to be a decision made by the last government which happened under this one, and TB had nothing to do with it at all. 'These fuckers cannot just make up stories and get away with it,' he said. I said unless he was prepared genuinely to do something, we could do nothing more than deny it and stop others following it. John H called me to say what he called 'Operation Chirac' – my briefings – was having some effect. Chirac had called TB to say that there was a briefing war and it had to stop. They agreed to have dinner before Christmas. John said Chirac had been polite with TB but he clearly resented some of the portrayals in our and the US media, for which he also held us responsible. TB agreed it was probably right that he had seen we would not just take his bullshit without fighting when we had to.

Monday, November 23

Richard Wilson sent me a note saying I had to watch it over some of the briefings on the Lords and Ron Davies. It was pretty clear from the papers attached that [Mike] Granatt [head of GICS] had put him up to it, I think. I had it out with RW at the government reception when I said if Mike had a problem he should come and see me and not get Richard to fight his battles. He said 'You're tired,' and it got a bit heavy with me saying 'Don't patronise me.' He said I was being very unfair if I thought Mike was hostile because he was determined to be an ally of mine. Charlie F's view was that Richard was just desperate to be the man closest to TB.

TB was worried, as was I, that the main focus of the Queen's Speech would be Lords reform and I worked up a briefing note to try to point up other issues. He felt people were perfectly happy for us to reform the Lords, but they would not see it as a priority and would not want to think we were operating out of some kind of ideology or prejudice. I met Jack C and Margaret B, who were doing the bulk of the media work on it, and we agreed the best approach was to say it was addressing people's priorities, as a way of indicating Lords was not one of them.

Bertie [Ahern] caused a bit of a flurry, which I had to damp down at the 11, when he said there would be a united Ireland 'in my lifetime'. I also had a go at the right-wing papers for their ludicrous coverage of the PES and Ecofin [EU Economic and Financial Affairs Council]. All they ever wanted to do was to present us as weak or isolated or caving in to a crazy EU agenda. It was comic-book stuff.

Today was a good day to go at them because we finally got the beef ban lifted, and I could argue it was as a result of a more co-operative approach. It led the news all day but we had to get Nick Brown to redo his clips, his main line originally being it was a great day for the EU and the Commission because it showed them being fair by us. Ludicrous. It was a win for UK agriculture.

At the Queen's Speech reception for ministers, I had a nice chat with Betty Boothroyd, who was supportive of me, and said not to worry about all the attacks, but she said she felt TB was attacking the Tories too much at PMQs, and he had to watch it.

Tuesday, November 24

Queen's Speech day. The overnight briefing had gone not bad, with welfare reform high up in the mix. But the story was bound to be Lords[1] after the reaction in the chamber when the Queen read out the relevant section and there was a mix of hear, hears alongside grumbles of disapproval. TB was working on the speech [for the debate following the Queen's Speech] mainly on his own and particularly after what Betty said last night, which I passed on to him, I was a bit worried we didn't have a big enough theme. We had been hoping to walk as per last year but the police advised against because of an animal liberation protest, so we went by car and with the streets all closed that would lead to more bollocks about being more remote and aloof.

I briefed the broadcasters as the Queen was doing her thing, and then TB came back to carry on working on his speech. He was in a bit of a grumpy mood. GB came in from next door, and TB said he was not happy at the way he was handling the tax harmonisation issue [taxation policies being decided at EU level]. They had a bit of an upper and downer about that, which didn't really go anywhere. TB felt we were being boxed in because GB was so nervous about the press on this, but he should not be threatening the veto the whole time. There may be some areas where tax harmonisation suits our purposes so we should not be totally blocking it off. He felt GB could afford to be more relaxed about the debate, and see where it went, without playing into scare tactics against us.

TB said he needed to talk to me about the Lords. He said Derry had had a lot of contact with [Robert, Viscount] Cranborne

[1] The Queen's Speech announced that the right of hereditary peers to sit and vote in the House of Lords would be removed, as the first stage in the democratic reform of the Lords.

[Conservative leader in the Lords]. How would it be, he said, if we cut a deal with Cranborne under which one-tenth of hereditary peers would stay for the transitional period; that three cross-benchers put down an amendment that made clear all of them would go apart from this block, that there would be a limited number of appointments to balance it up, and then we and then the Lib Dems would back it? TB seemed confident we could get Cranborne to do the deal without Hague, who was, seemingly, not expressing a view while others were totally opposed. I said it sounded fine, and if it was doable, the sooner the better. It would be even better if we could say at the same time that as a result there would be more space for other bills of greater relevance to people's lives that we could bring in.

We worked on interventions, but both Bruce [Grocott] and I had bad vibes. They turned out to be well founded. Hague was very funny, with some brilliant one-liners, whereas TB was a bit flat and wooden. He hammered the themes of modernisation, fairness, delivery, but it didn't work as a whole. We really needed to rethink how he did these Commons set pieces. Something wasn't right. He was a bit flat afterwards and knew he hadn't performed and that Hague had – added to which Hague was about to get the Parliamentarian of the Year award, to be presented by JP. Lords reform was dominating the news coverage and it was becoming a PR battle. We really had to go for it now.

On the plane to Belfast we were working on the Thursday speech for the Dáil [Irish Parliament] which he wanted to go big, and be about more than the usual stock of Anglo-Irish issues. He even threw out the idea of speculating that one day Ireland could join the Commonwealth, before John H and I persuaded him it was a barmy idea. Over dinner, he said he wanted to frame a context for the debate on decommissioning, that we had to break the ideological grip they had against the physical handing over of weapons. John H and Mo were worried about getting into that territory too. Seamus Mallon came up for a drink and did a doorstep saying the process was in danger unless we made progress before Christmas. I watched the late news and Hague was getting very good write-ups for his speech today.

Wednesday, November 25
Hillsborough. TB was worried that the process was in danger of moving backwards and felt we had to make progress soon on the North-South implementation bodies. He was also concerned at the feeling in the security services that the Real IRA would be going for a big assassination

soon. We headed for Stormont and there was a lot of tension between Trimble and Mallon at the first meeting. They could barely bring themselves to look at each other, and Seamus looked both hurt and angry whenever DT spoke. TB felt he was close to the end of his tether and after seeing them together he had a session with them individually, told DT he had to be more understanding of what SM was trying to do; told Seamus to keep going, not let the lack of progress get to him, keep working away. SM said DT saw the implementation bodies as a Fenian plot between us and the Irish. Then Adams, and TB trying again to push on decommissioning but getting nowhere, with GA constantly moving back to DT being obstructive. I ducked out of some of the meetings to work on the speech for the Dáil, marrying John H's draft with TB's comments overnight.[1] It was a strong speech which I started to brief. I particularly enjoyed briefing the 'new positive relations with the Republic' line with Ian Paisley sitting on the edge of my desk looking at a newspaper. He looked around at me, shook his head. I winked and he laughed.

Viktor Klima came in for the pre-summit meeting. His teeth looked whiter and bigger every time I saw him. He seemed to begin every sentence with a very ponderous 'In my opinion . . .'. He also seemed a lot more nervous than before, and I wondered if the enormity of the task of chairing the whole shebang was beginning to weigh on the Austrian system a bit. He did a good job stamping down on tax harmonisation. TB did the smaller [NI] parties pm, then left a group of UU, SDLP and Irish officials to work up new ideas on how we take forward the N-S implementation bodies. He did his third doorstep of the day, said he remained optimistic but there was a lot to do blah.

The Law Lords voted three to two to uphold the decision on Pinochet's immunity so that was a massive story. In truth we had been hoping he would just be sent home but now we had a no-win situation, with the left hoping he would be sent to Spain and the right, led by Thatcher and Hague, saying he should be freed to go home. TB was clearly of the view he should just go, that the point had been made, honour served and now he should be taken out of our hair. But it had some way to run yet. TB was exercised through the day about the possible deal on the Lords and raised it with me at several points. But the thinking was Hague would move against as it became clear what this might lead to. Most of the Shadow Cabinet were against and the question was really whether we could get Cranborne to deliver.

[1] In the first speech to the Dáil Éireann by a UK prime minister since 1922, Blair appealed for nationalists and Unionists to work together.

We got a meeting fixed for tomorrow with him and [Sir Alastair] Goodlad [front bench Conservative MP].

We had a ridiculous Blunkett problem today. He didn't want to do the debate in the House today because he said he had to be in Scarborough for a speech tomorrow. But David Willetts [Shadow Education Secretary] was doing it so what was the problem? With the Speaker getting agitated we ended up having to order DB to do it. Though he didn't like to admit it, and though he can shift as much work as any of them, I think he finds these set pieces real hard work and so the idea of preparing for both, and travelling, just got him down. We carried on with the speech for Dublin where the Tony and Bertie show was going well. I really like the Irish political class. They seem far less hidebound and of course they love talking about UK politics. They [the media] wanted a response to Bob Marshall-Andrews [Labour MP] saying I was Pontius Pilate's spin doctor. Ignored.

Thursday, November 26

Dublin. It was only as I filled TB in on the Irish media that it dawned on him how big and how historic this speech was being viewed in Ireland. We had a meeting with Ruairi Quinn [Irish Labour Party leader] who briefed him on the planned Labour/democratic left. We set off in a very long convoy for very few people and at the Dáil there was a real excitement in the air as he walked through, that buzz that you normally associate with weddings or big sporting events. The mood was really good. Fiona and I sat up in the gallery behind CB and Celia Larkin [Ahern's partner]. It was a good speech and he delivered it really well. The UK press picked up on the very positive mood music re the euro. But generally it was the history and the sense of occasion that dominated.

We left for a visit to Bertie's old school, St Aidan's, really bright kids, and did a computer link-up with other schools, then a walkabout, where the mood again was terrific. Over lunch they were crunching hard again on implementation bodies and also re Vienna – no to tax harmonisation, yes to dealing with unfair competition. TB said he was worried 'the crazies' would do something soon. Martin Mansergh [Fianna Fáil politician] said he was worried if the IRA moved to decommission, the Real IRA would strike. Mo called me out halfway through to say TB really must speak to Trimble to seal the deal on implementation bodies. TB and Bertie were really working together well but both agreed the whole thing was in danger of stalling unless they managed to get a shove forward soon. They did a short doorstep before we left for the plane. The *Mail* did another euro-scare splash story, the fourth in a few days. Then Schroeder said something about QMV [qualified majority voting] which our press decided to take up as another 'threat' to our veto. More comic-book stuff.

On the flight home, I showed TB the Margaret Cook [autobiography] extracts. 'They will harm her more than him,' he said. CB and Fiona were bending our ears on Pinochet. We got back and TB saw Cranborne and Goodlad. They pretty much did the deal – [Lords reform] amendment would go down in the name of three cross-benchers. They would support it whether Hague liked it or not. Very odd.

Friday, November 27

We got pretty good coverage for Ireland and now we were heading straight for Wales. TB spoke to GB early on, and I had a similar conversation with Whelan, re the way they had got up the story of the veto re tax harmonisation. We had played the card too early because of the noise being created by some of the papers, which would have passed. By the sound of his voice, I think GB knew he had screwed up but was having to defend the way he had handled it. On the train down to Wales, TB and I were going over the Lords deal. It seemed too good to be true but as it seemed to be there for the taking, we had to move quickly.

I was at a loss to understand how Cranborne felt he was in a position to say he would go ahead with it regardless of whether Hague supported it or not. TB said Cranborne seemed adamant, that he was so fed up of Hague's lack of judgement and leadership. TB was sure Cranborne could deliver. On timing, I said the optimum was 1. cross-benchers announce, 2. we welcome and say it could mean room for the Food Standards Agency and Rail Authority bills, 3. Cranborne welcomes and says Tories in the Lords will support. I spoke to Derry to say this was what we need to happen. He came back after speaking to Goodlad who said nothing could be done until Wednesday, when Cranborne was seeing his hereditaries. I spoke to Cranborne, and agreed we should both micromanage. I think we were both surprised to be dealing with each other. He said 'I hope you understand my need in this is to cover my arse. I am committing high treason just talking to you.' He said he had to put the proposal to his own people before we could progress, but he was confident of support.

Even if the Shadow Cabinet went against it on Wednesday, he would still press for peers to support it and he was confident of support. I said it would be better to move sooner because of the fear of leaks but he said he could not do that, it was not possible, so we would just have to keep things as tight as we could. He seemed very serious about the whole thing. My only concern was that he wanted me not him to approach Lord Carnarvon [hereditary peer, cross-bencher]. When I mentioned this to TB later, he assumed it was part of the arse-covering, that Cranborne did not want to be seen to be the prime mover.

Re Wales, we had agreed he might as well just go for it, that fence-sitting would be condemned as weakness and he should support Alun Michael, say the job is effectively the successor job to Welsh Secretary, and he has the right qualities. That seemed to be confirmed as the right decision when TB met the party people later. They were very warm and supportive though not surprisingly Rhodri [Morgan] looked a bit distant and nervous. TB got over the message that this was about what was best for the party, not what the media or London Labour thought. Alun was looking a bit bewildered by it all, and he definitely needed some new clothes and a bit of a makeover, but he was reckoned by those who knew him he to be a tough character.

The meeting with the Welsh editors went fine, though Alun probably interrupted too much and made points which would have come better from TB. TB spoke to Trimble again, who was cutting up rough re implementation bodies and TB felt he may need to go again soon. Pinochet was rumbling on with the Chilean foreign minister over here. Godric was also very exercised because after days and weeks of us saying it was all a judicial process, the Foreign Secretary and others were circulating papers on their assessment of 'damage to Anglo-Chilean relations'. TB just wanted him to go home but that would give us real grief in the party. We did badly in the Euro by-election in Scotland, coming third behind the Tories.

Saturday, November 28
Derry called, clearly suspicious that Cranborne no longer wanted to deal with the cross-benchers. He was also worried about leaks, as I was, with the circle of knowledge widening. TB had told JP, who was happy because if the deal was executed as planned, it would mean room for his Rail Authority Bill. He had also spoken to Margaret B, who was not happy because she felt the party would expect there to be no hereditaries left at all.

Derry said Goodlad and Cranborne had been leak-free so far, but he felt the more people on our side knew, the more they would discuss with each other and the risk of a leak and everything going half-cock was increased. He and I both felt we should keep pressing to do this pre-Wednesday, but I was not sure we could push Cranborne much harder. TB called, said he was worried re the way GB had handled the Europe/tax situation, felt he lacked subtlety in his dealings with these guys and they sensed it and exploited it. We are going to have to get a proper grip of this before Vienna, he said. He was fine re the Cranborne note, but said if we could get it done earlier, we should. He was relaxed about me being the one to approach the cross-benchers, but I had doubts, feeling they would think it inappropriate. I spoke to Derry again who picked Goodlad's brains, and they agreed it was not the best way to take it forward.

Peter M called, partly because he was worried the *Mail on Sunday*, who had been sniffing around Brazil for two weeks, were about to do him over, but also re GB. I could see the GB/Peter clash moving very quickly into the Europe debate and said he really had to stay shtum, let us handle the tax stuff pre-Vienna, and not make this a bigger deal than it needs to be. In the afternoon, David [Miliband] and Louise's [Shackelton, professional violinist] wedding, which was really nice. They are both so palpably decent and nice and happy with each other. I played the bagpipes for the first time in a while, and surprised myself at how well I played. TB made a nice little speech and then left early.

Sunday, November 29
Derry was calling fairly regularly re the deal on Lords reform, but we were going to have to wait for Wednesday whether we liked it or not. Peter was getting very worried re where we were heading Europe-wise, and TB was agitating re Ireland, but it was a fairly quiet day.

Monday, November 30
The papers were going through a berserk phase on Europe. The *Sun* splashed on a piece of bollocks that there would be VAT on kids' clothes if we joined the euro. They, the *Mail* and the *Telegraph* could sense indecision and doubt on our part re our European strategy and so they were going to go for it. TB and I discussed in the morning and agreed he and GB had to get on to the same page quickly, and sort the one or two big issues where they sensed vulnerability. We also needed to turn some heat on the papers. GB was still of the view we needed to be talking up the threats to our position, but we felt that helped justify some of the scare-mongering that was going on. I tried my best to be dismissive of all this Europe/tax stuff at the 11, but it was clearly going to be the main political story for the next few days. I denied the *Sun* story God knows how many times. Even the fact of the Franco-German summit was being seen as a 'snub to Blair'

for fuck's sake. They could not see beyond the old narrow lines set during the Thatcher era. We just had to keep our nerve on it.

I had a meeting with Cranborne, who Mark Bennett brought in through 70 Whitehall. I could tell the minute he walked in that he was enjoying the drama of it, the plotting, and the fact of consorting with an enemy, a subject he joked about frequently. He was wearing bright red socks and a very smart suit. We talked a bit about how brilliant the Number 10 switchboard were, and what secrets they knew, and got down to it. I said I didn't understand why he wanted me to be the one speaking to the cross-benchers. He said they would enjoy the drama of it, but more importantly it was part of him covering his own arse with his own side. He could not be seen to be a prime mover in this. I said I felt they might think it odd if I did it because I am not a peer, let alone a minister, and I suggested Margaret Jay. He said he could see what I was saying, that I was a 'big juju', whatever that is, in the eyes of the Tories and maybe non-Tory peers too, and he was happy with Margaret. Later I spoke to Margaret and squared her.

The loop was widening the whole time and the earliest we could do this was lunchtime Wednesday – the cross-benchers' statement, with Cranborne reacting. I drafted the statement for the cross-benchers while he was there, with Mark quietly typing it up from our scribbles. TB and Derry were both happy with it. Cranborne took a copy and said there were still a few people he would need to square but he was confident we could get support where we needed it. I still could not fully understand why he would do this – he didn't know me from Adam, and what he did know he probably didn't like and yet we had just sat down and agreed a line-by-line plan that he must know would damage his leadership, help us through a difficulty, and no matter how much I tried to take a rap and protect his arse, he was going to be implicated. He was certainly a different breed to what I knew, but I remember Alan Clark once saying to me the Tory toffs were fascinated by me because they thought I was brutal and understood power and its use. Cranborne had power going down through his family line, and was enjoying the game. As he left, after an hour or so, he said to me 'You do realise I am committing high treason, don't you?' 'Good,' I said, and he left. But I still could not fathom what was really in it for him. He didn't really care what Hague thought about this, said he was doing the thinking for him.

He was still going to oppose us on various things. He was going to call for a post-legislative referendum. His basic line would be that he had rolled us over, that he had wanted one hundred of his peers to stay so seventy-five (one out of ten) plus fourteen as cross-benchers plus two was a key part of it. TB was pleased with the way it was going, still felt it seemed too good to be true. He emphasised though we would still need to emphasise second stage to come after the next election, and also that this was about getting more space to do things the public really cared about, e.g. transport, food safety etc.

I did a foreign press briefing in the afternoon, and there was an on-off drama re whether we were going to NI again. TB was keen, but DT was so difficult at the moment, and also so under pressure from [John] Taylor and others, that it might prove fruitless. Eventually the decision was made for us when we were told Trimble had flu, though there were mixed views as to whether it was the diplomatic variety. TB said there is a real risk we lose this whole thing because these people are so impossible.

The other drama of the day was Peter M. The *Mail on Sunday* had established that the *Punch* story about his private life was not substantiated and the piece came out OK for Peter. We had agreed yesterday to get Martin Dowle [ex-journalist working for the British Council in Brazil] to put out words saying the *Punch* stuff was not true and Hague had been disgraceful to do what he did.[1] Peter was very low about the whole thing, and there was a lot of pressure on him to put out a statement saying he was gay and that he was hurt by his friends being hit by this. I worried that far from closing it, this would just get it up in lights even more and also that it would show the press having their cake and eating it. He would get short-term sympathetic coverage but long term become an even bigger target. But he was keen to do something.

While I was dealing with Cranborne, Derry and Margaret at 5, Anji, Lance, Ben [Wegg-Prosser] and Peter H met and agreed he should do an interview with Don Macintyre to say he was gay, so what, why did his friends have to be hounded because of it? I was strongly against. TB saw Anji and Co., and they pressed him to urge Peter to come out properly. I again advised against, said I felt it would have the opposite effect of what they thought, that Peter had always been more comfortable handling this the way he had, and that some big public statement would make him a bigger target – added to which I felt there was a thin dividing line between explanation and exhibitionism. Also, it would make the media and the Tories feel great that

[1] Hague had referred to 'Lord Mandelson of Rio' in the Queen's Speech debate, a reference to claims made in the satirical magazine *Punch* that Mandelson had visited gay bars and nightclubs in Brazil accompanied by Dowle.

they had dragged him kicking and screaming to a position he never wanted to be in. I got him to call [Richard] Stott [*News of the World* columnist, former tabloid editor] who felt much the same as I did. Richard felt Peter had come out of this OK, and that Hague had been disgusting and would pay a price, and we were best to leave it.

Peter and I had a lengthy conversation after all the others had seen TB. I said I felt he had the right line on this – his private life was his, he had never discussed it, didn't intend to start now. His main concern was that Reinaldo was coming from Brazil on Saturday and he worried whether they would be able to lead a normal life. Would they be able to go out? Would they be photographed? What would he do if he was doorstepped? I said the minute he started talking about his private life, they would feel it was open season and he was better where he was. He was not Chris Smith [Culture Secretary, first MP to come out as gay]. He was an established bigger political figure and bigger target and this would expand the target they would shoot at. He would set off another frenzy and he would not be the winner. I felt people would respect him more if he just maintained the line he always had, carry on with his job, don't let others push him around.

He sounded very low, and asked whether he might not feel better if it was all out in the open. I said in many ways it is, but on his terms and that is how to keep it. Keep your nerve, and do not let them feel they have won against you.

Tuesday, December 1

On more and more days, I was waking up and wondering how we were going to get through the day. There just seemed to be too many high-octane issues flowing through the system at once, and too few of us dealing with them. Europe was leading the news again, a classic case of a press agenda driving the broadcasters' agenda. GB was doing *Today* and his tone was a lot better, playing down the veto talk, sounding confident we could win arguments. It was much better.

Things were going fine until the afternoon when [Oskar] Lafontaine piped up somewhere, saying he wanted to 'break unanimity' on tax. It was clearly going to send them into convulsions and go mega. I felt we should start to go for him a bit, say he was becoming an embarrassment to Schroeder and to Germany but TB was still in 'relax' mode, all that matters is that his ideas do not have a cat in hell's chance of being accepted. He was nonetheless furious. He felt this was happening only partly because of our wretched media. The other factors were that Lafontaine was a jerk, and he was also sure the

November '98: AC urges Peter M to hold his nerve

French would be encouraging him. That is why he wished GB had not played the veto card publicly, because it would help the French game, which was really to try to split us from the Germans. He felt that deep down, indeed quite superficially, the French did not want us in EMU, so the more domestic problems Oskar could create for us, the better for them.

On the Lords, TB was having to be fairly devious, as we all were. My most devious piece of deviousness was probably saying at the top of the draft note that all this was subject to agreement by the PM and Lord C, which should it leak gave us the option of that being Lord Chancellor or Cranborne. Cranborne now wanted to change the text on the number of peers going, to delete the reference to the ninety-one remaining peers going at stage two. This was a breach of the deal we had reached so instead we offered a slight change of words though not substance and he was happy enough. We worked through four drafts in all. I spoke to Cranborne a couple of times. He said he was seeing Hague in the morning and he would be 'no trouble, I promise you'. TB was moving to the view that Hague might feel he had to sack him when it became clear, as inevitably it would, he had been negotiating with us direct. Cranborne also mentioned on a couple of occasions he might get the chop. Back to see JP to go over the rail stuff, and I got the impression he was on board. He was a bit like me, in that he liked these big hits. His worry was that Cranborne would make a big deal of being left with more than a hundred peers in total, that he had stuffed us and would say they could stay beyond the second stage. Derry was very excited by the whole thing, said that if we pulled it off we 'deserved the Order of [Labour firebrand Aneurin] Bevan' because we were purloining the right to damage the right.

Wednesday, December 2

Hysterical coverage on Europe, with Lafontaine front page everywhere. I got Julian [Braithwaite, press officer] to collate lots of the coverage from around Europe, which had next to none of the nonsense we were having to deal with. GB and Ed B came round to see TB pre-PMQs and we agreed a strategy to define tax harmonisation as potentially relating to income tax, VAT and corporation tax, then one by one get every other country to say they would oppose such a move. GB said to TB this was a real issue coming fast down the tracks and we had to 'get real' about it. TB said he was not sure what the proposal actually was. He was strongly of the view there was simply a French game going on, and we had to be careful not to play. They were simply trying to split us from the Germans. They fundamentally disagreed about whether the tax harmonisation issue was a real one to get so concerned about. TB felt we should be maintaining the focus on our agenda for economic reform, winning alliances for our position.

Cranborne called, said he had seen Hague, who was 'reeling – but not sufficient to sack me yet'. He asked me what he should advise Hague to do, and I said take credit for the idea. I got Jo Gibbons [Margaret Jay's special adviser] to start tipping off the press re the [convenor of the cross-bench peers Lord] Weatherill press conference. Now Hague knew, TB and I discussed the outside chance he would raise it in the Commons, oppose it, and leave Cranborne out to dry. TB felt that would still leave us in a win-win situation, because we would say we still had the deal with Cranborne, who was confident he could get it through his people in the Lords.

Over to the House and, hey presto, Hague did it. At first TB, like me, thought he was supporting the deal, but it turned out he wasn't. TB was very quick on his feet, said even Hague's own people were supporting him, was he on some kind of suicide mission etc.? He hit him again on how he always got the strategic questions wrong. It was a clear win in House terms, but obviously there would be a battle in the briefings to win too. Of course, apart from Charles Reiss, who we had briefed, the media were totally bemused by it all, which meant we had to get straight out explaining. Gregor Mackay [Hague's spokesman] and I were both swamped at either door out of the gallery, and I was at a big advantage knowing so much of the background. He looked flustered when I looked across. Clearly the whole thing raised the question of whether Hague had sacked, or was sacking, Cranborne. I briefed in very factual terms and did so again at the formal briefing at 3.45. Cranborne called Alison [Blackshaw] at 3.20, while we were still in the chamber, and left me a message 'apologising for Hague's behaviour and saying he felt he has let you down'. They are a totally different breed these people. He had just shafted his leader and he was apologising to me because he had refused to take the shafting. Hague seemingly went to Cranborne's meeting with his own people, which went in Cranborne's favour, but then Cranborne was sacked.

He called me afterwards, apologised re Hague. 'I'm really sorry. I made the mistake of thinking we were dealing with grown-ups, which sadly we are not.' He was very chatty, sounded a bit high. 'It has been very good doing business with you,' he said. 'We are doing the right thing, I'm sure of it.' Alan Clark called, said 'You've

lit the fucking touchpaper, and my party is in flames all around you.'
I did a note for the file on the various chats with Cranborne. Hague
wanted to appoint [Lord] Strathclyde as Cranborne's replacement,
but Lord S said he would only do it on condition he could support
the deal. Hague agreed, so looked like he was weak and climbing
down. I was beginning to worry we had destabilised him too much.
The more I thought about it, the more shocked I was that Cranborne
had consorted with us the way he did. It was always going to end
in tears for them.

Thursday, December 3

TB got back from Ireland at 3am after the talks on the North-South
bodies. They had been close to a deal and he thought it was to be
sealed but again, as he left the thing slipped away. By the time we
got to France it was all falling apart and there was a growing sense
of crisis. The Lords was still the big story though. Hague did a lot
of interviews and was fine as far as it went but did look faintly ridiculous having seemed to change his line. Kenneth Clarke and Alan
Clark were out being critical, more peers were set to resign. It was
a definite win-win situation for us. Margaret B was reluctant to do
clips because she had felt out of the loop yesterday, but we needed
to get up the message about the extra legislation that we would now
be able to get through. I met TB before he went to his teaching reform
speech. He was worried the Lords deal could still fire off in all sorts
of directions.

He had spoken to GB and told him he could not treat all the
European politicians the way he tried to treat the Cabinet. Cabinet
was Lords, tax harmonisation, Northern Ireland, education. TB said
our backbenchers had been brilliant in their reaction to the Lords.
Margaret B said only [Tony] Benn and [Brian] Sedgemore [Labour
MPs] had gone against it. RC said it was a spectacular blow against
the Tory Party. On tax, GB said we were in the midst of a hysterical
media campaign. The briefing afterwards was nearly all Lords. The
Tories were beginning to implode on it. Northern Ireland was a big
problem again, and TB was blaming Trimble and Taylor. 'I sometimes
wonder if they are just thick,' he said. 'They do not get it.'

On the plane to St Malo for the Anglo-French summit, TB was
working through the mass of briefing papers, and concerned at tax
harmonisation. The French laid on a good welcome, with some
decent bagpipers and Chirac doing the usual grandiose stuff well.
The crowds had turned out, the mood was good and Chirac was far
friendlier than of late, though there were still some big gaps on

substance. He was going through the motions of being supportive of our ideas on defence, but was clearly suspicious. TB said it was a humiliation for Europe that it took a power from another continent to provide the military muscle to deal with a problem on our doorstep, namely Kosovo. He had an open mind on the institutional arrangements. Chirac said an Anglo-French defence plan could lead Europe. 'C'est un grand objectif.' [It's a big objective.'] He said 'Nous ne voulons pas affaiblir l'Otan,' ['We do not wish to weaken NATO'] but in a tone of voice that indicated the opposite. TB was pressing for NATO as the main thing, but saying this could be developed alongside. I did a few French interviews re defence and though they could sense the differences between us on Iraq and tax, by and large it went well.

We set off for the dinner where again TB and Chirac seemed to be getting on better. Though he had been nervous, TB now felt a bit of hammering Chirac through the press had been worthwhile. He had to know TB would not just be rolled over. Chirac had said it was vital the UK was a part of the great European family. TB had urged him to develop better relations with the US, that positioning France as a rival was a mistake. I got a good look at Claude Chirac [younger daughter and personal adviser] telling her dad a lot of the time what to do, how to sit, how to hold his hands. He seemed to defer to her a fair bit. She was clearly a force in the land, at least on the presentational side, and probably the one he let his guard down with a bit. The dinner was in the main fairly social, all very jolly and the food a cut above the average. I got to bed very late.

Friday, December 4

The Tories were still leading the news. We were slowly getting up defence as the big story from St Malo, and the text had improved overnight, with a clearer reference to NATO's pre-eminent role. TB was still worried at the reaction in the US though, if they thought this was a distancing from NATO. TB was really pissed off re NI. Mo called to get me to get TB to call Trimble but he didn't want to in case he lost his rag. It's a joke he's off for the Nobel Peace Prize [won jointly with John Hume] next week. This thing could tip over. He felt generally that sometimes the NI politicians were more interested in being feted than getting the job done.

The main Jospin bilateral took place in a fairly dark and cramped room, and upstairs we could hear people walking over the uncovered floorboards. It was hard not to see the contrast with the smoothly run Chirac meeting yesterday, and we guessed it was deliberate. Jospin came over as a nice but rather careworn man, watching over his

December '98: Chirac much friendlier at defence summit

shoulder a bit too much. Although Jospin would never say a word out of turn re Chirac, you could feel the inbuilt tensions all the time. TB, Chirac and Jospin met to agree the amended defence text, with even more references to NATO. GB had turned up late for a 25-minute meeting with Dominique Strauss-Kahn [French finance and economy minister], and then he wondered why they didn't much take to him. The plenary session was the usual rather hackneyed going through what we all already knew but the mood was a lot better than it would have been a few weeks ago. [Charles] Guthrie and I were making a few non-PC remarks about what we ought to be doing to the French but in truth the difficult stuff had gone well.

TB was on good form at the press conference, particularly on defence and very positive on Europe, and Jospin kicked tax harmonisation very effectively into touch. Chirac looked like he was going to behave but then out of nowhere threw in a line about the UK rebate being up for grabs. I watched TB's face and he was trying very hard not to react, but he was pretty pissed off with it. In the absence of much else negative, it was obviously where our press would go, and it meant a lot of the good work undone. It was very Chirac, made TB feel it was all sweetness and light and then threw in a little firework and acted all innocent afterwards. Even with that though, it had been a good summit and TB felt there was a lot more to work on with them. TB and I both thought Chirac's rebate ploy was deliberate. John H gave him the benefit of the doubt, felt he would not necessarily realise it would play big as he had said it so many times.

On the flight home, we discussed whether we thought Dobbo could win the London mayoral elections against Ken [Livingstone] and or even [Conservative mayoral contender Jeffrey] Archer. He had some strengths but campaign-wise a lot of weaknesses. In the car TB spoke to Jonathan re NI and was absolutely livid they had let it slip back. We got in for a meeting with Mo who was convinced now we were going to miss the February deadline. She blamed the UUs straight out for moving the goalposts again.

I did the Sundays, during which Tom Baldwin, out of nowhere, asked whether I saw Cranborne in the build-up and whether he was wearing red socks?! He later told me he also knew Goodlad had been to see TB. They all latched on to me being involved, and being the devil-like figure that helped Cranborne shaft Hague. Baldwin seemed to know an awful lot. I didn't want him to overdo my role because it would make life even more difficult for Cranborne. Worried, I spoke to TB who said the main point was that Hague knew about the plan and allowed Cranborne to do the negotiations. I spoke to Derry who was due to see Cranborne and Strathclyde to ensure the deal was still on. He said he could not believe how well it had all gone. He had been working at it since October and it was marvellous to see it all fall into place.

Saturday, December 5

I was due to take Fiona and the kids for one of Mo's Hillsborough Castle weekends so I was hoping for a quiet time work-wise. The St Malo coverage, as feared, was OK on defence but totally overshadowed by Chirac on the rebate. The Tories were heading for a grim weekend. Alan Clark called and said he feared we had dealt a fatal blow. Maybe we had. He said the bad blood was beyond belief now and Hague was stupid enough to turn it into a 'toffs vs commoners' issue. On the way to the airport I earwigged a call between TB and Cranborne. 'Well done,' said Cranborne. 'You could not have come out of this better.' TB said he was sorry that it had cost him his job. Cranborne said he was looking forward to having more time to do other things. I explained that Baldwin knew both that we had met and also that Goodlad had seen TB. He seemed fairly relaxed now. He had taken the first wave of flak and anything else would be subsidiary. I spoke to Goodlad who did not want any coverage but after he spoke to Derry, we agreed he could be described as a facilitator. I rang round most of the Sundays to get over the point that Hague had authorised Cranborne to negotiate, and that it was only in the end that Cranborne did him in. TB was determined not to let Hague get away with the line that he had acted on principle, because he could have said no at any time in the last few months.

We got to Hillsborough and went straight out to a pub lunch nearby – Mo and Jon [Norton, Mowlam's husband] and his daughters, Will Hutton and family, DB plus his three boys and a girlfriend, Chris Smith and Dorian [Jabri, Smith's partner], Tessa Blackstone [Baroness Blackstone, education minister], Ross Kemp [actor] and Rebekah Wade [*Sun* deputy editor, engaged to Kemp]. Mo was a good host and everyone seemed to enjoy the whole weekend. Even the charades game, which was normally the kind of thing I hated, was good fun. I was called out of dinner God knows how many times as the papers dropped, and there was a lot of interest in my dealings with Cranborne. I said it had been important to have a presentational strategy and it was not about doing in Hague. That line was coming from the Tories who had now decided to do in Cranborne. TB was of the view we had nothing to lose from any of this. Any detail merely served further to expose Hague's failure as a strategist.

December '98: A weekend with Mo

Sunday, December 6

My meeting with Cranborne was running second on the news. Ridiculous. Lord Fraser [former energy minister] did a very good 'so what?' kind of interview on *Frost* which got it in the right perspective. I had breakfast with Mo, Will Hutton and Tessa B. They were all doing in Geoffrey Robinson, on whom there was more stuff in the Sundays. We touched on whether Mo should go for London mayor. She got a call from a UUP contact saying [Michael] Mates and [Brian] Mawhinney [Conservative MPs, former Northern Ireland ministers] were making calls in advance of Wednesday's debate on prisoners to stir things up and raise pressure on the UUs to be difficult. Mo was worried the Tories were preparing to end bipartisanship. They were even suggesting Hague might lead the debate for them. She was clearly worried at where things were. Trimble wasn't leading and the vacuum was being filled by troublemakers. It made it harder to put Adams under pressure.

I spoke to TB who was minded to speak to Major and line him up to step in if need be. They basically want us to end the Agreement, he said. We won't do that. It is despicable if they talk bipartisanship while trying to undermine the Agreement at every turn. I had a long chat with DB who seemed fairly relaxed for once. His boys were terrific with him, very solicitous but also taking no nonsense. Clare Short was in self-indulgent mode on *Dimbleby*, some nonsense about how she didn't see it as her job to help British companies. She could easily have made the same point without making news but she can't resist it. The kids really enjoyed the weekend and even though I had spent several hours of both days on the phone, I was really glad we went and felt refreshed by the time we got home.

Monday, December 7

Clare Short's 'gaffe' was big news but we maintained the strategy of playing it down. When I refused to react angrily, Charles Reiss said 'Oh drat – you've learned how to deal with these Clare Short situations.' At the office meeting, which Peter M seemed to want to turn into a DTI bilateral, TB's main worry was delivery. He remained unconvinced departments were properly managing and monitoring change. The tracking poll was fine, but arrogance was coming up as a problem. It was an inevitable by-product of the media prism being framed for us and we had to decide whether and how to make the media an issue.

TB spoke to Schroeder re the Vienna [EU] summit and agreed a formula for defusing the tax issue, making clear there was no support for uniform tax rates. He intended to hang tough on the rebate and felt in a way Chirac may have helped us. Was a quiet day for a Monday. The eleven o'clock was mainly Short and [Geoffrey] Robinson and I stayed low-key on both. We had a long meeting with Nigel Wicks pre-Vienna, and clearly tax harmonisation was the big danger, whatever they were all saying. TB also spoke to Bertie and Adams and was getting more and more fed up with it. I left early for parents' evening.

Tuesday, December 8

Clare Short was getting the usual post-outburst plaudits. Peter M got a bad press for Post Office policy proposals, including in the *Mail* a stream of Treasury quotes – all a disaster, rubbish, nothing to do with GB, etc. I called Whelan and said if Paul Eastham [*Mail*] was his handiwork, let it be the final word. TB was for once livid about a GB briefing operation, said it was unacceptable for one minister to undermine another's policy launch like that. Only the fact GB's dad [Revd John Brown] had died yesterday stopped him from going on the warpath about it. TB was determined – again – that Whelan should go. Peter M wanted to make a formal complaint to Richard Wilson. TB and I both urged him to leave it.

TB and I left for lunch at Cottesmore Gardens with Conrad Black [*Telegraph* owner], Charles Moore, Dominic Lawson [*Telegraph* editors] and Barbara Amiel [Black's wife], who was looking more and more odd. The food was almost as good as something offered up by the French. Europe dominated the discussion, Black obsessing with his dotty idea that we should be part of NAFTA [North American Free Trade Agreement]. There was a strain of opinion – and he certainly had it – that Europe was just a bed of left-wing lunatics and we should have nothing to do with them. TB stuck to a pretty pro-European line but I felt he could have demolished the arguments better. He felt it was pointless. He said these were seriously right-wing people. They were miles away from us politically and the best thing to do was just make them feel we were competent and not insane. That was about as good as it would get. We also had to listen to right-wing dogma on Ireland, tax, the economy, Pinochet, you name it. TB let out a large belly laugh when we got out of there. 'These people are crazy.' We were working away on Vienna [summit preparation] when word came through that Lafontaine had said in a speech that Britain had asked for them not to mention harmonisation but refer to co-operation instead. What a wanker. It also showed again Schroeder wasn't really in charge of his show.

December '98: A right-wing lunch with Conrad Black

Wednesday, December 9

TB saw GB in the flat first thing, GB still clearly very down about his dad's death. TB was sympathetic about all that, but adamant Whelan had to go. He said that to undermine deliberately the policy launch of a Cabinet colleague, and do it so blatantly, was the final straw. He said his whole modus operandi had to change. He was not served with good advice. Balls was a menace who often gave him the wrong advice. Whelan had alienated him from virtually every Cabinet colleague. He had taken that modus operandi to Europe with dreadful consequences for the arguments we were trying to win. GB was equally adamant Whelan should stay. Jack C meanwhile wrote to TB saying he had been done in through the press by Whelan on GB's behalf and suggested Wilson sack him if GB won't get rid of him. TB did fine at PMQs and Hague was off form. TB showed real confidence on Europe and our side visibly cheered up while the Tories looked pretty down. At the 4, I was asked if I knew when Pinochet was going to happen and I just danced around because I didn't want to get into it. Jack C came to see me to go over his speech to the press gallery but also to say he felt we really had to force Whelan out now.

Thursday, December 10

The press on Pinochet was pretty massive, and mixed. There was sudden talk around of Jack S as next leader! The German tax situation was bad in the usual places. Very irritating. TB agreed finally that we needed a more aggressive media strategy on this, that we were taking hits on Europe without properly fighting back. TB had an interview with an Austrian paper pre-Vienna and was OK but, as Godric and Jonathan immediately spotted from the transcript, he seemed to be linking CAP [Common Agricultural Policy] reform and the rebate, which could set a new hare running.

Cabinet was longer than usual, with a discussion on Europe the main thing, and what was interesting was that although a lot of it was on substance and policy detail, the whole time they were having to work round an impossible media that would not allow an honest debate, so it became as much a tactical as a strategic discussion. RC said the reality was that we were far closer to the European centre of gravity than Lafontaine but it suited our media to present someone like him as the reality. Peter M felt we had to get the whole thing focused at a more fundamental level – in or out of Europe. The other contributions didn't add much. George R blathered endlessly and I could see TB and others getting irritated. TB said we were more influential in Europe than Britain had been for years, but the media would not believe it let alone print it.

Dennis Carter [Lords chief whip] announced we had a deal on the Lords, which I announced at 11.30, and which caused a fresh wave of consternation for the Tories. Goodlad called to say there was a lot more press interest in him and he intended to carry on saying he was a facilitator, and always acted with Hague's authority, but Cranborne exceeded his brief. In the car to the airport, TB spoke to Peter M re the trade unions plan [based on the Fairness at Work White Paper], which he was having trouble squaring Ian McCartney [DTI minister] on. Peter was still seething re the *Mail* stuff on the Post Office. GB's latest claim to TB was that Peter had got Eastham to put in quotes against him so that he could blame Charlie and force TB to have another go at GB. This stuff was fucking madness.

On the plane out to Vienna, we discussed how best to deal with what was becoming a new and harsher press mood. The problem was not the bias, but their refusal to carry both sides of a story. Europe was just the most obvious area. But it had the potential to damage us. I was up for a properly organised full-frontal attack, supported by people from other walks of life, which made them an issue and forced them to explain their output more. TB felt we needed something more subtle but was not sure what. I saw the press who were trying to push the line that we had softened on the rebate and I had to hold firm on that. TB had pre-recorded with Sopel for *Today* so I was able to give his words which were pretty clear. They then tried to run the line either re confusion or that we were saying different things to different people. After the PES dinner, at which Schroeder was particularly laid-back, TB was more confident we would be fine on tax and the rebate.

Friday, December 11

The papers were absolutely ridiculous. Having been deprived of a story about softening on the rebate, they used my briefing to go for chaos and confusion. The editor of *Kronenzeitung*, the Austrian paper whose interview with TB started it, went on *World at One* and said he was bemused by the way the UK media played it. I was more convinced than ever we had to go for them. So at my first briefing I went for them, said the UK media coverage of Europe was a joke, tore into Boris Johnson [*Telegraph*], took the piss out of Trevor Kavanagh. What happened was that the right-wing tabloids set an agenda that the BBC and the other broadsheets couldn't resist.

TB's day started with a gloomy bilateral with Bertie. BA was really down, felt Trimble – either because he wanted to, or because of the

December '98: Need for organised attack on media madness

pressure from within the UUs – was holding up on North-South bodies, and this was stalling any progress on the debate inside the IRA. He agreed with TB that it was crazy they were going around collecting peace prizes when there was no peace. 'These people drive me crazy,' said TB. 'Sure, they're not easy,' said Bertie. Our intelligence on the IRA meeting at Cavan at the weekend was that basically they had decided not to decide yet, but it was going to be tricky to handle if word came out. I did a couple of big briefings through the day, with near on 300 hacks in there, and I think it worked going for some of our press in the first one. Come the second one, I was able to point to other leaders who were in exactly our position on the areas where we were constantly said to be isolated. Kok in particular was livid at some of Lafontaine's outpourings, and at Schroeder's inability to lead. As RC said, Schroeder had allowed a vacuum to develop and was allowing Lafontaine to fill it.

TB did a doorstep, at which Robert Moore [ITN] asked if he found the UK media coverage of Europe exasperating, so the message was getting through. I had a long meeting with Claude Chirac about pools and sorting pictures. She wanted to swap a few ideas after we had agreed St Malo didn't quite work picture-wise. She was smart, sexy and very French, and totally devoted to his interests.

I popped in and out of the summit meeting, which TB seemed to think was going fine. Neither Chirac nor Schroeder mentioned the rebate, and tax was going our way too, as on defence and duty-frees. I did another briefing to point that out, and raised the sarcasm levels a bit more. The French, Germans and Swedes all played up our attacks on our media, saying about time. Brian Bender [head of European Secretariat, Cabinet Office] was a terrific help at the briefings, which I think he enjoyed, and he said it was noticeable how more and more subdued they were getting through the day.

TB felt we were in a strong enough position to do a round of interviews, and the sense was growing we were on a bit of a roll. We had a secure line brought in for TB to speak to Bill C about Iraq. They agreed we would go in if there was more obfuscation over the weekend. RC was still totally opposed. The IRA's briefing led the news. Robin Oakley had tipped me off in advance and I put a note through to the office and the NIO that we must not overreact, and demand people keep it in perspective.

Saturday, December 12

The summit conclusions text had improved overnight for us, on tax, rebate and probably on duty-frees. TB was convinced that his interview with *Kronenzeitung* had made Klima much more favourably disposed. Their headline had been '*Dickes Lob für Presidentschaft*' (literally 'Thick praise for presidency') which was particularly powerful because Klima had in the past criticised our presidency. TB and I started to use '*dickes Lob*' as a term of agreement or praise in private discussions, and at one point he said 'the *dickes Lob* strategy is delivering all we need'. TB was virtually alone of the big leaders who did Austrian TV as well, and went on and on about how well the Austrians had handled things, which even they must have realised was bullshit. But Klima helped us on everything we asked for help on, so it worked. Both [Hans Göran] Persson [Swedish prime minister] and [Jean-Luc] Dehaene [Belgian prime minister] had a pop about the rebate on the radio and TB spoke to both, and warned Dehaene we would retaliate if he did it again. I had a series of sessions with the French and Germans to go over our media and explain why they had to be careful in what they said.

I did a Sunday lobby and [Tom] Baldwin [*Times*] and [Patrick] Wintour [*Observer*] pushed me into admitting that Goodlad was at the TB meeting with Cranborne. I felt bad confirming it but they could read me on it. I got Mark Bennett to get hold of Goodlad who said they had already been on to him and he was saying nothing. He was a privy councillor and not commenting on meetings he may or may not have had.

Once we got the final text, we set up TB's press conference, which went fine. He was on top of the arguments, and confident setting out the benefits of a pro-European position. Robin chipped in on a few questions and afterwards TB said RC did the EU nuances much better than GB. He said what Gordon had to understand was that he could just about get away with treating Cabinet ministers the way he did because ultimately he controlled their budgets. But these guys owed him nothing and if they wanted to shaft him, they could. GB hated mixing with them and saw everything as a battle for the next headlines. Robin loved all the mingling and the backslapping and the camaraderie. The press were subdued again and felt a bit bowed I think. None of the great dramas predicted had actually materialised and in some parts of the media we had raised questions about them. Whether it would change anything in the long term was doubtful but TB agreed it had been the right thing to go for them in the way we did.

TB had to go back for the lunch with the accession [EU candidate] countries. He had a very difficult conversation with Chirac over Iraq, with Chirac saying there was no way we could go in over a refused inspection. [Poul Nyrup] Rasmussen [Danish Prime Minister] and [Wim] Kok were a bit bruised re duty-frees[1] and as we flew home, TB said no doubt some of the other delegations would be staying behind to dump on us, but we had got pretty much everything we wanted. I was back too late to get to Fulham vs Burnley, which we lost 4-0. I got to bed early but at 1.30am the office called re a bizarre incident involving JP. He had driven home, totally sober, but someone had called the police, and then the press, to say he was drink driving. JP called all the papers himself to emphasise it was a lie.

Sunday, December 13

I tried to have a quiet day but TB wanted to do a piece for *The Times* on Europe, and we were back and forth on that through the day. Plus there was a bit of post-Vienna fallout to deal with. Clinton was in Israel, followed by calls for impeachment.

Monday, December 14

TB was called by Bill C early, his second call in thirty-six hours, and it was pretty clear he was gearing up for action on Iraq. [Head of UNSCOM inspection team Richard] Butler was due to report for UNSCOM tomorrow. If he said he was being obstructed, BC was clearly on for a strike. The problem was Ramadan was due – Saturday – so the strike would have to be soon. TB was supportive but worried that the public would simply think the whole thing was a diversion from impeachment; or that Butler would not be crystal clear, and we would be going to war on an ambiguity.

The post-Vienna press was OK, though as ever better overseas than here. At the office meeting, he was back banging on about delivery. PG said the [focus] groups were still basically fine, though beginning to think we should have done more by now on the public services front. On Europe, the worry was we were going in deeper and deeper by stealth, which is of course what the wretched papers were saying the whole time. Jonathan brought in a bottle of claret, and bet TB that Whelan would still be there by Christmas. If he was proved wrong, the claret was his. Peter raised worries re the party, felt the machine was in danger of atrophying and that with Margaret B as campaign co-ordinator, we would quickly revert to Old Labour, and lack any campaign or modernising drive.

[1] A number of EU member states, including the UK, called for a postponement of the abolition of duty-free sales within the EU while potential employment problems were examined.

Hague did a big press conference on Europe, saying Vienna was a massive act of integration and Britain's independence was at risk. It didn't really work because it was so over the top. We went over to the House for TB's [Vienna] statement, which went fine. He was always more on top of the detail by dint of having been there and lived with the arguments, and Hague came over as a bit ridiculous and certainly OTT.

TB said if the US were going in [to Iraq], we would support them and Guthrie was told he could put out a secret signal that we would be with them. The latest intelligence suggested Saddam did not believe he was going to be attacked. Guthrie said the US were being less open with us because of what happened last time. We reckoned Butler was going to say there had been clear and unambiguous obstruction. TB said he wished the background was not impeachment, but having said that, the Americans had been on record as saying that if he [Saddam] did not comply, he would be hit without warning. People will understand and support that, though there is no doubt Clinton's domestic problems complicate things. Guthrie was clearly up for it. He said there would be lasting problems if people felt they were led up to the top of the hill again. TB was worried how the Tories would react, given their recent buggering around on Northern Ireland.

Tuesday, December 15

AD was doing a good job on pensions which we could more or less leave to him. Northern Ireland was getting more and more difficult and TB was several times on the phone to BA, DT etc. Bertie wanted him to go out there and try to drive it on. We suddenly latched on to the fact that TB had a speech at AP [Associated Press agency] today and we didn't have a proper draft, so I quickly knocked out something on Europe-US. It wasn't brilliant but would do. We left for the lunch where the most important thing was editors hearing direct the basic argument, rather than the bullshit they got fed most days by their lobby people.

We had a draft of Butler which TB did not feel was as clear as we had been expecting. I disagreed, felt it would be seen by any fair-minded reader as a clear obstruction and a clear breach of his November undertakings. So while there were undoubtedly problems because of Bill's impeachment situation, which was worsening, equally you could not hold back from doing something in the international sphere out of fear of how it would be seen in relation to the domestic situation. The president called TB from his plane around 9pm and at this stage was still basically asking for views. TB and I were both sure they were going to go for it, and Bill C was clearly being advised in that direction, but he was very sensitive to the allegations there would be re impeachment and diversion.

Of all the meetings through the day, the most important was DOP which should have been in the Cabinet Room but for some reason ended up taking place in TB's overcrowded room. Things weren't helped when JP arrived late and sat at the back, which made him grumpy and probably more quizzical than he otherwise might have been. He was pressing on whether anyone had got Butler to harden up the language. TB had to massage him a fair bit during the meeting, and I could spot Guthrie keeping an eye on him the whole time. Robin C was a lot more bellicose than yesterday, and clearly felt Butler was reason enough. In the end, TB gave explicit authority for Guthrie to instruct the Yanks, and our own troops, that we would be there if the US decided to carry out the strikes. George R warned of the likelihood of loss of British life. RC talked through what we had to go through to try to get UK nationals out.

John Holmes, who had been at the Palace receiving his CVO from the Queen, was also a bit late, but he had the info on Butler's meeting with Kofi, who had expressed bewilderment at the behaviour of the Iraqis, so he was fairly clear what direction it was all going in. In public opinion terms the most important thing was going to be the report coming out on the right terms, with a sense of clarity about the breach. TB took JP aside at the end, said he would rather we didn't have to do this, but there came a time when the last chance really was the last chance. JP had mellowed a bit, and said he guessed there was never a good time, and it had been a long time coming. TB said much the same when Bill called again on his way back from the Middle East.

Wednesday, December 16

The briefings overnight went well and the sense in the morning media was that Butler was damning and now we had to show we were serious in the November pledge to hit without warning if he carried on obstructing. So by the eleven o'clock, the questions were all about why we hadn't hit him already, as the breach was so clear. I fed this through to Joe Lockhart, who was very different to deal with after Mike [McCurry]. The US were absolutely paranoid about security of information and I had to be vague bordering on misleading with the press. Charles Guthrie had really had to push to get the plans, said only five people in the UK knew and he was doubling the size of the net. TB was clearly having a bit of a wobble. He said he had been reading the Bible last night, as he often did when the really big decisions were on, and he had read something about John the Baptist and Herod which had caused him to rethink, albeit not change his mind.[1]

TB spoke to Bill C again and it was now very much when not if, and we were into working out the media management detail. I dug out the speech we had done for November 14, which was never delivered, and worked on that. I did a redraft, which TB then played with, and we had a very strong statement. He was still worried about the impeachment angle, but felt Butler was strong and clear enough to justify what we were doing. Guthrie was furious at leaks – we think through the FCO – of yesterday's meeting. He told me he 'got the horrors at the thought of Cook talking to his European cronies about all this'. He had a strong face, big expressive eyes and a wonderfully conspiratorial way of talking. I sensed him as someone who was a great ally and a terrible enemy, and I liked him instinctively. You would certainly go into the jungle with him.

TB was more nervous than usual, and wanted to do a proper run-through for once, and was constantly asking for reassurance we had the words and the tone right. I thought the statement was strong. He delivered it well. The MoD and FCO had produced a very good briefing pack which I took over to the gallery, full of drunken hacks who had been out on the Christmas party circuit. Everything went according to plan – operation launched, brief announcement from Lockhart at 10pm our time, TB 10.15, Bill 10.40. The general feeling was TB got the tone spot on. He was less worried about the impeachment situation now than the possible loss of innocent civilian life. He said he worried about our forces losing their lives, and he worried about the people on the receiving end too. 'I think if ever you lose that, you risk making the wrong decision, and you cease to do your job properly.' It was at moments like these you got a proper sense of the enormity of his job. Dealing with this, on the same day as the Irish were pressing him to get more involved in their problems, and with a stack of difficult domestic issues too, it was pretty impressive the way he kept these different issues under some kind of control, and was able to move from one to the other and box them off where he needed to. I could tell he was worried and would stay so until he got word the operation had gone well. He called some of the

[1] After John the Baptist denounced the marriage of Herod Antipas, Herod ordered him to be imprisoned and later beheaded.

Europeans. Schroeder was basically supportive, Chirac iffy while Klima said 'I will offer understanding or support depending on the outcome'!!

Thursday, December 17

I saw TB first thing and he went through the main points for me to take to the meeting at the MoD bunker, chaired by George R with CDS [Guthrie] alongside. I spoke to Guthrie earlier to make sure toppling of Saddam was not on the list of military objectives, as it would require tens of thousands of land troops. Likewise the SIS guys were emphasising we should be making clear no threat to Iraq's territorial integrity. We had a lot of material to get out re Saddam's actions in previous crises, the way they faked evidence etc. Charles did a very good job at the press conference, then we went up to George's room. He is a great guy but he has a real problem on the blather front, and it meant we kept having the same conversations to go over things already agreed. At Cabinet, too, I could sense him and Robin vying as to who was the minister most involved and most knowledgeable. TB said Saddam had had 'umpteen' last warnings and what happened overnight was the response to his latest deliberate and clear obstruction. He went through the Ramadan sensitivities. He said he had tried as hard as anyone could to avoid being in this situation, but he was sure we had to act in this way now to uphold the inspections regime. Robin said it was in no way a breach of the UN Charter. He warned the Iraqis would mercilessly play pictures of poor Iraqis being targeted by our bombs, and we had to point out past fraudulence and also the reality of the penury of their lives under the SH regime. In came Clare with a real stomach-churner: 'We know he is a bastard but can we help the poor people too?' She was calling for a new sanctions regime.

Peter M, out of nowhere, asked me if Geoffrey Robinson was being sacked. At lunchtime, it became clear why he was asking. Ben [Wegg-Prosser] called me and said Routledge's book on Peter was going to reveal that Robinson had given him a £300k loan to help buy his place in Notting Hill. Peter felt they should get it out through e.g. Bevins as part of a story about dirt being dug on Peter. I said hold fire. There was no way the story would be anything other than the existence of a loan that most people would find very odd. 'Do you think it is a problem?' asked Ben, knowing the answer. I do, I said. A big problem? Well, it sounds like it. I went round to see TB, who was in the loo. I took Jonathan into TB's room and waited for him to come back. He was in upbeat mood, which I was about to deflate. I told him the facts as I knew them, and he was horrified. First, what on earth was Peter doing taking out that kind of loan from Geoffrey, who was not an uncontroversial figure? Second, we were immediately on to the angle that Peter was ultimately in charge of the DTI investigation into Geoffrey. Third, it was bound to be – or certainly seen to be – part of the ongoing GB/Peter M nonsense. We assumed Geoffrey had told GB's lot, and someone had fed it to Routledge as a way of doing in Peter if Geoffrey was going to go down anyway. And all in the middle of a bloody difficult international situation which required us to keep our eye on a very different kind of ball. TB was not best pleased, but quickly calmed down and went into his usual 'we need the facts' mode. I found it astonishing Peter wanted to brief pre-emptively, which would never work on this. He [TB] wavered between anger and exasperation. 'I hate this. I cannot believe this. The Tories will murder us for it.' Yet when I spoke to Peter, he couldn't see it, or at least pretended not to. It was a loan between old friends who go back a long way. What about the DTI angle? I would not be making the decisions. Charlie F came to see me, and asked me what was wrong with Geoffrey lending him money? Possibly nothing, but the politics are fairly obvious and you can't just ignore them. Meanwhile we were finalising the Commons statement and TB was agonising over whether to deal head-on with the impeachment point, on the grounds it would be better to deal with it up-front rather than wait for a nasty pointed question likely to make the bulletins. Bruce and Sally, who both felt yesterday's tone was right, were against, but TB and I both felt you had to be up-front, and pre-empt the point that e.g. [Tony] Benn and [George] Galloway [Labour MPs] were bound to put.

In the car on the way over, TB said 'Christ, I hope our pilots are OK.' TB was constantly asking Jonathan and me to find out what was happening re our pilots. He was also a lot more concerned than I imagined he would be re Iraqi casualties. Calum brought that home to me when I got home and he had been watching the news, and asking why we were killing Iraqi children. I tried my best to explain, and also to point out that in the past they had faked pictures like that. But the truth was you could not escape the reality of bombs and deaths, and some of them unintended. By now the second wave of Tornadoes was under way. Oona Muirhead [MoD press office] called with the idea of TB doing a briefing tomorrow from the MoD crisis management centre. Good idea. In between Iraq, we were beginning to think through the Peter M situation, which had the makings of a disaster area.

Friday, December 18

Again, our press was going better for us than the US press was for BC. There was good news overnight in that there was finally agreement on North-South bodies, and we put out TB words of welcome. The broadcasters were really beginning to grate with their pro-Iraqi line, or if not pro-Iraqi, their refusal properly to communicate the level of restrictions they operated under – like if they strayed too far from a line acceptable to the regime, they would be out. At the 11, I put a gentle shot across their bows, whilst saying we understood the difficulties. TB meanwhile felt the US were not clear enough in their medium-term strategy, what actually happened when the strikes ended. We left Number 10 through the underground tunnel from the Cabinet Office and through to the MoD, met by GR and Oona.

On the way, bent halfway forward because the roof was so low, TB told me he had spoken to Peter and warned him his instinct was that the Geoffrey Robinson loan story was potentially very dangerous. We had asked Charlie F to do a report on the facts, and when I spoke to him later, he seemed to think it was pretty serious. Peter was still of a mind to brief on his terms, and later Ben W-P told me Tom Baldwin knew about it. Then Wilson came to see me, said Michael Scholar [DTI permanent secretary] had only been informed of the loan once Peter knew the book was going to divulge it. So there would definitely be questions about non-declaration as well. I felt it was a no-hope situation for him. It could easily be seen as bad as anything the Tories did, and it showed poor judgement, first to get involved, and then not to be up-front when there was the possibility of a conflict of interest re the DTI investigating Geoffrey.

Oona's idea of getting the cameras in for a TB bunker meeting worked well and after the cameras went, we had a proper meeting. PJHQ [Permanent Joint Headquarters] gave us a rather gloomy assessment of bombs that didn't work, or missed their target. It was 'potentially disappointing', they concluded, which probably meant a bit of a disaster area. Around half of the command and control targets had been hit, fifty-five per cent of air defence targets, only two out of eleven WMD targets definitely damaged. All the airfield attacks were successful. TB and I both emphasised that with the Iraqis now playing their usual games re engineering Western media coverage, we had to engage fully in a propaganda war. There were some excellent pictures of successful strikes which would form the centrepiece of the press conference. The intelligence guys said SH had been taken by surprise, and that there had been clear damage to his command structure. They said it was possible there would be a terrorist response, probably [Osama] Bin Laden [al-Qaeda].

George Robertson and Guthrie took TB down to the ops room for a morale-boost visit. In many ways, it was just like any other Whitehall office, only they were deep underground and tracking military action hundreds of miles away. TB was a bit downcast when we got back, felt the picture had been a gloomy one. Guthrie said we were making progress but the chances were we would need all four days to get the job done. I brought forward the lobby to 10, did that then went to the GR/CDS press conference. George was having a bit of a wood-for-trees day and we urged him to stay focused on the military side of things. They both did well, and the pictures worked well. We cut things to a halt at thirty minutes when the questions started to become predominantly political. Charles agreed to do the lunchtimes live, and was strong. We spoke afterwards and he had noted the broadcasters were beginning to refer to restrictions. It shows your bullying works, he said. 'I think you must have a military background in there some-where.'

The MoD targeting people came over pm and gave TB an update which suggested we were now doing much more damage. He wanted to be able to say we had set Saddam back several years in his weapons-making capability. TB did his doorstep in the Pillared Room, and was OK on the big argument, but used the line about keeping Saddam in his cage, which none of us really liked. I went home after the duty clerks' Christmas party, but then had to do a conference call with TB/John H after we heard the US were about to hit the Ba'ath Party HQ, saying it was being used for military purposes. Mike McCurry was on *Newsnight* having a go at Clinton. Another exhausting week was over, another busy weekend ahead, and we now had a real sleaze problem looming.

Saturday, December 19

The press was turning. The right wing so hated Clinton for winning twice that they were now going at him over this, and the *Guardian* were now going down the usual mealy-mouthed route. There was the chance we would get politically hurt by the damage to BC. I didn't think it was very wise that he was out dancing last night. I was in by 7 to prepare for the MoD Operation Bolton bunker meeting at 8. CDS and PJHQ explained what had happened overnight militarily. There had been a seventy-five per cent strike rate. When I said the main problems today would be diplomatic, Robin came in on cue, and was in a very spiky mood. I had real trouble with the FCO yesterday getting them to prepare proper briefing material on the regime. Finally, after a lot of resistance, I got Robin to agree it would be done, and he would front it. But he was in very difficult mood. At one point [Admiral] Alan West [Chief of Defence Intelligence], who probably irritated Robin because he had a bowler hat, was going through his brief and RC kept asking snide questions and then looking away. He asked the significance of one destroyed target, a Republican Guard maintenance area near Kuwait. West said it was to stop Saddam invading Kuwait. 'Was there any sign that he was going to?' asked RC. 'Not today,' said West.

The updates were much better than yesterday, though the MoD guys were getting angry, feeling the Yanks were not being as open as they should be re overall targeting strategy. Clinton's impeachment hearings were about to begin, which was an added complication. TB was talking to Chirac again and working up ideas for a forward containment strategy. Guthrie told us they were going to have to revisit some of the targets because they had not been sufficiently damaged. There was a mildly comic moment when George Robertson told us they had successfully hit Republican Guard targets and destroyed his radio-jamming capability. I said we should announce re jamming at the press conference and TB should do a World Service interview. Julian [Braithwaite] called the BBC WS to fix, and they said there had been no jamming for a year!

I had a long chat with Peter M, who claimed not to see what the problem was re the loan. He said what is wrong with a friend lending money to someone? I said it had the potential to be a big bad story and surely he could see that. He said I was overreacting, I had always been a bit of a Calvinist, and it was all a bit 'Alastair and Fiona-ish'. He was adamant it would not be much of a story. I said it had the potential to be the worst thing to hit us yet. 'Would it be the same if it was Sainsbury?' he said.[1] Probably not, I said, but politics is not science. So it is a Geoffrey problem, he said. I said it is a Geoffrey problem, but it is also a Peter Grand Panjandrum problem, and it is a GB/Peter M self-destruct at the heart of government problem. He was adamant I was overreacting. I began to wonder if I was and checked out how the others who knew about it saw it. John H, whose judgement was pretty solid, thought it was indefensible. Wilson, Charlie Falconer, Jonathan and most important TB all saw it as a major problem, and very hard to defend. John said to me he had noted in

[1] Lord Sainsbury, Undersecretary of State for Science and Innovation. Until July 1998, chairman of J. Sainsbury plc.

politicians that no matter how talented they were, they tended to be useless as their own advisers on their own personal affairs.

We had another meeting with the MoD targeting people, who had new pictures of the Ba'ath Party HQ being hit by missiles in ten different places. TB was seeming more anxious and he, Jonathan and I had endless circular conversations through the early evening. Bill C was due to do a press conference at 11 calling it [military action] to a halt. TB was worried that Bill was now going too far in terms of carrots – e.g. sanctions. They spoke and agreed the threat of force had to remain in place. They agreed they would go out soon, but Steinberg came on, very clear BC would take it amiss if we went out first.

We had TB at the door at one point, but John H came though to say hold fire. By the time he went out, flanked by Guthrie and GR, RC was on the phone complaining he wasn't there. I said he should have asked, like the others did. It was all a bit messy and scratchy. I stayed in the flat, and worked late on tomorrow's script. TB felt we were in the right place on the strategy of containment. We had to be able to show we had substantially set him back. His doorstep was carried live across the US and elsewhere and with Clinton still mired in the impeachment stuff, the sense was TB had handled things well, but he hadn't enjoyed it one bit.

Sunday, December 20

I stayed overnight at the flat and woke to a set of papers that were not that great. There was quite a lot of 'poodle-ism' around. TB said if this had been a Tory government supporting the US, the media would have been overwhelmingly supportive. They cannot stand a Labour government and a Democratic presidency working together. He felt we had done the right thing. He said he had found it really difficult to sleep these past few days, and he had worried the whole time about our pilots. It is one thing to make a decision in the comfort and safety of Downing Street, but you always have to remember there are people who then literally put their lives on the line. He was just relieved they were all back safe and sound.

CDS, George R and RC came over to prepare for the morning briefing. Charles was confident we could put over a very good case of the damage done. TB wanted us to emphasise our desire to work closely with the French on the forward diplomatic strategy. He wasn't satisfied with the MoD battle damage assessment paper, and wanted it reordered. Jonathan was arguing against him using the cage line again, but TB felt if we were saying he was worthy of being bombed, we had to be pretty strong in our language about him. We went over to the MoD, and the press conference was OK, with the defence guys in the lead, and questions to TB not too hostile, though I sensed the papers were going to be pretty down on us about the whole thing. The left-wing chatterers and the right-wing ideologues were for their different reasons moving to the same point. The Tories were now saying the aim should be to remove Saddam.

RW was heard complaining – at least I think it was a complaint – that the whole government show was run by TB, AC, Jonathan and John H. TB called several times through the evening. 'How do we stand?' 'The same as we did the last time you called.' He was in major circular-conversation mode at the moment. He spoke to the forces out there and then left for Sedgefield.

Peter M called, said he was worried the *Guardian* were about to do the Geoffrey loan story and he felt it important he get on record that he was removed from any responsibility in the inquiry into Robinson. He was still refusing to accept it would be an enormous story. TB said if Whelan had given the info to Routledge, he intended to have it out with GB when he got back from the States. Peter felt he could tough it out. TB called around 10, as I was going to bed, and said he was now really worried about it. He thought it was possible, but unlikely, that we could tough this out. I could barely bring myself to think about the next few days if this was about to land on us.

Monday, December 21

The BBC was grim, with the Baghdad line being swallowed pretty much wholesale, and though the print news media was OK, most of the comment, *Sun* and *Mirror* apart, was pretty hostile. Also the Tories were moving into a more difficult position, saying there was no long-term strategy and we should be going for Saddam personally. I spoke to TB and we agreed he should do Christiane Amanpour on CNN and TF1 [leading French TV channel]. He was less down about the reaction than I was. I felt there was very little sense of military success, a lot of international isolation, and more re impeachment than during the strikes. We had to keep up the arguments. I called Robin C and said he had to go wall-to-wall again, and agreed with Guthrie he would do an article for the *Sun*. A draft came over which we knocked into decent shape and David Yelland took it.

I went to a meeting on the planned Freedom of Information moves, which I feared were going to be a disaster, an excuse for the media basically to clog up the whole government machine with ludicrous enquiries the whole time. Charlie F leant to my view but Derry was driving it very hard. The eleven o'clock briefing was long and difficult. I felt real public opinion was more or less with us but for their different reasons most of the press had decided to go hostile. Added to which some of the questions were difficult to answer for anyone but the Americans and they had not thought them all through. I did OK, and felt comfortable with the big arguments, but it was tricky. I went then to a briefing for the foreign press, which was less hostile, but more focused on how we rebuild some of the diplomatic relations damaged over this. TB was back just before 4, went straight into the interviews which were OK though for some reason he said we hit every target, when we hadn't. And we were still struggling to get over the lines as to why this had been necessary now, because it was so easy for the media to compare negatively with the Kuwaiti invasion.

Then, the other problem was upon us. The *Guardian* put a series of questions to Ben W-P re Peter's loan. Charlie F and Lance [Price] went to see Peter, and then Geoffrey, and came back with a draft Peter statement, while I worked on a Number 10 line. TB was angry, at the bad judgement as much as anything, but also the way the thing had clearly been used in the Peter M/GB battle. Charlie said that when he went to see Robinson, Ed Balls came in in the middle and went through what CF was sure was a great charade of not knowing anything about it. Charlie, Lance and Ben came over to my office, where we were joined by Jonathan. I sent the draft line round to Richard Wilson and spoke to [Michael] Scholar. Our only real point of defence was that Peter was not directly involved in in the Geoffrey Robinson inquiry at the DTI, and had insulated himself from it. Apart from that, we didn't have much ground to stake out. The *Guardian* were asking about breaches of the code, and registration rules, and would doubtless get hold of Tories, and some of our own, to fuel it along. Derry joined us, and like the rest of us thought it was going to be difficult. Both he and Charlie F felt our major vulnerability was that Peter did not tell the permanent secretary [Scholar] about the loan when he was appointed to the job. I said you could also make the argument he should have told TB prior to accepting the appointment. The press and the Tories would be on to that angle in no time as well. Wilson's view was that it would be better if Peter were to admit he should have declared it earlier, and also to announce that he would pay back the loan. Peter was going to say that his mother would help him do that. He was dreading her being dragged into it, and also dreading the press hanging round the house and trying to get pictures of Reinaldo.

We all kind of felt he was not going to survive, but also felt we owed it to him to see if we could fight it out. That was going to mean him leading the fight, explaining himself, and seeing how party and public reacted. His problem was there would be a few enemies out to sort him. I told him I felt it was rocky but we would support him in a fight. We took an hour or so to sort the final statement, then heard the *Mirror* were on to it too, presumably via Routledge.

I had a number of calls with Peter to go over the tricky questions. He was a curious mix of nervous and steely. We were agreed it was going to be awful. The question was how awful. I fixed for him to go and do the Millbank rounds and given how sticky the wicket, he did OK. But Yelland and [Piers] Morgan were both straight on, saying it was a political and presentational disaster, which of course it was. All we could do was set out the facts, say it was a private loan, and emphasise the insulation from the Robinson inquiry. TB said either he goes, or we defend him robustly, there can be no in between. But he accepted it was likely to end in him going. I called Whelan and said I did not want to hear of a single Treasury comment, and I intended to ask every single journalist whether he was briefing on it. Needless to say he denied having anything to do with Routledge getting hold of the story in the first place. I persuaded Peter to say that with hindsight, he wished he had declared it earlier, but that did not change the fundamentals. He was in for an almighty kicking, and the next twenty-four hours would be crucial. Richard Wilson was making it clear he did not want to be set up as a kind of judge on this – ministerial conduct was a matter for the PM, Sebastian Wood [Richard Wilson's private secretary] reminded me – while Michael Scholar was equally not prepared to say he had 'cleared' it. The truth is he did not know until the press were on to it, and only then did Peter declare it to him. It was a very weak point and Peter knew it. I was beginning to lose the will to live, first days and nights on Iraq and now this when I was hoping to wind down pre-Christmas.

I called Tony Hall [Director of News, BBC] in between the Peter meetings and calls to say we had a lot of trouble with some of their coverage of Iraq – particularly [Jeremy] Bowen and [Rageh] Omaar [BBC correspondents]. He blathered on as he always did about how they always took our complaints seriously, but they felt their reporters were doing well in difficult circumstances. I said it was getting to a point where we would have to go public with our views that there was an inbuilt bias against us caused by their refusal to match their scepticism of what we said with scepticism of what the Iraqis said and showed them, in an environment where they were TOTALLY dependent on the regime for access and information. He said that would make it much harder to get any change in approach.

Tuesday, December 22

The Iraq fallout was bad enough but the Peter M situation was a wall-to-wall disaster area. Every paper led on it in later editions, and it was grim. Though Peter did OK on his broadcast interviews, as the day wore on the thing felt worse and worse. I went to see TB in the flat. Should we cancel the end-of-term meetings with editors? No. TB had seen GB last night who was on, finally, both for Geoffrey Robinson's dismissal, and Whelan too. But Robinson was fighting hard, saying it was absurd if he was to be dismissed for being generous, and was angry with GB every bit as much as TB now. Whelan was saying he would go if we could get him a job at the FA. TB said his antennae were twitching, the damage to be done was real, and he could not see a way through it. He felt the line to hold was the avoidance of conflict of interest, and that maybe Peter himself should ask for the registrar of Members' interests to look into it.

I spoke to Peter and Charlie F to go through the tricky questions again. Though the press scented blood, I felt the briefing went fine, I knew the ground to stand on and just stood there, and let them make their own judgement about everything else. I agreed Peter had made an error in not being open about it, but he had moved to avoid a conflict of interest.

After the lunchtimes, which were pretty ghastly, I went to see TB in the flat, where he was making lunch for the kids. He said he sensed the Tories and the media would not let up, and there was enough here to drive Peter out. I felt the Tories were missing the point – they were so mesmerised by Peter, but that story was taking care of itself. They would have been better going on the notion that Geoffrey survived everything because he provided TB with holidays, GB with funding and Peter with a loan to buy a swanky place to live. The party would hate it. I went to see GB and he asked what I thought was the worst part of it. I said choose any angle you want – Robinson problem; Peter M liability; TB/GB-ery; cronyism; sleaze; no better than Tories. There were a lot of hits in one go. He knew I would be gunning for Whelan again and was being very nice and charming, saying we had a problem, what did I suggest for getting out of it? I asked if there were any other ministers Geoffrey had given money to, also whether he had paid Balls' and Whelan's wages at any time. He said most of Geoffrey's money went into the leader's office and campaigns, in opposition. I said it would be better all round if Geoffrey resigned. GB said he had already put that to him, not saying it was what TB wanted, and he got very difficult about it. He felt he had done nothing wrong and was not prepared to be sacrificed.

I got a call to go back to Number 10 and TB asked me to go and see him, upstairs in the flat. He said wouldn't it be better if we asked both to go? I said you could make the case for that. Geoffrey had become more and more of a problem for the government, Peter had shown bad judgement, this had brought it all to a head. They could always come back at some point, he said. He then put the counter-argument as though he were now trying to talk himself out of it – Robinson had merely loaned a friend some money. It did not add to the difficulties he was already in, over which we had consistently defended him. Peter's judgement may be called into question but he had avoided a conflict-of-interest situation. And so on, then the other side, circular-conversation time.

Charlie F joined us and thought it was a bad idea, felt it was better to see if we could hold the line, not give in to hysteria. He was against Geoffrey going because that would make it much harder to keep Peter. I called JP. He said Peter's weaknesses were vanity and arrogance and they were the cause of his downfall. He used the word downfall, which suggested he felt he was a goner. I asked if he thought that. He said on balance I don't think TB should sack him, but it is bad and it could get worse. DB and Mo both called in, both appalled and clearly on the tough end of the market. JC agreed to do interviews but even he found it a tough wicket. He said the party would be appalled. He would defend him because he was a loyal team member, he said, 'but I find it very hard to defend at all'. It was interesting, however, how few of the hacks were saying he should resign. Little did they know that TB was getting to that point before them. The BBC was a bit better today, doubtless because of the bullying yesterday. TB saw a few editors, then headed to Chequers. I sensed he was going to wake up tomorrow and feel he had made a mistake in not following through his instincts on Peter. TB said 'I blame myself for this. We should have got rid of Geoffrey earlier.' I felt TB would wake up and decide he [Mandelson] should go.

Wednesday, December 23

The papers were absolutely ghastly for Peter, massive coverage and relentlessly negative. Sadly – and it was never going to be any other way – people's basic reaction was the same as ours had been, and with the usual venom on top. Yet despite all that the balance of opinion was that he should stay, which was a surprise. But I had dreadful vibes about the next day or so. I had a doctor's appointment, came back and Fiona said Ben W-P had been on the phone, there was some problem re an aspect to the mortgage that Peter thought could be a resigning issue. Could I go to a meeting at 10.30? I spoke to TB who, as I thought he would, had pretty much made his mind up. 'I'm worried what this is all doing to the public, never mind the press,' he said. He said in the end it was the concealment that was the main problem. Everything else was secondary but they would pick away. I said if Peter went, Geoffrey would have to go too. I know, he said. We had a conference call with GB, who was still asking if Geoffrey could stay. Re Peter, somewhat disingenuously I felt, he was saying maybe an apology and a reprimand would be enough. TB said that didn't do enough. He felt Peter could only rebuild from a fresh start. He had spoken to Peter late last night, and he sensed Peter was coming to the same view. Peter had spoken to GB this morning too, and one of the odder aspects of this was that as it got worse, he turned to GB for advice and support, despite being pretty sure he had been involved in setting the whole thing up.

I got a lift in with Fiona, feeling pretty stressed and depressed. I met up with Jonathan and Lance and we went to the DTI. Jonathan was scruffily dressed as he was due to go to the Lake District. Lance was due to be heading to Chile for a break. We were driven into the underground car park, met by a very pretty girl who took us upstairs to an outer office that was deathlike in its atmosphere and then in to see Peter, who was at his desk, reading the papers. He had done the office very much to his taste, modern and brightly coloured furniture, a minimalist desk, nice pictures. A Christmas card from Prince Charles had pride of place on his desk. I asked everyone else to wait outside and told him TB wanted to talk to him. I didn't listen in so only heard Peter's side of the call, that he knew he had made a mistake, wished he had handled it differently, but was it really a hanging offence? I could tell from the vibe coming back that TB was in steely mode, and saying that it was. His argument was that an apology would just be seen as a piece of spin. There had been a deception, or at least a concealment that could be construed as such. Added to which neither party nor public could really grasp the scale of it. I was pacing up and down by the window and after a while Peter's tone changed, became one of resignation. He said 'You have clearly made up your mind and I have to accept your judgement, which of course I do. I'm obviously very sorry.' The call ended, he looked at me, shrugged and then went out to see Ben.

I spoke to TB and began drafting resignation letters. I told Lance to put out a line that the PM was looking at the detail. I called Jack C, who was still manfully doing bids on it, and warned him it may end with his resignation, so change the tone. I spoke again to TB who said we now just had to put sentiment to one side, and deal with it. He wanted it made clear that we were not the Tories, and never would slide to standards as low as theirs. He, Jonathan and I worked out the reshuffle and agreed the sooner it was done the better. I felt desperately sad for Peter, who came back in looking wretched. I said this is not going to be easy, but we are just going to have to do it, and be professional about it. I know, he said, I know. He had clearly been crying. He collected himself and then amazed me by saying he felt he ought to call Gordon. Again, I only heard his side, but it sounded as though sympathetic noises were coming from the other end. Peter said he had been foolish, he was desperately sorry it was ending like this, and he hoped they would maintain some kind of relationship. It was extraordinary considering all that had gone on. GB was clearly saying he could trust him because Peter said on more than one occasion 'Yes, I know I can trust you, I know that.'

I wanted the letters done and dusted and out by the lunchtimes, and started to read the draft of Peter's letter to TB. The first line was 'I can scarcely believe I am writing this.' We were both quite emotional by now. I went over to him, said this is all absolutely dreadful but we just have to get through it. He kept saying why, why, why, but I was unsure whether he meant why did he do what he did, or why was he being forced to go. He felt if it was anyone else, we could have fought on. He made a few small changes, I got Lance to type it up outside, and then spoke to TB re his reply. Again, Peter startled me re GB. 'It's important Gordon sees them before they go out,' he said. He saw my surprise. I sat alongside him as he read through the letters, tears cascading down his face, and I gripped his shoulder and told him he had to be strong, and just get through the next ghastly few hours. I watched the news with Peter, who was calmer now, more focused, but still regularly bursting into tears. 'Please do your best,' he said. 'Don't let them portray me as some kind of felon.'

Michael Scholar popped in to say he was sorry, and seemed genuinely moved. Peter was fine when someone else came in like that but when it was the two of us, he kept breaking down. 'You don't deserve this Peter, you really don't.' Yes, I do. 'Well,' I said, 'even if you do, you don't really, if you see what I mean.' How many times had I warned him that what I called his 'lifestyle ambitions' would do for him? His desire to be famous and mingle with the rich and the great and the good. What the fuck was Charles' card doing there like it was the biggest thing in the mailbag? I really felt for him though, and felt wretched that I was having to act like some kind of undertaker to his ministerial career, doing the letters, shaping the media, telling them it was all over and soon he would be gone. We had had so many moments, good and bad, but when push came to shove, he was still one of the best and it was a dreadful fucking waste. I'd done Ron Davies' letters, and others, and it was just a job really, just helping sort things tidily, but I really felt this, and felt dreadful for Peter, for whom politics was wrapped up in everything he had.

As we left, I took him to one side and hugged him, and he me, and my mobile phone went off inside my jacket. We laughed. Be strong, I said. Do not let those bastards take any joy in seeing you broken. Stand tall and give every sense that one day you'll be back. I left feeling absolutely drained. TB called to go over the lines we should be pushing. It's grim, I said. Yes, he said, but we just have to get on with it now. I was back in the office and did a full briefing at 2, gave out the letters, took all their predictable questions. I felt OK, apart from when pressed on whether it was a breach of the ministerial code, and also why he hadn't moved on it earlier.

I had a bit of a flare-up with [Adam] Boulton because he quoted on air my 'fuck off' response to his bid for a TB interview yesterday, as though it were part of a briefing, and also gave the impression it was today. I paged Peter M and said don't do Sky which I regretted because it was petulant on my part, and I allowed that to affect Peter's efforts to get things in a better place. I told Nick Pollard [head of news, Sky] that if Adam called to apologise – which later he did – it would be forgotten. I spoke to Peter again, who said he felt better. He said 'I've done the right thing so I feel better about it.' TB called as I was going to bed. 'How's the BDA [battle damage assessment]?' It wasn't good, but it could have been a lot worse if we had kept hanging on.

Thursday, December 24

I was feeling pretty low, really tired after a hellish period, and reckoning I would be lucky to get anything near a rest in the next few days. I went for a swim. Peter called a couple of times 'to see how you are'. TB was of the view that it would blow over quickly, but that there would be an effort to say it tilted politics against New Labour. PH did a note on the same theme. I felt what was more worrying was the sense all Labour MPs were into big money and fancy houses

December '98: Saying goodbye to Peter

when in truth most of them work hard for not much reward. JP was poor on *Today*, and sounded tired. I got to the afternoon not having bought a single Christmas present and went shopping with Grace to get Fiona's presents.

Friday, December 25

I managed to avoid work most of the day apart from a couple of calls re bits of Peter fallout. The Kinnocks had been given the use of [theatre and film director] Richard Eyre's house and we went there for Christmas dinner which was fine, but I was tired. We basically just avoided politics as much as we could. I spent most of the time playing with the kids.

Saturday, December 26

Amid the fallout, some of the papers were saying Peter M would lead the euro campaign, or go for London mayor. We were due to go to Chequers for their Boxing Day do. TB was trying to calculate whether we had been really damaged or whether this was a one-off quickly forgotten. I felt there was a cumulative effect building at the moment re out-of-touchness and this was a part of that. He felt Peter personally was badly damaged but if he learned the right lessons, and changed his ways, he could emerge stronger from it. I didn't like these friends and family social dos, because truth be told you were never really off duty, and I didn't like the atmosphere at Chequers anyway. I think we were both glad to have a 'proper excuse' to go into TB's study and prepare for his BBC interview and talk things over. He played tennis for a bit then we went up to their bedroom to talk over the interview. He was in the bath, and CB was lying in the bed throwing out lines of argument, until he said it wasn't helping him and could she be quiet.

It went fine, short fairly factual questions, pressing mainly on why he didn't sack Geoffrey earlier. He managed to get some big-picture message into it and was reasonably happy. The top line was Peter had done something wrong and now we had to move on. That was a bit inconsistent with Peter's resignation letter which TB had not actually read, but had had read to him by me.

Peter was changing tack a bit. He was clearly being told by some that he should have toughed it out. He told TB he was getting lots of supportive letters and the feeling was we had allowed the media to force him out. TB told him he could only rebuild if he accepted he had made a big mistake and learned from it. He had to be more honest with himself. He said afterwards he was worried. Peter had gone from contrite to feeling somehow we had wronged him. I suspected it was just the after-effect. He had been hit by a truck and was now feeling the bruises. JP was very down on him, said he was pretty much a busted flush and had shown poor judgement. Little friendship and loyalty at the top. Peter was discovering that TB could be pretty ruthless when he had to be. Indeed, his only worry after the interview was whether he had been too obviously too ruthless. Then he did his jokey northern accent bit: 'Right you are, Ali, what a triumph eh?'

Sunday, December 27

The press were refusing to let go, keeping going on every detail. The Sundays didn't have much new but they were gorging on every spit and fart so the overall impression was bad. Also it was clear some ministers, including JP, were using it to diddle on the political front, saying it would herald a change in direction, less New Labour. TB called JP and asked him to stop the briefing, told him it was not a sensible response. TB was now adamant we had to be dismissive of all the soap stuff, but I said there would never be a better time to get rid of Whelan and he should seize the chance. TB said he would definitely be going, but surely today it would just become another huge story as this was dying down. Peter was also of the view not to do it today, presumably because he did not want to be too linked to Whelan in the public mind.

TB, who was due to leave for the Seychelles, said the most important thing was we all got a bit of a rest, and the last thing we needed was another great drama. I said fine, but he must not let him stay indefinitely. TB felt the public had absorbed the facts and now the media were just wallowing in it, but to little further effect. That was probably right. Our problem in the media was that the left-wing media thought we were too right wing and the right-wing media thought we were too left wing, and no paper or group had the intellect or self-confidence to develop themselves as New Labour. They were all trapped in the old prisms. TB set off in more upbeat mood than a few days ago, but we had a fair few problems lined up for the New Year.

Monday, December 28

I had spoken to one or two people re Whelan yesterday and the *Sun* were going for him today, while the *Mirror*, no doubt organised by Routledge, were starting what looked like a mini campaign to save him. I sent a note through to TB saying the problem here was weakness.

December '98: Peter learning about TB's ruthless side

Everyone knew we wanted him out, and yet we appeared unable to shift him. That was a very weakening position. TB called on receipt and said the difference now was that GB accepted he had to go, but we had to get the timing right. If we did it now, it would keep the Peter M story running and look like a minor form of disintegration. We had to calm things down. TB had sent JP a short fax reiterating the point about the need not to brief a change in direction and on the couple of occasions I spoke to JP today he joked about 'my fax telling off'.

I spoke to Peter a couple of times and he was now moving to my view that we should get rid of Whelan quickly. He sent a note to TB to that effect, saying it was becoming a TB/GB problem area and had to be resolved. He was worrying about the building-society angle on his mortgage and was due to speak to them tomorrow. But I sensed real concern. He also felt TB was being very 'wily' with him, that he was saying he could one day make a comeback, but actually hoping he might disappear. I said TB was being genuine, but he did need to heed the advice.

Tuesday, December 29

TB and I were working via fax on his New Year message, and talking about the best time to put it out. I took Rory and Calum to Chelsea vs Man U, and saw Alex F for a chat. He felt we'd handled the Peter M thing fine, and people were not talking about it any more. Then Clive Soley called and said the *Indy* were doing a story about how JP and GB have forged an alliance to push for more Old Labour approaches to PFI and spending. I called JP who said it was not about that; it was about core values. But it was going to be troublesome and the last thing we needed right now. I resisted the temptation to call GB again. Peter said even if I wasn't threatening, GB would take it as such and it would just feed his angst and paranoia. I really enjoyed the football, had a good laugh with [singer] Mick Hucknall. Frank Leboeuf [French footballer, then with Chelsea] and his wife and parents came up for a drink afterwards. Dickie Attenborough [director, actor and Labour peer] took me into a corner, very conspiratorially, and said only I could sort the TB/GB infighting, which had to stop or else we were finished.

Wednesday, December 30

RC called from Chevening [Foreign Secretary's country residence], asked whether there really was a new alliance between JP and GB. I suspected not, but JP was diddling post-Peter, and had been loose with his words. I spoke to Joe Irvin [Prescott's special adviser] and said we now had to ensure JP's New Year message to his party was very New Labour. Joe was on for helping and I think realised John had gone a bit far. *World at One* was priceless. MPs welcome JP shift of strategy. Audrey [Fiona's mother] called and said what on earth was JP up to? She said past Labour governments were always destroyed by themselves, by ego leading to division.

Thursday, December 31

The JP problem was worse. Lots of big page leads, lots of deliberate mis- and over-interpretation, and a silly story, in part fuelled by that tick Nick Jones [BBC], that we had rushed out the New Year message to take attention away from JP. I spoke to JP at 10.15 and he realised it had got a bit out of hand, said he would do whatever we needed to rectify it. We were entering a very febrile stage and we had to get off personality and on to substance and policy. I was worried that anything we did at the moment, unless of real substance, would just fuel the rubbish. Both RC and DB came on offering to do interviews or articles but if we were not careful they would just be seen as more evidence of division. JP had apologised to GB, saying he had not intended to push it as far as it went. But he said there was no point denying Peter leaving the Cabinet meant there would be a change. I said the problem now was that when TB came back on the scene, with all the press with us, in South Africa, they would be desperate to write a 'Blair stamps his authority' line and it would then be seen as a slap down to JP.

GB called. He felt we could only get back on the front foot through major policy, but it may be the climate would not take it and we just had to let this period pass. He then raised Whelan. He said where are we with the Charlie situation? I said 'You tell me.' He said that Charlie would not accept responsibility for the Peter loan story and if he was forced out on those grounds, he would put up a real fight and cause us real trouble. He said he had told him that when a press officer becomes the story, he ceases to be effective. I pointed out that a day earlier a survey showed I got more coverage than virtually every member of the Cabinet. He laughed and said I was in a different position, but got the point. GB was in his warm and friendly, almost pleading mode – you have to understand I am with you on this, he said, but we have to be careful how we handle it. He felt we should try to help get him a job, though of course he was getting a pretty bad press which was unlikely to help.

It was ridiculous that he and I were dealing with this on the day of the launch of the euro. We went over that, and agreed a strategy at least for being involved and in the picture, to avoid a fresh bout of 'isolated' coverage. My sense of the papers was that they knew a lot of this stuff was rubbish, but it didn't stop them. The Sundays were all calling for one-on-one briefings and were clearly going to be doing big numbers on Peter M, euro, looking ahead etc. We had to get back on to serious stuff, and the public to realise there was a media agenda – which is why they could not let go of the Peter story – and a government agenda actually focused on their concerns. I was feeling very down about the job – too much work, too much pressure, too many incompetents I was having to support or cover for, too much time doing things others ought to be doing, too many people looking to me for their answers. Today was meant to be something close to a day off and I would reckon I dealt with more calls than most people would deal with in a busy day. Neither Fiona nor I felt much like going out. We stayed in and watched *Gone With the Wind* with the kids.

Friday, January 1, 1999

I called TB on holiday. He was blissfully unaware of all the JP hulla-baloo, and he was not very happy about it, yet was clearly relaxing and basically of a mind it would blow over. He said JP had been daft, and was playing to too narrow a constituency. He said he was having a great time. Having virtually lost my voice, I said I was so pleased for him. He banged on again about the need for me to get more time off, but I couldn't see where it was coming from. Would you have been happy if I had gone away as well? Probably not, he said. I said if I had buggered off like everyone else, I suspect we would be in an even bigger mess. There was a fair old rash of Whelan stories around the place. He was banking on something at the FA but I had spoken to David Davies [Football Association chief executive] who did not sound very encouraging.

There was stuff in the press re JP backing Whelan. I called JP who said he had said nothing. He was not getting involved. 'I am not playing a double game here, I can promise you that,' he said. But he would not want to go against GB too much over it. It wasn't such a big thing in a way, not for him, and GB was backing some of his schemes for spending, and letting him have Dorneywood [usually the Chancellor's country residence] which he and Pauline [JP's wife] seemed to like. I said to him that TB wanted him to call him. 'Wants to bawl at me does he?' He said he knew he had ballsed up but we had to realise that Peter M's departure DID make a difference, and he wanted it too. 'The plates have moved a bit, that's all I'm saying. The balance has shifted.' TB was beginning to worry re South Africa, as was I. It was going to be a tricky visit in lots of ways.

Saturday, January 2

TB sent through a note saying he wanted a major focus on domestic policy as soon as we were back – Frank Dobson on nurses' pay, Blunkett on minister for inner-city schools. I called them both and they were on board for major statements. They were also totally supportive of any agitating re Whelan. I spoke to Frank while I was out on the heath. At one point I said the way things stand, Gordon has allowed Whelan to alienate so many of his colleagues that if Tony fell under a bus tomorrow, it is hard to think of any who would positively want to vote for Gordon to be leader. 'That's interesting,' said a passer-by. I had a long chat with Charlie Falconer, told him I was really fed up with things at the moment. He felt they were not as bad as they might be, though TB was weakened by recent events. We had to get him to a better place with the party and with the Cabinet. Charlie said he had heard from Michael Wills [Labour MP, close to GB] about the GR/Peter M loan six months ago, and felt sure it emerged from that inner GB circle – he was certainly in no doubt CW had to go.

Sunday, January 3

The Sundays were bad, as we anticipated. I went downstairs and Fiona was going through them. They are dreadful for Tony, she said. I had slept badly, and woke up determined that Whelan should go, preferably today. There was loads about him in the papers, including sympathetic profiles, and in the *Mail* two pages on who is for him and who's against. Others ran straight news pieces on GB backing Whelan. Anji called, said Sue Nye was asking whether we were getting anywhere with the FA [re Whelan job]. Anji had called David Davies who said he had no idea it was so urgent. I told Anji I felt GB was just buying time, and trying to see us through till we lost interest again. I was intending to say to TB that if Whelan didn't go, I was going, and she agreed with that approach.

This was a problem that had been allowed to become a crisis because for three years we had not faced up to it and dealt with it properly. Sally Morgan called, said she was worried because there was a sense of drift. People were looking for leadership and it wasn't there. She felt JP had handled the last few days dreadfully, and TB underestimated the damage being done. Is JP onside or not, she asked? Mo called, said she hoped I understood from the outside we look like a total shambles – JP on the rampage, Whelan unresolved, no replacement for Robinson, not clear who was in charge of the Dome, shambles. She said she was happy to organise a meeting with FD, DB, JC, CS and others to start a concerted Cabinet effort to get the show on the road next week.

I finally had a very difficult call with TB. He was out on a boat and it had taken an hour for Switch [Downing Street switchboard] to get through on a line decent enough to have a proper conversation. I said he was getting a dreadful press, there was a sense of drift and he was being weakened and damaged. 'What am I supposed to do about it from here?' he asked, sounding irritated to be bothered. I said one thing he could do was call GB and tell him it had to be resolved re Whelan. There was a boil to be lanced and it was time to lance it. He said that was difficult when there was no actual evidence he was responsible for providing the info which brought down Peter. The main call was ridiculous and summed up the nonsense of the whole fucking situation. He was out on a fishing boat and halfway through the conversation suddenly said 'Hold on, I think I've got a fish.' He handed the phone to Bill Lloyd [protection officer], who then gave me a detailed running commentary as he brought the fish in until I said 'Bill, I could not give a flying fuck about his fish.' I then listened to shouts and hollers and 'wows' until TB came back and said 'You should see the size of the fish I've just caught.' I said I was so pleased for him. 'Yeah, OK,' he said, now sounding hurt.

He said in his last conversation GB suggested Whelan would go tomorrow. If tomorrow, why not today? He said the papers were just determined to do us in and we had to keep everything in perspective. I said my perspective is too often having to deal with rubbish created by Whelan and I'm not prepared to do it a day longer, and you had better get that message. It was clearly OTT and he was taken aback, but I had decided he had to get the message. He said he would call GB and get back to me. I went for a swim, then took the boys up to the heath to play football.

GB came through. Another difficult conversation. I asked what was happening re Charlie. He said – nothing, he was due back tomorrow. I said I was not prepared to work with him any longer, that whether he was responsible for the loan story or not, there was enough of a track record for me to have reached that judgement, and I felt it was impossible to have him around. It was not just one thing – it was a modus operandi over years that made him an impediment to effective and professional politics or communications. Whelan had to go. GB said there was a basic justice question. If he went now, everyone would say he had leaked that information, and yet there was no evidence of that. He had to be able to clear his name. He said my approach – of saying today that he was going – would make him unemployable and everyone would say he was going because of Peter. I said they will say that whenever he goes.

I said if he was not going, one thing I was clear about was that he was not coming to any meetings I chaired. He added nothing on the economy, nothing on Europe, he was there to arm himself with information and then go out and act as an unofficial source thought to be in the loop. He said he knew there was a problem, and he would have to go, but we had to manage his exit so he didn't feel the need to go out writing columns and books and the rest. I said we were in danger of looking like a soap opera, immediately struck by the thought there was nothing more soap-operatic than me shouting down a mobile from the top of the heath in the howling wind, to GB in his garden in Scotland trying to save his mate's skin one last time. He said what was clear was that if the key people did not work together, we were finished. He, TB and I should always agree at a minimum on the big questions, he said, and I had to understand he agreed on the outcome but we had to be careful about the timing and the manner.

I was probably too open with him, but I had pretty much reached the end of the road on it. Whelan was a menace with few redeeming features and every day he stayed was a further weakening of TB and Number 10. GB and I went round in circles, him talking natural justice, me saying there was never a good time but we had to grasp it. He said we should have a private agreement he was going and give him time to look for work. I said with the media as it was if we did not have him gone soon, it was a major defeat for TB. He said he would call TB and then call me back.

I heard from the cops TB was taken aback at my 'get the message' call and there was more evidence of that when I got home. CB had called Fiona and said she thought I needed a holiday. Fiona said that was patronising, I was perfectly fine, but being asked to work in ludicrous conditions, in which we spent so much time having to fend off trouble from within. Then Peter called, back from Paris, and sounded much more like the old Peter, now saying – horror – he was minded to do a resignation statement. He sent me through a draft which was self-indulgent in the extreme and very counter to the 'learning experience' approach. He said, however, he realised he had caused a near disaster for TB and was not sure how we got out of it.

I called GB again. He said he was surprised TB had not called me. He said he had persuaded Whelan he would make a statement saying he had worked in Labour politics for several years, now he had become too much part of the story and it was time to move on. He said CW was feeling very bitter and hurt. There were loads of media outside his house when he got back from Scotland tonight. He said it was vital the story was not sacked but moving on. I said I could assist in that. The second I put the phone down, it rang again. It was Charlie. 'Happy New Year' – you had to hand it to him.

Monday, January 4

I called TB at 6.30 after a sleepless night. He said Whelan was going, but it was important we did not do him in, and that GB was not damaged. This was as much about a media obsession with spin doctors as anything else. With a mix of friendliness and sarcasm, he 'thanked' me for the cuttings I had sent out, and said he was grateful I had waited till his break was almost over before ruining his holiday. He knew it was right for Whelan to go, but coming after Peter and Geoffrey Robinson, he was worried the press would start to think they could decide who survived and who didn't. I pointed out that we had been arguing for Charlie to go. Most of the press wanted him to survive. He said GB had said to him 'We must not let this kind of thing happen again, and in future I will do what you say on these issues.' He was still basically of the view that GB was a force for good.

GB called as CW arrived. Charlie was remarkably cheerful, though if you looked closely, you could sense he was both hurt and nervous. Despite it all, there was something likeable about him. He kept his coat on for some reason, and stuck his feet on the table, an odd mix of relaxed and can't wait to get out of here. We were both pretty businesslike and perfectly civilised to each other. I said there was no point going over old stuff, we just had to sort today as best we could with minimum damage to him or GB, or TB. He had drafted a statement protesting innocence re the Peter M loan leak, and saying it had become impossible for him to do his job. He was reluctant to go for the media, presumably because that was where he saw his future living. He said he had become pretty fed up anyway, preferred opposition to government, where he felt constrained, and he hated a lot of the civil servants. He denied briefing against ministers. 'Come off it, Charlie,' and he did his look of injured innocence which I had seen so many times. We finished his statement and I got GB on the phone to go through it. He said it was important we got through today with Charlie's integrity intact, and with him being seen as effective and thus employable.

I was briefing at 12 and was making sure I had other things to announce for the week ahead, e.g. loose ends of reshuffle, stuff on the South Africa trip, going to Kuwait on Saturday. I had several calls with JP during the day who was sounding a bit subdued, and apologetic. Mo was calling a lot too, and putting herself up as a player, getting as involved as possible, and JP rightly resisted her idea that he phone round the Cabinet 'to settle things down'. Jack C and DB were also desperate to be more involved. JP spoke to TB, and said he knew he had fucked up but he had not planned some big deliberate thing. I spoke several times to GB who was in reflective mood. He seemed to be trying to build bridges and get the show back on the road. I said if you go back down the last few years, the times we have been most effective have been when we have worked together and we should try to do that now.

My briefing went OK. Ten minutes on South Africa, then endless questions on Whelan. They clearly felt he was pushed and I did my best to play it down and go on about the absurd priorities of the modern media. TB sounded more relaxed when I spoke to him afterwards. He had been out on a boat again and seemingly helped rescue some Dane [Hans Joergensen, a dentist] who had been in difficulty, and who seemed pretty shocked to see TB hanging over the side. He said we needed to get on to big policy and substance quickly. He intended to go for the media, and JP wanted to do likewise. Whelan was doorstepped and talked a bit and looked like he was enjoying himself. People thought it odd GB said nothing. I got home, feeling knackered. I hadn't had a day off for weeks, apart from Christmas Day really, and Fiona was pretty fed up with it all too. TB said I must get a rest, which was a brilliant order to give from his boat bobbing in the sea off the Seychelles while I was trying to sort his South Africa trip. He said he sensed a new approach from GB and it was vital I worked with him closely. PG did a couple of [focus] groups in Croydon, said they were dreadful, Peter M showed we were as bad as the Tories, TB weak in his handling of it, and they were moaning about delivery.

Tuesday, January 5

The papers were if anything even worse – wall-to-wall Whelan, and definitely a new mood of soap and negativism as the things they would push. The editorials were universally bad for us. Whelan got a better press than he deserved. I was being described as the winner of a bruising battle but it didn't feel like it, and I was exhausted at a time batteries should have been recharged. TB called early, said he was up for doing anything that moved us on, and we agreed I would put together a package on Africa to try to get him on to the morning broadcasts.

Richard Wilson was back after a break in California and he said I was TB's main person and I had to be protected. 'All the main tensions come down through you, because you are the one they all speak to.' He said I really had to watch for exhaustion. He was worried that TB did not involve his colleagues enough, which would leave him prone to isolation. He felt Whelan's departure meant we could finally leave the ways of opposition behind us. I saw Andrew Turnbull [Treasury permanent secretary] and said he should help GB find a good strong civil servant to front his media coverage, and reduce the political briefing. Turnbull had identified John Kingman, ex-*FT*, Treasury insider. GB said he would go along with a civil servant provided he could retain the option of a fresh political appointment later. Turnbull said GB had become a bit reclusive from the Civil Service of late, but he was sure 'some good can come of all this'.

TB sounded subdued when he called later, knew that his holiday was over and the first few days back would have a tricky feel. He wanted us to get over the message we were staying focused on the things that mattered, and let the media wank on in their own way. I fed back some of the comments, e.g. from Mo and Richard Wilson, that the answer was more collective and collegiate government. He was pretty dismissive. It's just a way of them saying they want to be more central, have more power. On the general reaction, he said the going had got tough and as ever too many in the party wet their knickers. We have been here before, he said. It will be tough for a while but we just rebuild. I spoke to Mbeki's[1] office to make sure they understood the especial need for the visit to go well, because of domestic difficulties. I got a particularly unpleasant death threat through the post today, dripping with blood, which Fiona took to the cops.

Wednesday, January 6

Seychelles. We arrived after an eleven-hour flight. Philip Barton, John Holmes and I got off the plane in thirty-degree heat and were taken to a waiting room. TB and CB arrived soon after. We had exchanged some fairly heavy words in the last few days, but as ever the tensions subsided pretty quickly. He came in, made a big beeline for me and said to the lounge staff 'Can I have some of your best coconut milk for my friend Mr Campbell, who has had a bad few days while I've been away.' Peter Wilkinson [Downing Street press office] was told by the *Sun* that Prince Edward and Sophie Rhys-Jones were announcing their engagement. We knew nothing about it. I called Geoff Crawford, who confirmed it. We agreed a line about when we were told, and I said it was a shame they hadn't announced it two days ago. TB and I worked through all the basic arguments and upcoming problems on the plane. There was no doubt we had taken a hit, he said, and people would be looking to see how we responded to that. It was all about perspective and staying focused on the right priorities.

---

[1] Thabo Mbeki, Nelson Mandela's deputy and leader of the ANC, was due to succeed Mandela as president in the spring.

We took him back to see the media on the plane and he was good, refusing to go back over Peter M/Whelan, refusing to fall into any of the traps re specific stories they were pursuing, good on big picture and context. He was worried about the NHS and the talk of bed shortages for the flu epidemic, which was provoking the usual 'winter crisis' talk. We worked on the South Africa speech for the rest of the flight. We arrived to a pretty impressive welcome and were driven to the presidential guest house. TB and CB had a private dinner with the Mbekis. TB felt he was charming and friendly but it wasn't easy living in Mandela's shadow. TB felt there was too much attachment to the policy of affirmative action to promote blacks and he wanted to get Mbeki to say black South Africa would not become rich by making white South Africa poor.

Thursday, January 7

TB was out early for a game of tennis and came back complaining of feeling ill. He was really getting agitated re the NHS, felt delivery was too slow and a flu epidemic could really set us back. Today was going to be Mandela/Mbeki day. I was in for the start of the bilateral forum but then, irritatingly, Mbeki's spokesman suddenly said they wanted to do a proper communiqué and we spent ages toiling over a long statement that few would read and even fewer would publish, and the main points of which could have been covered in a one-minute briefing. I put in a line about TB and Mbeki working on Third Way politics, which Mbeki's civil servants wanted out, and I took TB and Mbeki to one side to agree it should stay. He was very warm and friendly, with real charm in his eyes, and a wicked smile. He was puffing away at a pipe most of the time. He said it was true the Third Way was arousing a lot of interest so why not put it in there? Their meeting was largely about crime, education, Asian crisis, a tricky exchange on Iraq. I met some of Mandela's people, and others from the SA government who wanted to pick my brains on modernising communications.

I worked on a proper briefing note for the speech, which was coming into shape. TB read it and okayed it in the car on the way to see Mandela. He was looking pretty good, if walking more slowly. His ankles were visibly thicker than the last time we saw him, and his hearing was clearly going. They went straight into a tête-à-tête on Lockerbie. And when I got him to sign a book for Monica [Prentice, Downing Street messenger], he took an age to write it out in his elaborate, old-fashioned handwriting, then looked up halfway and said 'It's not THAT Monica, I hope.' The atmospherics at their doorstep were good but Mandela having dropped Lockerbie on them, we had to get our act together on it. It had been a difficult discussion because Mandela wanted to tell Gaddafi [Libyan leader] that sanctions would be lifted for good if the suspects were handed over for trial. Gaddafi's worry was that the two suspects would say he ordered them to do it and the US/UK would then have to go for him. They were looking for assurances that the Libyans would not be interrogated by our police over other crimes.

We left for the same Alexandra township we had visited in opposition, visited a health centre and then a domestic violence/rape project. The figures were terrifying. Any improvements on the last time we were here were fairly marginal, though as then the spirit was phenomenal. TB left for a business reception and I briefed the press on the bus, both on Lockerbie and on tomorrow's speech. By the end of it, with Lockerbie such a strong story, they were wondering whether to hold back on the speech till tomorrow. But we had already placed an article in the *Indy* based on it so in the end they went for a full meal – Lockerbie, Mandela/Mbeki, Third Way plus the leadership stuff which was obviously going to be 'I'm in charge' headline material. TB was looking wretched and when we got to the guest house went for a lie down.

Later, he and John H and I discussed the fallout from recent events. He said he intended to say on *Frost* that the media were determined to reduce us to the level of soap opera. John and I argued that the main characters fed it too much, and encouraged it with their behaviour. In different ways, JP, GB, Peter M, RC all did it. All Robin seemed to care about when I talked to him at the moment was his bloody wife's book and how far she would put the knife in. TB felt they had not all upgraded their mentality or their operation – and many were incapable – to a bigger and more important arena. Politics was the be-all and end-all for some of them. It was all they had. At the business reception, he said lots of the business people were saying it was a shame for business Peter M had gone.

Friday, January 8

TB was feeling dreadful, and looking not too good either. He was performing heroics in public for it not to be noticed just how ghastly he was clearly feeling. I was briefing Ewen MacAskill and made the mistake of telling him about the drowning Dane incident. It was a mistake first because it was a far better Sunday story and second because it would detract from the speech and TB's meeting with the AIDS victim he and CB sponsored. It was also wasted just on the

Guardian so having told him I then told the tabloids, and got Bill Lloyd to go and tell the story. They loved both the Dane and the AIDS sponsorship stories, and were getting on heat about whether they would get pictures of the girl.

TB did a session with the two black journalists travelling with us and one of them, Steve Pope [*Voice*], said he couldn't believe how awful the British travelling press were. He said it had made him wonder whether we deserve a free press. Once we reached Cape Town, TB called GB, who was back thinking he needed a non-civil servant to do his media. We went straight to Nazareth House, the home for kids with HIV, where the staff were absolutely superb. The nuns didn't want the press to name Ntombi (the girl they sponsor) but Reuters did so and it was obvious from the way she stuck to them that she was the one. TB seemed genuinely moved talking to her, and did a very good clip on the whole AIDS situation, the figures on which were mind-blowing.

The speech was signed off, and then I realised some of the words I had briefed yesterday, and which had been carried in the media, were not in the final version. It was a strong speech though and would carry well. But it was a fuck-up that put me in an irritable mood and at the briefing afterwards I should have just gone up front, said we briefed words that were taken out and sorry for the fuck-up, instead of which because the press were getting on my nerves I waited for them to raise it and said it was no big deal. I then did the Sundays and was even ruder to them. I had given up any pretence of holding the bulk of them in anything but contempt. But I was over the top and later apologised. We had a military medals ceremony, and there was a protest of Muslims outside, which turned nasty and shots were fired.[1] The media got very excited, the lobby suddenly behaving like war correspondents.

We got to the Parliament building for the reception, followed by the speech, which went well, and he did an excellent off-the-cuff peroration about noble causes/glittering prizes, the need to challenge cynicism, politics as soap opera. Robin Oakley managed to get three clips out of the speech on to the bulletins, and said the riots had helped take the trip higher up the news agenda. TB had done well to get through the speech, and by the time we got to the residence was in a bad way. He sat picking at a salad, with just a towel around him, muttering how crap he felt. I went for a swim, then spoke to

[1] Police had opened fire in Cape Town on a group of Muslims protesting at recent British and American military strikes on Iraq.

Peter, who said the Britannia building society were going to be clear he had done nothing wrong. On the plane to Kuwait, I had a session with some of the more grown-up journalists to get their take on the current media prism. Oakley thought things were getting worse not better, and it was becoming harder and harder to get serious coverage. I took a sleeping pill, slept for a few hours, and woke to find the crew really worried about TB, and even talking about diverting to land and get a doctor. He had been sick and looked wretched, but we agreed we had to plough on and just get through the next visit and then home. I half jokingly said the public have no sympathy with illness in politicians so we just had to get on with it.

Saturday, January 9

Kuwait. TB was looking like death warmed up but still the press hadn't latched on to it. We got very limited coverage for the speech and I was kicking myself for briefing re the Dane, who in any event was tracked down by the Sundays and they got him to say the whole thing was exaggerated. We were driven to the emir's palace for an odd meeting, in which TB did his best but provoked fairly monosyllabic responses, mainly re Iraq. TB said he was trying to build a consensus for a policy of containment. The emir [Jaber III al-Ahmad al-Jaber al-Sabah] said Britain always helped Kuwait. They chatted about South Africa and the euro, but without much energy.

I got the feeling that quite a lot of the Saudis were a bit grungy and not terribly grateful for the military support, looking at our presence as a bit of a problem. They said it would be better if we did not say strikes on Iraq came from pilots there. We pointed out that we had a free press and there were expectations in Parliament about information being divulged. They looked unimpressed. They liked the support in theory but in practice they gave the impression it was a bit of a pain. Still, they had put a decent visit together quickly so we had to hand them that. TB said he was of the view that the stronger we were with Saddam, the less likely we were to use force. They had a pretty scary exchange re Iran and the way it was developing militarily.

TB did a sales pitch on a defence contract we were chasing against the US, and then we were gone, a meeting that was neither friendly nor unfriendly, neither substantial nor insubstantial. Sally [Morgan] called and said there was a lot of anger around re Peter being back in Number 10 yesterday doing the Hombach meeting (Labour-German SPD meeting). JP and others were up in arms about it. She said the *Indy* was running a story too that JP, GB and Jack S were uniting to oppose the Lib Dem strategy. TB was livid with Peter. It had not been necessary to meet there and the whole thing was just to get him back in the political picture, he said, when the time was not right. 'He should just disappear for a few months.' He was getting exasperated again, not least by JP's overreaction – he had been on to Jonathan to say it was undermining of him as DPM that Peter was in there holding meetings!

TB was still feeling really rough, sweating profusely but just about managing to hold it together when he was in public. It was only the tan he had developed in the last few days that stopped it being obvious he was in a pretty bad way. I really felt for him having to do all the official stuff and the glad-handing. We went to see the pilots out at the airbase. They were a lot younger than I had expected, very friendly and professional, but when you got them talking openly, admitted it was a pretty tough place to work. TB got into a Tornado cockpit for the cameras, then did a doorstep with a very tough line on Saddam, who had been making more belligerent noises. The Kuwaitis seemed to think Saddam was weakening. Back at the residence, I played the bagpipes with my namesake, the defence attaché [Alastair Campbell, later defence attaché in Baghdad]. TB had gone to bed again, feeling dreadful. I was gathering all the briefing for *Frost*, but wondering whether TB would be able to do it. It wasn't a serious illness, but the effort he had to make to keep going when he was in public meant the second he stopped, he was in a state of virtual collapse, and had been sick again.

The Sundays were starting to get very excited re Margaret Cook's book serialisation, which was starting in the *Sunday Times*. I called the boys as we left for the airport. Burnley were at Bristol Rovers. It was 2-1 when the call started, 3-3 by the time we got to the airport, 4-3 when we took off. TB did a bit of a mingle with the press, but basically just wanted to get his head down. On landing, I had a message to call Robin C re the Margaret stuff. I still felt it best he stay right out of it. 'Is this survivable?' Robin asked. 'For fuck's sake of course it is. Stop being so melodramatic. TB will not give this a moment's thought. He backed you when it mattered and will back you now. It is personal and unpleasant but it is certainly survivable.'

Sunday, January 10

The Sundays were wall-to-wall Cook. Romola Christopherson [former Department of Health director of press and publicity] had a big piece in the *Sunday Times* saying I was the real DPM, which wouldn't help with JP, or with the soap bollocks. I was up at half six and in to see

TB in the flat. We agreed he would be saying NHS delivery was the thing he was most concerned about and intending to focus on, defend RC, go for the media over Europe, announce an appointments commission re the Lords, mild distancing from Peter (which in the end came out as the opposite). I agreed with *Frost* we would get Mrs Cook out of the way first and then go through policy areas.

He was on good form, really strong in parts though of course defending Robin would be the only show in town media-wise. What the interview showed again was that when the wicket was tricky, TB was far and away the best communicator we had, but there was no doubt recent events had changed the way we were seen, mainly by media but that would begin to seep through pretty quickly. TB said again in the car afterwards that ego and division were the big problems in Labour history and we had to learn from that. 'We are blessed with a useless Opposition but even they should be able to shift ground now.'

Monday, January 11

I was feeling really tired and decided to take a couple of days off to recharge, and to think a bit. The papers were full of the Cooks, but intelligent opinion was definitely moving our way on the soap stuff, and what kind of politics we wanted. Jack C was doing media and doing it well. Jonathan called to brief me on the office meeting, and said his view was no matter how much we loathed the media, we had to get into a better place with them post-Peter. TB wanted me, Anji and Philip to sit down and work out exactly what Peter could and could not do in the next phase. He was sure Peter could come back eventually, but he really needed some time out of the picture. Tam Dalyell [veteran Labour MP] did a stupid point of order suggesting Number 10 briefed against the Speaker and were pushing her to retire early. I drafted a letter of complaint to him. Tam had really taken against me.

Tuesday, January 12

The blitz of events and speeches for the return to the House was inevitably seen as a relaunch and got mixed reaction. Health was the one area that felt most worrying, but at least there was a sense we were on about the things people cared about, after all the soap and the rubbish. There was still far too much around re Peter M. He, TB and I spoke and agreed we would make clear he was not behind these stories about him making a comeback sooner rather than later, and that he was out of the front line for the foreseeable future. Peter was angry about a *Times* leader saying he didn't appear to understand why he had resigned. Philip called from a focus group in Edgware to say 'Shagger Cook is a hero, and they think she (wife) is fucking ghastly.' I called Robin, hoping to cheer him up a bit, and it seemed to cheer him up a lot. He said he felt 'she' – underlined four times – had gone too far and would have little public sympathy. I said the most important thing was he stopped thinking and talking about it, and got on with the job.

Wednesday, January 13

Bizarrely, as I'd only had a couple of days off, I had that 'first day back' feeling, slightly struggling to get into the flow. I travelled in with Jonathan who was worried about Robinson-funding questions for PMQs, as we had not been able to get to the bottom of everything. The worst kind of PMQ was the factual question to which you don't know the answer. The Mandelson-obsessed papers were still going on that, though it was by and large off the broadcasts. TB, Charlie, Derry and I met to go over all the difficult Geoffrey R, Peter M etc. questions. TB hated this kind of thing and was dreading it. He was most worried about direct factual questions on Geoffrey R. I was more worried Hague would be strategic and get into TB/GB. If I were them, I would be relentless on it. In the event, Hague was poor, though he had a couple of good lines that would carry. TB was pissed off with Peter because he felt he was probably behind the comeback stories. I believed Peter's protestations that he wasn't. At least not all of them.

The eleven o'clock was NHS, European Commission crisis, Peter M half-heartedly. I was trying to be friendlier and more relaxed and felt it a bit after a quiet couple of days. Robert Peston had a piece today attacking me over the 'mutual contempt' with the press. I needed to watch it. The post-PMQs was mainly about the Libs because Paddy had really gone for TB, which was a bit of a diversion. Jill Palmer [*Mirror*] called to say Piers Morgan was planning a 'Crisis what crisis?' front page based on my saying TB did not see an NHS in crisis. I went through the charade of a long chat with Piers, an agreement to have lunch, and then talked him out of it.

I had a meeting with TB and GB re the IPPR [Institute for Public Policy Research] speech. GB was still being unusually friendly, helpful and co-operative. He and I persuaded TB that a political Cabinet on Thursday would look like panic and we should call it off, and stick to a normal Cabinet. Some of GB's motivation was probably to stop any post-mortem of recent events, but it was the right decision, I was sure of that. Richard Wilson called to apologise on behalf of Romola, and to say it was absurd I didn't have a car and a driver. I said I was fine without. TB called later on and told me in confidence Paddy Ashdown was intending to announce he was standing down as leader.

Thursday, January 14

Peter Hyman came up with a decent top-line talking point for the speech at the QE2 [conference centre] – spreading power, wealth and opportunity to the expanding middle classes. We had done no advance briefing and it would play fine. Cabinet was OK, fairly subdued and GB still looking downcast. Margaret B made a very good point – that we called for and generally got good discipline from the PLP, and we had to show that kind of discipline at the top. TB said much the same thing. He said the last few weeks had been difficult, frenzied in the media, but this was an ideologically united Cabinet and we had to maintain that and drive it right through our staff and the party. Ann Taylor said the PLP demanded professionalism and discipline and expected ministers to have a grip of their staff. Frank said there seemed to be a cultural bent against talking each other up, and praising each other in public, and if we did it, there would be a greater sense of us operating as a team.

GB didn't really engage, but led a discussion on the economic crisis in Brazil. He gave a pretty upbeat assessment showing the UK better placed than most at the moment. Retail sales had been better than expected. Welfare to work was beginning to show results. Manufacturing was in some difficulty but the pound has fallen. He went through some of the upcoming benefit and welfare changes that were planned for the near future. We had to emphasise that we were steering a course of stability in a troubled world. Then Iraq, with the usual long spiel from George [Robertson] largely going through an account of events we already knew.

There was a comic moment when JP's mobile went off, despite it being a no-mobile zone, and it turned out to be Joan Hammell [JP's special adviser] saying they had found the papers he'd lost on his way to Number 10. Anji and Sally and I were counting the number of glasses of water Clare was getting through. She had downed two full carafes by halfway through. At the briefing, there was a bit of interest in the Libs coming in. Robin wanted to do a big briefing on it, which I persuaded him against. The Libs blew these things up into huge great events anyway and we should let them get on with it, but not go overboard.

I then left for what was going to be a difficult meeting, to discuss Peter, with him, Anji, Philip, Ben [Wegg-Prosser], at [Labour peer and media entrepreneur] Waheed Alli's office. There was the usual jokey small talk at the start, Peter talking himself down as a disaster area a bit, then I kicked it off properly, said we all started from the premise – and this includes TB – of wanting Peter back in the front line at some point. This meeting was about how we suggested he conducted himself in the meantime. My own judgement was that he should have a reasonable period of radio silence, at the end of which he emerged as a reformed character who had learnt from the experience, was more humble, less media-focused, more substantial. Peter said he agreed, then seemed to contradict that immediately by saying that he thought he should use the time to write a book about his personal journey in the party, his upbringing, his sexuality, his politics, his strengths and weaknesses, and that he should also make a film about the Third Way.

I knew about the book idea already because JP had mentioned it to me. He was pushing for Peter maybe to get involved with the ANC [in South Africa] in their elections – a [Richard] Caborn [regional development minister] idea. Re the book he said he thought 'later rather than sooner'. Peter said JP supported the idea. Ben said he didn't think Peter would be happy until he was out of politics. Peter said on the contrary he was only happy when he was in politics. 'I am not, contrary to what some of you think, interested in wealth. I was put on this earth to do what I've been doing.' When it was suggested he spend more time in Hartlepool, he said his constituents didn't want to see him in Hartlepool as much as they wanted to see him in the Cabinet. 'Indeed they do not think I should have left.' This was not making progress. When Anji suggested he did back-bench committee work, and Philip said other MPs found it interesting and satisfying, he said the vast bulk were bored out of their skulls. He then said, not really meaning it and exaggerating to make a point, 'If I can't come back and make a difference, then I may as well take my own life.' 'The Third Way,' I said, and he laughed, but we were getting nowhere. He then turned on Anji in particular, said she did not have his interests at heart and we were all just trying to find ways of keeping him out. 'Anji, if you want me to be a vegetable, to just vegetate, well I won't.'

He said he was fed up with being talked about, now he intended to do the talking, to let people see him as he is. We went on for an hour, by the end of which all we had concluded was that we all wanted him to make a comeback – apart from Ben – but there was little or no agreement about how to lay the ground for that. He had lost weight, as had Ben, and at times he looked close to the edge. Later he called Fiona and said he would like to come round and see us on Saturday. TB's worry was that he was incapable of living without the limelight. He couldn't do without it. He said he was getting fed up with the lot of them. There was too much to do without having to worry about all this the whole time. We had left the meeting, particularly Anji, in a state of some agitation. I had tried to be conciliatory re the book, though I was unconvinced it was a good idea, and TB was sure it was a bad idea. There was a bit of a feeling around, articulated by Peter Hyman, that if he was not careful, Peter was finished.

Friday, January 15

I had a session with Don Macintyre re his book on Peter. He didn't take much to my suggested title, 'Remaindered'. Peter was convinced Don had loads of bad stuff, but I had no sense of that from Don. He felt the [Paul] Routledge book had largely been a cuttings job, but with one big story in it, which is what these instant books were about. I was slowly getting a grip of the SCU and establishing its role through Whitehall in terms of reordering events. We were getting OK coverage on Education Action Zones but by the end of the day the political reporters had taken over from the education correspondents, so it became yet another 'Blair tries to draw the line under recent troubles', cue a run through all the recent troubles. Very irritating. GB called to say we should try to get up the working families tax credit over the weekend. He said Charlie was not planning to do much media, which I didn't believe. I had a meeting on the work I wanted done on a new strategy for the ethnic minority media. Talking to the two black guys in South Africa made me realise we were still far too driven by the male, middle-class Westminster lobby, and needed to define proper strategies for the non-news media and the various growing media out there. We were due to go to one of Michael Levy's Friday night dinners, which he took really seriously, prayers, skull-caps all round. There was lots of Peter talk inevitably, which I tried to stay out of, but generally it was all just chit chat. I was sitting next to Marianna [Hildyard], who is great fun and a breath of normal personology.

Saturday, January 16

Peter M and Ben W-P came round for dinner. Peter was much calmer than on Thursday, said that Anji had just rubbed him up the wrong way. She was rather clumsily putting what TB clearly wanted, but without the subtlety needed. He said he was in no doubt he should come back, because he saw politics as a vocation. He could not see himself doing anything else. Re the book idea, I said I could see no circumstances in which it wasn't seen as a bit of a problem. Was he doing it for money, therapy or as part of the comeback strategy? He had to be clear about its purpose. He said it was all three. He was going to sell the house, but he needed to live somewhere and needed £100k for a flat. It would also be therapeutic and allow him to sort out his mind and his political thinking, and it would allow him to maintain a proper political profile.

I said if he did a book that was self-indulgent, or too controversial and provocative, there was a danger it would kill him in the party. He would not be able to control how it was perceived as easily as he might think. He said he would listen to advice on the book, but he had to do something to fill his time. He could not vegetate. Ben wanted him to quit altogether but that was clearly a non-starter as far as Peter was concerned. Fiona asked if he thought he could change his ways. The answer suggested not – he said he was confident party and public felt he was different and special, lots of them thought it was wrong he resigned and they want him back. He denied leading the glamorous social life the press chronicled and of which we so obviously disapproved. The friendliness to GB on the day of the resignation had now totally gone.

He said he felt very bitter about him, basically blamed him for his downfall, and felt the sudden co-operation with TB was short term and totally tactical. He had felt for a long time GB wanted to force TB to choose one out of Peter M/GB, and he had chosen GB. GB had created the circumstances where that was the obvious choice. I said he had to accept some responsibility for that too. He was now worried that TB had made that choice fundamentally, that he was in the process of managing Peter to keep him sweet and quiet, but he was not as committed to a comeback as he said. He stayed till 11.30, and I forgot to tell him that TB wanted to see him tomorrow evening. He was on much better form than on Thursday, more relaxed and less aggrieved but it was not going to be easy. He said he knew TB was ruthless and that was worrying him.

Sunday, January 17

TB called early and I briefed him on last night, said Peter was much more open to proper advice, provided he was sure it was as much about his interests as TB's or the government's. TB said he DID want to get him back but he had to be prepared to listen to advice, and not go off in a fit every time anyone suggested something he disagreed with. He disagreed with Peter's analysis that the PLP wanted him back fairly soon. The PLP were pretty fed up with Peter and GB at the moment, and they hated the infighting.

Whelan did *Frost*, all cheeky chappy, very dubious re when he first knew about the loan, having another dig at me re friendship with Alex Ferguson, generally mixing it. The Sundays were not a disaster but there was a definite change in tone and tenor. I watched *On the Record* for once, and thought Jack S did well. The *Sunday Times* had stuff on Jack C's expenses. This would be the latest thing to do us in, and get away from policy. The Cabinet Office were dreadfully slow getting any rebuttal together and I had to kick arse later and finally got a line-by-line rebuttal worth using. Robin Mountfield [permanent secretary, Office of Public Service] said Jack C did constantly put them under pressure to get the expensive office options.

Monday, January 18

At the office meeting, TB was back asking why we were not doing better on delivery. I was back asking why it was taking so long to get agreed branding for new government projects, which would at least show the public new school and hospital buildings had something to do with government investment going in. These things took a fucking age to penetrate the cross-departmental jealousies and dysfunction-alities, and all the bollocks about propriety and politics. What on earth is the problem in putting up a board saying this school is being built by x with money from y? And Christ knows how many different arms of government would be commissioning different reports and ideas and designs for something I could do in five minutes.

TB said there was too much anti-GB chatter around the building which then emanated out in briefings and mood. He wanted weekly TB/GB team meetings to stay on a common agenda. The *Sun* splashed, accurately, on nurses' pay. The *Telegraph* led on 10p tax rate. I had no idea where these leaks were coming from, but we had to get a grip. There were too many people just talking for the sake of being seen to know what was going on. Vanity publishing. We had to use Whelan's departure to get more discipline injected. The eleven o'clock was low-key, a bit of heat on Jack C, who had come to see me earlier to go through the stuff on his expenses. He seemed pretty relaxed about it, saying he had no idea where it was coming from.

Kosovo was the main story of the day, with RC doing a statement and TB took a big meeting on it. They agreed we could not bomb at the moment because there was no political process and the KLA [Kosovo Liberation Army] were not much better than the Serbs, and just looking to NATO to be their defence arm and bomb Milosevic for them. George Robertson said there was a growing overstretch problem, with twenty-seven per cent of the army currently involved in conflict somewhere. The US are at eleven per cent. Guthrie said it would be difficult to sustain a long-term UK ground troop commitment if we ever get to that. The US are in any event opposed to ground troops, GR said. He said SACEUR [Supreme Allied Commander in Europe, General Wesley Clark] blamed everything on the Serbs. Guthrie said he didn't mention the Kosovars once when he briefed the NAC [North Atlantic Council] yesterday. TB said everyone accepts Milosevic is a dreadful man, but if we bomb as things stand, what is the process we are trying to bring about? If the KLA move back in and take over, what then?

TB was seeing the Garvaghy Road Residents' Association which had a big media crowd outside. I left early to go to Edgware with Philip who thought I should see for myself the way the mood had changed in the focus groups. It was very depressing, little awareness of delivery, in one group of eight Tory–Lab switchers, only two said they would definitely vote for us. Among the women, it was three out of eight. There had definitely been a turn for the worse. The NHS and asylum seekers were problems. They had lots of good things to say about Tony but did not warm to the government. But when Philip asked if TB was more like Major or Thatcher as a leader, they said Major, which is a problem. Mo, Blunkett and Straw were the only others seen in anything like a favourable light.

They didn't believe waiting lists were falling, were totally ignorant of child benefit increases and only just aware of the minimum wage. They were pro Clinton but anti TB being too close to him. What had happened was that they had stopped giving us the benefit of any doubt. That was in part poor perceptions of delivery, plus the media shift. There was one woman who said she hated us, could not understand why she voted for us, would never vote again. A lot of this was operating at an emotional level. When Philip probed, she had virtually no complaints at all. It was probably something in her own life that had made her anti everything. It was weird and all a bit worrying. People take the piss out of these focus groups – I used to – but I always get something out of them, this time confirmation the mood change was real, and some insight into how. We had to get back on their side, focused on their priorities, and making a difference.

Tuesday, January 19
I got a letter from Eric Jacobs [journalist and biographer] saying he was going to write a book about me, and would I co-operate? No. I was in early to get TB out and ready to leave for Liverpool Street with DB for a school visit. I told him about last night's dreadful

groups and he was sure it was all about health. He was less worried than I about the 'more Major than Thatcher' line, just felt we were going through a down phase. I had found the whole thing depressing, particularly the phenomenal ignorance about what we were doing. They were being fed a diet of shit by the press, and eating it. He said we were always going to be in this position two years in. A lot of the change has yet to show through in results. The visit went fine, the school was good.

TB was dealing with Sierra Leone on the way back, then in for a meeting on Scotland, and fretting re the Lords. We were about to announce that the public could nominate people for peerages. The *Sun* were on to the fact that [Prince] Andrew and Fergie [Duchess of York, Andrew's former wife] were at Chequers at the weekend but then, oddly, Trevor Kavanagh asked if Peter M was there and had they been for a swim? No and no. Irwin [Stelzer] told TB Kavanagh was trying the whole time to turn the *Sun* back to the Tories. I had a meeting with Saatchis [advertising agency] and Frank D re the nurses ad campaign. The idea was a young girl, clearly ill, ninety seconds into camera, with all the hospital noises around. It was clever but I wasn't sure it would have real impact in recruitment terms. I said I wanted them tested with real nurses. Pete Gatley [advertising art director] sent in a good idea for local election posters – go back to the bright colours and put up facts of delivery. He said he felt duty bound to explain why he left BMP [advertising agency]. Basically that he didn't find it creative, and he was kind enough to say I was a better copywriter than the whole army of people there.

Wednesday, January 20

For PMQs, we thought Hague would do health, Kosovo or maybe Jack C's expenses, which hadn't really taken off. In the end he did Northern Ireland in a way that was very tricky for us re prisoner release. At the 11, I didn't go overboard on Lords detail. I chaired a forward planning meeting, and though the process was improving, we were still struggling to drive themes through events. Departments were not on to delivery with the urgency we wanted. They still measure news in terms of policy announcements, not monitoring and driving change and progress. Over lunch I worked on the Lords document. I didn't feel I was on top of the detail at the moment.

At 2.30 GB called to say he wanted to announce John Kingman as new head of press, but hold open the option of a political appointment later. TB spoke to him and said it was a mistake. He needed his media act cleaned up and if he made something of that today, people would say he had learned nothing and not changed. It got a bit ratty and GB told him to grow up – probably because TB had been saying the same to him, more politely, in recent days. I saw GB as TB went into the chamber and he said it was important it was not spun as anti him. I said why on earth would we?

PMQs was OK, and TB on good form, but Hague got very close to busting bipartisanship on N Ireland. TB said afterwards he felt he was getting more into his stride. TB was also sure Hague was in trouble, and that the skids were possibly under him. I did a line on Paddy A's standing-down announcement, which we'd managed to keep quiet. I sent him over the draft TB words and he was happy enough. Only TB, Jonathan and I had known inside Number 10 so it was a bit of an 'oo-er' moment when the Press Association snapped it. TB was keen for the sense to go out there that Lib-Lab co-operation would not go into reverse. It got far bigger coverage than I predicted all day but then Paddy always said I underestimated the importance of the Libs.

Thursday, January 21

There was huge coverage of Paddy Ashdown stepping down and a lot of 'end of Lib-Lab' speculation, which TB didn't like. We arranged for him to do a doorstep as he arrived for the volunteering speech. He said people underestimated what a serious figure he was, how popular he was, what a good communicator, and he was sure any successor would realise party and public wanted a more mature politics.

At Cabinet, they went over Kosovo, Lords and general politics, with a bit on the Libs. JP kicked it off with a laugh by suggesting we had a minute's silence for Paddy's career. Jack S was reasonably positive re the Libs, which was a surprise. But one or two, e.g. Dobson and Blunkett, said people were not sure what the purpose of the Libs' strategy was, and David was unsure our people meant it when they said they wanted a new politics. Robin was unbelievably pompous and overbearing when he went through Kosovo, but good on substance. TB said the situation was serious, RC that it was 'very grave'. War crimes were being committed. There was a humanitarian crisis. Everyone including the Russians was united against Milosevic.

I left with TB for the European Publishers' Conference lunch. TB and I were seated either side of Murdoch and as the lunch wore on, he [Murdoch] got more and more right wing – tax, competition, BBC, Europe, pretty full-on mode come the end. I was called out halfway by GB. The *Daily Express* in Scotland had a story that the SNP were planning to announce a 1p tax rise for transport. Helen [Liddell] wasn't keen to go on it but GB felt we should motor. I agreed, felt it could be the turning point that allowed us to put real heat on the nationalists. We agreed we should do a press conference on it. Helen felt we risked giving too much profile to them. I called Donald D at the airport. 'I hear it's you agitating for a press conference,' he said. I said it was me, TB and GB and they ought to listen. It was ridiculous that it took Gordon and me several calls to persuade people of the blindingly obvious – that the SNP had exposed a flank and we had to make them feel the pain.

The lunch and TB's Q&A were OK. I don't think Murdoch much enjoys these big shindigs, even if he is the main man among them all. I noticed how quietly he talks when he is in little groups. I couldn't decide whether it was shyness, boredom or a way of forcing them to listen hard. We got back for the first of the TB/GB team meetings – TB, GB, Jonathan, SM, AC, DM, AH, Ed Balls, Ed Miliband, Sue Nye. There was a fair amount of false bonhomie which I suppose was marginally better than tension. GB was currently determined to be co-operative. We agreed we had to establish the idea of two tough years as a necessary foundation for delivery. We agreed we should be doing more to define the Tories as being more Thatcherite than Thatcher. It was a perfectly good meeting, far better mood than of late, but I doubted it would last. I did the four o'clock with Margaret B. I tried to get her wound up to weigh in against the SNP, but she was pretty half-hearted about it. In the afternoon, the story about Peter M maybe helping the ANC came out. Peter called and said 'Why can't they just leave me alone?' TB and GB had dinner with Murdoch, Les Hinton and Irwin Stelzer. The idea was to try to coax them into a less anti-European position, but when TB called later, he said it had been a bit small-talky and when they did get to Europe, he quickly realised it was pointless because Murdoch's position was so fixed and OTT. Murdoch said at one point he thought Britain could be like Switzerland. It was faintly obscene that we even had to worry what they thought, but we had to do what we could to get a better debate going on Europe. TB said he was 'really irritated' at the idea of Murdoch comparing Britain to Switzerland.

Friday, January 22

The *Guardian* ran a story, briefed we think by Andrew Mackinlay [Labour MP], that TB told the parliamentary committee [of the PLP] he would consult re any further advance on Lib-Labbery. The tone was that he was in retreat, so I put together a line to correct it. I saw him in the flat and we agreed I would brief the Sundays he was asking

Jack C and Alan Beith [Lib Dem deputy leader] to agree new areas for co-operation. He said last night's dinner had been disappointing and irritating. We had a *Mirror* interview, which Piers Morgan agreed in advance would be policy-based, but needless to say was peppered with questions that ranged from trite and trivial to stupid. I took the afternoon off to watch Rory and Calum playing football in Stepney. They lost, and at the end I was harangued by the dad of one of the other team's players, saying Labour had done nothing for the poor and he would never vote for us again. He looked and sounded like a Trot, and I asked him if he ever had voted for us.

Saturday, January 23

Lots of post-Ashdownery, and people making up stories about who we fancied as successor. The only work I did was a letter to Peter Wright [editor, *Mail on Sunday*], copied to the PCC, re a story they were chasing about Kathryn [Blair].[1] It was always the fucking *Mail on Sunday* who were trying to get into the kids.

Sunday, January 24

TB called as I was watching Hague on *Frost*, who also had Paddy on, and also did a very tough interview with Margaret Cook. Hague was pretty useless, though he had a good crack about TB being the opposite of Magnus Magnusson – 'I've started but I don't know how to finish.' TB was livid at the *Mail* doing Kathryn. 'I have those buggers in my sights, Mr Dacre and his big salary and his kids at Eton trying to lecture me about my kids.' I spoke to Cherie as well and agreed the PCC was the only route, but it was basically a tool of the press. But I briefed fairly heavily and was confident there would be basic public support for us going after them whenever they went for the kids.

TB was getting more and more concerned re delivery, particularly health, and felt Frank D just didn't have the drive or the zeal to make a difference. He said JP got oversensitive every time TB tried to make inroads on transport policy, but it needed a total sort out. Welfare to work was working, he thought. He was still not happy the office was functioning as it should. JP called, sounded very pissed off and I had to cheer him up a bit. He was very grungy re the Libs and felt TB and Paddy had cooked up some kind of deal about Cabinet jobs in the future.

[1] The story claimed that Kathryn, then ten, had received preferential treatment in the Blairs' choice of school, the Sacred Heart Catholic High School for Girls in Hammersmith. The Press Complaints Commission upheld the complaint by the Blairs against the *Mail on Sunday*.

Monday, January 25

Perfectly straight coverage for the PCC complaint. Only the *Sun* had a critical editorial. TB saw [Lord] Rothermere at [the late Lord Rothermere] Vere's memorial and he said he was appalled and embarrassed. At the office meeting, we were back on banging about delivery, going over various structural ideas for change that might help. PH had done a couple of notes basing a campaign on the notion of how we were making a difference. TB's concern was as to whether we really were, and he was lacking confidence in departments to make a difference, or tell us how it was being done. PG said when people listed our achievements they tended to be foreign or constitutional. We lacked the big symbolic changes to people's everyday lives. TB felt recent events had knocked people's confidence in us and they were denying us the benefit of the doubt.

Jonathan and David M felt the PCC re Kathryn was a mistake because it just drew more attention to the issue. Philip and Anji felt we had to take these fuckers on and make sure the public knew what they were about. I really wanted to go to war on the *Mail*, which is a poison in our national life, but TB was nervous about it. He said we had to be sure where it was going to end. I spent a lot of the day working on our submission to the PCC, based on speaking to CB and the head of Sacred Heart. She said the people quoted in the story as attacking TB were not even practising Catholics and one had not been to church at all. TB was still nervous though. 'We'd better win, or we are wrecked with these people.'

The *Mail* splash today was another grotesque distortion on the NHS. PG and Stan Greenberg came in at 2. Our lead and party ID were stable but we were being hit re sleaze and division. Hague was in the toilet. Stan felt overall we were in OK shape but vulnerable on delivery. Media-wise, it confirmed me in the view we had to ensure interviews were delivery-focused. I played the pipes at the Burns night do which was fine. I also set up a survey of editors' salaries and lifestyles and got Mike Foster [Labour MP] to front it, which was brave of him.

Tuesday, January 26

Fiona had to go to Liverpool so I stayed home late and took the kids to school, and was sorely tempted to stay home all day. I got in to finish TB's speech to Charter Mark [public service] award winners which took off as a message about pay not being the only thing that draws people into the public sector. Some of the media spun it, somehow, as an attack on the nurses over their pay claim. Alex [Ferguson] called and we discussed how I should handle the two or three book projects that appeared to be under way about me. He felt total non co-operation, including telling friends not to co-operate, without it ever being said that was the approach.

I had meetings with Al Gore's advance people either side of a very jolly lunch with David Frost at Le Caprice. He went for the joint TB/Gore interview idea, but then Barney [Jones] came on saying it was a problem as TB had been on so recently. The Gore people were fine, though less talented and less fun than Clinton's people, and a tiny bit Mormonic. They agreed to a New Deal event as part of the visit to Number 10, so we set in train plans to get some real New Dealers in. Guy Black [director, PCC] called, saying he felt we could get the *Mail on Sunday* on Clause 1 [accuracy] as well as the areas we had gone for. I went to a meeting with TB and GB, again focusing on how to get up a sense of delivery and direction. TB was veering to the view that maybe this is just what happens midterm, that there is a rhythm to it you can do very little about.

Peter Hyman went to a meeting at Health on the nurse recruitment ad campaign. The focus groups showed that the ones we are aiming at – former nurses we wanted back – didn't like any sense that pay would be the big attraction, so we reworked the script accordingly. I still doubted the concept was powerful enough as a direct recruiter but we agreed to give it a go. I got back to rewrite Mo's article on prisoner release for the *Telegraph*, which was tricky. Jonathan and I were engaged in the latest skirmish with Richard Wilson who felt I should not be going to a PES event in Vienna. Our argument is that there will be government-to-government, TB-to-other-PMs work going on, and it is totally justifiable.

I went to dinner at the French Embassy, hosted by their ambassador. John Birt warned me that the press were trying to build me up to become a big target to bring down. I think I had worked that one out but he had a good common-sense feel for it. Peter M was there and seemed reasonably happy. Christina Odone [deputy editor, *New Statesman*], Terence Conran [designer and restaurateur], a woman called Vicki, who I was mildly flirting with until she told me her kids were at Marlborough [College, public school]. It's a killer for me, can't stand private schools, but even worse are the people who use them. Richard Branson was there, who I noticed didn't take kindly to anyone making anything like a joke at his expense. I think the cool, laid-back image was all a bit spray-on. I didn't take to him really.

On the other side I had Arsène Wenger [Arsenal FC manager], who was clever and quite charming, but I think may have known of my friendship with Alex F, and was maybe a bit cool as a result. He likes living here, loves the football and clearly loves his job, but hates our press. I tried to enlist him in the battle against them, but he felt it was pointless, that we would never change it, that there is something in our psyche that wants to build up and do down and constantly deprecate and gossip.

Wednesday, January 27

Northern Ireland was the main story and Hague was diddling again, really trying to crank it up, and we decided to up the ante a little by saying he was being dragged into this by [Gregor] Mackay. The other main story was the draft bill on the Food Standards Agency, which MAFF totally fucked up, somehow managing to make the story the £90 flat charge on food businesses, immediately labelled a poll tax on food. TB spent much of the morning preparing for a PMQs attack on health which never came. I finalised our case to the PCC. Frank D had been done over by the *Mail on Sunday* re some visit to Barbados and I had the idea of doing something public comparing his earnings to Dacre's. Frank was initially keen, then cautious. TB felt it was a declaration of war and if we were going to do that we needed to be clear where we were ending.

I had a meeting with John Kingman, who seemed OK, but he said that already it was clear GB would always talk to Ed Balls before him. I said he needed to get in with GB, build up his confidence in him, and whatever help we could give, we would. Barney Jones came back with a firm no on a Gore/TB joint interview, so we took it to a delighted Adam Boulton instead. PMQs was dominated by Northern Ireland and the Tories got perilously close to ending bipartisanship. TB saw Hague afterwards and Jonathan said he looked pretty low. His confidence was not good. We then did a TB presentation for the regionals on the New Deal and how it was working area by area, which was strong, and would carry in all of them. Bradders [David Bradshaw] had done a localised TB article for all of them. We needed to do a lot more of these kinds of briefings and break open the bollocks of the lobby. It all went well and then even better when, totally unexpected, Paul McCartney popped his head round the door of the Cabinet Room. He was in seeing CB and Fiona about a charity event. He was funny and charming and the guy from the *Liverpool Daily Post* thought he had died and gone to heaven.

Thursday, January 28

We laid the ground pretty well for the Fairness at Work Bill, with a lot of the focus on family-friendly policy, less on the union recognition issues. PG called from Scotland, said last night's groups up there were dire. He felt it was possible we could lose [the Scottish elections] and we had to take it over. The Scots had got themselves into a mindset that 'London Labour' and TB were a problem. On the contrary, he felt unless TB got more involved, we were in trouble. They were scathing about virtually everyone else, with some making an exception for Gordon. I spoke to Douglas Alexander to get his feel for it. We agreed we should get into the theme of divorce, that ultimately however much the Scots moaned about London, they did not want the divorce from the rest of the UK that the SNP represented.

Cabinet went over pay, Kosovo, NI and Iraq. TB stopped any discussion of Cabinet pay. He and GB stressed that the message on pay must be linked to reform and modernisation. We wanted results, and extra pay per se was not a result. Nurses were doing best, so DB pitched in again for teachers. Kosovo was getting heavier by the day. RC briefed on that. The North Atlantic Council would meet on Friday and trigger the ACTORD [activation orders for air strikes]. He and [Javier] Solana would go to Belgrade to deliver the message. He said we had to perform a very delicate balancing act between warning of military action as a threat and at the same time not having to use it. On NI, TB said the Tory shift was really unhelpful. Prisoner release was difficult and unpopular and it made it harder for the Unionists to move. The more the Tories made it an issue the harder it was. If the Tories move to the right of the UUs, it will be very hard for Trimble, who has a tough enough time as it is. At the 11.30, I briefed on pay, confirming that the rises [between 3.5 and 4 per cent for 1.25 million public sector workers] would not be phased. GB had warned there may be inflationary consequences but by and large he was happy and the coverage came out fine. After a very long eleven o'clock, I had a meeting with women Asian journalists, then another meeting on nurses' pay.

Frank and I agreed the text of a letter to Dacre, which signalled we may go after him on his own pay, etc. It would be interesting to see what reaction we got. PG had depressed TB re Scotland and he was really starting to agitate about it. Chirac was in at 7 and in his usual form. John Holmes and Jean-David Levitte [Chirac adviser] had agreed a statement on Kosovo which mentioned ground forces for the first time, designed to raise the pressure. Earlier, Michael Levy came to see me, very touchy-feely and conspiratorial, said he thought 'Wilson is trying to dick you', that he wanted to do me in to leave me weakened and chastened and bolster his own position with TB. I wasn't wholly convinced, though I knew he was on my case the whole time, and in some respects right to be. Michael had also been talking to Peter M, who had announced today he was selling the house.

Friday, January 29

TB, the one who had decided we ought to go to Vienna for the PES, now couldn't understand why we were going. Viktor Klima was desperate for him to go because so few of the big guys were there. Kosovo was big news in advance of the statement. Frank D was out and about on the NHS bill. Charles and Camilla [his long-time girl-friend] being seen out together last night was the main story of the day. I briefed Godric who was doing the Sundays while I was away. He was beginning to hate them as much as I do. We went out in a small, uncomfortable plane. TB was telling us about his conversation with JP re the Libs and his calling Menzies Campbell 'Campus Mingie' and how TB wanted to put Campus Mingie in the Cabinet.

Klima greeted TB, really keen to be filmed with him. TB did a clip on EMU – 'must be accompanied by economic reform' – and on Kosovo, the contact group having done its stuff, which was another step towards intervention. At the lunch, TB looked bored. TB came over and said he would like to boil in oil the person who decided to come to this meeting. I said it was him. In which case I will boil myself, he said. Just as TB was bored, so was I. TB went off to the dinner so Jonathan and I went out with Oakley, Sopel and some of the BBC lot and we had a for once decent discussion about the nature of the press. Oakley was pretty sympathetic really, and had his own worries re the way the political debate was developing. He said the problem was that if specialists were doing policy, all Millbank had left was gossip, analysis and raw politics.

Saturday, January 30

I ballsed up the time difference so got very little sleep. TB, though still joking about boiling in oil, was now saying it had actually been useful to have a proper discussion e.g. with Oskar Lafontaine, [Antonio] Guterres [Portuguese Prime Minister], one or two others. Neil [Kinnock] was urging us to set a date for EMU entry, but TB was pushing back pretty hard, whilst making positive long-term noises. TB had to do a press event with Klima and [Rudolf] Scharping [now German defence minister]. Both were all over him like a rash. 'Dickes Lob' ['big praise'], TB whispered to me as they came off the platform, joking about the smarm strategy we had deployed re Klima's presidency, which TB was convinced got us what we wanted out of the summit and had prompted a 'Dickes Lob' newspaper headline.

We set off for home in a six-seater, cramped to buggery. TB was raving about how much the PES people loved Robin. They thought he was absolutely terrific, and had run rings round them on the PES manifesto. We got back to Number 10 to wait for Al Gore. He arrived late from JP, so TB and CB worked the crowds in the street. Gore arrived, did a bit of glad-handing and we went into TB's room to prepare for the business meeting. He was wearing the most extraordinary boots. He was still a bit wooden, but more relaxed than before, and showed the odd flash of humour, e.g. when I warned him pre-press that there was a situation to be aware of re the Falklands and he said 'Falklands, that's what I have to call the Malvinas, right?' I looked horrified, he started laughing. 'Got you.' Asked by TB what he could say that was helpful, he said Jefferson, Kennedy, Clinton, Gore. He was good on Europe, really pro the argument that Britain strong in Europe was good for the US/UK relationship. The media were in for the business meeting and I thought he did well. We then had a meeting with kids from the New Deal, and once the media were out, he was really relaxed, good with them.

Like Clinton, he was excellent on policy detail and more focused on the ends of policy than the means. We had agreed to do two joint interviews, Sky and CNN, and as with Bill C, Gore was good at taking a brief, wanted to know the goal of the interview and then would go out and deliver. We went over some of the areas that might be tricky – death penalty, Ireland, Falklands – and he was pretty much up to speed. The Boulton interview was good, a mix of the political and personal and I thought both came out well. CNN was almost all Kosovo, with RC out there today. Gore and TB set off for dinner at Chequers. JP, who had been unbelievably status-conscious in the planning of the visit, was going too.

Sunday, January 31

TB said the dinner went really well, that once JP relaxed a bit, they had a great time, the right mix of politics and just letting their hair down. He found Gore more impressive this time, and Gore felt we had pushed the boat out. TB was keen we stay out of the elections when they come, but he felt we had done enough for Al to be a friend for life if he got in. TB's comments about him had seemingly played well. I went with Rory to Charlton vs Man United and had a moment of panic when John Gorman [coach and friend of England manager Glenn Hoddle] sat beside me in the stand. I assumed Hoddle would be with him. The media were desperate to see Hoddle because he was in the middle of a great row about something he was supposed to have said about the disabled.[1]

Monday, February 1

As expected, the *Mail* and the *Sun* were hostile re what we were saying re the press, and the ante would be seen as being upped with TB doing *Richard and Judy* today. We were hoping to get up the nurses' ad campaign, but they were bound to ask him about Hoddle's comments on the disabled, which TB really didn't want to get into at all. I spoke to David Davies [FA] who said he had had the kind of weekend I was always complaining about. My sense of what he was saying was that it was moving to Hoddle going, but it wouldn't be decided till tomorrow. I agreed with TB we would simply say it was being dealt with by the FA, and it all depended on what he actually said.

The interview started on the stories about us taking a new media approach, then a bit of nurses, then Glenn Hoddle's comments on the disabled, where he went a bit further than we had agreed and as far as the press were concerned strayed into 'Hoddle must go' headline territory. I knew as he said it that he had gone further than he wanted and that the last thing he would want to do was fuel a frenzy about Hoddle, but that was what he did. He rowed back a bit by saying Hoddle must be given the chance to put his side of the story, but it was hard to balance it up. When he came off, re the strategy of going on programmes like this rather than the more conventional political outlets, he said 'God, the press will kill us for this.' 'Fuck them,' I said, 'we have to reframe the terms of the debate. They believe that they helped do for Thatcher, did for Major, and that they can do for us, and we have to stop them.'

At the office meeting, the euro was on the agenda again, TB looking to the National Changeover Plan [on how, if it should choose to do so, Britain could join the euro] as the next step forward, and possibly with an indicative date for entry. His basic approach was that we would go in, provided the economics were right, and that we would not go in if they did not take the path of economic reform. He was definitely moving on it but others, mainly DM, PH and I, felt we had not really thought it through. On delivery, he was getting more and more frustrated, not just with the media, who were loath to give any coverage to progress at all, but above all with ministers like FD and

---

[1] Hoddle had been quoted in *The Times* saying disabled people were paying for sins in a previous life.

JP who were not properly communicating a sense of progress and direction.

The *Standard*, predictably, went on 'Hoddle must go, says Blair', so I called Hoddle to say he had said no such thing, and it had been taken out of context. Glenn said he had never said what he was quoted as saying. I spoke to his agent Denis Roach as well, who then went on Sky to say TB had assured Hoddle he was not calling for his sacking. TB was not keen to get too involved, but did not want to pile any more pressure on Hoddle, who he thought was basically a decent bloke. The lobby were also getting agitated re our 'new media strategy'. I made the point that a lot of people were turning off from the Westminster village coverage and we would not be doing our job properly if we didn't try to get our message out to people who were switching off from politics. I said as well that they could give it but they couldn't take it and they better get used to us drawing attention to the reality of modern political coverage. I pointed out that a fifty per cent fall in youth unemployment did not make a line in the national press, so forgive us if we tried to get it covered elsewhere. When did you ever feature people benefiting from the minimum wage or the WFTC [working families tax credit]? Never. Bevins was about the only one who openly agreed.

Tuesday, February 2

Comment on TB was critical, feeling he should have kept out of it. I sent the full transcript to Hoddle last night so that he could see the full context, but Godric had a pretty torrid time at the 11. Also, Tony Banks had said Hoddle's position was untenable, and the feeling was TB had given him licence to get involved, and raise the pressure. I called Banks in Lausanne and said no more interviews. I met up with TB at Paddington, then we waited for Wim Kok. They did a bit of football talk, then on to EMU, with TB saying, as he had to Lafontaine, that we were moving in that direction. They had a good run round the block on Agenda 2000, and economic reform. The Hoddle situation was still big, and TB provoking comment. John and I had a session with him saying he should be saying he wished he had said nothing, that he is PM not head of the FA but the problem was he was engaged and it was hard to disengage. The atmospherics with Kok were good. I liked him, very blunt and straight-talking and he had a sharp sense of humour. We had to be careful re Hoddle banter though, because I think I read somewhere Kok has a disabled daughter.

Kok asked what I was in a previous life. I said I was a German shepherd. I was beginning to feel sorry for Hoddle, as the firestorm continued on the media, and with no real understanding yet as to what if anything he actually said. On the way to Wales, I was gently ribbing TB, suggesting his intervention against another Christian had not been very Christian. TB did a stack of interviews. The tone of all the questioning was that Alun Michael was heading for a disaster [government nominee for first minister of the Welsh Assembly, Michael was not popular in the principality]. We launched a poster campaign and then got the train back, with TB pretty worried re the Alun M campaign. David Davies called to say Hoddle would be gone by 7. We had a few calls saying TB should never have got involved, which was right. Jim White of the *Guardian* was suggesting I was engineering Hoddle's downfall. Twat.

Wednesday, February 3

I had a sleepless night. Fiona woke up at 5 and said not to worry, but I felt I had overcooked the row with the press, and the new media strategy, and that the overblowing of TB's comments re Hoddle was a kind of revenge. Peter M called, said I should put it behind me, but he was unsure where we were heading with our media strategy. He was sure we were right to take them on, but what was the endgame? TB felt wretched that he was in the story, let alone the thought he had done for Hoddle, and kicked him when he was down. So we were both very down when we were preparing for PMQs. At 9.30, Hilary Coffman and I met Wakeham and Guy Black re the PCC complaint. Wakeham said he wanted to make it stick but he felt we were on stronger ground re accuracy than going on the clause re children. If we could establish the story was inaccurate, it would make the wrongdoing of intrusion worse. You always had to be very careful with Wakeham, but he may well be right. I didn't like his 'fallback' idea of an article to rebut. It needed to be accepted the story was wrong. We agreed the PCC should speak to the headteacher, she would confirm the admissions policy was applied fairly, that the detail of the parents' complaints was wrong. I agreed to go on accuracy as well. At the 11, I closed down the Hoddle story OK, even though they said we were retreating a bit, which TB didn't mind. Hague was useless and silly, and the first question – who did TB think would be next England manager – left people bemused.

Thursday, February 4

Apart from the *Mirror*, we didn't get too badly hit re Hoddle, but the truth was we were saved by Hague being so dreadful. TB was still feeling a bit raw and we were both pissed off at having handled it badly. I had a meeting with Donald Dewar pre his TV debate with Alex Salmond. Salmond was vulnerable to a sense of being slippery. I suggested to DD he find an opportunity to say at one point 'You are not being honest, Alex,' but DD, as ever with anything involving risk or conflict, was ultra cautious and reluctant. At Cabinet, DD gave a pretty downbeat assessment of the situation, despite a very good poll for us today, at the end of which TB said 'For those of you who don't know Donald, that was a very rosy assessment for him.' DD said the SNP were doing well to establish themselves as 'Scotland's party'. There was a lot of cynicism about politics generally. And we had suffered a few self-inflicted wounds. Having said that, the polls were moving our way and support for independence was falling. Our aim was to put over the cost of separatism. TB then went over pretty much the same ground, but far more clearly and effectively.

The Cabinet went over Iraq, Kosovo and the legislative programme. RC said both the UNSC and the NAC had endorsed our approach re Kosovo. TB said things were looking worse not better. Interest rates were cut by 0.5 per cent and I had a real argument with GB and Ed B who didn't want anyone to go up on it – least of all TB. The problem then, for something as important as this, was that the move was defined largely by our opponents. GB said it was just good news that would speak for itself, but that was ridiculous. These things can always be presented in different ways, and if we leave the field, others will define it negatively.

We were also arguing re EMU, over the extent to which the changeover plan on EMU should be presented as a major move towards it. TB was still muttering about setting a date, which most of us felt we were not ready to do. PG did groups tonight. People did not blame TB at all re Hoddle, and thought it unfair he was being maligned over it. DD did well in his debate with Salmond. Then news came through that King Hussein [of Jordan] was flying home to die, and as he would be buried soon after, we had to decide quickly whether TB would go. Most of the big cheeses were intending to go, so he would probably have to. He spoke to Clinton re Kosovo, and the tone of both was much much closer to military action being when, not if.

Friday, February 5

DD's debate with Salmond had gone well, which was a good context for TB's visit there today. Donald had finally gone for the jugular, and showed some real leadership. Pat [McFadden] had done a good draft speech for TB's Q&A in Glasgow, which we finalised on the plane.

Interest rates got good coverage and there was a lot of 'Hague is useless' around the place. We arrived in Glasgow and went straight to the College of Music and Drama, where we were unveiling a poster on the theme of divorce, Scotland divorcing from the rest of the UK, so we could start to put over the cost of separation. I watched the press as it was unveiled and I could see beneath the usual cynicism a few nodding heads. It would definitely be a strategic hit and I was confident the Nats would not respond well.

TB did a good mix of Nat-bashing and positive vision stuff. His best answer, which was clipped on the news, came when he was forced to defend the Nat-bashing and he really got going on what a threat to the country they were. He also got a good question from a bloke who said could he make sure Cherie never changes the colour of the loo paper in Number 10 – because if she did, it would get more coverage in papers like the *Mail* and the *Telegraph* than anything the government did. There were still rumblings through the press about my recent attacks on them, but I still felt I was ahead on points, and the fact of that question suggested it was getting through to the public too. TB had a stack of Scots interviews to do, which went fine, and he said he felt totally confident in the argument. We visited the Western Infirmary where TB got a very tough time from a group of nurses. One or two were clearly political activists, but even accounting for that, it was a heavy and aggressive scene. The visit as a whole felt better than last time, though the media up there was still a problem and DD and Co. hadn't really worked out how to deal with it.

Back at the office, I called in Bradders [David Bradshaw] and Siobhan [Kenny] who I knew were unhappy at my being open about our media strategy, feeling it undermined the sincerity of the approach to the non-news media. I explained it was a risk but one worth taking, because we had to have some sense in the public of what the media in Westminster was like. King Hussein was the main story all day and we were still on standby, black ties packed, to go to Jordan for the funeral. I went to the Ivy for one of the farewells to Syd [Young, former *Mirror* colleague]. He got a good turnout, including Mike Molloy, Richard Stott, Bill Hagerty [all former Mirror Group editors], and loads of the reporters and execs from my time there. Piers Morgan made a very funny speech about how crap the *Mirror* was since he took over – light, trite and shite.

Saturday, February 6

It was obvious that Jordan was just being shaped to get used to the notion of the King being dead, so we were pretty sure we would be heading there soon. The only domestic story I got involved in was some bizarre thing about Chris Woodhead of Ofsted who said at a seminar that it could be 'educative' for teachers to have relationships with pupils. The *Indy* led on it, others followed, and TB and DB were both a bit alarmed about it. I spoke to Woodhead, who I found generally very creepy. He agreed to a line that he regretted his choice of words, he supported our plans to deal with this and of course such relationships were wrong, and in the media world people in positions like his had to be careful how they expressed themselves. It had the potential to go quite big. He said he would try to calm it down in interviews. DB was having to swallow his loathing of him to express general support. I agreed the line with Woodhead, who had the added problem in this of stories claiming he had a relationship with someone who was once a pupil.[1] Peter M and the Stotts came round for a very nice dinner. Peter was a lot more relaxed, and Stott was in any event puncturing his pomposity and making sure he didn't get too la-di-da.

Sunday, February 7

Woodhead did OK on *GMTV* – apologised, good tone. But what the fuck had he said it for in the first place? There was something about him I really didn't like and I could not fathom TB's support for him. TB called to say it was about to be announced officially King Hussein was dead. We were taking Hague, [Sebastian] Coe [Hague's chief of staff, former athlete] and Ashdown out to the funeral with us. JP said 'Keep TB away from Paddy.' The flight out was fine, and I got through a stack of work, including the speech I was doing to a BBC seminar on Tuesday, which I had to get right. TB was reading through the GM papers [on the genetically modified food question] he had asked for, and getting more and more agitato re the Opposition. Derek Plumbly [FCO Middle East director] briefed TB, Hague and Paddy over dinner re what was likely to happen in Jordan. Hague looked very low and out of place. I could tell his confidence was a bit down and ended up feeling a bit sorry for him. I could remember from opposition what a pain these 'tag-on' events were as well, but he seemed particularly down. At one point, when Paddy was talking to TB I thought I should make sure Hague got the chance to see him too if he wanted, but

[1] Claims that Chief Inspector of Schools Woodhead had a relationship with a schoolgirl when a teacher in the mid-1970s were refuted by both, who claimed the relationship had begun only after the girl had left school. This was disputed by friends, colleagues and Woodhead's ex-wife.

went down the plane to find him and Coe, fast asleep. We arrived in Amman, greeted by the PM, straight to the hotel, a bilateral, a doorstep and more interviews. The media were keen to push the line it meant crisis in the Middle East, but TB played it dead straight, said he was confident a post-Hussein Jordan would play the same kind of role. We agreed a statement from DB saying he accepted Woodhead's statement and now move on. TB said it was important to keep Woodhead because 1. he was good at the job, and 2. it was important given where we were with the media that we did not allow them to 'win' a witch-hunt.

Monday, February 8

We were out and about at 8. There was a fair bit of hanging around, and when you saw the list of leaders attending you realised the enormity of the logistical and security effort. We set off for the residence to meet Prince Charles. I thought his suit was a bit light for a funeral. After a bit of small talk he and TB travelled together to what can only be described as a 'holding palace', where we spent two hours just wandering around bumping into people and having a mix of small-talk chats and vaguely useful bilaterals. If a bomb had been dropped on there it would have been quite a hit. Clinton and Chirac on the stairs, TB chatting to them, then the emir of Bahrain, then Crown Prince Abdullah, Crown Prince of Kuwait, then Jimmy Carter dropped by, there with [Gerald] Ford and George Bush [Sr] [former presidents of the USA]. We were one of a tiny number of countries who at least had our own room, and once we settled in there, a succession of people came in for a chat, including the King of Spain and Sultan of Brunei to see Charles. Charles taps his feet on the ground the whole time. He has very stubby fingers, which he is always tapping together, and he is constantly fiddling with his pinkie ring. Hague and Ashdown pretty much stayed in there and Hague looked very fed up. TB wandered around the place now bumping into all sorts – Kok, then [Poul Nyrup] Rasmussen, a proper sit-down chat with Yasser Arafat, who was boasting he had personally stopped two attacks on Israel.

Once the word came to go to pay respects, the atmosphere was almost like kids being let out of school. Clinton said it was like a world leaders' day out. I watched Chirac jostling the whole time, and he clearly understood if he was around BC he was likely to get in a lot of the TV coverage. TB tended to hang back a bit. There was a long rambling queue up to the coffin and when we got to the top of the stairs I realised they were going to usher all of us in there to pay respects, including officials. Hague was hanging back and I grabbed him and pushed him up with TB and Paddy. Partly it was for him, but also the last thing I needed was for me to be in the shot and him out of it. The young king [Abdullah II] and the old crown prince [Hassan bin Talal], who must have spent most of his life thinking he would one day be king,[1] had to stand there and watch delegation after delegation go by. Neither was really allowed to show emotion, other than a certain steely hurt. As we went out, the first people we met were the Israelis – [Ezer] Weizman, [Shimon] Peres [former leader of the Israeli Labor Party], [Binyamin] Netanyahu – which must have pissed a lot of the Arabs off. There was a bit more hanging around as the other leaders paid their respects, then we were corralled again to follow the coffin on a fairly long passage up to the burial. Chirac got himself in pole position next to Bill and some of the others were starting to notice and make little jokes about Chirac's new-found pro-Americanism.

It was a funny mix, the procession of world leaders all showing respect but also working out what they needed to do with the time they had and the access to people it was normally a real hassle to meet, the locals organising it who were just the efficient types you meet all around the world at big events, and a population that was clearly moved and yet also fascinated by the spectacle. I bumped into [Gerhard] Schroeder. *'Wie geht's?'* ['How's it going?'] he asked. *'Es könnte viel besser gehen.'* ['It could be better'] *'Ja, immer.'* ['Yes, always.'] TB had spoken to him a couple of times and felt he was really down, almost beaten. At the mosque, TB had a little chat with [Keizo] Obuchi, then the South Korean prime minister [Kim Jong-pil], a little conflab with Charles, and then on up the winding hill to the mausoleum. The Jordanian security people tried to limit it to one per delegation, but the security people of all the main guys were having none of it and in the end just about everyone went through.

It was warm now, and fairly dusty, and the combined noise from the feet shuffling along was fairly loud, so people had to raise their voices a little to be heard in the little chats taking place as the snake wound up the hill. Paddy came out at one point and said it was crazy in there. Eventually TB emerged and we walked back to the holding palace, having fixed a session with Chirac. On Kosovo, he was pressing for a new UNSCR, but TB was worried Milosevic would be able to drive a wedge through the process, and we could go on what we had, should that be needed. Chirac's point was not made in a hostile way

[1] Shortly before his death, King Hussein had disinherited his brother, Hassan, in favour of his son, Abdullah.

and there had been a definite improvement in the way TB and JC talked to each other. You had to watch him the whole time but he was becoming easier to read. He had also been waxing lyrical in Portugal seemingly about what a star John Holmes was and how lucky they were to have him.

Prince Charles introduced us to the 'king' of Yugoslavia [Crown Prince Alexander of Yugoslavia], exiled of course, who was giving us his views on Milosevic. Clinton had suggested a bilateral so we went up to the American room, where he was having a nap but his people felt he wouldn't mind being woken up. He was the one most into the whole atmospherics, 'What a day, what an amazing event, how many bilaterals you done, Tony?' kind of thing. We did Kosovo then Ireland, with BC clear the IRA had to decommission real weapons before Trimble should be expected to have Sinn Fein on the executive. He thought it was 'amazing' they would not even think of doing something symbolic. We were called out because we now had a session with the new king, Abdullah, so we walked up the winding hill again, and in for a fairly brief session. The poor guy must be having to do every world leader going, so TB did not stay too long, talked about what a great man his father was, how important Jordan was, and how we would do whatever we could to help. Abdullah was short and stocky, less impressive than his father, but that may just be an age and authority thing. He had a mild twitch, but he definitely had the makings of it and it was easy to see why Hussein had chosen him ahead of his brother, who was looking really hurt and sad.

TB was struck by his chats with Chirac and felt we should start to brief the improvements in the relationship, and get the French press to pick up on TB feeling JC and he were working together well. On the flight home, we got Hague and Paddy to come and have dinner with us. Hague said it had been one of the most surreal days of his life. He struck me as basically a nice and intelligent man but who had got in over his head, surrounded by problems he couldn't resolve, and his confidence was low. Paddy was full of it, had really enjoyed the day and was asking TB for his take on all the characters who had been there. We were late getting out and the RAF told us we would have to land beyond the late-flying threshold. We looked at Hague. 'There will be no complaints from the Opposition,' he said, and laughed. The policy guys later briefed us on Libya. TB asked how Gaddafi stayed in power. 'Terror, a better economy and a pretty useful secret police.' 'Sounds OK,' said TB. Hague laughed, Paddy shook his head. Hague went back to his seat, leaving TB and Paddy to have a bit of a chat on Lib-Lab co-operation, wanting to take it into areas of health, education, pensions. I asked Paddy who would get his job. 'Charles [Kennedy] – it's his to lose,' he said. He said he was a very attractive personality but he could be lazy and foolhardy. He surprised us later on by saying he had kept a diary and he would like to publish it at some point, and would I like to see it? I said I would. He said he had done thirty minutes every day, and that he did it so his grandchildren would know what their grandad did. 'And there's the serialisation,' I said.

Tuesday, February 9

I went in to see TB who was doing the *Jimmy Young Show*. It went OK, though most of the calls in the phone-in were fairly negative. Similarly, the response of *Saga* readers to a piece on TB had been negative. The Foreign Affairs select committee report on Sandline was due and TB was very dismissive, just refusing to take it as seriously as the media were. We bumped into Alan Freeman [veteran disc jockey] on the way out. He said 'Those that can – do. Those that can't – criticise. Keep going.' There was definitely an anti-media feeling out there to be tapped into. The lobby were working themselves into a lather about TB's dismissal of the Sandline report.

I had a meeting with Alan Sugar [businessman] who clearly felt that he was being discriminated against re honours because he was openly supportive and because he was active doing things with GB etc. He saw others getting honours who had done nothing like he had for the British economy. I liked the fact he was so straightforward about it, but said we were not allowed to make promises at all. He said he was just making a point. I was doing my Fabian Society speech on the BBC. I tried to do a proper argument and I felt the MPs in particular latched on to it. Alan Duncan [Conservative MP] said he found himself agreeing with virtually everything but it was hard taking it from me when they knew how I operated. Q&A, and I think the best answer I gave was a defence of politics and politicians. Two-thirds of the points from the floor were direct responses to my speech, and I felt it had been the right thing to take it on in that forum.

I had a cup of tea with Alan Clark back at Number 10. He was in good form, but really down re the Tories. 'It's sooooo nice sitting down and talking to someone successful in a successful organisation,' he said. 'The Tory Party as we know it is dead. You killed it.' He said he knew nobody who thought Hague could win. I said if he positioned himself as an on-your-side leader, sorting out a mad party and making it sane, he could do it. Alan said the problem was every time they tried to camp on new ground, we were there.

We had the farewell dinner for John Holmes, which Sandy Berger flew over for. John was unassuming as ever, but I think even he was moved by TB's speech, which really laid out how important he had been. He said TB, JH, Jonathan and AC would always have the bonding of the Good Friday Agreement days to remember. He spoke with real warmth about John's commitment and expertise. Richard Wilson said to John that he had heard a number of insincere farewell speeches, but that one was as genuine as it got. In *The Times*, Max Beloff [historian and Conservative peer] compared TB to Hitler.

Wednesday, February 10

The *Today* programme had David Hill and Boris Johnson on re my speech yesterday. DH did a great job while Boris was quite funny talking about the dwarves in our grotto who write all these TB articles. But I sensed from Jim Naughtie's questioning that he accepted at least some of the argument I was putting. Annie Stewart, editor of the *Voice*, came in. She said she used to be a secretary at the *Mirror*. She was chippy and spiky and very cynical about our efforts with the ethnic minority media. Kelvin MacKenzie [now chairman of Talk Radio] came in, said he thought we were on track, and he felt I was right to take on the media. He had the idea of TB doing a radio broadcast like the US president and he would run it every week if we produced our own.

We had Amy Allen in, the fourteen-year-old who had been on the *Richard and Judy* phone-in, and agreed she could travel with him to PMQs. TB, Jonathan, John Sawers [new foreign policy adviser] and I met re the [euro] changeover plan. TB wanted to go for it on Feb 22, then have a joint committee with Schroeder on Feb 23 to push the reform agenda. But he wanted it kept very quiet because he may want to pull back from it later. It was not possible to be sure yet. PMQs was OK, then Alistair Darling and I did a joint briefing on welfare. He was superb, the right mix of message and detail, and totally not taking any of their bullshit arguments. Jonathan and I went to the Palace for [Sir Robert] Fellowes' farewell. There was a huge Establishment turnout. I had a longish chat with the Queen re Jordan, and her memories of the King. She was smiling a lot tonight, and seemed genuinely to be enjoying herself. Guthrie and I had a good natter and he was raging against the FCO. Thatcher was there, I had a session with [former Conservative Cabinet minister] Ken Baker, who was as jovial as ever. The speeches were a bit lame and tired, and the all-white Establishmentism of it all was a bit much to bear. But I said to Fellowes as I left that I had always enjoyed working with him, and felt he had always played fair with me, which he had. Tim Allan and Ian Hargreaves [former *Independent* and *New Statesman* editor] were on *Newsnight* re a speech I'd done on the BBC and I thought it went fine. Tim did well, Paxo [Jeremy Paxman] was pretty laid-back about it and Hargreaves was just whining away about me, and I thought came over as a bit bitter, about what I know not.

Thursday, February 11

A meeting with TB, Jonathan and Charlie F, who totally disagreed with my approach to the media, and felt it was unwinnable. Re delivery, Charlie felt that as a government we had not adapted to the fact that departments were their own power bases. They were not jumping when we shouted, unless we shouted really loudly and then they rather resented it. The important thing was having ministers who bought into a Number 10 agenda, and then knew how to drive their departments. He felt DETR was a bit of a disaster area and intended to see JP to say so. TB felt we needed new structures and a team centrally based dedicated to pursuing departments and chasing delivery. TB also felt Richard Wilson needed to be more on the inside track with us. TB felt our overall cause would be helped if he had a better understanding of it.

Cabinet was mainly Kosovo, enlivened by Clare asking how much a military operation would cost. George R said £120m for six months. She said she was being blocked for an extra £20m to help sort the civil war in Sierra Leone. Alan M [Milburn, now chief secretary to the Treasury] and GR stood up for themselves, but she was clearly gearing up for an 'I'm the only one who cares' period (always run alongside an 'I'm the only one who tells the truth' media strategy), and at the end of Cabinet she told Alan he was responsible for children dying and women being mutilated. At one point TB said 'We [i.e. the government] have provided help for the military [in Sierra Leone].' 'No you haven't,' she said. 'We have.' In other words, in her mind DFID was not part of government, but her own thing. GB led a discussion on the economy, and he warned the next few months would be difficult. Gibraltar was a big story again, the Spaniards were going through another angry phase and I had to have a tough line for the 11.

I had lunch with Piers Morgan and Kevin Maguire. Heseltine and [Norman] Fowler [former Conservative Cabinet minister] were at the next table, which allowed for a bit of friendly banter. Re the *Mirror*, I felt they resented us having a relationship with the *Sun*, but they had to understand we could not rely on the *Mirror*. Piers felt it was personal with me, that I still felt bad at the way I left the paper.[1] It wasn't that, but I felt the *Mirror* was not an instinctively Labour paper any more, did not feel any especial need to be supportive, and instead tended to go with the anti-government flow. He said he wanted to wipe the slate clean, get more politics in the paper, get involved more. Maguire asked how I would do things differently if I was there. I said I would exploit the *Mirror*'s unique selling point more, be more firmly identified as the Labour paper. And I would push hard at the frontiers of New Labour, stop politics from being defined by an outmoded left/right, Old Labour vs Thatcherism prism.

I got back to get George R to do a statement on troops being put on zero hours alert re Kosovo. Peter M was in South Africa and we had to sort a little flurry because some in the ANC were saying they never asked for him, and we dug out the letter from them. I was asked whether I wrote the [Oskar] Lafontaine article in the *Telegraph*, and had to dance around it because by and large I had.

Friday, February 12

To try to develop the press/SCU operation, I'd arranged for a joint awayday at the Civil Service College. I did a fairly scripted opening about what I wanted from the next phase, what I meant by strategy, how I believed they fitted in to it. Philip [Gould] did an excellent polling presentation, distilling both quantitative and qualitative. His summary was that we were OK, but doing badly with women, not breaking through on delivery, and we should not underestimate the levels of ignorance about what government policies were. He said afterwards he was impressed by the general quality of the people I had drawn together. I think they enjoyed the day and felt at the end of it that they had a better understanding of what we were trying to do.

We came up with a stack of specific new ideas for further change, including re the website. But more than that it was good for morale, and also good that they saw the big picture and understood some of the difficulties we faced. GM food was a growing media problem, with several of the papers vying with each other to be THE anti-GM paper. This was another problem we faced – that these campaign issues were treated as campaigns rather than policy debates, so the policy tended to get lost in the noise. TB called from Sedgefield, saying that we had to get scientists up making the case.

By the time we got back to the office, Clinton winning his impeachment battle was the big news. Godric did the Sundays. We were

[1] AC had resigned as political editor of the paper after another executive had been put in charge of politics.

basically just letting the Sunday lobby wither on the vine. They were a waste of time, and wrote whatever rubbish came into their heads anyway. They were gearing up for a few attacks on me re the BBC speech. Can give it, can't take it.

Saturday, Friday 13
We were in Suffolk at Philip and Gail's place for the weekend, and I was looking forward to a few quiet days. TB called a couple of times. He was worried at the way the GM debate was developing. He had done an interview with Tom Baldwin for the *Sunday Telegraph*. Tom was trying to do a story that TB would have put Ashdown in the Cabinet had there been a hung Parliament, which we didn't really want, and I persuaded him to go on TB calling on Ken Clarke to stay and fight in the Tory Party, and take the challenge to Hague to take on the right. We had a nice dinner, and agreed re the various books being done on me that I should have nothing to do with them. I felt there was a chance some of them would drop it once they realised I was serious about no co-operation at all.

Sunday, February 14
We went for a long walk out in the countryside, in an area where the phone didn't work, and it was nice to be right out of it for a while. We had lunch at the local pub. The papers were full of GM-ery. PG was much more relaxed than TB. He felt it was one of those issues that fascinated fanatics, filled reams of papers, but did not really shift votes. There were a few pieces in the papers attacking me, but fairly half-hearted.

Monday, February 15
We were clearly in for a GM insanity week, but TB said he was determined we would not get pushed off our position on it.

Tuesday, February 16
I went north to see Mum and Dad, who was not looking too great. They had the telly on in the afternoon and on one of the quiz programmes, there was a question 'What does Alastair Campbell do?' Good question.

Wednesday, February 17
I took Rory to Man U vs Arsenal. It was an OK game, 1-1, with [Patrick] Vieira [Arsenal footballer] superb. We had a drink with Alex afterwards who needless to say was totally on my page re the attacks

on the media. They are out of control, he said, and doing a lot of damage. TB called, said the GM situation was becoming ludicrous.

Thursday, February 18

We got the 10.30 train back, and having been fairly chilled on the newspaper-reading front, read a few on the train down. The GM coverage was a fucking joke. TB had decided he needed to do an article to put the other side of the story, and I worked on that a bit. We had not really handled it well. We had let the issue develop its own steam, and not really had a strategy for how the public debate developed. It was now reaching the stage of hysteria and it was hard to row back to a normal place once that happened.

Friday, February 19

I was beginning to feel a bit more rested and sat down to write out a longer-term strategy paper. We were seeing things too much on a day-to-day basis, at a time the media were turning hostile, and it meant both morale and effectiveness were being affected. Also, TB had to be much more strategic in his modus operandi. I totally understand why he gets pissed off with departments and with the press, but we just have to practise what we preach, stay focused on a bigger picture and basically keep going. If we are confident we are doing the right thing, it will come good. But it was hard when a lot of the time it felt like hand-to-hand combat with opposition, media or someone inside the government who didn't get it.

Saturday, February 20

I took Calum to Wycombe vs Burnley, a dreadful match which we lost 2-0, and then hours getting out of the car park. Peter Wilkinson called me early evening to say that Tom Baldwin had somehow got hold of the Macpherson Report [Sir William Macpherson's inquiry into the murder of Stephen Lawrence, branding the Metropolitan Police as institutionally racist] and Jack S was going for an injunction, which was duly granted. TB was not terribly happy that we weren't consulted re the decision to go for one, but we agreed to the line that it was a decision taken by Jack, and the right decision to take. The argument was that this was not a White Paper, Green Paper, run-of-the-mill policy speech that was being leaked, but the outcome of a judicial inquiry into events that had an enormous impact on people's lives. There was the usual whining from some in the media re the fact of an injunction but by and large it was OK. Lawrence was leading the news by the end of the day and apart from more GM crapola, there wasn't much in the Sundays.

Sunday, February 21

We had a meeting in GB's room at Number 11 – TB, GB, Nigel Wicks, Jeremy Heywood, John Sawers, Ed B, Jonathan, AC, re the changeover plan re preparations for the euro. We were still not totally decided when we would do the statement, or who, TB or GB. TB had done his own draft statement, which was definitely a shift to a pro position. GB, who was clearly anxious at the thought of TB doing the statement, felt it was too pro and would be seen effectively as a change of policy. TB's argument was that it articulated the policy according to current events. GB felt the policy he had set out on October 27, 1997 was a robust position and one that would get us through the next election, given there was next to no chance of us going in before. I proposed that we speak about a change of gear, not a change of policy, and they both seemed OK with that. We had to admit that we were warming up on the issue, because time was passing, but still the basic policy framework set by GB applied. TB kept saying he felt we needed greater clarity about the direction of travel, whereas GB was wedded to the position as he had set it out. We agreed it would not be sensible to set a date but the fact of TB fronting it, and the fact we would be talking about public expenditure implications, would be seen as a pretty big signal. GB felt it would be enough just to set out what the preparations were. There was a clear difference of emphasis, but also I sensed GB basically trying to maintain control of a process that he rightly felt TB wanted to push along now.

The truth was, given the complexity of the issues, that a lot of it would be in the spin, and how we decided to frame it and brief it afterwards. If they wanted it seen as a big step, that would not be difficult to achieve, but we needed clarity and agreement that was what we wanted. The Tories and the sceptic press would do the rest to deliver definition. It was a perfectly good-natured but tense meeting. TB was pretty determined to signal the change of gear but GB was cautious. Afterwards, he and Ed Balls came round to my office, and he emphasised he felt it would be a disaster if it was seen as a change of policy. I didn't think that was what TB wanted, but they were suspicious, and unspoken – till I mentioned it – was their assumption that Peter M would be in the background promoting it as a huge step towards the euro. I said what was important was that we and they agreed absolutely the line and stuck to it.

I went to see TB to reiterate GB's point. He said it was a role reversal from October '97, when he had been effectively holding back GB. This time it was GB wanting to add the sceptic touches. As ever, TB thought there were good reasons and bad in his argument. The good was that we didn't necessarily need the shift and it would signal to the pro camp they could push us into positions ahead of the time we might want to adopt them. The bad was that he was worried about loss of face, or loss of control of the policy, the idea 'his' policy was being changed.

There was a fair bit of running around on it through the day, at the end of which we agreed we would be saying yes to going in principle, conditions as set out in October '97 had to be met, not going to happen this side of an election but certain preparations have to be made, and meanwhile keep pressing for economic reform. That was a perfectly sensible and realistic position. What we had yet to agree was where we put the emphases. Jonathan felt even with TB's push that pro-EMU business would not think we were going far enough. For once TB seemed to be as much worried by them as by Murdoch and his merry men.

Monday, February 22

I was back in full-time harness again, and what a week lay ahead. The chances are we could be going to war against Serbia. We had the Macpherson Report, the national changeover plan, the Agenda 2000 summit. The papers were full of predictable outrage re Jack's injunction, but Roy Greenslade [*Guardian*] had an excellent piece on it, and the phone-ins were by no means one-sided. The *Sun* front page said we were the most arrogant government in history. A lot of this was still payback for my whacks at the national press. I felt we had to keep going, ensure the public conditioned their response to media attacks with an understanding of the game being played, but TB was losing his nerve a bit. He called me at 7.20, said the front pages were ghastly. 'We are in trouble on this.' He made the same point at the office meeting, said he wasn't sure where this war with the media ends. I said it doesn't end, you have to fight the whole time, or they make sure you never get heard properly. Philip was the only one totally supportive of where I was, saying the public would be with us over time, and there was never a better time. But people were getting jumpy. They were finding lots of things to kick us with and kicking hard, and TB was feeling a bit scarred. He said PG and I were so anti-press we were beginning to sound like constituency surgery cases. 'It's reaching the point where John Burton [agent in Sedgefield] pops his head round the door and says "You have another appointment."' I argued for confidence and boldness, taking them by surprise, always staying a step ahead of them.

On EMU, we had to show we were bold and confident and unafraid of the frenzied response there would be in the sceptic press. TB was desperate for us not to announce in advance but I felt we had to as part of our 'week ahead' briefing. Otherwise they would argue we had cooked it out of nowhere to detract from the row over Lawrence. He raised again the need to involve Richard Wilson more if we were to get the machine focused properly on delivery. Between 10 and 11, I was mainly dealing with Jack S. We agreed, after talking to TB, that he should do a statement in the House saying why he went for an injunction. We agreed I would announce it at the 11, and say that [Sir Paul] Condon [Commissioner, Metropolitan Police] and the Lawrences [family] would see the report today. Jack was going to take a hammering but the more he explained it, the better the position with the public. At the 11, there was plenty of indignation but I just stayed calm, though I was overly dismissive of a leak inquiry, which was a bit of a problem later when JS announced one. I had a meeting with GB, Ed and Jeremy to go through the latest draft of the changeover statement for tomorrow, and was trying to persuade GB to do a briefing with me tomorrow. He was not keen. I told the eleven o'clock TB would be doing the statement and there was a bit of excitement at that, which would grow as the day wore on.

Jack was unsure whether the Lawrences would call for Condon to go. He said he had no particular brief for Condon, and this wasn't about the Home Office defending its back but he didn't think the police would be best served by him going. It was clear that Richard Wilson and David Omand [Home Office permanent secretary] were going to defend Condon, and didn't like the tone of any criticism of him. TB was with them. TB was worried that the whole thing would be used as a stick to beat all the police, and we had to be very careful. I said there had to be something we could point to as a lasting testament to Stephen Lawrence – new laws, changed attitudes, a changed Britain. Jack was on for that, but not for piling pressure on Condon who may soon be dealing with riots. The civil servants thought there was a chance Condon would sue if he was sacked anyway. We agreed that when Jack saw the Lawrences tomorrow, he should try to win them over for something bigger than just calling for Condon to go. Later Peter Hyman and I told TB we felt he was losing some of his politics and instinct because he was constantly having to calculate according to other positions being put to him. The values part of his politics was going missing sometimes.

TB asked me again if I was sure about taking on the press in the way we were. I said he had to show who was boss, him not them. Later he spoke to Murdoch. Anji listened in and said it was a very chilly conversation. Trevor Kavanagh had clearly being pouring vitriol into Murdoch's ear and they had decided tomorrow meant we were going into the euro whatever, regardless of economic reform. It also made TB think we should not have trailed it. I said we would never get the *Sun* or the *Mail* on board for this but if he thought it was the right thing, he had to do it, and go for it. I said the public will back him in any fight, as long as they think he is doing the right thing. If we are going to win re Europe, they had to understand the press were players not spectators. TB said he was worried my sense of injustice about what they did was clouding my judgement about how to deal with them. I said we had to be much more systematic and brave about it, decide a strategy and stick to it.

Tuesday, February 23

The JS story was back in proper perspective. I drafted a new peroration for Jack's statement, and suggested that real emotion was the way to get it off Condon's fate being the issue. He took in some but not all of the points and in the end it was a bit lawyerish and flat. The overnight briefing on EMU went fine. TB saw Michael Heseltine early on, while GB saw Ken Clarke. TB also called Chirac and Jospin. They welcomed what we were doing but Jospin asked 'What's new?' TB agreed with Hezza [Heseltine] that he would say it was our 'intention to join' if conditions were met. It wasn't remotely a problem, and was the policy, but GB didn't like it. He was worried we would be pushed into an 'in come what may' position and it would define the next election. I put together an agreed script for me to use at the 11, which included 'change of gear not change of policy', which ran well throughout the day.

The discussions on it went on right up to 2.30, when Peter M, by phone, and I finally persuaded him to simplify the message. I think John Sawers and Jeremy Heywood were both a bit shocked by the modus operandi, for example the fact it had been squared with the Cabinet with a ring-round. In the car on the way over, TB was more nervous than he had been for a while. 'Are we OK on this? Are we in the right place on this?' Going over the arguments etc. The statement went fine. Hague was funny but ultimately all over the place and as [Sir Edward] Heath [former Conservative prime minister], Clarke and Hezza all piled in, he ended up in a pretty dire position on it. I did a briefing at Number 10 afterwards which was open to European and US journalists and they all sensed it was a big moment and potentially defining. I called round a few editors, including Dacre who had basically decided we were going in by stealth, and was also convinced the Macpherson Report would lead to a load of political correctness piled on the police. TB called later, said he felt we were in good nick, but was a bit put out when I said Paul Johnson [journalist and historian] had accused him of 'betrayal'. I couldn't understand why he bothered with people like him, but he said 'I don't like losing my little friends on the right.'

Wednesday, February 24

The euro coverage was pretty poor, the sceptic papers predictable and the pro papers pathetic, not even making the *Guardian* splash or the *Mirror* front. Interestingly the *Times* leader was pressing on the economic reform argument, so it wasn't all over on that front. Simon Jenkins had a pretty nasty piece about me in *The Times*, on the Rasputin theme, and I suspected he had been given a bit of help from someone in the Cabinet Office. Guthrie was over for a meeting on Kosovo and had seen it. They're jealous, he said. He said he was pleased I attended key military meetings because he felt I gave objective and sound advice re media and public opinion, which they had to take into account.

The main event today was going to be Jack's statement on the Macpherson Report. TB saw the Lawrences [parents Neville and Doreen], who were clearly nice people surprised to be caught up in something that seemed, and was, so important. We got the sense they were unlikely to call for Condon's resignation, but there was a real hurt there, albeit with a dignity that was to the fore. I felt really moved seeing them, and hearing them, and when I went to the loo a bit later found myself crying briefly. TB was worried, however, that we would lose the support of the police if we weren't careful. As Liz [Lloyd] said, 'He speaks less about values these days than he does about groups of supporters.' He said the point was it was an appalling crime, and the investigation not handled well, but there will be good decent people around the country who feel they are being branded as racist.

David M, Peter Hyman and Liz all, in their different ways, said that they worried TB was 'losing soul', that he was so immersed in policy and different difficult areas that he was being forced to make calculations the whole time, and values were not always the driving force. He did some of the black media re the Macpherson Report, then Channel 4, when they linked him to Doreen Lawrence in the studio. His interviews were OK but he was not really engaged. On everything at the moment, he seemed to be asking 'Where are we on this?' rather than going for issues and driving them through. I hoped it was a phase. One of the things I like about working for him is that he stakes out difficult ground and we go for it. He is too calculating at the moment.

Thursday, February 25

Wall-to-wall, and very moving, coverage of the Macpherson Report. I said to TB that I didn't think he really connected yesterday. I was unsure whether he felt it as deeply as most people did. He insisted he did, but he was worried about the impact on the police. He did not buy the line that most policemen were racist, and he was worried this would hit their morale and recruitment. He said it was a dreadful waste of a young talent but it should not lead to an over-the-top mass of new laws and procedures. He felt we had been too emotional yesterday, not rooted enough in an understanding of the impact on the police, and veering towards the politically correct. He looked almost hurt in saying it, knew what people in the office were saying and didn't like it. He felt there was overt racism and covert racism and we had to deal with both, but not by going over the top.

That view was endorsed by Cabinet discussion where several said they didn't like the idea of 'institutional racism' and both DB and FD said it was important millions of public servants weren't tarred as racist. Just before Cabinet though we had news that Stephen Lawrence's memorial had been desecrated and the CCTV camera was not working. Disaster 1. Disaster 2 came just before we left for Germany when it emerged that one of the appendices had names and addresses of people who had tipped off the police about the killers, and who would need protection. It was clearly the fault of the inquiry team, Jack said when he called me to tell me, but in the current atmosphere we would get savaged. I said to Jack surely someone at the Home Office had been through the whole report in detail, and spotted it. They had had it for almost ten days.

Cabinet also did EMU and Kosovo, where TB said Robin had done a 'quite brilliant job' getting an agreement on the way forward. We were discussing internally whether TB should do a speech on race at the weekend. He and Anji felt the moment would pass. I thought we should establish first what he would want to say. I was meanwhile trying to get my head round Agenda 2000 and the mass of briefing from the Cabinet Office. I had a meeting with GB re the Budget, where he was intending to go for a tax cut by scrapping MIRAS [mortgage interest relief at source]. I had a meeting with Victor Blank [chairman, Trinity Mirror] and went through both that day's copy of the *Mirror* and the *Record* to show the hostility that was coming through the whole time now. I like Victor but I wonder how much clout he has to get anything done. PG had wound up TB by telling him that in the groups the Scots were starting to get comfortable about the idea of the SNP being in power. Our attacks had just not hit home. On the plane [to Germany] Stephen Wall [UK representative to the EU] and David Bostock [head of European Secretrariat, FCO] briefed us on Agenda 2000 and duty-free and it was clear both issues were going to be difficult. That became even clearer at the Aznar [Spanish Prime Minister] dinner at which he and TB chatted first about Gibraltar, then about the general political scene.

Aznar was in a rage about the German government and dismissive of the French. I didn't get the feeling Chirac would be top of his Christmas card list. He felt much more comfortable with TB and it was fairly mutual. They agreed to do a big joint number on economic reform at the Chequers seminar on April 10. It was his birthday and we had a cake and he told us how important it was to get it into ¡Hola! magazine, with a big laugh. He had a very sharp sense of humour. TB meanwhile was persistently worrying re EMU that we had set ourselves up needlessly for a war we couldn't win. We were staying in a really nice place in Petersburg.

Friday, February 26

We got a real kicking over the Macpherson Report cock-up. *The Times* had us slipping a bit, which had TB back asking if we were doing the right thing going for the media. Scotland had showed how hard it was to get out a positive message if the press didn't want to hear. He had a bilateral with [Jacques] Santer [president of the European Commission], who strikes me as hopeless. It is as though he is surprised to be there. TB did his usual number on the [CAP] rebate. Then Ahern, and decommissioning, which was at a difficult moment. There was a wonderful moment which cracked everyone up when TB, exasperated, said 'If it is in the Agreement, I cannot see why it should not be in the treaty, and if it is in the Agreement it NEEDS to be in the treaty,' to which Paddy Teahon [Ahern adviser] replied 'You are applying logic, Prime Minister, and that has no place in this process.'

Then to the main meeting, doing a doorstep on the way in and somehow managing to avoid a question on the Lawrence fiasco. The meeting itself was in a beautiful mountaintop hotel, where TB did a bit of the usual schmoozing. These early moments were an important part of the deliberations, where you had literally a few seconds to try to square the people who needed to be squared on the issues that were difficult for you. I left for a local school which had been designated as the briefing centre and Nigel [Sheinwald, FCO], Bostock and I briefed on where things were. It was all about budget abatement but I did manage to get up the differences of opinion between France and Germany. They had been picking up on it anyway, not least because there had been some talk about Chirac 'bringing his own furniture' with him because the French didn't like what had been provided.

As at other recent summits, we were getting the biggest crowds for the briefings but we didn't have the biggest room, and the Germans annoyed Jack S by refusing to let us borrow theirs. The French were almost openly saying how poor the German presidency was. I got back to the meeting to learn only Chirac had gone for us over the rebate, and there had been few takers to pile in behind him. One of Chirac's problems was that his people didn't always do the legwork to organise for that kind of thing to happen. As summits go, it was fairly low-key, a warm-up for the main event in Berlin. The only real stories were the rebate and the row over duty-frees but by the time we got to TB doing the press, even our lot were more interested in the row between France and Germany which of course it was in our interests to fuel.

On the flight home, TB said it was worth making the effort to get the French to turn down the volume on the rebate. We had a long session with the experts who were saying there was a chance we would not get the deal sorted by Berlin. TB said he had been trying to persuade Kok to go for Commission president but he was doubtful Chirac would let it happen.

Saturday, February 27

It was the first summit I could recall where the UK press were covering other countries, i.e. France and Germany, and not just the UK. TB called a couple of times over the weekend re the press, and where we were going on it. He asked if I felt we were basically going to war with them. I said no, but we are not going to let them set the agenda and where they distort and invent we are going to make sure the public know that is what is going on. I said it would get a lot worse than this.

I also felt it was important for TB's own position that he exuded strength not weakness, and they sensed his excessive concerns about the damage they could do as a weakness. In opposition, we had needed them more than we do now. The best way to maintain any support is keep the public with us and that is about having an agenda, seeing it through and ensuring the results are clear to see.

Sunday, February 28

I managed a quiet day. The Sundays were harmless and dull and the only bad story over the weekend was a row kicked up over Jack S taking a three-day break to France and avoiding questions over the Macpherson Report.

Monday, March 1

Jack's break, ridiculously, was still leading the news, the Tories jumping on the bandwagon by calling for his resignation (always a mistake if there is no chance of it happening). It was a silly story, and further evidence the BBC was getting more and more tabloid in its news judgements. I spoke to Jack and we agreed a line that politicians have obligations to their families as well. At the office meeting, TB wanted us to think through a way of dealing with the David Owen/Denis Healey [former Labour ministers] anti-euro [New Europe] group. He was concerned now that our shift of gear had unnecessarily given the Tories a platform – a point GB had made in warning against going too far – and we had given the antis at the *Sun* the opportunity to turn things generally against us.

He was still going on about my approach to the press, said he felt we were now between two stools, not at war but not at peace. I said that was because he signed up to one approach and was now pulling back and we had to get agreement for a strategic pitch. PG and I were still arguing for a more aggressive and confident posture, but he was clearly worried. I said another way of pitching it was that we had one agenda and the press had another and we would not get side-tracked from the issues that matter. But then we had to see that through, be dismissive of the rubbish, not let the frenzies distract us, let them work themselves into a lather and blow themselves out. He said if the *Mail* are at us the whole time, fine. But add in the *Sun* and the *Mirror* as well, and it is a tough place to be. I said it was not just about the papers, but their influence on the broadcasters which were going downmarket the whole time. A year ago there is no way Jack taking a weekend off would have led the news. It is a press-driven agenda.

We had another example later today, when Prince Charles and Alun Michael 'accidentally' ate some beef on the bone. Years ago it would have been a diary lead and maybe an 'And finally' on the news. It led the bloody bulletins, like it was some earth-shattering event. TB kept me back at the end and said he thought our difference was that I was saying provided we pursued our own agenda successfully, they were not as powerful as they thought. He felt they still had the ability to knock us off course, which is why he liked to keep as many on board as possible. I felt part of the problem was his desire to be liked and the press aggression was in part driven by people who for whatever reason just didn't like him. I had no trouble not being liked by people for whom I have little time or respect myself.

Later, he said in his meeting with RW he felt the Civil Service were feeling we were going through a rocky period and that meant an opportunity for them to get back to their way of doing things. Jack C told TB the Cabinet Office civil servants were stultifying, found ways of stopping any new ideas from taking off. We had meetings with GB and DD re Scotland, which were pretty depressing affairs. TB was getting more and more livid re the Scottish campaign, which just wasn't doing the basics well, let alone really taking the fight to the Nats. TB told DD he had to get it – that the SNP would always outflank us on the left, so we had to be in the centre ground, hit the New Labour line harder. 'I don't care what your activists are telling you. I'm talking about people who instinctively will reject nationalism and who want us to be a moderate and sensible force.'

Neither DD nor Helen [Liddell] seemed capable of delivering a message at the moment. GB was complicating things too, wanting to shift to 'Scotland leading in Britain' as our main message. I felt we were far better on delivery and divorce. By the end of it, TB was very dispirited. He said he was really worried about Donald, felt he had lost his confidence and his fight.

Tuesday, March 2

I was in early to meet up with TB and head to the airport for Milan. We talked re the Civil Service. He thought Wilson was trying to help but he was more a shop steward for the Civil Service than a real driver of change. He said he was surprised at how few genuinely talented people there seemed to be in the government machine. There were a lot of quite good people but a lot of mediocrity. He was in no doubt we had to keep strengthening the centre but the stronger it became the more resistance there would be elsewhere. On Budget strategy, I wasn't convinced a basic rate cut would be as welcome as he imagined, particularly if MIRAS and MCA [married couple's allowance] were being cut.

On the flight out, we wrote the PES speech pretty much from scratch, eighty per cent of it his, and got it pretty much done by the time we landed. We chatted with Sally and Margaret [McDonagh] re who could be Peter's replacement, as an extra brain at the centre, and whether it could be Charlie [Falconer]. TB made the observation: 'He is clever and though he doesn't have all that much natural political skill, you can learn it – I did.' I think that understated both Charlie's skills and TB's. We had a totally crazy police escort into the city centre, outriders, sirens and guys hanging out of the windows waving sticks at people. The more we travelled, the more I realised Scotland Yard had the best, most efficient and most economical escort system. These guys were fucking maniacs and it's a wonder we got there without a major accident. Added to which it is virtually impossible to have a conversation with the sirens raging away and the car careering round corners. I almost thought of telling the driver TB got carsick but feared it was a lost cause.

The overnight briefing – that we could learn a lot from America – ran well on the broadcasts, but irritated e.g. Glenys [Kinnock] who was a bit frosty when we bumped into her at the Marriott. TB had bilaterals with [Poul Nyrup] Rasmussen, then [Massimo] D'Alema. He did clips on the murders in Uganda which was the main story of the day, and ghastly. After the lunch, a meeting with MEPs which was a lot friendlier and more constructive than before. Then to the main conference centre and his speech went down well. As well as the US bit, he had a powerful section on social justice which really connected.

It was clear that so far as the European media were concerned they were seeing it as Blair vs Lafontaine, two different visions of Europe. I saw Lafontaine arrive. There is something very odd about him and he lacks presence. I watched the audience during TB's speech. Though not all of them agree, and some couldn't disguise it, he is the one they listen to most intently, and the one who has the presence or charisma or whatever. Maybe because of the shift on the euro, he was received much more warmly than we might have expected.

Julia Hartley-Brewer [*Sunday Express*] was the only British press reporter to go so we gave her a lift back and an interview on the plane. She got him to say he would love to be mayor. He was good defending Jack, and strong on the Tories. Once we got rid of her, TB wanted to go over young up-and-coming MPs and ministers. I went to the other end of the age scale and said I thought Gerald Kaufman [Labour MP, former minister in the Wilson and Callaghan governments], who coincidentally had a very good piece on the Tories in *The Times* today, would be a good addition to the government, assuming he wanted it. TB said he was desperate for new political rigour and brains around the place. He said whatever else people said about GB, at least he thought deeply about politics and saw things through. Too many of our people were just caught up with the flow of things.

Wednesday, March 3

Very scant and negative coverage of Milan. I got Julian [Braithwaite] to get together the European coverage, which was big and generally positive. Charlie F, DM and PH thought we were being hit on Europe because we were losing the argument with the chatterers. I was more relaxed about it. Maybe that was because, as according to Godric some of the hacks had started to observe, I was becoming more disengaged. We got crap coverage on waiting lists. At the 11, I took them through some of the European coverage and asked if they were all wrong, and 'you people' all right to ignore yesterday's event? Equally, I showed some of them the European coverage on the New Deal. It was absurd that we got better and more detailed coverage overseas for a policy whose impact was exclusively domestic.

I had an excellent meeting with Balls and [John] Kingman re Budget strategy and a focus on tax reform for families, work and enterprise. We agreed top-line messages, plus a pretty impressive rollout of statement in the days following GB, focusing on the obvious main areas. TB and GB were still mulling re whether to go for a base-rate cut. Ed was a lot better without Charlie [Whelan] round his neck and we were able to shape and agree a robust strategy that left me feeling a lot more confident. I felt economic competence was the single most important strategic message to develop, and the single most important electoral factor for us, and this was definitely a Budget to help in that direction. It would show we had delivered on sorting debt, beginning to invest properly in health and education, welfare reform, dealing with youth unemployment. Now we could start to give more tax help to families and enterprise as well as keep investing in our priorities.

At PMQs, Hague did tax and health and TB did fine, and went big time on boom and bust, another strategic message we had to hammer day in, day out. The four o'clock was pretty desultory. They were trying to get me going re a Denis MacShane [Labour MP] article in *Le Monde*, which probably was a bit forward on policy but I didn't see the point of getting into a great lather about it. I spoke to him just to say be ultra careful, but in truth it showed how hard it was to have a sensible debate. I saw Charlie F at 6, and re the media I said it was not about taking them all on, but it was about making the good feel they had to take on the bad, because at the moment the bad had the upper hand in terms of style, tone and agenda.

Thursday, March 4

The bananas dispute took a turn for the worse with US sanctions to be applied and, with us heading to Scotland, trouble for the cashmere industry too.[1] Extra money for class sizes was going well on the broadcasts but on the way in, Jonathan said yesterday DB and GB had a screaming match because GB had told him for the first time, as a done deal, plans for education in the Budget. TB was not sure GB was spending on the right things, e.g. a massive computer scheme. He was a bit gloomy when I showed him the *Scotsman* poll which, while good on the party figures, said sixty-one per cent wanted him to stay away during the campaign. That would fuel the negativistas in the campaign, but I still felt it was wrong, media-led rather than thought through. Scots were not that different.

Later, when we were up there, he was beginning to think we could lose and said 'This could really fuck the government. Can you imagine how bad it will be, the sight of the Queen opening a new Parliament with Salmond in charge?' He was a bit discombobulated at the moment, had been off form yesterday and was off form at Cabinet (incidentally the first at which JC presented a grid for the week ahead, in a very Jack-ish way).

Cabinet did Iraq and NI, then we had a meeting with DD and Byers re bananas and cashmere. GB joined us. Steve ran through the detail. I said there was a case for us making this the issue for the Scotland visit, showing we could fight and win for Scottish interests. I suggested a meeting was fixed with the cashmere industry. GB and DD argued it meant lost jobs would be the backdrop. But Byers was already having to do a PNQ [Private Notice Question] on it so the question was whether we could frame on our terms.

At the 11.30, I got a lot of Northern Ireland and said we were likely to miss March 10 – there was a bad poll today – and a Good Friday Agreement Mark 2 was now more likely. Mo had told the Cabinet March 10 wasn't going to happen. On bananas, the hacks just laughed, and refused to take it seriously as a story. Sad but true. We left for a school visit in Ealing and TB went live into the one o'clock news. But he looked and sounded weak and a bit all over the place. Not one of his best. He did some clips for the others and we left for the plane. In the car, I said he was off form and he said he knew. He was letting things get to him a bit, worrying about Europe, GB, the media, usual stuff. And he was seriously worried we could lose in Scotland.

He wasn't totally sure what the message for the visit [to Edinburgh]

[1] A trade dispute in which the US wanted the EU to stop giving preferential treatment to former African, Caribbean and Pacific colonies at the expense of Latin American growers and their US backers. Threatened sanctions would target EU goods including Scottish cashmere.

was. We had both pretty much lost confidence in DD, who had virtually collapsed. It meant TB wasn't taking his advice seriously. We were relying on our own instincts and the occasional input from GB, but it certainly wasn't a campaign in good shape. We arrived, spent a few minutes doing the usual piss-taking of Pat [McFadden] and Scots in general, then to Marconi [electronics company]. It was a good visit, good hi-tech jobs, good pictures, TB's mood lifting a little. We got to the hotel where Anji, Pat and I had a real heart-to-heart session with TB. He was saying he couldn't see how we turned it round, that something had changed irreversibly. We said that was bollocks, but we had to show some fight and leadership. Donald was a lovely man but he had lost it for the moment and it was up to him.

We fixed a Clinton call for later to make the case re cashmere, then to a Q&A at Carluke, with Helen [Liddell] in the chair. He was OK, though he went on far too long on GM foods. But his peroration was excellent and hit all the right notes. In the car he said he felt totally comfortable with the arguments and if he could have three or four days up here he was confident we could turn it round. I worked on the speech till 2 with Pat and Douglas Alexander. The basic argument was fine and the line, fighting for Scotland's future, OK. But the whole thing was unnerving TB and making him question the whole policy of devolution. I wondered if there was anything else going on that was getting him down because he was as low – and low performance – as I could remember. He said he would get out of it. Bananas ran as the main story. Byers 'summonsed' Phil Lader [US ambassador] which we felt was a bit OTT. When TB spoke to Bill, he started by saying 'Bill, as you might say, I'm up to my ass in alligators.'

Friday, March 5
The *Record* did a front-page nonsense on the fucking Dome for the second day running. So much for Victor [Blank] calming them down. We worked a bit more on the speech, while he left for his Radio Clyde phone-in. Listening back at the hotel, I felt he sounded nervous and unsure. But the programme said later they had a massive and generally positive response. I decided to stay away from his meeting with [Martin] Clarke, because I would not be able to hold back, and it was better TB tried a bit of the charm first. Of course Clarke loved being the centre of attention and a bit courted. TB said it was up to them how they covered things but we were being denied a fair crack of the whip. Clarke seemingly went on about how they had to reflect

the readers' views. TB said he thought the readers would expect a bit more scrutiny of the SNP.

He did the political editors, then an STV phone-in which was excellent. The speech was in good shape, but DD was really irritating me with a host of really tiny points. The mood at the [Scottish Labour] conference was good, and they were up for a proper message. I said just before he went on that it was all about confidence and demeanour. He nodded and then strolled around backstage going over some of the key lines in his head. He really went for the SNP on economic incompetence, did a terrific unity rallying call at the end and all in all it was pretty good. TB wondered afterwards if I shouldn't go up there for a while, but there would be big Civil Service objections to me getting more directly involved in the campaign. He did a pep talk for candidates, then saw some business people. Earlier David Murray [Rangers FC chairman] said he would come over to us during the campaign.

On the plane, TB said we had to find a strategist to work alongside DD. He said Donald was clever and smart and popular but at the moment he was like blancmange. He also wanted a plan for a TB/GB double-act visits programme. He thought we could turn it around but said it was going to be difficult and it would be a big blow to the government as a whole if it went to the SNP.

Saturday, March 6

TB saw GB at Chequers for another Budget discussion. He told him he had to improve his modus operandi with colleagues and at least involve them more in decision-making for the Budget re their departments. Tax cut was on. Peter Oborne [writing a biography of AC] called, said he was doing my Cambridge days at the moment and was I a football hooligan? I repeated that I was having nothing to do with his silly book.

TB said I had to speak to DD to get him to do a leadership number and really take apart the SNP on their education plans, which were a joke. I worked over the weekend on three papers – one on the press, one on problems we were facing inside the government and a third suggesting an action plan for both. Piers did a very funny piece on page 2 of the *Mirror* about my complaints re the coverage from Milan, 'Tony Blair is a genius' in lots of different languages.

Sunday, March 7

Other than a bit of pre-Budget planning, it was fairly quiet, the Sundays full of the usual pre-Budget fiction. Blunkett called re Woodhead whose ex-wife was in the *Mail on Sunday* accusing him of lying. I spoke to Byers re the rash of articles saying TB spoke European but acted American. We went to a party at the [Richard, architect, and Ruth] Rogers' house for John Diamond [journalist battling throat cancer] and Nigella [Lawson, food writer and broadcaster, Diamond's wife]. A mix of media and le beau monde. Totally not my scene really. I spent most of the time talking to Noreen Taylor [former *Mirror* colleague] and Natascha [McElhone, her daughter, actor].

Monday, March 8

The pre-Budget coverage was picking up, leading to accusations of systematic leaking. The truth was there was precious little leaking, certainly compared with some of Whelan's operations. I woke up to 'U-turn on right to roam', saying we had gone back on our pledge. It wasn't true but Meacher didn't want to brief so it was running away as a bad scene for us. The Tories were chasing us re leaks from select committees to the government following Ernie Ross admitting leaking the Sandline report to the FCO.[1] Meanwhile, NI was coming back up the tracks and at the office meeting, Jonathan said it was needing TB's attention. Gerry Adams claimed we were in crisis. On the press, we agreed there was no point going to war, but we did need a proactive strategy for putting over arguments about them and about the nature of political debate. TB had more or less bought into the proposals I put up over the weekend. PG was pretty alarmist re delivery and said people would not understand if there was a tax cut because they wanted more investment in public services. TB's worry was different, that there was so much in the Budget people would end up confused. I felt it was a really strong package and would bring to an end this rather difficult and unsettling period we had been through. But we did need to make an economic case for tax cuts. We should not expect them just to be seen as an unqualified good for us. We had the best possible context-setter in an IMF report saying how well we had managed the economy so far.

TB was getting more and more worried re the capability of the Civil Service, and also sensed RW was offside. I saw Richard and told him TB was serious in wanting him more not less involved but he had to feel he was pushing in the same direction re reform and

[1] Ross, Labour MP and a member of the Foreign Affairs Select Committee, had resigned from the committee in January after admitting sending a copy of the report to the Foreign Office.

delivery. Richard moved to a different point, having been tugged by Mike Granatt [head of GICS] re my comments on the SNP at a briefing. He said he thought it was a difficulty that Anji and I went with TB on Scotland campaign visits. I said it was no different to civil servants going to conference. He said the difference was I was helping with the politics. I thought the rules were too strict. It was as though politicians and governments could not be political.

I went back to sit down and read through the Budget and the background notes properly, and get my head round it all. At the briefings, I was doing a big number on TB's NATO speech, European defence initiative plus the warning to Milosevic. I saw TB for a chat re Budget positioning. Say what you like, he said, but GB can deliver. He was worried Jonathan wasn't handling RW well and it would have bad consequences for us. I had another fight with the *Record* over their dishonest stitch-up. They had done an interview with Mo, she had talked about the importance of integrated education and they had presented her comments as though about Scotland, not NI. I spoke to Mo who wrote a letter to Clarke and suggested there was now malice in their coverage of us. Word then came back they were going to splash on the letter, and attack her. The guy [Clarke] should be a down-table sub on the *Mail*, not editing what was once a decent newspaper. I suggested to Mo we pre-empt with a statement put out generally. DD was worrying the row with them was escalating out of control. I said this was the result of not standing up to them when it started.

Tuesday, March 9
The pre-Budget stuff was running fine, and there was not a whiff of the 1p tax cut. Donald Dewar came to see me before Cabinet. He looked tired and shambolic and was hobbling more than usual and he seemed just sad really. His sparkle was going, which was sad to behold, and the more we tried to raise his spirits or generate stomach for the fight, the closer to collapse he seemed to be. At Cabinet, GB rattled through the outlines of the Budget, basically a shortened version of the speech, as ever firing figures at them, so fast those who were taking notes could barely keep up. As ever, the overall impression was strong. He knew what he was on about, and he was confident. Their reaction was pretty good. TB let most of them have their say but it was all a bit otiose, given the thing was a done deal and had been at the printers for days.

TB went through the broader political context and emphasised the key messages that all of them needed to be communicating over time.

Blunkett made one or two noises that could be seen as anti the tax cut, and I had a word with him at the end to say I hope that didn't find its way into the press. Not from me, he said, laughing. At the lobby I stuck to the basic advance messages but also used some of the material from AD who had gone through the extra savings e.g. from income support. We went over to the House. GB delivered it brilliantly, the right mix of light and heavy, figures and argument, and it went down a storm with our side. I felt a real sense of relief we were back on big message and major substance after a bitty period. Ed and I briefed in the lower gallery and I could tell from the mood and the questions they thought it was strong. They were asking whether we were going for an early election. The Tories and the Lib Dems were nowhere on it, just didn't have an argument.

I went back for a meeting re Scotland. I said DD had to have a lot better support than he was getting. We needed to work up a proper strategy that played to his strengths and then see it through. I said they needed a strategy and systems to implement it. The Budget was going down well, the bulletins were good. Jonathan said Jeremy was finding a few worms in the detail, even to do with widows' bereavement benefits. But it was going down a storm and should help us on the Wales and Scotland fronts too. TB was a lot happier tonight than he had been for a while. I said it had worked because it had been strategic and substantive and though you can't have a Budget every day, we should stop worrying about the bits and pieces and focus much much more on the big connecting moments. The bad news was we lost 6-0 at home to Man City.

Wednesday, March 10

GB got a phenomenal press for the Budget. Only the *Mail* and the *Telegraph* were sniffy, but overall the effect was fabulous. Ed Balls called at 7.30 to go through the tricky questions pre *Today* programme. I assumed they would go on stealth taxes. After TB's PMQs meeting I went over to the Treasury for the GB/Byers briefing. GB was on good form, knew he had done a good job and we had regained momentum. The game the media was playing was to get us to say 'some people are worse off'. GB brushed them aside, took it to the big picture about the economy, many not few etc., and I worked up a decent script to put round.

We got a terrific press in Scotland which should help get us on track, and I persuaded GB to make a big campaign speech up there on Friday. Alex Ferguson called as he arrived for the Chelsea match, said it was a great Budget, everyone was saying so. For PMQs, TB thought the Tories would go for the idea of redistribution, which was still seen as a negative and we had not yet fully recalibrated the tax-and-spend arguments. In fact he was fine, good on the big arguments and nobody really got near him. Ed B and I did another joint briefing afterwards, and they were starting to say there was a better Number 10/11 joint operation post-Whelan.

We had a moment of light relief with Trevor Kavanagh. The *Sun* had asked for one of their white-van drivers to do an interview with GB. It turned out the guy was living with a benefits fiddler. We urged Trevor to make a citizen's arrest. By the end of the day, they had settled on the tax burden as their point of obsessing, but I still think we won the day with big economic message and direction. I ended up saying it would go up because there would be more people in work and paying tax.

Thursday, March 11

We were now doing a daily conference call with the Scottish campaign team and a fairly depressing affair it was too. Helen Liddell sounded panicky. Donald had a list of problems and no real ideas for solving them. I asked what the plan was for today, a few seconds of silence followed, then a cacophony of different ideas. GB came on halfway through and had one or two ideas, like getting David Murray up pre-SNP conference, but he too sounded a bit deflated. TB said he was going to have to put a rocket up Donald.

I left with TB and GB for Talk Radio, and the joint phone-in. Kelvin MacKenzie was loving it. The questions were fairly hostile but they did some good answers, both political and personal, and we got decent pooled TV footage out of it too. Kelvin was relaxed about me wandering in and out of the studio and we fed them a few lines as they went, e.g. it's goodbye from me, and it's goodbye from him, and jokes about dealing with noisy neighbours etc. We got back for Cabinet, where GB warned there could be trouble ahead on the jobs front. He went over what he thought was the Tory plan re the Budget – which had not been discernible on the day. It was to suggest financial ill discipline.

Then TB saw DD and claimed he really put it to him. But the worry was Donald had just lost the stomach for the fight. His confidence and his appetite seemed low. The CAP deal reached overnight wasn't everything we wanted so the 11.30 briefing was mainly about that, plus continuing post-Budget stuff. Alex F came in for a cup of tea and while he was there we got Walter Smith [former Rangers manager, now managing Everton] on the phone who agreed to come out for us in the Scottish elections too. I told Alex I was beginning to feel the pressure a bit more, and also feeling that I wasn't putting in the hours at home like I should be. He felt the press were going to go for me because they knew I was important to Tony, and I had to take that as a compliment, and live with it. He wondered if I shouldn't go up-front on TV so that the public could make up their own minds, not just rely on the press. He said I keep hearing people talk about you and a lot of them haven't a clue what you sound like and they only know pictures that are used the whole time to make you look nasty and dangerous. He felt re the family I just had to do my best, get there whenever I could, and be there properly when I was there. He said he never gave the kids the time they needed but he had Cathy [his wife] looking after them full-time. But as adults they understood he had a total-commitment job and my kids would be the same.

I had a meeting with Gerald Kaufman to enlist his support re the press. He loathed them, felt broadsheet and tabloid alike were debasing politics with their coverage of it, and agreed we should fight back harder and better. I showed him the file on Budget speculation, the vast bulk of which, presented as fact, had been total bilge. He said there was never any comeback. Nobody ever went back to them – e.g. their editors – and asked why they had got it all so wrong. I was paged during the afternoon briefing with the message Lafontaine had resigned. I briefed that it showed modernisers were on the up in Europe, and that the battle on economic reform could be won. We got terrific TV coverage from the joint phone-in. Kelvin sent me a bill for the free advertising.

Friday, March 12

The big story overnight was the SNP briefing they would oppose the 1p tax cut. As ever the press were giving them an easy ride on it, but the public would be in a different place and it was potentially a big moment for the campaign. TB said it was the moment to kill them, to make the economy and living standards the issue, to say they could not take away the tax cut without making compensating changes elsewhere. I said I bet DD doesn't see it like that. Sure enough, on the conference call, he said he felt the SNP would get credit for boldness. Thankfully GB came on the line and we were able to drive the line and the tactics to where they needed to be. Again, till now we had put nobody up against them so they were getting away with it. We needed political and business voices out there now.

I suggested to DD he write to Salmond asking if he would vote against the tax cut and reverse it if he won. It was virtually impossible to get him to do anything quickly. It was like swimming through mud. GB injected a bit of urgency. He said he would activate David Murray. I called Alex F and Walter Smith to get their go-ahead to bring forward their joint statement urging a Labour vote. Walter said his dad was a real socialist, whereas he was New Labour. He said he felt the SNP were old-fashioned tax and spend and the Scots would reject them. The SNP needed to feel they had made a big mistake and the strategic plates were shifting against them. But it meant, as I said to DD, that we showed aggression and confidence.

Lafontaine's resignation was big in the papers, if a bit OTT with people saying champagne corks popped in Downing Street. I sent a note through to Uwe [Uwe-Karsten Heye, Schroeder's spokesman] saying we were trying to play it down, suggesting we do the joint document between Labour and SPD on the 'Neue Mitte' [Third Way manifesto] soon. TB called, worried we were overdoing it, and I explained we were trying to haul it down. The Guardian had a story saying TB wanted Mo to be London mayor. She called in a huff about it and I said she should ignore all reshuffle stories. TB chaired a meeting on office structures. Jeremy [Heywood] felt we needed more people. I felt the media side needed to expand if we were genuinely going to move to 24-hour cover. David M wanted four more policy people. John Sawers thought the foreign side was understaffed. Jonathan was a bit sensitive about it all, feeling each department would become its own and carve him out. TB said he wanted to ensure Jonathan retained a role in the domestic and foreign side, which was right. There was a discussion about whether to move the main offices to the Admiralty Buildings, and then why can't we take over Numbers 11 and 12?

Alistair Darling came over to do a joint briefing for the Sundays on various elements of welfare reform. He is a very solid performer, serious and assured, and takes no shit from them. I played a straight bat re the Lafontaine story, welcomed the [Hans] Eichel nomination [as Germany's new finance minister] and said it made no difference to the abatement situation. For the rest of the day I was mainly motoring on Scotland. With DD still umming and aahing, I got GB on World at One and he was excellent. Alex and Walter basically said I could say what I wanted on their behalf, and I was really pushing them at the tabloids.

GB came on with the number of an Aberdeen businessman willing to do interviews attacking the SNP policy and I spoke to him and got him up and about. I briefed Martin Clarke several times, and just pretended the recent past had never happened. I was calling the editors up there all day, really trying to get them to see this as a turning point. It was like being back in the campaign. GB was motoring too, all over the Scottish media thank God.

I got a call from Neil McKendrick [Master of Gonville and Caius College, Cambridge, AC's alma mater] saying they had been approached by Oborne and he was minded to 'give a dinner for him' to help with his book on me. I said I would rather they told him to bugger off. I was being approached the whole time by people who said they were being contacted by researchers for this book or that. DB called re GB's jobs briefing, said he was behaving like he was PM, tramping on everyone else's departments. TB called a couple of times from Chequers, where he was working on Kosovo.

Saturday, March 13

GB and I spoke several times through the day to keep pushing on the SNP and tax, and we carved up the Sundays up there between us. We had more business people to push their way. TB called re Kosovo, which was taking up a lot of his time at the moment, and was pretty sure it was getting worse not better. I said GB had been terrific in the last few days and he said it was important I maintained that working relationship with him. He said he was the best there is when he played as a team, and he was probably feeling a bit liberated with Peter not there, and may even have seen he was wrong about Whelan. We went for dinner at the Foots' [former Labour leader Michael and his wife Jill], with [Salman] Rushdie [novelist], Martin Woollacott (and wife) and Jonathan Freedland [both *Guardian* journalists]. They were all of the view we should go for Ken Livingstone for mayor.

Monday, March 15

Philip sent through the latest polls from Scotland. DD was on the slide on an attributes poll vs Salmond. TB was worrying again that we could lose. Donald had done a really poor interview yesterday and Salmond had got away with his. GB called me at 7 and said we had to ensure we got another day of business hitting the SNP. We were planning for Schroeder tomorrow on Agenda 2000, and the eleven o'clock was dominated by questions on the CAP rebate again. TB and I were going to the *Sun* for lunch with the top executives and writers and on the way I said he really just had to make it clear we were never going to agree on Europe. He couldn't be all things to all men. The lunch itself was dominated by Europe. TB was fine, pretty dismissive of their agenda and set out his stall clearly. They were by and large very right wing and I can see that it really irks them to be thought of as a Labour paper. Richard Littlejohn [columnist] ranted on about political correctness, they had a go re marriage and the family, tax of course, but TB was pretty strong. I was taking the piss out of Littlejohn most of the time, with him giving as good as he got. He had become fantastically egotistical. He was definitely starting to believe his own blurb, but he could still make me laugh.

The real problem politically was Kavanagh and [Chris] Roycroft-Davis [leader writer], who were clearly desperate to get the paper back to the Tories. Trevor was easily the more intelligent and because he had a good manner, and authority, I think he held more sway over Rebekah [Wade] than she should allow. On the way back we got a call about the car bombing of nationalist lawyer Rosemary Nelson.[1] Grim. I put together a TB statement which we released on return.

I had a meeting with TB and GB first re jobs, and how we handle unemployment rising on Wednesday, then re Scotland where GB felt they had taken the foot off the accelerator today, and if we were not on their case the whole time, it stopped. Both of them were really worried re DD and we had to find a better strategy for him but also people who could ensure he delivered it. He had so many strengths but we just weren't playing to them. And of course the more TB and GB and I harangued him, which is probably how he saw it, the more his confidence went. TB said he had become obsessed with DD and how to get him to improve his performance.

Hague was at the Press Club awards and launched a big attack on me. Piers called and said it was pathetic. Late on, the EU fraud report came out and put real pressure on Santer and others to resign. Jan Royall [Neil Kinnock's office] called to say Neil was totally clean. The whole Commission was likely to resign and be reappointed. She said it would help if we could say the UK commissioners were not criticised, which we did.

Tuesday, March 16

I was up at 6 to work on TB's script for the Caledonian Club [London club for Scots] lunch, which we would be pushing big time up north, and Anji had persuaded them to let the cameras in. The Commission was huge as a story, and TB not too happy that we were inserted so

---

[1] Leading human rights solicitor Nelson was killed by a car bomb in Lurgan, County Armagh. The murder was claimed by a shadow loyalist group, the Red Hand Defenders.

prominently into the story, defending [Leon] Brittan and Neil, which the media were presenting as us defending the whole show. He felt we should be arguing far more strongly for root and branch reform, sleazebusters, the works. We felt RC would have to do a statement and then Hague put down a PQ which meant TB would have to do a statement in the House. GB was suggesting Anji and I go up to Scotland full-time, Anji on DD and events, me on media, but Civil Service-wise it was impossible. At the 11, I started to use some of the lines from TB's statement [on the EU summit]. We had strong words re Santer and TB was in danger of creating an enemy for life. The Caledonian Club speech went OK, pretty crusty audience, but it would make the bulletins up there with the attack on the SNP on the economy. George R stayed to do the Q&A and we got back to prepare for the statement. TB didn't like the draft John Sawers had done. Nor was he impressed by [David] Bostock's negotiating skills. He thought he didn't make enough effort to get into the German mindset. We did a rewrite and it went OK. I gave him a line, which he delivered with brilliant timing, re the Tories having an unfortunate record with compromise candidates that seem a good idea at the time.

At the briefing, I was making clear our view that Santer should go sooner rather than later. Kok called TB and it was fairly clear he would be willing to be drafted in. Prodi was also a strong candidate. We got back for Schroeder's arrival. He turned up in a small bus, with his entourage, had a great big smile as he stepped off the bus, did a few pictures then in they came. They did one hour forty minutes, just the two of them with interpreters, at the end of which TB said they were hoping Kok would do it. He said he had been totally unyielding on the rebate and Schroeder seemed to understand we were not going to shift on the rebate.[1] Uwe-Karsten Heye had sent his Number 2, Béla Anda, who was not quite as laid-back. We agreed that on the rebate we would say our position had not changed but of course Schroeder was always looking for compromise.

TB said the private session was perfectly friendly 'but it's not much fun having your balls squeezed by a German who is being wound up by a Frenchman'. He had said that the rebate could not be applied to new countries coming in and if TB resisted change, he would look

---

[1] Urged on by Jacques Chirac, German Chancellor Gerhard Schroeder (as holder of the EU presidency) was pressing to scrap the £2bn British rebate from the EU, arguing that EU spending had changed since the rebate was negotiated in 1984 by Margaret Thatcher.

like Thatcher. Schroeder was almost as strong as TB on Santer, but said that on his pre-summit tour of the capitals so far, he had come up against a lot of complacency. TB's view was that it was time for a real heavyweight in the Commission presidency, even if it meant Heads felt a bit threatened. At the press conference, had it not been for Santer, the rebate would definitely have been the story. Schroeder was pretty clear he was going for it, so we were set up for a big fight in Berlin.

TB gave the negotiating team a bit of a rocket, said he didn't think we were coming at them in the right way, that we had to be giving them solutions as well as problems. 'I want you to camp in Germany from now on.' He was clearly missing John Holmes and Brian Bender and of course this one was a really big one, because it was about money, big money, and who got what. He said he had the collywobbles re the rebate, because he sensed they were all going to come at us on it.

Wednesday, March 17

Wall-to-wall EU, a lot focused on Santer's 'arrogance'. We did OK, though there was a lot of pressure on Neil K and Leon Brittan too. TB had spoken to Klima and D'Alema and was pushing hard on the line Santer should go soon. Re Scotland, TB and GB were going well in the press there but Donald was barely on the radar, even though he was in the States and seeing Clinton tonight. When I asked whether they had made sure all the Scottish media were there for it, David Whitton [DD's special adviser] said 'Well, we're trying.' When GB asked if I could speak to the White House to ensure there was a photograph of the meeting, I said I couldn't believe it hadn't all been bolted down already. I learned later Fiona Ross [STV] had not even been told he was going to the bloody White House. GB and I gave them a script, that pitched it as a mission to save Scottish jobs by lobbying re cashmere. It was not bloody rocket science.

TB held a meeting re his Beveridge lecture tomorrow. Peter H had the idea of 'popular welfare' which would fly a bit. Trevor Kavanagh came in with my lunch. He was at pains to say he was not a committed Tory, but they had an agenda at the paper based on the readers' views. I said re Europe the views were those they pushed at them the whole time. He said in any event he saw no way back for the Tories. Santer announced he would go soon.

TB did OK at PMQs but he kept muddling his words. I got back for a meeting with Richard Wilson, Mike Granatt, Alun Evans, Godric, Lance Price and Bill Bush [Downing Street Research Unit] re rebuttal which was really what I wanted Bill to be doing. RW clearly saw it as a totally political concept, and it was a struggle to persuade them it was a necessary part of any organisation constantly being written about, a lot of it nonsense which had to be challenged. Granatt, as ever talking a good game, kept saying everything was covered, which was nonsense. Wilson was more sympathetic in a way, said he knew ministers were not happy and there had to be changes and possibly more resources too, and asked for a paper on it.

Piers Morgan called trying to get me wound into the Joe Ashton massage parlour story, which we had successfully stayed out of.[1] I went into my 'all you do is trivia' mode and he said well give us something serious and after a bit of toing and froing he agreed to splash on a trail of TB's welfare speech. Philip called after doing some groups in Scotland. He said the problem was they were thinking Salmond would get more for Scotland. The Donald/Clinton fiasco was beyond belief. He had lost his nerve and none of the people around him could sort it.

Thursday, March 18

There was a good poll in the *Record* but virtually zero coverage of DD seeing Clinton. Unbe-fucking-lievable. TB's speech was duly splashed in the *Mirror* but was running low-key on the broadcasts. GM labelling was going wrong and we decided to invoke Mike Granatt's cross-cutting departmental plan for the first time. This was a system I had been pressing for for ages, where when issues straddled departments we bought those departments' media operations together and ran them from the centre. Cabinet was mainly EU crisis then Kosovo. TB was worried the public were not remotely prepared for what might be coming, namely a pretty difficult military operation. Ireland was bubbling up and we finished the joint statement, which was still weak on decommissioning.

David Davies came in to see me. 1. Could I float with the Germans the idea of a joint 2006 World Cup bid? And 2. he was not going for the chief executive job at the FA because he had no business experience. The four o'clock was mainly about Ireland, George Jones [*Telegraph*] in particular giving me a really hard time re the lack of toughness of decommissioning. I met [press officer] Lucie McNeil's ethnic squad, people in each department assigned to focus on the

[1] The Labour MP had been questioned by police, after being found in a Thai massage parlour in a raid. The police announced Ashton had done nothing illegal.

ethnic media, to gee them up a bit. Kavanagh made a complaint to Colin Brown [*Independent*, chairman of the lobby] re David Peel [press officer] spying on what they were writing. David took me too literally, so when I said wander round the gallery and find out what they were all up to, he tended just to look over their shoulders at what they were writing.

Friday, March 19

The *FT* splashed on a story that the Germans were going soft on the rebate. Europe still going big, ditto the NI joint statement, even though people realised it was all just words to get us through a gap. TB was doing a doorstep on NI in Sedgefield when the Fiona Jones verdict came through.[1] She was guilty and he was asked about that too. It was a bad story and I was pissed off we had let him be drawn right into it. I had a conference call with TB and Margaret McDonagh. Margaret was against an appeal, but TB said there would be a lot of candidates of all parties thinking there but for the grace of God.

On Kosovo, he said there is a chance we will be launching bombing raids next week, at the same time we are trying to sort Ireland and negotiate a good deal for Britain in the Agenda 2000 talks. Another depressing Scotland conference call, this time without Donald. GB and I wanted DD up making a big speech over the weekend. Helen said he would be tired after the US. I said yes, it must be exhausting generating all that wall-to-wall coverage of a meeting with the US president. I spoke to Ian McCartney and got him out generating some proper attacks on Salmond, e.g. Scotland needs a future not an ego.

Saturday, March 20

Another desultory Scottish conference call, then TB on re Kosovo, which was really preoccupying him now. We managed to get the inner-city schools stuff up in the Sundays but their calls were all dominated by Europe. The Kinnocks, Foots, Goodmans [former *Mirror* colleague Geoffrey and his wife Margit] and Matthew and Vivian Lewin [neighbours] came for dinner. Neil was in full flow re Europe and going on a bit too much, but it was a nice enough evening. He was really angry re Santer – spineless, useless – but was too emotionally caught up in it, and often talking about people the others had

---

[1] The Labour MP was convicted of fraudulently failing to declare the full amount of her election expenses. She was disqualified from membership of the House of Commons for the offence, but the Court of Appeal overturned her conviction and she was reinstated.

March '99: Could be bombing in Kosovo next week

never heard of. I was in and out a bit dealing with the *News of the World* doing some story about a crank chasing Kathryn [Blair]. I got them to take it out on the basis it was a crank and would just spark copycats.

Neil stayed on after everyone else and said we must get a new president for the Commission out of Berlin, preferably Kok, if not Prodi. He said to watch Pauline Green [Labour MEP and PES group leader], who had a different agenda, namely to get all the commissioners to resign and become the Labour commissioner. A ridiculous proposition. Glenys was at last admitting to the gravy-train problem. Neil was clearly anxious and was letting it show by going over the same thing again and again.

Sunday, March 21
The papers were dull. TB was at Chequers, had a long chat with Clinton re Kosovo, then Schroeder re Agenda 2000. Another bad Scotland call. GB said the press were still letting the SNP get away with a lot and we had to be more imaginative about how we tackled them. I read all the Agenda 2000 briefing which was bloody complicated, but what was clear was they were going to come at us big time on the rebate and we were going to have to show a lot of balls to hold on.

Monday, March 22
I woke up with a bad cold, went back to bed and missed the morning meetings. Philip by all accounts gave TB a bit of a kicking for 'no longer finding your voice' on the big social issues. We were also in my view in the wrong place on the education stuff with too much focus on help for the talented and gifted, rather than a classic 'many not few' position. We had the usual crap Scotland conference call on which my cold was making me even more bad-tempered than usual. It was the Scottish Grand Committee [Commons committee of all Scottish MPs] today but they had no clear plan for it. GB came to the rescue a bit, saying Sam Galbraith [Labour MP for Strathkelvin and Bearsden] could announce a doubling of the number of one-stop health clinics to help against cancer.

GB called me from Scotland, where he was visiting his eye doctor. He said things were really bad up there. Both of us were getting fed up with the whole thing. We were having to carry people who didn't want to be carried but had no alternative of their own. Fiona, Rory and I went to look at William Ellis [secondary school], which seemed OK, even if we heard far too much bad language around the place. I could hardly believe Rory would soon be at senior school.

I got in to see TB before his Europe interviews. He delivered strong lines on Prodi, economic reform, Kosovo, and I used some of the lines in my 3.30 briefing, namely Prodi the man, need for faster reform, praise for Schroeder, tough on Kosovo. We had a TB/GB plus teams meeting, which largely consisted of GB and I telling them how ghastly the Scottish situation was. TB was constantly saying we had to fix it. We were doing all we could but it was hard. I wondered if we shouldn't put up three or four bright young things to front the whole campaign. GB said it was exasperating and hopeless, especially as the strategy was fairly clear – 1. hurt the SNP with business, 2. beat them on fairness, 3. make clear there was a process and this was the first instalment. TB spoke to Chirac and agreed that we would be side by side on Kosovo, possibly going in as early as tomorrow.

Tuesday, March 23

GB called pre the Scotland call and said he and I really had to start putting pressure on them to deliver, so both of us adopted a much tougher posture on the call. We were trying to get the SNP's small-business policies up in lights. I went with David M to the *Independent* for one of our press plus policy Q&As. They were the usual mix of cynicism and arrogance, stunned at our temerity in suggesting the press was anything but perfect, but at least these longer sessions gave them the chance to hear arguments at length and see that we at least had a coherent approach to policy. I think David and I are a good double act, because he does the heavy policy stuff while I fit it into a strategic narrative.

We agreed early that TB should do a Commons statement on Kosovo, so that dominated the morning briefing. Sandy Berger had sent over a good note on arguments for getting involved, and we worked some of that into the statement. TB had a meeting to go over the whole scene – RC, GR, CDS [Guthrie], RW, Jonathan, AC – and it was pretty gloomy. Charles Guthrie made clear it was a difficult operation being considered and nobody could be quite sure when or how it ended. It could be very bloody indeed, he said. TB's statement went fine and Hague was poor again. They were beginning to look really pissed off behind him now. The Germans briefed that they would be looking at the UK rebate regardless of this being about the costs of enlargement, which TB took as a worrying sign.

We had another session with Donald D, TB and I trying as gently as we could to get him to understand the need for a clear message in Scotland, a clear and agreed strategy, and some energy and aggression. TB said afterwards he felt dreadful, as though he was kicking a dog, so downcast did Donald look. But we had to grip it. TB did a clutch of Kosovo interviews, then we set off [for Berlin]. On the flight we sat with RC, David Bostock and Stephen Wall and went through the real nitty-gritty.

We arrived, got to the hotel then had a long session with Bertie Ahern and team which was pretty gloomy. Bertie said he was not sure it was worth holding talks in Belfast because we could be up seven nights and still not get them to say they would decommission. TB said if we didn't go, and it subsequently all collapsed, we wouldn't be forgiven. He felt we had to inject a real shock into the system. TB was sitting in the only comfortable armchair in the room, the rest of us on hard-backed upright chairs, and he was clearly the man calling the shots. Bertie ended up agreeing they should go next week, but he was down about things. TB said if the two of them, plus Bill C, all made the same points powerfully, it would have a big impact on public opinion. Joe Lennon said the IRA never gave two hoots about public opinion. TB said yes, but we have to separate the moderates from the extremists.

TB spoke to Bill C re Kosovo. He said afterwards it is ridiculous trying to juggle all these things – Kosovo, NI, Agenda 2000 – every one of them required real care and attention. I said that was his job and we just had to do it. But the pressure was intense at the moment, and it was affecting us in different ways.

Wednesday, March 24
Kosovo was still the main story and TB did a doorstep at the start of the day largely about that. We were now very close to action. We had a breakfast meeting with Wall and Bostock and TB set out our principle aims again – Prodi; abatement protected; progress on CAP; good deal for Northern Ireland and Highlands and Islands [Scottish rural area requiring special subsidy]. It was not going to be easy though. The summit itself was at the InterContinental. Our briefing room was in a cinema a short distance away and we had big crowds with the expectation of some pretty big bust-ups.

The German text was kicking around and I felt the words on the abatement were difficult for us. Our line was that we would not countenance paying the cost of the abatement ourselves and that we could not object to a review provided it was clear we were talking a 'kicking into the long grass' situation. I got back from one briefing to learn the Heads had suddenly decided to talk about the Commission presidency and Prodi had got the job. TB had been at the heart of the discussion, keen on Kok but it was clear that wasn't going to happen, then pushing Prodi. We were going to be pretty well tied to him, good or bad. We talked him up as a reformer and placed a piece from TB on him in an Italian paper.

He was still worrying re the abatement. Most countries had attacked it to a greater or lesser extent, but there was no way we could budge. I had a meeting with GB who could barely hide his loathing of these events, though he always managed to switch on the light – hi, how ya doing? – if any of the politicians or hacks walked by. He was downcast re Scotland and re Europe. He also felt we had not sustained our advantage post-Budget and were losing the argument on tax. I spent part of the afternoon working on TB's Kosovo broadcast, and a script for a press conference. I was in and out of the deliberations which Schroeder seemed to be chairing really well, not letting people stay too long on their pet projects. John Sawers took me to one side and said Kosovo was definitely on and action was set to start at 7pm. SACEUR [General Wesley Clark] had the key. We went back to the hotel and TB worked on the draft I'd done, and wrote a strong ending. He said D'Alema was wobbly re air strikes. Chirac and Schroeder were sound. Once it started, we were nervous until we heard the four Harriers were back safe and sound. TB did his statement here, JP in London, and I felt we had the arguments strong enough to carry public support for what we were doing.

The official dinner was effectively scrapped so foreign and finance ministers could carry on the negotiations. Santer had made two big attacks, first on the abatement, then re Highlands and Islands. TB talked of 'Santer's revenge'. But Schroeder was being pretty helpful all round, and the ongoing sense of difficulty between him and Chirac was getting a lot of play. Chirac was also doing a *déclaration aux français* [declaration to the French people] re Kosovo.

Thursday, March 25

TB was trying to talk to Schroeder for ages after he woke up, but even by 8 we were told he was in bed. This on the day he was meant to be solving the mass of problems still outstanding. The next thirty-six hours just melded into one long day, reminiscent of the Good Friday Agreement talks in a way. Our biggest worries were the attacks on the abatement, pressure on the extra help for Highlands and Islands, CAP, stabilisation. Kosovo was of course the main news, and Sally M called to say there was a bit of a head of steam building re questions of legality. TB did British forces radio, then a short doorstep, and most people felt we were in the right place on this and that his statement last night had been strong.

The mood pre the summit meeting itself was tense. Every single country had their own specific interests to protect and it was going to be impossible to satisfy everyone. The first session ended fairly quickly, Schroeder obviously deciding he was going to achieve more in bilaterals. He had a long one with Chirac, and with us. Though it was all reasonably good-humoured, there was a tension there. I think Schroeder had felt TB might give something on the rebate, but wasn't, and TB was now pushing in other areas, and looking for a bit of help. GB was taking part as well and was good, spraying the jargon all around to show he knew what he was on about, VAT/GNP, own resources, no windfall gains, which is where we ended. We were winning on most points, lost on a couple but we were running rings round the others in the briefing game. D'Alema's wobbles re the air strikes were seeping out so we spoke to him, pinned him down and got him to agree we could say we had spoken to him and he was NOT calling for an end to the strikes. We decided to go ahead with a TV broadcast and I got Lance Price to talk to Anne Sloman [BBC chief political adviser] to fix.

TB then had a second long bilateral with Schroeder. We had reshaped what we were asking for and where we saw how others could change and Schroeder seemed pretty on board but some of his people were wheedling at him. Later, when TB had another go at Schroeder, he totally lost it, basically told TB to fuck off, and stormed off, and his interpreter turned to me and said 'I don't think we need to translate that one.' TB said 'I think we've pushed him as far as he'll go.' Chirac was digging in re CAP and at one point TB was asked to have a go at Chirac, which he did, though to what effect was unclear. Chirac was playing hardball and gently doing in Jospin at the same time. Kok stopped short of really going for Chirac on CAP. Truth be told though, a very good deal for us was emerging, and it was others who were in trouble now.

TB, GB and I went for a walk, during part of which TB took a call from [Yevgeny] Primakov [Russian Prime Minister]. We decided we should ignore the advice of officials and go direct to Schroeder with our own proposal for resolving this, which would include a better deal on the safety net, and getting Objective 1 for Highlands and Islands. TB had slightly lost faith in the negotiating team and wanted to do it himself from now on in. The Commission officials were reasonably up for it. TB got Kok and [Hans Göran] Persson [Swedish Prime Minister] pretty much on board. Schroeder said he was grateful we were being constructive. Then, PR-wise at least, a breakthrough in the form of a French error. Pierre Moscovici [French minister for

Europe] did a briefing saying the UK rebate was a permanent obstacle to good UK-Europe relations. This was our moment. I went straight out to brief. We were being attacked for not giving in just at the moment we were constructively offering to make concessions. I dropped in the pre-accession points. Someone had briefed John Palmer [*Guardian*] re the row with Schroeder, which we were not keen to play up now we were trying to help sort the whole show. GB was keen to leave but TB wanted him around. It was now just one meeting after another in one or other of the ghastly rooms at the InterContinental. By about midnight we felt pretty safe but it wasn't till gone 5am that it was finally sorted.

Friday, March 26

As we walked from the conference centre to the hotel, crowds milling about, delegates mixing with drunks and people going to work early, it seemed such an absurd way to do business. TB said it kind of worked after a fashion. You needed these moments to bring things to a head. Officials could toil away forever but in the end politicians had to make deals. We had done well on the Highlands and Islands and I was on to the Scottish lot making sure they made the most of it.

The feedback from the Kosovo attacks was not great. As well as the Harriers failing to hit their targets, our TLAMs [Tomahawk land attack missiles] from [HMS] *Splendid* [nuclear submarine] failed too. The Yanks who sold us the missiles were not surprisingly in a bit of a flap about it. I suggested we just say it was a joint operation and not get into who did which bit of the operation. TB had about an hour's sleep while I worked on the broadcast speech. The summit coverage was going well, but dwarfed of course by Kosovo.

On the plane back, we had the usual joking re the other leaders. TB felt Chirac had really hung tough, Dehaene had been tough, Schroeder had been pretty cool apart from his fuck-off moment. 'I thought he was going to hit me,' he said. 'It's war' would have been the headline, I said. We worked on the Kosovo broadcast. He asked me to do a passage re the suffering of the Kosovo people. We both felt like heading for home but he was speaking to the Welsh Labour conference. We stopped at Northolt to drop off the EU team and pick up Sally M, Pat McF and Hilary [Coffman]. Pat had done an excellent draft of the Welsh speech which we barely needed to change, just slot in bits re EU and Kosovo. The main event was going to be his broadcast and by the time we landed at Hawarden [airfield], we were happy with it. We were driven to Llandudno, getting a bit of sleep on the way, then to St George's hotel where the TV people were set up for the broadcast to the nation. It was an odd setting but would do.

The conference speech went fine, though he was really tired by now. The recording went fine, but we were two minutes over. It was supposed to be 4.40. We got it down to 4.48 and I called Anne Sloman and said they would have to make do with that. We slept on the plane back, but were both pretty shagged by now. TB was really worried re Kosovo. The Tories and some of the papers, mainly the *Mail*, were positioning themselves for it going wrong, whilst on the surface being supportive. I did a conference call for the Sundays, which was a mix of Europe and Kosovo.

Saturday, March 27

I slept solid for twelve hours then took the football club at school. I was also working on a joint TB/Bertie Ahern article, the Irish as ever trying to get a bit weaselly on the decommissioning issue. The Europe coverage was excellent, most of them saying we got pretty much everything we wanted, one or two saying the benefits of a more positive approach were now showing. The BBC coverage re Kosovo was bad, with them basically taking the Serb line ahead of ours and without any context re the pressures they're under there. We were finding it virtually impossible to get Kosovar Albanians on to the TV and radio here. I spoke to Paddy Ashdown about it, suggested maybe an intervention from him would have more impact than another blast from me. George R did a good press conference on the Serb attacks and there were some really powerful pictures coming out of the refugees on the Macedonian border.

The US fixed a TB/Bill C call for 7pm so I had to leave the kids' school disco to get home and listen in. They agreed to an intensification of the campaign and I briefed that TB had said we would increase our contribution, GR to announce details tomorrow. They also went over the yardsticks by which they would judge it right to talk to Milosevic again. There was no real clarity about an endgame at the moment. There was also a presentational problem in the way Serb attacks on Kosovar Albanians were now being seen as a response to NATO attacks, and of course our media were swallowing their line. As TB said to BC, if Milosevic had a BBC to deal with, he would not be getting such an easy ride. As it is, our media is helping him with his own public opinion.

They also did a bit of NI, BC saying he would do whatever it takes and we briefed that too. Good call, and he sounded a lot more sharp and clear than last time they did Kosovo. Then we heard a stealth bomber had been shot down and there was a race on to get to the pilot first – thankfully won by the Americans. But because the stealth bomber was supposed to be undetectable by radar, it would have a bad effect on morale. The press was not so bad, but we had a real problem with the BBC and we talked over whether we should go for them publicly. They made no effort to balance the fact that they were reporting democracies and a dictatorship, virtually taking the dictatorship propaganda at face value while putting everything we did through a far more intense scrutiny.

Sunday, March 28

On Kosovo, the press was pretty supportive and there were three good polls out today. The problem would come with casualties. Also, the strike success rate so far was not good. TB said he wanted to take a far more active interest in targeting and I fed that message through to Charles Guthrie. GR and Guthrie did a press conference and we had to use Day 1 pictures because last night had not been great. George's main lines were that Arkan [Zeljko Raznatovic, Serbian paramilitary leader and organised-crime boss wanted for genocide and crimes against humanity] was in Kosovo, and the details of the extra Harriers and Tornadoes being deployed. The MoD wanted TB to do the briefing tomorrow but he wasn't sure.

The news was dominated by the stealth bomber, more UK planes being deployed and NATO saying it was the worst genocide since WW2. Paddy A went up on Kosovar Albanians not being heard. TB called, worried at the delayed reaction to the Budget, felt GB should have been more open about some of the changes now out there. Burnley beat Macclesfield 4-3.

Monday, March 29

Another day from hell really. The refugee situation was getting worse, and there wasn't much sign the military campaign was getting better. Some of the papers, especially the *Mail*, were positioning for failure. Another ghastly Scotland call. Salmond was to do a broadcast on Kosovo and I said we had to be ready to pounce if there was the slightest equivocation. Back came the line he might get support. Added to which NI was upon us again, at another crisis point. I asked Julian [Braithwaite] to do a proper report on how the Serb media worked, so that we could start to inform our own media as much as anything else.

The question had really moved from justification – there was widespread support for the idea of action – to competence and efficiency and ability to deliver the policy. At 9.30 RC, CDS, GR, RW came over for a meeting and Charles [Guthrie] gave a pretty gloomy assessment. Bad weather and poor weapons performance meant we were not really hurting Milosevic as planned. TB looked pretty downcast. CDS was fulminating re the TV armchair generals and later vowed he would do none of it when he retired. I was asking why they were not hitting transmitters, if our argument was that his media machine was part of his military machine. Charles said even if the Yanks had the stomach for a ground war – doubtful – the Italians wouldn't. TB said we had to do such damage to Milosevic, the regime and the personal assets that he would sue for peace. He too couldn't understand why we were not taking out his transmitters. At the 11, I reflected TB's line that we now needed strength not weakness, that we would see it through, and I went for those who were pursuing the line that the humanitarian disaster was a consequence of the attacks rather than his ethnic cleansing and genocide. TB's statement on Agenda 2000 went fine. Hague, who was off form again, did not even attack us on the abatement or structural funds. He stayed onside re Kosovo. I spoke to Gerald Kaufman to plant a question re the way our media was covering it, and that turned out to be fairly effective. [Tony] Benn was a bit calmer. [Sir Peter] Tapsell [Conservative MP] was mad, calling TB 'the kaiser'.

Once we got Salmond's weaselly statement GB and I drafted a statement which we got RC to put out, with the line that Salmond would be the toast of Belgrade. He made the mistake of comparing the air strikes – targeted at a dictatorship – with the Blitz of London or Clydebank. Silly boy. Bad judgement and we went for him.

Plane to Belfast. TB asked me to work with George R on plans to neutralise or turn the negative effects Milosevic's media machine was having on our media. We helicoptered to Hillsborough, where TB did a fairly downbeat doorstep, less 'hand of history' than 'we have come too far to stop now'. TB saw Bertie, then Trimble, then Mallon, then he and Bertie met Adams and McGuinness together. Everyone seemed to think we were in the shit. I had a chat with McGuinness re Kosovo. He said he [Milosevic] would be a hard nut to crack and 'bombing into submission' isn't always a sensible policy. Pots and kettles. The only breakthrough of sorts came when Adams said to us 'Look, we know the score, there has got to be decommissioning.' It was the first time he, rather than we, had been that blunt. It had also been announced where nine of the 'disappeared' were. The downside of that was it reminded people the IRA were killers. As TB said, are we really expected to be hugely grateful that years after they did it they told us where they killed and disposed of a few people?

TB worked through past 11, then spoke to Clinton, agreeing we needed a strengthening of resolve all round re Kosovo. Salmond was running big time in Scotland, and it was registering as a mistake. We still couldn't get Donald to pile in properly, but RC did fine, and GB was up doing a big number on poverty, on which we said Salmond had nothing to say.

Tuesday, March 30

Kosovo was not looking good. The humanitarian crisis was becoming a disaster, and another night of bad weather meant another night of military failure. He said we had to start doing some real damage. He felt we had two days before things turned against us. TB said Milosevic will only move if he senses we are in a position of over-whelming strength. He saw the Orange Order before we left for Stormont for talks mainly with the smaller parties. He and Bertie saw [General John] de Chastelain, who must live a very weird life, backwards and forwards to NI, with large periods of literally nothing happening to bring him into the picture. But TB stressed de Chastelain's credibility was vital to the process. He felt we might get something, possibly an act of decommissioning, videotaped by SF, verified by them. Paisley was out and about rowing with the Irish, but the one TB really couldn't stand was Brendan McKenna [Garvaghy Road residents' spokesman]. He said he was making things worse and people would die as a result.

I watched the GR, CDS, Clare press conference, which was OK but we really needed signs of the military campaign working. Joe Lennon and I suggested that we impose a deadline of midnight and that if there is no progress by then we leave. They were nervous. Then a school visit, which was a way of trying to get through to public opinion direct. We flew back to Hillsborough and over lunch TB and BA agreed they would really try to work on Sinn Fein. They went into a two-hour meeting with Adams and McGuinness, while I put together another vacuous space-filling briefing about it all being 'difficult but doable'. We were literally having to just dream up lines to keep the news guys busy whilst TB and Bertie tried to put the pressure on. The BBC ran a story, based on God knows what, that the UUs were now saying an act of decommissioning was not required. John Taylor [UUP deputy leader] went straight out and said it was nonsense.

GA and McG were basically saying they would decommission – not least because they knew they had to – but they could not be sure how the IRA would react to that idea. We set up a Sinn Fein/UUP meeting for 8pm, beforehand TB/BA seeing GA/McG again to suggest the UUs were not as insistent on prior decommissioning as a precondition. He tried to get them to have a drink, but they refused. Even Taylor had said he could see it was a problem for SF if they were seen to be responding to pressure on this. Taylor wanted to delay but we were saying we had to move on it now. I felt TB was being too open with them and that they would brief the SF position and then move SF back. John Sawers came in with tonight's [Kosovo] targets, mainly defence ministry buildings. There was a North Atlantic Council meeting going on and Italy was getting more and more nervous. The truth was we were not in control of events. TB was keen to get more and more involved 'but I'm here having to deal with this nonsense.' He said if it was left to him and Bertie, they could sort a deal that most people would support in five minutes. But the NI politicians were a nightmare. They delight in being prisoners of their own history. There were meetings going on all over the place but the one that mattered was SF/UUs. Adams and McGuinness were always on their own, Trimble always with a huge entourage to keep an eye on him. The aim was to try to get some kind of sequencing agreed. GA/McG agreed there would have to be decommissioning within two years, which was an advance. TB felt Trimble was keen to get off the precondition hook but he needed at least the sense of a timetable and we were not able to get it.

About 9, they came through into the big lounge where we were just chatting and Adams said 'I'm afraid that rather than wasting everyone's time we thought it best to tell you we have a real problem.' Trimble said 'We are not in the same ballpark.' Very calmly, GA went through the main difficulties – the UUs need some kind of act, and we cannot deliver it in that way, while we cannot have decommissioning as a precondition for joining the executive, and political realities make that impossible for David. There was a long silence, TB a mix of frustration and anger, and he just sat there stony-faced for a while.

We talked round the problems for a while, but it was impossible. We met the SDLP delegation who had been hanging around getting more and more impatient. Seamus Mallon said he had to 'fight his way in to see the prime minister'. TB explained that he was not the problem, and charmed him round. Seamus said it was not sensible to keep the other parties feeling uninvolved. He felt de Chastelain's remit should be widened to give him control over a timetable. Officials were put to work on drafting overnight a proposal to kick things off in the morning. Earlier, we had been genuinely optimistic. TB said we should stay another night to give it a go, but there was a sense of deep gloom. TB was pretty much fed up with the lot of them. We were saying progress had been made but in reality all that referred to was SF acknowledging they had to decommission sometime in the future, but without a commitment it took us nowhere with the UUs. Even they accepted it wasn't enough for DT.

TB's only hope was GA and McG were off seeing the IRA guys to say 'Do we really want to be the people who bring this crashing down?' There had been something pathetic about the way they came through to TB and BA to say they couldn't sort it. It made you worry they could never work in government together, which was meant to be the aim. TB called Clinton to brief him. A group of loudmouth Loyalists appeared at the gates to abuse just about anyone who came near the place.

Wednesday, March 31

I had a bad call with Fiona first thing because she said it was impossible for her to plan anything when she never knew if I was going to be there. It put me in a foul mood for the day. Kosovo had had another night of bad weather so military frustration. TB was worrying about that, and about NI, where he said at the first meeting he just felt we were too far apart. We're wasting our time here, he said. I had a brief chat with McGuinness in the corridor and said I thought TB was getting to the end of his tether on this, so they needed to work out their lines for failure. He said it was all down to Trimble (or Trumble as he says it). TB saw the UUs. BA saw SF and gave them a hard time, said TB had a 'war to fight' and they were keeping him here, buggering him around and getting nowhere. 'I told them in Dublin Central language to "stop fucking about".' Obviously nobody wanted to be seen to bring the whole thing crashing down, and they had to feel more pressure. That did require us to stay a little longer, whatever the frustrations. I agreed with Bertie that when we left we would say if left to the two PMs it would be sorted in minutes, and people had to face up to their responsibilities, to give the sense there was a solution but the two sides would not embrace it. TB was a bit worried leaving Mo in charge of the talks, as her relations with the UUs were so poor. Yesterday she asked him what job he was going to give her post-devolution. She was making clear she felt she deserved one of the big ones. TB felt Cabinet Office was probably the best he could offer her. He had not been impressed by the way she had let the UUs stray more and more offside.

March '99: 'We're wasting our time here' – TB on NI

Bertie and Liz O'Donnell [Irish foreign minister] came in after a meeting with Adams and McG who had said the IRA were issuing a 'helpful' statement. We eventually got it and what was helpful was that it did not say there would be no decommissioning. It put in all the usual stuff but did say they wanted peace and that the IRA guns are silent. We had the usual analysis chat re what it meant and agreed it was broadly positive. We had another session with the UUs and I could see DT reading the draft declaration upside down on Bertie's footstool. I motioned Joe [Lennon] to go and drop something on top of it without it looking too obvious. DT did not go bonkers, but did say he would have real difficulties with the parts about SF being on the Shadow executive. While we were in the meeting, Mark Bennett paged me to say Sky were quoting a Trimble spokesman [David Kerr] as saying the talks would adjourn for two weeks, and TB was not able to focus properly because of Kosovo. I was pretty pissed off at that, told DT it was a low blow, and went out to deal with it. Bertie was getting more and more impatient.

We had to leave for PMQs. Re the *Mail* and the Tories, TB said their patriotism is as deep as the next opportunity to attack a Labour government. We got to Northolt, were driven straight to the House, where we were expecting Kosovo and NI to dominate. He got very little on either. On Kosovo, we worked up a line re the damage being done to Milosevic. The word from Belfast was not good. McG had basically said piss off to the paper. Bertie was threatening to go home. TB's view was the IRA were just unable to move. We also had intelligence reports on their worries the Real IRA would move if the IRA decommissioned.

We had a Kosovo meeting with RC, GR, CDS, RW etc. Charles [Guthrie] said the military side was not going brilliantly. TB said he couldn't believe the weather could be such a factor when we were talking about supposedly sophisticated weapons. He said the generals had to understand they should really be going for it, no holding back. In fact [Javier] Solana [NATO Secretary General] had vetoed plans to hit military buildings yesterday. Charles was still trying to get them to hit broadcast transmitters. Robin was very gung-ho. TB said we had to do a lot more damage before we could even think about peace moves. CDS was raging about armchair generals again, 'rats who should be shot'. He told me as a result of his press conferences he was starting to get hate mail and fan mail. His favourite was one that said he was a hapless poodle to a demented Jock. I said we needed to do more stuff in the papers with him. He said the one in the *Sun* made him sound like a lager lout. He had a fantastic sense of humour which we needed at the moment with things not going according to plan. He said the problem with targeting was that the plans were being discussed too widely e.g. in the NAC, with the ambassadors of countries not really keen on the whole enterprise.

We left for Northolt again. We met Bertie at [RAF] Aldegrove, got a helicopter to Hillsborough, then took stock. Clinton wanted to speak to Adams but he was away 'consulting' IRA members, which meant we couldn't get hold of him, as he went without a mobile, presumably because he knew he could be tracked on it. DT was at Stormont, telling everyone he intended to go to the opera. You sometimes wondered if they were serious. We started the next round around 8, first BA/TB, then the UUs and then a possible breakthrough meeting, just TB, Bertie, Adams and McGuinness. TB called us in after a while, saying 'I think we are in go mode.' He said they had definitely moved on decommissioning, however dressed up. By now most of the top IRA guys were in the building, including [Thomas] 'Slab' Murphy. 'Don't give him your home number,' Bertie said. Alongside the supposed shift, they had put down a list of demands on so-called 'normalisation'. It went too far, as did the stuff agreed earlier while we were away between the Irish and the NIO, all about the dismantling of the police and security apparatus which, when you set it against a vague and unspecified act of decommissioning, did not look that great. Mo was getting really steamed up that we were trying to water down what she had agreed, but it would tip the UUs off the other side. John Sawers was arguing against some of the specifics she had agreed, and she virtually stormed out. But he was right. They had gone too far. TB felt the SF meeting went well though, and GA went off on another round of whispered conversations and walks in the garden.

The news from Kosovo was dire, with the refugee crisis getting worse. TB saw Trimble and Taylor. DT was down because Adams was being quoted as saying there would be an agreement in the morning, and they would take their seats, which was not where DT was. But he was misrepresenting what SF were saying. They had been talking about 'no precondition', not 'no to decommissioning'. I was briefing the BBC that DT was hanging tough for deeds not words, to try to help him with his own people on the later bulletins. We were obviously set for the talks going into the night. McG was due to come back with specific comments on the paper and all the various objections to it but came back around 1.30 to say there was a problem, they had political difficulties and needed more time. I did a fairly positive briefing because I think they sensed things were moving, though SF were trying to move without saying they had. DT and Taylor said their Assembly people were getting very fractious and maybe TB should speak to them.

Ken Maginnis gave me a real bearding about how awful Mo was, how she didn't understand where they were coming from at all. He said there was no way they would accept all these normalisation measures 'and remember I am relatively speaking one of the liberals'. They all later surrounded TB and monstered him with the same kind of message. John Taylor said Mo was a liar. TB said afterwards, I think now I understand better why Trimble is like he is. While SF were away again, I had a very nice quiet chat with Bertie and Mo. Bertie said even though it is all so frustrating, it is worth remembering that not long ago, people inside this building were trying to kill each other. He was right. Earlier, I had briefed the PUP on what was going on, and they had gone to seek out some of the SF people to get clarification on one or two points. TB was less sanguine than Bertie. 'We are in a fucking madhouse,' he said as the next round wore on. Yet somehow I thought we would get there.

Thursday, April 1

We rolled into the early hours. Taylor said his troops were getting more and more fractious and wanted to go home. TB talked them into staying. I said to Taylor why don't you go up for a nap? I suggested he take TB's bed to which he said 'I could not possibly use a bed reserved in the main for the Queen and the PM.' So he took my room instead, and Maginnis, clearly no possessor of false modesty, took TB's. When I wandered up later he was snoring loudly at the ceiling. We had another mad moment shortly afterwards when McG was talking us through a SF statement as though he had literally nothing to do with the IRA, 'the other people who are being chased about the other thing'. BA, TB and I had a very jokey conversation re having conversations between various parts of your body but pretending they were not part of the same thing. By 5 or 6, there were people kipping in chairs and lying out on sofas. The staff were providing an endless supply of food and coffee, and somehow we kept going.

Bertie was convinced there was a real and substantial discussion of the [seven-member] IRA Army Council, inside the building, and that GA and McG were genuinely trying to win them round. At 5.55 we had a meeting with the Irish and it was gloomy as hell. Bertie felt they were at the bottom line. TB felt we were going nowhere but was striving to find another way of moving it forward. TB was looking a bit grey by now though, and the briefings on Kosovo weren't helping his mood or morale. TB had another session with Adams and McGuinness. I went in, and later got DT in, and said we had to publish something today, or else people would feel we were totally hopeless and this was all going nowhere. Mo and I were both getting really pissed off at the way the SF people were handling it all. Mo said they have got two PMs totally tied up in this, and a US president, yet they are giving nothing at the moment. It reached a low point when we got Clinton up at 5am US time to speak to Adams, who was busy delivering a history lesson to TB and too busy to take the fucking call. [Sandy] Berger was raging about it. We were moving to the idea of publishing the document and simply saying the parties would have to consult on it, and we would give them ten days to do so. Then, cheek of all cheeks, McGuinness said 'You realise we will be bound to oppose the delay.' Bertie, by now getting fractious, said 'That's a good one – you'll oppose it when you've been calling for it.'

Joe Lennon and I were now both imploring TB to go for them, put some real heat on. He said he was, but it was all still a bit matey. The PUP said we were kidding ourselves if we thought they would do something in ten days that they couldn't do now. Around 12, TB, Bertie, Paddy [Teahon] and I went for a walk in the garden at the back. TB said we had to get DT signed up to the text, then work on the smaller parties, then publish. TB spoke to Clinton at 12.30, who was also preoccupied with the three US soldiers being paraded on Yugoslav TV. TB said we were going to put down the declaration – d'Hondt [voting system], act of reconciliation, full devolution – and we wanted him to say to GA he should go for it. Bill spoke to him, then to TB again and we could see the SF people getting very tetchy and feeling the pressure. The BBC did a story that SF were asking for an adjournment, which pissed them off, but Joe and I both felt they should stew a bit. TB asked me to draft a positive press statement, which I did, and there was enough to build up into something. Mo liked it. TB thought it went too far and needed toning down a bit. Adams was saying to TB that they would get there, but not today.

The important thing was to give at least some sense of progress and movement. We did a joint TB/BA press statement, probably too positive, with a bit of TB emotional uplift at the end. I got Tom Kelly and Sheree Dodd [NIO] to get the press in place at the back of the castle, and told Mo and Liz O'Donnell this should just be TB and BA. They were very pissed off but what I was trying to do was create a sense of occasion, because the fact was the agreement itself would need to be carried by more than the words. What I didn't want is for it to look just like any other NI doorstep mess. From the look Liz gave me, I think I made an enemy for life, and Mo was steaming too. The last meeting was with de Chastelain to go over what he would do. We went through the difficult questions in the pre-briefing. People were reasonably upbeat apart from SF. I got them to agree an order in which they went out, so that everyone could hear everyone else. Everyone was very tired and the mood at farewell and handshake times was not great, though the TV were just about buying the line. We got a helicopter to Aldegrove and then flew home, TB and I impersonating the main players for much of the flight. What a crazy place to work. TB was still worried that if we pushed SF too hard, they would be unable to shift at all. I got home, and crashed out.

Friday, April 2

I was very tired still, and starting to get that achy feeling that exhaustion brings. We were losing the propaganda battle with the Serbs. The three US soldiers were wall-to-wall. The press for NI was OK without being great. TB called early on, and wanted a real sense of urgency injected into things. He had spoken to Clinton about the timidity of the military strategy. He had spoken to Thatcher last night who was appalled that the NAC and NATO ambassadors discussed targeting plans. He wanted the message out that we were intensifying attacks. I said we said that on Wednesday.

I drafted him a detailed note that was a draft strategic briefing, which we would probably give to *The Times*, which I sent to him, RC, GR and CDS for comments. TB was worried it would provoke talk of NATO splits, but agreed we should say NATO had moved to a real war-footing command/control structure, and that meant the generals would have far more flexibility and authority for their attacks. It was a tricky briefing, and I agreed with Phil Webster exactly how far he could push it. John Sawers was also worried re the prospect of it engendering talk of a NATO split, but TB was clear we had to inject the sense that this job was going to be seen through, however long it took. I set it in the context of a battle between a dictator and democracies, that he had all the levers at his disposal and we didn't.

Webster was in Norfolk and I was out on the heath with the kids when he called through with his final version, which was good and got the nuances right. I said to him we wanted to avoid a split story whilst at the same time getting out the message the generals had to be given their head and stop feeling they were being run by complex committee and bureaucratic structures. The TV coverage of the refugees tonight was hideous. Switch said they were getting inundated with calls after every bulletin asking what we were doing about it. The *Times* splash headline was 'Allied generals cleared to bomb at will', which was picked up straight away. The only worry was if NATO denounced it. But we really had to start showing some results on the military front.

Saturday, April 3

We left Saturday morning for France. I was worried about going, particularly because I felt the Kosovo communications were not going well, but Fiona would be off the radar if I cancelled and the kids were really looking forward to it. I had given TB plenty of warning and asked him several times whether he was OK with me going. But we had not even reached the shuttle when he called. There had been a series of big and successful attacks on Belgrade, for once. We agreed he should go up on it and fixed interviews for 12, the main message that we were making progress, were in for the long haul and would prevail in the face of barbarism and genocide. It totally fitted the message in *The Times*, which had gone well and was being picked up all over the place. Julian Braithwaite called with his usual long list of mainly good ideas to keep the message going. He knew the area well, was really committed and was a real help at the moment.

Sunday, April 4

TB was calling the whole time, more and more anxious and exasperated. I suggested he speak to Solana again. 'I can't see much point to be honest.' We had another problem arising from his *Sunday Telegraph* article, which Julian B had drafted. It was basically a straight military piece, 'must win, will win' kind of thing. But it had the line there could be no question of spreading refugees around Europe. But then Germany (40k), USA (20k), Turkey and others all said they would take refugees and we were being pressed for a number. I sent through a note to TB, RC, JS, Clare and set out a plan and a message note which focused on our commitment always to be there for the weak and dispossessed, and which meant helping those most in need, which made clear we would take some without a commitment to a specific figure. Jack S called to say he really was against giving a number.

We had Clare S out in Macedonia looking at the refugee situation and ended up having to say we would take 'thousands'. Even then I emphasised that we saw this as a temporary measure and that they would hopefully eventually go back but it was enough for our media to say it was a U-turn. We were staying at a Pierre et Vacances holiday centre, nice but fairly basic, and the TV had CNN which meant I spent a lot of the time on the phone and then making sure things were followed through. It was pretty hopeless though and TB and Godric were telling me the whole time we were being caned in the domestic media. I did a conference call to agree a media plan for the next few days but clearly the humanitarian picture was going to take precedence.

Monday, April 5

Jamie Shea [NATO spokesman in Brussels] made the refugee situation worse for us by listing those NATO countries prepared to take refugee quotas. TB had now started every day of my 'holiday' phoning up with a downbeat assessment of where we were. The lack of military success, the dire pictures of the humanitarian situation, the briefing on 'a failure of imagination', today the so-called U-turn on refugees. The *Sun* were doing a front-page editorial saying no to ground forces and I had to speak to Rebekah and Trevor K to stiffen them up a bit. I was beginning to feel very anxious not being there, and the amount of calls I was getting, and TV I was watching, I might as well have been. Fiona was getting pissed off with me constantly being on the phone but I had a real feeling this thing could run away from us on the public opinion front if we weren't careful.

TB said we could deal with the humanitarian crisis but we had to be able to show military success. The two strategies had to work in tandem and at the moment, day after day, the sense was of the military machine not clicking because there were too many people and organisations with the ability to interfere in the process. We agreed he should do another interview and I sent through a note on that. He had to say we would take refugees but I suggested we say that if they moved away from Kosovo permanently it was a victory for Milosevic. I was beginning to think I should be there.

TB said there was no strategic capacity across the whole machine unless he or I was driving it. The 'U-turn' headlines came, he felt, because officials do not get the importance of language. They lacked the subtlety to deal with it. He said I'm at Chequers, you're in France and we're losing grip on message. We decided to do a BBC pool plus Montenegro RTV and I was pissed off the BBC sent Nick Jones, who they claimed was the only one available. I watched a very good guy on CNN called David Scheffer, US ambassador-at-large [for war crimes issues], and got Julian to chase him.

TB called after the interviews, said they were fine, but very much refugee-focused. He was not happy at the way NATO was operating. He felt the Big Four foreign ministers should be speaking every morning and setting the tone for the briefings. The NATO frontmen, Shea and [Air Commodore] David Wilby [military spokesman] were both Brits and that should be helping us, but the more I watched their briefings, the more I felt they were reactive rather than strategic, though Shea's knowledge was impressive. TB spoke to Bill C who was also worrying that the co-ordination between capitals involved was not good, and he was not impressed with the NATO operation.

Tuesday, April 6

I was really beginning to think I should go home. The main problem was an obvious lack of co-ordination within and between the NATO governments. I spoke to John Williams [FCO] and said we needed to start thinking about changing the cross-government handling structures because what we had currently wasn't working. TB called at 9, said the overnight action had been better, the refugee situation was still dire. The right-wing commentators were in full cry and we agreed to try to get Thatcher and Charles Powell [former foreign policy adviser to Thatcher] out saying the right hate the left fighting wars but they should be supporting what we are doing. The swimming pool at the holiday centre was closed because of a problem with the chlorine so Fiona took the kids off to a different place and I spent two or three hours on the phone starting to talk through what structures we might put in place. NATO might baulk but we were going to have to get a grip of their communications and make sure capitals were more tightly drawn in to what they were saying and doing. Mo called to say Jon Norton [her husband] worked [in banking] with a Serb who knew Milosevic's son Marko was in Crete and it might help if we use the media to put him under pressure. Why were his kids getting out? I spoke to Jon then got Julian B to go and see the guy.

I was now spending much of the day trying to keep on top by phone and then watching the various press conferences. Clare was getting a good press for kicking ass and sorting out a few blocks on refugees. We had a mini drama as I was going to bed. Godric called and said Milosevic was making a unilateral ceasefire offer for Easter. I said we should just reject it out of hand. It was clearly just a ploy and in any event we had to make clear our demands went way beyond Milosevic stopping the violence and the persecution.

Wednesday, April 7

Godric said the papers were going from seven pages a day to three or four on Kosovo. We were having some effect with the strategy for the right, e.g. Charles Powell and David Hart [former Thatcher adviser] were both going up, but the right-wing papers and commentators so hated us that they were determined to do what they could to help anything fail. If this was a Tory war, they would support it every inch of the way. We were beginning to hit better on the military front and following our instigation in the call with Clinton, Jamie Rubin [US State Department chief spokesman] was now chairing a daily conference call with us, France and Germany. I was reading [former Clinton adviser] George Stephanopoulos' book [*All Too Human: A Political Education*] which threw up a few interesting parallels re relations with the press but also between adviser and principal. I spoke meanwhile to Joe Lockhart re trying to get a Bill C piece into one of our Sundays.

TB called and said he was very keen that I get some proper rest. He said he was sorry to have been calling the whole time, he now felt we were beginning to improve our handling of it and he thought I should switch my phone off for a while and have a couple of days off. He knew that I wouldn't switch the phone off but I did take it as permission to duck out of all that day's events. He said I think you'll find this thing going on for a while yet and your skills are going to be in a great deal of demand, so rest now.

Julian went to see Jon Norton's Serb friend, said he was a typical Serb, weeping at the state of his homeland. He said he had set up a lot of the Milosevic bank accounts and he was credible enough for us to put the agencies on to him. We were also trying to get a closer fix on the son in Crete.

Thursday, April 8

It was a beautiful still day, quite cold but sunny. We visited the Chinese [World War One] cemetery at Noyelles-sur-Mer, which like all of these war cemeteries in France has the capacity to move and inspire. I couldn't work out why so many Chinese died.[1] The big story was the sudden disappearance of thousands of people who had been queuing to get into Albania. We agreed on another round of TV interviews. Milosevic's ceasefire offer, however hollow, was at least a sign he was looking for a way out. TB was up in Scotland for the campaign, and in between the stuff on Scotland did some very strong message work on Kosovo. He was hitting the right messages hard, and it would help if we could get the other leaders out in similar vein in a more co-ordinated way.

I was finding it impossible to switch off from it, and was starting

---

[1] 838 Chinese Labour Corps workers, recruited by the British between 1917 and 1919, mainly died in the post-war Spanish Influenza epidemic.

to map out more changes I felt we should be making to the communications effort. A lot of this was about communication now. Militarily, NATO is overwhelmingly more powerful than Belgrade. But Milosevic has total control of his media and our media is vulnerable to their output. So we can lose the public opinion battle and if we lose hands down in some of the NATO countries, we have a problem sustaining this.

TB called as he was leaving, said the only thing that mattered was winning this now. If we won, we could sort the refugee situation, and it wouldn't matter a damn what any of the wretched right-wing commentators were saying. Mike Elliott [*Newsweek*] called, said people were beginning to notice TB's leadership and they would love a piece from him, to go in all editions around the world. That could be a real opportunity. I drafted an outline and sent it through. Julian called to tell me NATO had made the idiotic decision to ANNOUNCE they were going to hit transmitters. What on earth was the point of that? It had taken us all of two weeks to persuade them they were legitimate targets and now they were bungling the job by making it a big issue in advance.

Julian had done a very good paper on the role of Milosevic's media in his military machine and we had to start deploying some of those arguments. Julian had also worked up a good note on the family, and in a psychological warfare skirmish we told Reuters we were looking to do Milosevic and his family through Interpol and other international organisations, which would include targeting those who were not currently in their country. Lance [Price] called from Scotland to say the SNP launch had not gone well. The media were beginning to turn on them over unanswered questions and uncosted policies.

Friday, April 9

I had gone the whole week without seeing a British newspaper which was bliss, and was beginning to think the media summary was all I needed. The military campaign was really picking up and he was being hit hard. Yeltsin made an apocalyptic noise about World War Three being started out of it all. Rupert Murdoch's bid to buy Man Utd was rejected by Byers which led to a rash of calls – Rebekah, Tony Banks, Peter M. Byers felt, instinctively, as I did, that it was a bad idea. TB was worried it would simply turn Murdoch against us. He worried what we got out of it apart from a bit of populist support which will evaporate quickly. In his view, football clubs are rarely owned by saints, any more than newspapers are. He wasn't convinced

April '99: TB stresses importance of military victory

of the anti-competitive arguments but couldn't really intervene, but felt it was not impossible the Murdoch papers would turn as a result.

Saturday, April 10
We were back home by lunchtime. I can't say I felt rested and Fiona and I had a couple of bad scenes as I had been working so much of the time, but we had spent a fair bit of time together, out every night and the kids had a good time. The Sundays were broadly under control, but we had a rough few weeks ahead.

Sunday, April 11
TB called a few times, first to go over things in general on the domestic front, but also because when he was channel-hopping during the FA Cup semi-final breaks, he came across the NATO briefing with Jamie Shea and [Colonel] Konrad Freytag (standing in for the rested Wilby who had fucked up announcing the bombing of transmitters). TB said it was amateurville, and unless we got a grip, we were going to lose the PR war. We put out his *Newsweek* article which got a fair bit of play.

Monday, April 12
The need to grip the Kosovo media operation was now a running theme, though our press had settled down a bit. Today was manifesto launch day in Scotland and DD sounded up for it. The talk in the press was now of the SNP in crisis, with senior figures not talking to each other. At the office meeting, TB seemed a bit more relaxed re Scotland. Ireland and Kosovo were the big worries. He wanted new structures on the Kosovo operation, and wanted to get more directly involved himself.

The 11 was fairly desultory but a useful opportunity to make clear we were not going to get drawn into 'what if' scenarios the whole time. Prodi was coming in at 12.30 and there was a bit of interest in the rubbish about him wanting to get rid of UK passports, which was in some of the papers today, and easily dealt with. The meeting itself was fine, but Christ does he meander. Added to which he has a tendency to whisper, and the combined effect is a bit like trying to listen to a fish. TB kept trying to pin him down to deal with one point at a time but he was all over the place. I had a separate meeting with Ricci Levi, his press guy, to say we would help in any way we could. I then met with Oona Muirhead [MoD] and John Williams [FCO] to go over meeting structures and to ensure better internal co-ordination. There were now daily calls of the QUINT [US, UK, France, Germany,

Italy] and I emphasised they had to make sure there were people on there who were properly plugged in, not just space-fillers.

At 2.30 TB, GR, CDS, RW, John S, Jonathan, AC and David Fisher [MoD]. First, on air food drops, which was clearly not being well handled by foreign ministers, with all kinds of different lines out there. TB said he was not averse in principle but I pointed out there was a danger we would look very silly – the bombs don't land in the right place but the fruit and nuts do – or not. The refugees on the border were easily identifiable. But for those travelling it was not so easy. TB felt we needed to do what we could and also that we needed some kind of cover when we went in and found starving Kosovar Albanians. He emphasised nothing should be done that might limit the military campaign.

Charles Guthrie said the weather was still not great and the Americans were not being totally open about their operations, but damage was definitely being done. On ground forces, though the public line had not changed, he said we were doing more and more detailed work on it. It would take ninety days to get there in sufficient numbers to do the job. The debate was also whether once Kosovo was taken, we would go all the way to Belgrade.

TB was anxious re Russia and the extent to which they were helping the Serbs. He was also asking for an assessment of whether the bombing had worsened the refugee crisis. On one level, it was obvious that it would, but the word from the refugees was they still wanted the operations to carry on. They knew it was shit or bust basically. The press were asking for another briefing and I used it to put out a more strategic message re Kosovo. Guthrie agreed that the NATO operation was far too media-friendly, done with the media's as much as NATO's interests in mind. He felt some of the coverage was a disgrace and we needed to show a bit of anger. Bad news with a stray bomb hitting a train.

The TB/GB political meeting was OK, ranging all over the place – Scotland, local elections, petrol prices (more demos today, and GB didn't look too chuffed when I told him how cheap it was in France) plus how we needed more money for cruise missiles. TB nipped out to see a child with motor neurone disease whose family had asked if they could come in. TB was genuinely moved by them, and said as he came back it put any problems of our own in perspective.

I had a meeting with Charlie F and others re office structures, and we were discussing whether TB needed more foreign policy support when we were called through to see him. He was with Jonathan. He had just learned Jack S, in his 'quasi-judicial' capacity, wanted to send

Pinochet to Spain. TB felt he shouldn't, that it wasn't worth the aggro, and he should intervene. I had to leave for the MoD 7pm meeting. CDS wasn't there and it was a long rambling run round the block. Edgar Buckley [MoD] was just back from Brussels where he said the talk was all of peace plans and air drops. He said RC was determined to do something. GR let the meeting run on far too long and without any clear decisions. Kevin Tebbit [MoD permanent secretary] had crinkly hair and eyes that kept fixing on me, saying the whole time how grateful they were for my input. He said some of the people there were getting tired and needed stiffening. I said the humanitarian all had to be dealt with but the main focus had to be on the military operations and making a success of that. Everything would flow from that. [Lord] John Gilbert [defence procurement minister] virtually said out loud what TB and I had been thinking – the military campaign was not as effective as we were being told. It had to be stepped up. TB's worry was that we were pushed into a deal before we were really in a position of strength which could only come from sustained and major damage to his military infrastructure. The NATO media operation clearly wasn't working though. Air drops just emerged as an issue, it wasn't forced by them. Likewise the way they handled the refugee quotas last week. I watched [General] Wesley Clark on *Newsnight*. It wasn't good. TB said our media operation was good only by comparison with the others, which were awful.

Tuesday, April 13

The 7.30 Scotland call was all about Kvaerner [shipbuilders], due to announce Govan [shipyard] sale and possibly shut down. It was being seen largely as an industrial story but there were obvious political implications. We had to be out saying it was not a decision about Scotland or the Scottish workforce, and meanwhile Gus [Macdonald, industry minister, Scottish Office] was setting up a jobs task force to respond. The SNP were loving it but we just about managed to contain the political fallout. I went over for the 8.30 MoD meeting in the bunker. RC arrived at 9, very hoity-toity today – I think it was the military intelligence guys who got his back up – and we discussed air drops. Robin was totally in the 'something must be done' camp. I was pleased that John Vereker [International Development permanent secretary] was making a lot of the practical points Charles and I had been making yesterday.

I said my big worry was that what sounded like a good idea, and one that would have popular support, would be used to tear us to shreds if anything went wrong – if the drops landed in the wrong places, and went to Serb troops, or killed refugees, or whatever. Unless we could be sure this was an effective way of getting food to the right place, why risk it? Robin seemed to pull back from such an aggressive push for it. The military assessment was that it would be very hard to pull off. They also did a colour bar assessment of the damage done so far. The bulk of the colours on the chart were 'sufficient' or 'poor'. There were hardly any 'severe'. We agreed that for the morning briefing RC should trail that TB would be announcing further deployments, but agreed we should not give any sense it was about land troops.

I decided to pre-empt a little at the 11, making clear we were not talking ground forces. I cleared it with the Speaker's office after the event. The last thing I needed was a row with Betty [Boothroyd] about pre-empting Parliament on troop announcements. The announcement of more troops would take us through the day but we also needed Kosovar Albanians out saying the bombing must continue. I called Jamie Shea for a chat, said I thought he was doing a great job in unbelievably difficult circumstances, but could I make one observation – I felt that he didn't go into his briefings with a clear idea of what he wanted the media to take from them. He gave them all the information they needed, and then they decided the story. I felt we had to decide the story, not them. He was very receptive, said as far as he was concerned, I was 'the master of this kind of thing, so I would be grateful for any advice'. I was worried he would take offence at me calling but on the contrary, he seemed relieved. He asked that we keep in regular touch.

TB was out on a visit and worked on the draft statement for the House on the train back. He arrived at the Commons just as news broke of a border incursion which Ceefax [BBC teletext service] headlined 'Yugoslavia invades Albania'. TB was on good form in the House. He hit at media manipulation. Alan Clark called to say he thought TB was 'splendid' today, but he worried for us on this, felt it could go very wrong. We went back for a TB meeting with RC, GR, CS, CDS. I found myself joining forces with Clare to argue on air drops that we should be making this Milosevic's problem not ours. Vereker said we were trying to reconcile getting in effective humanitarian help with an effective military campaign and they were currently not reconcilable. The defence intelligence people had produced a map of displaced Kosovar Albanians and Clare and I agreed it would make a good backdrop to a press conference on the humanitarian side of things.

TB finally agreed on air drops. He also wanted Montenegro ports blocked and couldn't understand how, if we were successfully bombing his oil dumps, he [Milosevic] was still getting oil into Serbia. At the later MoD meeting, which again meandered for ages, I got them to agree we should get Clare to front a press conference on the info their intelligence team had got. I talked to Charles afterwards and asked if we couldn't cut the size of some of the meetings. George was too keen to let everyone have their say, and the MoD officials were too deferential to GR which meant nobody cut through the crap. Charles said that was my job. He was joking about how Clare interrupted virtually every single intervention with 'Tony, Tony, can I say . . . ?' I said he was seeing her at her best and most engaged because on this she supported what we were doing. In fact, later she asked me to write her statement for the press conference, a first.

Wednesday, April 14

Another of those days when you wonder how we get through them. TB was off at 6.30 to meet Kathryn [Blair] off a plane after she had been involved in an accident and was suffering from whiplash. Magi [Cleaver] was advancing and the press were already on to it. We got good coverage for TB's statement yesterday but both of us were now tearing our hair out at the NATO media operation. SACEUR had done a briefing at which they showed film of the bombing of the train, in which Wes Clark opened himself up to a hammering. Then Clark let himself get drawn into a messy walking doorstep. I called Jamie [Shea] re both. Again, he said he was pleased to hear from me, and welcomed advice. He said he was getting exasperated with SACEUR's media operation on the military side. TB said to me later 'What on earth are they thinking of showing film of how they killed innocent civilians?'

Clare was back to her usual self today. Having asked for a script on the rape centres and the displacement etc., now she wouldn't read it, and instead just waffled generalities. It was bizarre. Yesterday she was all up for it, and agreed it with TB, and now she was back to being the bitch from hell. I was particularly pissed off because I'd had to square the MoD to let her take the lead on it. GR was doubly pissed off that TB was seeing MoD officials without him being there, but it was all part of TB getting more directly involved in the whole military side.

TB spoke again to Thatcher, who said she couldn't understand why Clinton was not more exercised and hitting the buttons harder. George Robertson and CDS came over to do a presentation on ground troops. Charles taped a map up to the mantelpiece above the fireplace and went through the three routes in – Albania, Macedonia, Montenegro?

– and explained why all three were difficult. He said there were two options for invasion – limited, which meant three months and involving around 80,000 troops at least; or unlimited, which would mean 200,000 troops, and no idea yet where they would come from. TB was nodding silently, occasionally sighing loudly, and clearly taken aback at the scale of what it would require to be sure – and even then you wouldn't be that sure. He said we had to carry on making the preparations and in the meantime hope the air campaign improved in effectiveness and intensity.

I then had a meeting with the Home Office Security Unit re my own security. They said the current Security Service assessment was that I was moderate risk but that it would rise to significant if things went backwards in NI. He said it meant I needed protection mainly focused on home and cars. He said, in a very matter-of-fact way, that in some ways Jonathan and I were at greater risk than the PM because the terrorists know he is so heavily protected whereas they know we are one layer out and not subject to the same level of protection. Very cheery. I was a bit worried about Fiona's reaction. She was OK about it, though it was going to mean work on the house, blinds on all the windows and cops wandering up and down the street every few hours.

I drove out to Northolt with TB who was banging on about how to grip NATO. He had spoken to Schroeder who like us did not like [German foreign minister Joschka] Fischer's approach on Kosovo. In Brussels, the first bilateral was with Kofi Annan, who was pretty supportive. I liked him, and I liked his style. TB stressed the importance of reversing ethnic cleansing. Kofi said he wanted the UN to play its part, and he was keen to keep the Russians involved in some way, positively. They went over the relative 'permissiveness' of any environment for any international force to go in there. It would not be totally permissive. Kofi said he didn't see Milosevic weakening easily. 'He is desperate and would happily take everyone down. He is a tactician not a strategist. He is clever but not intelligent.'

TB felt we would discover real atrocities when we got in there and our public opinion would not tolerate deals being done with Milosevic. Kofi asked how long could we keep bombing. 'You can run out of targets you know.' TB said we had to do real damage before we could consider the next steps. TB then saw a very depressed Bertie [Ahern], really down about things. He was coming under a lot of attack but more than that, he said he couldn't see where the next bit of progress was coming from. All we would get out of the EU meeting was a bit

April '99: Guthrie spells out ground-force options

of solidarity re Kosovo. The Serbs were claiming NATO bombs had hit a convoy of refugees, killing many. I called Jamie Shea and said while the facts were being established, we had to have ready a history of the lies the Serbs told about casualties. It was not clear at first whether the claims were true or not and it was proving hard to get the info out of the military. TB came out for a Clinton phone call. Both were now hitting the panic buttons quite hard. Bill said we had to work on Chirac to support attacks on Phase 3 targets, and we had to help Solana and Wes Clark on presentation. He felt Jamie was OK as a frontman but the operation needed building up. TB said the methods of operation were too diffuse and both of them needed to be driving this more directly. Yes, we have done some damage but we are not there and yet here I am, at an EU meeting where they are talking about the future of the Balkans as if this thing is won. Clinton said he would lean on Chirac, and say that if we ended up unable to take the decisions that the military believed were necessary, and the suffering went on longer than it should, we would all pay a price for that. TB said he would send me to see Solana re the presentation issue.

TB did a press conference which was pretty strong, and re the convoy we were simply saying until the facts were clear you could not take the Serbs' word for it. TB saw Chirac and just about won him over to going for the riskier targets. Chirac felt it was important we gave some kind of concession to the Russians. TB said Bill was finally all systems go, and on the way home he seemed a bit more at ease. He said it might be best if I went out there, and ran the communications operation. I felt at a minimum we should send Julian after I had seen Solana.

Thursday, April 15

The convoy attack, now virtually admitted by NATO, was clearly going to be the main story, and all kinds of different versions were flying around. I went to the MoD bunker meeting to hear another gloomy overnight assessment of military operations. I got back through the linking tunnel for DOP, where TB said there were two main problems: 1. a military operation with too many people able to call shots, and a resulting lack of intensity and effectiveness, and 2. poor presentation, which was hurting us in NATO countries' public opinion. Jack Straw said we needed 'some good old-fashioned Millbank discipline instilled in them'. Quite, said TB. He was very fired up and I used some of the words and feelings to harden the line personally against Milosevic as being responsible for all the suffering.

TB called Solana to discuss presentation, thinking they would resist a UK takeover. But Solana said, almost as soon as TB raised it, 'If you can send me your man Campbell, that would be best.' He said I was the best in Europe and, listening in opposite Jonathan, I felt myself blushing. TB said I would go out tomorrow. CDS was in Brussels so I got a message through to him that he emphasise to [Wes] Clark that he needed to find time to see me and have a proper discussion about the importance of getting the presentation right. Charles called later, said he told all of them that I was the man to sort them out and they had better bloody well listen. It was a huge help having someone as blunt as him, and more important who got the need for the media side of things to be right. He said Clark had seemed tired and distracted. TB said I should go there, assess it, work out the structures needed, then put them in place. He would then go out on Tuesday next and follow through, reading the riot act if necessary.

Cabinet was nearly all Kosovo, TB warning we were in for a long haul, then basically the various ministers updating. The mood was fairly gloomy. I was now starting to get focused on tomorrow, working out the best way of ensuring I got Solana and Clark onside for change. I spoke to Jamie S again and he sounded genuinely pleased I was going out. He said Solana was desperate to see me, really wanted to put the thing on a different level. So at least I was entering what Charles Guthrie would call a permissive environment.

I said the problem was the obvious gap between the military and the governmental or civilian at NATO and we had to close it, make the operation come together as one. I confess to feeling a real excitement, almost exhilaration, at the thought of a new challenge, and one that both BC and TB had asked me to do. I had been feeling a bit jaded of late, tired of the same old arguments and issues and at least this was a genuine big challenge with the potential to make a difference. PB said in his note to our people at NATO that I was to be seen as a special envoy from the PM, on a par with a senior Cabinet minister, and I should see anyone I wanted to see in the time I was there.

Just how bad things were became graphically clear today. Shea was saying NATO was making no comment till things were clearer just at the time Clark was telling the Pentagon to say that it was all the work of the Serbs. There was a sense of the whole thing unravelling. Again, it underlined to me that I had a big challenge to rise to. I sat down and wrote out what I hoped to achieve – a communications operation co-ordinated across the NATO capitals and beyond, and how to approach the different personalities I was going to have to get on board. Unlike a lot of the stuff we do on the media side, this felt like it mattered and I was determined to be properly prepared and win them over. My only worries were tiredness, and how Fiona and the kids would react if I was out there the whole time.

I went over to the MoD to see Charles, Tebbit and Edgar Buckley and get their take on how to handle it. Charles said he had given Wes the message but I would find him nervy and a bit shaky. I asked how frank I should be. Totally, said Charles. I got home to watch the news, leading on the convoy, and it was wall-to-wall dreadful. The attack was bad enough, but the handling of it was truly awful and made things a whole lot worse. The only good thing, re tomorrow, was that with this backdrop it would be hard for anyone to resist change. I was thinking we probably needed to put in an entirely new operation, with people from all the main capitals, and all the functions you would expect of any big campaign.

Friday, April 16

Pretty extraordinary day. I was up at 5.30, out to meet Julian [Braithwaite] and got the 6.53 train to Brussels. I called Joe Lockhart who was on Air Force One and went through the kind of thing I was thinking of proposing. He said if we needed people, they would help provide. I spoke to Michael Jay [UK Ambassador in Paris] about the best way of dealing with the French, what with the complexities of cohabitation. He felt it best just to deal through Catherine Colonna [Chirac's press secretary]. My main message for the NATO lot was that a military campaign had to be founded on simple concepts, and so did any supporting media campaign; that they should not be having to deal with media the whole time and needed to let professional media advisers take the strain so they could concentrate on the military; that the morale and effectiveness of the operation could be enhanced by the feeling of a strong and co-ordinated media message going out around the world. But it needed new systems and greater discipline.

I was met and taken to see Sir John Goulden, our ambassador [to NATO]. He was nice but I sensed a bit nervous of the kind of radical change I felt was needed. But he did say to be very frank with Solana. I was. The main discussion was over lunch with him and Jamie Shea. He said he knew the problems – lack of co-ordination, lack of proper information from the military. I said I thought it went deeper than that, because it wasn't just the media operation here but in the capitals too that had to be gripped. The different reactions to the convoy attack had shown that graphically.

Shea said he had been fascinated how we had changed our approach to the media as New Labour and he was sure there were lessons they could learn. I said we didn't have much time. I felt we needed more people, better integrated. We needed a strategic approach to communications, greater centralisation, so that all capitals felt involved in what we were saying and doing, and also felt obliged at least to know what the line here was, even if they then felt unable to toe it. And we needed to improve links with the military. Jamie said he despaired of some of Clark's interviews, which were set up without regard to him and often created as many problems as they were designed to solve. He looked tired, which was hardly surprising, and the fact that he and his deputy took notes while I was speaking made me think they were a bit out of their depth. They were nice though, and definitely up for change.

I went through what I saw as a proper structure – a strategy owned by Solana and Clark, signed up to by the Heads, monitored at least twice daily by conference calls between the spokesmen of the main Heads of Government, with a media war room here staffed by people from all the main nations, with direct links to the military, and all the functions – a grid, hour by hour, of all the main events; message development; story development; articles; interview preparation; speech-writers; rebuttal team; media monitoring etc. Solana said he wanted it asap. I said it would need proper premises – preferably one room – and equipment. He said he would ensure that was all done. I asked if he thought Clark would buy it and he said yes, provided he did not feel his role as the main military commander was in any way threatened, and he retained a big role in communications. It was pretty clear SACEUR was the dominant partner.

We went up to the pre-briefing room and joined a surly American three-star general, a mustachioed Italian one-star, and an assortment of odd-looking individuals. It was afternoon, and yet this was clearly the first time they had had this kind of meeting to go over what was likely to come at the briefing. The Italian wanted to give some new information about the convoy incident, which others felt would be a mistake. It was a very odd meeting, which made me think George [Robertson's] MoD meetings were a triumph of strategy and competence by comparison. It reminded me of some of the awful by-election meetings in opposition.

Jamie Shea was scribbling notes, and clearly basically wrote his own scripts and lines to take without any proper drafting by others. It meant he had too much to do. I said we should try to shut down the convoy incident as best we could, though it would be difficult. I said to Solana afterwards that they should have a meeting like that the night before a briefing, and again in the morning, and make sure proper materials are prepared for it. I told Solana if he wanted me to come out again, he just had to say. He said he loved the way we had 'tamed' the media. I said we hadn't, we'd just made them think we had. Goulden emphasised the need to keep the small countries involved in any changes I made. Julian and I then left with Colonel Konrad Freytag for SHAPE [Supreme Headquarters, Allied Powers Europe] at Mons, with Julian subtly interviewing Freytag on the way. He clearly felt the whole operation was OK, and that kind of complacency was pretty apparent on the military side.

Ahead was the most extraordinary part of a pretty extraordinary day. We arrived at the rather soulless building, parked, went up a very narrow passage and waited for SACEUR to finish a meeting. He was running late and the atmosphere was a bit frenetic. As Rupert Smith [UK general, Clark's deputy] told me, his personal organisational skills were not what he was most renowned for. Smith's was the only office where I didn't feel the sense of suppressed panic that prevailed elsewhere. At one point, as I waited in the waiting room, I could hear Jamie Shea's voice on the speaker of a conference call, telling SACEUR's people we had to shut it down, and they were saying 'We'll get murdered in the US press.' All too frenetic and no grip. I met David Wilby, and a nice Brit called John Duncan [FCO, seconded to NATO] who was a political adviser to SACEUR. They were all clearly tired and overworked but when Freytag said that Clark worked nineteen-hour days and 'six were on the media', I said he shouldn't be doing any more than one on the media, top whack.

As Clark's meeting wore on, Smith took me to his altogether more calm office for a chat. He was impressive. He said he only spoke to the press if he had to 'but these guys are different'. He said Clark saw himself as much answerable to Washington as to NATO. He had travelling secure communications with him and was always a call away from the Pentagon. He said NATO's problems were too many chiefs, not enough Indians. He said SACEUR was suspicious when he heard I was coming out, but Rupert had told him I was the guy who took a useless political party and somehow got everyone to sing from the same hymn sheet through basic discipline. He advised me to be frank but build up to my plan for change, and be gentle.

After twenty minutes, I got the call. Clark, a diminutive man for a general, was standing at the door waiting to shake my hand, warmly and with a big smile. He had very lively eyes, well-groomed hair, more presence than I expected, but a bit of a wild look too. 'You're looking pretty good considering,' I said. 'Only way,' he said. 'Just got to keep going.' We sat down, on a kind of corner sofa, then were joined by an array of uniforms, and he said 'Right, what do you think of our media operation?' 'No diplomacy required,' said the woman next to him. 'Good,' I said. I said I felt it needed a total revamp. I went through the script I had prepared and memorised, but then added in a few observations from the day, like the lack of proper preparation for briefings, the lack of a grid or strategic map, the fact he was required to do so much of his own media-handling.

I said the refugee convoy incident had exposed basic weaknesses and they needed help. He was not unreceptive, though as I got more critical, I noticed his knee jerking up and down, and pulled back a bit. I felt some of the uniforms getting a bit agitato but he seemed to take it in. I said he was the main man in the most important single event happening anywhere in the world at the moment and that meant he needed proper communications support. An operation designed for peaceful times when NATO is just ticking over is not adequate for a major military campaign. So what do you want to do, he asked?

I said we had to be proactive, be strategic, set the agenda on our terms, not the media's, take them by surprise. His eyes lit up when I said if we have something big to announce at 3am, get them out of bed so they know that it's big, and they can stop talking about the convoy. 'Hey I like this,' he said. 'I like the sound of this guy.' He let me talk for a fair old while and at the end he seemed to be pretty well won over, though I could feel a few hackles rise when I said I thought they should have more military people in the Brussels media set-up, and more civilians here. He said 'Well, I like a lot of what you're saying. And I kid you not, we have to get something done, because we are on the brink of a disaster.' It was pretty alarming to hear him say it so bluntly, just as I found it alarming when, as I was leaving, he took me by the arm and said 'Good luck, Alastair, we're all counting on you!' I said 'Shouldn't I be saying that to you?'

I found him likeable, much more impressive than I had been led to believe I would, but I found it a bit scary that at the height of a military campaign, I was sitting down telling a general how to run it, or at least run the media side, and complaining that the media campaign lacked the discipline we expected of a military campaign. I also assured him I was no Freedom of Information freak, and indeed felt they were sometimes giving out too much. I said I would not have shown the bombing of the train. It did not benefit us at all. If you are fighting a war, it has to be fought like a war at every level.

As the meeting drew to a close, SACEUR leant back and said 'Well, they tell me you're the man who can do it, so I'm happy. Go for it.' He had his own idea, though, about a 72-hour forward-planning cell headed by Wilby. That apart, he agreed with all the specific proposals I put and said he would support me in putting the plan into action. The meeting had lasted an hour and I felt with his and Solana's backing, I should be OK. He showed me out, and as I walked out, John Duncan told me SACEUR was desperate to go on an all-out war footing. They were really pleased TB was coming next Tuesday because they felt he had the same urgency.

On the train back, I wrote up the meetings with Solana, Wes Clark, etc. and then prepared a detailed plan to put to TB, CDS, GR, RC, etc. TB discussed it with Bill C, who said he thought I should base myself there until it was over. I told TB he was right to be anxious. They did not feel like they were in charge of a winning campaign. They felt they had hands tied behind their backs, and they struck me as a bit desperate and demoralised. I felt that Clark would be in a bad way if it went on too long like this. TB said we are going to have to take this show over.

Saturday, April 17

TB had read my note and agreed with the plan to take it forward. He said I should send a sanitised version to all my main counterparts. I reworked a version to send to Solana and SACEUR, Joe Lockhart, Catherine Colonna and Uwe-Karsten Heye. I was tired, and feeling a bit stressed but excited I had a new challenge to confront. I felt yesterday went as well as it could have done. I spoke to Anji and Julian to get them out to Brussels tomorrow. I wanted Julian to get charge of the grid and essentially be my eyes and ears when I wasn't there. I also wanted Jan [Royall] from Neil's office, and Anne Shevas from the Scottish Office to do the management and personnel side. Bernard Gray [MoD special adviser] called and I suggested he come out with us on Monday. Goulden called to say Solana was very excited by yesterday and he wanted to move quickly. Philip G came round. I showed him my various notes and his feeling was I should go out there and take it over, hopefully without undermining Jamie S. The *Telegraph* did something on the front about me being there yesterday but it was pretty straight and not a big problem.

I fixed a conference call with Joe, Catherine, Uwe, SACEUR's office, and everyone signed up to the plan. They were all pretty enthusiastic, though Uwe said it would only work if the military told us the truth. We went through all the different areas where we could co-ordinate better. I said we should get to the stage where we are all making the same points in all our briefings, through real co-ordination and message discipline. TB called after speaking to Bill again, who had asked to see my note and was saying I should go out there full-time if I could. TB had also sent him a personal and private note which he said had focused him better. TB's take on Clark was that he is very clever but probably worries too much what people think of him, and is in danger of being overwhelmed.

Peter M was worried my role would become too big a story and 'spin' would be a problem. TB said he was fed up with all the bollocks about spin. He said nineteen democracies were at war with a dictatorship and we needed the best media operation available, which up to now we sorely lacked. He was desperate for some real grip and discipline. He was, however, telling me I had to get some rest, which as ever he followed with half a dozen ideas or instructions he wanted me to put into action.

Sunday, April 18

TB called before his *Meet the Press* [NBC] interview at Chequers, and we agreed the line had to be no let-up and no compromise. His big worry was how to answer the question re whether we were making plans for ground troops. Trevor Kavanagh called to say he had insisted to Yelland that the *Sun* should not be painting us into a corner. We had our first Kosovo group conference call at 12, fixed by Switch. Mike Phillips at SHAPE and Ken Bacon [Defense Department chief spokesman] at the Pentagon led the charge, half backed by Jamie, for a US general to go up tomorrow and do a detailed briefing on the convoy incident, including how the Serbs were using it to make it seem even worse than it was. I was worried it would simply open up new avenues and we would start the week on the back foot again. It was a close call though. Joe, Catherine and I all felt if we could genuinely show the Serbs had manipulated the truth on it, fine, but otherwise we risked an own goal. Phillips said the media currently had a bad taste in their mouths because they felt we had not been totally open about it. I sensed they wanted a bit of a mea culpa to get it out of their system. Ken Bacon said they could show why the pilot thought it was a military truck, and how the Serbs made the scene worse afterwards. Jamie Rubin, maybe having a dig, I don't know, said we had to be careful these NATO reporters didn't think this was all just the new spin meisters at work. We agreed to wait till later to decide. We agreed Jamie [Shea] should go up on the Serb media and the humanitarian side of things.

I went off to watch Rory in his Cup Final. They won 6-0 and he scored an awesome goal. TB called, having sent round a note on ground forces which basically said it was almost certain to happen, the question was when and how. Julian and Anji were already in Brussels commandeering space and pushing for the proper links to SHAPE. I said to JB there was a case for me seeing SACEUR again tomorrow to go over where we were taking things and ensure we were able to get into his operation properly. I thought maybe Julian or Bernard Gray should be alongside him the whole time.

On the 8pm conference call, the Americans in particular had hardened in favour of doing a full broadcast/explanation of the convoy incident tomorrow and we had a thirty-minute discussion on how best to frame it. Ken Bacon in particular felt we had to do it to regain credibility with the press, then move on. I liked the sound of Ken, who was very dapper and bow-tied on the box, and very calm and composed on the calls.

I was won over by the line that we could only move on once all the detail was out there to be gorged upon, to show mistakes were made, and by our side at least admitted. I also felt that as it was in part loose briefing that led to it being a bigger problem than it should be, this would be a good test of how strong and co-ordinated briefing could have a positive impact, even when a negative story. I was a bit worried it would leave a few loose ends which would trail into TB's visit on Tuesday, but subject to agreeing scripts tomorrow, we agreed to go with it, and get the top guy up from the region to do it. The White House were making clear they would send us good people who were properly plugged in. Jamie Rubin was pressing SHAPE for greater clarity. His contributions were laced with a little bit of scorn for the NATO operation.

TB saw Guthrie and he basically levelled and said we were likely to have to put in ground troops. TB said he was aware of all the sensitivities but he wanted the preparations to go on. Guthrie called me later and said according to Rupert Smith I had scored a direct hit with Clark, who told everyone he wanted my plan put into action, and every co-operation given. Charles' assessment was that Clark was not a 'proper' general, also that he [Clark] was suspicious of Rupert because he was a 'proper' commander. I said I was reasonably impressed by him and Charles said yes, Tony said that, but he is not what you think. A good general looks upwards and sideways, delegates and then protects the people he has delegated to from the politicians. Clark won't delegate so he risks being swamped by events. And he is not good at explaining strategy when there is one. Why those targets? What are we trying to achieve? You always need the answers to those questions. Guthrie said he was really pleased with the way Number 10 and the MoD were working. He was getting proper leadership and decision-making from TB, which made life relatively straightforward. All we ever want is clarity, he said. 'I could not be happier. It is amazing, considering he is not a military man at all, that he is so clear and decisive with the military.' He said he felt what I was doing in Brussels was vitally important and he would keep pressing Clark to ensure all doors were open. He complained about the quality of ministers at press conferences, felt that apart from RC and GR it was all a bit weak, and he was no fan of Robin's anyway. Ed Miliband called to say Alex Salmond had said in a Sunday newspaper that TB would 'sell his granny to a glue factory'. Later TB recalled he had said it before.

Monday, April 19

I met Alison [Blackshaw] and Bernard Gray at Waterloo and we headed for Brussels. Danny Pruce [FCO], just back from Macedonia, met us on the train and we went over what he might do. He seemed on the ball. TB had done a very impressive note and that, allied to the Clinton call, all suggested we were heading to ground troops. Julian, Anji, Anne [Shevas] and Jan [Royall] were all there when I arrived and showed me the various offices we were being offered. In the meantime we just camped. I got Danny working on an article for Solana, others working on lines to take for the briefing, as we pressed for better premises. On the conference call, Joe [Lockhart] said Clinton's *Sunday Times* article and TB's [NBC] interview had all blown back big in the US media, so that was great.

Julian, who was really motoring, spotted from BBC monitoring [Caversham] a fake transcript of the F16-AWACS [aircraft Airborne Warning and Control System] conversation re the convoy, which the Serbs had simply invented. JB moved heaven and earth to get audio of the real conversation to show it was a fake. I had a difficult meeting with Jorge Domecq [director of Solana's private office] at which the political problems were clear. He was clearly worried about upsetting the French and obviously felt this was a UK takeover. I said that was why we needed people from other capitals to get involved. I met General Mike Byron [US general, deputy chairman of the NATO Military Committee] and liked him. He was a bit gnarled and growly but he seemed to be competent and calm.

Earlier I had a good chat with Mark Laity [BBC defence correspondent] who made several good points: 1. don't undermine Jamie, 2. try to keep my own profile low because the press won't be able to resist building me up as a story to undermine the others, 3. have briefings am as well as pm to fill a vacuum currently filled by the Serbs. He struck me as someone I could call on for fairly good advice from the media side of the fence. He was totally contemptuous of the John Humphrys and John Simpson approach to the story.

We had a draft of the [USAF Brigadier General] Dan Leaf presentation re the convoy which had already been through SACEUR's office and which, at SACEUR's request, had been shown to a guy from the *New York Times*. It was ridiculous they were trying it out on a journalist, however friendly, before the NATO civilian side. Byron said to me 'None of the people round SACEUR tell the people here the truth – or know what they're doing.' Dan Leaf was an absolute central casting US military type. Leather bomber jacket, chewing gum, square-jawed, clear-eyed, tense and taut but overall impressive. 'I cannot tell you how nice it was to fly here this morning over a country where the houses aren't all on fire below you.' He was also looking for direction, said he had never done anything like this before and he needed a bit of guidance. We agreed he would go up at 4pm. I suggested he did a proper rehearsal and he went to the lectern and started to take us through his twelve-page script. They had gone over all the footage, all the tapes, all the debriefs and done a very thorough job. Apart from tightening the script in places, it didn't need that much work. I got the feeling now that it would work, that it was the right time to draw a line on a story that had dragged on for days, and he was the right guy to do it, having been in charge.

There was an illuminating moment in the difference between their world and ours when I mentioned the fake transcript and how it could be useful. He said 'I've seen that and I can assure you it is bullshit.' I said that is the whole point. He agreed it was worth doing. We also tried to get him to drop the expression collateral damage. He was wary of changing too much because Clark had already cleared it. I had a good meeting one-on-one with Byron. He said Solana didn't command total respect. It was obvious my plan had to work, he said, but there will be a lot of resistance and people will be after me. Clark will be suspicious and he will always want a piece of the media action, which you have to give to him. The real action and info and decision-making was at SHAPE and you should get inside there. I sensed he was an ally. He said he would give me all the support I needed in terms of support staff etc. He said I was doing the right thing getting people from lots of different countries 'but only the US and the UK are any good. We are the only ones who really know how to fight a war.'

I saw Leaf again before he went out to the briefing and he seemed overemotional. I said don't pick a fight with them. He said 'I won't. My fighting happens in the sky,' and I could sense him welling up a bit. I said be calm, and imagine you are explaining to a friend. Julian and I had to leave for SHAPE and only saw the start of the presentation, but he was impressive. It would definitely work. I had a meeting with David Wilby and we managed to get people into his 72-hour forward-planning cell. The word was the real inner circle were the people who went up to SACEUR's chateau in the evening and watched the screens and chewed things over and that was clearly where we needed someone. I was also urging him not to let SACEUR do so much media-handling himself. A call from him should be a special event.

I had a good meeting with John Duncan, first planning TB's visit and then on how to get Clark to focus better. John said there was very little strategic thinking. He warned me Clark was suspicious my plan was designed to boost Solana, and he had to feel it was about the military role. The more time I could spend with him the better. He advised I tell TB to give it to him straight. I did a long note to TB on the way back to Brussels. He was going to have to cut through the crap with Solana, and impress upon Clark, who was clearly worried about being made a scapegoat, that he needed help if he was to avoid that.

The conference call was good. People felt Leaf did well, and we agreed TB's visit would be the main event for all of us tomorrow, while Ken Bacon would do the main military briefing. There was nobody from SACEUR's office on the call and I sent a note through to General [Dieter] Stockman [Clark's chief of staff] to complain and say Clark had given an assurance he would always be represented on the call. I had a good chat with [USAF Colonel] PJ Crowley, who was pretty senior in the National Security Council and was being sent over. We were also getting Jonathan Prince from the White House and Lee McLenny from the State Department, plus a couple of military guys. I called home and had a bad call with Fiona, who was piling on the pressure, saying there would be a price to pay with the kids if I was basically out of circulation till this whole thing ended. I went back to John Goulden's residence and we had a good chat over a late-night cup of tea. He was pretty scathing about Clark, said he was always worrying about his own position, and people sensed that vulnerability. I said I was determined to get on with him because we could not carry out a proper communications plan without him.

April '99: All-American Dan Leaf does well in briefing

Brussels. The Dan Leaf presentation went well, just about drew a line. I left for Mons airfield to meet TB. I briefed him in the car and he was alarmed at some of the points in my note – e.g. Solana and Clark being at odds the whole time, Clark doing his own media. We arrived at SHAPE, met by [Rupert] Smith, and TB was taken straight to the video-conferencing centre, where Clark talks daily to the commanders in the field. Clark 'compered' it, and asked TB to say a few words. He spoke really passionately, and powerfully, about the job they were doing, and I could feel a positive effect around the room. He also went out of his way to build up Clark. On the way out, Clark was effusive in his thanks. TB got the impression Clark was very nervous, and unsure about whether we were winning. Milosevic's military capability was at seventy per cent, so degraded but still fairly strong. As he had with me, Clark went on about Milosevic in a very personal way, and TB felt he saw it a bit too much as a personal mission, rather than a military leadership task. 'If we don't win, all our asses are on the line,' TB told him. They went over ground troop options, which was becoming the most talked-about likelihood, but one that was worrying the US in particular. Guthrie called and said the feedback from my intervention so far was totally positive. Rupert told him I had 'electrified' the place and that Clark had made it clear that when I said jump, they had to jump, so hopefully so far so good.

Clark took me in for a chat after TB left. I thought it would be about his meeting, or about his profile, on which I had sent him a note earlier. Instead he took me to a raised dais and opened a book that was lying on it. It contained satellite photos of targets. In particular he showed me various pictures of RTS [Radio Television of Serbia] in Belgrade and the Socialist Party HQ, which was used as a broadcasting centre run by Milosevic's daughter. He said the French would let him hit one but not the other. Alongside the picture of RTS was a strapline 'collateral damage risk very high'. It was next to a church and other buildings. The party HQ was more open. He would like to hit both because his media machine was a legitimate target, but the French would be very iffy. He was intending to hit the TV station. I said we had been arguing for that for weeks. But he said there was another problem. This was the place where some of the Western journalists did their broadcasts. Ken Bacon had been saying there were no safe places in Belgrade, which was as near as we could get to warning them, but how big a problem was it? he asked. It suddenly dawned on me I was being asked whether the significance of the target was sufficient to live with the fallout of outrage and possibly deaths among the Western media. 'So can I do it?' he asked. Not like 'Do I have permission?' but 'Is this doable?' He said: 'I need your answer within the hour if that's OK.' Then Solana called. Clark said 'Alastair and I are discussing whether to hit it. The French are being difficult but I'm in favour.' I said after the call had finished it was not difficult to make the case it was a military target, and that unless we feared there was a human-shield situation, there was no difference between a working journalist and any other civilian who might be hurt. He said if he could hit TV today, electricity tomorrow, we would really start to make progress. I bumped into Rupert Smith, told him of the conversation, and he said it was typical of him. 'He should just do it. His decision, nobody else's. The right call.' I discussed it with TB. He said it may be he was just trying to flatter me by making me think I was centrally involved. Equally, I had clocked he couldn't resist telling Solana I was there and involved in the discussion. TB said I should say to him that I was there to be used but this was not a responsibility I expected at this time. Fortunately, in our party media-monitoring report, I clocked a line of John Simpson saying he had been 'invited' to the TV station but didn't go, which suggested the media realised it may be a target. TB had had a pretty dispiriting chat with Smith, who said the operation wasn't focusing ruthlessly on the job in hand. I rejoined TB and while I was doing the noon conference call I got him to come on and say how well Jamie was doing, and how the co-ordination was already beginning to improve, which cheered everyone up a bit.

We arrived at NATO, met by Solana and TB was emphasising to him that we had to hit the targets that mattered, and the military could not be expected to operate with hands tied behind their backs, a reference to the French vetoing certain targets. He was also saying the NATO summit should not all be about ground troops, but it was going to be hard to avoid. I worked up a script for the press confer-ence, based in part on the SHAPE overnight report. TB was on good form, his only slip-up when he said Milosevic must 'step down' when he meant 'back down.' After TB left, I was taken up to the US dele-gation offices to make a secure call to Ken Bacon. I went through my lines of defence for hitting the TV station. I faxed through the note and also Julian's note on the links between Milosevic's military and media machine, which I also sent through to SACEUR's office. I was then taken to a secure line for a chat with the SIS Yugoslav desk, and told the secure room inside the registry was the only guaranteed safe area, that the Russians were pretty much all over the place.

PJ Crowley, Jonathan Prince and Co. arrived and it was clear to me they were going to be superb. They just got it. I really felt things coming together. We had sorted excellent premises at the heart of the building, the equipment was going in, the people were arriving, and we were already making a difference. PJ was middle-aged, bald, quiet but authoritative. Jonathan was lively and witty and a bit zany. Catherine Colonna said she would send people from Paris. TB called from Germany, worried about the 'step down' line, but it wasn't running and we were getting great media out of the visit. I sent through another note to Clark on his own media profile which had to become more substantial, based on a less-is-more strategy.

Wednesday, April 21
We got terrific press from TB's visit, right round Europe and the US. The press were also beginning to say the media operation was improving. I had a bit of a lie-in, took the kids to school, then straight to the Kosovo meeting. TB was now of the view, encouraged by SACEUR, Smith and Stockman, that there was no way we were going to win without ground troops. The US were behind us on the issue. He got John Sawers to talk to Sandy Berger in advance of us leaving for Washington, to get their take. I exploded at the meeting when GR said Bernard Gray was coming out of SHAPE because he was being given the runaround by Wilby. I said he had to stay and fight for the proper access and I would speak to Clark to ensure he got proper access to paper and meetings.

TB's only worry for PMQs was ground troops, but he did fine. He gave a good answer on Simpson – he should be free to report as he sees fit. We should also be free to speak as we find. Afterwards he said of Simpson 'What a precious arsehole. Thinks he should swan around criticising as he pleases but if anyone speaks back it is an attack on civilisation as we know it.' On the plane to Washington, TB said if we didn't win this, it was curtains for the government, and not just ours. He was going over the argument he intended to use with Bill – if we the politicians say we cannot afford to lose, and they the generals say they cannot do it without ground troops, then we have to go for it. Invasion. Simple as that. Bill was kidding himself if he thought the politicians would win a great briefing war with the military. They would say their hands were being tied, and it was true. He asked if I thought Clark was up to it. I said he's the only one in charge so we have to build him up. He was worried if he pushed too hard on ground troops, he would risk his relationship with Clinton. Joe Lockhart called with two points: 1. the Italian general screwed up when he said the Serbs would target the summit, and 2. the American papers were full of reports TB would be pressing the president on ground troops. They were picking up on the different nuances but I could tell from his tone they thought we were pushing this in briefing. I assured him we weren't and we were trying to stay on the same pitch publicly.

Berger complained to Sawers about a *Wall Street Journal* story that TB was flying out to stiffen Clinton's resolve. We spent part of the flight working on TB's speech for Chicago tomorrow which he wanted to be seen as a big one. It was a big opportunity for a major rounded foreign policy argument but it meant a lot of work, with the current draft nowhere near the job. We were driven straight to the White House, TB and Guthrie in the back row of the car, John Sawers and I in front. John said they were very, very cool on ground forces and I think we all knew it was going to be a difficult meeting. Guthrie had just come from speaking to [General Hugh] Shelton [Chair of the US Joint Chiefs of Staff] who was of the view they had to go for ground troops. TB said the bottom line was that all the military appeared to be advocating ground troops. TB said his goal was to stiffen US resolve and at least get commitment to proper planning of ground troops. Shelton also asked us to speak up for Clark. CDS felt [US Defense Secretary] Bill Cohen was muttering about getting rid of him, which would be a disaster at this juncture.

Bill C arrived, went round everyone shaking hands and then took us up in the lift to one of the bigger lounge rooms upstairs. Madeleine Albright [US Secretary of State], Berger and [Jim] Steinberg [Berger's deputy] were already there and the mood was pretty stiff, other than with BC. Clockwise, BC and TB in chairs, Madeleine, Sawers and Chris Meyer on a sofa, Jonathan and I in chairs, Steinberg and Berger on a sofa. The small talk didn't last very long. They went through the NATO summit agenda, then into the detail on Kosovo. TB laid out a very tough case. 1. NATO/SHAPE is a mess. 2. The air campaign is OK but not much more than that. 3. All the military seem to be saying air power alone won't do the job. TB said he knew how difficult this was, not least because we had all said we would do it without ground forces. But 'I start from the assumption we cannot afford to lose. So we must do whatever we have to do to win.' He thought Milosevic was unlikely to cave unless he thought there was a realistic prospect of a ground troop invasion. He was worried if we waited and waited and waited we would suddenly find we were close to winter and near-impossible conditions. He said of Clark he was doing a heroic job but he needed help. He was swamped. They were very unkeen on ground troops, or even saying there were contingency plans. It would require an invasion force of 150,000–200,000, the bulk of them from the US. TB said the bottom line was we had to win, and if the military said it couldn't be done just by air, we had to listen. Bill was fairly mild throughout, chewing on a cigar, drinking Diet Coke, grumbling about the French a lot. You could feel the eyes of his advisers on him the whole time. He seemed more relaxed than they were. Jonathan said it was win-win for the French. If we fuck up, our fault. If we win, they are part of a great victory. BC said he felt we were probably damaging Milosevic more than we thought based upon their public statements. We were hitting him harder than he ever imagined we would. The question was whether we could hit him so hard he looked for a diplomatic way out. BC was talking both about Milosevic being indicted for war crimes, and at the same time about whether we could do a deal with him. Berger was pretty grumpy and saying the summit was going to be all about ground forces now, that the world's media was here 'waiting to salivate on the idea we have given up on the air campaign'. He said a summit designed for unity could become the summit that fell apart over ground troops. We argued the way round that was for the story to become one of military success. We needed to hit big psychological targets systematically, one after another.

Bill said we had to bomb like hell, be more creative diplomatically, maybe arm the Albanians, sort the presentation. He was very nice about my plan, a copy of which Joe had shown him. Bill went off to get some drinks as it became obvious this was going to drag on a bit. TB said the worst-case scenario was we lost and the generals were out saying they were prevented from doing what was needed to win. Berger said there should not be a whisper about ground troops. TB said we have to generate more uncertainty in Milosevic's mind re whether we would use ground troops. Bill said he was not as negative as Sandy but he didn't really know what Cohen and Shelton thought. He said it would be irresponsible not to do some planning, but in a way that doesn't split the Alliance.

TB realised we had to work on Berger more and at one point he was addressing him as much as Bill. Berger said we had to be careful of communicating a mindset to SHAPE that said even the politicians have given up on the air campaign. Jonathan said how does air power alone win? Berger said as the rubble mounts he realises he has to shift course. Madeleine put a slightly softer version of Berger's thesis. Berger said the military operation is broke and we can fix it. Alastair is fixing the media. We have to fix the military. Bill said at one point the Republicans would probably support him on ground forces 'because it might destroy me'. They may not think it is Vietnam, or Hitler and Tito, but they think we will be there for a long time and with a lot of casualties. BC and TB had a short session on their own, during which I filled them in on how bad NATO/SHAPE was, at the end of which Berger said 'I will now jump out of the window.'

In the car TB was very gloomy. He felt we were a long way apart, and there was a danger of a US/UK rift being the background, which of course Chirac would love. He said to me and Jonathan 'I am not usually prone to panic but I am starting to panic. This could finish us. If we lose, or even if it ends in a messy deal, we are in trouble.' We had been in there for two and a half hours. 'I think I failed in my mission tonight,' he said. I felt BC had been far more receptive than Sandy but it was true we were a long way apart and it was going to be a struggle to get through the summit without a few divisions here and there.

Thursday, April 22

TB woke up more resolved, and quite angry. As far as he was concerned, this was a moral challenge and a moral issue. TB hadn't liked what he heard last night. Bill was rehearsing the pros and cons. Berger was trying to keep him on the cons. Madeleine Albright was trying to give herself room to negotiate with Milosevic. TB was back to being mega worried, constantly asking where do we stand, where is this heading? He said Bill seemed to be hoping Milosevic would just crumble and shove off but when Jonathan had asked how air power alone could make that happen, Berger just served out waffle. TB kept coming back to the central point – if all the generals were saying we could not win by air power alone, we had to listen. And if Bill is unsure, and I go all out to persuade him, as this cannot be done without the US, how much are we putting our relations at risk? Jonathan reminded him of the time Thatcher told Bush this was not the time to go wobbly. The difference, TB pointed out, was that 'she had been PM a long time, and I have only been here two years'. But he said he wanted to see BC again and emphasise we could not live with a messy deal. He felt strongly that there was a fresh place in history for BC here that blew away all the rubbish about his personal life. He said repeatedly it was a moral question. He was really fired up and even though he was wearing just socks and underpants, it was hard not to take seriously what he was saying, though I was constantly chivvying him to get dressed.

The US press were saying not just TB but also Chirac was pressing Clinton. I raised this on the conference call, during which Catherine

[Colonna] said 'off the record' that Jospin could not deliver the government for ground troops. He would lose the Communists and others and he would be gone. We are not there 'yet', she said. It was interesting she said 'yet', and also significant that she sent me an advance copy of Chirac's address to the French people, which was very strong, *'Presque blairiste,'* ['Almost Blairite'] she said.

The conference call was largely about ground forces. Ken Bacon wanted to be able to say there was no question of a ground force invasion. I said it would be better to say our line had not changed. So we would say as the PM has said, the position has not changed. They would say as the president has said, etc. That was agreed. I spoke to Julian to draft a Wes Clark article which we should place in papers all over the world to show him the kind of service we could give him without him even having to be bothered. I said I was convinced we needed up to fifty people involved in this, to meet all the functions round the clock.

Before we left the residence, TB spoke to Yeltsin, who was banging on about World War Three, and we then left for the Senate to see Trent Lott [Republican Majority leader] and the other ghastlies who run the place. But they loved Tony, absolutely, gushingly, totally over-the-toply loved him. He could do no wrong. Jesse Helms [Republican chair of the Foreign Relations Committee] of all people told him he was the greatest political leader alive today. We had a brief meeting with [Senator Edward] Kennedy and a few others, a quick doorstep with a strong line on ground troops, then off for the flight to Chicago. I briefed on the speech,[1] did some rebuttal of Milosevic's interview, and was grilled relentlessly on ground troops and just about held the line. I read the transcript of the Milosevic interview and it was obvious he was obsessed with our media, and probably following it closely. BBC, CNN, Sky, they were all being paid to lie apparently. I felt we should be doing more to reach direct to him, stories about some of his soldiers selling us information, stuff about his family being under threat. I was becoming obsessed with the media war, as he clearly was too, saying it was more important than bombs and bullets. He obviously realised if he could maintain public support at home, and divide opinion abroad, there was a chance NATO would strike a deal that kept him there.

---

[1] Blair's speech to the Chicago Economic Club, entitled 'Doctrine of the International Community'. With a focus on events in Kosovo, the speech set out Blair's principles for military intervention against tyrannical regimes and pre-emptive war against perceived threats.

TB was getting more and more steamed up at the idea that we were asked to help in an operation that may end in just such a messy deal. If it did, he said he would never again lend our troops to such an operation. I felt most people in Britain would want to see Milosevic in a box or toppled and wouldn't understand a deal. I broke off for another conference call. Bernard [Gray] was still getting the runaround [at NATO] and Julian said SHAPE forward planning was still the hardest nut to crack. We arrived at the Hilton and TB had a number of interviews planned, including Larry King [CNN TV host], which was easily the strongest, and he made clear all NATO demands had to be met in full. He wasn't happy the way the US were handling it. The interviews went well, and then off to the speech which was going down with the press as serious, substantial and interesting. He was getting a rave press in the States and pretty good at home at the moment.

On the plane back, though he knew the speech had gone well, he was growing more irritated and angry. I worked through a mountain of paperwork, then wrote another strategy paper re NATO. Anji said that whenever I wasn't there the resistance crept back in from both military and civilian. Back at the hotel TB spoke to Bill C again by phone and was more reassured afterwards. I was listening in with Charles Guthrie, who had just seen [General Hugh] Shelton and said he told him to stiffen spines.

Friday, April 23
We were hitting our stride on the media front, so much so the *New York Times* did a piece about Blair's media blitz, saying we were ahead of BC on the public opinion front. The good press he was getting here was now beginning to blow back in the UK media. On the conference call I tried to get Jamie Shea focused on big message, unity, resolve. We had hit the broadcast station RTS and so were coming under attack from the usual quarters. Schroeder arrived for breakfast. He was totally up for it, total resolve, and was clear in his total contempt for Milosevic. He wanted tougher attacks, but he was determined that 'Bodentruppen' [ground troops] should not be discussed. Neither his government nor his public opinion would support it. TB gently took him through the logic – that if we were not prepared to lose, we had to prepare for every eventuality that may be required to win. I asked Schroeder if he would help ensure they send four of his best media people to Brussels and he agreed. I got the strong impression he wanted this to be over soon, which is why he too was pressing for more intense attacks.

Clark did a good briefing for the North Atlantic Council and I suggested he use some of the material for a media presentation with the line 'We're winning, he's losing and he knows it.' Then Chirac told TB that Clark had said we didn't need ground troops – the exact opposite of what he said to TB. I had a long meeting with Peter Daniel [director of information and press, NATO]. He was very laid-back, said he was moving slowly to a life on the golf course. He said he had not seen my plan because nobody had shown it to him. Solana's people were putting in blocks at every level. He said he was keen to help but I should not worry too hard about merging the old and the new. He said a lot of the staff were useless. They were the same people doing the same job since the 80s. I said we wanted more people still. Julian was suggesting it was imperative I went out there on Monday. For the Sundays, we put over a picture of Milosevic living in a bunker surrounded by TV screens, watching for signals we would cave in and getting the opposite.

Saturday, April 24

TB was getting a terrific press in the States and the *Sun*, the *Mail* and *Telegraph* all saying he was taking the place by storm. I was worried BC would be getting pissed off TB was getting a good press at his expense, and we had to watch it. Overnight there was an SIS report on a number of Yugoslav generals under house arrest. At the morning briefing, I batted off ground troops, pushed hard on Milosevic cracking, did more on his hideous propaganda machine, and when the Serb apologist from the Belgrade media asked me a question, I tore into it. I got someone to ask Jamie S about the house arrests, he said he had heard those reports, and away they went with that as the main story. Julian was painting a pretty bad picture of lack of access, and Bernard Gray was getting nowhere. I got TB to make clear to Solana that if the blocks remained we would just pull out. TB wanted a QUAD [US, UK, France, Germany] meeting on ground troops. Charles Guthrie felt the US were coming our way and TB wanted to test it. BC was furious with the French again who were still vetoing certain targets at the last minute. CDS said the security re targeting was hopeless. There had been plans to hit Arkan's casino bunker. They took so long umming and aahing, with the French fucking around, that by the time they went for it the place had emptied. Guthrie wanted me to meet Shelton, a big, friendly man but who also had that same hard look that Charles could summon when he needed to. He said he would make sure Wes Clark knew the importance of what we were doing.

At the NATO lunch, TB and Chirac had a spat re targeting. Primed by Bill, TB raised the way targeting was agreed and both he and Schroeder said it was crazy that we were not hitting him harder, and pulling back from military targets the generals wanted to hit. TB said it was ridiculous that the targets were subject to a kind of committee discussion after the military had decided what was needed, and Chirac said it was preposterous if we thought the military should have sole decision-making power. TB said they didn't, they were given general authority and specific authority where it was particularly sensitive, but too many people were claiming a veto. TB was disappointed that Bill having set up the row, he then positioned himself somewhere in the middle, but it was probably sensible management of Chirac.

After the lunch, TB and I went for a walk around the park at the back. It was a lovely warm day and nice to get away from the hothouse, though the security was a bit OTT and guaranteed to draw attention, so we didn't really get the chance for a proper chat. We bumped into Kok and Aznar so I took the opportunity to ask them for decent people for Brussels. Chirac and Schroeder were both pretty sound at their press conferences. We went back to the hotel where TB was doing *Meet the Press*, and again was strong. He was very strong making it a moral argument. The stuff on the Yugoslav generals was running well. Fiona and I went out for dinner. I bumped into one of the White House guys who was making it clear Sandy Berger was very pissed off with us, more than BC I think.

Sunday, April 25

There had been bad weather again so not all the planned targets had been hit. On the conference call we agreed to get the focus on the front-line states who were coming in to see the NATO leaders today. TB/CB had been out at the White House dinner till 2.30am and Bill had said to TB 'Don't worry, I'm not going to go wobbly on you.' TB had replied he wasn't worried about him going wobbly, but he worried the way the operations were structured meant there were too many pressures to stop us really going for it to get the job done. Cherie said that BC had said I ought to go out to Brussels and stay there till the job was done, because the co-ordination was definitely improving and it was improving overall performance as well. Cherie called it 'being the anointed one', and took the mick, saying once I had saved NATO I should come out and save Bill. I spent part of the day working on a note for TB, for him to discuss with BC, re how some of these structures, founded on UK/US, could become semi-permanent so that we had something in place ready to go if a crisis blew up.

Jonathan and John S felt TB was pushing Bill too hard, that the US system would rebel once we had gone home, and that in the cold light of day Clinton would resent the way TB had dominated the agenda. One by one, the front-line states had been saying we had to stay the course. I got a lot of questions on oil and also again had to justify why we saw media targets as legitimate military targets. Jonathan [Prince] and I saw Jamie before his briefing, trying to get him to focus on the message from the front-line states and the line that Milosevic was a pariah in his own backyard. He was frantically scribbling notes to the end, but he was less resistant to ideas now.

TB was doing a doorstep with the Albanian president [Rexhep Meidani] and I got him to use the same lines as we had done for Jamie. Then a rather more difficult meeting with the president of Macedonia [Kiro Gligorov], who had huge swollen ankles and a couple of holes in his head from a 1996 assassination attempt. They were pretty clear they did not want a ground invasion but TB was equally clear we had to do whatever it took to win. Julian was fixing my next visit to SHAPE and suggesting we go with Clark on his visit to Bulgaria and show how we can generate coverage without him doing anything at all. I talked to Clark and he sounded receptive to the idea of me shadowing him for a while to see how we could improve his own media.

TB felt he should engage Hillary C and get her engaged in pressing Bill to be more urgent. TB's main focus now was 1. US urgency and ground troop preparations, 2. help for SACEUR, 3. maintain improvement re communications. We had to go to a Third Way event organised by the Democrats. Schroeder asked me how my disinformation campaign was going. I said it would go a lot better if we had a few more Germans in it.

TB had a long session in a quiet corridor with Bill and Al From [Democratic Leadership Council], and then took Bill into a private room, just the two of them, where he pressed him again on ground troops, saying we really needed a proper fix on where we were heading, that it could only be done if the US were clear they would be there when the time came. He said afterwards Bill was much more amenable. He also said I should basically run the whole media operation.

Monday, April 26
I slept pretty much the whole way home. Fiona and I went home to see the kids and then I headed into the office later. The general coverage from the summit was positive and we were well set up for TB's

statement. So we had plenty of positive messages to push at the various briefings through the day and from the conference call circulated basic scripts for all of us to use through the day. I left fairly early to take Rory to a Cup match, which they won, and then back for the 8pm conference call, thinking ahead to SACEUR's press conference tomorrow. I sent through some lines on Milosevic's miscalculations, which I knew would appeal to Wes.

Jill Dando was murdered, which was a real shock. I had always got on with her really well when I did breakfast telly and she was easily one of the nicest people in TV. The immediate assumption was that it was *Crimewatch*-related, someone her programme had done over, but then I worried whether it was Serb retaliation for our attacks on their media machine being part of their military machine. Given that Milosevic said much the same about the BBC, I wondered whether they were going to start thinking BBC journalists were fair game. When I mentioned it to TB, he said 'They would be far more likely to try to take out you.' Thanks.

Tuesday, April 27
I left home early to get the 6.53 train to Brussels with Mark [Bennett], and spent the journey working out how to break down the barriers that were clearly still there between civilian and military. The facilities were superb. Anne, Anji, Hilary, Jan and Julian had done a brilliant job getting the thing up and running. Anne filled me in on all the various people who were arriving and what we could best do with them. There were some very good people there and it was now a case of matching people to specific tasks. I did a general pep talk, told them how the leaders from BC, TB, Chirac etc. down had all signalled their commitment to what we were doing, that Solana and Clark wanted this to work, that as democracies we had inbuilt disadvantages against the Serb lie machine and we had to be clear, imaginative, flexible, cleverer than his people.

I then saw Solana, said the facilities were terrific but there were still a few walls we had to break down. I said it was imperative we had someone at his overnight planning meeting. Jorge [Domecq] said Peter Daniel would need to clear that. I went straight to see Daniel at the end of the meeting and by the time I got there Jorge was already on the phone, no doubt putting in another block. I got Solana to visit the media ops room, and later Clark too. Jamie had had an attitude transplant since the weekend. I had got both TB and Clinton to seek him out and tell him how well he was doing and I think that buoyed him up.

Brian Steel [friend, journalist] called to say Tom Condon [journalist] was doing a book on me. That was three or four now. Fucking ridiculous. I told Brian I was not co-operating with any of them.

Wes Clark arrived at 4.45, was very warm and friendly, on his way to see Solana, then we walked together to the media ops room where he did the rounds, said hello to people individually, then said they were doing an important job, then off we went. He said he was finding the whole modus operandi frustrating, too many masters, not enough clarity, no way to fight a war, he said. His briefing was poor. Then there was the usual mess on the way out, a scrum of TV and radio reporters trying to get him to say in a messy way what he had said in a controlled way inside. I walked out of the side of the building with him and into the waiting car. The door was easily as heavy as the one on TB's car, possibly even heavier. He had moderate security and secure comms travelling behind. What did you think of that? he asked when we set off. 'No diplomacy required?' I asked and he said, sure. I said mobiles were ringing the whole time during the press conference. They should all be switched off and people should be listening. He should be got in and out without a scrum, no crews allowed to swarm. There had been no crystal-clear message so they fished around. He said he had read my note about his own profile and found it 'insightful'. I said but it wasn't being acted upon. You have to understand not everyone understands the media like you, he said.

His big problem was the way the war was being conducted. Key principles of war are clear objectives – we don't have them; tactical surprise – we have lost it; and clear command structures – we have nineteen countries who all think they can be boss. Clark's basic complaint was rooted in the reality of NATO, an essentially political structure running a military campaign. Yet he was sure we were going to win. How long? Maybe more than a year, maybe less than a week, no way of knowing. As we drove along, I noticed again how much he jiggled his legs, which didn't fill you with confidence, but I found him likeable and open. He talked about his wife, who was clearly influential, his son, a scriptwriter in Hollywood, a bit about his politics. He had much kinder eyes than you would expect for a general, and a warm smile. He would not look out of place in American politics. He told me of a bomb they were intending to use that could destroy an area the size of four football fields, and then grenades would go off, and spread further. He said the Serbs don't know we have it. The question is do we warn them or just use it? Not easy. I said if you do end up using it, make sure we have enough time before you do to have a proper explanation for its use.

We drove past Waterloo [battlefield], which I think was the first foreign place I visited, on a school visit. It was a nice drive through some pleasant scenery and I felt we would get on.

We arrived at a beautiful chateau in its own grounds, and his wife came out to meet us. She clearly saw herself as part of the deal, and she protected him fiercely. When he went off to take a call, she said to me 'Let me tell you something: he is a great general, and even when he's bad, he is better than most.' I said I wanted to help fix his media operation because he should be getting a better profile and he should not be having to spend so much time on it. When he came back, I said we had to be more aggressive in stopping the Serb media from dictating the agenda of ours. He said the Serbs were masters at intelligence. They certainly tracked UK diplomatic traffic. He had studied Milosevic and the people around him, went through the key people, said they were weaklings, would never stand up to him, but if they had to kill anyone else they would, every single one of them. I nipped out for the conference call. We had already learned there was a stray bomb in Surdulica [small Serbian town]. We agreed to get as much information as we could and go up front with it before the Serbs swung into action on it. Joe Lockhart led the charge against being too open though, saying we should emphasise we had carried out a successful attack on an army barracks. Then the Serbs started putting out the line that we had targeted and killed children. Jamie had told his night staff only to put out a more robust line if pressed so nothing was going out.

We carried on over a dinner of cheese salad, chicken and pasta, fruit salad, all pretty healthy and he wasn't hitting the wine hard either. He said that because of Vietnam and Watergate, the media assumption was that people in power deceived them. In fact most people strive to be truthful but that is not how they see it. The people's views came through on that. In his own surroundings, and these were nice surroundings, he relaxed a bit. He gave me a tour of the house, which had been a command and control centre during the Second World War. But though there were plenty of pictures and statues of soldiers, it didn't feel oppressively military, and they both made an effort to make a home of it. But downstairs there were a couple of guys poring over the intelligence stuff coming in. We ended up chewing the fat in his little study upstairs, where one of his guys was keeping an eye on the overnight military action. He said war is about clarity, politics is about compromise and when they meet it can get messy. This is messy at the moment, but I promise you we're going to win. Solana had hinted to me about a possible deal and he had asked me to start thinking how we sell a deal with Milosevic still there. With difficulty I said, but that was clearly what Clark was referring to. Both of us felt, and I know TB did, that after all he had done, and after all we had said about him, our publics would not tolerate a deal that kept him there. Clark was pretty positive re Clinton, very impressed by TB, but said it was a nightmare fighting a war with so many politicians involved. Clark went to bed fairly early, said he had taken on board what I said and he intended to act on it because he knew that part of modern warfare is fought through the media. I said Clinton showed the media mattered less than was assumed. If the media had real 'power', he would not still be there.

Wednesday, April 28

I was up again at the crack of dawn, but Clark was already gone. I was tired, but had to keep going. We had gone backwards and forwards on how to handle Surdulica and we'd finally settled on a fairly minimalist line, but now there were pictures and we were going to have to establish the full facts and engage. I had breakfast with [retired] General [Edwin] Burba, Clark's friend and mentor, ex-Vietnam, four-star general. Seemed a very nice guy, and clearly close to Clark. He was also doing a bit of freelance planning for him. He had done info ops in the past and felt we had to raise the game on it. He was totally on board for what I was trying to do but advised that Wes liked the people round him and I should work with them, not circumvent. He was a kindly, quietly spoken man, old enough not to worry about his reputation too much, and he was keen to stay in the background. But I sensed he was an ally in the effort to get a proper media operation running. He said Wes liked and trusted me and felt I was already making a difference, so I could build on that quickly.

Once at SHAPE I went to my first Clark 'desk-side meeting'. He chaired it crisply, though as Rupert Smith had warned me, he could go from talking about a tree we hit to a discussion about the oil embargo with the same level of intensity. I then went with Clark to the VTC [video teleconference] meeting where the commanders in the field were all beamed in. It was hard to work out whether what they were describing was a success or not but there were a stack of stories there which I would write up and get Clark to OK for release. I had a session with Smith who said he was already feeding in ideas through Burba. Clark called me in for his inner-circle meeting which again was a good sign. I had a session with [General Dieter] Stockman to go over much the same ground re a basic media operation. He agreed we should send media people with Clark on his trips and generate clear storylines around them. He said there were too many rival voices giving advice on the media and it would be good if they could centralise through me, he said, so again it was all going in the right direction. He said Clark likes and trusts you and respects your judgement, and the whole place had taken on a new energy since I came over. It would be great if you could be here full-time. I feared that would be a political problem. Not for us, he said. The truth was I didn't want to be away from the family on anything like a permanent basis, and felt a bit of a heel for thinking that, given how many of these guys were away from home for long stretches, but also I did not feel I should get too detached from the domestic front too, and from TB's trips etc. When I spoke to TB later, he said if Clark asked for me full-time, he would probably say yes, because winning this thing is all that matters at the moment. He said he would speak to Fiona and try to square her too if that became a problem.

There were people at the North Atlantic Council, and not the usual supportive ones, saying we had handled the stray bomb better than previous such incidents and they were definitely noticing the co-ordination. Lee McLenny was now in day-to-day operational charge of the media ops room, and was a terrific progress-chaser. Bruce Mann from the MoD was our main resident defence expert and was making real inroads on liaison with the military. It was getting there. I went back to Brussels, spoke to TB pre-PMQs, where he was on storming form, and then had a meeting of the key people at the new NATO set-up. If someone walked in there now, they would have no idea it had emerged from nothing in days. We'd done a fucking good job getting it up and running. Peter Daniel was engaging properly, Bruce Mann was going to be terrific, I could tell. The foreigners from other capitals were arriving.

Thursday, April 29

Mark [Bennett] and Julian [Braithwaite] came out to meet me at Mons and we were driven to SHAPE. I had sold Julian effectively as Clark's special adviser and he had to establish himself pretty quickly as indispensable. We went to Clark's desk-side meeting, where the mood was a lot gloomier than yesterday. The weather had again affected operations and nobody really knew what Milosevic was thinking. [UK General] Mike Jackson was the clear star on the video conference. He had a great way with words and also always had his boots and shoes in shot, because he was working out of a shoe factory.

There were real problems down in Greece, with troops being attacked and some lorry drivers refusing to take loads for NATO. At

April '99: UK General Mike Jackson 'star' of video conference

11, I got Julian in to see Clark. Julian did pretty well, conveyed to Clark both knowledge and commitment and a clear obsessiveness re Milosevic which Wes clearly liked. He said he also wanted daily strategic scripts as discussed and he wanted Julian working on his own ideas, e.g. both Clark and I had said we need a blitz on the Greek media but, to use his words, 'it just kind of drips through fingers', so we would be looking to Julian to do that kind of thing too. He said to Julian 'You only have to work here seven days a week, twenty-four hours a day. You don't get time to eat or sleep, but please take care of your personal hygiene.' Wes kept me back at the end, said he had been bollocked by Bill Cohen for the way his briefing came out in the *New York Times*. I said don't pay attention to individual articles. Look for the centre of gravity.

After the meeting, Wes asked me to sit down, and said something very quietly, and very interesting. 'I like you, and I like your prime minister. And you and your prime minister need to be very careful. Because if I hear the noises out of Washington right, I can hear the sound of saws being sharpened. They are preparing to make a deal, and if they make a deal they will cut through the tree and you and your prime minister are going to be stranded on the bit they cut.' He said he totally supported our position, but we needed to be careful about the endgame. I wrote up some of the remaining problems with Mark on the drive to Lille. Guthrie called when we were on the train home, said Dieter Stockman was keen I base myself there. I said we were going for Option B, with Julian there full-time and I would go in and out. I emphasised we had to stop people talking down Clark, even internally, because he was feeling undermined and vulnerable and I was sure if we could generate better coverage for him, he would perform better on the military front.

I got to the office and saw TB, who was still pissed off at the lack of US razor-sharp focus. He had not even had a reply to the note he sent about a US/UK nerve centre. He sensed no progress at all re ground troops and he was worried, particularly after I relayed Clark's comments, that there was some dreadful deal in the making. He said he could only live with Milosevic still there provided we then helped neighbouring countries to do him in and boost democratic forces there. He was stuck on this being a moral question which required a different order of response. We went out into the garden and strolled around a bit. His frustration was more intense even than when we had been at the summit.

I pointed out in BC's defence that most of the others were in the same place on ground forces – Schroeder, Chirac, Yeltsin. But the military say it can't be won without it, he said. I called Ken Bacon to say Clark needed bolstering, and Cohen's bollocking had really undermined him. He agreed we needed to bolster Wes.

Friday, April 30

I did a note to TB on the idea of getting BC to see Clark one-on-one to get his genuine take, as opposed to what was being filtered through a seemingly hostile Cohen. We had hit some important Belgrade targets overnight. I was working on TB's speech for the Glasgow Newspaper Press Fund lunch, where he did a big whack on the SNP, during which Salmond raised a 'bluff' card from *Call My Bluff*. Quiz shows are about his level. I got home to see Jamie Shea's briefing, which wasn't great. Jonathan Prince said he was tearing his hair out again. I said we just had to keep plugging away. During the evening conference call came news of a third nail bomb in London, this time at a gay pub in Soho. TB called and we agreed for now he should leave the response to Jack [Straw]. I got home for Grace's birthday party and I noticed how some of the adults were a bit alarmed about the security stuff. It was meant to be reassuring! I worked on TB's *Sunday Times* piece on race pre his speech tomorrow, as well as having to sort the bomb reaction.

TB called again. Though we had just about gripped the media operation, he was worried there was not the same urgency militarily because of all the mixed signals. He was confident we could maintain support in the UK, but was less sure about other NATO countries. He was worrying about Ireland too, and anxious that with us so focused on Kosovo, Ireland and international stuff we'd drift on the domestic front. I said to him that two years ago, tomorrow was election day '97. Christ, he said, nobody could say we haven't done a fair bit. 'Is it really two years?'

To be continued.

Index

and Ecclestone donation 202; drafts
TB's letter on reform 240; questions him
on honours list 247; shields AC from
calls 249; prepares excellent note for
BBC seminar 273; tries to help RC 273;
on Diana death industry 295; sends
wrong document to paper 335; at
farewell 374; on Murdoch/Man U deal
495, 498; on *Newsnight* re AC speech 658
Allason, Rupert: case against AC 371, 458,
460, 461–2, 463, 464, 472 *and n*
Allen, Amy 657
Alli, Lord Waheed 631
Amanpour, Christiane 603
Amiel, Barbara 588
Amsterdam, Treaty of (1997) 14*n*
Amsterdam European summit (1997) 57–61
An Phoblacht 148
ANC *see* African Naional Congress
Anda, Béla 685
Andrew, Prince, Duke of York 637
Andrews, David 276, 347
Andrews, Irene 91*n*
Annan, Kofi 70; and Iraq 298, 299, 301, 302,
303, 304, 305, 306, 358, 560, 561, 566,
595; and Kosovo 716
Anne, Princess 506
Appleyard, Sir Leonard 75
Arafat, Yasser 365, 367–8, 369, 380–1, 382,
538, 653
Arbiter, Dickie 129
Archer, Lord Jeffrey 234, 585
Ashdown, Paddy: and reform of PMQs
11–12, 13; not keen on Lib Dem/Labour
merger 12; and TB's offer of Cabinet
committee places 12, 19, 20–1, 22, 98,
246, 247; and PR 25, 496, 499, 502, 518,
541, 545, 547, 557, 567; in Hong Kong
77, 78; and Draper's revelations 101,
102; on top of things 198; and party
donations 211; NI visit 386–7; 'in a
paddy' 519, 541; Lib-Lab project 559–60,
655–6; stands down as leader 631, 638,
640; at King Hussein's funeral 652, 653,
654, 655; keeps a diary 656; and Kosovo
695, 696
Ashton, Joe 687 *and n*
Associated Press (AP) 246, 594
Astaire, Jarvis 25
Attenborough, Lord Richard (Dickie) 25, 613
Attlee, Clement 85
Ayling, Bob 26
Aziz, Tariq 303
Aznar, José María 356*n*, 357, 412, 413, 668,
738

BAA (British Airports Authority) 21, 22
Bacon, Ken 724, 725, 728, 729, 730, 735, 746
Baker, Kenneth 227, 657
Balcombe Street Gang 388, 389, 394, 396
Baldwin, Tom 34, 515, 585, 586, 592, 599,
660, 661

Balls, Ed: 6; and Bank of England 8, 10, 30;
as source of stories 52, 165, 277, 453;
and EMU 179, 180, 184, 187, 190; and
privatisation 196; 'fairly open' 215; and
ISAs 221; briefs on Euro X 227;
wedding 258; Helen Liddell on 289;
politically 'not fully grown up' 296;
becoming a menace 300, 589; AC lets
lead briefing 421–2; and minimum
wage debate 422–3; and CSR 445, 454,
455; denies *Observer* claims 447; briefs
on GB's statement 551; agrees strategy
on tax harmonisation 581; and PM/
Robinson loan affair 604; at TB/GB
team meeting 639; and GB 643, 650;
and euro 662, 664; and Budget 673, 679,
680
Bank of England: independence of 5, 7, 8,
9, 10, 27, 28
Banks, Tony 8, 19, 22, 102, 103, 147, 163,
172, 283, 424, 495, 541, 648, 710
Barak, Ehud 367
Barber, Brendan 122, 146
Barber, Lionel 419, 423
Barber, Professor Michael 252
Barton, Philip (PB) 300, 367, 398, 409, 475,
476, 523, 623, 718
Bassett, Phil 236, 249, 408
Battle, John 222
BBC 9, 28, 61, 80, 94, 98, 204, 227; *The
World This Weekend* 35, 240; *The Chair*
47*n*; *Panorama* 58; follows AC around
101; Jimmy Young 105, 656; seminar
273, 274; *Woman's Hour* 307; *The World
Tonight* 315; *Question Time* 411, 525; *Any
Questions* 429, 537; *Dimbleby* 587;
coverage of Iraq 405, and Kosovo 695,
696, 707; AC's Fabian Society speech
656; *see also Newsnight*; Oakley, Robin;
On the Record; *Today*; *World at One*
Beckenbauer, Franz 252
Beckenham by-election (1997) 212
Beckett, Margaret (MB): in Cabinet 4, 5; 'a
real grownup' 16; and Lib Dems 20;
and Millennium Dome 63; as possible
Foreign Secretary 110; and union rights
10, 315, 389–90, 394; and ministerial pay
153; on EMU 187; in Cabinet 235; on TB
255; blocks BNFL contracts 255; dislikes
Fairness at Work plan 405; and Cabinet
reshuffle 412; and minimum wage 415–16,
417, 422–3, 427, 428; and GB 422, 427;
announces large science allocation 452;
and Cabinet reshuffle 428, 445, 464, 465,
467, 468; on legislative programme 472;
at Chequers Cabinet awayday 500; and
Neill committee 530; and Lords reform
570, 583; on PLP 631; and SNP 639
Beckham, David 426, 438 *and n*, 507–8
Beckham, Victoria (*née* Adams) 426
Beckwith-Smith[?], Anne 136
beef *see* BSE

Beith, Alan 154, 640

Belfast *Newsletter* 405, 480, 481, 494

Belfast Telegraph 64, 351, 383

Bell, Martin 205

Bell, Mary 374 *and n*

Beloff, Max 657

Bender, Brian 29, 57, 61, 318, 332, 591, 686

benefits: child 168, 237, 302, 323, 325, 450, 636; disability/incapacity 232, 242, 264, 317, 324, 528; housing 329; single-parent 215, 216, 220, 225, 226, 227–8, 307; widows' 527, 528, 568, 679

Benn, Tony 102, 104, 456, 583, 598, 697

Bennett, Mark 482–3, 529, 543, 544, 545, 548, 578, 592, 701, 740, 744, 745

Berger, Sandy 66, 67, 287, 288, 289, 355, 396, 475, 491, 493, 562, 563, 565, 566, 657, 690, 704, 731, 732, 733, 734, 738

Berlusconi, Silvio 200*n*, 325

Berry, Chuck 68

Berry, Roger 515

Bestic, Richard 524

Bevins, Tony 4, 8, 33, 59, 115, 151, 176, 205, 278, 280, 299, 368, 430, 469, 470, 648

Bhutto, Benazir 397

Bickerstaffe, Rodney 497

Bingham, Revd William 449, 452

Birt, John 432, 642

Bishop, Tony 167

Black, Conrad 251, 588

Black, Guy 642, 649

Blackpool 333, 334, 335, 505

Blackshaw, Alison 3, 6, 32, 45, 212, 272, 288, 319, 420, 430, 446, 470, 582, 726

Blackstone, Tessa 586, 587

Blair, Cherie (*née* Booth) (CB): opposed to Anji Hunter 4, 7, 8 (*q.v.*); worries Irvine 5; moving-in pictures 9; and Humphrey the cat 11, 14; walks with TB to House 19; at Chequers 24; offers AC a haircut 39; and Clinton visit 18, 42; plans invitations for children 46, 69; cold-shoulders journalist 53; in US 66, 69; and press coverage of new bed 73–4; on *Britannia* 76; rows with staff 81; 'loose' on mobile 81; and the press 81–2, 83–4; has problem with money 83–4, 90; her role discussed 83, 106–7; and Carole Caplin 84, 142; and new kitchen 89; and Noel Gallagher 106; bored at school visit 122; and Diana's funeral 130; asks Queen about John Brown and Queen Victoria 144; getting 'a bit grand' 150; annoyed with TB for not taking pay rise 153; birthday dinner 156; calmer than usual 162; nice to AC about his stalker 164; advises Lib Dems on getting more women MPs 170; has bottom pinched by African leader 192; gives AC a big kiss 209; advises TB to change his ways 209–10; defends a rapist 218; submits bill to Cabinet

Office for new bin 220; at Chequers 245; horrified by Cabinet Office bill for use of car 251–2; and use of No. 10 notepaper 254; on AC as Goebbels 256; on GB and leadership 258; rows with AC 262; and Hillary Clinton 286; in Middle East 361, 367, 369; on GB's lies 364; at Ellie Merritt's funeral 428; attacks media 429; her pendant 458–9; and BC/Lewinsky affair 483, 506; in debt 483; at TUC conference 505; lunches with Prince Charles 505–6; and Princess Anne 506; angry with *Mirror* 514; at *Mirror* lunch 517; at father's wedding 519; on China trip 524, 525, 527; at Dáil 574; helps prepare TB for BBC interview 611; suggests AC needs a holiday 620; in Seychelles 623; on South African trip 624, 625; and daughter's school press report 640, 641; and Paul McCartney 643; on AC as 'the anointed one' 738

Blair, Euan 4, 17, 78, 83, 157, 314–15

Blair, Kathryn 78, 106, 220, 640, 641, 642, 643, 689, 715

Blair, Katie 76, 527

Blair, Leo 212

Blair, Nicky 4, 8, 17, 78, 83, 106, 157

Blair, Tony

1997

appoints Cabinet 3, 4, 5, 6, 7–8; and AC and his role 6, 12, 15, 101, 103, 120, 152–3, 213, 303, 338, 373, 393, 430, 440, 502, 709; insistent on keeping Anji Hunter (*q.v.*) 7, 8; could 'cheerfully kill' Robin Cook (*q.v.*) 7; and independence of Bank of England 8, 9; at birthday do 9; believes in communication 10; PLP speech 10–11; pictured with women MPs 11; and reform of PMQs 11–12, 13, 14, 15, 47, 194; wants Lib Dems in Cabinet 12, 19, 20, 21, 24, *see also* Ashdown, Paddy; first Cabinet 12–13; and IGC 14–15; at birthday lunch 15; feels he can sort Northern Ireland problem 16, *see* Adams, Gerry; Ahern, Bertie; McGuinness, Martin; Trimble, David; plans Queen's Speech (*q.v.*) 17; One Nation message 17, 29, 48; on Tory leadership 17, 19, 53, 56; on Gordon Brown (*q.v.*) 17–18, 25 93, 120, 121, 165, 182, 184–5, 186; walks to the House 19; and PR 25; worried about John Prescott (*q.v.*) 25; at FA Cup Final 25; and Sarwar bribery case 26–7, 28, 29; at NEC 28; first PMQs 28–9; meeting with Mrs Thatcher 31–2, 34, 35, 36; at Noordwijk European Council 27, 29, 30, 32–4; plans for Amsterdam summit 34, 35–6, 48, 51, 52; at NATO Paris summit 35–8; and BSE 38–9; and Clinton's (*q.v.*) visit 39–43, 44; welfare speech 44, 45;

and Scottish devolution (q.v.) 45; at PES conference 48–50; in Berlin 50–1; sells house 51–2, 104; and EMU (q.v.) 52, 88; photographed by Snowdon 53; and Chirac (q.v.) 54–5; worried by Dobson (q.v.) speech 56; and Millennium Dome (q.v.) 57, 62, 63; at Amsterdam summit 57–61; and RUC murders 59–60; wins cycle race 60–1; and Mandelson's (q.v.) outburst 63–4, 65; at Denver G8 65–9; and Kohl (q.v.) 66; speaks at Tina Brown's party 69–70; speaks at UN 70; and Gore 70–1; and *Sun* story on new bed 73–4; and Clare Short's (q.v.) gaffe 74; at Hong Kong handover 54, 74–8; meets Prince Charles (q.v.) on *Britannia* 76; and security in Sedgefield 81; entertains Diana at Chequers 48, 51, 78, 81, 83; at Madrid NATO summit 84–5; and hunting 85–6, 88; and Bosnian war criminals 86, 87; leans to right on moral choices 88; football at Chequers 89; and No. 10 kitchen 89; and nanny-state 90; in Wales 93–4; and Uxbridge by-election 93, 96, 101, 107; and arms sales 100; on Hague (q.v.) 99; and Draper 101–2, 103, 105; and press stories 103–5; on Irvine (q.v.) 104, 225; and peerages 105–6; and No. 10 reception 106; and RC affair 109, 110, 111, 112, 113, 117, 121; enjoys holiday 119–20; and Cabinet reshuffle 121, 165, 197; and Shayler 122, 123; and Diana's death and funeral 124–8, 131–2, 134, 135–7, 138–9, 140, 141–2, 143–4, 145, 146; and Scottish referendum 144, 145, 148–9; worried about pay 150–1; forgoes pay rise 152–4; and Charles Spencer 154; TUC and speech 122, 145, 146; positive ratings 155; prepares Conference speech 147, 155, 156, 157, 158, 159; at Conference 159–62, 164; and Murdoch (q.v.) 164, 165; rethinks policies 165–6; Moscow trip 164, 165, 166–7; and Yeltsin (q.v.) 167; and EMU 167–8, 176, 179–81, 182–3, 184, 186, 187, 188, 189, 190–2; pop star welcome at Holland Park 168; at Luxembourg Council of Europe 169–70; and India 177; bad in CSR 178; on Kohl (q.v.) 184; chairs Edinburgh CHOGM 188–9, 192, 193; and Mandela 191, 192–3; and EMU (q.v.) 190–1; and Ecclestone donations 198–9, 200, 201–10; disagrees with Chirac over Iraq 200, 201; at Queen's Golden Wedding celebration 212; and father's stroke 212; discusses AC's strategy unit 214; and Humphrey the cat 214; and ban on tobacco advertising 214–15, 217; getting measure of Hague 216, 235; in Bosnia 217–19; worried about ISAs 221, 222; and BSE and beef ban 222–3, 224, 234, 235; gaunt

and tired 223, 224, 225–6; and British European presidency launch 224; and Euro X 226–7, 228, 231; opposes policy on single parents 227–8; speaks at driver's funeral 228; at Luxembourg European Council 231–2, 233, 237; further plans for reshuffle 233; PLP speech 235; and welfare reform 236, 237, 238, 242, 245; angry with Blunkett's attack on CSR (q.v.) 239; has bad haircut 240, 245; on tax relief 243; at Chequers 244–5; and Seychelles holiday 244, 245, 246, 247

January–August 1998
rested and ready for battles ahead 249–50; worried about image 250; and bill for use of car 251–2; and European Commission meeting to launch presidency 252, 253, 254–5; on GB 155, 158, 159, 261, 266, 267, 290, 316, 439; in Tokyo 256–7, 258, 259–60, 261; finds Harriet Harman (q.v.) impossible 263; on Hague 263; on welfare 264; in Dudley 264–5; and reference to GB's 'psychological flaws' 266, 267, 268; and EMU 270–1; sees through a hoax 271; enjoys Chequers meeting without Balls 273; concerned at attacks regarding perks and fripperies 274, 275; discussion with Clinton (q.v.) on Iraq 275–6; supports him re Lewinsky 275; and Blood Sunday inquiry 278, 279; and Sheffield protesters 280; and Iraq (q.v.) 280, 281, 291, 292, 296, 298, 299, 300, 301, 302; and minimum wages 281–2; and Whelan (q.v.) 282; looked upon as 'smarmy' 283; hawkish with Yeltsin over Iraq 283–4; in USA 284–9; Enoch Powell tribute 289; and Budget leak 289–90; and New Deal (q.v.) 291, 292; on Diana death industry 295; and disability organisations 297, 309; and *Guardian* lunch 298–9; and Budget 302, 303, 313–14, 320, 324–5; briefed by Annan 303, 304, 305; and calls from BC 304–5; Millennium Dome speech 306, 307; current angsts 309; and countryside march 310; angry with Irvine over refurbishment 312–13; and Catholicism 313; reads riot act on leaks 315; and Euan's mugging 314; in Scotland 315–16; and welfare 317; and hunting 317; and gifts from politicians 317; and Scottish Labour Party 318, 334; and World Cup bid 318–19; on defects in his team 319–20, 323; and Jonathan Powell (q.v.) 323; thinks HH and FF not up to it, 324, 326, 331–2; and PMQs 325–6; wants to move office 326; in Germany 327–9; in Paris for National Assembly speech 329, 331–3; at ASEM 339–40, 341; and signing of Good Friday

Blank, Victor 534, 667–8, 675
Blatherwick, David 361
Blatter, Sepp 541
Bloody Sunday 170, 175, 263, 268, 278, 279
Bloom, Jonty 189
Blumenthal, Sidney 509
Blunkett, David 4, 16, 18, 21, 28, 52; at
    Murdoch do 53; and assisted places 54;
    against Dome 63; school visit with TB
    84; dines with AC 86; on GB 157; good
    in strategy meeting 178; and EMU 182;
    and Ecclestone donation 204, 222;
    obsessed with GB 222; wants awayday
    236; attacks DSS proposals in CSR 238,
    239–40; Richard Wilson's view of 263;
    on GB 268, 499; and post-Budget state-
    ment 324; dinner with AC 392; state-
    ment on schools angers JP 410; on the
    economy 474; worried about TB 498–9;
    and Old Labour thinking 549; ordered
    to do debate 574; at Hillsborough
    Castle weekend 586, 587; and
    PM/Robinson loan affair 607; and
    inner-city schools 617–18; and Whelan
    618; public opinion of 636; does school
    visit with AC 636–7; on Lib Dems and
    new politics 638; alarmed by
    Woodhead's remarks 652; rows with GB
    over Budget 674, 679; and GB 683
BMP (advertising agency) 637
Bolland, Mark 129, 134, 135, 147, 447, 507,
    531, 541
Booth, Gale 209, 356
Booth, Lauren 299
Booth, Mark 496
Booth, Tony 519
Boothroyd, Betty (Speaker) 10, 79, 222, 223,
    226, 278, 393, 438, 471, 483, 549, 571,
    574, 629, 714
Bosnia 31, 66, 68, 81, 86–7, 101, 217, 218, 461
Bostock, David 668, 669, 691
Bostock, James 474
Bostock, Tom 335–6, 474
Boulton, Adam 66, 68, 87, 527–8, 559, 610,
    643, 646
Bowen, Jeremy 605
Boycott, Rosie 215, 388n, 498, 531n
BP (British Petroleum) 115, 166
Bradby, Tom 50, 527
Bradshaw, David 103, 236, 392, 460, 462,
    504, 568, 643, 651
Bragg, Lord Melvyn 176
Braithwaite, Julian 427, 581, 601, 673, 696,
    706–10, 717, 719, 721, 725, 726, 728, 730,
    735, 736, 737, 739, 740, 744, 745
Bramall, Field Marshal The Lord Edwin 127
Branson, Richard 423, 642
Bremner, Charles 237
Britannia, HMY 76, 78
British Nuclear Fuels (BNFL) 255
Brittan, Sir Leon 227, 233, 339, 340, 341,
    685, 686

Brown, Colin 688
Brown, Craig 419
Brown, Gordon (GB)
1997
5; announces independence of Bank of
    England 5, 8, 9, 10, 27, 28; and CW 5–6;
    in team photo 12; rules out ministerial
    pay rises 13; critical of JP and RC 14;
    on VAT 15; thinks PM a menace 19; and
    BT's fight against windfall tax 21, 25;
    and Eddie George 30, 31, 32; prepares
    first Budget 30–1, *see* Budgets; and
    public spending 31, 56; and TB/
    Thatcher meeting 31, 34; and BC 39, 41;
    worries Butler 43; jobs initiative 47, 48,
    57; finds Europe a nightmare 48; and
    Stability Pact 57, 58; does own thing at
    summit 58, 60; and Millennium Dome
    57, 62, 63, 158; and Hague's election as
    Tory leader 64; at Denver G8 65, 68;
    wants to 'bury' interest-rate rises 87;
    clashes with PM 88, 133, 135; starts
    debate on single currency 92; doesn't
    keep TB informed 92; and Scottish
    devolution 92, 93, 146; feels lack of
    strategy 101; at Chequers with
    Spielberg and Connery 103; as one of
    the four musketeers 115; has good
    summer 120; discusses strategy with
    AC 134–5; and Spencer's attacks on
    Royals 143; chairs Diana Memorial
    Committee 144, 146, 147; a different
    person in Scotland 144; and pay
    restraint 152n, 153, 156, 158; talks with
    TB re EMU and health spending 159–60;
    at conference 160, 161, 162, 165; backs
    Alexander for by-election 161, 164; told
    to get grip of CW and Balls 165; at
    strategy meeting 168; and public
    spending 170, 171; in Rome for football
    match 171, 176; and Darling interview
    171–2, 173; gives interview on EMU
    179–80, 181, 182; Stock Exchange speech
    182, 183; hurt and embarrassed by TB's
    criticism 184–5; friendly and construc-
    tive 186, 187; and EMU 186–7, 188, 189,
    190, 191, 193, 195; and privatisation of
    NATS 196; on Ecclestone donation 201,
    202, 204, 205, 206, 207, 208, 209, 210;
    offhand with TB 215; as the real power
    215, 216, 219; wins *Spectator*
    Parliamentarian of the Year award 216;
    suggests TB deal with benefit cuts
    217–18; denies leaking story on royal
    tax avoidance 219; and ISAs 221; and
    single-parent benefits 227, 228; at Euro
    X 227, 231, 232; clashes with RC 236;
    and welfare reform 236, 237, 242, 243,
    248; as common link in recent fiascos
    237; and DB's attack on DSS proposals
    238, 239–40; paranoid 241, 242; on
    Frank Field and HH 242; leaves bad

impression 242; on taxation 243; dislikes Chequers 243

1998–99

'a problem' 253; on meeting pledges 253; and press stories re 'pact' with TB 255, 256, 257, 258, 265; fetes Routledge 258; and 'gay smear' story 258, 259, 263; and CW 258, 259, 262, 263, 274, 289–90, 316, 321–2, 410–11, 529, 589, 590, 614; Wilson on 263–4; and 'psychological flaws' comment 265–8, 270, 271; JP's views on 269–70; on TB and Budget 274; on pay 279; at strategy meeting 281; impossible 289, 290–1; charming at *FT* lunch 295; looks 'tortured' at Chequers dinner 295; defended by Sarah Macaulay 295–6; and carpet at No. 11 299, 300; more engaged 305–6; and single-parent benefit 307; and union recognition 315; upstages TB 315; on best behaviour 327; hosts Ecofin 327; co-operative 327–8, 334; Pym biography 359–60, 363–4; agrees to NI victims compensation 385, 388; on *Frost* 388, 527; and CSR 408, 409, 418, 419, 422, 434, 436, 440, 449–50, 453–5, 456; and minimum wage 416, 417, 422–3, 426, 427, 428; on *Richard and Judy* 433; and ad campaign on euro 433–4; and PM 321, 436, 439; sets out Strategic Defence Review 440; and Cabinet reshuffle 462, 464, 465–6, 468, 469; broadcast does not impress TB 463; defends CW 466–7; wants to keep Geoffrey Robinson 468, 469; has teeth capped 498; at Chequers awayday 500; accepts his modus operandi harms him 501; TUC conference speech 513–14; praised by BC 522; in US 522; and interest rates 525, 528; opposed to world summit 529, 560; gives impressive presentation 536; and publicaton of G7 statement on economy 548, 549, 550; on Nick Brown 555; does *On the Record* 557; screws up on tax harmonisation 571, 573, 574, 575, 576–7, 580, 581–2, 583, 585, 587–8, 589; on *Today* 580; and death of father 588, 589; told to change modus operandi by TB 589, 676; and press report on PM 590; and PM/Robinson loan affair 606, 607, 608, 609; and CW's resignation 619–20, 621, 633; tries to build bridges 621–2; and new press officer 622–3, 626, 637–8, 643; unusually friendly 630; and the economy 631, 644, 650; and tax credits 633; tells TB to grow up 638; and SNP 639; and euro changeover 662–3, 664, 665, 670; rows with DB over Budget 674; and Scottish campaign 674, 682, 683, 684, 685, 686, 689, 690, 698; at Berlin summit 692, 693

Brown, Revd John 588

Brown, Nick 14; and Sarwar bribery affair 26, 27, 28; stuck in lift with AC and Jonathan Powell 47–8; at Murdoch do 53; and McMaster inquiry 118; 'operating factionally' 215, 216; and Labour rebellion 228; critical of Flynn 245; as source for Routledge book on GB 263, 268; and Cabinet reshuffle 445, 459, 462, 464, 465, 466, 467; and BSE 470, 571; trapped by *News of the World* 553–7, 558

Brown, Tina 69, 144

Browne, John 166

Brunson, Michael 20, 46, 66, 67, 80, 122, 138, 210, 214, 221, 226, 243, 337, 348, 351, 356, 431, 491, 536

Bruton, John 12, 13, 59–60, 70, 71, 80

BSE (bovine spongiform encephalopathy)/beef ban 13, 14, 21, 38–9, 100, 169, 222–3, 224, 225, 234, 241, 265, 470, 497, 540; ban lifted 571

BSkyB 495, 496

BT (British Telecom) 21, 22

Buckley, Edgar 301, 561, 713, 719

Budge, Sir Richard 220, 222

Budgets: 1997 15, 30–1, 75, 78, 79–80, 81, 82, 84, 215; 1998 264, 274, 289–90, 291, 302–3, 307, 308, 313–14, 320–1, 322, 323, 324–5, 326, 327, 551; 1999 667, 671, 673, 676, 677, 678, 679, 680

Bullen, Anne 275, 277, 283

Burba, General Edwin 743

Burnley, David 376

Burnley FC 124, 149, 150, 196, 198, 238, 280, 295, 372, 376, 495, 519, 532, 549, 569, 593, 628, 661, 679

Burns, Sir Andrew 526

Burns, Sir Terry 192, 218, 277, 414–15

Burton, John 81, 505, 663

Bush, Bill 686–7

Bush, George, Sr 653, 734

Business Age 468

Butler, Brian 552

Butler, David 93, 453

Butler, Eddie 388*n*

Butler, Richard 305, 593, 594, 595

Butler, Sir Robin (RB): and TB's arrival 3–4, 5, 6; against AC attending Cabinet 11, 12; complains about cost of special advisers 38; meeting with AC 43–4; and Jonathan Powell 46; suspicious of PM 46; on Whelan being responsible for Budget leaks 84; on British people in Bosnia 87; and TB's use of RAF plane 90; and Barbara Mills 103; 'amiable but out of date' 104; opposes Irvine's idea of splitting Cabinet Secretary's job 105; to be replaced by Richard Wilson (*q.v.*) 108; asks AC's help in finding source of Snow story re funeral 145, 146–7; and Prince Charles and Fellowes 151; calls meeting on pay 157; and modernisation of the GIS 158; and Jason Campbell

furore 169; appears before select committee hearing 193, 194; asks AC to help Fellowes 196; suggests next head of GCHQ 197; and lobby changes 203; and Ecclestone donation 203–4, 206, 210; and new strategy unit 207, 214; and GIS review 211; and Humphrey the cat 214; and BSE inquiry 223; not happy about TB's message to PLP 231; his farewell 237
Butler, Trevor 175
Byers, Stephen 101, 178, 264, 271, 412, 459, 464, 468, 528, 531, 674, 675, 677, 679, 710
Byrne, Patrick 478
Byron, General Mike 726, 727

Caborn, Richard 632
Caines, Jean 16
Caledonian Club, London: TB speech 684, 685
Callaghan of Cardiff, Lord James 35, 98
Camelot: pay rises 39
Campbell, Betty 35, 51, 238, 240, 336, 532, 660
Campbell, Calum: misbehaves 99; birthday party 103; and RC's affair 113; in France 116; at football matches with AC 124, 149, 196, 198, 211, 238, 245–6, 372, 519, 613, 661; and Ferguson 184, 460; plays football with AC 202; upset at his leaving 209; out with AC 157, 219, 225, 244, 246, 304, 406, 501, 569; at birthday party 357; in play 386; and Ellie Merritt's death 422, 423; falls off bike 489; upset at AC and FM going to Blackpool 512; and bombing of Iraq 598; at football match 640
Campbell, Donald 35, 51, 238, 240, 532, 660
Campbell, Grace: taken to school by AC 146, 428; goes skating 304; birthdays 374, 746; at the fair 406; Christmas Day 1998 611
Campbell, Jason 169, 170–1
Campbell, Menzies (Ming) 154, 645
Campbell, Rory: misbehaves 99; and RC's affair 113; at football matches with AC 149, 196, 203, 372, 373, 438, 552, 613, 646, 660; out with AC 157, 244, 246, 304, 406, 569; football matches 141, 640, 724–5; and Ferguson 184; at birthday party 357; AC at his assembly 420; and Ellie Merritt's death 422; prize-giving 440; on security measures 478; fights with FM 489; fine about AC and FM going to Blackpool 512; birthday party 548; visits new school 689
Canavan, Dennis 559
Cantona, Eric 22
CAP see Common Agricultural Policy
Caplin, Carole 7, 74, 84, 142
Cardiff: G8 summit 333, 383, 413, 416, 419, 420, 423–7
Cardoso, Fernando 402

Carey, George, Archbishop of Canterbury 146, 276
Carnarvon, Lord 576
Carter, Denis 590
Carter, Jimmy 653
Carville, James 186
Cash, Bill 101
cashmere industry, Scottish 673, 674, 675, 686
Cassidy, Jim 517
Castro, Fidel 402–3
CBI (Confederation of British Industry) 27, 204, 408, 409, 541, 549, 550
Charles, Prince of Wales: and TB/Diana meeting 48, 51; and reflected glory 57; at Hong Kong handover 75, 76, 78; and Camilla Parker-Bowles 94, 102, 103–4, 645; and Diana's death and funeral 126, 128, 129, 131, 132, 133, 135, 137, 139, 140, 145, 147, 150; Fellowes defensive against 151; and Charles Spencer 154; Manchester speech 154, 155; at Hillsborough garden party 412; opposed to travelling on buses 447; and Omagh bombing 477, 480; meets Salmond 487; lunches with Blairs 505–6; and possible programme on 531; Penny Junor's biography 539–40; PM treasures his Christmas card 608, 610; at King Hussein's funeral 653, 654, 655; eats beef 670
Chequers 15, 24, 88, 244, 511; Cabinet awayday at (1998) 496, 498, 499–500
Chernomyrdin, Viktor 166, 167
Chicago Economic Club: TB speech 735n
Child Support Agency (CSA) 440–1, 442
child benefit see benefits
Chinese People's Daily 520
Chirac, Claude 584, 591
Chirac, Jacques: personality 201; and TB 32–3, 34, 38, 66, 67, 68, 170, 328; and Yeltsin 37; in photograph 37; makes grand little speeches 38; OTT at Paris summit 54–5; makes grand statements 61; and NATO 85; and Diana's funeral 130; and Iraq 200, 201, 306, 308, 309, 311, 332; supportive over EMU 201; clashes with TB at Euro X 232, 233; gives TB a watch 317; in 'second-hand-car salesman' mode 332; and ECB presidency 332, 375, 376, 377–9, 380; at Asia-Europe summit 339, 340, 341; at G7-8 summit 397, 398, 400; at European pre-summits 413, 420; at Cardiff summit 424, 425, 426; and World Cup 452, 463; TB calls 486; opposes TB at Austrian summit 538, 539, 540; and bombing of Iraq 559, 565, 566, 592–3, 597, 601; and 'briefing war' 569, 570; at Anglo-French summit 583–4; and Jospin 585; and UK rebate 585, 586, 588, 669, 685n, 693; at King Hussein's funeral

116, 121, 255–6, 257; her *A Slight and Delicate Creature* 503–4, 568, 575, 625, 628

Cook, Robin: appointed Foreign Secretary 4, 5; and media 7, 12, 14; 'mission statement' 15–16; and Lib Dems 20; and GCHQ 21; 'diddling around' 25; and AC's briefing note on Europe 30; on border controls 30; sacks secretary 32; and slogan for Amsterdam 34; 'going native' 32, 48; at NATO summit 35, 36, 37; worries TB 50; and IGC 53; and GB 58; and Dome 61, 63; at Denver G8 65; at UN 70; in Hong Kong 77, 78; brings in film crew at NATO summit 85; and capture of Bosnian war criminals 86, 97; and arms sales 100, 101, 104, 158; and European presidency 100, 224; affair 109–15, 116, 117, 118, 186, 247; announces Diana's death 125; and her funeral 132–3, 135, 136–7; cannot understand Clare Short 152; at meetings with Lib Dems 154, 198; in New York 157; conference speech 162; depressed over Queen's visit to India 177; and 'outing' of Gaynor Regan 186; on CHOGM 187; warns against Saddam Hussein 200; and Euro X 232; clashes with GB 236; and Scottish Executive 251; on welfare-to-work 254; and story about AC ordering him to end marriage 255–6, 257; and Gaynor 259, 260, 263, 272, 274, 275, 277; and the media 277, 278, 279, 280; goes to Saudi Arabia 282; on Iraq 298, 301, 302, 304, 308; in Israel 326, 332; wedding plans 335, 336, 342, 343, 345; supports AC 339; Third Way speech 370; wedding party 370; and FCO 374; greets Arafat 382; and Sandline 385, 386, 387, 388, 390, 391, 392, 394, 396, 399, 403, 415; being briefed against 386; at Chequers dinner 411–12; and PM as TB's representative at PES 423; at Cardiff summit 426; and landmines 433; and Lockerbie 461; worried about ex-wife's book 503–4, 568, 625; and Kosovo 516–17, 519, 520, 529; on *Frost* 539; and Falklands Islands 550, 559; and bombing of Iraq 560, 562, 564, 565, 566, 591, 595, 596, 597, 600–1, 602, 603; at Anglo-French summit 589, 592; asks about GB/JP alliance 613; and serialisation of ex-wife's book 628–30; and Lib Dems 631; and Kosovo 635, 638, 644, 650, 667, 690, 697, 701, 705, 713, 714; loved by PES people 646

Cordy-Simpson, General Sir Roddy 218

Coronation Street 336

Country Landowners Association 307

Countryside Alliance 306

Countryside march (1998) 309, 310

Cousins, Jim 54

Craig, Jon 284

Cranborne, Viscount (Robert Gascoyne-Cecil, 7th Marquess of Salisbury) 411, 413–14, 571–2, 573–4, 575, 576, 577, 578–9, 581, 582, 583, 585–7, 590, 592

Crawford, Cynthia 533

Crawford, Geoffrey 26, 44, 136, 145, 150, 159, 212, 531, 539–40, 623

Creation Records 106

Crickmay, Anthony 542

Crime and Disorder Bill 461

Crowley, Colonel P. J. 728, 730–1

Cruddace, Martin 461

Cruddas, Jon 101, 241, 370

CSA *see* Child Support Agency

CSR *see* Comprehensive Spending Review

Cunningham, Jack: and Food Standards Agency 10, 13; and Friends of the Earth 15; and BSE/beef ban 21, 222 *and n*, 223, 234, 238; pro Dome 63; fancied by Chris Smith 95–6; and whaling 177; on EMU 187; and press officers 199; makes silly remarks in press 309; and Cabinet reshuffle 235, 412, 445, 459, 463, 464, 465, 466, 468, 469; chairs morning meetings 469, 470, 471; has taste for the high life 470, 485–6; happier in role 473; excellent on detail 485; on *Question Time* 510; as campaign co-ordinator 510–11; and Neill committee 530; and Hague 534; bad on *Today* 569; and Lords reform 570; and CW leak 589; and PM/Robinson loan affair 607, 609; does media well 629; expenses questioned 635; on civil servants 671; plans for the week ahead 674

Cuomo, Mario 491–2

Curwen, Peter 171, 172, 215, 221, 445, 461, 549

Cusack, Sinead 106, 303

Dacre, Nigel 280, 314

Dacre, Paul 11, 163, 530, 569, 640, 643, 644, 665–6

Daily Express 334, 375, 388, 433, 435, 445, 504, 531*n*

Daily Mail 11, 30, 334, 342, 359, 442, 452, 455, 525, 551, 556, 574, 577, 588, 647

Daily Mirror 6, 79, 83, 90, 101, 103, 104, 105, 114, 136, 145, 163, 207, 240, 243, 244, 246, 247, 249, 273, 275, 306, 327, 334, 341, 402, 406, 407, 410, 425, 450, 514, 517, 658–9; *see also* Morgan, Piers

Daily Record 99, 213, 215, 433, 517, 558, 675, 678

Daily Telegraph 13, 24, 30, 35, 46, 49, 55, 59, 117, 131, 136, 176, 193, 200, 257, 359, 362, 373, 375, 464, 567, 577, 635, 723

D'Alema, Massimo 539, 540–1, 672, 686; and Kosovo 692, 693

Dalglish, Kenny 398, 527

Dalyell, Tam 275, 337, 629

Dando, Jill 227, 740
Daniel, Peter 737, 740, 744
Darling, Alistair 10; good on *World at One* 56–7; and JP 153; and GB 171, 172, 454, 464–5, 468; runs CSR 407; against Dome 63; and welfare 470, 498, 528, 594, 657, 679, 682; and FF 471
da Silva, Reinaldo 548, 580, 604
David, Wayne 554
Davidson, Lorraine 457–8
Davies, Chris 543, 545
Davies, David 617, 618, 647, 649, 687
Davies, Gavyn 284, 288
Davies, Ian 424
Davies, Liz 513
Davies, Ron 21, 63, 91, 94, 100, 149, 223, 235, 417, 500; his 'moment of madness' 542–7, 548–9, 550, 551, 552–3, 554, 569
Davis, David 430
Day, Air Marshal John 301
Deans, John 525
de Brún, Bairbre 484
de Chastelain, General John 72, 95, 489, 490, 698, 699, 705
Dehaene, Jean-Luc 379, 419, 425, 426, 592, 694
Democratic Unionist Party (DUP) 90, 175, 279, 385
Demos: report on monarchy 494
Denham, John 412, 464, 470, 471
Department of Trade and Industry (DTI) 16, 138, 170, 171, 176, 222, 225, 339, 435, 436, 461, 464–5, 468, 495, 507, 587; and PM/Robinson loan 598, 599, 604, 605
Derham, Katie 338
devolution *see* Scottish devolution; Wales
Dewar, Donald (DD) 13; has problem with press 19, 21, 38; and Sarwar affair 26, 28; and Dome 63; and devolution 91, 92, 93, 96, 98, 99, 100, 101, 127, 145, 149; and ministerial pay 153; at committee meeting with Lib Dems 154; and Jason Campbell furore 169, 170–1; and Ecclestone donation 204; attacked by Liz Drummond 246–7; goes for seat in Scottish Parliament 255; rejects knighthood for Connery 304, 306–7; plans to get more Scots women MPs 313; losing his nerve 315, 316; complains of lack of resources 318; and welfare-to-work 327; at discussion on Scottish Labour Party 334; JP on 417; worried about Salmond 433; savaged in press 436, 440, 442; and TB's visit to Scotland 455, 456; criticised by Lorraine Davidson 457–8; 'hollow-cheeked' 559, 561; TV debate with Salmond 650; incapable of delivering message 671, 675, 676, 678, 679, 680, 681–2, 683, 684, 685; sees BC in US 686, 687, 688; downcast 690–1; and manifesto launch day 711
Diamond, John 677

Diana, Princess of Wales 48, 51, 78, 81, 83, 102; death and funeral 124–44; 'death industry' 295; anniversary of death 481
Dini, Lamberto 60
disability benefit *see* benefits
Di Tella, Guido 550
Dixon, Don 494*n*
Dixon, Pat 238
Dobson, Frank 6; and tobacco ban and sports sponsorship 28, 34; sets off screaming headlines on NHS 56; opposes Dome 63; and RC 116; and publicity re Health 171, 173; not a reformer 178; on *Frost* 182; and Ecclestone 202; and Formula 1 exemption 211; and Health White Paper 223; on pay 279; on Iraq 292–3; and NHS waiting lists 301; post-Budget statement 324, 325; supports AC 339; and Cabinet reshuffle 407, 459; on NHS plans 434, 436, 439, 458; at Chequers awayday 500; and Lord Mayor election 585; and nurses' pay 617–18, 637; and CW 618; on the benefits of praising each other 631; no zeal or drive 640; and press report of Barbados trip 643, 644
Dodd, Sheree 704
Doherty, Hugh 388*n*
Doherty, Pat 174, 268, 484
Domecq, Jorge 726, 740
Donaldson, Jeffrey 97, 168, 345, 353, 355, 384, 385, 394, 395, 396, 405, 414, 484
Donohue, Brian 7–8
Donoughue, Lord Bernard 7, 199
Dounreay (UK Atomic Energy Authority) 370 *and n*, 371
Dowle, Martin 579 *and n*
Downey, Sir Gordon 199
Doyle, Vera 230
Draper, Derek 92, 101–2, 103, 105, 183; and 'Lobbygate' 443, 444, 445, 447, 448
Drumcree marches: 1997 82–3, 84, 86, 88, 96; 1998 370, 435, 437, 438, 441, 443, 444, 450–1, 458, 460
Drummond, Liz 246–7
DTI *see* Department of Trade and Industry
Duggan, Harry 388*n*
Duisenberg, Wim 270, 332, 375–6, 377–9, 380, 386
Duncan, Alan 656
Duncan, John 721, 723, 728
DUP *see* Democratic Unionist Party

Eappen, Matthew 196*n*
Earl, Robert 213
Earth Summit (1997) 68, 69
Eastham, Paul 588, 590
ECB *see* European Central Bank
Ecclestone, Bernie: and Labour Party donations 199, 200, 201–2, 203–9, 213
Ecofin (EU economic and financial council) 58, 226, 231, 268, 327, 570

Edinburgh, Duke of *see* Philip, Prince
Edinburgh Evening News 461
Edmonds, John 146, 505
Education Action Zones 254, 633
education and schools 20, 31, 54, 80, 81,
    121, 138, 165, 167, 252, 255, 309, 549–50,
    567, 635, 688, 689; and spending 52, 78,
    79, 454, 551, 674; and honours 104, 235,
    247, 422; *see also* Blunkett, David;
    Woodhead, Chris
Edward, Prince 623
Edwards, Anne 37, 285
Edwards, Martin 474, 495, 496, 507
Eichel, Hans 682
El-Baz, Osama 361
Elder, Murray 38, 96, 318
Elizabeth II: delivers Queen's Speech 19–20;
    press reports on 26, 44, 105; and TB 54;
    and Diana's death and funeral 125, 126,
    128, 129, 131, 133, 134, 135, 137, 138,
    139, 140, 141, 143; frosty with CB 144;
    and modernisation of Royal Family 145;
    and Snow story about funeral 147;
    alleged not to want Diana stamps 152;
    and royal yacht 159; Indian visit 177; at
    CHOGM 189; AC introduced to 190;
    50th wedding anniversary 211, 212; and
    TB 356, 432, 447, 487; Golden Jubilee
    447; approves Cabinet reshuffle 470; and
    Queen's Speech (1998) 571; at
    Fellowes' farewell 657
Elizabeth, the Queen Mother 137, 275
Elliott, Larry 289
Elliott, Mike 710
Empey, Reg 344, 351
EMU (Economic and Monetary Union) 41,
    49, 50, 52, 62, 65, 98, 158, 159, 166, 167–8,
    169, 176, 178, 179–80, 183, 184, 186–8,
    189, 190, 191, 192, 195, 255, 256, 270–1,
    375, 376, 424–5, 432, 437, 445, 497, 550,
    581, 645, 648, 650, 663–4, 665, 667, 668
English, Sir David 11, 32, 138, 143, 306,
    422, 569
Ervine, David 91, 276, 353
European Central Bank (ECB): election of
    president 332, 375–80, 383; launch 437,
    438
European Commission 251, 252, 254, 684;
    presidency 691–2
European Convention on Human Rights
    297
European Court of Human Rights 89
European Elections Bill 567, 568
European Publishers' Conference 638–9
euro/single currency 52, 92, 121, 165, 176,
    188, 410, 574–5, 614–15, 647, 657, 665,
    666, 670
Euro X 221, 226, 227, 228, 231–3
Evans, Alun 225, 227, 236, 249, 250, 252,
    253, 290, 338, 686
Evans, Harry 69
Evans, Sir Richard (Dick) 527

Evans, Steve 101, 178
Evening Standard 12, 40, 139, 221, 246, 291,
    299, 315, 436, 464, 537, 648
Eyre, Richard 611

FA *see* Football Association
Fabian Society 118; AC's speech 656, 657
Fabius, Laurent 332
Fabricant, Michael 455
Fahd, King of Saudi Arabia 360*n*, 362
Fairness at Work 138, 405, 410, 502, 590,
    643–4
Falconer of Thoroton, Lord Charles
    (Charlie): on AC 330, 498; and Cabinet
    reshuffle 436, 459, 465; and JC 470, 473;
    and Murdoch bid for Man U 498; first
    morning meeting 528; 'Tony crony' 540;
    and Lord Rothermere 569; on Richard
    Wilson 570; and PM/ Robinson loan
    affair 598, 599, 601, 604, 606, 607, 618;
    and Freedom of Information 603; and
    CW 618; opposed to AC's media
    strategy 658, 673; TB's view of 671–2
Farr, Christopher 223
Fatchett, Derek 77, 296, 298, 299
Fawcett Society 289–90
Fayed, Dodi al 124, 126, 127
FCO *see* Foreign and Commonwealth Office
Fellowes, Lady Jane 128, 143
Fellowes, Sir Robert: and Diana's death
    and funeral 125, 129, 130, 131, 132, 133,
    135, 136, 137, 141, 143; and Snow's
    report 145–6, 147; attacked in the press
    151, 196, 197; introduces AC to the
    Queen 190; in restaurant 198; and
    Queen's 50th wedding anniversary 212;
    and Prince Philip story 392; lunches
    with AC 447; on Prince Charles's
    meeting with Salmond 487; and film on
    Prince Charles 531; farewell 657–8
Ferguson, Alex: gets Giggs to help with
    Welsh Assembly campaign 90; and
    Mellor's Football Task Force 116–17,
    118; and referendum campaign 123;
    and AC's sons 184; gives encourage-
    ment 188, 213, 341, 432; pre-match
    nerves 203, 326; forgets wedding
    anniversary 319; picks up AC's mood
    373; on Beckham 426, 507–8; visited by
    Calum Campbell 460; a difficult
    summer 474; and Murdoch bid for Man
    U 495, 496, 498, 507; TUC visit 502; on
    PM 613; advises AC on unwanted biog-
    raphies 641–2; agrees with him re
    media attacks 660–1; praises Budget
    679; supports Labour in Scottish elec-
    tions 680–1, 682
Ferguson, Cathy 319, 507, 511, 681
Ferris, Martin 229
Field, Frank (FF) 4; denies press story 18;
    'a maverick' 25; worries AC with
    welfare plans 44; at Murdoch's do 53;

223, 310, 357, 390, 497; in France with AC 117, 118, 119; on RC 117; on AC 118, 194, 337, 389, 453; on PM 119, 139–40; on modernisation 147; on targets 178; on GB 202; on CB's image 212; worried about TB/GB dynamics 215, 216; on TB 223; worried by press report 252; speaks to Stephanopoulos 273; on Dome 294; at AC's with the Kinnocks 296; his *The Unfinished Revolution* 322–3, 429, 513, 531; feels Labour has a problem 336; and NI 402, 403, 404; dinners with AC 409, 451; at Chequers dinner 411–12; at Ellie Merritt's funeral 428; frightens TB 459; gives presentation at Chequers 499; on economy 528; not good on *Newsnight* 535; Scottish focus groups and polls 644, 668, 683, 687; does excellent polling presentation 659; with AC in Suffolk 660; on GM foods 660; supports AC on media strategy 663, 670; criticises TB 689; tells AC to take over NATO media 723

Goulden, Sir John 36, 719, 721, 723, 728
Government Information Service (GIS) 27, 44, 46, 51, 193, 218–19; review 147, 148, 152, 156, 176, 178, 179, 194, 197, 198, 210, 211; and politicisation 158, 168, 178, 194, 334; 'a sad little bunch' 410; PASC inquiry into 414, 427, 430–2, 473–4; staff meeting 567
Gradi, Dario 214
Graham, [Sir] Alistair 370
Graham, Tommy 494*n*
Granatt, Mike 44, 152, 428, 570, 678, 686, 687
Gray, Bernard 723, 725, 726, 731, 736, 737
Gray, Charles, QC 460, 462
Green, Pauline 49, 689
Greenberg, Stan 155, 641
Greenslade, Roy 412, 663
Grice, Andy 25, 34, 35, 81, 123, 158, 159, 170, 171, 435, 458, 511
Griffiths, Nigel 461, 462, 465
Grocott, Bruce 8, 12, 27, 317, 430, 449, 465, 467, 549, 572, 598
Guardian 6, 11, 46, 52, 60, 99, 105, 145, 158, 170, 208, 211, 217, 220, 223, 234, 236, 237, 242, 244, 248, 255, 256, 298–9, 341, 375, 414, 437, 496, 519, 553, 604, 639–40, 682
Guterres, Antonio 645
Guthrie, General Sir Charles: briefs TB on Bosnian war criminals 218; supports GIS changes 218–19; and media coverage of Iraq 293; briefs on Iraq 296, 297, 301; plans attack 301, 302; and defence review 436, 437; and Kosovo 519–20; and Iraq 560, 561, 562, 563, 564, 565, 566, 594, 595, 596, 597, 600, 601;

non-PC 585; rages against FCO 657; and Kosovo 636, 690, 696, 697, 701, 705, 712, 714, 715–16, 732, 736, 737; and AC 718, 719, 729, 735; on General Clark 725, 726

Hagerty, Bill 651
Hague, Ffion 77, 273
Hague, William: becomes Tory leader 17, 53, 56, 57, 59, 64, 71; at PMQs 73, 79, 86, 99, 216, 235, 263, 291, 370, 383, 455, 471, 637, 638, 649; not making an impact 74; names wedding day in Hong Kong 77; does not worry TB 80; suspends devolution campaign 127, 130; tribute to Diana 133; Cardiff flat 149; on *Frost* 150, 649; gives dreadful speech 152; and DT 154; and media 155, 166; 'dying on his feet' 158; 'a foetus' 163; at conference 168; TB and AC on 170; and Alan Clark 197, 432; and Ecclestone 205; and party donations 211; and NI 219, 300, 383, 386, 404, 643; wedding 230; and Iraq 337; Boothroyd on 393; doing well 448, 449, 497; announces EMU ballot 497, 499; not to be underestimated 500; and Clarke and Heseltine 519, 520; gives poor speech 525; and economy 532–3, 534, 535; and European Elections Bill 568–9; and Lords reform 572, 573, 575, 581, 582, 585, 586; gets Parliamentarian of the Year award 572; and Pinochet 573; digs at PM 579 *and n*, 580; sacks Cranborne 582, 583; critical of Vienna summit 594; at King Hussein's funeral 652, 653–4; attacks AC 684; poor in the House 690
Hain, Peter 16, 18, 83
Haines, Joe 160, 429
Hall, Phil 108–9, 110, 113, 556
Hall, Tony 273, 605
Halligan, Liam 392
Hamilton, Archie 47
Hamilton, Christine 41
Hamilton, Neil 41, 176, 446
Hammell, Joan 631
Hanson, Lord James 452
Hardman, Robert 150
Hargreaves, Ian 658
Harman, Harriet 4; pro Dome 63; and AC 92; and press reports 158, 215 *and n*, 294; and TB 235, 263, 264, 309, 326; and welfare reform 168, 236, 237, 238, 252, 258, 307, 326, 330, 332, 333, 335, 336, 337; in 'party set' 258; walks out of interview 307; 'shot to pieces' 324; and AC's letter 335, 336, 337, 431; offers to help AC 338; praises him on *Frost* 341; and Cabinet reshuffle 407, 412, 445, 462, 465, 466, 467; on pensions 415; and CSA 440–1, 442; leads bulletins 458

Harrington, Claire 347
Harris, Robert 95, 464
Harry, Prince 51, 78, 125, 131, 137, 139, 140, 141, 541
Hart, David 708–9
Hartley-Brewer, Julia 672
Hashimoto, Ryutaro 65, 259–60, 261–2, 340, 341, 396, 398, 537
Haslam, Jonathan 3, 4, 29, 178, 194
Hassan, Crown Prince of Jordan 364, 654, 655
Hastings, Max 315, 337
Hatter, Maurice 121
Hattersley, Lord Roy 102, 104, 291, 300, 373
Havelange, João 318–19
Haworth, Alan 15, 150
Healey of Riddlesden, Lord Denis 670
Healy, David 331
Heath, Sir Edward 278, 665
Heffer, Simon: *Enoch Powell* 568
Hellawell, Keith 226
Helm, Sarah 323
Helms, Jesse 735
Henderson, Douglas 7, 103, 561
Hennessy, Patrick 445
Henney, Sandy 134, 135, 137
Henry, Lenny 106
Herald 99, 183, 318, 456
Herald Tribune 128
Heseltine, Michael 20, 54, 62, 78, 227, 306, 519, 520–1, 658, 665
Hewitt, Patricia 465, 470
Heye, Uwe-Karsten 550, 682, 685, 723
Heywood, Jeremy: and Robinson 234, 237; impresses TB 273, 280; at Budget meeting 320; and welfare Green Paper 329, 330, 334; at Wilson's meeting 462; on TB/GB relations 488, 502, 508; and euro changeover 662, 664, 665; and Budget 679; and need for more staff 682
Hibbs, Jon 193, 200, 526
Higgins, Stuart 101, 120, 135, 141, 163, 261, 262, 331, 402, 403, 410, 415, 531
Highlands and Islands subsidy 691, 692, 693, 694
Hildyard, Marianna 569, 633
Hill, David (DH) 9; and Sarwar bribery affair 26, 27; deals with press story 35, 47; in Scotland 145, 148; optimistic about Welsh Assembly referendum 155; finds life dull 169; and Ecclestone donation 202, 203, 205; BBC letter leaked 232, 234; and Tory support on welfare reform 263; with AC at Nuffield College seminar 273; and Budget 324; leaves 335, 374; AC bumps into 421; supports AC on *Today* 430, 657
Hill, Robert 88, 279
Hinton, Les 101, 429, 556, 639
Hipwood, John 401

Hoddle, Glenn 412, 438, 646–7, 648–9, 650
Hoey, Kate 394
Hoffman, Michael 541
Holborow, Jonathan 122, 123, 124, 294
Holbrooke, Richard 527, 528–9
Hollick, Clive 406, 435, 488, 490, 531–2
Hollis, Patricia 240
Holme, Richard 154
Holmes, [Sir] John (JH) 9, 12; and NI talks 16, 18, 20, 22, 23, 59, 64, 73, 91, 94, 95, 174, 250, 257, 276, 292, 293, 317, 340, 347, 348, 351, 352, 353, 355, 357, 385, 392, 393, 394, 398, 403, 404, 405, 435, 488, 489, 490–1, 492; and TB 20, 22, 50; prepares for Noordwijk summit 29, 30; at NATO summit 35, 36; disagrees with Chirac 55; in US 66, 68; in Hong Kong 77; praises AC 99; invited to dinner with TB *et al.* 104; and Diana's death 126, 130; on Prince Charles 150; at discussion on ministerial pay 153; plays golf with AC 191; speaks for old guard on Christmas carols 234; drafts TB's PLP speech 235; and DT 250, 276; and leak on NI 257; beats TB at tennis 258; at JIC briefing 301; and *Sun* 'top secret' story 330, 331; in Paris 332; on Netanyahu 366; and MEPP 362, 365, 366, 383; and release of IRA prisoners 389; and Drumcree march 443, 444, 450, 451; and Lockerbie 460; and Omagh bombing 476; urges caution with Russia 487; and Kosovo 520, 644; in Beijing 522, 523, 525; at Austrian summit 538; note on lunch with Menem 559; and bombing of Iraq 560, 561, 562, 565, 595; on 'Operation Chirac' 570; in NI 572, 573; receives CVO from Queen 595; on PM/Robinson loan affair 601–2; on the media 625; farewell dinner 656–7; missed by TB 686
Holmes, Kate 106
Holroyd, John 199, 247, 422
homosexuality 89, 90, 166, 461 *and n*
Hong Kong: 1997 handover 25, 54, 65, 74, 75–8, 339; 1998 526–7
honours lists: 1997 46, 47, 105, 108, 199, 214, 235, 247, 304, 306–7, 310; 1998 422, 534; 1999 656
Hope, Bob 286
House of Lords: and Irvine 297–8; and age of consent for homosexuals 461 *and n*; reform 314, 570, 571–2, 573–4, 575–7, 578–9, 581, 590; and European Elections Bill 567, 568
Howard, Michael 17, 19, 283, 300, 520, 568
Howarth, Alan 194
Howe, Geoffrey 77, 189
Howells, Kim 337
Hucknall, Mick 295, 613
Hughes, David 205
Hughes, Roy 105

that AC needs a holiday 620; fed up 622; takes AC death threat to police 623; and PM 634; in Liverpool 641; looks at secondary school for Rory 689; and Paul McCartney 643; cannot plan ahead 700; on holiday 706, 707, 711; and AC's security 716; in US 738

'millennium bug' 216

Millennium Dome 57, 60, 61–4, 74, 121, 158, 252, 294, 306, 307, 675

Milligan, June 543

Mills, Barbara 103

Mills, David 200 *and n*, 203

Milne, Seumas 434, 437, 502

Milosevic, Marko 708

Milosevic, Slobodan 424, 527, 529, 635, 636, 638, 654, 655, 678, 695, 697, 698, 701, 708, 709, 710, 714, 715, 716, 717, 729, 730, 732–7, 740, 742, 743, 745

minimum wage 225, 241, 281, 411, 416, 417, 420, 422–3, 424, 636

Ministry of Agriculture, Fisheries and Food (MAFF) 10, 13, 57, 223, 235, 412, 464, 470, 643

Ministry of Defence (MoD) 132, 170, 171, 203, 219, 241; and Iraq 293, 298, 302, 564, 596, 597, 598, 600, 601, 602, 603; and SDR 441; and Kosovo 696, 711, 712, 713, 715, 717, 719, 726, 744

MIO (meeting of information officers) 10, 45–6, 52, 89, 91, 152, 210, 220

MIRAS 667, 671

Mitchell, George 89, 97, 173, 340, 341, 342, 343, 346, 349, 351, 353, 355; 'Mitchell principles' 148 *and n*

Mitterrand, François 328

Molloy, Mike 83, 651

Monde, Le 673

Monks, John 146, 370, 390, 391, 505

Monopolies and Mergers Commission (MMC) 495

Montgomery, David 326, 371, 403, 433, 440, 517

Montserrat 152 *and n*

Moore, Charles 131, 135, 193, 403, 588

Moore, Robert 591

Moore, Roger 310

Moratinos, Miguel 364

Mordechai, Yitzhak 365

Morgan, Piers 101; TB interview 104, 105; and Charles Spencer 141; on PM as source of Snow report 145; and AC's stalker 163; and Will Straw's arrest 241, 243; on GB 292; goads AC 326; 'a slug' but clever 327; takes Kabbah article 392; angry at *Sun* getting BC article 402, 403, 410; at Rebekah Wade's party 410; clashes with AC over BC 504; criticised at *Mirror* lunch 517; at Women in Journalism event 517–18; attacks TB 526; and PM/Robinson loan affair 605; talked out of NHS piece 630; interview

with TB 640; on *Mirror* 651; lunch with AC 658–9; writes funny piece 676; on Hague 684; trails TB speech 687

Morgan, Rhodri 334, 430, 431, 554, 557, 559, 576

Morgan, Sally 3, 8; and Anji Hunter 7; and Sarwar affair 26, 28; on NEC 156; at Conference 162; on Nicola Pagett 164; on GB 215; and TB's office change 326, 330; and unions 390; and landmines 433; and Margaret McDonagh 433; on MB 467; upset by TB 472; and the press 512; on Nick Brown 555; on Labour Party 560, 618; BC impeachment 598; on JP 618; warns of questions of legality re Kosovo 692; at Welsh conference 694–5

Morley, Elliot 177, 309

Morris, Estelle 470, 567

Morris, John 247

Mortimer, John 411

Moscovici, Pierre 693–4

Mosley, Max 198–9

Mossad 316

Mountfield, Sir Robin: GIS review 147, 148, 152, 156, 176, 178, 199, 216, 217, 220, 428; and David Clark 177; and strategy unit 207; on JC's expenses 635

Mowlam, Mo 5, 13, 21; and TB's NI visit 23; and BC 41; pro Dome 63; gives draft article to press 64; optimistic 67; and Drumcree march 82, 83, 84, 86, 87, 88; attacked by DUP 90; and IRA ceasefire 94; and DT 96, 97, 173, 275; wants to announce Sinn Fein talks 122; and Jason Campbell case 171; and TB's visit to NI 171, 172; at talks 174, 219, 228, 229, 230, 268; resignation called for 245; announces visit to the Maze 253–4; wants Bloody Sunday announcement 263, 268, 278, 279; on GB 268; works with AC on response to IRA 271; angers TB 277; accused of lying by Maginnis 291; and IRA killings 292, 293; suggests Clare Short do an article on Iraq 301; and Sinn Fein expulsion 303; and further talks 343–4, 347–8, 352, 353, 354, 355, 373; and TB 360, 371; and Belfast shooting 361; public opinion on 363; tells AC about Sinn Fein bugging 371–2; and IRA statement 374–5; insensitive to UUs 384; releases IRA prisoners 388, 389, 394; with TB at Balmoral Show 394; and NI prison medals 397; and imprisonment of Scots Guardsmen 415; against TB going to NI 440, 441, 442; and Jonathan Powell 442, 444; and Omagh bombing 477, 478–9; worried by DT/Mallon relations 483; pressured by GA 492; gets standing ovation at TUC conference 515; angry at BBC memo on PM's sexuality 548; and decommis-

629; and Kathryn Blair story 641; with AC and BBC people 645; at euro discussion 662, 663; and NI 677; and Wilson 678; sensitive about his role 682; and security 716; at Kosovo discussions 712, 732, 733, 734, 739

Prentice, Monica 624

Prescott, John: happy to be Deputy Prime Minister 4, 5; and the media 6, 12; and ministerial pay 13; worries GB 14; thanks AC for help 19; and deal with Lib Dems 20; thinks Clare Short 'bonkers' 21, 31; worries TB 25, 121, 122; his transport White Paper 47; ministerial committees 52; doesn't go to Murdoch's do 53; leaves papers in *Panorama* studio 58; and Dome 62, 63, 64, 70; at UN 70; and Bosnian war criminals 86, 87; and European elections 92; a possible Foreign Secretary 110; his PM joke front-page news 119, 120; sticks up for PM 122; and Diana's funeral 130, 135; and pay 151, 153, 154, 156, 157; thinks TB should go to rail crash scene 155; on PM 156–7; and GB 157, 238, 240–1, 243; conference speech 162, 164; council tax statement 221; at Kyoto talks 225, 227, 287; on *Frost* 225, 233; and Old Labour 235; 'loud' 236; on state of Party 247–8; and Education Action Zones 254; to chair welfare group in TB's absence 264; gives his views on TB/GB situation 269–70; and CW 276; angry at TB's planned local government pamphlet 279; amused by GB 308; and Rowntree Trust donation 316–17; talks of vendetta against him 318; rages at press on *Frost* 322; post-Budget statement 324; and local elections 339; and Midlands floods 358; and Meacher 358; agrees to do one-year-on speech 371; and PM's speech 375; and wife's 'secret child' story 387; on RC 387–8; and unions 391; and Fairness at Work 405, 502; and CW 410–11, 429; on relations with TB 417; thinks Liddle should go 447; and transport White Paper 459–60, 465; and Omagh bombing 475, 480, 481; attacks *Sun*'s coverage of transport 490; at Chequers awayday 498, 500; says GB should marry Sarah Macaulay 518–19; and Nick Brown affair 555, 557; and Menem 559; happy with Lords reform deal 576, 581; accused of drink driving 593; and Iraq 595; and PM/Robinson loan affair 607, 612, 613; poor on *Today* 611; and press report on alliance with GB 613–14, 617; and CW 617, 618; exasperated by PM 628; his lost papers found 631; and PM's book idea 632; and transport policy 640;

and Lib Dems 640, 645; and Gore's visit 646

Prescott, Jonathan (son) 316–17
Prescott, Michael 316, 481
Prescott, Pauline 387, 617
Press Association (PA) 26, 54, 125, 151, 232, 256, 278, 313, 398, 432, 444, 446, 547, 558, 638
Press Complaints Commission (PCC) 143, 235, 297, 315, 640 *and n*, 641, 642, 643, 649
Preston, Peter 299
Preston, Roz 7, 17, 46, 144, 176, 190, 320
Price, Lance 444, 537, 545, 554, 579, 604, 608, 609, 686, 693, 710
Primakov, Yevgeny 500, 501, 693
Prince, Jonathan 728, 730–1, 739, 746
Prisoners of War, Far East (FEPoWs) 257 *and n*, 260, 262, 398, 408, 409, 411
Private Eye 237
Prodi, Romano 32, 33, 85, 243, 275, 325, 331, 417, 486, 508, 509, 685, 690, 691–2, 711
Progressive Unionist Party (PUP) 91, 276, 348, 353, 703
proportional representation 496, 518, 537, 545, 547, 557–8, 567–8
Pruce, Danny 726
Punch 579
PUP *see* Progressive Unionist Party
Purnell, James 498
Pym, Lord Francis 105
Pym, Hugh and Kochan, Nick: *Gordon Brown...* 359–60, 363–4, 411, 450, 453

Queen's Speeches and debates 11, 12, 13, 17, 18, 19–20, 570, 571
Quin, Joyce 470
Quinn, Ruairi 574

Rabin, Leah 364
Rabin, Yitzhak 364
Radice, Giles 437
Rae, Maggie 15, 51, 150
Railtrack 315
Randall, John 107
Rasmussen, Poul Nyrup 593, 653, 672
Rawnsley, Andrew 265, 266, 267, 268, 271, 519
Rayner, Terry 23, 506
Raznatovic, Arkan Zeljko 696
Read, Rob 235, 326
Reagan, Ronald, 328
Real IRA (RIRA) 476, 480, 487, 497–8, 538, 572, 574, 701
Rebuck, Gail 74, 118, 296, 409, 411, 451, 660
Redwood, John 497
Reed, Jane 131
Reform Club 220
Regan, Gaynor (later Cook): affair with RC 32, 109–15, 116, 186, 247, 259, 260, 263, 272, 370

Scottish Football Association 133
Scottish Labour Party 113*n*, 144, 318, 502–3, 644, 675, 676; *see also* Dewar, Donald
Scottish National Party (SNP) 318, 334, 339, 383, 420, 433, 457, 458, 485, 503, 558, 559, 562, 638–9, 651, 668, 671, 676, 681, 682, 689, 690, 710, 711, 713; *see also* Salmond, Alex
SCU *see* Strategic Communications Unit
SDLP (Social Democratic and Labour Party) 72, 97, 173, 250, 257, 276, 277, 278–9, 342, 344, 349, 350, 352, 354; *see also* Mallon, Seamus
SDR *see* Strategic Defence Review
Seddon, Mark 207, 513
Sedgemore, Brian 583
Senior, Doug 509
Sereny, Gitta: *Cries Unheard...* 374*n*
Sergeant, John 218, 376, 544
Sha'ath, Nabil 367
Shackelton, Louise (Miliband) 266, 577
Shand, Jimmy 534
SHAPE 721, 724, 725, 727–34, 736, 739, 743, 744
Sharif, Nawaz 402
Sharon, Ariel 365
Shayler, David 121–2, 124
Shea, Jamie 707, 708, 711, 714, 715, 717, 718, 719–20, 721, 723, 724, 736, 737, 739, 740, 742, 746
Shearer, Alan 424
Sheinwald, Nigel 30, 33, 291, 299, 301, 374, 669
Shelton, General Hugh 564, 732, 733, 736, 737
Shersby, Sir Michael 85*n*
Shevas, Anne 726
Shinseki, General Eric 218
Short, Clare: on Channel 5 11; in Cabinet 12, 13, 21, 31; 'bonkers' 31; opposed to Dome 63; in US 69, 70; invites Sinn Fein to Lancaster House 74; attacks FCO 123; AC wants sacked 152; has too much to drink 164; and strategy unit 216; doesn't feel involved 216; 'witters on' 236; 'ludicrous' 272; does BBC documentary 291, 293 *and n*, 294; on Iraq 292, 301, 308; as the great purveyor of truth 300; does 'Mother Teresa bit' 500; at TUC conference 505; criticises BC on *Question Time* 525, 526–7; and Hurricane Mitch 558; gaffe on *Dimbleby* 587, 588; and bombing of Iraq 597; drinks water 631; on Sierra Leone 658; and Kosovan refugees 706, 708, 714, 715; 'waffles generalities' 715
Sieghart, Mary Ann 53, 558
Siemens 473
Sierra Leone 383*n*, 399–400, 658; *see* Sandline
Simon, Lord David 105, 106, 107, 115, 116, 233

Simon, Siôn 263
Simpson, John 520, 522, 523, 727, 730, 731
Sinatra, Frank 396, 397
single currency *see* euro
single-parent benefits *see* benefits
Sinn Fein (SF) 16, 18, 20, 22–3, 60, 62, 64, 72, 73, 80, 91, 96, 148, 257; expulsion 296, 300, 302, 303; bugged 371–2; votes on GFA 388; and TB's speech 393–4; *see also* Adams, Gerry; McGuinness, Martin
SIS (Secret Intelligence Service) 367, 597, 730
Sixsmith, Martin 330
Skinner, Dennis 205, 337, 518
Sloman, Anne 548, 693, 695
Smith, Chris 39, 62, 63, 64, 95, 126, 235, 309, 411, 456, 500, 580, 586
Smith, Delia 83
Smith, Baroness Elizabeth 144
Smith, Godric (GS): as press officer 15, 17, 57, 66, 67; and changes needed 53; on TB's travel schedule 84; warns re ministerial pay 152; good note on Moscow trip 164; and David Clark 181; alarmed at DB's letter to GB 239; briefs from Porton Down 294; and welfare Green Paper 333; as AC's deputy 371, 373–4; and Kabbah 392; tries to restrain AC 392; on CW 410–11; and GIS report 474; and Omagh bombing 476; does press briefing for AC 537; and Ron Davies affair 553; and Pinochet 576; and TB and UK rebate 589; hates Sunday papers 654, 659–60; on AC 673; on reports on Kosovo 707, 708
Smith, Iain Duncan 263
Smith, John 255
Smith, Jon 547
Smith, Plum 348
Smith, Rupert 721, 725, 729, 730, 731, 743
Smith, Walter 680–1, 682
Smyth, Hugh 91
Snoddy, Ray 334
Snow, Jon 145, 146–7, 224, 504
Snowdon, Antony Armstrong-Jones, Earl of: TB photo 53
Soames, Nicholas 7, 226
Social Exclusion Unit 224–5, 226, 502
Solana, Javier 87, 644, 701, 706, 717, 718, 720, 721, 723, 726, 727, 728, 730, 737, 740, 741, 743
Soley, Clive 236, 446, 557, 613
Sopel, Jon 115, 446, 524, 537, 590, 645; TV profile of AC 427, 428, 429, 430
Southall train crash (1997) 155
Spacey, Kevin 106
Spectator 150, 292
Spencer, Charles 129, 131, 136, 137, 139, 140, 141, 142, 143, 146, 147, 154
Spice Girls 83, 124, 426
Spielberg, Steven 103, 373
Splendid, HMS 694

Illustration
Acknowledgements

Picture research: Amanda Russell

Section 1

p. 1   Author's private collection; Martin Cleaver/AP/Press Association Images; Topfoto
p. 2   Topfoto; Peter Marlow/Magnum Photos
p. 3   All author's private collection
p. 4   Topfoto; Topfoto; Press Association Images; Topfoto
p. 5   All author's private collection
p. 6   Topfoto; Reuters/Ian Waldie; Topfoto
p. 7   Topfoto; Press Association Images; Author's private collection; Author's private collection
p. 8   Topfoto; Author's private collection; Author's private collection

Section 2

p. 1   Topfoto; Bruce Adams/Daily Mail/Rex Features; Chris Bacon/Press Association Images; Barry Batchelor/Press Association Images; Barry Batchelor/Press Association Images
p. 2   Topfoto; Author's private collection; Author's private collection
p. 3   Topfoto; Topfoto; AFP/Getty Images
p. 4   Topfoto; Author's private collection; Author's private collection
p. 5   Topfoto; Author's private collection; Author's private collection; Author's private collection
p. 6   Author's private collection; Author's private collection; Topfoto
p. 7   Topfoto; Topfoto; Rex Features
p. 8   David Cheskin/Press Association Images; John Stillwell/Press Association Images; Hidajet Delic/Press Association Images